Michigan Real Estate Law & Practice

A Complete Guide for Exam Prep, Practitioners, and Consumers

Jack K Waller, J.D.

NCI Associates, Ltd.
publisher of
Michigan's Top Real Estate Textbook

Please support the legal and appropriate use of copyright protected materials by using only legitimately purchased textbooks.

Do not participate in the illegal and/or unauthorized photocopying, scanning, uploading or downloading, link sharing, distribution, and/or subsequent use, via the Internet or otherwise, without consent of the publisher.

Piracy of copyright protected material is illegal. Your support is appreciated.

Copyright © 2021 by NCI Associates, Ltd.

All rights reserved.

No part of this publication may be reproduced, stored, and/or transmitted in any form or by any means whatsoever, including but not limited to electronic storage and retrieval systems, photocopy, facsimile, or recording, without the prior consent, in writing, from the publisher and author.

Printed in the United States of America.

10 9 8 7 6 5 4 3 2 1

Published by:
NCI Associates, Ltd.
P.O. Box 180758
Utica, Michigan 48318
Contact: 586-247-9800
U.S.A.

ISBN: 978-0-9678462-2-4
Library of Congress Control Number: 2015933391

Contributors: Thomas Kotzian, J.D., Ann Millben, and Marguerite Walker II, J.D.

Cover photographs: The homes featured on the front and back covers were constructed by Lombardo Homes. As a strong, family-owned building company, Lombardo Homes features distinctive, single-family homes, condominiums, and apartments for the buyer or resident who is searching for the perfect merging of style, features, and affordability. Further information about Lombardo Homes is available at <www.lombardohomes.com>.

Book design, cover design, and cover photography: Jack K Waller, J.D.

Printing: July 2021

NOTICE

The information contained in *Michigan Real Estate Law & Practice* is designed to help the reader better understand the material covered on the Michigan Real Estate Salesperson's and Broker's License examination. Any specific language of a contractual or legal nature that is discussed or appears in this textbook is for educational purposes only. Any and all references to specific policies and procedures, including commission rates or amounts, are merely provided for purposes of illustration. While this textbook does provide information pertaining to real estate laws and rules as well as real estate brokerage practices, it is not designed or intended to be relied upon by an actual real estate broker or salesperson, or a buyer or seller, to guide him or her through any specific real estate-related transaction or dealings.

Take notice that serious rights, duties, and responsibilities can arise when entering into real estate transactions and/or engaging in specific real estate activities. Therefore, you are strongly recommended to seek the advice of competent legal counsel prior to engaging in any such activities. Other professionals may also need to be consulted who possess special expertise in one or more of the following areas: (1) Appraisal; (2) Environmental concerns; (3) Finance; (4) Distressed property transaction rights and remedies; (5) Property inspection; (6) The negotiation of residential or commercial purchase, sale, or lease transactions; or (6) Taxation.

Special care has been taken in this edition to accurately reflect the current state of the laws, rules, and regulations affecting the real estate industry. Nevertheless, all ideas and concepts contained within are subject to local, state, and federal laws and regulations and any revisions of same. Further, references to financing issues such as interest rates, qualification limits, and regulations are also subject to frequent change. Therefore, this textbook is not designed, nor is it intended to be relied upon, as a substitute for legal counsel. Should any questions arise as to an actual or perceived legal matter, you are again strongly recommended to consult with competent legal counsel. No representations or warranties whatsoever are made, either express or implied, with respect to the information in this textbook or any instruction that is provided based on its content.

MEET YOUR AUTHOR

Jack K Waller, J.D. is the president and co-founder of a successful education development, delivery, and consulting company based in Michigan. He specializes in creating exceptional educational materials and programs for the real estate and construction industries. Waller is a Professional Real Estate Broker, Attorney, Educator, Author, Business Advisor, and Risk Management Consultant who has worked with numerous individuals and groups on a local, state, and national level. His undergraduate degree in public education allows Jack to perfect the right programs and materials to assist all learners. As a real estate attorney, Jack serves in an Of Counsel capacity with the law firm of Linnell & Associates, PLLC which is located in the metropolitan Detroit area.

Jack believes that serving as a real estate professional is more challenging today than at any other time in history. The abundance of real estate information on the Internet has spawned a knowledgeable and sophisticated buyer and seller corps. As a result, real estate professionals are being asked to offer more targeted advice, vigorous advocacy, and skilled negotiation services than ever before. Jack is proud to help real estate professionals meet these demands.

As you read or study from this textbook, Jack invites you to learn from the wisdom that being a real estate "professional" is more than obtaining your license, fulfilling basic continuing education requirements, and staying out of trouble. It means you recognize that you are part of an honorable profession. You understand that you are being called on to assist buyers and sellers in the fulfillment of the American Dream–that of home ownership. You strive to reach the heights of this calling by subscribing to high ethical standards built on honesty and integrity. You diligently expand your own personal knowledge and skills each year. To do this is to serve your clients in the noblest manner.

Once you receive your real estate license, Jack would like you to join him in spreading the message of professionalism throughout your practice, your office, and your community. Be the example and demonstrate to other real estate professionals that there is no greater gift we can receive from the public than that of respect and trust.

Jack may be contacted by calling 586-247-9800 or email at <info@teamnci.com>.

DEDICATION

To all who are using Michigan Real Estate Law & Practice...

Whether you are a future real estate professional preparing for your new career, an existing real estate professional who uses this book as a reference, or a buyer or seller educating yourself in anticipation of working with a real estate professional, may the truth of who you really are, the gift of your inner wisdom, and your vision of a bright future light the path of success!

CONTENTS

- Preface 1
1. Introduction to Real Estate 7
2. Brokerage Concepts 21
3. The Listing Agreement 47
4. Appraisal 69
5. Deeds and Title Transfers 83
6. Interests in Real Property 97
7. Forms of Ownership 107
8. Title Verification 117
9. Real Estate Settlement Procedures 127
10. Legal Descriptions 145
11. Land Use Controls & Real Estate Development 153
12. Contract Law 171
13. Leases 195
14. Property Management 211
15. Financing Considerations of Ownership 219
16. Financing Instruments 241
17. Financing Options 269
18. Fair Housing 307
19. Real Estate License Law 331
20. Administrative Rules 367
21. Michigan Specific Statutes 379
22. Real Estate Mathematics 407
- Practice Exam and Answer Keys: Sharpening your test-taking skills 427
   - Diagnostic Practice Exam: 100 question review 429
   - Answer Key, Chapter Practice Questions 439
   - Answer Key, Diagnostic Practice Exam 440
- Appendix 441
   - Agency Disclosure 443
   - HUD-1 Settlement Statement ... 445
   - TRID Loan Estimate 448
   - TRID Closing Disclosure 451
   - Seller Disclosure Statement 456
- Index 459

"INSIGHTS & INSPIRATIONS"

Throughout this material you will encounter a number of Simple Thoughts . . . Stimulating Ideas . . . and High-Performance Recommendations designed to improve your business, feed your spirit, and empower your life.

Read, Heed, and Enjoy!

Preface

Do you want to pass the state licensing exam? Then carefully read and study "every single word" in this Preface. It is that important!

We live in what experts refer to as the Digital, Electronic, or Computer Age. Our lives are bombarded with billions of information bits that cover an unimaginably wide range of subjects. Most of this information is pushed to our electronic devices in the form of short messages and through social media outlets. As a result of this digital bombardment, we have conditioned ourselves to skim read and filter out more information than we take into our awareness.

The method of information processing (and dismissal) used in the Digital Age must not be applied to the content in this textbook. This is especially true if you are using it to prepare for the Michigan real estate licensing exam. <u>Take your time</u> and methodically <u>read everything</u> with the intent of truly learning it. This means <u>slow down</u>, <u>eliminate distractions</u>, <u>read for understanding</u>, and <u>concentrate</u> on what you are studying in a focused manner.

Keep in mind that nobody can guarantee you will pass the state exam. However, if you follow the recommendations in this textbook, you will place yourself in the best possible position to do so!

In your hands, you are holding *Michigan Real Estate Law & Practice*. It is absolutely the most comprehensive and up-to-date textbook on the practice of real estate in Michigan. If you have purchased a personal copy of this excellent resource, it is a safe bet you have a serious interest in real estate. You may also be interested in obtaining your Michigan Real Estate Salesperson's or Broker's License. If so, passing the licensing examination in the shortest time possible, and with the least amount of effort, is the prime goal. While such an outcome requires a firm commitment, effort, and disciplined study, having the right textbook can make the job easier and more enjoyable.

The beauty of this powerful resource is that it is the only one that gives you full control over the information you need. *Michigan Real Estate Law & Practice* is created for those students who want a comprehensive exploration of likely test topics in an easy-to-learn format. There is no other textbook that provides so much information in such a learning-friendly design.

As you read the balance of this Preface, keep the following thought in mind:

Nearly every student who learns from this textbook and passes the salesperson's or broker's exam says the same thing... If you really want to pass the licensing exam, make sure to pay close attention to all of the suggestions in this Preface!

If you want to pass as they did, follow their advice. Each of the powerful recommendations in this Preface are designed to add valuable points to your score on the state exam!

USER-FRIENDLY COVERAGE OF TEST POINTS

The terms and concepts explored in *Michigan Real Estate Law & Practice* are designed to show you a comprehensive picture of how real estate is actually practiced. Attention is also focused on those terms which have the greatest likelihood of appearing on the Michigan real estate licensing exam as set forth in the PSI Information Bulletin. PSI is the company that delivers real estate examinations in Michigan. The highest degree of care possible has been taken to provide you with the most complete and concise coverage of test topics. Here are your keys to success.

EXAM SUCCESS KEY 1: <u>Know the terms thoroughly.</u>

The real estate salesperson and broker examinations are designed to test the depth of your understanding of various real estate subjects. You will be presented with a number of questions that have a fact pattern or story problem format of varying length. You could also encounter a lengthy fact pattern with multiple questions tied to it. Regardless of the question type, each one includes four possible choices designed to assess your understanding of the issue or issues being tested.

The good news is that answering questions correctly on the state exam simply comes down to having a thorough understanding of the concepts and terminology. Merely looking over the terms and definitions in this textbook a few times, however, is not enough. All elements must be understood sufficiently to apply them correctly to the range of fact patterns that you might see on the state exam. If you attempt to shortcut this process, you will only shortcut your exam results.

By way of analogy, think of each real estate term or concept as a child's wooden block with six sides. Each side of the block represents a particular aspect, or element, of the term or concept. Questions on the state exam could cover any one of the six sides. If you only learn one side, and the exam question tests your understanding of a different side, the question will be confusing. Learn all sides of each term or concept and you will be prepared to confidently tackle whatever question you are facing.

EXAM SUCCESS KEY 2: Put the tools of the text to use.

Each chapter in this textbook was written in an outline format to enhance your ability to see how each topic or term relates to the overall chapter topic. This has proved to be a highly effective way to learn a large volume of information. To make the most of your textbook, apply the following suggestions as you read, learn, and study.

1. **Start by reviewing headings and subheadings:** When you first approach each chapter, review just the headings and subheadings without actually reading the accompanying text. This will give you an overall picture or feeling of how the subject of each chapter is organized. Mentally say the headings and subheadings to yourself and notice how they relate to one another within the outline structure. Be aware of the logical flow of the headings.

2. **Read and research the text:** Next, return to the beginning of the chapter and actually read the accompanying text. Anytime you encounter a term or definition that you do not clearly understand, spend additional time re-reading and thinking about it. If you need additional help, feel free to conduct an online search. Be aware that for exam purposes, any conflict between what this textbook says and an online resource should be resolved in favor of this textbook.

3. **Pay attention to the examples:** As previously noted, your textbook is an effective learning tool that delivers the key concepts needed for exam preparation in an easy-to-learn and easy-to-remember manner. The information is enhanced with numerous examples designed to strengthen your understanding. As a result, you will encounter two key abbreviations:

    E.g. (e.g.): This is an abbreviation for *exempli gratia* which simply means "for example." You will typically see it immediately following discussion in which an instructional example is provided. The information that follows the abbreviation contains the example.

    I.e. (i.e.): This is an abbreviation for *id est* which means "that is" or "that is to say." It is another expression for the phrase "in other words." When an author is teaching a concept, it is often helpful to express it in more than one way. The abbreviation "i.e." alerts the reader that an alternate expression is being provided immediately following.

    Note: Remember that examples are excellent tools for reinforcing understanding. As you prepare for the exam, pay close attention to any additional examples and illustrations provided in this textbook.

    Use of gender-specific terms: Anytime the pronoun "he" is encountered in this textbook, it is understood to be gender-nonspecific and mean both "he" and "she." This is done merely for grammatical efficiency. If a term or phrase is gender-specific as it is defined in the law, it will be noted in the discussion.

"SIX CRITICAL STEPS FOR PASSING THE STATE EXAM"

1. **Complete all regularly-scheduled education sessions and promptly make-up unavoidable absences.**

    During each session, focus your full physical, mental, and emotional energy on the material and program content. Take advantage of this excellent opportunity to learn the subject matter. Do not distract yourself during the program by text messaging and checking emails. This will put your success at risk!

2. **Complete all recommended pre-reading and at-home assignments.**

    Do not fall prey to the all too common excuse that you do not have the time to study. Last minute cram sessions are not as effective as sustained, long-term preparation. Study early and often!

3. **Develop the habits of Focus and Discipline with your preparation.**

    Some students allow themselves to be distracted by other priorities or commitments that slow down their preparation. Interestingly, the same non-productive excuses can deter a steady income once they are in the business. Make the time to study. You are definitely worth it!

    Good habits developed at this point in the process tend to carry over into the business world and translate into consistently-earned commission dollars. Top producers know the importance of focusing on prospecting and other dollar productive activities. Staying focused means eliminating all distractions while you are studying outside of your program.

    Turn off all smartphones, computers, tablets, radios, and televisions. Some students think these background "noises" help them focus. Contrary research confirms that these devices do not help anyone who is trying to memorize items for later recall. Distractions make it more difficult to retain information.

Try studying in shorter intervals with breaks in between. Be one-minded and of single-purpose as you prepare. Train to become an "Exam Warrior" rather than an "Exam Worrier." If you look for distractions, you will find them. If you look for quiet time, you will find that too.

4. **Review the material in this textbook on a frequent basis.**

    It cannot be repeated enough that those students who commit the terms to memory are most likely pass the exam with the least amount of difficulty. Constant repetition, almost to the point of boredom, is central to solidifying your understanding of and ability to recall the information on the state exam.

    It is important to note that the environment in the actual test center will be different from your favorite desk or lounge chair in your home. The comfort level you create via constant review at home can be used to create an important level of confidence at the test center.

    In addition, remember to spend as much time with your textbook as you can. Use it, read it, and know that it provides your quickest path to passing the state exam. Here is an interesting thought to ponder, "You show me a textbook that looks frayed and I'll show you a student who does not!"

5. **Answer the practice questions in the textbook, but only as recommended.**

    Do not attempt to memorize questions. Instead, use them to gauge your understanding of the material and to diagnose weak areas. If anyone tries to tell you they have the actual questions that are on the exam, they are sadly misinformed. Nobody knows what will be on the exam ahead of time. We do know, however, that there are a limited number of question types that can be used. If you know the terms, know how to apply them, and view the process as a fun discovery process, you will be in the best shape possible.

6. **Watch for subject areas or terms where your level of understanding may require extra preparation.**

    Weak areas will be uncovered as you work through this process. To create a feeling of strength and confidence, keep reviewing the material and use the resources provided through your education delivery system. Repetition is the key to success.

The days leading up to the actual state exam

Use your textbook to review the information on the days leading up to the state exam. If you have faithfully employed the approach recommended in this Preface, light review may be sufficient to reinforce what you have already learned. This will avoid any last minute panic studying which, as noted, typically yields disappointing results. Being in full command of the definitions is the best way to ensure success on the exam. Keep up the good work and know that your newfound success habits can carry forward to the actual real estate business!

NCI's BEST EXAM-PASSING STRATEGY... EVER!

What you are about to read is the most important advice this textbook will give you on how to approach an exam question. It is a process developed by your author based on solid research, testing, and experience. It is strongly recommended that you apply it: (1) to every practice question in this textbook, (2) to your program mid-term and final exams, and ultimately, (3) on the state exam. Do this without shortcut or fail.

Students who use this textbook to prepare for the state exam sometimes wonder if they will remember enough of the required information at the testing center. Assuming they studied as recommended, the majority of students have little difficulty remembering the information needed to pass. If a problem occurs, it generally relates to careless (and avoidable) mistakes in how the question is approached. The strategy you are about to read will help to prevent this from occurring.

Every great professional athlete knows how important it is to master the mechanics of their sport and repetitively apply them when practicing. As you learn, so shall you practice. As you practice, so shall you perform. Remember this as you work with the practice questions in this textbook!

1. **Read the entire question. (Don't stop to think!)**

    As you approach an exam question, read the <u>entire</u> question before you attempt to process any portion of it. Questions sometimes contain information that is not necessary for selecting the correct response. The question writer may be testing your ability to sift through multiple facts. Sometimes the only fact or facts needed to answer the question are located at the end of the story problem.

    If you stop halfway through your reading to process a question, you could inadvertently overlook or ignore the end where the key facts are located. You would then be tempted to pick the choice that conforms to your incorrect assumption of the question without realizing what you overlooked. The solution is simple–always read the <u>entire</u> question (without stopping to think half way through).

2. **Identify the objective of the question. (What am I solving for?)**

    Every question has a specific objective that you are asked to address. Before you look at the four possible answer choices, you must know the question objective. By mentally (meaning, quietly) verbalizing the question objective before looking at the possible answers, you will dramatically enhance your chance of answering it correctly. When the objective is not clear to the test-taker, the answers will appear to be confusing. A question will rarely be confusing to a student who has studied properly and knows the question objective.

3. **Read all four question choices. (Don't consider any one until all have been read!)**

   a. If one answer appears to be an "obvious" choice, select it and move on to the next question. Don't look back!

   b. If you are uncertain about two or more choices that initially appear to be correct, then eliminate the "obvious" wrong choices. (Doing so can literally double your chance of getting the answer correct. In other words, you have a 25% chance guessing with four possible choices. Eliminate two of the choices, and the odds double to 50%.)

4. **Repeat steps 1 through 3. (Only focus on the remaining choices!)**

   a. This step is really important because it helps you refocus your attention on the question objective. Wrestling with a challenging question for a minute or two causes the test-taker to possibly lose sight of the question objective. This step gets you back on track.

   b. If you have reduced the remaining choices to two (which is common), treat it as a True–False question.

5. **Note if the question is a 1T – 3F or 1F – 3T option.**

   a. Some questions ask for the one correct (i.e., TRUE) answer and provide three choices that are not correct (i.e., FALSE). An example of this question type might read, "A deed in which no warranties exist is known as... ." In this question type, you have one TRUE answer and three FALSE answer options.

   b. Another question type could ask for the one answer that is FALSE and provide three TRUE options. The wording might be constructed as, "All but which of the following are types of agents?" In this question type, you have three TRUE answer options and you must select the one FALSE answer option.

6. **Additional tips.**

   a. The approach discussed in the Preface is designed to help you answer the question correctly the first time. Do not return to previously-answered questions and change your answer. Test-takers who second-guess their answers often do so based on false assumptions. This forces them to mentally "rewrite" the question which leads to a new, and wrong, answer. The only exception is the rare instance where a later question triggers a firm memory recall and you are absolutely positive you need to make a change. Otherwise, do it right the first time and leave it alone!

   b. Leave all math questions to the end of the exam. When its time to answer them, you can enter a "math frame of mind" and tackle one after the other. Doing so will also stimulate recall of the formulas needed to answer them correctly.

   c. Do not ignore a hunch. If you are deciding between two choices, and have followed this process exactly, you will likely have a hunch or an impulse to select one choice over the other. Know that everything you learned and studied is stored somewhere in your head. The impulse is that part of your brain "hollering at the top of its lungs" to select the correct choice. Call it wisdom, intuition, or your inner guide, it can help you in these moments.

   d. Create a flash card with the key points from this exam strategy and read it prior to every practice question. Here is an example:

How to pass a licensing exam... The NCI Associates, Ltd. way!

Copyright © 2020 by NCI Associates, Ltd. All rights reserved. For use by authorized purchasers of this textbook only. Call NCI for purchase information 586-247-9800.

1. **Read the entire question.** (Don't stop to think!)
2. **Identify the objective of the question.** (What am I solving for?)
3. **Read all four choices.** (Don't consider any one until all have been read!)
   – If one is obvious, take it. Go to next question.
   – Eliminate obvious wrong choices.
4. **Repeat steps 1 through 3.** (Only focus on the remaining choices!)
   – Treat as a T – F question.
5. **Note if question is a 1T – 3F or 1F – 3T option.**

INFLUENCES THAT CAN AFFECT SUCCESS

Although life can be simple, our interpretations of the experiences we encounter can make life appear to be a struggle. For many individuals, these interpretations are based on the false idea that we are all victims of our circumstances. It is important to note that this idea stems from a chosen belief rather than reality. The good news is that you have the power to change your beliefs.

If you want to pass the real estate exam, choose a belief that says, "I will pass!" Then adopt the habits and behaviors that support this goal. The even better news is that the exact same process can be used to become a successful and financially-secure real estate professional.

EXAM SUCCESS KEY 3: Create a "model" for success.

To become successful at something, simply duplicate what other successful people have already done. Identify their behaviors, their habits, and their beliefs. This process is called modeling. The core of modeling is the replication of excellence. To model a skill such as passing an exam, learn "what" other successful students have studied–which identifies the behaviors. Learn "how" they studied–which represents the habits. Then identify what "motivated" them to study on a regular basis–which shows their beliefs.

This textbook simplifies the "what to study" part of the model. The "how to study" part is covered in the section titled "SIX CRITICAL STEPS FOR PASSING THE STATE EXAM." As far as "why it is important to study," only you can determine that for yourself. One suggestion is to make a list of every reason you are obtaining your real estate license. Include everything, no matter how insignificant the reason may seem at the time. Do not judge your reasons. Once you have completed this list, rank the items in decreasing order of priority with your most compelling reason at the top. If you have taken the time to do this properly, you should end up with a list of your personal beliefs and values in life. This powerful exercise can be used anytime you need to re-energize yourself.

One thing is certain–successful students have formed the clearest mental pictures and feelings as to what they will experience when they pass the exam. They have visualized the experience of passing, including what it will be like seeing their "pass" results. They repeat this process daily until the experience is so ingrained in their minds, that they actually experience strong feelings of exhilaration. Know this for yourself: If one person has passed the exam using this process, you can too!

Managing distractions

Successful people also have another common thread that binds them to good outcomes; they effectively deal with anything that distracts them from their goals. The best laid plans for success are often subject to temporary derailments such as the following:

1. **Outer Influences**: Friends, co-workers, acquaintances, or family members can become jealous of your goals and subtly seek to undermine what you are doing by casting doubts. Even those who love and support you may unwittingly pull you off your path.

2. **Inner Influences**: We all have multiple "inner voices" that seem to pop-up from out of nowhere and cast doubts as to our capabilities. Sometimes they show up as "mental recordings" of negative affirmations that nag us incessantly. As everyone has experienced at one time or another, these "inner voices" can be powerful influences on our present state of emotion.

3. **Bad Habits**: Bad habits are old, worn-out, repetitive behaviors developed years, and in some cases decades, ago that no longer serve us, but seem to have total control over our present thoughts and actions. The amazing thing is that some of these habits may even have been "borrowed" from persons we observed long ago.

Regaining control

Fortunately, there are fairly simple techniques that can be employed to deal with each of the above distraction sources.

1. **Outer Influences**: When dealing with outer influences such as individuals who are not supportive, be polite, but gently and quietly move away. Do not take on the role of "fixer-upper" by pointing out how unhelpful their attitudes and behaviors are. Just remember... as they have the right to their opinion, so do you have the right to your privacy and freedom from their influences. Instead, focus your energy and attention on your dreams as a top-producing real estate professional. Seek strength from those who truly have your best interests in mind as well as your inner wisdom. The support you need is out there.

2. **Inner Influences**: Just as our psychological make up includes the inner voices of doubt, worry, and anxiety, so does it absolutely include wisdom, intuition, and intelligence. To confirm this, move within your own awareness and do the following: Every time a negative inner voice speaks up, sit quietly with your eyes closed, take a few slow, deep breaths, and as your mind clears, gently ask wisdom, intuition, and intelligence to assume control and describe your true reality. With practice and a firm willingness to let go, this inner guidance system will clearly show you the appropriate thought or action. Be ready as wisdom usually speaks in the whisper of a gentle thought or idea.

3. **Bad Habits**: A habit is a tendency or practice that is often difficult to discontinue. Interestingly, many of our habits are actually based on observations of those with whom we interacted at the earliest stages of life. Fortunately, habits can be changed by becoming aware of the decisions made in each moment of the present. To do this, make a conscious decision to change, and then couple the decision with a positive affirmation of the specific desired outcome. Repetition is the key to your freedom.

SUCCESS KEY 4: <u>Make the Decision to Succeed.</u>

Success on the state exam, like success in the real estate business, begins with a conscious decision. This textbook and program represent a new beginning for you. If you have demonstrated good study habits in the past with good results–continue them. If you have chosen in the past to de-focus yourself when studying, and were not pleased with the results, you get to start over with a clean slate. How many times have you lamented, "If I could only go back and do it over!" Well, now is your chance...

Make the Decision to Succeed and You Will.

PSI Content Outline

Connecting your textbook to the state exam.

If you purchased *Michigan Real Estate Law & Practice* to prepare for the Michigan Real Estate Salesperson's or Broker's examination, this section is designed with your success in mind. The information in this powerful textbook follows a logical progression through a typical real estate transaction. This helps with learning and retaining the information. The subjects tested on the state exam are listed in a separate Content Outline created by PSI which is located in the PSI "Candidate Information Bulletin."

The PSI Content Outline lists the exam topics under 16 headings. These headings are reproduced below along with the chapter (or chapters) in *Michigan Real Estate Law & Practice* in which the discussion is located. Each PSI exam topic is "flagged" in your textbook with the ▶ icon. As you read the textbook, this ▶ icon tells you to pay extra close attention. If you encounter the ▶ icon at the beginning of a topic discussion, make sure to thoroughly cover all subsections (and paragraphs) associated with that topic. It is also important to note that any and all subjects covered in this textbook, whether or not they are flagged with the ▶ icon, can appear on the state exam.

As you read, study, and review the information contained in *Michigan Real Estate Law & Practice*, make sure to adequately cover everything. When you encounter the ▶ icon, take a few extra moments to thoroughly absorb the information. Keep in mind that nobody can predict the specific questions or question topics that will appear on your exam. Therefore, studying everything in this textbook is a good practice. In many instances, surrounding paragraphs can significantly enhance your understanding of topics flagged with the ▶ icon.

Use *Michigan Real Estate Law & Practice* with confidence knowing that it is a well-rounded and up-to-date resource. Not only does it give you a full, comprehensive understanding of the real estate industry, it also sharpens your ability to successfully complete the state exam. This is an unbeatable combination!

(REAL ESTATE PRINCIPLES AND PRACTICES)

Property ownership
See icons ▶ Chapters 1, 4, 5, 6, 7, 10 and 13

Land use controls and regulations
See icons ▶ Chapters 5, 11, 15 and 21

Valuation and market analysis
See icons ▶ Chapter 4

Financing
See icons ▶ Chapters 16 and 17

General principles of agency
See icons ▶ Chapters 2 and 3

Property disclosures
See icons ▶ Chapters 2, 9, 10 and 21

Contracts
See icons ▶ Chapter 2, 3, 12 and 13

Leasing and Property Management
See icons ▶ Chapters

Transfer of Title
See icons ▶ Chapters 3, 5, 8, 9, 15 and 16

Practice of real estate
See icons ▶ Chapters 2, 3, 9, 12, 14 and 18

Real estate calculations
See icons ▶ Chapters 4, 5, 9, 16, 17 and 22

(MICHIGAN SPECIFIC PORTION)

Duties and Powers of the Department and State Board
See icons ▶ Chapter 19

Licensing Requirements
See icons ▶ Chapters 19 and 20

Statutory Reqs. Governing the Activities of Licenses
See icons ▶ Chapters 19 and 20

Contractual Relationships
See icons ▶ Chapters 19 and 20

Additional State Topics
See icons ▶ Chapters 18 and 21

Chapter 1
Introduction to Real Estate

Defining real estate from both a practitioner's and a layperson's perspective.

I. **Foreword**: All parties to a real estate transaction need a sufficient working knowledge of what the term "real property" means. In the case of real estate brokers and salespersons, an even higher professional degree of understanding of real property laws is required. This is due to the fact that today's educated buyer and seller frequently ask licensees to explain how the law defines and affects real estate. Although licensees cannot give legal advice, they are expected to provide guidance and general education on real estate matters. This chapter begins this process by exploring how real estate is precisely defined.

II. ▶ **Real estate defined**: Real estate consists of a number of component parts. It is especially important that the parties to a purchase agreement thoroughly understand what is being purchased and sold. This includes understanding the legal difference between real property and personal property. Many lawsuits have been initiated over what each party thought was included, or not included, in the sale. Licensees can help avoid some of these problems by educating the parties in advance.

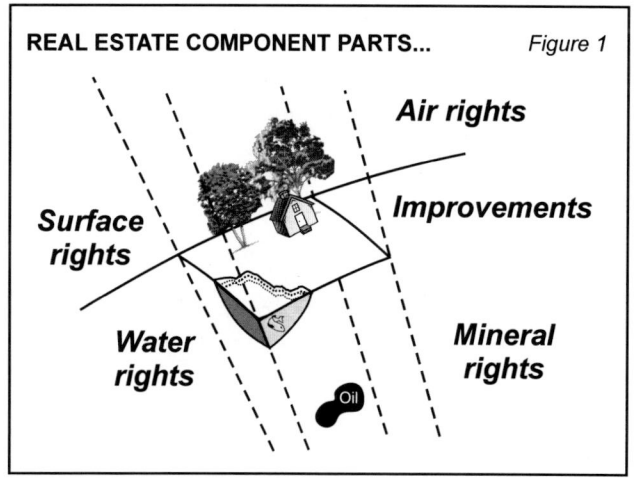

A. ▶ **Real estate components–land and improvements**: When real estate is sold, all component parts are deemed to be included in the sale unless stated otherwise in the purchase agreement or addenda. Accordingly, a seller can either withhold certain elements from a sale or sell them separately. See Figure 1.

1. **Land**: As a specific component part, land includes the immediate surface area, subsurface area, and air above to a reasonable distance. A buyer should determine the extent of the seller's interest in any sale property prior to submitting an offer to purchase rather than making assumptions as to what may or may not be included. This can be accomplished by asking questions, making careful pre-purchase observations, inspections, surveys, and possibly obtaining a preliminary title search.

   a. **Surface rights**: The surface rights to real estate include ownership and use of the actual surface area, the underlying soil, and any physical objects permanently attached by nature such as boulders, trees, and landscaping.

   b. ▶ **Mineral rights**: The owner of real estate is further entitled, at least theoretically, to the surface extending downward to the center of the earth including the rights to any minerals located therein. It is important for a buyer not to assume the mineral rights are automatically included. They may have been conveyed by a prior owner in the chain of title.

   c. ▶ **Air rights**: The air rights associated with land ownership are generally considered to be limited to a reasonable distance above the surface area rather than being unlimited. Air rights typically become an issue with (1) condominium developments, (2) high-rise buildings constructed over roads and railways in urban areas where a small portion of the land may be required for caissons, i.e., supports, and (3) for approach patterns next to airports.

   Air rights may also be the subject of easements such as an easement for air, light, and the right to a view. For example, an easement on a lakefront property prevents the erection of a structure beyond a certain height to prevent a back lot owner's view of a lake. A neighboring property owner may bring a cause of action for a nuisance or trespass when his air rights have been violated.

d. ▶ **Water-related property rights**: Most states in the eastern United States follow similar riparian rights laws that limit the right to use water and watercourses to those lands that actually border the body of water. Further, a waterfront owner's use must be reasonable and consistent with other owners' uses, subject to the public's right of navigation. The land owner generally owns the right to use the water without actually owning the water itself which is held in a public trust for all citizens.

(1) **Classification of lands associated with water**: Land that is associated with water-related rights are commonly classified as either riparian or littoral in nature. *See Figure 2.*

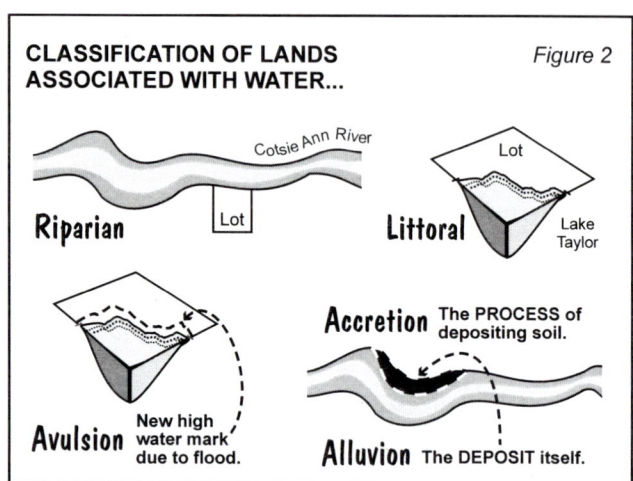

(a) **Riparian land**: Riparian land is that which is bounded by or touches a natural watercourse such as a river or stream. To qualify, the land must actually contact the water in some respect. The term riparian is sometimes applied generally to all types of water whether it is a lake, river, or ocean.

(b) **Littoral land:** Littoral land is a specific term referring to property that borders an ocean, sea, or one of the Great Lakes. It means of, related to, or situated on the shore of the sea or a major lake. For real estate exam purposes, you may be asked the difference between the terms riparian and littoral. If the question merely refers to water rights, then it may only use the term riparian.

(c) **Prior appropriation**: "Grandfathered" Prior appropriation is a legal form of water control that does not require the water to actually contact a landowner's property in order for rights to arise. It is based on a principle that water rights are unconnected to land ownership. Under the doctrine, the first person, i.e., the prior appropriator, to use water from a source for a beneficial use has the right to continue doing so. It is used primarily in the western United States where water scarcity is an issue.

(2) **Extent of rights**: As discussed earlier, riparian owners acquire the right to use the water without actually owning the water itself. As a general rule, water which is navigable is deemed to be owned by the state in a public trust. The right to use or enjoy something in which the person has no actual ownership is legally known as a usufruct.

(a) **Bottomland and high water mark**: A riparian owner typically owns to the center of an inland lake. Under common law, a littoral owner of property that borders a large body of water owns to what is known as the high water mark. This high water mark has historically been defined as the line to which water normally reached. As will be seen, the Michigan Supreme Court created a new term called the "ordinary high water mark."

i) **Historic use, control, and trespass issues**: Historically, the area from the high water mark down to the wet sand by the water's edge has been controlled by the state government with exclusive use granted to the littoral owner. The public only had a highly limited right of passage on the area between the wet sand into the water (since wet sand is part of the bottomland and the state government holds all bottomland in a public trust).

ii) **Shoreline boundary changes**: Shore, also known as beach, is the land located next to a body of water. Littoral owners gain new shore when water levels drop, but generally do not lose it when water levels rise.

iii) **Ordinary high water mark**: In 2005, the Michigan Supreme Court rejected the common law definition of high water mark in favor of a new one which expanded the public's right to use the upland beyond the water's edge. According to the Court, the ordinary high water mark is "the point on the bank or shore up to which the presence and action of the water is so continuous as to leave a distinct mark either by erosion, destruction of terrestrial vegetation, or other easily recognized characteristic." The Michigan Supreme Court definition further goes on to state that if the ordinary high water mark is impossible or difficult to ascertain in one location, reference can be made to the ordinary high water mark at another point of the bank or shore of the same lake or stream.

To summarize, the public is able to walk anywhere from the water, upland to the ordinary high-water mark without constituting a trespass. The public only has a right to walk across this area, but not to do anything else such as picnic, swim, camp, etc. Refer to Chapter 11 for additional information on water rights pertaining to wetlands and shorelands protection.

(3) **Changes to land resulting from the motion of water**: As noted in the examples below, the washing motion of water can alter the actual boundaries of an owner's land.

(a) **Accretion of land**: Accretion is the process of gradual and imperceptible accumulation or buildup of land by natural causes. It can occur, for example, from the continual washing motion of water as may result with a river or large lake. It adds to the land that is already owned. There are two kinds of accretion; (1) alluvion and (2) dereliction.

　i) **Alluvion**: Technically speaking, alluvion is the name for the actual sand or soil that is deposited by the process of accretion. The terms accretion and alluvion are sometimes used or defined synonymously.

　ii) **Dereliction**: The process of gaining of land when a body of water shrinks below the usual water mark is referred to as dereliction. The actual land that is uncovered from the water receding is called a reliction. Dereliction and reliction are frequently used synonymously in practice.

(b) **Avulsion**: Avulsion is the sudden and perceptible loss of land from one parcel by the action of water; for example, from quick and unexpected flooding. The lost land is usually deposited on the parcel of another. It also refers to a sudden change in the course of a stream. Avulsion does not cause any legal change to original land boundary lines.

(c) **Erosion**: Erosion refers to the eroding or wearing away, usually of soil, often by the gradual running or washing away action of water. Various laws have been enacted to prevent soil erosion and resulting pollution of lakes and streams from sediment such as Part 91 of Michigan's Natural Resources and Environmental Protection Act (formerly known as the Soil Erosion and Sedimentation Control Act). This law is discussed later in Chapter 21.

2. ▶**Improvements**: An improvement is any item or group of items that is permanently attached to land or the buildings located thereon. The term improvements may also be used to refer to permanent land development structures such as streets, sidewalks, and sewers.

　a. ▶**Fixtures**: A fixture is one type of improvement. It is technically defined as an article of personal property that is attached to land or to a building so that it can legally be regarded as part of the real property. When real property is sold, the buyer not only assumes ownership of the land and buildings, but also all of the improvements unless they have been specifically excluded in the purchase agreement. Raw land itself is never considered to be a fixture.

(1) **Legal tests of a fixture**: Three common tests for determining whether an item is personal property or real property include the "intent of the party," the "method of annexation," and its "adaptation to the real estate." Any combination of these tests may be applied to determine whether an item is a fixture or personal property. Disputes often arise over items such as drapes, blinds, custom light fixtures, and wall-mounted flat screen television sets.

(a) **Intent of party annexing the object**: This test examines whether the intent of the person placing the item was to have it be removable or forever attached to the structure. For example, an outdoor wood deck or patio structure is intended to be a permanent structure and part of the real estate. By contrast, a standard refrigerator or washer and dryer are intended to be removable and are not fixtures.

(b) **Method of annexation**: This test examines the actual means of attachment. For example, an expensive dining room light fixture which is directly wired into a ceiling junction box is deemed permanent and part of the real estate while a plug-in floor lamp is not. Consequently, if the seller removes the light after the closing, leaving exposed wires dangling from an open ceiling junction box, a violation of the purchase agreement has occurred. The seller must return the fixture or provide a replacement fixture of like kind, price, and quality.

   i) **Will removal damage the real estate**: Another form of this test looks at whether a permanent bond has been created between the item and the real estate. If not, then it should be easily removable without causing sufficient structural damage to warrant leaving it as part of the real estate. For example, a special order refrigerator unit built into a custom basement bar will likely be deemed to be a fixture.

(c) **Adaptation to real estate**: This test examines whether the item has become so adapted to the real estate that it is being used as real property. For example, a central furnace is a fixture as compared to a portable space heater which is not.

(2) **Other fixture examples**: Other common examples of fixtures include curtain and drapery rods, blinds and other wall-mounted shades, wall-to-wall (also known as attached or tacked down) carpeting, plumbing fixtures, mechanical systems such as a central air conditioner, and elevator equipment in commercial buildings. Anything that does not meet the fixture tests is likely an item of personal property. For example, a professionally-installed direct vent gas fireplace heater is a fixture and must remain with the property. The owner may, however, take the decorative fireplace tool set sitting on the hearth next to the fireplace since it is personal property.

(3) **Facts, circumstances, and custom**: The question of what qualifies as a fixture is usually resolved by a judge or jury based upon the particular facts and circumstances of each case and the above-described tests as they may be applied. A fixture in one case might be deemed to be personal property in another. Some items, however, such as furnaces, are nearly always deemed to be fixtures.

(4) **Importance of a written agreement**: To avoid confusion and post-closing lawsuits, the parties to a purchase agreement should always address questionable items, in writing, during the negotiation and drafting phase of the purchase. As another option, the seller can remove any non-negotiable fixture prior to marketing the property for sale, and replace it with a suitable fixture of lesser value. This is often an appreciated recommendation by a savvy listing agent.

b. ▶ **Trade fixture**: A trade fixture is any article which is attached to a leased structure by a tenant and used to advance the tenant's trade or business for which the premises has been rented. Common examples include store shelving, display units, walk-in refrigerator units, bar and restaurant equipment, and bakery ovens.

   (1) **Treatment**: Even though a trade fixture meets the definition of a fixture, it is legally treated as the personal property of the tenant. A tenant can remove any trade fixtures before expiration of his lease providing the removal process does not damage or impair the property in any way.

3. ▶ **Personal property compared to fixtures**: As compared to real property, personal property refers to those items which are movable such as furniture and other non-attached items. The terms personalty and chattel are also used when referring to personal property.

   a. **Conversion of one form of property to another**: One form of property can be converted to another form. For example, a growing tree (which qualifies as real estate due to its attachment to the ground) can be severed (i.e., cut from the land) thereby becoming personal property. Once a purchase agreement is executed, however, property cannot be converted without the (mutual) consent of all parties.

   b. **Bill of sale**: A bill of sale is a specific document that is used to transfer ownership of personal property items from the seller to the buyer. It accompanies the deed to the real property at the closing of a real estate transaction. Buyers and sellers sometimes negotiate various items of personal property in their real property transaction. If, for example, a buyer cannot encourage a seller to lower his sale price, the buyer may ask the seller to include the kitchen and laundry appliances.

B. **Characteristics of real estate**: Real estate has certain characteristics that add to its allure for the public. These characteristics help create a sense of uniqueness for real property. This is an important reason why real estate traditionally maintains its value long-term. Even factoring in the significant shift in sale prices resulting from

Chapter 1: Introduction to Real Estate   11

the mortgage meltdown of the 2000s, property values eventually recover over time. Real estate has both physical and economic characteristics.

1. ▶ **Physical characteristics**: The physical characteristics of real estate include heterogeneity, immobility, and indestructibility.

    a. **Heterogeneity**: Real estate is heterogeneous in nature. According to the concept of heterogeneity, all property is different with no two parcels being identical. By definition, heterogeneity refers to a state or condition of dissimilarity. Heterogeneity also positively affects the value of real estate because people tend to be drawn to properties that have a unique look and appeal.

        (1) **Homogeneous**: Homogeneity, also referred to as homogeneous, means same or similar. It is the opposite of heterogeneous. Properties in a common subdivision may appear to the eye to be somewhat homogeneous. Even if the exact same set of prints was used by a builder to construct an entire subdivision, each property would still have a separate and unique geographic location, address, and parcel identification number. This is why real estate is ultimately considered to be heterogeneous.

    b. **Immobility**: Immobility refers to the fact that the geographic location of land is fixed and stationary. The fact that real estate is immobile also contributes to its stability as an asset.

    c. **Indestructibility**: Land is also considered to be indestructible. While a building or its fixtures may be removed or destroyed, the raw land itself is indestructible. This is another characteristic that leads to the strength of real estate as an asset.

2. ▶ **Economic characteristics**: The value of real estate is impacted by a set of economic characteristics. They include conformity, regression and progression, highest and best use, situs, stability of investment, substitution, supply and demand, and scarcity. Refer to Chapter 4 for an explanation of these important characteristics.

C. ▶ **Types of real estate**: As noted in the examples below, parcels of real estate tend to be differentiated based on their specific uses. These uses can also be affected differently by real estate laws, rules, regulatory agency determinations, and court cases. As you study the balance of the chapters in this textbook, notice how the law often applies different standards to different property types.

1. **Residential**: The term residential relates to that property which is used to fulfill housing needs. Residential can be single- or multi-family in nature as with detached single-family homes, apartment buildings, and condominium and cooperative developments.

2. **Commercial**: Commercial property is that which is owned specifically for its income-producing ability; for example, office buildings, shopping or strip centers, and parking structures.

3. **Industrial**: Industrial property is similar to commercial property by definition, but is more closely related to manufacturing production enterprises; for example, factories, plants, industrial parks and districts, and warehouses.

4. **Agricultural**: Agricultural property commonly refers to farm and farm-related land; for example, various types of farms, ranches, timber farms, and orchard lands.

5. **Special purpose property**: In general terms, special purpose property includes churches and other places of worship, parks and recreation-use areas, day care centers, schools, cemeteries, and any other municipal or government-owned land.

6. **Manufactured housing generally**: Applying a broad definition, manufactured housing encompasses different types of production-built structures that are constructed at an off-site factory and then transported to a destination site or lot for final assembly. The term may include manufactured homes (formerly known as mobile homes), modular homes, and panelized construction.

    a. **Manufactured (mobile) homes specifically**: As a type of housing, a manufactured home is a structure, transportable in one or more sections, which is built on a chassis and designed to be used as a dwelling with or without permanent foundation, when connected to the required utilities (at the destination), and includes the plumbing, heating, air-conditioning, and electrical systems contained in the structure. A manufactured home may be constructed in one or more sections in a factory on a permanent steel undercarriage (consisting of a chassis assembly with wheels, braking system, and towing hitch), and then delivered to a private site or manufactured home community (formerly called a mobile home park). The steel undercarriage on a manufactured home is an actual structural component and, therefore, not typically removed.

- (1) **Federal construction standards**: As of 1976, the Department of Housing and Urban Development (HUD) is responsible for the regulation of manufactured housing construction. Manufactured homes are readily identifiable because they must have a red aluminum plate known as a "HUD Label" permanently attached to it at the taillight end of each transportable section. Local inspectors are responsible for checking any destination work such as electric and sewer connections, leveling, tie-down, and skirting.
- (2) **State law**: In Michigan, the Mobile Home Commission Act (MHCA) governs the licensing of manufactured home retailers, communities, installers and servicers, warranties, and titling. Many manufactured homes are located in communities in which the homeowner obtains a lease to the land upon which the manufactured home is located.
- (3) **Modular home distinguished:** A modular home is constructed at an off-site factory in a manner similar to a manufactured home, with the key difference being that the undercarriage or frame is designed to be removed when the home is installed on a permanent foundation. Modular home construction must conform to the state and local building codes of the final destination.
- (4) **Panelized or prefabricated home distinguished:** Prefabricated homes are typically comprised of multiple components and/or sections which are prefabricated inside of an off-site factory and then shipped to the building site for final assembly. This form of construction is preferred by some larger builders because it is not as affected by weather stoppages, labor or materials shortages, or other common obstacles to site-built homes.

b. **Title to manufactured homes:** Ownership of a manufactured home is transferred via a Certificate of Manufactured Home Ownership (formerly, Certificate of Mobile Home Title) rather than a deed. In Michigan, it is processed by the Secretary of State. When the owner sells the manufactured home, he indorses the back of the certificate of manufactured home ownership and gives it to the buyer, who then delivers it to the Secretary of State along with a specific application for issuance of a new certificate.

- (1) **Sales and use tax:** Sales tax is paid on the selling price of a manufactured home when purchased through a licensed retailer. In the case of a private sale of a previously-owned manufactured home, a use tax is paid instead of a sales tax.

c. **Manufactured homes as real property:** A buyer may permanently attach his manufactured home to a foundation on land in which he has an ownership interest. The wheels, towing hitch, and transportation running gear are permanently removed. After attaching the unit, the owner delivers an Affidavit of Affixture (along with the certificate of manufactured home ownership) to the Secretary of State. A copy of the affidavit is delivered to the local register of deeds for recording. If the owner subsequently detaches the unit, an Affidavit of Detachment is recorded and a new certificate of manufactured home ownership is issued.

d. **Manufactured home sales**: The sale of new manufactured homes is handled by a retailer licensed issued under the Mobile Home Commission Act. The sale of previously-owned manufactured homes can be handled by a licensed retailer who brokers the transaction for the owner. Private sales between owners and buyers are also permitted.

- (1) **Sale by a real estate licensee**: An owner may contract with a real estate broker to assist the owner of a manufactured housing unit which has been anchored to a permanent foundation on land in which the homeowner has an ownership interest.
- (2) **Attorney General Opinion**: A licensed real estate broker, or salesperson on behalf of his broker, may handle the sale of a manufactured home which is affixed to a permanent foundation, providing it is part of the sale of the real property on which the mobile home is situated. In such case, no additional MHCA license is needed. Any such agent must have a real estate license if the manufactured home is taxed as real property (unless it is directly sold by the owner on a for-sale-by-owner basis).

e. **Security interests in manufactured homes:** If the purchase of a manufactured home is financed, a security interest (which is similar to a mortgage-lien) is created in the manufactured home. If it is not

Chapter 1: Introduction to Real Estate
13

permanently attached to the land, the security interest is perfected according to the MHCA which requires that the interest be noted on the actual title.

If an affidavit of affixture has been recorded (meaning that the home is permanently attached to the land), the security interest, typically a mortgage, attaches to the manufactured home and land and is recorded in a manner nearly identical to any other financed residential home.

D. **Basic construction types and materials**: A practicing real estate licensee should be familiar with basic construction types and materials. This knowledge allows the licensee to communicate more competently with sellers and buyers about subject properties. Further, listing licensees need this knowledge to complete multiple listing service, i.e. MLS, property data sheets. A data sheet is typically an online form that a licensee fills in after entering into a listing agreement with a seller. Once completed, the data sheet is available on the MLS website for exclusive viewing by other licensees who participate in the MLS.

1. **Property styles**: There a number of different construction styles to suit just about every need and taste. Some of the more common and popular styles are briefly defined in this section. While the choice of style is mostly a personal preference, some styles are better suited to particular functions. To assist with learning what these styles look like, you can conduct an online search and see pictorial representations of each one. As used in this discussion, the word elevation refers to a drawing that shows the front, rear, and sometimes the side of the home.

    a. **One-story styles**: The one-story design is the most common construction style. An advantage of a one-story home is its efficient design since everything is on a common floor with no wasted space for upper-level staircases and extra bathrooms. Other advantages include lower heating and cooling costs, safety for exiting the home in the event of a fire, and ease of navigation for elderly family members or those with a disability. The most prevalent one-story design is known as a ranch.

        (1) **Ranch**: A ranch home is a popular choice for first-time buyers, buyers with smaller families, and empty-nesters, i.e., those families whose children are grown and have moved out of the home. Ranch styles are characterized by rectangular, simple plans, cost-effective construction, and low-pitched roofs.

    b. **One and a half story styles**: One and a half story (1½ story) styles include the bungalow and cape cod to name a few. Today, there are so many style variations that it is often difficult to tell the difference between one specific style and the next. A quick online search will evidence this point. The definitions in this section are merely provided to show the basic features of each style.

        (1) **Bungalow**: A bungalow is a residential structure with, possibly, a smaller finished living area such as a bedroom constructed in the roof or attic space. Bungalow designs can be single story or 1½ story with an upper-area living space. A 1½ story bungalow can be identified by a dormer window that is set in the roof. A traditional bungalow is also characterized by a large front porch that is supported by heavy columns. Floor plans are open and simple. The bungalow, also known as the American Craftsman, was a popular style in the early 1900s and remains a viable option today.

        (2) **Cape cod**: A cape cod house is close in design and function to the bungalow, but usually with smaller, distinct rooms versus the more open floor plan of a bungalow. Cape cod design options tend to be symmetrical and include one or 1½ stories with a steep roof and a small overhang in the front. A cape cod lacks the larger, fuller porch of a bungalow. Dormer windows in a cape cod style home may interrupt the roof space to light an upper story bedroom. Many cottages are cape cod-style dwellings.

    c. **Multistory styles**: Multistory styles are designed to maximize square footage by "stacking" two stories over a common foundation and under a common roof. This is why two-story construction tends to be less expensive to build per square foot as compared to a one-story home. Two-story homes are also better suited for use on smaller lots.

        (1) **Colonial**: A colonial home plan is one of the most common two-story home style. It features a rectangular, often symmetrical, front elevation. A colonial may contain two or three stories and a gable roof. A gable roof is one consisting of a single, continuous roof ridge at the top of a steeper roof. The two sides of the roof then slope in opposite directions. The gable roof on a colonial often runs from one side of the house to the other rather than from front to back. A variation of the colonial-style home is the dutch colonial. This style uses a gambrel or barn-style roof, dutch doors, and a porch or entry way with a decorative hood.

(2) **Split level**: Split level homes represent a variation of the traditional multi-story home that became popular in the 1950s to 1960s. They include the bi-level, tri-level or triplex, and quad-level or quadraplex home designs. The intention of a split-level design is to create separate, yet smaller, floor levels of interior space that serve distinct functions. With a typical split-level plan, half of the house looks from the front like a traditional ranch (with or without a basement beneath it) and the other half looks like a two-story home that is sunk into the ground at mid-height. While split-level styles offer interesting design potential, they are often shunned by buyers who do not like the multiple half-height stair cases which are necessary to navigate from one level to the next.

d. **Other styles**: Along with manufactured housing which is discussed previously in this chapter, other common styles include contemporary and log home designs.

(1) **Contemporary**: This home style has been around since the 1940s and features both one story and split-level designs that have clean, angular lines, and minimal decorative elements. Home shapes are often irregular and unconventional. Contemporary homes often include sweeping or flat roof lines along with multiple, over-sized windows. Interior space is comprised of large, open room designs.

(2) **Log home**: Log homes represent one of the earliest styles that existed in this country. They utilized the plentiful, indigenous trees in the region in which they were built. While present-day log homes are often romanticized versions of their earlier counterparts, the thermal mass of natural wood provides excellent insulating qualities and heat retention. Elevations of log homes generally accentuate the rustic appeal of the building material.

2. **Foundations and basements**: Since all structures constructed on land settle over time, a foundation is necessary to evenly distribute the weight of the home to the raw ground beneath it in such a manner that settling is minimized with no negative impact on the structural integrity of the structure. Just about all foundation types, whether a basement is included or not, rest on what are known at footings. A footing is a trenched area around the perimeter of the structure that is filled with concrete. The foundation walls will eventually rest on the footings to evenly distribute the weight of the structure to the bottom of the trenched soil.

a. **Slab-on-grade construction**: Slab-on-grade is the least expensive type of foundation since there is no basement or crawl space. Footings only need to extend to a depth below the frost line for the area. A concrete slab is then poured directly on a bed of crushed stone that extends to the footings. The structure is built on the dried concrete slab. Slab-on-grade construction is common with commercial buildings and residential structures in which a basement is not required. If a crawl-space or full basement is desired, another type of foundation will be necessary.

b. **Crawl-space foundation versus basement foundation**: Rather than constructing a full basement, a structure can be built on what is known as a crawl-space. The process used to construct a crawl-space is nearly identical to the process of constructing a foundation with a full basement. The only difference is that the crawl-space below the main floor is minimal, often 18 inches in height. A crawl-space design also saves money compared to a basement since fewer building materials and less labor are required.

Crawl-space construction allows for greater design flexibility compared to slab-on-grade construction because heat ducts and plumbing and electrical lines can be run beneath the main floor. It also allows floors to be insulated and provides extra storage space if desired. If a full basement is desired, however, additional considerations come into play, such as what type of foundation walls to construct.

There are several basement options available in Michigan. The term "full basement" refers to a basement that has the same square footage as the main floor. The term "common basement" generally refers to a shared basement such as may be found in a multi-unit condominium building. In other words, the basement is a common element to be legally and physically shared with other condominium unit owners. Other condominium units may have a private, separately-walled full basement.

c. **Block foundation**: For years, concrete block was the preferred method used to construct basement walls. The hollow blocks are masonry in nature and manufactured using a mixture of cement and aggregates such as fine stone and sand. The first course of blocks rests on the concrete footings previously installed. Each succeeding course of blocks is laid upon the last and bonded with mortar. The mortar is a mixture of cement, lime, and sand that must be strong enough to withstand the ordinary pressures exerted on foundation walls.

c. **Poured wall foundation**: A poured wall foundation is constructed on site after the footings are laid. Instead of courses of concrete blocks, the wall is constructed of wet concrete that is poured into temporary wall forms. These wall forms are often composed of plywood panels or sheathing that are installed on the footings and braced from the outside. Metal tie rods are also used to hold the forms together during the curing process.

d. **Permanent wood foundation**: Permanent wood foundations represent another foundation option. Lumber and wood sheathing or panels are used instead of concrete. All wood used in this foundation is pressure-treated to resist fungus, rot, and insect damage. The outside of the walls are protected with waterproofing and a barrier of polyethylene film which is a thicker sheet of plastic-like material. Many builders like wood foundations because the walls can be fully insulated thereby creating a more comfortable living environment.

3. **Types of framing**: Depending on the length or width of the structure, steel beams and supporting posts are installed as part of the foundation to support the house itself. Once the foundation is in place, the structure is built on it. There are a few framing options available to builders including platform framing, balloon framing, and post-and-beam framing. A simple online search of these framing types will provide illustrations to aid in understanding their differences.

    The actual architectural drawings used to construct the structure will specify which type of framing is to be used. This decision is based on factors such as the house style as well as other conditions including whether the home is constructed in a cold-weather climate in which the house may have to bear the weight of heavy snows on the roof. Homes may also need to be resistant to high winds or seismic activity.

    a. **Platform framing**: Platform framing is the most common form used in residential construction. In platform framing, the first story is constructed as a separate platform that rests on top of the foundation. If the structure has a second story, it will rest as a platform on the first story. The process of platform framing typically begins once the foundation has been constructed. A wood sill is anchored to the top of the foundation wall.

        Horizontal floor joists are then installed by resting them on the sills and beams to form the support for the floors. Plywood sheathing is installed on top of the floor joists to create the actual base of the floors. Exterior and interior walls are constructed using vertical wall studs and bracing. Wood is the most common building material used in residential applications and steel framing members are commonly used in commercial buildings.

    b. **Balloon framing**: In a two-story structure with balloon framing, the vertical wall studs run continuously from the foundation sill of the lower floor to the top of the upper story wall or rafter plate (rather than as separate platforms). Balloon framing results in a home with less weight and, arguably, less structural integrity. It is no longer used today due to how quickly fire can spread from one floor to the next through the outside walls. Heat retention is another potential problem with balloon framing.

    c. **Post-and-beam framing**: Post-and-beam framing is an older framing method that relies on heavy timbers as opposed to normal framing members such as 2" × 4" dimension lumber. Since the framing members are larger and stronger, fewer building materials may be necessary. This also allows for higher ceilings with exposed beams and more design flexibility. Post-and-beam construction would be more likely used in larger, more expensive homes.

4. **Exterior wall finishes**: Exterior finish refers to any building material that is used to enclose and, ultimately, protect the structure. The choice of materials is important from both structural and aesthetic perspectives. Structurally, the exterior finish protects the interior living areas from the elements. Aesthetically, the choice of finish helps to establish the curb-appeal of the structure. The term curb-appeal refers to the attractiveness of the exterior of the home.

    There are many different types of exterior wall finishes available to a builder and his clients. The choice of which one to use varies by things such as design preference, local climate, and budget. Here is a partial list:
    - Brick, stone, and other masonry veneer.
    - Horizontal aluminum or vinyl siding.
    - Wood or plywood siding.
    - Cedar shingles and shake panels.
    - Stucco and synthetic stucco (which is also known as exterior insulation and finish systems or EIFS).

III. **Real estate law**: There are many different sources of law that affect real estate ownership, sales, transfers of title, leasing, financing, and construction.

   A. **Law defined**: A law is any body of rules of action or conduct which are handed down from some controlling authority, such as a legislature, to have binding effect. Such laws are enacted pursuant to the police power of the state government. The subject of police power is discussed further in Chapter 15.

   1. **Sources of law**: Common sources of laws include statutes and court decrees.

       a. **Statute**: A statute is a formal, written enactment of a state or federal legislative body. A statute is also known as an Act. Statutes are the primary laws by which society regulates its conduct.

       b. **Common law**: Common law is that body of law stemming from judicial decisions such as judgments and court decrees. In a constitutional sense, a legislature creates the law and the courts interpret the law. In the absence of a specific controlling statute, a higher or appellate court's decision is deemed to create binding precedent.

       c. **Administrative law**: Administrative law is the body of law that agencies, such as licensing departments, use to carry out their regulatory functions. An administrative agency is a governmental body charged with implementing a specific statute; e.g., Michigan's Department of Licensing and Regulatory Affairs.

IV. **Professional affiliations**: Trade associations are the primary conduit through which professionals affiliate with one another. Membership in such a professional organization is always voluntary. In other words, it is not automatic upon obtaining a license nor can it be mandated by law. Even though membership is voluntary, a broker-member is generally assessed a membership fee based upon the number of licensees affiliated with his firm. As a result, the broker-member may require his salespersons and associate brokers who work for him to join the association. This is actually a good practice, since members of the National Association of Realtors®, for example, must agree to abide by a code of ethics.

   A. **National Association of Realtors® (NAR)**: NAR is the best-known real estate professional organization. Dedicated to the preservation of private property ownership, it is also the world's largest trade-based association. Membership is divided into state and local Realtor® associations which may also be called Realtor® Boards. Michigan's important state association is known as the Michigan Realtors® (formerly the Michigan Association of Realtors®). According to its website, "Michigan Realtors® is an integrated advocacy and communications force for the real estate professionals of our State."

   1. **Realtor®**: The term Realtor® is a trademark-protected mark used specifically to refer to a member of the National Association of Realtors®. Consequently, only members of NAR may use the term in the course of business. As noted, Realtors® are bound to a comprehensive Code of Ethics.

   2. **Trademark**: A trademark is a mark consisting of a word, symbol, or graphic depiction through which the owner of the mark differentiates his products (or services in the case of a registered service mark) from those of others. The mark must be truly distinctive and used in commerce to obtain federal registration protection. See also, "Copyright considerations" in Chapter 2.

   3. **Code of Ethics**: A code of ethics is a body of self-imposed regulations and ethical standards of conduct which are imposed upon the members of a group such as an association (in addition to applicable state statutes and common law). NAR's Code of Ethics is designed to eliminate trade practices that may damage the public or bring dishonor to the real estate profession through the use of questionable practices.

   B. **National Association of Real Estate Brokers (NAREB)**: NAREB is the nation's oldest minority-owned real estate professional association. According to the NAREB website, it was formed in 1947 by African American real estate professionals out of the need to secure the right to equal housing opportunities regardless of race, creed, or color. For more than 60 years, NAREB has participated in meaningful legal challenges and has supported legislative initiatives that ensure the availability of fair and affordable housing for all Americans.

   1. **Realtist®**: NAREB uses the Realtist® membership mark to refer to its active members. Real estate licensees who use this mark distinguish themselves as members of this important and respected association.

   C. **Ethical considerations for licensees who are not members of an association**: At one time or another in their careers, all real estate licensees are confronted with situations that require the application of integrity and ethical principles. Today's buyers and sellers are more knowledgeable and sophisticated than ever before. They recognize, and are no longer willing to accept, unprofessional behaviors from their real estate professionals. Licensees who are not bound to an association's code of ethics, should still aspire to offer a level of professional service that exceeds the minimal standards set by license laws and rules.

DIAGNOSTIC PRACTICE QUESTIONS – CHAPTER 1

IMPORTANT STUDY TIP!

Step 1: Carefully review the information located in this chapter.

Step 2: Take the following Diagnostic Practice Questions. Review any question you answered incorrectly by researching the topic in this textbook. If you are still uncertain as to why the question is answered as it is, consult your program provider.

NOTE ON CHAPTER PRACTICE QUESTIONS

The following questions are representative of the type encountered on the Michigan real estate licensing examination. While some of these questions may be similar in nature and style, there is no way of predicting the exact wording of a question that will appear on the exam. Spending time memorizing these questions is, therefore, not recommended.

These questions are designed to help you determine how well you comprehend the material in this chapter. They are also intended to help you develop problem solving skills and to become comfortable with question formats.

Do not attempt to answer these questions until you have attended the lecture corresponding to this chapter and spent the appropriate time studying the material.

1. Lydia Landowner has a 10 acre parcel of land that she wishes to sell to Barry. The mineral rights to the parcel had been previously transferred by Lydia to Mega Oil Company for a substantial sum. The back 4 acres of her parcel were undeveloped and had recently been declared a wetlands by the local municipality. Which of the following statements applies to Lydia's transfer of her 10 acre parcel to Barry?
   A. Mining operations must cease upon sale of the property due to the wetlands restriction. As a result, Barry must pay Mega Oil for lost profits.
   B. Barry cannot build upon the area designated as a wetlands but is entitled to use the remaining 6 acres in any lawful manner.
   C. The mineral rights and wetlands restrictions only apply while Lydia is the owner and does not apply to any subsequent buyer such as Barry.
   D. Since Barry was not a party to the transfer of mineral rights to Mega Oil, the mineral rights revert back to Barry at the closing.

2. Buyer Able purchases property with lake frontage on one of the Great Lakes. Which of the following statements best describes the extent of Able's ownership?
   A. Since the body of water is subject to prior appropriation, ownership of any adjacent land is controlled by the state rather than Able.
   B. Able owns the water and bottom land out to a distance of 100 feet.
   C. Able may use the shoreline for his personal enjoyment.
   D. Able has no rights whatsoever with respect to the water since the lake is over 5 acres in size.

3. Lots "A" and "B" share a common border. An old tree growing on lot "A" has branches which extend over a portion of lot "B" including "B's" garage and driveway. "B," who recently moved into the neighborhood, notices that sticky sap has begun to drop from the tree onto his new sports car. Which of the following statements best applies to this situation?
   A. If "A" ignores "B's" requests to correct the problem, "B" may carefully trim the tree back to the property line since "B's" air rights have been violated.
   B. "B" must first request that the city attorney file a lawsuit in district court.
   C. "A" must destroy the tree since it constitutes a nuisance and violation of air rights.
   D. There is nothing "B" can do. He was aware of the existence of the tree when he purchased the property and, therefore, assumed the risk of falling sap.

4. Salesperson Johnson is showing another broker's listing to Buyer Karsen. Johnson was not aware that the Seller was planning on removing a large crystal ceiling chandelier in the dining room when he moved. Karsen purchased the property, and after taking possession 30 days later, found a replacement bulb screwed into a plastic socket instead of the chandelier. Karsen called Johnson and demanded that the original chandelier be replaced immediately or she would take legal action. Which of the following statements

is true?
- A. As long as the Seller installed the chandelier himself with the intent that it be removed if he ever moved, there is nothing that Karsen can do.
- B. Karsen is entitled to the value of the chandelier from salesperson Johnson. Since Johnson was working directly with Karsen, it was his responsibility alone to determine the Seller's intent with respect to the chandelier.
- C. Under the doctrine of "buyer beware," Karsen has no recourse since it was her responsibility to ask about the chandelier which she failed to do.
- D. Karsen is entitled to either the chandelier or its value from the Seller since she viewed the property and signed a purchase agreement with it in place.

5. A neighborhood is referred to as homogeneous by an appraiser. This means that the homes located within it are:
- A. Varied in architecture and style.
- B. Similar in value regardless of any differences in size.
- C. Multi-family dwellings which share certain characteristics.
- D. Similar in design and function.

6. Broker Tara is a broker-member of the National Association of Realtors®. Romeo is a newly licensed salesperson who begins working for Tara. Which of the following statements is true?
- A. A licensed salesperson must join a real estate trade association within 2 years of licensure.
- B. Romeo can be required to join the association by his broker as a condition of employment as an independent contractor.
- C. Romeo is automatically a member of the association as a result of being licensed in Michigan.
- D. Tara cannot require an affiliated licensee to join a trade association due to antitrust laws.

7. Which of the following statements is true regarding the sale by a licensed real estate salesperson of a manufactured home?
- A. The salesperson must be licensed under a broker who is also licensed as a manufactured home installer.
- B. A salesperson may only sell a home which has been built using panelized construction.
- C. The salesperson would first have to obtain an additional license under the Mobile Home Commission Act.
- D. The salesperson, through her broker, may assist the seller of a previously-owned unit which has been anchored to a permanent foundation.

8. All EXCEPT which of the following would be considered a generally recognized type of real estate?
- A. Commercial.
- B. Heterogeneous.
- C. Agricultural.
- D. Manufactured.

9. A person is walking along the shoreline of a lakefront owner's property. This would be considered a trespass under which of the circumstances?
- A. Only if the person stops to engage in any activity that constitutes loitering.
- B. If the person steps out of the water onto any area comprised of beach.
- C. If the person walks upland toward a dwelling beyond the discernible vegetation line.
- D. There is no trespass unless the person actually enters the lakefront owner's dwelling.

10. Tip Top Tyler Bakery is nearing the end of a 5 year commercial lease. Brianna, the bakery owner, is moving to a new location and wishes to take a floor-mounted oven with her. Which of the following statements is true?
- A. Brianna may take the oven even though it is anchored to the building because it qualifies as a trade fixture.
- B. Brianna is not able to take the oven because it was anchored to a part of the building owned by the landlord.
- C. By taking the oven, Brianna must compensate the landlord for the loss of the use of the building as a future bakery.
- D. Brianna may take the oven providing she replaces the entire floor in the leased premises.

11. Real estate includes an interest in all of the following types of property EXCEPT:
- A. Air rights above land.
- B. Tractors and farm equipment.
- C. Growing maple and elm trees.
- D. Barns and windmills.

12. An owner who is preparing to place his house on the market would like to take a special refrigeration unit that he purchased at the time of construction. The unit was built into a space cut out of the kitchen wall so that the refrigerator would be flush against the wall. All EXCEPT which of the following statements is true?
- A. The unit must be left with the property at the time of sale because it qualifies as a fixture.
- B. The intention of the seller at the time of installation was to have it become a permanent part of the house.
- C. The unit can be taken at the time of sale because refrigerators are personal property.
- D. The seller can exclude the unit in the purchase

Chapter 1: Introduction to Real Estate

agreement and remove it providing the wall is repaired.

13. A purchaser acquires a property through which a stream passes. What are the new owner's rights with respect to the stream?
    A. The owner can use the water for any purpose he desires since it passes directly through his property.
    B. If the owner has a legitimate irrigation need for his crops, he can dam the stream to divert the water flow.
    C. The owner can use the stream to carry unused pesticides away from this land.
    D. Although the owner does not own the water, he may use it for recreation purposes and may exclude others from coming ashore.

14. Two farms share a common border. Farmer A is a dairy farmer and raises cattle while Farmer B grows crops. Farmer B is out crop dusting one afternoon and takes a convenient short-cut over Farmer A's land to continue his dusting operation. The noise from the aircraft scares the cows who then stop giving milk. What are the rights of the parties?
    A. Farmer A has no rights since the air is held by the state under a public trust.
    B. Farmer A can sue Farmer B for a trespass due to a violation of Farmer A's reasonable air rights.
    C. Farmer B was within his rights since his use of the air was reasonable under the circumstances.
    D. Farmer A can take no action because he failed to give prior notice of his intent to assert air rights.

15. The definition of land naturally includes which of the following?
    A. The rights to any precious metals that may be in the ground.
    B. Unlimited rights to any water that may touch the land.
    C. Trade fixtures.
    D. Accretion rights to adjoining properties.

16. An owner leases a commercial unit in a shopping mall to a tenant. The tenant purchased several display units which he then installed in the building by anchoring them to the floor. Two large refrigeration units were also purchased and then installed against the back wall. Upon expiration of the lease, which of the following statements applies?
    A. The refrigeration units can be taken, however, the display units must remain since they were anchored to the floor.
    B. Regardless of how long the units remain in place after expiration, the tenant will always be able to assert his ownership to the units.
    C. Providing the display units can be safely removed, the tenant can do so. However, the refrigeration units will revert to the landlord due to the electrical connection that was necessary at the time of installation.
    D. All units can be removed providing no structural damage occurs during the process. *Trade Fixtures*

17. A builder constructs several homes in a neighborhood which are all similar in size and architecture. The character of these homes can best be described as:
    A. Unsalable.
    B. Homogeneous.
    C. Immobile.
    D. Heterogeneous.

18. Which of the following documents is delivered to the Secretary of State when a mobile (manufactured) home is attached to a foundation on land?
    A. Warranty Deed.
    B. Affidavit of Removal.
    C. Certificate of Attachment.
    D. Affidavit of Affixture.

19. A seller and a buyer execute a purchase agreement that does not mention a shed built by the seller to contain his lawn equipment. The shed is constructed on a concrete slab poured for the purpose of anchoring the shed. Which of the following statements best describes what will occur at the time of closing?
    A. The seller may take the lawn equipment and the shed because they both qualify as personal property.
    B. The seller may take the lawn equipment since it qualifies as personalty but must leave the shed because it qualifies as real property.
    C. The seller may take the lawn equipment but must remove the shed since it was not originally part of the property.
    D. The seller must leave the shed and lawn equipment since he neglected to reserve any rights to either in the purchase agreement.

20. A bill of sale is accurately described as:
    A. A document which is used to transfer title to personalty.
    B. A document used by a purchaser to acquire title to unattached buildings.
    C. The documents used by a title company for preparation of the closing statement.
    D. The document that sets forth the terms of sale of personal property in a real property transaction.

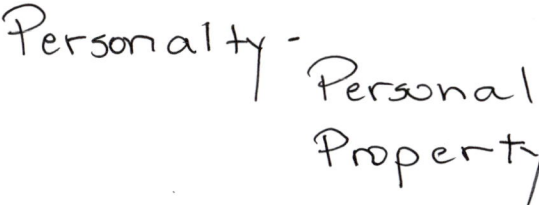
Personalty — Personal Property

*"Imagination" means image-in-action. Put your dreams into action
and watch them magically appear in your life.*

Chapter 2
Brokerage Concepts

Understanding agency relationships.

I. **Foreword**: The law of agency has undergone a number of important changes over the years. From the addition of mandatory agency disclosure, buyer's agency, and transaction coordinator status in 1993, to the passage of statutory fiduciary duties and limited service agency in 2008, Michigan agency law has helped licensees deliver contemporary real estate services to their clients. The agency relationship is one of the most important legal connections that a licensee can establish with a buyer or seller. Understanding the nature of agency relationships is the focus of this chapter. A copy of Michigan's agency disclosure statement titled, "Disclosure Regarding Real Estate Agency Relationships," is located in the Appendix at the back of this textbook. It may be helpful to refer to this form when learning about disclosure requirements discussed in this chapter.

    A. ▶ **Scope of advice must be properly limited**: While modern licensees provide a wide range of critical real estate services, they must take care not to provide advice outside the scope of their authorization under license law. For example, a licensee who provides legal advice may be found to have engaged in the unauthorized practice of law. A simple referral to a competent legal professional can avoid this problem.

        1. **Examples**: Licensees must refer questions on (1) tax consequences to a CPA or tax attorney, (2) legal matters to an attorney-at-law, (3) appraisal to an licensed appraiser, (4) home inspections to a home inspector, and (5) construction-related issues to a licensed builder.

        2. **Expanded need for policies**: Brokers and their management teams should consider expanding their company policies and procedures to cover what advice can be provided by their affiliated licensees. This is equally important as it pertains to errors and omissions insurance coverage.

    B. **Service provision agreement**: Listing agreement and buyer's agency agreement are common industry terms. In 2002, the Michigan legislature created a new term called "service provision agreement" to collectively refer to all types of agency agreements. Since the needs of sellers versus buyers can vary significantly, the phrases listing agreement and buyer's agency agreement will continue to be used in this textbook. Further, since a service provision agreement creates an agency relationship, it does not include any agreement or memorandum that creates a transaction coordinator relationship. The concept of transaction coordinator is discussed further in Chapter 3.

        1. **Historical role–Represent sellers only**: Real estate licensees have historically earned their commissions by functioning exclusively as agents for sellers in the search for and negotiations with a buyer. Historically, all buyers were customers and had no agency relationship with any licensee.

        2. **Modern role–Represent sellers, buyers, or both**: Current real estate practices now include the individual representation of sellers or buyers as well as dual agency representation. Under buyer's agency, a broker enters into an agreement with a home buyer to exclusively represent him in the location of a suitable property. Other concepts and directions in agency law are discussed at the end of Chapter 3.

II. **Basic agency concepts**: An agency relationship exists between two persons when one of them (the agent) acts on behalf of, or represents, the other (the principal). It is actually a three-party relationship because the <u>principal</u> hires the <u>agent</u> to represent the principal's interests to <u>third parties</u>. In terms of a traditional listing agreement, the seller hires the broker to represent the seller's interest to potential buyers.

    A. ▶ **Creation of agency–authority**: The term authority refers to the granting of permission. In the context of an seller's agency relationship, a licensed real estate broker (acting as an agent) is granted authority (permission) by a seller (the client) under the terms of a listing agreement. This authority allows the broker to represent the seller's interests to third parties (buyers). The agency relationship is created via this authority.

B. **Parties to the agency relationship**: As noted, the primary parties to an agency relationship include the principal, agent, and third party. These terms will now be explained in greater detail. As the items in this section are studied, keep in mind that multiple terms may be used to refer to an individual. For example, a seller in a listing agreement might be called the client or the principal. Depending on the nature of the relationship, a buyer may be a principal, a client, or a customer.

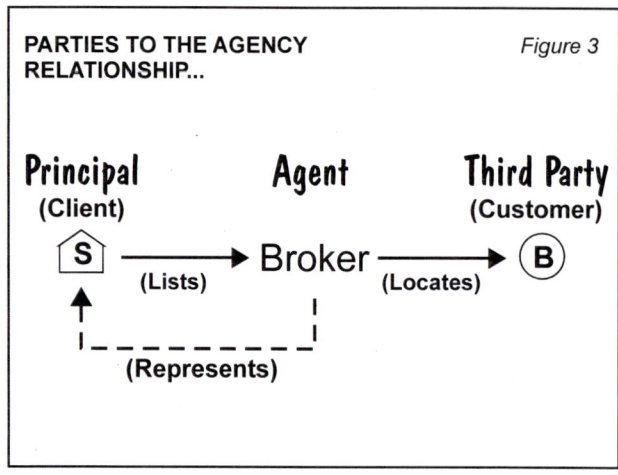

1. **Principal**: In a real estate transaction, the principal is the one who hires the agent. Historically, the principal was always the seller. Today, buyers routinely become a principal by hiring a buyer's broker to represent the buyer pursuant to a buyer's agency agreement. *See Figure 3.*

2. **Agent**: By definition, an agent is a person who is authorized by another (the principal) to act on the principal's behalf. The agent formally represents the principal pursuant to a written contract. Depending on who does the hiring, a broker can act as an agent for the seller under a listing agreement or the buyer under a buyer's representation agreement. As will be seen, a broker can also act as a dual agent.

   In the context of lease relationship, a landlord can hire a broker as an agent to locate a qualified tenant or a tenant can hire a broker to locate a suitable property to lease. It is important to note that the broker rather than the salesperson acts in the capacity of an agent for clients. As will be seen, a salesperson acts strictly in the capacity of an agent for his broker when dealing with consumers.

   a. **Types of agents**: There are many different types of agency relationships that can be created in the marketplace. Each one varies by the extent or amount of authority the agent is granted. Typically, the agent's employer (the principal) is the one who decides what level of authority is desired.

   (1) **Universal agent**: A universal agent is one who is empowered to conduct every lawful transaction that a principal can delegate, meaning to entrust to another, including the right to represent, negotiate, and sign contracts on behalf of his principal. A power of attorney is often used to create a universal agency.

   (a) ▶ **Power of attorney**: A power of attorney is a written instrument which is used to create a universal agency by appointing an attorney-in-fact to act as a universal agent. The agent is appointed to perform any number of specified acts which may include executing legal instruments on behalf of the principal. The principal delegates (i.e., transfers) the authority (i.e., permission) to the agent.

   (b) **Attorney-in-fact**: The formal name for the agent named in a power of attorney is attorney-in-fact. The attorney-in-fact acts for the granting party with the legal power to execute a contract on the granting party's behalf. This binds the granting party to the contract as if the granting party had personally signed it.

   i) **Not an attorney-at-law**: The terms attorney-in-fact and attorney-at-law are not synonymous. An attorney-at-law, i.e., lawyer, is a person who can officially engage in the practice of law. Real estate licensees must never engage in the practice of law. If a buyer or seller raises a legal question or issue, it must be referred to an attorney.

   ii) **Licensees should avoid acting as attorney-in-fact**: While it is not illegal for a real estate licensee to act as an attorney-in-fact on behalf of a client, issues can arise for the licensee should a contract problem later arise. It is generally best for licensees to focus on providing traditional real estate services and not add the responsibility of obligating the client to the very contract the licensee helped negotiate. Most brokers' policies specifically prohibit affiliated licensees from accepting a power of attorney and executing a document such as a purchase agreement on the client's behalf.

   (2) **General agent**: A general agent is given, i.e., authorized with, broad negotiating power to act for his principal in all matters concerning a particular business venture. Some property managers act

as general agents when fulfilling their duties. A property manager is typically given broader powers to negotiate and execute leases with tenants along with the power to negotiate and execute agreements with contractors for the maintenance and improvement of the landlord-client's property.

  (3) **Special agent**: A special agent is employed to conduct a single transaction or a series of transactions that, once completed, cause the agency to end. A real estate broker is an example of a special agent. The reference to a "series of transactions" could arise in the context of a master listing that a real estate broker has with a lender-client who lists all of its bank-owned properties within a geographic area for sale through the broker.

    (a) **Limited authority**: A special agent has the most limited authority of any agent type. A broker typically acts as a special agent pursuant to a service provision agreement and cannot do any more than what has been authorized in the listing agreement or buyer's agency contract.

    (b) **Real estate broker as special agent**: The authority that a seller-client grants to a broker via a listing agreement is usually confined to holding out the seller's price and terms to buyers and presenting all offers to the seller. The broker is not authorized to actually negotiate any price and terms for the seller other than what is specified in the listing agreement. Similarly, a buyer-client authorizes a broker to locate a suitable purchase property. In neither case is the broker-agent authorized to bind his client to a purchase agreement through a power of attorney.

3. ▶ **Third party**: The third party is considered to be a stranger to the relationship created between the principal and agent through the listing agreement or buyer's agency contract. Under a seller's agency, the third party is typically the buyer-customer. With a buyer's agency, the third party could be a seller-customer who is marketing his home on a for-sale-by-owner basis.

4. **Customer or client**: Customer and client are common labels used to refer to the parties to a real estate sales transaction. It is important to understand the meaning of and difference between each.

    a. ▶ **Customer–non-agency relationship**: A customer is any non-represented party. At the onset of an agency relationship, and before entering into a representation agreement, the status of any seller or buyer is that of a customer. A customer is not considered to have an agency relationship with a broker. Therefore, there are no agency-level duties such as disclosure owed to a customer. License law does require licensees to be honest to everyone.

       Example: A broker is aware of a proposed municipal trash landfill to be created approximately one mile away from a residential home in which a buyer-customer is interested. The broker owes no duty to disclose the proposed landfill to the buyer since there is no agency relationship. If the buyer-customer were to ask if the broker is aware of any such development in the area, the broker would have to answer the question honestly. Failure to do so would constitute a misrepresentation.

    b. **Client–agency relationship**: In a general sense, a client is one who hires a professional for advice and special assistance. The client in a real estate transaction hires a broker to perform representation-level services including advice and advocacy. Advocacy involves the presenting of a case for another, or the arguing for, or pleading for the position of another. Using the previous example, if the broker is representing the buyer as a buyer's agent, the broker would have to disclose what he actually knows about the property including anything in the vicinity such as the landfill.

       (1) **Payment of the fee is not conclusive**: Payment of a brokerage fee, i.e., commission, may provide evidence of who the client is, but is not absolutely conclusive. For example, a buyer's broker can represent a buyer while seeking compensation from the listing broker through the Multiple Listing Service (MLS) offer of compensation.

C. **Single agency, dual agency, and subagency.**

  1. **Single agency**: A single agent is authorized by one principal to represent the principal's interests on an exclusive basis. The single agent

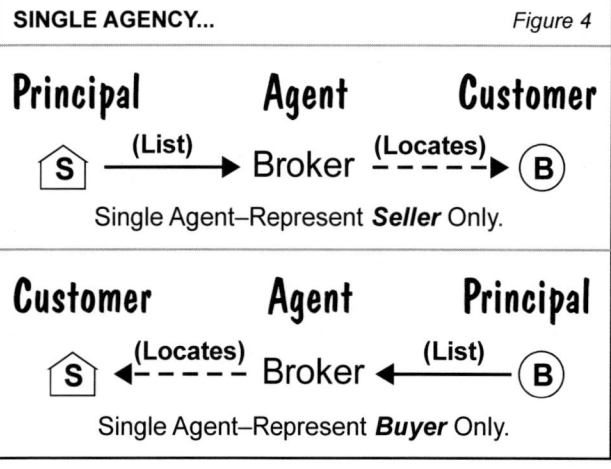

represents and acts in the best interest of his principal. A single agent can represent either the seller under a listing agreement or the buyer under a buyer's agency contract, but not both in the same real estate transaction. *See Figure 4.*

2. ▶ **Dual agency**: A dual agent is authorized to act for two principals in a single transaction; in other words, to represent both a buyer-client and a seller-client who are negotiating a common transaction. The full range of fiduciary duties must be adjusted because the duties of confidentiality and disclosure (of material facts) cannot be fully afforded both clients. For example, the secret of the buyer may be a material fact that the seller wants disclosed. The parties, therefore, agree in advance that any confidential information will not be disclosed despite the fact that it may be material. Michigan license law permits dual agency relationships provided they are based on informed consent and in writing. Dual agency must be thoroughly understood in the practice of real estate as well as on the licensing examination. *See Figure 5.*

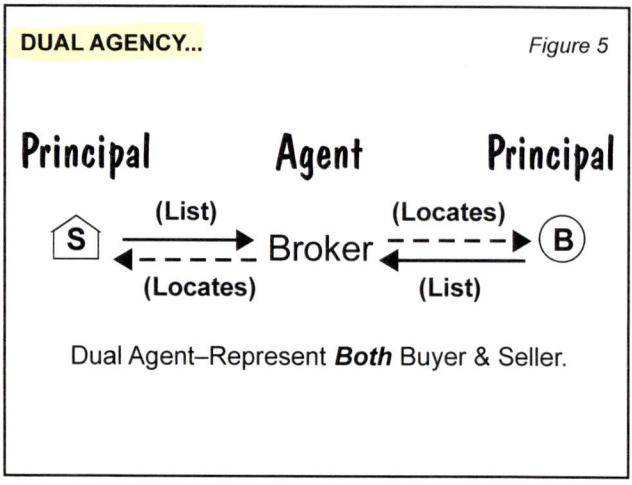

  a. **One broker–Two salespersons**: A broker also becomes a dual agent under the following circumstance. One affiliated salesperson works with the seller under a listing agreement and another affiliated salesperson works with the buyer under a buyer's agency contract in the same transaction. The broker is the dual agent since both salespersons are affiliated licensees under the same broker. The discussion pertaining to designated agency in Chapter 3 will expand on this concept.

  b. **Notice requirements**: Michigan agency disclosure is based on informed consent. One Michigan Court summarized that a broker must provide adequate disclosure, in writing, that the possibility of a dual agency may arise during the course of the transaction. A broker likely meets this requirement by (1) discussing it when agency disclosure is made, (2) using a clause in both the listing agreement and buyer's agency contract that the possibility of a dual agency exists, and (3) making sure that both parties execute a written dual agency agreement. This would not apply to a broker who only offers single agency services and does not act as a dual agent.

3. **Subagent**: A subagent is an agent to whom another agent delegates and shares his authority to represent a particular principal. Typically, a listing broker creates a subagency via an MLS offer of compensation to subagents who are often called seller's agents in the MLS system. Subagents in this respect are seller's agents because they assist the listing broker in finding a buyer for their seller-client. If a selling agent is acting as a subagent, any buyer with whom he works would be a customer. *See Figure 6.*

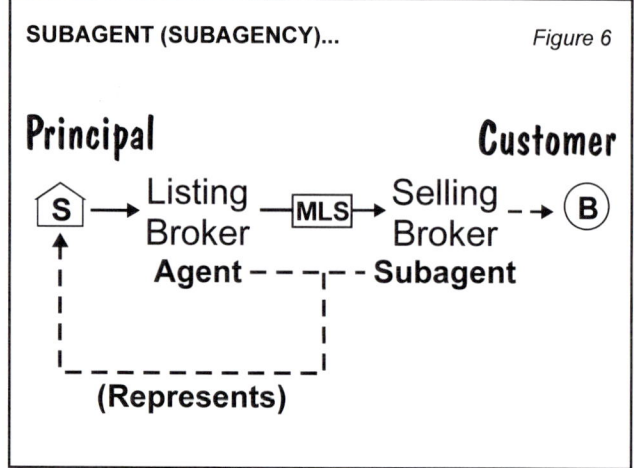

  a. **Responsibility for the actions of a subagent**: Depending upon the circumstances, an agent may be vicariously responsible for the actions of a subagent. While not necessarily likely, it is legally conceivable that the principal (seller) may also be vicariously liable to a buyer for the conduct of a subagent. The potential for vicarious liability resulting from the actions of a subagent in a real estate transaction has, and continues to be, a source of debate.

    (1) **Vicarious liability**: By definition, vicarious liability is the legal responsibility that one person acquires from the actions of another. Legally, a principal is liable for the actions of an agent, but that liability typically arises only when the agent is acting within the scope of his authority. If a

Chapter 2: Brokerage Concepts

seller authorizes an agent and his subagents to misrepresent the condition of the seller's property to prospective buyers, then the seller can be held vicariously liable for the statements.

Some brokers and their attorneys have expressed concern that subagency exposes sellers and their listing brokers to a high risk of vicarious liability for the actions of a careless subagent. Others are not concerned since listing agreements and MLS cooperation agreements do not contain authorizations to engage in unlawful conduct.

(2) **Alternatives to subagency**: The concern over vicarious liability has caused some brokers to avoid offering subagency to other brokers through the MLS. Instead, they offer compensation to only buyer's agents and transaction coordinators. A transaction coordinator is a licensee who does not act as a seller's agent or buyer's agent. A buyer's agent owes a duty to the buyer only. In either case, there is no agency and fiduciary relationship between the seller, listing broker and selling licensee, therefore, no vicarious liability. Many if not most brokers today still offer compensation to subagents. See Chapter 3 for further information on transaction coordinators.

b. **Confusion over whom the subagent represents**: Buyers often believe that all selling licensees, regardless of their agency status, work for them in the acquisition of a property. This results from the close relationships that subagents frequently develop with buyers, as they attempt to sell the listings of other brokers. Michigan's agency disclosure law was passed to require brokers and salespersons to disclose their agency status to all parties with whom they work. Agency disclosure is discussed in detail in Chapter 19.

III. **Practical aspects of an agency relationship**: There are several practical considerations for licensees who enter into agency relationships. They include (1) the creation of the relationship, (2) the duties that arise from their creation, (3) broker–salesperson employment, (4) the role of the salesperson, and (5) administration of a brokerage operation.

A. **Creation of an agency relationship**: An agency relationship can be created (1) by the intention of the parties, (2) inadvertently through words, actions, and/or conduct that implies an agency has been created, or (3) by a court of law when circumstances warrant it.

1. **Actual agency**: An actual agency arises when an agent has literally, and in fact, been employed by a principal, whether by express or implied authority. The best example of an actual agency is that which is created by the execution of a listing agreement between a seller and a broker. Actual means that it is real, exists in fact, and is enforceable by a court.

    a. **Express agency/express authority**: In this context, the word express means that a writing is involved. Since a listing agreement is in writing, the relationship thereby created is classified as an express agency. The listing agreement gives the broker what is known as express authority.

    b. **Implied agency/implied authority**: An implied agency arises from the words, actions, and/or conduct of a party (known as an implied agent) rather than a written contract. These words, actions, or conduct are said to imply to the client that an agency relationship, if fact, has been created. A court will treat an implied agency as if a writing had been created and enforce it against the implied agent. An implied agency creates what is known as implied authority.

    (1) **Example–implied agent**: A broker is working with a buyer who is reluctant to sign a buyer's agency contract. Fearing the buyer will go elsewhere for services, the broker tells the buyer, "Don't worry about a thing. I'll personally take care of everything for you and make sure your needs are met." The broker check marks "Buyer's agent" on the agency disclosure form, hands it to the buyer, and proceeds to advocate on the buyer's behalf in the search for a suitable property.

    (2) **Implied agency problems**: From a court's perspective, an implied agency is enforceable against the implied agent, but not against the client. Under an express agency, the terms of the written service provision agreement establish both the extent and limits of the broker's duties to the represented client. If an implied agency is inadvertently created instead, there is no such writing, and potentially no such limits. Additionally, if an implied buyer's agent performs and finds a home for a buyer who purchases it and then refuses to pay a commission, the agent cannot collect in a court of law since there is no written contract.

2. **Agency by estoppel**: An agency by estoppel is created by operation of law rather than a written agreement or conduct. For example, a principal allows an agent to exercise considerably more authority when dealing with a third party than had actually been granted. A court may protect the third party by binding the

principal to the agent's fuller actions as if authority had been granted. The principal is estopped, meaning prevented, from denying it. This typically does not arise in the course of a traditional real estate transaction.

    a. **Ostensible agent**: The word ostensible means that which is apparent or merely seems to be. Consequently, an ostensible agent is one who only appears to have actual authority, but in reality, does not. Ostensible agents and agency by estoppel situations rarely, if ever, arise in a traditional real estate setting.

3. **Agency coupled with an interest**: While not common, a real estate broker's agency relationship with a client can be coupled with an ownership interest in the listed property. The broker, as agent, obtains an estate in the property that does not end with the death of the principal. For example, a real estate broker assists with the financing of a developer-client's subdivision and receives security interests in the newly-constructed homes along with the exclusive right to sell listing agreements.

B. ▶ **The fiduciary relationship**: An agency relationship is based on an important bond of trust that is established between the agent and his principal. The term fiduciary is used to describe the trust-related responsibilities that the agent owes his client. Fiduciary also refers to the person who owes the trust, that is to say, the agent. A fiduciary must always act with the highest degree of care and in the best interests of the client.

As a result of this special relationship, certain duties and responsibilities are created for each party. These duties are owed to all clients in an agency relationship whether the client is a seller, a buyer, a landlord, or a tenant. When the term client is used in this section, it also means principal.

1. ▶ **Duties and services that arise from agency relationships in Michigan**: From the beginning of agency law until July 1, 2008, Michigan real estate licensees have been guided exclusively by common law fiduciary duties. These duties have been carved out by judges evaluating cases in which plaintiffs, generally sellers and buyers, alleged that a licensee acting as an agent failed to provide the required level of duties and services under agency law. The common law fiduciary duties have been supplemented by a set of statutory fiduciary duties presently set forth in real estate license law. The license law itself is discussed in Chapter 19.

The discussion in this chapter pertaining to Michigan's fiduciary duties is still relevant as it applies to the practice of real estate. This stems from the fact that Michigan license law defines a seller's agent and a buyer's agent as licensees who undertake to accept the responsibility of serving the seller or buyer in a manner consistent with those fiduciary duties existing under common law. The reference to "common law" in the statute means that common law is still valid. See Figure 7.

FIDUCIARY (TRUST) DUTIES *Figure 7*
AGENT OWES TO THE PRINCIPAL...

- **Loyalty**
  - Fidelity
  - Confidentiality
  - No profit outside of agency
- **Disclosure (notice) of material facts**
- **Reasonable Care**
- **Obedience**
- **Accounting**

2. ▶ **Statutory duties**: Michigan's agency disclosure form was significantly changed on July 1, 2008 to set forth seven statutorily-prescribed duties that all agents owe their clients. It also sets forth five services (three of which can be waived by the client) that are owed. These duties and services are in the language of Michigan's required agency disclosure form. Agency duties are sometimes referred to using the simplified acronym COALD. The letters stand for Care–Obedience–Accounting–Loyalty–Disclosure.

According to the agency disclosure form, an agent who provides services pursuant to a service provision agreement (i.e., a listing agreement with a seller-client, a buyer's agency agreement with a buyer-client, or an agreement to represent a landlord or tenant as an agent) owes the following minimum duties to the client. The word minimum allows for additional duties to be created via the terms and conditions of the service provision agreement. Many of these duties also have a counterpart in Michigan real estate license law and rules as well as the Code of Ethics of the National Association of REALTORS®.

    a. **Reasonable care and skill**: An agent must exercise reasonable care and skill in representing the client and carrying out the responsibilities of the agency relationship. This means that the agent is expected to perform in a manner that would be reasonably expected of any competent real estate agent who is acting under like or similar circumstances.

b. **Performance of the terms of the service provision agreement**: An agent is expected to abide by all terms and conditions set forth in a listing agreement or buyer's agency contract. As a general rule, an agent can only exercise the authority granted in the service provision agreement. It is possible, however, for an agent to act outside of this authority, and the client to later approve the actions. This is known as ratification (which is discussed further in Chapter 12).

   (1) **Obedience**: The duty to perform the terms of a service provision agreement may also be referred to as the duty of obedience. Agents must obey all legitimate instructions including the preparation of all documents necessary to close the transaction and providing copies to the client.

   (2) **Unlawful conduct excluded**: Obedience does not flow to a client's request for the agent to perform an illegal or unethical act or service. For example, a seller-client cannot ask his agent to lie to a buyer on his behalf or commit a crime or a fraud. If the agent complies, the agent is directly liable for the wrongdoing and the client is vicariously liable since he authorized it.

c. **Loyalty to the interest of the client**: The term loyalty refers to fidelity and faithfulness. Agents must always act in the best interests of the principal. Placing the principal's interests above all else means that the agent must not use his knowledge and expertise to his principals' disadvantage. Loyalty applies equally to brokers and their salespersons. Branches of the duty of loyalty can include the following concepts.

   (1) ▶ **Fidelity**: An agent generally pledges fidelity to one person, i.e., the client as opposed to the unrepresented customer. However, this duty can legally be expanded to both buyer and seller in the same real estate transaction via a dual agency with the written, informed consent of both.

   (2) ▶ **Conflicts of interest between agent and client**: An agent should work to avoid conflicts of interest between himself and his client. When this may not be possible, the agent should at least disclose any actual or potential conflict. Depending on the nature of the conflict, it may also be advisable to afford the client an opportunity to terminate the agency relationship if the client is concern about the perceived conflict. This is part of a sound risk management strategy. Disclosure and termination decisions should be handled by the broker or company manager.

      (a) **Profit outside of the agency**: Generally, brokers acting as agents may not accept payments, commissions, or referral fees from anyone other than the principal without written authorization from the principal (and possibly the third party paying the fee). Care must be exercised since some of these payments may be illegal under RESPA (discussed in Chapter 17).

      (b) **Agent acts as a principal**: An agent who acts as a principal (i.e., is the property seller or buyer) in a real estate transaction must disclose his relationship to the client before the client enters into a purchase agreement. Michigan Administrative Rules requires such disclosures to be provided to the client in writing. Further, if the agent will receive a commission as a result of the transaction in which he is a principal, the client must consent to the commission. Even though it is not specifically required in the Administrative Rules, it may be advisable for an agent to provide written disclosure of any ownership interest in property he leases to a client.

d. **Compliance with the law**: Compliance with the law requires an agent to abide by all laws, rules, and regulations of Michigan and any applicable federal statutes or regulations. This is why brokers and their affiliated salespersons must continually keep abreast of all applicable laws and regulations to make sure that they are followed. Many continuing education programs are designed to assist licensees with this important task.

   (1) **Duty to present all offers**: There are a number of different license law requirements pertaining to the duty to present all offers. For example, as a general rule, a listing agent must present all offers made on a represented seller's property. One variation could arise where a seller empowers the agent to reject offers below a certain amount. This instruction should be in writing to protect the broker against potential claims from selling brokers that the listing broker is improperly refusing to present all offers to the seller.

   (2) **Withholding of offers**: Some listing agents have unilaterally withheld the presentation of low offers from selling (i.e., cooperating) brokers believing that it is in the seller's best interests to do

so. This is incorrect and constitutes a breach of license law and the duty to present all offers to the seller-client.

e. **Referral to other professionals**: Agents must refer their clients to other professionals for expert advice related to material matters that are not within the expertise of the licensed agent. Examples of other professionals who provide potentially necessary advice or services outside the scope of what a real estate licensee is able to perform include an attorney, finance or tax advisor, environmental engineer, surveyor, appraiser, loan officer, home inspector or other construction expert, and commercial real estate expert (if the agent is experienced only in residential real estate).

   (1) ▸ **Practice within area of competence**: In a related issue, an agent is expected to confine his activities (i.e., practice) to his specific area of competence and expertise. For example, a real estate specialist who only has experience with residential transactions should not attempt to assist a client with the listing or purchase of a complex commercial property. Real estate licensees commonly refer such business to other licensees who possess the necessary knowledge and expertise. The referral of business to other licensees should be handled by the company broker or manager.

f. ▸ **Accounting and responsibility for earnest money deposits**: An agent is responsible for an accounting, in a timely manner, of all money and property received by the agent in which the client has or may have an interest. This duty pertains to money or property that belongs to others that come under the agent's control. A client's funds must never be commingled or mixed with the agent's personal funds. Doing so could lead to the intentional or inadvertent theft of the money by the agent.

   Theft, in this context, may be referred to as conversion. Legally, conversion is the wrongful and unauthorized exercise of ownership over the personal property of another. The fiduciary duty of accounting most frequently involves the handling of earnest money deposits. See Chapter 12, as well as license law and rules, for further discussion.

g. ▸ **Confidentiality**: An agent must preserve the secrets and confidences of his client. This duty pertains to all information about the client obtained within the course of the agency relationship that the client does not want disclosed. Disclosure would only be permitted with the client's written permission, or as provided by law. An agent should not even disclose confidential information to other licensees within his company if the company practices dual agency.

h. ▸ **Disclosure and notice of material facts**: An agent must disclose all material information to his principal that could affect the principal, his property, negotiating position, or the agency relationship. The duty of disclosure is also known as the duty to provide notice of material facts. While this chapter discusses material facts in an agency context, it is important to understand its broader definition.

   (1) **General meaning of material**: Facts are considered to be material if their disclosure is capable of influencing the decision-making process of a reasonable seller or buyer who is acting under like or similar circumstances. In other words, if the disclosure of a particular fact would impact a reasonable buyer's decision to buy or affect the price and terms of his offer, then the fact is material and must be disclosed. The fact that a basement leaked in a listed property once five years ago is material to a buyer since he may decide to purchase a different home, make a lower offer due to the possibility of a repair after moving in, or make his offer contingent on an inspection by a basement waterproofing contractor. The question of what is material is primarily economic in nature.

   (2) ▸ **Examples of material information**: Examples of information that could be interpreted as material under the appropriate circumstances include: (1) the true market value of a property, (2) the financial condition of a buyer in the case of a represented seller, (3) the status of an offer in the case of a represented buyer, (4) the broker's policies on cooperation with subagents, buyer's agents, and transaction coordinators, (5) the status of an earnest money deposit, (6) accuracy of lot and building dimensions such as square footage, and possibly (7) property taxes, zoning restrictions, building codes, land use restrictions, encroachments, easements, land or soil conditions, environmental hazards, and representations of school districts.

   Illustration: A buyer's agent shows a property to a buyer-client who is thinking about making an offer on it. The buyer's agent subsequently learns that the seller had filed an insurance claim for damage to the property a few years earlier. The buyer's agent must inform the buyer-client of this discovery, and should recommend that the buyer investigate it prior to making the offer.

(3) **Coverage on the agency disclosure form**: While not included in the list of minimum duties on the agency disclosure form, disclosure is discussed in the paragraphs titled "SELLER'S AGENTS" and "BUYER'S AGENTS." For example, the "SELLER'S AGENTS" section states, "Seller's agents and their subagents will disclose to the seller known information about the buyer which may be used to the benefit of the seller." This informs unrepresented buyers that the listing broker, i.e., seller's agent, has a duty of disclosure, and warns the buyer not to disclose any information that he does not want shared with a seller.

3. **Services**: As with fiduciary duties, the agency disclosure form also contains a list of services that a real estate broker or salesperson must provide when acting pursuant to a service provision agreement. There is one key distinction, however. Three of the five services, (b), (c), and (d), may be waived in the case of a limited service brokerage relationship. The fact that only five services are listed does not, however, prevent a broker from providing additional services to clients. Brokers frequently use their individual full-service packages to distinguish themselves from one another.

   Some brokers may elect to serve as a limited service broker and provide fewer services. The most likely scenario involves a seller who is marketing his property on a for-sale-by-owner basis and wants to have his home listed on the MLS while still attempting to sell his property on his own. While limited service is legal in Michigan, most sellers have historically chosen a full service broker to market their homes. Chapter 3 contains further discussion of full service versus limited service brokerage.

   a. **Marketing**: A client's property must be marketed in the manner agreed upon in the service provision agreement. This service cannot be waived which means that even a limited service broker must perform marketing services according to the terms of his limited service listing. This should not present a problem since a limited service, or MLS-only, broker places his client's property in the multiple listing service which is a form of marketing.

   b. **Presentation of offers**: An agent is responsible for acceptance of delivery, and presentation of offers and counteroffers to buy, sell, or lease the client's property, or the property the client seeks to purchase or lease. This service may be waived by a client who is working with a limited service broker.

   c. **Assistance in developing and communicating offers**: An agent must provide assistance in developing, communicating, negotiating, and presenting offers, counteroffers, and related documents or notices until a purchase agreement is executed by all parties and all contingencies are satisfied or waived. This service may be waived by a client who is working with a limited service broker.

   d. **Complete the transaction**: After execution of a purchase agreement by all parties, an agent must provide the necessary assistance so his client can complete the transaction under the terms specified in the purchase agreement. This service may be waived by a client who is working with a limited service broker.

   e. **Furnishing a closing statement**: A broker or associate broker who is involved at the closing of a real estate or business opportunity transaction must furnish, or cause to be furnished, to the buyer and seller, a complete and detailed closing statement signed by the broker or associate broker showing each party all receipts and disbursements affecting that party. The broker signature requirement is waived if the closing is conducted by a licensed title insurance company. This service cannot be waived.

   f. **Other services provided by a seller's agent**: In the case of a traditional full service broker, other services are typically provided to seller-clients. They include (1) discussing market trends and making suggestions to improve saleability, (2) estimating the net proceeds due the seller, (3) protecting unoccupied properties with security measures such as lockboxes, (4) keeping the seller updated on the results of marketing efforts, (5) maintaining records of all inquiries and showing activity, and (6) making sure all fair housing laws are strictly followed.

      (1) **Conducting open houses**: An open house is essentially a sales tool that many full service listing agents offer their seller-clients as part an overall marketing strategy. A diligent agent will obtain the names, addresses, and telephone numbers of all potential buyers who attend the open house not only to inform the seller-client, but also to use as a potential source of future business leads.

      (2) **Property crime and open houses**: In order to help safeguard valuables, a listing agent should always recommend that the seller-client take appropriate action prior to the house being held open. This may include the seller removing any high value items to a different location. The agent holding the house open may wish to register all prospective buyers and ask for identification as a

security measure. It may be prudent to limit the number of persons who are able to tour the house at any one time and to conduct a final walk-through at its conclusion to make sure all windows and doors are securely locked.

(3) **Premises liability and open houses**: The law of premises liability states that a property owner owes a duty to protect those who enter the property with permission from unreasonable risks of harm. Maintaining the property in a reasonably safe condition means taking simple steps such as: removing trip, slip, and fall hazards; keeping the walk and driveways clear of ice and snow; maintaining adequate lighting; and maintaining safety features such as stair and porch rails in good working order.

   (a) **Broker liability**: Normally, the land owner is the one who is responsible to those who enter his property. To address the question of whether a broker is liable for damages flowing from a buyer who suffers an injury while previewing a seller's home the law looks to (1) the purpose for which the injured person was on the property and (2) who was in control of the property at the time the injury occurred. The law uses specific terms when referencing individuals who enter the premises of another. Note that the term "licensee" used in this section is a specific legal term pertaining to premises liability and not a real estate licensee.

   i) **Invitee**: As an overview, a person is an invitee if he enters the land or property of another by invitation and does so for a business purpose from which the owner somehow benefits. The owner owes the highest duty which includes inspecting the premises, maintaining it in a safe condition, and correcting or warning about those that cannot be corrected. The classic example of an invitee is a shopper who enters a grocery store to purchase an advertised sale item and trips over a buckled floor mat thereby sustaining an injury. Real estate examples might include a seller who enters a real estate office to talk about listing his home or a potential buyer who enters a broker-advertised open house to preview a home.

   ii) **Licensee**: A licensee is one who enters a property of another with permission, but not for a business purpose. A license is a form of legal permission. A landowner owes a lower duty to a licensee than to an invitee. That duty essentially is to exercise reasonable care to either fix or warn of known hazards which are not obvious to the licensee. This means that a licensee is expected to exercise his own reasonable care regarding open and obvious hazards. Examples of a license would include permission to park a car on a lot, permission to hunt on the property of another, and the invitation of social guests into a home.

   iii) **Trespasser**: Since a trespasser enters the property of another without permission, the only duty is to exercise care to protect the public from a known dangerous condition (also known as an attractive nuisance), especially where children are concerned. For example, a homeowner with an in-ground pool should consider installing protective fencing around the pool (if local ordinance does not require it). Also, a builder should install temporary barrier fencing around the perimeter of an open excavation for a basement in an area in which children are known to live and play.

   (b) **Determining control and possession**: In the case of an open house, a host broker is likely to be deemed in control and possession of the property. Most brokers request that the seller vacate the home to afford the buyers freedom when touring the property. A listing licensee may also wish to require the seller to inspect and remedy any hazards before the open house.

   i) **Insurance**: A broker should make sure that he has adequate liability insurance coverage for accidents that may occur in the ordinary course of operating a real estate business. Similarly, a seller should make sure he has insurance coverage for his property.

   ii) **Liability for selling licensees**: Michigan courts have ruled that a selling agent who is working with a buyer on the showing of another broker's listing does not control and possess the property and, therefore, is not liable for injuries the buyer may suffer while previewing the home.

g. **Other services provided by a buyer's agent**: In addition to the basic services set forth on the agency disclosure form, a buyer's agent and his affiliated salespersons will (1) consult regarding property availability and set showings, (2) qualify buyers and consult regarding the desirability of properties based

Chapter 2: Brokerage Concepts

on market conditions and amenities, (3) consult on financing availability, rates, and obtaining credit/loan eligibility, (4) assist in purchase strategies, (5) negotiate purchase agreements, and (6) adhere to all fair housing laws.

4. **Duties a principal owes to the agent**: When a seller-client or a buyer-client enters into a service provision agreement with a broker, the client has certain duties or responsibilities he owes to the broker. These duties include cooperating with the agent as the agent performs his functions and paying the agreed upon commission if the broker successfully brings about the desired result.

   a. **Cooperation**: A listing agreement and buyer's agency contract contain either an express (meaning written) or implied (meaning deduced) promise that the principal will cooperate with the agent and not hinder his ability to perform. For example, a seller-client cannot intentionally frustrate his listing agent's efforts in order to avoid having to pay a commission by trying to negotiate privately with a buyer who was procured by the broker.

   b. **Compensation**: A broker is entitled to the commission negotiated in the listing agreement or buyer's agency contract upon fulfilling all required acts. In a listing agreement, if a buyer makes an offer with a price or terms that differ from those specified in the listing, the commission is deemed earned only upon the seller's acceptance of the varied terms. A buyer's agent earns a commission when the represented buyer purchases a property during the term of an exclusive buyer's agency contract.

5. ▶ **Duties an agent owes to the third party**: An unrepresented party, such as a customer, is not entitled to any fiduciary duties whatsoever since no agency-level services are provided. Nevertheless, certain basic requirements and principles come into play when licensees work with customers.

   a. ▶ **Honesty and integrity**: While a licensee does not owe a fiduciary duty to customers, the licensee cannot engage in any act that would rise to the level of fraud, deceit, or dishonesty. Integrity is a term that is sometimes used synonymously with honesty. There is a technical difference between honesty and integrity, however. Honesty refers to truth-telling while integrity refers to a state of moral soundness and incorruptibility.

   Examples of dishonesty include: (1) a listing agent lies to a buyer-customer about the market value of the listed property to induce the buyer to make a higher offer; (2) a listing agent who knows that the seller's basement leaks during heavy rains is asked about water problems and tells the buyer that the basement is watertight; and, (3) a listing broker knows that a member of the seller's family died in the home years ago, and answers "no" when asked by a buyer if anyone died in the home.

   b. **Caveat emptor**: Caveat emptor is a Latin phrase that means, "Let the buyer beware." Under this legal principle, a buyer assumes the responsibility and risk for discovering obvious defects. This is why the buyer, whether represented or not, should inspect a potential purchase property himself and hire a professional inspector to ascertain the structural integrity of the property and look for possible defects and repairs that might be necessary. Caveat emptor is discussed further in Chapter 12.

6. ▶ **The issue of property defects and disclosure**: The issue of property defects and who is the responsible party remains an ongoing source of concern for buyers and sellers alike. Property condition disclosure laws have been enacted to reduce the chance that a defect will go undisclosed to a buyer.

   a. ▶ **Licensee responsibilities**: A licensee has no duty in Michigan to inspect for (or discover) property defects. A listing licensee will recommend that his seller-client accurately complete the seller disclosure form for distribution to prospective buyers. If the listing licensee suspects that a property defect may exist, he should recommend that the seller investigate it further. A selling licensee (whether working as a buyer's agent or non-agent) who suspects that a property defect exists should recommend that the buyer explore it with the appropriate expert or inspector prior to making an offer on the property.

   b. ▶ **Seller is responsible for disclosure**: As between the seller-client and his listing broker, the duty to disclose property defects to a buyer belongs to the seller. A listing agent has no duty to disclose defects to an unrepresented buyer unless the agent created or participated in the active concealment of the defect. Recall, however, that if a buyer-customer asks about a defect of which the agent is fully aware, the agent must answer the question truthfully (as part of the requirement of honesty).

   c. **Latent versus patent defects**: A patent defect is obvious and one which a reasonable buyer is expected to discover. Hidden or latent defects are those of which only a seller may be aware. While all jurisdictions require a seller to disclose hidden defects of which the seller is aware, a large number such as

Michigan require a seller to disclose all defects of which the seller is aware whether they are latent or patent. The details of Michigan's Seller Disclosure Act are explored in Chapter 21.

d. **Seller disclosure statements**: Most state legislatures, including Michigan, require a seller to complete and distribute a property condition disclosure statement to potential buyers, at least on residential property. A property condition disclosure statement is designed to place prospective buyers on notice as to the condition of the property especially as it pertains to the structural, mechanical, and appliance systems. The seller specifies, to the best of his knowledge, any known irregularity, any item which is in need of repair, and the history of certain problems and/or repairs including water in a basement or crawl space, problems relating to a well, insect infestation, and environmental issues such as mold.

e. ▶ **Stigmatized property**: Certain events can occur at or on a property that do not affect the structure, but can stigmatize it. These events have the potential for high psychological impact for some buyers. Examples of stigmatizing events include murders, suicides, illegal drug or other illicit activities on the property, or even a claim that the house is haunted. The legal controversy over stigmatized property is whether these events amount to material defects thus requiring disclosure to potential buyers.

   (1) **Question of material defect**: Michigan law does not recognize stigmatized property situations as being a material defect unless it has a material effect on the condition of the real property or its improvements. According to Michigan license law, Section 2518(b), a licensee's failure to disclose that a property was the site of a homicide, suicide, or other occurrence prohibited by law, which had no material effect on the condition of the real property, is not a violation of the law.

   (2) **Disclosure is required if there is an accompanying defect**: If stigmatizing drug activity on a property includes manufacturing, the property may also be environmentally contaminated. This does rise to the level of a property defect. See also, Chapter 11 and the discussion pertaining to "Clandestine 'meth' labs and the environment" for additional discussion.

7. ▶ **The issue of fraud**: The subject of fraud and other forms of misrepresentation are discussed in Chapter 12. For purposes of an agency relationship, a licensee must always be truthful and never lie. Especially harmful lies are those lies perpetrated for the purpose of inducing another to take action in response to the falsehood. Fraud is also known as an intentional misrepresentation. A licensee generally is allowed to engage in puffing.

   a. ▶ **Puffing**: Statements of opinion made during the sale process are known as puffing, puffery, or puffing the goods. Puffing does not amount to a misrepresentation since such statements are not intended to be a representation of fact upon which a person can rely. For example, a listing agent tells a buyer that a home is located in a "beautiful" neighborhood. The concept of beauty is subjective and does not rise to the level of a material fact.

   b. **Puffing versus statement of fact**: A licensee is generally allowed to express his opinion through statements such as "good shape," "great price," or "nice home," but care must be exercised to make sure such statements are not capable of being interpreted by a buyer as a fact. For example, a licensee who is working with a buyer states, "The schools in this area are absolutely the best." It might be better to say, "Many buyers who have purchased in this area say they really like the schools." Assuming this latter statement is true, it avoids the buyer taking what the licensee says as an affirmative statement of fact.

C. **Broker responsibilities–Employing sales associates**: To employ means to hire. Brokers are hired in real estate transactions by seller-clients and buyer-clients. Real estate salespersons are also hired by their brokers to represent the broker in the broker's real estate dealings. When a broker hires a real estate salesperson, he almost always enters into an independent contractor agreement. It is critical for brokers to understand the difference between employees and independent contractors.

   1. **Employee status**: An employee is a person who is hired, either by written or implied contract, to work for a salary or wages. The employer retains the right to control and direct the significant details of how the employee's work is to be performed. This "control and direct" aspect of the employment is a key difference between an employee and an independent contractor.

   2. **Independent contractor**: An independent contractor is a person who is hired to perform a specific task or service, according to the independent contractor's own methods and often using the contractor's own resources, subject to the control of his employer only as to the final result. The independent contractor is generally employed for a particular and limited purpose, the completion of which causes the relationship

to end. An independent contractor such as a plumber can be hired to complete a short-term task or the contractor can be hired on a continuing basis such as a real estate salesperson.

    a. **Compensating an independent contractor**: Compensation is generally contingent on the successful completion of the task for which the independent contractor was hired. For example, a real estate salesperson earns his agreed upon share of the broker's listing commission upon the transaction successfully closing.

    b. **Salespersons (and associate brokers) as statutory independent contractors**: Michigan license law creates what is known as a statutory independent contractor. To qualify, a written agreement must exist setting forth that the real estate broker does not consider the real estate salesperson (or associate broker) to be an employee for federal and state income tax purposes. Further, at least 75% of the annual compensation paid by the broker to the salesperson (or associate broker) must be from commissions from the sale of real estate. Following the statutory guidelines creates a "safe harbor" for a broker against claims that the salesperson, for example, was actually an employee and that the broker should have been paying federal withholding taxes to the IRS.

    c. **Income tax considerations**: As suggested above, an independent contractor is responsible for payment of his own withholding taxes to the IRS rather than the employer. Self-employed individuals are required to file an annual return and pay estimated tax quarterly. In addition to income taxes, self-employed individuals pay a self-employment tax (SE tax). This is similar to the Social Security and Medicare taxes withheld from the pay of most employee wage earners. Beginning with the receipt of their first commission check, new licensees should discipline themselves to pay their required taxes on time (subject to the advice of a financial expert).

D. ▶ **Role of the salesperson and commission programs**: As noted earlier, a real estate salesperson acts as the agent of his broker. State license laws require a real estate salesperson to be licensed under a broker, subject to the broker's supervision. The broker's license law duty to supervise all affiliated licensees is one of the key distinctions between brokers and salespersons. *See Figure 8.*

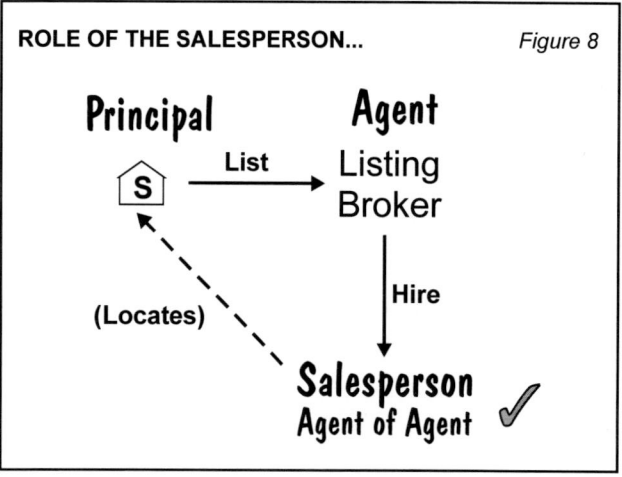

ROLE OF THE SALESPERSON...   *Figure 8*

    1. **Agent of an agent**: As his broker's agent, a salesperson owes his fiduciary duty to the employing broker (who is his principal). Consequently, a salesperson owes the same level of care to clients as does his broker since the salesperson is the legal representative of the broker.

    2. **Execution of contracts**: A salesperson executes, i.e., signs, listing agreements and buyer's agency contracts on behalf of his broker. Even though the salesperson uses his own name, the signature appears in an agency capacity for the broker. The agent of record is the broker and not the salesperson. Therefore, if the salesperson transfers to a new broker, the listing stays with the former broker.

    3. **Commission programs**: Historically, many brokers split or shared the individual commission checks generated by their affiliated licensees on a 50/50 basis. The broker uses his portion to pay the cost of running the brokerage operation which may include the mortgage payment or rent on the building, insurance, utilities, telephone bills, etc. This sharing formula tends to work out well today with new or lower-producing licensees. The exact commission formula varies from one broker to the next since antitrust laws do not permit independent brokers to discuss or set pricing programs with one another.

        a. **Accelerated commission program**: A large number of brokers also use incentive arrangements such as an accelerated commission plan. Under these commission programs, the broker splits each individually-earned commission on a 50/50 basis until an annual income cap or base is reached by the affiliated licensee. Thereafter, the affiliated licensee either earns increasing percentages as the number of transactions increase during the year or the majority of the commission once the cap is met.

        b. **100% or desk rent program**: Other brokers, especially those who hire only experienced agents, may use a straight monthly rental fee that allows the affiliated licensee to retain 100% of their commission dollars. A licensee who is a member of a franchise operation may have to pay a modest additional franchise fee per transaction for the services provided by the franchisor.

4. **Managers**: A manager is a person who assists a broker with the administration of a real estate operation. Most medium-to-large size brokerage operations, especially those with multiple offices, hire managers to assist the broker in running the company. In smaller single-office companies, the broker often serves the dual role of broker and manager. Some brokers employ their managers as employees to strictly manage without personally listing or selling properties. Other brokers allow their managers to list and sell while also performing managerial functions.

According to Michigan license law, a branch office in excess of 25 miles from the nearest boundary of the city where the main office is must be under the supervision of an associate broker. This implies that a licensed salesperson can be appointed manager for any office within this 25 mile boundary (because the broker is still the supervisor). Managers play a vital role in the day-to-day operations of a real estate company.

E. ▶ **Broker's responsibilities–Administration of a brokerage operation**: A broker acts as the central coordinator of all activity that takes place within his office. Although there may be other persons licensed to carry out the functions of a broker, such as an associate broker, the broker of the company is the one who is ultimately responsible. Michigan license law and rules require a broker to supervise the work of all licensees. One way brokers can supervise is by creating the state-mandated written operating policies and procedures. Additional supervisory duties are discussed in Chapters 19 and 20.

1. **Policies and procedures manual**: A well-written policies and procedures manual addresses all facets of the brokerage operation including highly specific requirements that all affiliated licensees must follow. These requirements are not designed to create an employee relationship, but rather, to set the appropriate standards for meeting the company's legal and ethical requirements. This is part of a good risk management strategy for brokers. These standards can also help with a broker's defense if he is sued for the actions of an affiliated licensee who engaged in wrongful conduct.

    a. **Sets the scope of authority**: Written policies and procedures set forth and limit what an affiliated licensee can do as a representative of the broker. We have already learned that when an agent acts outside of the scope of his authority, the principal is not automatically liable. A broker obviously wants all affiliated licensees to abide by all applicable laws, rules, and regulations. When an affiliated licensee acts outside of the scope of his authority, he risks not being covered under his broker's errors and omissions insurance policy.

        (1) **Limiting liability**: Plaintiffs in court cases often attempt to implicate the broker in any cause of action against one of the broker's licensees. This forces the broker into a position of having to defend himself in court for something of which he may not be aware. A policy manual can be helpful in this respect.

        (2) **Incorporation by reference**: It is a good practice for a broker to connect or link the contents of the policies and procedures manual to the requirements of the independent contractor agreement that an affiliated licensee signs prior to becoming licensed to the broker. This is accomplished by placing a clause in the independent contractor agreement that incorporates, i.e., includes, the terms of the policy manual into it. By executing the independent contractor agreement, the policy and procedures manual is agreed to as well.

        (3) **Regular policy update and review**: As new issues arise whether from statutes, court cases, or business practices, policy and procedures manuals should be re-evaluated and updated on a regular basis. At the very least, an annual policy "check-up" makes sense for brokers.

    b. ▶ **Employee manual and supervision requirements**: A broker is also responsible for the supervision of all company (unlicensed) employees. Along with a policies and procedures manual for affiliated licensees who are independent contractors, a broker should develop a company employee manual for employees such as secretaries, clerical staff, and other administrative personnel. This manual deals with issues that pertain exclusively to employees such as hourly compensation, overtime, holiday pay, sick days, and vacation days.

2. ▶ **Education and training**: Along with supervision, a broker should also provide regular education and training for his staff. This includes both affiliated licensees and staff employees. Monthly office meetings present a great opportunity to make sure that everyone in the company knows the company policy and

Chapter 2: Brokerage Concepts

to keep licensees abreast of changes in local, state, and federal law as well as market trends. Every licensee should make attendance at all office meetings a high priority. Attendance can be an intelligent risk management strategy for salespersons and associate brokers.

F. **Additional areas that affect a brokerage operation**: There are a number of important areas that potentially impact a brokerage operation. Some of them are regulated by specific laws that carry stiff financial penalties for non-compliance. As a result, it is in the best interests of all real estate licensees to understand how they are applied. New technologies represent one of the greatest areas of change for real estate practitioners.

1. **Laws affecting real estate marketing and consumer protection**: Several pieces of legislation have been enacted over the past decade under the banner of consumer protection. Licensees must be aware of these acts due to their potential impact on real estate marketing efforts.

    a. ▶ **Telemarketing and Do Not Call registries**: The purpose of these statutes is the prevention of telemarketing fraud and other perceived abuses. Both state and federal Do Not Call registries have been authorized and funded. A consumer can request that his number be added to the list to prevent further calls from telemarketers. The primary concern for real estate licensees is whether or not their prospecting activities qualify as telemarketing for purposes of these acts.

        (1) **Telemarketing under Michigan law**: Classic telemarketing involves a telephone solicitor who seeks to obtain a financial commitment from a consumer during the course of a telephone call. In seeking an exemption under the state Do Not Call law, the real estate industry successfully argued that telephone calls placed by licensees are designed for purposes of requesting a face-to-face meeting and not to encourage the recipient of the call to make a purchase decision during the call.

            (a) **Preemption**: In spite of the exemption afforded Michigan real estate licensees under state law, the federal Do Not Call rule was subsequently amended to preempt, meaning overrule, any state law that is deemed less restrictive. This means that the provisions of the Federal law apply to calls made within the state of Michigan whether or not the licensee limits his calls to Michigan residents only. Michigan has now adopted the federal registry as its own.

        (2) **The FTC Telemarketing Sales Rule–Federal law**: The Federal Trade Commission (FTC) rule was originally created to prevent deceptive or abusive telemarketing practices and was later amended to include a national Do Not Call registry.

            (a) **Activities subject to the rule**: The rule defines telemarketing as a plan, program or campaign which is conducted to induce the purchase of goods or services, by use of one or more telephones, and which involves more than one interstate call. As noted above, intrastate calls are also regulated by the federal Act.

            Prohibitions include:

            i) Calling a person whose number is on the national Do Not Call registry or who has specifically asked not to receive further telemarketing calls.

            ii) Misusing the Do Not Call list for any purpose other than compliance.

            iii) Denying or interfering with a person's Do Not Call rights.

            iv) Calling outside the hours of 8:00 a.m. to 9:00 p.m. (local consumer's time).

            v) Abandoning an outbound telephone call (meaning the telemarketer does not respond within 2 seconds of the consumer answering the outbound call).

            vi) Failing to transmit or otherwise blocking Caller ID information.

            vii) Using threats, intimidation, profane language, or obscene language.

            viii) Repeated calling or causing the consumer's telephone to ring with intent to annoy, abuse, or harass.

            (b) **List scrubbing requirements**: Qualifying telemarketers are required to scrub their call lists every 31 days by accessing and searching the national Do Not Call database, typically for a fee (the first five area codes are free), and then drop any consumer whose number(s) is registered. Scrubbing in this context means updating a call list to remove any newly-registered consumers or telephone numbers.

(c) **Penalty for non-compliance**: A consumer may file a complaint with the FTC, either on-line or by calling a toll-free number. A recipient who receives more than one illegal call from the same business during any 12-month period can sue for up to $500 per violation. If the illegal calls were willfully and knowingly made in violation of the Rule, the consumer may be entitled to treble damages of $1,500 per call. The Federal government can also bring an action for up to $16,000 per violation. Violators may also be subject to a nationwide injunction.

    i) **Safe harbor requirements**: A business that makes an inadvertent mistake as a telemarketer may escape liability if it can show that, as part of its routine business practice, it has a policy to honor consumer's requests not to be called, has trained personnel to assist with "do not call" compliance, maintains records, routinely scrubs its lists, and has a low incidence of errors.

(d) **Exemptions**: A few notable exemptions to the Do Not Call Rule exist. Even if a real estate licensee believes that an exemption exists (and company policy permits calls to be made to these exempt categories), the broker or manager should be consulted if any doubt exists as to whether a particular call qualifies for an exemption.

    i) **Existing business relationship (18 months)**: Upon the conclusion of a business transaction, calls may be made to the past client or customer for up to 18 months, even if the past client's or customer's numbers are on the federal registry. Requests not to receive further calls must be honored even if the consumer was a past client or customer within the 18 month period.

    ii) **Consumer inquiries (3 months)**: If a consumer places an inquiry call to a business, the business may continue to call the consumer for up to 3 months after the inquiry. This includes calls from sellers about real estate services as well as buyer inquires about existing listings and other real estate services. A request not to receive further calls, however, must be honored.

    iii) **Consumer permission**: A consumer may grant written permission to receive calls from a business or telemarketer. It is becoming a common practice on the conclusion of a real estate transaction or at an open house for licensees to have consumers sign a consent form giving permission to contact the consumer via telephone, fax, or e-mail. A request not to receive further communications, however, must be honored.

    iv) **Other**: Exemptions are also afforded to charitable organizations (with some limitations), political organizations, and companies that conduct surveys providing the purpose of the survey is not to sell goods or services. Business-to-business calls are not covered under the Rule.

(e) **Application to For Sale By Owners (FSBO) and expired listings**.

    i) **For sale by owner calls**: A person who is selling his house on a "for-sale-by-owner" basis, and whose name is on the Do Not Call list, may not be called by a licensee for the purpose of obtaining a listing. While the law does not specifically mention it, the licensee is most likely able to call the seller on behalf of an actual buyer who is specifically interested in previewing the property. Setting an appointment on behalf of a potential buyer is not telemarketing. The licensee should keep a record of the buyer and note the details of the call in case a complaint is filed by the seller.

    ii) **Expired listings**: There is no special Rule exemption for calling the sellers whose listings have expired. Applying the regular exemptions, the following calls would be permissible (pending a request to discontinue calling):

        a) The former broker or his affiliated licensees can call the seller of a company listing for up to 18 months after expiration under the existing business relationship exemption; and,

        b) A licensee can call the seller of an expired listing for up to three months providing the seller made an initial inquiry with the licensee about re-listing the property.

b. **Use of facsimile and recorded messages**: While the following statutes are not specifically directed at real estate licensees, they can affect the manner in which licensees market their services or the properties of their clients.

   (1) **State law**.

   (a) **"Facsimile Machines" Act**: This Act was passed in 1990 to prohibit the use of facsimile machines to transmit unsolicited advertising messages to a person or business entity. A licensee may not send advertisements via fax without prior consent. Consent for present and future fax advertising can be obtained during the course of a standard telephone or in-person contact. At the very least, licensees who send general and unsolicited advertisements via fax should include instructions on how the recipient can have his name removed from the licensee's distribution list.

   i) **Penalties**: A person or business who receives an advertisement in violation of the Act may file a civil suit in court to recover actual damages or $500, whichever is greater, plus reasonable attorney fees.

   (b) **Advertising via commercially-recorded messages**: While the use of commercially-recorded telephone advertising messages is no longer widespread, some licensees relied on them in the past. Several requirements were enacted pursuant to Michigan's "Telephone Companies As Common Carriers" Act that limit the use of such recorded messages to market properties or services.

   i) **Consent**: The recipient must have requested the information, provided a telephone number, or otherwise consented to the call.

   ii) **Equipment**: The equipment used to deliver such messages must disconnect the line if the recipient hangs up the telephone. This applies to calls made to a residence, business, or a toll-free number.

   iii) **Blocking Caller I.D.**: When making such calls within Michigan, the caller cannot block the caller identification information otherwise available to the recipient. This means that the caller blocking feature, *67 on most systems, cannot be used.

   (2) **Federal law**.

   (a) **Facsimile restrictions**: Rules issued in 2003 by the Federal Communications Commission (FCC) specifically prohibit unsolicited advertisements to be sent to facsimile machines without an express invitation for permission.

   i) **Junk Fax Prevention Act**: This Act applies to fax advertisements sent by businesses to consumers as well as those sent to other businesses. It does not, however, apply to consumers who contact businesses via fax. Unsolicited faxed advertisements may be sent according to the following rules.

   a) The business possessed the recipient's fax telephone number prior to July 9, 2005 (the effective date of the Act).

   b) If the fax number was obtained after July 9, 2005, the business must prove that consent to fax was given via a voluntary communication.

   c) The advertisement contains a cost-free opt-out mechanism by which future faxes may be declined. Opt-out requests must be processed within 30 days of receipt, and remain in effect without limit on its duration.

   ii) **Licensees must obtain consent**: As a result of the FCC's rule, real estate licensees must not send unsolicited fax messages without first obtaining the written consent of the recipient. Written consent can be obtained through interaction with individuals, mail, websites, and e-mail communications. The consent must include the recipient's signature and fax telephone number. It is illegal, however, to transmit a request for permission using a fax machine.

   iii) **Penalties**: Recipients are entitled to collect statutory damages of $500 per violation. If the violation is willful or knowing, the recipient is entitled to treble damages equalling $1,500 per violation. Court injunctions can also be obtained.

2. ▶ **Technology issues in advertising and marketing**: Real estate advertising is a crucial client service as well as a necessary business marketing tool. From a legal perspective, all licensees, especially brokers, must work diligently to make certain that all forms of advertising comply with existing laws and rules. This applies equally to marketing via the Internet; social media sites; smartphones, tablets, and other wireless communication devices; as well as traditional channels such as print, signage, radio, and television.

   a. **Internet–definitions, impact, and issues**: The Internet is a global network of local and regional computer networks that is open to the public. It links multiple computing devices on a worldwide basis and delivers content to these devices in the form of text, graphic images, video, and audio. The impact of the Internet evolution on the real estate business has been immense. It is estimated that well over 90% of buyers and sellers prefer to use some form of electronic communication to exchange data and information with real estate professionals. These professionals should not, however, lose sight of the value of verbal and face-to-face communications, especially when negotiating or managing challenging situations.

      (1) **World Wide Web (Web)**: The Web, which historians estimate was developed around 1989–1990, is an area of the Internet consisting of a network of documents housed on separate, interlinked computers. A person with an Internet-enabled device and a web browser can access this network locally on their device. Web pages typically contain text, images, videos, and other multimedia. These pages are navigated through the use of hyperlinks. A hyperlink is an embedded electronic marker that leads the viewer from one page to another page located anywhere on the Internet.

         (a) **Real estate websites and search engine optimization (SEO)**: The number of real estate related websites has grown dramatically. For example, a search for "real estate agent" on one of the popular search engines today will return a results page in excess of 1.4 billion pages or locations within pages containing the search parameters! Any individual real estate agent who is trying to get noticed will be buried in this avalanche of data.

         Search engine optimization, or SEO, is a highly complex process used to make a website more visible on the Web. This is accomplished by having the site be ranked and appear higher on the search results page (compared to other sites with similar content). The higher a site or page appears in the search results, the more visitors clicks it tends to receive from individuals who conduct searches. Most consumers today do not take the time to scroll through voluminous search results.

            i) ▶ **Broker sites**: A real estate broker who promotes his company's services on the Internet through a private, corporate Web site must comply with all laws and rules, especially those governing real estate advertising and fair housing. All listing information must be accurately reflected with current information. Nothing is more frustrating to a potential buyer than to call about a listing he saw on the Internet that was sold 10 months ago. If the broker's site also includes a directory of affiliated salespersons and associate brokers, it should also be current.

            ii) ▶ **Salesperson (and team) sites**: The majority of active licensees now use a personal website to promote their real estate services. According to Michigan license law, all real estate advertising by a salesperson, associate broker, or team must identify the employing broker by name (including the broker's telephone number or street address) and be supervised by the broker. Further, the type size of the broker's name cannot be smaller than the name of the affiliated licensee or team appearing in the advertisement. As a matter of policy, each website should also be periodically reviewed by the employing broker or manager for compliance. This applies to all Internet-based tools that advertise or promote real estate including all social media outlets.

         (b) ▶ **Social media and real estate advertising**: The use of social media sites by licensees to promote their services and listings is growing exponentially. Social media is a type of electronic communication through which an online community of registered users exchanges information, personal messages, pictures, videos, and digital files. Popular social media sites include Facebook, Twitter, LinkedIn, Pinterest, Instagram, and Google Plus+.

         Licensees must understand that any and all forms of real estate advertising, including on social media sites, are governed by real estate license law and rules. If a licensee posts a new listing on a social media site, for example, the post should contain a hyperlink to the broker's corporate website to identify not only that the person posting is a real estate licensee, but also the broker under whom he is licensed. Using social media to promote listings is still relatively new to the industry. A broker, therefore, should make sure that company policy pertaining to advertising (and compliance with license laws and rules) extends to social media.

(c) ▶ **Internet advertising of listings**: Internet advertising is both preferred and expected by the majority of sellers. Some sellers, however, may be wary of perceived privacy issues and should be afforded an opportunity to individually "opt out" of Internet advertising. This would include opting out of advertising on the broker's website as well as the many sites connected through Multiple Listing Service affiliations.

(d) **Linking other businesses**: A real estate broker may wish to provide consumer information on its company website regarding specific lenders, attorneys, title companies, or home inspectors. By clicking on a hyperlink to the company promoted in the broker's site, the consumer can visit the linked company. It is prudent for a broker to seek written permission from any other company before creating a link to its website. A salesperson who does this on his personal website should first obtain the permission of his broker to make sure no conflicts of interest are unintentionally created.

i) **Hyperlink considerations**: If a broker desires to create a link to the website of another company or organization, it would be a good idea to have it reviewed by someone such as legal counsel. The broker may be advised not to create the appearance of a specific recommendation or endorsement. Further, the linked company or organization may provide information that could cause an issue for the broker such as a fair housing violation or RESPA. The broker may also wish to include a written disclaimer on his site relating to the products or services of the linked company.

(2) **Copyright considerations**: As the ease of accessing and providing information on the Internet has expanded, so have copyright violations. Licensees must not use someone else's copyright-protected material for a commercial purpose without first obtaining written permission from the author. Generally, one does not copyright an idea, only its form of expression. For example, a person could not copyright protect the idea of a real estate textbook, but could write one and then copyright protect the specific textbook so authored.

Any direct copying or duplication of copyright-protected materials by anyone other than the owner is an infringement under federal copyright law. In the real estate industry, MLS photographs and data are generally protected with the MLS holding the copyright. For example, Broker Able from ABC Realty lists a property that was previously listed with Broker Cain at XYZ Real Estate. Able cuts and pastes the photographs taken by Cain into Able's MLS entry for the new listing. This is a copyright violation and Able is subject to penalties.

(3) **Trademarks and cybersquatting**: Trademark law protects brand recognition by preventing others from mimicking a registered distinctive mark, for example, a company's business logo. Infringement of a trademark, like that of a copyright, is a violation of federal law. Cybersquatting is the illegal act of registering or using an Internet domain name that contains a trademark belonging to someone else. Typosquatting is a form of cybersquatting whereby the infringer registers variations or common misspellings of a competitor's trademark-protected name. When a consumer accidently misspells the intended company's domain name, he is redirected to the infringer's site.

b. **E-mail:** E-mail is an abbreviation for electronic mail. As electronic transactions, marketing, and communication continue to evolve, so will the laws governing them. It is important for licensees to stay abreast of legal developments in this arena. Brokers should also update their policies and procedures manuals with guidelines on conducting business via electronic means.

(1) **Electronic Communications Privacy Act**: With the prevalence of smartphones, wireless devices, and e-mail in the marketplace, security and privacy issues have grown in importance. The Electronic Communications Privacy Act sets forth provisions for access, use, disclosure, interception, and privacy protections of electronic communications including e-mail. Electronic communications are defined as any digital transfer of signs, signals, writing, images, sounds, data, or intelligence.

(a) **Prohibitions**: The act prohibits someone from (1) intentionally intercepting, using, or disclosing any wire, oral, or electronic communication, or (2) accessing the messages while they are in temporary, intermediate, or backup storage. For an interception of an electronic message to be illegal, it must occur at the same time the message is transmitted.

(b) **Exception for providers**: A provider of wire or electronic communications services may access messages while they are in storage. Accordingly, if a broker provides an e-mail service for his company, he may access all of the stored messages without being in violation of the Act. The broker should, however, verify compliance with legal counsel before actually accessing e-mail messages of affiliated licensees.

The key to this exemption is found in the phrase "provides the communication service." If the broker merely makes Internet access available via a wireless, i.e., WiFi, router, he cannot intercept or access any e-mail housed on a licensee's personal computer or e-mail the licensee stores using his own Internet Service Provider account such as webmail.

(c) **Penalties**: Violations can result in an injunction being issued and civil fines of $500.

(2) **Control of commercial e-mail messages and spam**: The digital age has also ushered in new and cost-efficient methods for delivering electronic messages to a wide range of recipients. Legislatures at the state and federal levels have attempted to grapple with problems associated with bulk electronic messages that may not be requested or desired by the recipient. The key to find a way to balance the right of businesses to advertise with consumers' right to privacy.

(a) **Spam defined**: Spam is defined as unsolicited commercial e-mail messages which are dispatched, meaning sent, to multiple recipients on a bulk basis. The act of spamming is the sending of such e-mail. While commercial e-mail can be a legitimate form of advertising, some instances can be annoying and potentially malicious.

(b) **Federal law–Can-Spam Act**: In 2004, Congress passed a law designed to control deceptive and fraudulent commercial e-mail messages by creating a uniform set of national standards. Commercial e-mail includes any electronic mail message "the primary purpose of which" is the commercial advertisement or promotion of a commercial product or service.

i) **Exceptions**: The Act does not apply to the following examples. This means that they are not considered to be spam.

a) Commercial e-mail messages which are purely informational and do not carry advertisements; for example, electronic newsletters and articles.

b) Commercial messages pertaining to ongoing or transactional relationships that exist between the sender and the recipient.

c) Commercial messages sent with the consent of the recipient.

ii) **Meaning of "primary purpose"**: In a Federal Trade Commission (FTC) interpretation, the primary purpose of an e-mail is deemed to be commercial under the following circumstances. This means that they are considered to be spam.

a) The message is devoted entirely to the promotion of goods or services.

b) The message contains both commercial (i.e., spam) and transactional or relationship content (i.e., not spam); the subject line is commercial in nature; and the transactional or relationship portion appears at the end of the message.

c) The message contains both commercial (i.e., spam) and informational content (i.e., not spam); the subject line is commercial in nature; and the informational portion appears at the end of the message.

iii) **Requirements**: The Act applies to all commercial e-mail messages whether solicited or not. Any commercial e-mail message must include all of the following:

a) A clear and conspicuous notice that the message is an advertisement or solicitation.

b) A legitimate return e-mail coupled with a physical postal address.

c) A clear and conspicuous notice that the recipient may decline to receive future messages, i.e., an opt-out provision.

Chapter 2: Brokerage Concepts

d) A mechanism by which the recipient can actually decline future messages, or an e-mail address to which the recipient can send a declination (i.e., opt-out) message.

iv) **E-mails containing multiple advertisers**: Only the sender has to comply with the requirements. For example, a real estate broker sends e-mails to clients containing advertising for the broker along with an advertisement from a loan officer with whom the broker works. Only the broker as sender must comply.

v) **Penalties**: Significant penalties exist. Fraudulent activities and repeat offenses may result in imprisonment for three-to-five years. Violators are subject to actual damages, statutory damages, or fines of $250 per violation. Each unlawful message may constitute a separate violation with damages up to $2,000,000. Additional penalties may be issued if an individual gains unauthorized access to the computer of another, i.e., hacks it, to either relay spam or to harvest the e-mail addresses of the hacked person for the purpose of spamming his addressees.

vi) **Impact on real estate licensees**: Licensees must be aware that any e-mail messages they send have the potential to fit, or be interpreted as fitting, the definitions of the Act. A good practice is to strictly adhere to all requirements of the Act.

(c) **State law–Unsolicited Commercial E-mail Protection Act**: In 2003, Michigan adopted its own law governing unsolicited commercial e-mail messages. The state Act only applies to commercial e-mails sent to Michigan residents or those sent via an e-mail service provider located in the state.

Requirements for e-mails include:

i) The subject line must include "ADV:" as its first four characters. Note that the colon (:) counts as a character.

ii) Conspicuously include the sender's name, street address, Internet domain name, and return e-mail address.

iii) Establish a toll-free telephone number, return e-mail address, or other electronic method for notifying the sender not to send further messages.

iv) Conspicuously provide a notice that the recipient may conveniently, and at no-cost, be excluded from future e-mail messages.

3. **Personal safety and property crime considerations**: Real estate is an honorable profession in which sellers, buyers, and licensees work to facilitate mutually beneficial outcomes. Nevertheless, the business still involves human interaction in which personal safety and property crime issues can arise at any time. By adopting a policy of awareness, vigilance, and common sense, licensees may have little reason to fear working with the public.

    a. **Personal safety**: Regarding personal safety, most crimes are initiated during daylight hours and involve the selling side of the transaction, i.e., working with buyers, as opposed to the listing side, i.e., working with sellers. A few general safety guidelines include pre-qualifying all buyers by gathering personal information prior to working with them, not meeting strangers at vacant properties at night, not riding in cars with strangers, not wearing expensive or flashy jewelry during appointments outside of the office, and always carrying a cell phone with a fully charged battery.

    b. **Property crime considerations**: Property crime is also an issue for real estate agents, especially when a large number of vacant and distressed properties are on the market. Keys, lockbox combinations, and other means of accessing vacant properties should never be provided to buyers or any other unauthorized individual. Some common sense property crime prevention suggestions regarding open houses were provided earlier in this chapter.

4. **Administrative requirements for brokers**: Real estate brokers must fulfill many key supervisory, managerial, recordkeeping, and reporting requirements under license law and rules requirements. A sound risk management policy is also essential. Insurance policy provisions may also require a broker to fulfill other requirements such as periodic internal audits.

    a. **Business matters**: A real estate brokerage operation can be established under a number of different business arrangements or legal entities such as a sole proprietorship, partnership, corporation, limited liability corporation, or professional corporation. The choice of which one to use is up to each individual broker after careful consultation with both legal and financial advisors. Chapter 7 discusses these various business entities.

    b. **General recordkeeping, bookkeeping, and reporting requirements**: Recordkeeping is central to a brokerage operation. Various requirements exist for things such as: IRS income tax, payroll, and business filings; state business filings such as the Michigan Annual Report; trust account recordkeeping; employee and personnel records management; open and closed transaction files that include copies of all disclosures, contracts, and addenda; and general accounting procedures and records including profit and loss statements, banking statements, and accounts payable and receivable.

    c. **Insurance**: All businesses face certain risks for which insurance should be purchased. A brokerage operation is no exception. Brokers should consider the following types of policies: General Liability Insurance; Professional Liability/Errors and Omissions Insurance; and Commercial Property Insurance including coverage for lost income and business interruption. Since many affiliated licensees also conduct business out of home offices, they should consider adding a form of home-based business insurance. Umbrella policies are also available to fill in gaps in other liability policies. The distinctions between these types of policies are discussed in Chapter 15.

    d. **Compliance with license law**: Several license law requirements exist that can impact a brokerage operation including supervision of affiliated licensees, maintenance of trust accounts including recordkeeping requirements, compliance with requirements as to license renewals, transfers and terminations, advertising, and other issues relating to practice and conduct. Pursuant to a 2015 change in license law, the broker may also wish to ascertain that all affiliated licensees have fulfilled their annual continuing education requirements, and to keep a copy of the licensee's proof of attendance.

    e. **Personnel management**: A broker will not only hire and supervise numerous affiliated licensees, but may also hire and manage clerical assistance for the office including administrative personnel, secretaries, and receptionists. Proper management of employees requires the meticulous maintenance of personnel records. Additionally, the broker is also ultimately responsible for licensed assistants who work for an affiliated licensee.

5. **Recruiting and training of sales staff for brokers**: The most important element of any successful brokerage operation is a team of productive and ethical sales associates. Building a sales team depends on the broker's ability to recruit, train, and retain licensees who are energetic and anxious to excel.

    a. **Recruiting**: Some companies seek to hire and then train individuals who are new to the business. Other brokers prefer to focus on hiring mostly experienced licensees who are seeking a transfer from another company. Most, however, seek to balance their hiring practices by recruiting both new and experienced licensees. Newly-licensed salespersons should resist any temptation to change employment from one broker to another until they have had an opportunity to thoroughly learn the business. Switching brokers early in a career is not a productive way to learn the business.

    b. **Sales training**: Sales associates typically look to their broker and manager for education, business advice, counseling, and direction on business practices. A comprehensive in-office sales training program is the primary tool used to prepare new salespersons to become successful and existing salespeople to reach new levels of production. Sales training also adds value to a broker's risk management practices. This is due to the fact that non-productive sales associates might be more likely to cut corners and bend the rules out of desperation.

    Sales training is sometimes referred to as post-license training. There are a number of different resources available to brokers to train staff. Some brokers have developed their own training programs built around their company contracts, forms, and addenda. Others use outside resources such as DVDs or online, web-based training modules. Franchise companies typically provide online training modules that independently-owned and operated broker-franchisees can utilize. Regardless of the tools used, nearly all brokers incorporate them into a classroom-style multi-day program conducted by the company broker, manager, trainer, attorney, and/or veteran affiliated licensees to make sure that the culture of the broker's company is embedded in the program.

DIAGNOSTIC PRACTICE QUESTIONS – CHAPTER 2

IMPORTANT STUDY TIP!

Step 1: Carefully review the information located in this chapter.

Step 2: Take the following Diagnostic Practice Questions. Review any question you answered incorrectly by researching the topic in this textbook. If you are still uncertain as to why the question is answered as it is, consult your program provider.

NOTE ON CHAPTER PRACTICE QUESTIONS

The following questions are representative of the type encountered on the Michigan real estate licensing examination. While some of these questions may be similar in nature and style, there is no way of predicting the exact wording of a question that will appear on the exam. Spending time memorizing these questions is, therefore, not recommended.

These questions are designed to help you determine how well you comprehend the material in this chapter. They are also intended to help you develop problem solving skills and to become comfortable with question formats.

Do not attempt to answer these questions until you have attended the lecture corresponding to this chapter and spent the appropriate time studying the material.

1. Listing Broker is contacted by a local Buyer's Agent who is inquiring about one of Listing Broker's advertised properties. Listing Broker recalls a previous deal with Buyer's Agent that went sour and, as a result, refuses to deal with him on his current listing. Which of the following statements is true?
   A. Listing Broker should obtain the name of the buyer and contact him directly to show the listed property.
   B. Buyer's Agent must immediately inform his client of the Listing Broker's refusal to set the showing appointment.
   C. Listing Broker has acted in his client's best interests due to the increased chance of another failed deal.
   D. Buyer Agent should take his buyer-client to the property on his own and insist that the buyer be given access.

2. Depending on the nature of the relationship between a buyer and a real estate broker, the buyer may be referred to as a "client." This means that the buyer is:
   A. Working with a broker who owes the full extent of fiduciary duties.
   B. Being represented by a transaction coordinator.
   C. Not being represented by an agent.
   D. Working with a general agent as opposed to a special agent.

3. Salesperson Yankim signs a listing agreement with the owners of a home in Low Heights. The Low Heights property is placed in the multi-list in the hope of attracting a qualified buyer. Buyer Branford drives by the property and notices a "For Sale" sign with Yankim's name and telephone number on it. Branford calls Yankim to see the property, but Yankim suggests that they first meet at his real estate office. At the office, Branford reviews the agency disclosure statement and signs a buyer's agency contract with Yankim. Which of the following statements applies to this situation?
   A. Because no purchase agreement has been signed yet, Yankim is merely a single agent acting for the seller on the listing agreement and a single agent working for the buyer under the buyer's agency agreement.
   B. Since Branford called using the number on the "For Sale" sign in seller's front yard, Yankim should have first shown the property as a seller's agent and then given Branford the option of being represented as a buyer's agent.
   C. Yankim should have asked another agent in the office to show the property to Branford in order to avoid any conflict of interest claims by either the seller or the buyer.
   D. Yankim has created a dual agency relationship and must act in the best interests of both the seller and the buyer according to the terms of their respective agreements.

4. The fiduciary duties that an agent owes her client include all of the following EXCEPT the duty to:
   A. Tell the client anything that might influence his decision to make or accept a particular offer.

B. Obey absolutely every instruction issued by the client so long as the request involves the transaction.
C. Inform the client of the true market value of the property regardless of the owner's desired sale price.
D. Keep confidential any reasons for selling or buying that might prove to be a negotiating advantage for the other non-represented party.

5. Agent Apol is staying in touch with several buyers who have expressed an interest in one of his listings. Heathcoat, a licensed salesperson working for another broker, calls Apol to present an offer on the listed property that Apol's other buyers are also considering. Apol should:
   A. Present the offer to the seller upon receipt and inform the seller that other buyers might still be interested.
   B. Have the offer dropped off at his office and retain it until the other buyers can be contacted to determine their seriousness.
   C. Contact the seller informing him that an offer has been received and then immediately disclose the offer amount to the other buyers to see if he can get a higher price for his seller.
   D. Hold off presenting the offer for 72 hours to give the other buyers a fair opportunity to make their best offer and then present all offers at the same time.

6. Darlonna, a top-producing salesperson, regularly contacts potential customers via telephone. According to the federal Do Not Call law, which of the following statements applies to her activities?
   A. Darlonna can call anyone that she has previously contacted within a 24 month window.
   B. Real estate licensees are exempt under federal law since Michigan has its own Do Not Call statute.
   C. Darlonna must check her contact list against the federal registry and may call anyone whose telephone number is not currently registered.
   D. Darlonna must comply with the federal law in all cases.

7. An agent who has authority to perform all lawful acts for a principal is referred to as a(n):
   A. Special agent.
   B. General agent.
   C. Universal agent.
   D. Implied agent.

8. When a broker enters into a listing agreement with a seller, which of the following statements is most accurate?
   A. The seller is the fiduciary.
   B. The seller is the principal of the buyer.
   C. The broker's salesperson is the agent.
   D. The broker is the agent of the seller.

9. Brokers must submit offers which are:
   A. issued for full price and terms only.
   B. below the listing price, but not above.
   C. above the listing price.
   D. of any amount.

10. Broker Brown works under an agency policy that does not permit the practice of buyer's agency. Brown, who is acting as a subagent, is showing another broker's listing to Buyer Green. When Green suggests that he might be more comfortable working with a buyer's agent, Brown states, "Do not worry Mr. Green. Since the seller has the listing agent on his side, I will look after you." Which of the following statements best describes the relationship between Broker Brown and Buyer Green?
    A. Brown is an implied agent.
    B. Brown is working under an express agency with Green.
    C. Brown is an actual agent.
    D. Brown is operating under a single agency.

11. One who engages another to act for him under a contractual agreement is referred to as:
    A. a principal.
    B. an agent.
    C. a grantor.
    D. a third party.

12. A For-Sale-By-Owner classified advertisement is placed in a local newspaper with the words "Buyers Only" included in the advertisement. What do these words most likely mean?
    A. Only persons who unquestionably have sufficient capital to buy should inquire.
    B. Only persons with serious intentions to buy should inquire.
    C. Only persons who intend to occupy the property should inquire.
    D. No real estate agents should inquire.

13. Which of the following applies to a limited service broker?
    A. The fiduciary duties owed the client are limited.
    B. A limited service broker may not participate in a multiple listing service.
    C. No statutory services are owed to a client.
    D. An agency relationship exists between the limited service broker and her client.

14. A fiduciary relationship exists between which of the following:
    A. A buyer and a seller.
    B. A buyer's agent and a principal.

Chapter 2: Brokerage Concepts

    C. Two listing agents.
    D. A seller/customer and a licensee.

15. A salesperson is informed by a listing seller that there is a problem with a leaky roof and termites. The salesperson must immediately do which of the following?
    A. Report the situation to his broker.
    B. Report the situation to the multiple listing service to warn prospective purchasers.
    C. Inform prospective buyers in all instances.
    D. Require that the roof be repaired and that an exterminator be hired before any showing.

16. Which of the following persons most closely fits the definition of a subagent in a real estate transaction?
    A. The salesperson.
    B. The cooperating broker.
    C. The listing broker.
    D. The escrow agent.

Study:

Fiduciary

9th 14

Agency examples

Just as the body requires rest after workouts, so too does the mind require periods of silence. Spend time each day unplugged from technology. Text messaging and social media will survive without you for a few hours.

Chapter 3
The Listing Agreement

Creating the agency relationship.

I. **Forward**: In Chapter 2 we explored agency law and the various relationships that brokers and salespersons can have with clients, customers, and each other. This Chapter delves into the mechanics of service provision agreements as well as the evolving face of agency relationships. A listing agreement is one type of service provision agreement. It is the primary employment contract for a broker. It protects both the broker and his principal since it clearly spells out the duties, responsibilities, and expectations for their relationship. Equally important to the broker, the contract also limits what the broker and his affiliated licensees are expected to do. Recall from Chapter 2 that a buyer's agency contract can be viewed as a form of listing agreement between a broker and a buyer-client.

All licensees must have a complete and detailed understanding of the nature of service provision agreements. This essential body of knowledge is used by licensees to explain to seller-clients and buyer-clients what they are agreeing to when signing a service provision agreement. Further, it is used to explain what is occurring as the duties in the service provision agreement are being fulfilled. A licensee should not ask his prospective client to sign a contract the licensee does not understand himself.

II. ▶ **Listing agreement**: By definition, a traditional listing agreement is a contract entered into by the seller of a property and a real estate broker in which the broker is hired as the seller's agent. This contract is actually an agreement to market the seller's property through the broker's efforts in exchange for the payment of a commission upon successful conclusion of the contract. As the essentials of a listing contract are discussed in this chapter, assume that they apply equally to a buyer's agency contract unless stated otherwise.

   A. ▶ **Buyer versus seller representation**: We learned in Chapter 2 that a buyer can hire a broker to represent the buyer in the purchase of a property by entering into a buyer's agency contract. Buyer's agency and buyer representation are, essentially, identical terms. So are the terms buyer's agent and buyer's broker. A buyer's broker provides the same duties and services in representing the buyer as a seller's agent provides to his seller-client.

   B. **Basic contract considerations**: A listing agreement has a basis in both agency law and contract law. Agency and contract principles actually merge in a listing situation. This chapter contains a discussion of agency principles coupled with some principles of contract law. For a deeper analysis of contract law, refer to Chapter 12.

      1. **Unilateral versus bilateral agreement**: Modern listing agreements are viewed as bilateral in nature. A bilateral contract contains two promises which are exchanged for one another. In a traditional listing agreement, the broker promises to use best efforts and due diligence in the performance of his duties to locate a suitable buyer for the seller's property in exchange for the seller's promise to cooperate in the agreement and pay the agreed upon commission. In the case of a buyer's agency contract, the broker promises to use best efforts and due diligence to search for a suitable property.

         a. ▶ **Need for a written agreement**: A listing must be in writing for a number of important reasons such as (1) to avoid confusion and disagreements that can flow from oral agreements, (2) to comply with state license laws that require a listing agreement to be in writing before a broker can sue for nonpayment of a commission, and (3) to satisfy the statute of frauds which requires certain contracts to be in writing to be enforceable in a court of law.

            (1) **Drafting (preparing) the contract**: Since a real estate broker is a party to the listing contract, he may draft it without necessarily being accused of practicing law without a license. Nevertheless, using standardized pre-printed forms is prudent. Whether or not a standardized form is used, the broker is still treated as the drafting party from a legal perspective since he controls its contents. This means that any uncertain, vague, or ambiguous provisions could be construed, meaning

interpreted, in a light most favorable to the seller and against the broker. When contracts are ambiguous, courts first try to ascertain the intent of the parties before deciding against the drafting party.

2. ▶ **Parties to the contract**: There are two potential issues involving the parties to a listing agreement that could impact a broker's ability to collect a commission. These issues include making sure all owners sign the listing document and that the owners have legal capacity to enter into the contract.

   a. **All owners should sign**: Many of the properties that brokers list are owned by more than one title holder. To protect the broker in the event of a commission dispute, the listing should be signed by all owners. For example, if the sellers are a married couple, both the husband and the wife should sign. As will become clear in later chapters, this holds true even if the property is titled in the husband's or wife's name alone. Unfortunately, there are times when a married couple may not be in complete agreement about selling their property. Getting all parties to agree to the terms of the listing and sign it assures the broker that each one intends to sell and pay for the broker's services.

   b. **Legal capacity**: All parties to the contract must be of sound mind and legal age. A contract entered into by a minor is legally voidable by the minor should he change his mind about listing the property. Similarly, the broker may not be able to enforce a commission payment against a person with a cognitive disability or impairment. A physical disability, formerly referred to as a handicap, does not disqualify a person from listing his property.

3. ▶ **Listing agreement considerations**: As noted, brokers and their affiliated licensees must be sufficiently familiar with their company contracts and forms, including all key provisions and legal details, so they can discuss them with seller-clients and buyer-clients. They must also know how to fill in all blank spaces so they meet each client's expectations in a legally-appropriate manner. Some brokers use standard forms provided either by local real estate associations or MLS service providers. Other brokers prefer to use forms that have been drafted by their company attorneys. Whichever form is ultimately used, there are key provisions common to all listing agreements.

   a. **Key provisions**: The provisions of a listing agreement are important since failing to include or sufficiently describe some terms and conditions can invalidate the listing along with the clause that entitles the broker to his commission. Listing contract terms and conditions can vary somewhat from one broker to the next. Most of the following items are included in one of the listing-related forms prepared by the broker or his affiliated licensees.

      (1) Names of the parties to the agreement, i.e., the broker and the client;

      (2) Legally sufficient description of the property;

      (3) Type of listing, e.g., open, exclusive, non-exclusive, limited service, etc.;

      (4) Sale price and other essential terms;

      (5) Items such as fixtures to be excluded or personal property such as appliances to be included as part of the sale;

      (6) Brokerage fee and protection period details;

      (7) Nondiscrimination clause;

      (8) Earnest money deposit with disbursement language if the buyer defaults and signs a mutual release of deposit;

      (9) Right to submit the property to a multiple listing service and fee-splitting policy with cooperating brokers, right to erect a "for sale" sign, right to post the listing on the Internet, and right to use a lockbox on the property; and

      (10) Mandatory disclosures, certifications, and inspections that may be required.

   b. **Other listing details**: A number of other details must be considered in connection with a listing agreement. The accuracy of the following details depends on the licensee's knowledge of real estate and his ability to obtain it either from the seller or another reliable source.

      (1) Type of property construction and property age for purposes of lead disclosure requirements;

      (2) Lot size;

Chapter 3: The Listing Agreement

(3) Physical dimensions of the structure (which may have to be physically measured by the licensee);

(4) Appurtenances such as easements and water rights;

(5) Presence of utilities which can include electricity, gas, water, sewer, cable, etc.;

(6) Compliance with health and safety building codes;

(7) Encumbrances such as easements, liens, etc.;

(8) Whether or not the property is subject to a homeowner's or condominium association by-laws and association fees; and

(9) Amenities that may be present, i.e., features that increase property attractiveness or value such as location, view, and unique design features of the house itself.

c. **Additional provisions unique to buyer's agency agreements**: While a buyer's agency agreement is a type of service provision agreement, it contains certain provisions that are unique to representing a buyer in the acquisition of a property. The same holds true if the client is a tenant who hires a licensee to search for a rental property.

(1) **Property**: In a seller listing, a specific, identifiable property exists that the listing broker will market. In a buyer's agency agreement, the buyer sets forth the criteria (i.e., range of features) of the type of home he would consider purchasing. For example: type of house, type of construction, price range, and geographical location.

(2) **Commission**: Some buyer's agency agreements include an option for payment of a retainer fee to the buyer's agent (in addition to a purchase-based commission). This is due to the fact that a search for a unique property may involve hours of research only to yield no sale and commission. The buyer's agent can also agree to apply the retainer to any commission should the buyer purchase a property.

(3) **Conflict of interest**: The contract will typically include a clause authorizing the buyer's agent to represent multiple buyer-clients, show them the same homes, and prepare offers on the same home without constituting a breach of fiduciary duty to any individual buyer-client.

(4) **Dual agency authorization**: A buyer's agency agreement often contains a dual agency authorization that allows the buyer's agent to assist a buyer-client in making an offer on a property listed with the company.

(5) **Limitations of liability**: The agreement typically contains one or more sections in which the buyer's agent limits the expectations of the buyer-client as to what a buyer's agent is expected to do. For example, the client acknowledges that the broker is not acting as an attorney, tax advisor, structural engineer, home inspector, environmental expert, etc. Another clause may indicate that the buyer-client is not relying on the broker to decide what property is best suited for the buyer-client.

C. ▶ **Compensation for real estate brokerage services**: There are several different types of compensation formulas that can be used in a listing agreement. While the broker gets to choose which formula to offer and ultimately accept, commissions are always negotiable between the broker and the client.

1. ▶ **Method of calculation**: Commissions are commonly based on a fixed percentage of the actual sale price rather than the list price. Even within this formula, other variations exist. The nature of the commission and how it is calculated must be specified in the contract. It can be a contingent fee, non-contingent fee, or variable rate.

    a. **Contingent fee**: From a legal perspective, when something is contingent, is tied to the occurrence of a condition or event. A contingent commission is, therefore, tied directly to the sale of the property meaning that no commission is deemed earned unless the property is actually sold. Depending on the terms of the agreement, the commission may also be contingent on the transaction actually closing. In this sense, the sale (and possibly the closing) becomes a condition to payment of the commission. Contingent commissions may be negotiated as a percent, or less commonly, a flat fee.

    (1) **Percentage fee**: In the case of a percentage fee, the commission is a calculated percent of the sale price of the property. The actual percent, while set by the broker, is negotiable. Further, the negotiated percent with one client can vary from the negotiated percent of another. A salesperson who negotiates a different percent with a prospective client needs the prior consent of the broker.

(2) **Flat rate fee**: With a flat fee, the parties negotiate the commission as a fixed dollar amount or flat rate which does not vary based on the actual sale price. Due to the risk of uncertainty in how much effort will be required by the broker in procuring a buyer, flat fee commissions are not common. They would be more likely used by a limited service broker with a limited service or MLS-only listing.

b. **Non-contingent fee**: A non-contingent fee is one in which the client pays the commission whether or not the property sells. In other words, the commission is not conditioned on the sale of the property. Non-contingent fees tend to be calculated on an hourly basis or as a prepaid retainer. Care must be exercised with respect to other prepaid fees as some of them may be illegal; e.g., a mortgage assistance relief service fee (MARS) charged in connection with a distressed property transaction (see Chapter 16 for details). A non-contingent commission would more likely be assessed by a limited service broker.

c. **Variable rate**: A variable rate commission is a negotiated fee that changes if certain conditions occur during the sales process. For example, Broker Smith charges a seller-client a 7% commission if the sale is consummated on a cooperative basis with another broker in the MLS. This is due to the fact that Smith has to share the total commission with the selling broker. Smith's commission rate lowers to 6% if the selling agent is a licensee within Smith's company. It lowers again to 5% if Smith personally locates the buyer. The savings of not having to split the commission is shared with the seller-client. A variable rate commission may also be called a dual rate commission.

2. ▸ **Enforcement of a commission payment**: The precise commission language in a listing contract must be thoroughly understood as it determines the conditions under which the commission is earned. One listing, for example, may specify that the commission is earned when a buyer is found who makes an offer acceptable to the seller. Another contract may state that the commission is earned when the transaction actually closes.

   a. **Commission conditioned on closing**: If the commission is conditioned on the closing rather than merely procuring a ready, willing, and able buyer, the seller is protected against unexpected financing or title problems that may arise for the buyer which prevent the buyer from closing.

      (1) **Financing problems**: A buyer acting in good faith may not be able to qualify for the type of loan needed to purchase the property. As discussed in Chapter 12, purchase agreements typically contain contingency clauses to protect buyers under these circumstances.

      (2) **Title problems**: The seller acting in good faith may not be able to convey clear title to the property at the closing due to circumstances beyond the seller's control. For example, a lien is filed against the home days before the closing. While the seller may be able to contest the validity of the lien, it is still a problem that may take some time to resolve.

      (3) **Unfavorable inspection or sudden defect**: A buyer may elect not to complete the purchase due to a property defect that is discovered by a home inspector. Or, the buyer of a vacant property conducts a final walk-though before the closing and sees damages of which the seller was not aware.

      (4) **Bad faith by a seller**: The seller may not attempt to avoid paying a commission by failing to cooperate with property showings or by frustrating the closing without just cause. If a seller acts in bad faith, the broker may still be able to bring a legal action for payment of an earned commission.

   b. **Buyer with full price offer cannot force seller to sell**: Assume that the broker locates a ready, willing, and able buyer who makes a full price offer, but the seller refuses to sell the property. Under these circumstances, the buyer cannot force the seller to sell because the buyer is not a party to the listing contract. A seller makes no promises to potential buyers in a listing agreement or by marketing the property on a multiple listing service (MLS). Depending on the seller's reasons for refusing to sell, however, the broker may be able to sue the seller for the commission since the terms of the listing have technically been met.

   c. **Salesperson's right to sue**: A salesperson acts as an agent of the broker and, consequently, has no direct contractual relationship with a seller. Therefore, a salesperson cannot sue a seller for nonpayment of a commission. If the broker collects the commission and refuses to pay his salesperson the agreed-upon share, the salesperson may bring an action against the broker for payment of his portion of the commission.

3. ▸ **Antitrust considerations**: State and federal antitrust laws protect free trade by prohibiting certain acts that interfere with free and open competition in the marketplace. Antitrust laws affect how real estate

brokers establish their commission structures and conduct their businesses. Compliance is a critical part of a broker's risk management program. Consequently, the broker should include compliance requirements for all affiliated licensees in the broker's policies and procedures manual.

a. **Full service versus limited service brokers**: Traditionally, most buyers and sellers work with brokers who provide full, which may also be called bundled, real estate services. A seller hires a full service broker to handle all aspects of the transaction including advertising, showings, presentations of offers, negotiation of a purchase agreement, and management of all transaction details through completion at the closing. Some sellers, however, seek out brokers who provide limited or unbundled services in exchange for reduced fees. Descriptive terms for these services include limited service, fee-for-service, or unbundled service. Michigan law refers to such broker as a limited service broker.

It is important to remember that all licensed real estate brokers in Michigan are bound by the same real estate laws, rules, and regulations. It does not matter who the broker is, what agency relationships are offered, the commission structure, or service provision agreements that are used. For example, a limited service broker acting pursuant to a limited service listing owes his client the same level of fiduciary duties that a full service broker owes to his client.

b. ▶ **Commission rates are not set by law or mutual agreement between brokers**: Commission rates and/or amounts (1) are not set by law and (2) cannot be established or modified by agreement between competing brokers. This is a critical aspect of antitrust laws which are designed to prevent price fixing. Even the mere discussion of commission rates between competing brokers can serve as evidence of a plan to engage in price fixing.

(1) **Commissions must be negotiable**: Even though an individual broker is allowed to set the desired fee for his services, commissions are always deemed negotiable between the broker and his clients. Similarly, an individual broker is absolutely free to establish the nature of his specific business practice; for example, whether to offer a "full service-full commission" structure, a "full service-discount commission" structure, or a "limited service-limited fee" structure.

(2) **Independent business judgment**: An individual broker can establish his preferred commission and service structures. This is called the exercise of independent business judgment. It is a violation of antitrust law, however, if a broker tells a prospective client that commission rates or service levels are set by industry agreement or the real estate association.

c. ▶ **Price fixing**: By law, the marketplace must be free and open so consumers can benefit from competition among businesses. Any attempt by two or more businesses to set prices at higher levels deprives consumers of this benefit. Federal law, in particular, Section 1 of the Sherman Antitrust Act, prohibits any "contract, combination, or conspiracy" that sets or attempts to set a common pricing structure among otherwise competing businesses. This is known as price fixing and is an illegal restraint of trade. The term trade, in this context, refers to competition.

When an individual licensee discusses his company's commission structure with a potential client, the licensee should sell the benefits of the company's services and why it charges the fee it does. No reference should be made to what other companies offer or charge. This also holds true if the prospective client were to ask, "Why do you charge 6% when Broker X only charges 5%?"

(1) **"Per se" violation**: Acts of price fixing are considered to be per se illegal. A per se violation is any wrongful act which is actionable in and of itself without the defendant being able to offer an explanation or justification why the act was committed. Any discussion regarding raising commission rates or agreeing not to lower them between independent brokers is a per se violation of antitrust law.

(2) ▶ **Brokerage cooperation and referral fees may be discussed**: Two brokers may discuss MLS or private compensation sharing arrangements since it represents a separate agreement between the brokers. For example, a listing broker can discuss the fee he offers to selling brokers via the MLS. Brokers can also discuss or negotiate referral fees among themselves. For example, Broker Jones from Grand Rapids has a seller-client who is moving to the Detroit area and needs to purchase a home. Jones calls Broker Smith, a relocation specialist from Detroit, and asks about Smith's referral policy. Smith may tell Jones that he pays a 20% referral upon the successful closing of any purchase without triggering an antitrust violation.

d. ▶ **Boycott**: A boycott is also known as a concerted refusal to do business or deal with a particular person or business. Concerted means combined or planned. The purpose and intent of a boycott is to cause harm to the boycotted person or to get him to change his trade practices. For example, several full service brokers discuss not showing the listings of a new limited service broker who just opened a brokerage operation in the area. Their purpose is to drive the limited service broker out of business, force him to stop offering lower rate-limited services, or make it so no consumers will list their properties with him. In a manner similar to price fixing, boycotting is treated as a per se violation.

e. ▶ **Dangerous phrases**: There are certain phrases that, when uttered by a real estate professional, may be used as evidence that an alleged antitrust violation has occurred. Phrases such as those listed below must be carefully avoided. Even the most innocent of questions can pose a potential problem. The fact that the uttering broker harbored no ill intent is irrelevant. Even if the group of brokers eventually change their individual rates independently of one another, the conversation could be used as evidence of price fixing.

Any licensee who finds himself in a conversation where potentially dangerous phrases are being used should immediately withdraw from the discussion. Some commentators also recommend telling the group the reason for the withdrawal. The licensee should also consider noting the pertinent details of the event and that he left the discussion promptly. If the licensee is a salesperson, he should also mention it to his broker.

(1) **Price fixing**: Here are some example phrases suggesting that price fixing has occurred.

(a) **Example 1**: A salesperson tells a prospective seller-client, "We have to charge 6%, it's the law" or "6% is the going rate charged by everyone."

(b) **Example 2**: One broker talking to a competing broker, "Let's keep our commission rates at 6%. Between the two of us we'll make enough money without having to compete with the discount broker down the street."

(c) **Example 3**: One broker talking to another broker, "The accelerated commission splits I have to give my sales associates just to keep them happy are making it so I can't make any money as a broker. Do you have the same problem at your company?"

(d) **Example 4**: One broker quietly tells another broker at an association meeting, "I'm going to lower what I offer other brokers in the MLS to 2% since they really don't do that much to help my sellers." Note: This could be evidence of price fixing because the discussion pertains to general pricing policies between competing brokers rather than an independent negotiation involving a single-transaction commission split between a listing broker and a cooperating, i.e., selling, broker.

(2) **Group boycott**: Here are some example phrases that can implicate acts of boycotting.

(a) **Example 1**: A salesperson working for a full service broker tells a potential listing seller who is also interviewing discount and limited service brokers, "Go ahead and list with those cut-rate companies, no other agent will ever show your home! List with me at 6% and everyone will show it."

(b) **Example 2**: Several full service brokers are having coffee at a restaurant. One broker says to the group, "Maybe we should send a message to the discount brokers by refusing to show their homes. They'll get the idea and come around to our way of doing business."

(c) **Example 3**: Several brokers openly and collectively agree not to place advertisements in a local newspaper until the company agrees to lower its advertising rates. A broker could, however, unilaterally elect to not to place advertisements based on the newspaper's fee structure.

4. **Broker transaction, administrative, and document preparation fees**: A number of years ago, some brokers began charging a modest flat fee in addition to a traditional percentage fee. These fees are commonly labeled "transaction fees," "administrative fees," or some similar name. They are typically charged by the broker to offset the rising costs of doing business. Not only have business costs risen, but brokers have also offered increasingly generous commission splits to attract existing licensees to join their firms.

a. **Not RESPA violation**: The federal Real Estate Settlement Procedures Act prevents settlement service providers, including real estate brokers, from paying kickbacks to other settlement service providers and from charging unearned fees. RESPA is discussed in further detail in Chapter 9. As long as a

Chapter 3: The Listing Agreement

transaction fee is part of the broker's ordinary commission fee structure, it does not necessarily violate RESPA. For example, an individual broker establishes his contingent commission structure at 6% of the selling price plus a flat transaction fee of $150. A broker should check with legal counsel before charging transaction fees to make sure that they are legal under the circumstances.

- (1) **Fee can be negotiated by the seller**: Since a client can attempt to negotiate a broker's commission, the client can also negotiate any transaction fee the broker wishes to charge. Recall, however, that a broker has the right to establish or set his company's minimum commission fee structure. This holds equally true for additional transaction fees.

b. **Document preparation fees and the unauthorized practice of law**: The Michigan Supreme Court has held that the charging of a fee for the preparation of documents, especially when they are standard forms, does not necessarily constitute the unauthorized practice of law. A licensee should take care when discussing the reasons why such fee is charged whether it is labeled a transaction, administrative, or doc prep fee.

c. ▶ **REO or short sale compliance fees**: During the subprime mortgage crises, some brokers began charging a fee called an REO or short sale compliance fee. REO stands for "real estate owned." An REO property is one taken back by the lender through foreclosure who then lists it for sale through a real estate broker. Compliance fees essentially follow that same guidelines noted in this section. However, many listing brokers included a provision in the MLS that the fees were to be paid by a buyer who made an offer to purchase the listed property. Since a buyer is not bound to a provision in the MLS, the buyer is free to include or exclude its payment in the offer.

5. **IRS cash reporting requirements–Form 8300**: IRS Form 8300 must be completed by any person who is engaged in a trade or business and receives more than $10,000 in cash whether in a single transaction or two or more related transactions. Transactions conducted between a payer and a recipient within a 24-hour period are considered to be related. Reporting requirements pertain to qualifying money received in one lump sum or installments paid over the course of one year. Cash includes cashier's checks, traveler's checks, and money orders.

a. **Example**: A licensee who receives a cash commission payment, or cash to rent a building, that exceeds $10,000 is required to file the IRS form by the 15th day of receipt. The licensee should consult a CPA for advice on the latest in tax rules and filing requirements.

b. **Exemption**: An exemption exists for a real estate agent who receives qualifying cash from a principal and then applies the cash, within 15 days, to a second transaction where the cash is reported on Form 8300.

D. **Term of listing**: A listing agreement must include a definite expiration date that concludes the agreement by operation of law. If the broker wishes to extend the agency relationship, he must negotiate a new contract. Brokers can also use a listing extension form which operates like a written mutual agreement to modify the original listing and extend the expiration date. Michigan license law does not allow a listing to contain a provision that causes it to automatically renew unless cancelled by the client.

1. ▶ **Carryover provision**: A carryover clause in a listing agreement states that if anyone to whom the property was shown during the listing period purchases it within a certain period of time after the listing agreement expires, the seller is liable for the commission. It protects the broker's efforts when dealing with a buyer who previews the listed property during the term of the listing, but makes an offer shortly after expiration. It also discourages a seller-client from attempting to sidestep the broker and commission payment by negotiating a deal directly with the buyer to purchase the property shortly after expiration. The clause is also be referred to as a protection period, extender period, or extender clause. Buyer's agency contracts may also contain similar language.

2. **"Sells" versus "sold"**: Some protection periods specify that the broker is entitled to a commission if he "sells" the property during the protection period. In this case, the broker is entitled to the commission if the procured buyer executes a purchase agreement with the seller during the period. Other contracts entitle the broker to a commission only if the property is "sold" during the protection period. In this stricter instance, the closing must actually conclude during the protection period for the broker to have earned the commission.

E. ▶ **Types of listing agreements**: There are several different types of listing agreements that brokers can use. Most brokers tend to rely primarily on one type of listing based on the business model they use to conduct their respective businesses. However, nothing prevents a broker from entering into different listing types to accommodate the varied needs of their clients.

From a seller-client's perspective, the type of listing is a matter of choice. This choice may be dictated by the seller's goal. For example, one seller may be interested in working with a broker who offers a limited service brokerage. Another seller may desire an exclusive right to sell listing with an excluded party. The listing types will now be explored in more detail.

1. ▶ **Open listing (non-exclusive):** In an open listing, the seller is able to list his property with any number of different brokers at the same time. This is a non-exclusive form of listing. The individual broker who locates the ready, willing, and able buyer is considered to be the procuring cause of sale and is entitled to the total negotiated commission. In a truly open listing, each broker signs a separate, non-exclusive listing with the seller and only the broker who is the procuring cause of the sale earns the commission.

    a. **Owner reserves the right to sell**: An additional characteristic of the open listing is that the owner reserves the right to personally locate a buyer without becoming liable for a commission. This represents an additional form of competition for the listing brokers. Open listings, while legal, are not common in the industry due to the investment of time and money brokers make in marketing listed properties.

2. ▶ **Exclusive listing:** The word "exclusive" means that only one broker is hired to handle the transaction as a seller's or buyer's agent. In the case of a listing agreement with a seller, should another broker find the buyer, the listing broker is entitled to payment of the commission even though he is technically not the procuring cause of the sale. An exclusive listing may also be referred to as an "exclusive agency" listing.

    a. **Owner reserves the right to sell**: As with the open listing, the seller in an exclusive listing reserves the right to personally locate the buyer and avoid paying the commission to the listing broker.

    b. **Example–Limited service (MLS-only) listing**: A seller is attempting to market his home on a for-sale-by-owner basis without much luck. A limited service broker offers to list the seller's home on an exclusive basis. The broker markets the seller-client's home by placing it on the MLS and handles all license law requirements pertaining to the preparation of the closing statement. The seller manages the other services that a full service broker would ordinarily provide. In exchange, the broker charges a non-contingent flat fee rather than a percentage-based commission. This may also be known as an MLS-only listing. Compare this to the one-party listing discussed later in this section.

    c. **Protecting selling brokers in cooperative transactions**: The selling, i.e., cooperating or coop, broker in a traditional listing agreement is the one who locates the buyer for the listed property. Since the listing broker under an exclusive listing is entitled to the full commission upon sale, a cooperation agreement is needed through which the listing broker agrees to compensate the selling broker. This agreement exists within the cooperation and compensation rules of the MLS. Compensation is typically reflected as a percent of the selling price offered by the listing broker to the cooperating broker who eventually becomes the procuring cause of the sale. This is discussed further later in this section.

    d. ▶ **Exclusive buyer's agency agreement**: While not common, a buyer-client can enter into a buyer's agency agreement with a broker in which the buyer reserves the right to negotiate directly with a for-sale-by-owner. In such case, the buyer does not owe a commission to the buyer's broker. The for-sale-by-owner is, in essence, an excluded party. This agreement operates like an exclusive listing between a seller-client and a listing broker.

3. ▶ **Exclusive right to sell listing:** The exclusive right to sell listing entitles the listing broker to a commission no matter who sells the property during the listing period. It is the most desirable and common form of listing for brokers. The following listing arrangements represent potential variations of an exclusive right to sell agreement. They may be used in special circumstances, such as attempting to list a home currently being marketed by the seller on a for-sale-by-owner basis.

    a. **One-party listing**: With a one-party listing, the seller's obligation to pay a commission is limited to one party, i.e., an interested buyer the listing agent has already identified and would like to introduce to the seller. A for-sale-by-owner seller might find this arrangement acceptable because it allows the seller to continue marketing his property without being obligated to a long-term listing.

    b. **Excluded party listing**: The broker under an excluded party listing agrees to exclude certain identified buyers with whom the seller has already attempted to negotiate a sale. If one of these buyers purchases the property during a specified period of time, the seller is relieved of his duty to pay a commission.

Chapter 3: The Listing Agreement

This listing variation is another tool that can be used to encourage a seller who attempted to sell on a for-sale-by-owner basis to list without worry that he will owe a commission if one of the seller's previously procured buyers purchases the property.

    c. **Shared listing**: Occasionally, a prospective seller may have a difficult time deciding between two independent brokers when listing his property. The two brokers can agree to co-list the property under one exclusive listing agreement. They share the commission regardless of which broker is the procuring cause of the sale. This type of listing is likely an exclusive right to sell listing rather than an open listing since it entitles the brokers to a commission regardless of who sells the property.

4. ▶ **Net listing**: In a net listing, the owner establishes a dollar amount he wants to net from the sale. The broker then sells the property for any amount he can, without cap or commission limit, and retains the portion exceeding the owner's net as his commission. For example, a seller tells a broker to net him $150,000 from the sale of his house. The broker is able to locate a buyer who is willing to pay $190,000 since this is the true market value. The broker retains the extra $40,000 as his commission. Since a licensee's superior knowledge of market values places him at an unfair advantage over an uninformed seller, a net listing is illegal in Michigan to the extent it is used to procure a commission.

5. **Multiple Listing Service (MLS)**: In basic terms, an MLS is an information-aggregating service through which a group of participating member brokers list and sell their properties within a common market area which can be as large as state-wide. The broker who works with the seller is called the listing broker and the broker who works with the buyer is referred to as the selling or cooperating broker. If a selling broker submits an offer on another broker's listing, the two cooperating brokers share the commission on a previously agreed upon basis. See Figure 9.

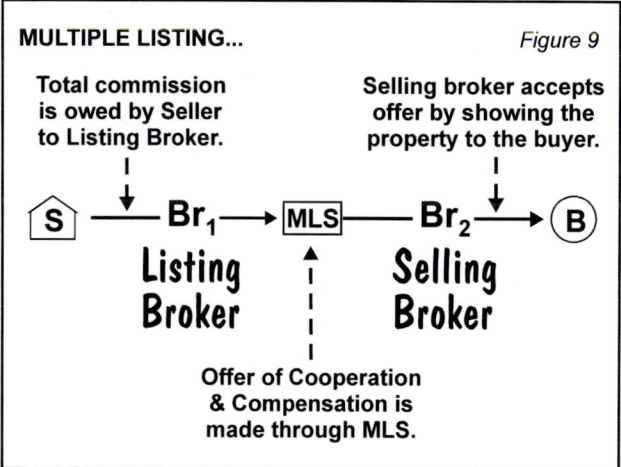

Figure 9

    a. **Unilateral offer of compensation**: Through the MLS, the listing broker makes a blanket unilateral offer of compensation to all participating brokers in exchange for their cooperation in locating a buyer. The compensation is typically a percent of the agreed upon selling price of the property. It is a unilateral offer meaning that the listing broker makes a promise to compensate without receiving a return promise from any of the MLS participant-brokers to locate a buyer. The listing broker's offer is deemed accepted if and when a participating broker actually procures an acceptable offer from a buyer. The payment of the commission is typically contingent on the closing.

      The listing agreement between the seller and the listing broker contains language authorizing the listing broker to share the commission. The listing broker actually controls the amount of compensation offered to selling brokers. Each broker then splits his specific share of the commission with any of his affiliated licensees who were involved on behalf of the broker. As one example, on a 6% total commission, the listing broker gives 3% to the cooperating broker and retains 3% for himself. The two brokers then split their commissions with their respective salespersons based on their commission sharing agreements.

    b. **Underlying rationale of MLS**: By submitting a listing to an MLS, the property receives significantly wider exposure which can result in a quicker sale. In this sense, MLS is synonymous with cooperation. Michigan license law does not require a broker to cooperate unless he has indicated or implied that he does. When a broker participates in an MLS, he advertises to the public that he cooperates with other brokers who participate in the MLS.

    c. **How an MLS works**: Upon listing a property, a special property data form is prepared which contains all essential details of the property. Upon receipt of the data form by the MLS, the information is entered into a computer database and broadcast via the Internet to all participating brokers. These brokers pay a monthly subscription fee for the right to access this information. Internet-based MLS databases have been the industry standard for a number of years. This allows for extraordinary information portability and search capabilities.

d. **Resolving commission disputes**: Commission disputes, while not an everyday occurrence, can result whenever multiple brokers work in a competitive marketplace. While disputes most frequently arise between two competing/selling brokers, they can occur between a buyer and a seller or a broker and his client. When a salesperson is involved, the matter is brought to the attention of and resolved by the employing broker. This is due to the fact that the broker, and not the salesperson, is the agent of record.

(1) ▶ **Procuring cause of sale**: Sometimes, a buyer will work with more than one broker on the same property. A dispute can arise between these brokers over entitlement to the selling share of the commission The primary objective is to determine which broker was the procuring cause of the sale. By definition, the procuring cause is the broker who originated the series of events, which without break in their continuity (meaning without interruption), resulted in the sale of the property. If the dispute is between two members of the National Association of REALTORS®, its Code of Ethics mandates that the brokers arbitrate it rather than litigate it in court. See Figure 10.

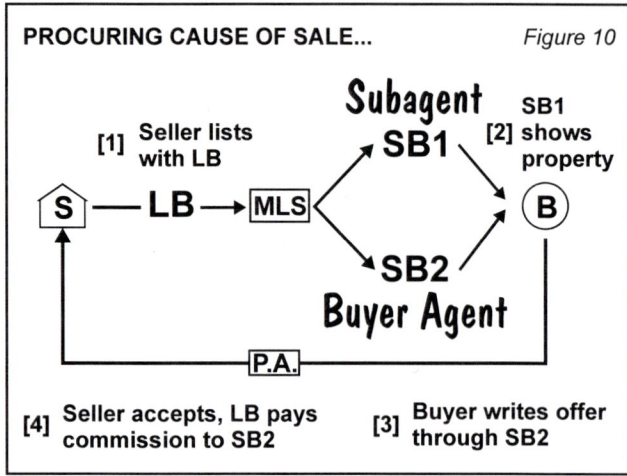

(2) **Act in the best interests of the transaction**: When brokers are involved in a commission dispute, they must do what is in the best interest of the real estate transaction. In other words, the clients should never be held hostage to a commission disagreement between their brokers. The closing should be allowed to proceed as scheduled. A hearing can be conducted thereafter to resolve the commission dispute. Arbitration or mediation is most often used rather than litigation. These forms of alternative dispute resolution are discussed further in Chapter 12.

6. ▶ **REO/bank-owned property**: When a lender forecloses on a property that is subject to a mortgage, it may become the high bidder at the sheriff's sale and own the property after expiration of the statutory redemption period. Once this occurs, the property is referred to as bank-owned or REO (which stands for "real estate owned"). Properties that have been taken back by secondary mortgage market participants Fannie Mae and Freddie Mac are also referred to as REO properties.

The lender, or secondary market participant, often lists its REO properties with approved licensed brokers to recoup as much of its mortgage investment in the property as possible. The broker may enter into a traditional exclusive right to sell listing, or a Fannie Mae Master Listing agreement, and market the property to potential buyers. REO property sales helped to maintain a degree of stability in the housing market as it recovered from the subprime mortgage crisis.

III. ▶ **Termination of an agency relationship**: A listing may be terminated in a number of different ways. As a general rule, the termination of an agency relationship releases the parties from any further obligation under the contract. However, an attempt by one party to terminate the agreement unilaterally may leave that party open to a claim for breach of contract. If the termination is deemed to be legally appropriate, the agent's authority to represent the principal ends. A termination may flow from the action of the parties or by operation of law.

A. **Action of parties**: Termination resulting from the action of the parties includes, performance, mutual consent, discharge, and resignation.

1. ▶ **Performance**: When the purpose of the listing has been fulfilled, the contract has been performed and ends naturally. The broker procures the ready, willing, and able buyer who makes an offer on terms acceptable to the seller, the seller formally accepts the buyer's offer, the transaction closes, and the broker is paid for his efforts.

2. ▶ **Mutual consent**: Since a listing agreement arises from the mutual agreement of the parties, they may also mutually agree to terminate it. Any release should be in writing. Mutual agreement may also be referred to as a bilateral termination.

Chapter 3: The Listing Agreement

a. **Conditional versus unconditional release**: When a broker excuses a seller from a listing agreement, he may issue either an unconditional release or a conditional release. In the case of an unconditional release, the seller is totally relieved of any further commission obligation. No restrictions are imposed on the seller as to any future marketing of the property, even through a different broker. With a conditional release, the seller is relieved from the contract providing he does not re-list with another broker for a stated period of time. The broker agrees to cease marketing efforts, but the listing contract remains enforceable should the seller sell it during the original term of the listing. This protects a broker who has invested time and resources marketing a seller's property.

3. **Discharge**: If the principal justifiably believes that his broker is not fully performing the contract duties in the listing agreement, the principal may discharge, i.e., fire, the broker. For example, the broker totally fails to market the property as promised or abandons all efforts in promoting the listing. The principal cannot unilaterally discharge the broker without cause, however.

4. **Resignation**: Just as a principal can discharge a broker who does not fulfill his fiduciary duties, the broker can resign from a listing. This could arise, for example, when the seller fails to meet his duty to cooperate with the broker by refusing to allow the property to be shown in a reasonable manner. Other examples could arise if the seller (1) orders the broker to lie about the physical condition of the property to potential buyers, or (2) violates fair housing laws by refusing to show the home to a particular buyer on the basis of the buyer's national origin. Resignation by a broker must be in good faith.

B. ▶ **Operation of law**: Termination resulting from operation of law includes expiration, destruction of the subject matter, material change in circumstances, and loss of capacity.

1. ▶ **Expiration**: An agency relationship is deemed to have expired, i.e., terminates, at the end of the specified term. Recall that the listing cannot contain a provision that causes it to automatically renew unless cancelled by the principal prior to expiration. Instead, the agent must enter into a new listing agreement with the client with a new expiration date.

2. ▶ **Destruction of subject matter**: When the subject matter of an agency is destroyed, the reason for its existence is lost. For example, a broker lists a residential property and the house is destroyed by fire prior to the broker procuring a buyer. The purpose of the listing is frustrated by the fire.

3. **Material change in circumstances**: When an agency is created, it is based on a set of facts known to the parties at that time. Should any of these facts change in an extreme and unforeseeable way, it may not be fair to enforce the continuation of the relationship. For example, a seller lists a property at market value and then discovers an oil reserve beneath the property that dramatically increases its value. The seller will likely be able to terminate the listing based on this significant change in circumstances.

4. **Loss of capacity**: According to contract law, all parties must have legal capacity; that is, they must be of sound mind and legal age. If the principal or broker had a mental or cognitive disability at the time of entering into the contract, the agency relationship could be terminated. A subsequent change may also terminate the relationship. Bankruptcy and death are two other events that impact capacity.

a. **Bankruptcy of either party**: Bankruptcy is a federally-authorized procedure that can be used to either liquidate or reorganize unpaid debt. In the case of a Chapter 7 bankruptcy, the debtor is relieved of nearly all his unsecured financial obligations. Under a Chapter 11 bankruptcy which is reserved for businesses, or a Chapter 13 bankruptcy which is reserved for individuals, the debtor enters into a longer-term reorganization plan that reduces the amount of debt to the extent the debtor is deemed able to repay it.

(1) **Ends the agency relationship**: The bankruptcy of either the principal or the broker generally terminates the agency relationship because the continuation of the relationship depends on the financial solvency of both parties. Since the principal's contractual relationship is with the broker, the bankruptcy of a salesperson does not affect the listing contract.

(2) **Effect on mortgage**: The bankruptcy of a property owner whose property is subject to a mortgage will liquidate or cancel the note which is the personal obligation, but not the mortgage which represents the lien. The mortgage can eventually be foreclosed by the lender.

b. ▶ **Death**: Since an agency relationship is a personal service contract, the death of either the principal or the broker destroys the relationship. Similar to bankruptcy, if a salesperson dies, the listing is not interrupted since the agency exists between the broker and the principal. If the broker's license has been issued to a business entity such as a corporation and the principal associate broker dies, a different associate broker is usually designated as the new principal and the listing continues without interruption.

Assume that a natural person is licensed as an individual broker, and that broker dies with pending offers awaiting acceptance or pending executed purchase agreements awaiting closings. Michigan's licensing department will allow all affiliated licensees a reasonable time to either wind up the business of the real estate broker or designate a new principal associate broker to the company.

IV. **The evolving face of agency law and brokerage practices**: Agency law has changed dramatically over the past couple of decades. This is due, in large part, to the development of new information technologies and the reliance on the Internet by consumers when looking for properties and real estate services. Real estate licensees must keep abreast of these changes and integrate them into their practices as warranted.

  A. **Agency-specific concepts**: Beginning in the 1990s, real estate brokers expanded and clarified their agency practices and policies. This was triggered by new agency disclosure mandates, statutory recognition of buyer's agency for the first time, new options such as designated agency, and the authorization of limited service agency.

   1. ▶ **Agency disclosure requirements**: State agency disclosure regulations require brokers and salespersons to discuss all agency alternatives with prospective buyers and sellers in a timely fashion. Agency disclosure requirements are part of Michigan's real estate license law. The elements of agency disclosure are specifically discussed in Chapter 19.

   2. **Company policies on agency**: Every broker can establish whatever agency policy he desires. For example, a broker can offer all forms of agency or limit his practice to that of exclusive buyer's agency. These decisions are then formally set forth within the broker's policies and procedures manual. The policies become binding on all affiliated licensees within the company. Policy decisions are solely those of the broker rather than his affiliated licensees.

      a. **Single agency**: The practice of single agency involves representation of only one party in a transaction. A single agency broker does not represent both the buyer and the seller in the same transaction. Single agency brokers can represent either the seller or the buyer as part of their business practices, just never in the same transaction.

         (1) **Single agency–Represent sellers exclusively**: Under this policy, the broker elects to list properties and represent sellers while always working with buyers on a customer basis. No buyer's agency is offered. If a buyer wishes to become a client, the broker refers the buyer to a company that offers buyer's agency services. This is not a common practice since most companies provide buyer's agency along with seller's agency.

         (2) **Single agency–Represent buyers exclusively**: Under this policy, the broker elects to exclusively represent buyers. Sellers, who are never represented in the listing of their homes, are treated as customers. If a seller wants to list his home, the exclusive buyer's broker refers him to a company that offers seller representation. A small number of brokers nationwide practice exclusive buyer's agency.

         (3) **Single agency–Represent buyers and sellers**: Brokers who engage in this practice represents both buyers and sellers, but never in the same transaction. Generally, the party (for example, the seller) who contacts the broker or his affiliated licensee first is the one who is represented. The other party to the transaction (for example, the buyer), if procured by an affiliated licensee, will automatically be a customer. If the customer later wants to be represented, the customer will be referred to a different company. This is why this form of single agency is not widely practiced.

         (4) **Dual agency is avoided**: Dual agency is avoided in all forms of single agency. If a buyer-client wishes to purchase a seller-client's property, one of the represented parties is released from their agency relationship and treated on a customer basis. This release may concern a previously-represented party which is why a large number of brokers allow for the practice dual agency.

      b. **Dual agency**: When a broker practices dual agency, both the buyer and the seller can be represented in the same transaction. It is important to a successful dual agency transaction that each client's fiduciary duties be balanced, especially the duties of disclosure and confidentiality.

         (1) **Disclosure**: Dual agency practice is authorized under Michigan license law providing prior written consent is obtained from both the seller-client and the buyer-client. Notice is typically given

via the agency disclosure form coupled with some form of dual agency agreement. A dual agency agreement or authorization must be signed by both parties. The authorization can be in a separate form or incorporated in the company's basic listing and buyer's agency contracts.

3. **Imputed knowledge generally**: To impute means to attribute, credit, or charge a person with something. Generally, information that is known by an agent is legally imputed to his client, the principal. In other words, the principal is legally treated as if he knows what his agent knows. The same can be said about the relationship between a broker and all of his affiliated salespersons. What a salesperson knows is imputed to the broker, and vice versa. This can create a potential issue in any real estate company where multiple agency relationships exist, including dual agencies.

    a. **Imputed knowledge in a dual agency**: While dual agency is legal, care must be exercised not to inadvertently disclose the confidential information of either client. This is easy to manage providing the licensee who works with the seller-client and the licensee who works with the buyer-client exercise care not to disclose or provide access to confidential information. Some legal experts believe that having the information of both clients imputed to every licensee in the entire brokerage operation creates an unnecessary legal risk. This concern motivated the creation of a designated agency policy.

4. ▶ **Designated agency**: Some members of the legal profession have historically been concerned that dual agency creates a conflict that cannot be fully resolved. Not every expert shares this belief, however. In an attempt to help mitigate this concern, the Michigan legislature enacted designated agency as a policy elective by a broker. Once adopted, all affiliated licensees within the entire company are subject to it. This material merely describes, but does not take a position either in favor of or against, designated agency. The decision to adopt a designated agency policy is up to a broker after consultation with legal counsel.

    a. **Non-designated versus designated agency**: Under traditional non-designated agency, when one licensee obtains a listing contract or a buyer agency contract, all licensees affiliated with the firm are deemed to have an agency relationship with the client. With designated agency, only one licensee within the company is designated as the exclusive agent for the seller-client or buyer-client. This limits the number of affiliated licensees who have a fiduciary duty to clients of the brokerage firm. See also Chapter 19, Article 25, Section 2517, for details on Michigan's designated agency statute.

    b. **Affiliated licensee defined**: Affiliated licensee refers to any individual who is licensed as a salesperson or associate broker under the broker. When a seller-client or buyer-client enters into an agreement naming a specific licensee as his designated agent, the client does not have an agency relationship with any other affiliated licensee except the broker and supervisory broker(s).

    c. **Designated agent defined**: A designated agent is the individual salesperson or associate broker who is designated, meaning named, in the agency contract as the only person responsible for providing agency services to the client (along with the broker and any named supervisory brokers). The designated agent provides the full range of agency duties and services required under Michigan license law and the terms of the service provision agreement.

    d. **Supervisory broker defined**: Supervisory broker is a term which is specific to a designated agency policy. It is an associate broker who is named in the agency agreement to provide supervisory assistance. The supervisory broker helps one or more designated agents with the representation of clients. A supervisory broker becomes a disclosed consensual dual agent (along with the broker) for any transaction in which two different designated agents, affiliated with the same broker, represent the seller-client and the buyer-client in the same transaction.

        (1) **Imputed knowledge in a designated agency policy**: A designated agent's knowledge of confidential information about a client is not automatically imputed, meaning attributed, assigned, or charged, to other affiliated licensees in the company (providing the same designated agent is not representing both the seller and the buyer in the same transaction). The fact that a designated agent is the only company affiliated licensee besides the broker who represents the client is the key to reducing concern about dual agency representation. Even under a designated agency policy, however, affiliated licensees must take care when representing their respective clients.

            (a) A designated agent must not disclose confidential information about his client to another licensee whether that licensee is affiliated with the same broker or not.

            (b) A designated agent may disclose confidential information to the broker or a named supervisory broker when seeking advice or assistance that benefits the client.

(c) There is no breach of duty if a designated agent withholds confidential information from his client that is obtained through a present or prior agency relationship with another client. All listing and buyer's agency agreements typically include important language to this effect.

(2) **Dual agency disclosure still required**: Designated agency does not eliminate dual agency because the broker and named supervisory brokers continue to act as disclosed dual agents. The agency disclosure form makes it clear that "[i]f the other party in a transaction is represented by an affiliated licensee, then the licensee's broker and all named supervisory brokers shall be considered disclosed consensual dual agents." Whether or not an additional written dual agency agreement is needed under these circumstances is a question for a broker to resolve with the advice of legal counsel. Certainly, if one licensee is the designated agent for both the seller and the buyer in the same transaction, then a separate dual agency agreement is likely warranted.

e. **Designated agency agreement**: A designated agency agreement is the actual written agreement between the broker and the client in which the affiliated salesperson or associate broker is named as the client's designated agent. In the absence of a designated agency agreement, a traditional non-designated agency relationship exists.

(1) **Creation of a designated agency policy**: The decision to create a designated agency policy is made by a broker. Once this decision has been made, it applies to all listings and buyer's agency relationships. As a reminder, (1) fiduciary duties in a designated agency relationship are only owed to a client by the designated agent, broker, and any supervisory broker, and (2) a broker is free to decide whether to provide designated or non-designated agency services as a matter of company policy. Traditional non-designated agency remains an acceptable practice in today's marketplace.

f. **Agency disclosure form**: The existence of designated agency and a brief discussion of what it means is contained in the agency disclosure form. The paragraph titled, "Designated Agency" defines the practice in general terms. The paragraph titled, "Affiliated Disclosure," allows a broker and his licensees to indicate to a prospective seller or buyer whether or not they practice it.

5. ▶ **Broker acting in a non-agency capacity–Transaction Coordinator**: A transaction coordinator is a broker who elects to act in a strictly non-agency capacity while assisting sellers or buyers. To act as a transaction coordinator, a broker should obtain authorization or permission from either the buyer or the seller. Transaction coordinator status is used in situations in which a seller or a buyer does not want the broker to represent him. As will become clear, it allows the broker to provide real estate services that do not rise to the level of agency representation. While completely legal, transaction coordinator status still is relatively untested in the courts.

a. **Agency services must not be provided**: Since agency level services are not provided, the seller or buyer is treated strictly as a customer. The broker cannot perform any fiduciary duties or provide the same type of representational services that are provided to clients. This includes not providing advice, acting as an advocate, or negotiating on behalf of the party with whom the broker is interacting.

b. ▶ **Form of authorization–creating the agreement**: If a broker is working with a buyer-customer on the selling side of the transaction, the broker can have the buyer sign a "Memorandum of Transaction Coordinator" or similar form. If the buyer is reluctant to sign such a form, the selling broker can be authorized by the listing broker through the MLS if an offer compensation to transaction coordinators (sometimes referred to as Non-Agent in the MLS). When the selling broker accepts this compensation, authority has arguably been given by the seller (through his listing broker) for the selling broker to act as a transaction coordinator.

B. **Personal assistants**: The use of personal assistants by real estate licensees has grown tremendously since the 1990s. A personal assistant is person who is specifically hired by a real estate licensee to assist the licensee in furthering his real estate business objectives. A personal assistant can either be licensed or unlicensed as a real estate professional. By delegating certain tasks to an assistant, especially those which are administrative in nature, the hiring licensee can focus more time on the dollar-productive activities of prospecting, listing, selling, and negotiating contracts.

1. **Unlicensed assistants cannot perform regulated real estate acts**: As with any other unlicensed person, an unlicensed personal assistant must not perform any acts for which a real estate license is required by license law. If the unlicensed assistant is hired by a salesperson, for example, to exclusively provide administrative

support, the assistant can be employed and paid directly by the salesperson (providing the broker's policy permits it).

   a. **Examples**: Unlicensed assistants may not: (1) Solicit for business, e.g., make prospecting calls for new listings or sales; (2) Show properties or hold houses open by themselves; (3) Answer specific questions or provide advice on matters relating to contracts, title insurance, financing, or closings; (4) Execute listing agreements or other agency contracts; (5) Advocate for or negotiate contracts on behalf of clients; (6) Provide information to consumers which is not included in general promotional materials prepared by the hiring licensee; or (7) Hold themselves out to the public as a licensed agent.

   b. **Employing licensee's responsibilities**: An affiliated licensee who hires an assistant must abide by the broker's policies and procedures as it pertains to the hiring of assistants. Further, as an employer, the affiliated licensee must abide by applicable IRS withholding and reporting requirements as well as state and federal employment laws. While hiring an assistant sounds like a simple thing to do, inadvertent violations of key laws can be very expensive.

2. **Licensed personal assistant**: If a personal assistant is actually licensed as a real estate salesperson, the assistant can perform any act described in real estate license law under the definition of real estate salesperson. The limitations pertaining to an unlicensed assistant described above do not apply. It is important to remember that, while the licensed assistant may have been hired by an affiliated licensee, every licensed person within the firm must be licensed under the employing broker. In other words, the licensed assistant is still deemed to be employed and supervised by the broker and cannot receive any compensation directly from the hiring licensee. As discussed in Chapter 19, all real estate compensation earned by a salesperson must be paid directly by the broker.

C. ▶ **Avoiding the unauthorized practice of law**: A real estate licensee is statutorily authorized to provide a wide range of real estate-related services. While these services include providing advice about buying and selling properties, licensees must be very careful not to provide legal advice. Understanding this subtle difference can be challenging, especially for new licensees. When a non-attorney provides legal advice, it constitutes the unauthorized practice of law.

   1. **Original standard**: A Michigan Supreme Court case dating back to the 1950s held that a real estate broker may (1) fill in standardized or preprinted forms, (2) if doing so is incidental to his real estate business, and (3) is done without charging additional compensation. This definition was modified decades later by the Michigan Supreme Court.

   2. **Current standard**: In 2003, the Court held that a person engages in the unauthorized practice of law when counseling or assisting another in matters that require the use of (1) legal discretion and (2) profound legal knowledge. This new standard appeared to open the way for certain practices by non-attorneys including charging a fee for the simple preparation of documents. As to what constitutes "legal discretion" or "profound legal knowledge," a licensee should not provide specific counsel on the legal validity of a document. Further, a licensee should not answer a question if the answer would constitute a conclusion as to best legal outcome.

      a. **Example**: Two potential buyers who are business partners ask their real estate agent what the best form of ownership would be to protect the business in the event of the death of one of the partners. The licensee should refer the buyers to an attorney for the answer. In this instance, the licensee could provide a basic overview about the different forms of ownership providing the discussion does not conclude with the licensee advising the buyers on the best form to meet their goals.

      b. **Use standardized forms**: The standardized forms used by real estate licensees have generally been reviewed by the company's attorney. Licensees then assist clients and customers by filling in the blank spaces with the transaction facts and details. This process is permissible. In some instances such as a personal property addendum to a purchase agreement, large sections of the addendum may be filled in with a licensee's help without constituting the unauthorized practice of law.

D. **Errors and Omissions (E&O) insurance**: Errors and omissions insurance is a specific type of insurance policy which is purchased by brokers to cover potential liability for errors, mistakes, and negligence that may arise from the ordinary practice of real estate. Most E&O policies cover the broker as the primary insured and the broker's business practices which, as noted below, include the hiring of affiliated licensees as well as administrative staff members. Every broker who conducts business should strongly consider purchasing an E&O policy with adequate coverage as part of his risk management strategy. One source of legal exposure flows from the affiliated licensees who are licensed under and serve as agents for the broker.

1. **Basis of claims**: The most common claims typically involve alleged fraud, breach of duty, breach of contract, and negligence. Another common claim involves misrepresentation of the condition of a property. For example, a real estate licensee is showing a company listing to a prospective buyer who desires a natural, wood-burning fireplace. The licensee was unaware, however, that the "fireplace" was actually a vent-free, gas firebox which cannot burn wood. While a number of variables can affect the outcome if the buyer makes a claim against the licensee, as long as the licensee did not intend the statement to be false, the errors and omissions policy could protect the company.

2. **Exceptions and qualifications**: Certain acts are excluded from E&O policies, meaning that they are not covered. If a listed exception arises, the broker must pay for his own defense and will be responsible for any financial outcome. General exclusions include intentional acts or willful misconduct on the part of the insured. Property damage, bodily injury, environmental hazards, and fair housing violations may also be excluded in some policies. Since insurance policies and coverage can vary from one insurance carrier to the next, a broker should thoroughly read and understand the terms of any policy prior to purchasing it.

3. **Coverage for affiliated salespersons and associate brokers**: Since salespersons and associate brokers are authorized representatives of the insured broker, any policy that protects the broker likely also protects the acts of these affiliated licensees. E&O protection, however, extends only to those activities authorized by the broker via the independent contractor agreement and company policies and procedures manual. In other words, the policy covers the activities of affiliated licensees when those licensees act within the scope of their company policy.

4. **Keep current**: The real estate industry is in a constant state of change. As business evolves, so do risk management needs. This is why brokers should periodically review their insurance coverage. Some E&O carriers may be willing to offer more competitive insurance rates for brokers whose businesses are guided by comprehensive, up-to-date policies and procedures manuals.

E. ▶ **Safeguarding confidential information**: Data security and identity theft are a growing problem in the information age. Many businesses, especially those operating in the financial sector, routinely collect sensitive personal information on its consumers. To a lesser degree, so does the real estate industry. Unfortunately, there is no single, fail-safe way to prevent a hacker from breaching a database. However, there are some simple measures that a real estate company can adopt to prevent, or at least reduce, a hacker's ability to read or use a client's sensitive information for malicious purposes.

1. **Michigan law**: Two Michigan data security laws can potentially impact a brokerage operation. They include the Identity Theft Protection Act and the Social Security Number Privacy Act. All real estate companies need to consider the importance of data security from both a practical and a policy perspective.

    a. **Identity Theft Protection Act**: This law prohibits the use of an individual's personal identifying information for fraudulent purposes. The statutory list of what constitutes personal identifying information is comprehensive. Some of the information items that a real estate licensee might obtain in the course of a real estate transaction include a client's or customer's: name; address; telephone number; and/or place of employment. The list is even longer for lending institutions which means that a licensee should probably let the loan officer handle any data collection in connection with a mortgage application.

    If a data breach occurs, the business must send a notice to all persons whose information might be compromised informing them of the breach. This notice requirement may not apply if the business determines that the breach is not likely to cause injury. One way to protect sensitive data is through encryption or other means such as a complex password that renders the information unusable.

2. **Wire fraud**: For years, hacker's have been employing sophisticated email-based scams that target real estate agents who are involved in cash transactions. In a typical scenario, the buyer's funds are wired from his lender to the seller's title company. In wire fraud, the hacker illegally gains access to the email server of either the buyer's agent or title company. A bogus email is sent instructing the buyer to redirect the money to the hacker's account instead. Shortly thereafter, the hacker sends the money to an offshore account. A sampling of steps that can be taken to limit wire fraud include:

    a. Protect email by using a password manager (or complex passwords) and Internet security software.

    b. Do not act as an intermediary for wiring instructions (let the buyer communicate directly with the lender or title company).

c. Consider using the transaction management software included with most MLS systems for delivery of all transaction forms, documents, and communications (rather than the agent's email account).

d. Provide a company-approved notice to all of the parties in the transaction warning them of the scam.

e. Do not use public Wi-Fi when entering passwords or communicating personal, sensitive information.

*When judgement and anger fail to produce positive results,
give love and forgiveness a try.*

DIAGNOSTIC PRACTICE QUESTIONS – CHAPTER 3

IMPORTANT STUDY TIP!

Step 1: Carefully review the information located in this chapter.

Step 2: Take the following Diagnostic Practice Questions. Review any question you answered incorrectly by researching the topic in this textbook. If you are still uncertain as to why the question is answered as it is, consult your program provider.

NOTE ON CHAPTER PRACTICE QUESTIONS

The following questions are representative of the type encountered on the Michigan real estate licensing examination. While some of these questions may be similar in nature and style, there is no way of predicting the exact wording of a question that will appear on the exam. Spending time memorizing these questions is, therefore, not recommended.

These questions are designed to help you determine how well you comprehend the material in this chapter. They are also intended to help you develop problem solving skills and to become comfortable with question formats.

Do not attempt to answer these questions until you have attended the lecture corresponding to this chapter and spent the appropriate time studying the material.

1. When preparing a listing agreement on a prospective client's property, a listing agent is expected to be familiar with and consider which of the following items?
   A. The measurable dimensions of the exterior and interior building components as well as the size of the lot.
   B. The existence of any homeowner's associations including any fees which may be involved in owning a property within such association.
   C. Easements, liens, or other encumbrances.
   D. All of the above.

2. A broker and a seller sign a 6-month listing contract on Monday morning to market the seller's property for $230,000 with all financing terms being acceptable. Since the seller desires a quick sale, she prices the home 5% below current market value. As a result, the listing broker receives a full-price, cash offer later that afternoon. Since the full-price offer came in so fast, the seller refused to accept it believing that she should have held out for a higher price. Which of the following statements best applies?
   A. The seller may refuse the offer but may owe the broker his full commission for securing a buyer at price and terms.
   B. Seller must accept the offer since it was for price and terms otherwise the buyer can sue for breach of contract.
   C. Seller must accept the offer but will not be liable for any commission because the broker knowingly underpriced the property.
   D. The seller may refuse the offer without penalty providing she agrees to accept the next offer if it is 5% higher.

3. An owner has unsuccessfully attempted to sell his home on a for-sale-by-owner basis. Frustrated with his results, he contacts Bill, a broker with Done-Rite Realty, to list his property. During the time in which the owner marketed his property, he was able to obtain the names of three couples who were somewhat interested. The owner is willing to list, but would like to reduce the commission in the event any of these parties buys the property during the term of the listing agreement. What variation of an exclusive right to sell listing allows for this?
   A. One-party listing.
   B. Variable rate listing.
   C. Excluded party listing.
   D. Net listing.

4. Broker Marco with Progression Realty has an exclusive right to sell listing on a property. Marco is not a member of any MLS. Agent Liz with Infinity Properties sees a sign on one of Marco's listings and determines that it may be perfect for one of her buyer-customers. Liz cannot find any information regarding Marco's listing in the MLS. Which course of action would be in everyone's best interest?
   A. Liz should disregard the property and tell her buyer that brokers who are not members of the MLS are suspect.
   B. Liz should contact Marco and seek a cooperation

agreement to split the commission before setting the appointment.
   C. Liz should make the buyer sign a buyer's agency contract for the purpose of protecting her right to a commission.
   D. Liz should contact Marco with an application to join the MLS at the time of setting an appointment on the property.

5. A listing broker has two months left on a listing agreement with a valued client who has referred business to the broker in the past. A family member of the seller passes away and the seller decides to take his home off of the market to be near his children instead of moving to Arizona. Which of the following options would be best for the broker and his client under these circumstances?
   A. Force the seller to continue marketing the home since the death of a family member does not change the underlying listing agreement.
   B. Cancel the listing with a requirement that the seller pay a prorated amount of the full commission for the time the property was marketed.
   C. Give the seller a conditional release which relieves him of any further commission obligation providing he does not re-list the property with another broker for a certain period.
   D. Terminate the listing if the seller agrees to pay the broker any out-of-pocket expenses including advertising and administrative costs.

6. The broker for Pink-Lyte Realty acquired an errors and omissions insurance policy. Which of the following statements is true?
   A. The policy will likely not cover an act of willful misconduct by a salesperson.
   B. The policy will cover a fair housing violation by one of Pink-Lyte's salespersons.
   C. The policy covers all activities engaged in by affiliated licensees.
   D. Coverage extends for 12 months when a licensees transfers to another broker who is not covered by a similar policy.

7. Broker Murphy in a local multiple listing service has elected to offer radically discounted commission rates as part of a menu of separately-priced services. This is contrary to the traditional practice of most brokers in the area who offer full-service agency. Which of the following statements applies to this situation:
   A. Murphy's practice is not illegal but is highly unethical because it tends to make the other brokers in his marketplace look overpriced.
   B. Since the commission rates and services offered by brokers is an individual matter, there is nothing wrong with Murphy's pricing policies.
   C. Innovative commission structures such as Murphy's are subject to prior approval by the licensing department.
   D. Multiple listing services are designed, in part, to foster cooperation by preventing practices such as this.

8. Broker Hixson lists the property of Frugal Seller under a 6 month listing. During the first 5½ months, Hixson advertises the property in the local newspaper, holds several open houses, shows the property to all interested buyers, and mails special marketing pieces on the property to his extensive prospect list. Unimpressed by Hixson's efforts, Frugal Seller fires his agent due to the lack of a firm offer. All EXCEPT which of the following statements applies to the firing by Frugal?
   A. Frugal's termination was premature under the circumstances.
   B. Frugal may be liable for the reasonable expenses incurred by Hixson in marketing the property.
   C. Hixson's inability to find a buyer under the circumstances amounts to a breach of the listing contract.
   D. Hixson has been wrongfully discharged.

9. A broker enters into a buyer's representation agreement with an interested buyer. After searching the MLS inventory, the broker finally decides to show one of his company listings. Prior to doing so, however, the buyer is released from the buyer's representation contract for the showing and possible sale. Which of the following agency policies is the broker most likely operating under?
   A. Single agency, seller only.
   B. Single agency, buyer only.
   C. Single agency, seller and buyer (not in same transaction).
   D. Dual agency.

10. Salesperson J.T. is interested in expanding his ability to prospect for client and customer leads. He hires personal assistants to help build his business. Which of the following statements is true?
    A. The full-time assistants should probably be hired as independent contractors.
    B. J.T. can use unlicensed assistants to be the only company representative at open houses providing they do not negotiate contracts.
    C. The licensed assistants must be licensed under J.T.
    D. J.T. should hire only licensed assistants to handle the telemarketing aspects of his business.

11. A seller desires protection against owing a commission in the event a buyer backs out of a signed

purchase agreement before the closing. Which of the following listing clauses would best protect the seller?
   A. "Payment of the commission is contingent on finding a ready, willing and able buyer."
   B. "The broker is authorized to retain the earnest money deposit upon default by the buyer".
   C. "Payment of the commission is contingent on the closing".
   D. A combination of "Caveat emptor" and an "As is" clause.

12. The rate of commission in a listing agreement is typically established by the:
    A. Board of Realtors®.
    B. Broker.
    C. Seller.
    D. Salesperson.

13. Salesperson Greg has listed properties for clients A and B, one on an exclusive basis and the other on an open basis. Without previously inspecting each other's properties, clients A and B exchange properties one week after the listings expire. Under these circumstances, Greg is entitled to:
    A. Two commissions.
    B. The commission from the exclusive listing only.
    C. The commission from the open listing only.
    D. No commission.

14. Which type of listing agreement gives the broker the maximum protection against financial loss?
    A. A net listing.
    B. An exclusive agency listing.
    C. An exclusive right to sell listing.
    D. An open listing.

15. Which of the following statements about an open listing is true?
    A. An open listing may be terminated by the owner at any time prior to performance.
    B. An owner may not enter into an open listing contract with more than two brokers in the same city.
    C. The owner will always be obligated to one of several brokers.
    D. An open listing is illegal to the extent it is used to secure a commission.

16. Mr. King, a licensed real estate broker, had a listing recently expire on a property. ACME Realty, members with Mr. King's company in the MLS, relists the property. Tom, a salesperson working for Easy Realty Company, also a member of the MLS, has a customer who would like to inspect the property and calls Broker King for an appointment. Broker King should:
    A. Call and make the appointment.
    B. Attempt to relist the property on a one-party basis.
    C. Encourage the inspection and then claim a commission under the carryover provision in the prior listing agreement.
    D. Explain to the salesperson that the property is no longer listed with his company and to contact the new listing agent.

Use each day as a gift graciously received.
Give thanks by sharing it with others.

Chapter 4
Appraisal

Determining the value of real estate.

I. **Foreword**: Part of a real estate licensee's role is to determine the likely worth of real property. At the time of listing a seller's property, the broker or his salesperson estimates its market value to help set an appropriate selling price. Likewise, a buyer may hire a buyer's broker to locate a suitable property and request that his agent perform a market analysis to determine if the home is properly priced. This chapter examines the various ways in which the value of real estate can be estimated.

II. **Concepts of valuation and appraisal**: There are several different terms that must be understood as they pertain to real property valuation. The difference between some of the definitions is subtle, so read carefully and make sure that you understand how they are applied in the field. Real estate licensees can provide a market analysis under certain limited circumstances. They cannot, however, provide or hold themselves out as providing appraisal services unless they have a separate appraiser's license.

   A. ▶ **Value principles**: The term value refers to the usefulness, meaning utility, or ability of an object to satisfy the needs and desires of human beings. It is the worth of an object, typically in terms of money. It may also be expressed as the power that a good or service has to command other goods and services in exchange. Value is a reflection of someone's idea as to what something is presently worth.

   1. ▶ **Multiple types and characteristics**: Depending on how the term is applied and who is applying it, value can take on several different meanings. For example, it can reflect reproduction or replacement value, sale or market value, taxable value, insured value, or investment value. The most common of these applications in the real estate business is market value.

      a. ▶ **Market value**: The term market value can be defined as the (1) highest and most likely price a ready, willing, and able buyer would pay, and (2) an unrelated, but equally ready, willing, and able seller would accept, (3) when both parties are fully informed as to market conditions, (4) the transaction is arm's length in nature, and (5) the transaction has had sufficient time to mature.

         (1) **Analysis of elements**: It is important that all of the above elements are present when determining market value. If any one of them is not part of the equation, the calculated figure may not properly reflect a property's true market value.

            (a) **Ready, willing, and able parties**: Both buyer and seller must be ready, willing, and able to perform. While it is not difficult to locate a buyer who may be ready and willing to purchase, not all buyers are financially able to do so. For example, a buyer with poor credit is not able to obtain a mortgage loan. The buyer asks the seller if he will accept a land contract. Since the buyer has questionable credit, the seller agrees to accept the increased risk of default if the buyer is willing to pay an additional $2,000 for the property. The new price does not accurately reflect market value.

            (b) **Fully informed**: Parties to a transaction must be aware of current market conditions and how they potentially impact value. For example, a buyer who has not researched the market or consulted with an expert may wind up paying more for a property than the market would otherwise command for the property.

            (c) **Arm's length transaction**: An arm's length transaction is one negotiated between two independent and unrelated parties, each working to protect his own best interest, without one being under the influence or control of the other. The importance of arm's length negotiations became an especially important issue during the subprime loan crisis. For example, on a potential short sale property, the lender holding the mortgage does not approve an offer to purchase from the seller-mortgagor's sister. The bank feels that the sister's offer is intentionally low to help her brother obtain a higher forgiveness of indebtedness. The offer is, therefore, not arm's length since it does not reflect the present market value of the property. The mechanics of short sales are discussed in Chapter 16.

    (2) **Other examples not reflecting market value**: There are a number of transactions that generally are not thought to reflect true market value. For example, (1) the price an owner might obtain at an auction sale, (2) forced sales such as foreclosures, and (3) time-pressed sales in which one party does not have the time to negotiate and must concede on his price in order to bring about a sale more quickly.

  b. ▶ **Value versus price and cost**: The terms price and cost, while related to value, are not necessarily synonymous with it. As will be seen, these figures can differ significantly depending on the economic conditions in existence at the time each is determined.

    (1) ▶ **Price**: The term price, which may also be referred to as market price, refers to the actual amount of money, including valuable goods or services, which is given in exchange for a property. For example, a property is appraised to have a market value of $150,000. A buyer offers the seller $148,000 which is accepted. The price is $148,000.

    (2) ▶ **Cost**: As a value-related term, cost is the actual amount of money, labor, and other sacrifices expended to bring a property into existence. In this sense, it is the past measurement of what it took to acquire a lot and construct a home. Using the figures above, assume that the property which was appraised at $150,000 was constructed in 1990 for $85,000. The $85,000 figure represents the property's cost.

B. ▶ **Purpose and use of appraisals**: An appraisal is a formal estimate or opinion as to the exact value of a commodity. As it pertains to real property, an appraisal is prepared by a licensed appraiser of suitable qualifications. Appraisals are essential to the home buying process since a lender will not approve a loan unless it knows the exact value of the property. The appraised value serves as the basis for calculating the loan-to-value ratio. When a lender orders an appraisal for this purpose, the lender is considered to be the client of the appraiser (rather than the buyer who is applying for the loan).

C. ▶ **Appraiser**: An appraiser is a person who is specially trained and licensed to formally determine (technically, he estimates) the value of real estate or other property such as automobiles, jewelry, and equipment. Appraiser licensing requirements are imposed on a state-by-state basis. Michigan's appraiser license law is found in Article 26 of the Occupational Code (which is otherwise known as Public Act 299 of 1980, as amended).

  1. **Appraiser independence**: Appraisers should not have an interest in either the property being appraised or the outcome of the appraisal. While nearly all licensed appraisers are professional and ethical, requiring this level of independence reduces any temptation to adjust an appraisal figure to suit an agenda other than calculating the true market value of the property.

    Appraisers are legally required to resist any undue influence or request by a property owner, lender, buyer, or real estate licensee to artificially adjust an appraisal report for any reason including helping a buyer qualify for a loan. Not only does this influence improperly impact market value, it may also constitute illegal mortgage fraud. See Chapter 17 for further details pertaining to mortgage fraud.

    a. **Real estate licensee contact with appraisers**: Questions often arise as to whether a real estate licensee can have any contact with an appraiser during the appraisal process. Current law does not prohibit such contact as long as appraisal independence requirements are met. Therefore, a real estate licensee could be present during the appraisal process and give the appraiser information pertaining to comparable properties along with a copy of the purchase agreement. The real estate licensee must not, however, compensate, coerce, instruct, or intimidate the appraiser in an attempt to influence the final appraisal figure. A real estate licensee should check with his broker before attempting any permissible form of contact to make sure that it is permitted under company policy.

    b. **Appraisal Management Company (AMC)**: An appraisal management company is a business entity that is formed to work with lenders by helping administer the process of ordering, completing, and delivering appraisal reports. A lender is not required to use an AMC to obtain an appraisal, but doing so may help the lender meet today's stricter requirements pertaining to appraiser selection and independence.

Chapter 4: Appraisal

All appraisals ordered by an AMC are completed by an appropriately-licensed appraiser. In other words, the AMC does not perform the actual appraisal.

2. **USPAP**: The acronym USPAP stands for "Uniform Standards of Professional Appraisal Practice." USPAP is a set of universal guidelines for appraisers that was adopted in 1987 by the Appraisal Foundation. The Foundation was formed by nine professional appraisal organizations in the U.S. and Canada. Two years after its adoption, USPAP was incorporated into federal legislation by Congress with the passage of FIRREA.

3. **Financial Institutions Reform, Recovery and Enforcement Act (FIRREA)**: In 1989, FIRREA was enacted by Congress in response to the savings and loan crisis of that decade. One important goal of the Act required states to enact licensing statutes that subjected appraisers to regulatory control. The information in this section is only an overview. Refer to Michigan law for complete details on appraiser licensing provisions.

   a. **Appraiser's license law**: There are four categories of appraiser licensing under Michigan law. As will be seen, only a state licensed or state certified appraiser can prepare appraisals for transactions that involve federally-related loans. A loan is federally-related if it is government insured (FHA), government guaranteed (VA), or to be sold to a government-sponsored enterprise (such as FNMA) in the secondary mortgage market. These loans are discussed further in Chapter 17.

      (1) **Limited Real Estate Appraiser**: A Limited Real Estate Appraiser is licensed to assist a State Licensed Appraiser, a Certified Residential Appraiser, or a Certified General Appraiser in the development of appraisals relating to federally-related and real estate-related financial transactions, but may not personally sign an appraisal report. If a Limited Real Estate Appraiser signs a report to be used for any other purpose, the client cannot later use it for a federally-related or real estate-related financial transaction.

      (2) **State Licensed Real Estate Appraiser**: A State Licensed Appraiser may appraise real property involving any non-federally-related transaction for which he has expertise as well as appraisals involving federally-related transactions for 1–4 family residential properties. He may assist a Certified Residential Appraiser or Certified General Appraiser in appraising properties where the transaction value is over $1,000,000, but his reports must have the signature of the supervising appraiser on the report to certify it.

      (3) ▶ **Certified Residential Real Estate Appraiser**: A Certified Residential Appraiser may appraise residential 1–4 family real property of any value, any other property for which they are authorized by the federal financial institutions regulatory agencies, and for non-federally related transactions for which they have expertise. He may not sign a report when the assignment is outside his scope of licensure.

      (4) ▶ **Certified General Real Estate Appraiser**: A Certified General Appraiser may appraise real property of any type or value.

4. **Professional appraiser organizations**: There are several professional and trade-based organizations that serve appraisers and the appraisal industry. These organizations provide advocacy and industry services similar to those provided for the real estate industry by the National Association of REALTORS®.

   a. ▶ **Appraisal Institute and the MAI**: One well-known appraiser organization is the Appraisal Institute. The Institute confers the following designations: MAI, SRA, and SRPA. The acronym MAI stands for Member Appraisal Institute. According to their website, the MAI membership designation is held by appraisers who are experienced in the valuation and evaluation of commercial, industrial, residential, and other types of properties and who advise clients on real estate investment decisions.

D. ==Informal estimates of value==: Not all estimates of value are considered to be formal appraisals for which an appraiser's license is required. In Michigan, for example, a licensed real estate broker may provide a homeowner with an estimated market value range based on similar properties that have recently sold. This is the essence of a comparative market analysis as discussed in the upcoming subsection titled, "Methods of valuation."

1. **Michigan definition of appraisal**: Michigan appraisal license law defines an appraisal as "any opinion, conclusion, or analysis relating to the value of real property." As we will see, this definition also carves out a couple of limited but important exceptions for real estate licensees.

2. ▶ **Fee-based comparative market analysis (CMA) prepared by brokers**: Michigan's original appraiser license law prohibited a real estate broker from charging a separate fee for performing a simple competitive market analysis unless they also had a Real Estate Valuation Specialist License. The law was amended

to allow a licensed broker or associate broker (but, not a licensed salesperson) to charge a fee for a market analysis providing it does not involve a federally-related transaction, it is in writing, and it contains the following statement, "THIS IS A MARKET ANALYSIS, NOT AN APPRAISAL AND WAS PREPARED BY A LICENSED REAL ESTATE BROKER OR ASSOCIATE BROKER, NOT A LICENSED APPRAISER."

3. **Non fee-based comparative market analysis**: Appraisal license law was also amended to allow any licensee, including a salesperson, to perform a CMA as long as no separate fee is charged and it is limited to certain circumstances. Accordingly, a market analysis can be performed by a broker, associate broker, or salesperson providing: (1) it is solely for the purpose of assisting a customer or potential customer in determining the potential sale, purchase, or listing price of real property or the rental rate of real property; and, (2) no separate fee or other valuable consideration is charged for the analysis. Note the following:

    a. **Example–Working with a listing**: As long as no fee is charged, a real estate salesperson can prepare a CMA to assist a seller-client in determining an appropriate sale price for his property pursuant to a listing agreement. The salesperson could also prepare a CMA to induce a potential seller to enter into a listing agreement with him.

    b. **Example– Working with a buyer**: As long as no fee is charged, a real estate salesperson can prepare a CMA to assist a buyer-client in determining an appropriate offer price for a property pursuant to a buyer's agency agreement. Recall that client-level services such as providing pricing advice on properties cannot be provided to a buyer-customer without risking the creation of an implied buyer's agency relationship.

    c. **Property management example**: As long as no fee is charged, a real estate salesperson can prepare a CMA to assist a landlord-client or a tenant-client in determining an appropriate rental rate.

4. **Attorney General opinion**: In 2012, the Michigan Attorney General issued an opinion (known as an OAG for Opinion of the Attorney General) that a fee-based CMA performed by a licensed broker must also be limited to assisting a customer or potential customer in determining the potential sale, purchase, or listing price of real property, or the rental rate of real property. The Attorney General further indicated that any other circumstance for which a valuation is requested must be performed by a licensed appraiser.

    Accordingly, a broker could not provide a CMA for a non-client bank that is considering a short sale offer, for a homeowner who is appealing his taxes, for an individual who is settling a decedent's estate, or in connection with a divorce and property settlement. A broker could, however, perform a fee-based CMA if the decedent's estate or divorce also involves an actual or potential property purchase, sale, or lease. It is important to note that this OAG contains a different, and more limited, interpretation on the circumstances under which a broker can perform a fee-based market analysis.

    a. **Not law**: When the Attorney General issues an opinion, it does not have the full force and effect of law as would a statute or appellate court opinion. Certainly, attorneys who give their broker-clients advice on matters pertaining to an OAG should strongly consider what the Attorney General has to say. Other knowledgeable and experienced real estate attorneys feel that the appraiser license law amendments are valid as currently written and a broker can provide a fee-based market analysis to individuals under the circumstances mentioned above.

    b. **Can provide comps**: Even if the OAG is ultimately confirmed in a future court opinion, a licensee can probably provide information pertaining to comparable properties, also known as comps, to anyone whether or not they are clients or customers. Since an appraisal is defined as an opinion, conclusion or analysis, the person who receives the comps is drawing his own opinion rather than the licensee doing it for him.

    c. **Real estate examination**: This information on the OAG is only provided so licensees, especially brokers, are generally aware of its existence. For purposes of the real estate broker's or salesperson's examination, do not factor the opinion into how you answer questions on a broker's or salesperson's ability to provide a CMA (unless instructed to do so by your course provider).

III. ▶ **Specific elements of value**: There are a number of different factors that create or influence the value of real property. Their influence can be seen in a variety of ways.

   A. **DUST**: The acronym DUST has historically been used to refer to four key factors that affect value. Real estate must possess these elements to have value.

Chapter 4: Appraisal

1. **Demand**: The element of "demand" refers to consumer desire. There must be a ready, willing, and able buyer who is interested in owning or possessing a property for that property to have perceived value.
2. **Utility**: The element of "utility" refers to the usefulness of property. The more useful a property is to any particular buyer, the more value it is likely to command.
3. **Scarcity**: As an element of value, "scarcity" refers to the availability or actual supply of goods or property. To create value, there must be a finite supply of any saleable item. Generally, the higher the scarcity, the more value a property commands. This also relates to supply and demand concepts.
4. **Transferability**: The element of "transferability" refers to the ability of a seller to transfer his legal property rights to a buyer. A buyer's ability to acquire all legal rights to a purchased property is generally a condition of his paying value for it.

B. **Conformity**: The maximum value of land is realized when its use is consistent with, and conforms to, existing land use standards such as zoning ordinances, building codes and restrictions, and wetlands ordinances.

1. **Regression versus progression**: As noted in the following examples, nonconforming properties can affect each other's value in either a negative or a positive way.
    a. **Regression**: In this first example, the value of a large, expensive property is negatively affected by its location in a neighborhood populated with smaller, older, and less valuable homes. The value of the larger home, in concept, regresses to that of the other smaller homes in the neighborhood.
    b. **Progression**: In a second example, the value of a smaller, less expensive property naturally increases if it is located in a neighborhood with larger, more expensive homes. Similar to the principle of regression, the value of the less expensive home, in concept, progresses to that of the other more expensive homes.

C. **Highest and best use**: Highest and best use is an important consideration for appraisers, especially when valuing commercial properties. Although there are many uses to which land may be put, the highest and best use is the one that results in the greatest amount of income for the longest period of time. The appraiser makes a determination of what the highest and best may be, and then appraises the property from that perspective.

1. **Example–Highest and best use**: A vacant lot located in a busy urban area is currently being used as a privately-owned parking lot. The owner is more likely to realize the highest and best use of his lot, and a better financial return, if it is marketed for sale and appraised as a building site for a large commercial building.
2. **Anticipated changes and interim use**: Since use affects value, the appraiser often considers anticipated, meaning future, changes in use or zoning. Rather than waiting for the actual use change before appraising a property (which is not currently at its highest and best use), the owner can label the present use, for instance, the parking lot in the above example an "interim use" pending the anticipated change.

D. **Improvements**: As discussed in Chapter 1, the improvements on land significantly affect its value. For example, an unimproved parcel of property, i.e., vacant land, generally, does not command the same value as a similar parcel with an expensive custom-built home built on it.

E. **Situs (location)**: The term situs is Latin for location. However, it means more than simply where a property is geographically situated. As an appraisal concept, situs considers the preference or desirability for a particular location. The fact that some areas are more desirable than others creates value for the properties located there.

F. **Supply and demand**: As previously discussed in connection with the term scarcity, supply and demand are closely related to one another. For example, when the supply of a saleable item increases, the demand for it generally decreases. This creates a corresponding decrease in its price. Conversely, prices are generally driven up when supply decreases due to higher demand and more purchasing.

1. **Location affects demand**: Demand can be heavily influenced by the location of property. Buyers are often willing to pay more for properties situated in what are considered to be prime locations. This relates to the concept of situs.
2. **Population influences demand**: Population growth and shifting affects the available pool of buyers in any given area. Similarly, local economic conditions relating to employment and wage levels can influence the amount of money that is available for real estate purchases.

IV. ▶ **Economic cycles, trends, and challenges**: Economic cycles and trends are frequently taken into consideration when determining the value of real property. The economy is cyclical in that it goes through periods of growth (meaning expansion) and decline (meaning contraction). In basic terms, a market cycle is the time period during which prices expand, contract, and then move back to expansion. The housing market experiences similar cycles with stages that may include growth (or boom), stabilization, correction (or slump), and recovery. Sometimes, severe changes resulting from regional and national housing bubbles can dramatically affect property values.

A. **Housing bubble defined**: A housing bubble is a rapid and unsustainable increase in housing prices, to the extent that a sudden drop in value (or bursting of the bubble) can result in a widespread and significant loss of equity. Historically, housing bubbles were viewed as localized economic issues. In the 2000s, however, a number of factors turned a once local phenomenon into a national problem with significant and long-term consequences. If anything positive resulted from the subprime mortgage crisis of that decade, it was a growing understanding of the importance of real estate to the overall health of the United States economy.

B. **Factors necessary for a housing bubble**: Economists, real estate experts, and pundits will likely debate the causes of the housing crisis of the 2000s for years to come. Nevertheless, several common factors tend to trigger housing bubbles. While the information in this section is likely beyond the scope of a real estate examination, it is important for those who are interested in real estate to understand what may have contributed to the problem. Only by applying understanding, common sense, and a willingness to exercise restraint can the next crisis be averted.

Note: No specific position is being advanced in this textbook as to the precise cause of the housing crisis. Instead, interested readers are encouraged to conduct their own research using multiple, independent resources and then draw their own conclusions.

1. **Phase 1–Prices rise and inventory falls**: First, the area affected by the bubble experiences a rapid and sustained rise in home values (typically exceeding the median home price rate of growth for the area). In statistics, the median is the number in the exact middle of a sequence of numbers. The median home price, therefore, is the home whose price is in the exact middle of all home prices for the geographic area. Sudden spikes in home prices usually occur when buyers and investors bid-up values by competing for a dwindling supply of available housing. As properties are purchased, the supply decreases with a corresponding increase in demand and prices. In the years preceding the crisis, the spike was dramatically different and due to a variety of reasons.

   Historically, if someone could not afford the payments on a particular property, he either downsized his expectations to a home which was more affordable or waited and saved the money necessary to purchase the subject property without going deeply into debt. In the lead up to the mortgage meltdown of the 2000s, numerous changes in both lending practices and government policies likely caused what many experts called a perfect financial storm.

   These changes included things such as: An increase in government policies enacted during several administrations that advocated affordable housing and deregulation of the banking industry; A widespread lowering of lending standards involving things such as credit scores, employment verification, qualifying documentation, and debt-to-income ratios; Increased reliance on unsustainable loan products from zero down payment loans to burdensome adjustable rate mortgages; Appraisal fraud in which properties were intentionally overvalued to increase the amount of the loan; Mortgage fraud in the loan application process; Securitization of mortgage-backed loans and credit default swaps in the financial markets; and Homeowner speculation.

2. **Phase 2–Prices fall and inventory rises**: The second phase of a housing bubble begins when prices start to soften and eventually decline. There are a number of factors that can trigger this, and while history may provide some guidance, no economic cycle can be predicted with absolute certainty. In some cases, investors who believe that prices have peaked begin to withdraw their investment dollars by halting their purchasing and begin to sell their property assets. A declining job market can also contribute to consumers' inability to purchase homes at rising prices.

   Eventually, the contributing factors begin to take their toll on the continuity of real estate purchases and sales. This leads to a glut or oversupply of homes followed by a steep and sudden drop in prices. Sometimes, the mere slowing down of the rate of appreciation gives the appearance of falling prices and investors react swiftly by moving their financial resources out of the housing market. Eventually, changes of this magnitude have an impact on the entire economy.

C. **Problems related to local housing bubbles**: There are a number of issues that property owners and local real estate professionals encounter during a housing bubble.

Chapter 4: Appraisal

1. **Property owner issues:** The last home buyers to purchase at or near the peak of the bubble cycle generally have the most to lose. Some of these buyers acquire high dollar value mortgages. When the drop in regional values is experienced, they often find themselves "upside-down" on their loans, meaning the balance on their mortgage loan is more than the present day value of the property. As long as these buyers do not need to sell their properties soon, the impact will be minimized over time as values eventually return to their pre-bubble levels. The problem, however, is that this recovery time can be measured in years or decades.

2. **Short sale and foreclosure issues:** As more "upside-down" home owners began to default on their mortgages due to job losses and increasing loan payments on adjustable rate mortgages, for example, lenders begin experiencing rising defaults and foreclosures. Rather than getting stuck owning thousands of foreclosed properties, numerous lenders and their investor partners allowed alternative recovery remedies such as short sales. In a typical short sale, the lender allows the property to sell for present market value and may forgive, cancel, or waive all or a portion of the balance owing on the loan. These settlements have resulted in millions of dollars of losses for lenders and their investors.

3. **Lending issues:** Lenders who lost money on short sale loan settlements and foreclosures became wary about the financial health of future borrowers and fluctuating property values. This led to conservative lending practices by underwriters and their secondary mortgage market partners which made it more difficult for buyers with less than perfect credit to obtain loans. This may also be a sign that lenders are returning to more traditional, less risky lending practices.

4. **Appraisal and valuation issues:** Eventually, the market begins to recover and new challenges arise during the initial recovery phase. A lender will not give a mortgage loan without first ordering an appraisal on the subject property. This is due to the fact that the lender will only issue the loan for a certain percent of the appraised value. When the appraiser examines the property, he will typically look for comparable properties that have recently sold (see the next section for details on the market data approach to appraising).

The "snapshot" of the market examined by the appraiser tells him what occurred during the preceding 3–6 months or so. As the market recovers, the "bubble effect" begins to reverse. People spend more, properties are purchased, inventory falls, demand rises, and prices begin to slowly increase. As prices first begin to increase, finding past sales that reflect this new price point is difficult. Buyers, sellers, and real estate professionals frequently lament the lower appraisals they receive during this period. The reality is, however, that this is a natural consequence of a recovering market.

V. ▶ **Methods of valuation and steps in the process:** There are three basic methods for estimating value that are available to an appraiser. The nature of the subject property typically determines which method should be applied. In some cases, an appraiser may actually employ more than one method to verify the accuracy of an appraisal. It is important for real estate professionals to understand how these approaches work and are applied. While real estate licensees are not allowed to formally appraise property, they often interact with sellers, appraisers, and lenders in the context of property valuation.

   A. ▶ **Market data approach:** Under the market data approach, the subject property is compared to similar properties that have recently sold. Since no two properties are identical, there will be physical differences between the subject property and the comparable properties. The appraiser will make adjustments to the sale price of each comparable based on these differences. The "market data approach" is also known as the "sales comparison approach" or "market approach."

   1. **Application:** The market data approach is the most reliable appraisal method for single-family residential and unimproved, i.e., vacant, properties. Since the subject property is not being rented out, the income approach would not be appropriate to apply. Further, in the case of unimproved property, there is no way to apply a cost analysis because there are no improvements on the property.

   2. ▶ **Comparable properties:** The key component of the market approach involves comparable properties. Comparable properties may also be referred to in the industry as "comparables" or simply "comps" for short. As noted in the introduction to this subsection, the question of similarity will be critical to the appraiser. In some cases, finding appropriate comps is difficult, especially in the case of neighborhoods with a high rate of foreclosures and short sales or when appraising a completely custom-built home.

      a. **Substantial similarity is required:** At the very least, a substantial similarity between the subject property and the comps is necessary. Features that are compared include location of the property, lot size, property condition compared to other homes in the neighborhood, building square footage, type of construction, architectural style, number of bedrooms and bathrooms, size and attachment of garage, foundation, dining room, family or great room, and other on- and off-site amenities. If there are no comps within the immediate neighborhood, the scope of the search may be expanded to a wider geographic radius.

    b. **Must involve sold properties**: The appraiser looks for comps that have been sold. This is the figure that tells the appraiser what a ready, willing, and able buyer was willing to offer and an equally ready, willing, and able seller was willing to accept. Comparable properties that are merely listed with a broker only indicate what a seller is hoping to receive from a buyer, but not the actual market value. Listings that have expired are not accurate reflections of value and cannot be used. The fact that the property did not sell may reflect problems with overpricing or the condition of the property.

    c. **Must be recent**: Finally, the sale price of each comparable property must be recent because market conditions can change within a few short months. This held especially true when the market experienced the dramatic value swings resulting from the housing crisis discussed earlier. Ideally, the closing date of each comparable property sale would be within weeks of the appraisal, but this is not always possible. As a general rule, appraisers will look back to sales no further than one year and prefer to limit the search to sales occurring within the past three-to-six months.

    d. ▶ **Adjustments are made**: The appraiser will make adjustments to the recent sale prices of the comps to bring them more in line with the subject property. For example, "Comparable Property A" is 1,500 square feet and the subject property is 1,300 square feet. The appraiser might deduct $10,000 from the recent sale price as an adjustment. If the subject property has an extra full bathroom as compared to "Comparable Property B," $5,000 might be added to its recent sale price. There is no absolute book or table to which an appraiser can turn and look up the value of these differences. Instead, they mostly use market-supported judgment.

3. **Appraised value is selected**: Once the comps have been selected, the appraiser has a probable range of sale prices for the subject property. After making the necessary adjustments to the recent sale prices, the appraiser can assign a single market value which is delivered to the client in a report with supporting documentation.

4. ▶ **Comparative market analysis (CMA)–a value range**: Licensees frequently prepare a simplified version of the market data approach called a comparative market analysis or CMA. These are generally provided at no cost to a prospective seller in anticipation of obtaining a listing agreement. They may also be provided by a buyer's agent to a buyer-client to help the buyer set a fair offer price. The biggest difference with a real estate licensee's CMA is that no adjustments are made for differences between the subject property and the comps. This results in the owner receiving a value range rather than an exact figure as would be provided by an appraiser.

    a. ▶ **Competitive versus comparative market analysis**: A full comparative market analysis includes comparisons to: (1) "Currently listed properties" to show the seller-client what competing sellers are asking for their properties; (2) "Recently sold properties" to give the seller-client a current market value range; and (3) "Properties where the listing has expired" to show what may be over-priced homes. A competitive market analysis, on the other hand, only includes a comparison to currently listed properties without the other details.

    b. ▶ **Not considered a formal appraisal**: Any real estate licensee who prepares a CMA must take care not to refer to it as an appraisal. As noted earlier in this chapter, doing so could create a violation under appraisal license law.

    c. **Broker may charge a separate fee for a CMA**: As noted earlier in this chapter, a licensed broker or associate broker (but, not a salesperson) can charge a separate fee for a CMA providing it does not involve a federally-related transaction, is in writing, and contains the appropriate disclaimer.

    d. **BPO**: The acronym BPO stands for "Broker's Price Opinion." This relatively recent term has been defined in slightly different ways. It basically refers to a comparative or competitive market analysis. The fact that the name BPO is different from CMA does not exempt it from appraisal license law. The preparation of a BPO is subject to the same regulations governing the preparation of a CMA whether or not a fee is charged by a broker. A consumer who seeks a BPO should first determine exactly what information it includes.

B. ▶ **Cost approach**: When an appraiser uses a cost approach to appraisal, he actually calculates the cost of rebuilding the subject property using present day construction techniques, materials, and costs. This establishes a replacement cost which is then adjusted by subtracting the cost of any necessary repairs, deferred maintenance, or depreciation that may be affecting the subject property. Using a market approach, the value of the raw land is estimated as if it were vacant and then added back to the adjusted replacement cost.

The process involved in the cost approach will now be broken into separate elements for ease of understanding. The "cost approach" may also be referred to as the "replacement cost approach." At one time it was also know as the "summation approach" because the depreciated value of the structure was added to the market value of the land. This term, however, is no longer used.

1. **Application**: The cost approach is typically more accurate than the market approach when applied to custom-built or very new properties in less populated areas. This is due to the fact that locating similar comparables for these types of properties may be difficult.

2. ▶ **Steps involved in the process**: There are five basic steps that an appraiser uses when using the cost approach to appraise real property.

    a. **Step 1–Determine land value**: First, the appraiser determines the value of the land as if it were unimproved (meaning vacant). This is the only way to appraise the lot since there is no way to "reconstruct" the raw land. The market approach may be used to accomplish this step.

    b. **Step 2–Calculate cost of construction**: Next, the appraiser reconstructs the home on paper. Depending on the goal of the client, either the reproduction or replacement cost can be calculated. For example, if a custom home is being appraised for insurance purposes, reproduction cost may be warranted. If, on the other hand, it is being appraised in anticipation of a potential future sale, replacement cost might be more appropriate. For the reasons mentioned below, reproduction cost tends to lead to a higher final figure as compared to replacement cost.

        (1) ▶ **Reproduction cost**: If a reproduction cost is desired, the appraiser calculates what it would cost to produce an exact duplicate of all improvements and fixtures. For example, if the subject property has premium wood casement windows, marble counter tops, premium hardwood floors, an all-weather wood foundation, and a geothermal heating and air conditioning system, today's construction and materials costs would be calculated to duplicate it. This figure tends to be higher than replacement cost.

        (2) ▶ **Replacement cost**: When a replacement cost is desired, the appraiser's only concern is duplicating the same living space, room functions, and amenities as are found in the subject property. More common, and generally less expensive, construction methods, materials, and techniques are applied when calculating construction costs. Replacement cost would most likely be used if the purpose of the appraisal is to determine the present market value of the property.

        (3) ▶ **Cost (price) per square foot**: In some instances, a "cost per square foot" figure is provided or requested. This is calculated as "Sale Price ÷ Total Square Footage." Cost per square foot may also be stated as price per square foot. Care should be exercised since the cost per square foot is generally not considered to be a good indicator of true value. This is especially true when trying to compare different home styles such as a ranch and a colonial home, two home styles of different square footage, or two homes on radically different lots.

    c. **Step 3–Estimate depreciation**: Now that the appraiser has the cost of a new home estimated on paper, it is time to calculate any depreciation on the subject property. There are several different forms of depreciation that can affect a property. Some of them can be physically remedied or cured, others cannot. Some remedies make financial sense to apply, others do not.

        (1) ▶ **Depreciation defined**: As a concept, depreciation is any decline in property value due to wear or obsolescence. Since raw, i.e., vacant, land does not deteriorate in the same manner as a structure, depreciation under the cost approach only affects the value of the improvements, meaning buildings, on the land. Vacant land values can fluctuate based on market conditions. Depreciation resulting from the causes listed below should not be confused with IRS depreciation which is discussed in Chapter 15.

            (a) ▶ **Physical deterioration**: One form of depreciation results from physical wear and tear. For instance, the floor plan of the home and its intended function are fine, but structurally, there is a problem that requires repair. Examples of physical deterioration include improper or deferred (meaning delayed) maintenance, weather damage, insect infestation, damage from water infiltration, mold, problems resulting from improper construction, and owner-caused damage.

    i) **Curable deterioration**: A problem is considered to be curable if the cost of repair is lower than the resulting increase in value if the repair is made. Physical deterioration is usually curable since the deduction an appraiser might make will be based on the cost of repair. Even if the deduction and repair cost are the same, it makes psychological sense to have the repair done. Some buyers, when faced with a property that needs a repair, will make a large deduction from the offer due to the inconvenience of having to make the repair themselves. A leaky basement that was professionally water-proofed with a long-term warranty might even be more desirable to a buyer than a basement that has yet to leak.

    ii) **Incurable deterioration**: A problem is considered to be incurable if the cost of making the necessary repairs exceeds any resulting gain in value. Incurable deterioration occurs most frequently with a property that suffers from economic obsolescence.

(b) ▶ **Obsolescence and functional obsolescence**: When something is obsolete, it is out of date or is no longer used or is useful. Obsolescence, therefore, is the state of becoming obsolete. Functional obsolescence is a form of depreciation.

    i) **Definition**: Functional obsolescence refers to a loss in value resulting from a structure, improvement, or component part that if or has become inefficient, outdated, or outmoded. Something that is functionally obsolete typically needs updating or replacement. Examples would include a four-bedroom home with only one bathroom, or a 2,500 square foot home with a detached one-car garage.

    ii) **Includes a superadequacy**: Functional obsolescence also include a superadequacy or over-improvement. A buyer is only willing to pay for what is deemed to be of value to him personally. For example, the owner of a subject property installed 24k gold-plated plumbing fixtures and Macassar ebony hardwood flooring (which costs $150 per square foot as compared to $8-$20 per square foot for typical hardwood flooring). The owner will not likely recoup the value of these improvements when selling the property to a typical buyer who is not going to pay extra for the house merely because it contains these items if standard plumbing fixtures and flooring are all the buyer desires.

(c) ▶ **External (economic) obsolescence**: As a form of depreciation, external obsolescence results from factors outside the property and is considered to be incurable.

    i) **Definition**: External or economic obsolescence is the only category of depreciation that is caused by factors which are external to, meaning outside the boundaries of, the subject property. Common examples include properties which experience a lower value due to being located in a deteriorating neighborhood or in proximity to a perceived or actual nuisance such as a landfill, shoot range, farming operation, industrial complex, or airport. The subject property is valued lower due to the surrounding condition. Economic obsolescence is nearly always incurable due to the impossibility of eliminating the surrounding negative conditions.

    ii) **No such thing as social obsolescence**: Social depreciation is not a recognized form of depreciation. Therefore, an appraiser cannot adjust the value of a property due to the composition of a neighborhood's inhabitants. To do so would violate civil rights laws. An appraiser may consider the fact that homes in a neighborhood are in disrepair, but to suggest that a particular inhabitant or group of inhabitants has anything to do with it is false, inappropriate, and illegal.

d. **Step 4–Deduct depreciation**: After calculating the actual dollar amount of depreciation, the figure is deducted from the estimated construction cost of the new building and site improvements calculated in Step 2. This figure represents the depreciated cost of the subject structure as it actually exists at the time of the appraisal.

e. **Step 5–Add back value of land**: The final step is to add the estimated value of the land from Step 1 to the depreciated cost of the structure from Step 4. This final figure is provided to the client in a report that explains the process and details the steps undertaken.

Chapter 4: Appraisal

C. ▶ **Income capitalization approach**: The income capitalization approach is exclusively used to estimate the value of income-producing properties such as apartment buildings, commercial and office buildings, and shopping centers. An income property is purchased for the purpose of generating a profit by leasing it at a high occupancy rate to financially secure tenants. The income approach expresses the present worth of the subject property as a function of its ability to produce this income. It factors in any risk that may associated with the ability to generate income. As investment risk decreases, income-producing potential increases, and so does its value.

1. **Capitalization defined**: Capitalization is the process of converting the anticipated future income stream of an income property into a present market value. This future income stream is simply the anticipated rental income expressed as net operating income. Net income is calculated by taking the total or gross income derived from the property and subtracting any expenses related to its ownership. The income capitalization approach accomplishes this by applying an appropriately-selected capitalization rate to the net income.

2. **The process of capitalizing income**: The process of capitalizing income for real estate examination purposes can easily be demonstrated through the use of a simple mathematical formula. This process is also described in more detail in Chapter 22.

    a. **Step 1–Determine net operating income (NOI)**: First, determine the gross annual income of the property. If an examination question supplies monthly income, multiply it by 12 months to arrive at annual income. Next, deduct fixed operating expenses (again watching for monthly versus annual figures that you may be given in the question). The amount remaining is the net operating income or NOI.

    b. ▶ **Step 2–Apply the capitalization rate**: Selection of a capitalization rate by an appraiser is a technical process involving a number of different variables. The appraiser can select a capitalization rate based on market data culled from comparable income properties, or construct an overall rate by examining factors specific to the subject property. For purposes of the real estate broker's or salesperson's examination, calculation questions will either supply the rate or provide the net operating income and market value so it can be calculated (as described in Step 3, below).

    c. **Step 3–Determine value**: The three components of the capitalization approach are Value, Net Operating Income, and Capitalization Rate. Using these variables, the formula is expressed as Value = Income ÷ Rate. For purposes of calculation, it is best to use the "PRB Diagram" which is discussed in Chapter 22.

D. ▶ **Gross rent multiplier (GRM)**: The gross rent multiplier is another appraisal method that expresses the value of a property as a multiple of its rental income. It is the ratio of the property's value to its annual rental income before expenses. Since it relies on gross rental income, and different properties can have different debt and expense loads, a GRM-derived value is relatively imprecise. Therefore, it is often used to make a quick, preliminary assessment before applying a more sophisticated appraisal approach. For example, a gross rent multiplier (GRM) of 115 on a property means that it is worth 115 times its rental income.

1. **Monthly income is used**: Monthly income is used with gross rent multipliers. Make sure to read any examination question on income property valuation carefully to determine whether you are being asked about the income capitalization approach (in which annual income is applied) or the gross rent multiplier method (in which monthly income is applied).

2. ▶ **Calculation of GRM**: The appraiser researches the recent sale prices and gross income information about comparable properties and then applies a formula represented as:
GRM = Sale Price ÷ Monthly Gross Rent Income

3. **Gross income multiplier (GIM)**: If a portion of the income used in the calculation is derived from sources other than rental income, some appraisers refer to the approach as gross income multiplier, or GIM for short. Other individuals appear to use GRM and GIM interchangeably.

VI. ▶ **Reconciling the appraisal figures**: As noted earlier in the chapter, a formal appraisal often involves the application of more than one appraisal method. Reconciliation is the process used to analyze and then weigh the findings from each approach to arrive at an even more precise value. It represents a weighted average of the approaches used. This is an advanced technique used by experienced appraisers.

VII. ▶ **Measuring square footage and gross living area**: Knowing the square footage of a home is important in a number of different situations. In the construction process, for example, builders work from a set of drawings. The drafting architect includes the exact dimensions of all aspects of the home including total square footage. Local assessors use the square footage of all properties located in the city or township as part of the assessing process for taxation purposes. Further, a prospective lender with whom a mortgage application has been made will require that the subject property be appraised. The appraiser carefully measures the property which is incorporated into the final report.

While one would expect that all square footage calculations are based on a uniform system of measurement, such is not the case. There is no uniform system that is used in all situations. This does not suggest that great discrepancies will be encountered from one figure to the next, but some variation may exist. In some cases, human error contributes to any differences between figures.

A quick Internet search shows there are several recognized methods for determining the square footage of a home may be used. While the precise differences are beyond the scope of the Michigan licensing examination, it is important for real estate professionals to have a basic understanding of the process. Most importantly, real estate professionals must be careful not to make specific representations as to the accuracy of any one square footage measurement when listing and selling homes.

A. **Calculating square footage**: According to most standards (including ANSI), the square footage of a detached single-family finished home is calculated by using the exterior dimensions. A finished area in a home is any enclosed space with walls, floors, and ceilings that incorporate building materials which are suitable for interior construction. Further, finished areas must be suitable for year-round use by the occupants. This means that the area is heated by conventional heating systems.

Experts sometimes use the term gross living area (GLA) when calculating square footage measurements via exterior wall dimensions. As noted in Chapter 22, Real Estate Mathematics, the area of a two-dimensional square or rectangle is calculated as width x length. Using exterior walls makes this process fairly straight forward. It is important, however, to avoid measuring certain areas including those described below. See Chapter 22, Real Estate Mathematics, for more information on using area measurements to calculate square footage.

1. **Areas not included in the calculation**: Certain areas cannot be included in the calculation of finished square footage. Examples include: Areas not accessible from other living areas through a heated hallway, door, or staircase; Unfinished attic areas; Basements; Garages; and Areas that do not meet minimum ceiling height requirements. The square footage of these areas is subtracted to arrive at the gross living area.

2. **Above- versus below-ground finished areas**: The square footage calculation of a home only includes above-ground areas. These are floors which are completely above-grade. The grade is the final level or surface of the earth after all work has been completed. An area is considered to be below-ground if it is entirely, or even partially, below the finished grade. A below-ground area can be noted as a separate figure from the above-grade calculation (including mention of whether it is finished or not).

B. **Risk management considerations**.

1. **Real estate licensees**: Care must be exercised when transmitting square footage numbers for listed properties through the MLS and individual advertising. The source of the reported numbers, even public record data (PRD), is no guarantee of accuracy. When referencing square footage, it is prudent to note it as "estimated" or "approximate." Service provision agreements as well as purchase agreements should also contain standard release or disclaimer clauses. Through these clauses, the parties to the agreement acknowledge that they are not relying on any agent representations concerning the property. Also, the parties, especially buyers, should be encouraged to independently verify the square footage and be offered ample opportunity to inspect and measure the property prior to purchase.

2. **Sellers**: Any seller who is working independently of an agent may wish to avoid including square footage numbers on advertising pieces. Or, the seller can mention that the figure is provided per public record data or a recent appraisal. If in doubt, the seller can always refer to the advice of legal counsel on how to proceed.

3. **Buyers**: Buyers should not assume that any square footage representation is accurate. Instead, they should independently verify the numbers if accuracy is an important purchase consideration.

The shortest path to receiving is through giving.

DIAGNOSTIC PRACTICE QUESTIONS – CHAPTER 4

IMPORTANT STUDY TIP!

Step 1: Carefully review the information located in this chapter.

Step 2: Take the following Diagnostic Practice Questions. Review any question you answered incorrectly by researching the topic in this textbook. If you are still uncertain as to why the question is answered as it is, consult your program provider.

NOTE ON CHAPTER PRACTICE QUESTIONS

The following questions are representative of the type encountered on the Michigan real estate licensing examination. While some of these questions may be similar in nature and style, there is no way of predicting the exact wording of a question that will appear on the exam. Spending time memorizing these questions is, therefore, not recommended.

These questions are designed to help you determine how well you comprehend the material in this chapter. They are also intended to help you develop problem solving skills and to become comfortable with question formats.

Do not attempt to answer these questions until you have attended the lecture corresponding to this chapter and spent the appropriate time studying the material.

1. The Jasons drew up plans to build a residential dwelling for $300,000. Due to several cost overruns and changes to the original drawings, they actually spent $425,000. One year later, the Jasons were offered $500,000 for the property by a prospective buyer. The Jasons hired an appraiser who informed them that they could hold out for at least $550,000 based upon current market conditions. Which of the following statements is true?
   A. The value of the property is $550,000
   B. The cost of the property is $300,000
   C. The price of the property is $500,000
   D. The market price of the property is $425,000

2. Of all the following factors that can affect the value of residential real property, which is the most important?
   A. Improvements.
   B. Heterogeneity.
   C. Location.
   D. Supply.

3. The Towners have owned a 2-acre undeveloped parcel of land for several generations. The property is located within a major downtown area and has been used as a daily parking lot. Due to favorable market conditions in the area, one of the family members has proposed selling the lot and splitting the proceeds equally between the three surviving siblings. An appraiser should research and consider all EXCEPT which of the following when determining the value of the Towner's property?
   A. Anticipated changes in zoning in the area.
   B. Possible changes in use that might create a higher value.
   C. Interim uses to which the property can be put.
   D. Linking the appraisal fee to the appraisal figure.

4. An appraiser is hired to calculate the value of a small retail strip center located in a thinly populated, rural area. The appraiser is concerned that any potential buyer may have trouble attracting enough business tenants to make ownership of the strip center financially viable. Which of the following is the appraiser taking into consideration with this property?
   A. Economic trends.
   B. Highest and best use.
   C. Substitution.
   D. Modification.

5. Approximately five years ago, a property owner noticed water stains on the upper part of his family room ceiling in the east corner. Since it did not seem to be a problem, nothing was done to either investigate the stains or take corrective measures. Unfortunately, the stain was a sign that substantial damage was occurring in the attic due to a leaky roof. The property suffers from which of the following?
   A. External obsolescence.
   B. Physical deterioration.
   C. Economic obsolescence.
   D. Functional obsolescence.

6. A broker may prepare a non-fee comparative market analysis for all of the following purposes EXCEPT:
   A. To assist a buyer in arriving at an acceptable offer price.
   B. When assisting a landlord in determining a suitable rental rate.
   C. When it is promoted as a substitute for a formal appraisal.
   D. For the purpose of helping a seller determine a competitive listing price.

7. When an appraiser estimates the value of a single-family home, the most reliance would probably be placed on which of the following sets of factors:
   A. Cost and income.
   B. Highest and best use.
   C. Rent capitalization and market.
   D. Cost and market.

8. A young couple decided to build their first house rather than purchase an existing property. After ignoring suggestions by their builder, they settled on a poor floor plan. Upon resale of the property, the couple was not able to recover the estimated value of the property. The property suffers from which of the following forms of depreciation:
   A. Functional obsolescence.
   B. External obsolescence.
   C. Physical deterioration.
   D. Neighborhood decay.

9. Physical depreciation is most frequently associated with:
   A. Eccentric design.
   B. Obsolescence.
   C. Changing function.
   D. Ordinary wear and tear.

10. Utilizing a property to its greatest economic advantage is commonly referred to as:
    A. Economic utility.
    B. Highest and best use.
    C. Functional optimization.
    D. Maximization of profit.

11. An income property has a $10,000 rent per month. If the GRM is 72, what is the estimated value of the building?
    A. $10,000
    B. $720,000
    C. $72,000
    D. $7,200

12. Which of the following represents the basic formula used in direct capitalization to estimate the value of income producing real estate?
    A. Value = Income divided by Capitalization rate.
    B. Value = Capitalization rate divided by Income.
    C. Value = Income × Capitalization rate.
    D. Value = Income divided by Factor.

13. An appraiser is asked to establish the estimated value of a residential property that was constructed during the past 6 months by a person who installed all custom features throughout the house. The house is located within one mile of a developing commercial area. Which of the following methods of appraisal would be best suited to the property:
    A. Market approach.
    B. Gross rent multiplier.
    C. Cost approach.
    D. Income approach.

14. Of all the following statements, which best applies to the concept of market value:
    A. The price a ready, willing, and able buyer offers to an equally ready, willing, and able seller who accepts it in an arm's length transaction.
    B. The price which a ready, willing, and able buyer might be willing to offer to a seller who is ready, willing, and able to sell when neither party has knowledge of the market.
    C. The most likely price which ready, willing, and able purchasers offer and sellers accept under the pressure of time.
    D. The price that two reasonable parties agree on in the exercise of independent business judgment.

15. An appraiser performs which of the following functions:
    A. Determines value.
    B. Estimates value.
    C. Sets market value.
    D. Estimates the home price index.

16. An appraiser's reconciliation is used to:
    A. Obtain recertification under the new federal licensing requirements for appraisers.
    B. Determine a weighted appraisal figure when two or more appraisal methods are applied to a subject property.
    C. Verify appraisal data that is collected on properties with questionable or difficult to estimate features.
    D. Establish a direct average of multiple appraisal methods as calculated on a property.

Chapter 5
Deeds and Title Transfers

How ownership is transferred.

I. **Foreword**: As we have learned, real estate licensees assist buyers and sellers in the acquisition and sale of real estate. There are specific laws that control how real estate is owned and transferred. In this chapter we will examine the concept of ownership, voluntary transfers of ownership, involuntary transfers of ownership, and transfers that occur upon the death of an owner.

   A. **Real estate law generally**: Ownership of real property is central to the American way of life. General real estate laws define the rights associated with property ownership and set forth a system of enforcement. This helps to protect the integrity of our system of property ownership.

   B. **Transfer law**: Some real estate laws regulate the conveyance of property ownership or possessory rights from one person to another. Private property rights need to be uniformly applied and consistent in their enforcement so the public knows what to expect when entering into a real estate transaction. This reliability is an important part of what makes real estate so crucial to the health of the U.S. economy.

   C. **Constitutional protection**: Private property rights are so important that they are protected by the centerpiece of our legal system–the U.S. Constitution. The Constitution protects individual rights including the right to own property and freedom from unreasonable government interference.

II. **The concept of ownership**: The term ownership refers to a group of rights that govern real property use and enjoyment, including the right to convey it to others. Ownership itself is a legal concept and intangible. In other words, ownership cannot be seen or held. Being intangible, a mechanism is needed to recognize it and transfer it. As we will see, ownership can be with or without restriction.

   A. ▶ **Bundle of rights**: Ownership includes a package or bundle of rights. In addition to the rights of possession, use, and enjoyment, this bundle includes the right to control, mortgage, lease, physically exclude others, subdivide, and sell or otherwise dispose of by will, gift, or dedication. Unless specifically excluded or limited by contract or conveying document, a person can expect to receive the full bundle of rights when purchasing real property in most instances. *See Figure 11.*

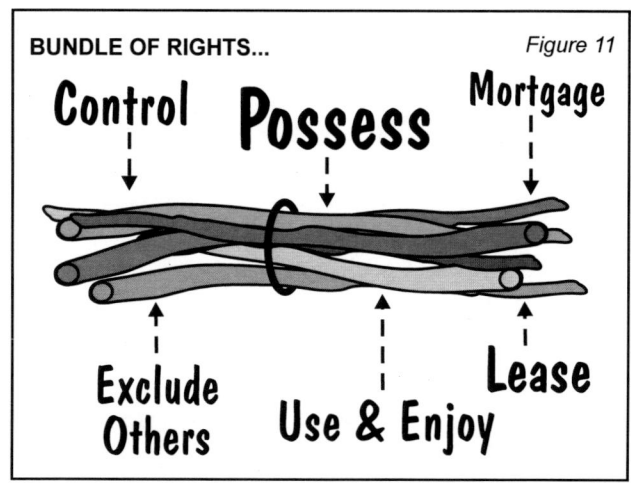

   B. **Title**: The word title is an abstract or conceptual term used to refer to the union of all elements that comprise ownership. Simply put, title means ownership. One who holds all rights to property is said to hold title.

   1. **Title as a tangible thing**: The term title is also used to describe the document or paper that evidences ownership of something such as a car title. The specific paper or document that evidences title or ownership to real estate is called a deed. By way of analogy, it could be said that "Deed is to Title, what "Birth Certificate" is to "Birthday."

III. **Voluntary transfers of title**: This section examines transfers that occur via sale, gift, or other grant during the lifetime of the owner. The term grant is used to refer to a transfer of property. In this sense, all transfers of real property are a grant. When the transfer of title is voluntary, a deed is almost always used.

A. ▶ **Deeds and their purpose**: A deed is the specific written instrument that an owner of real property uses to intentionally and voluntarily transfer or deliver his rights, title, and interest in the property to another person. Once this grant or transfer has been made, the deed serves as the tangible document that evidences the fact that title (meaning ownership) is now being held by the recipient.

   1. **Parties to a deed**: The parties to a deed are the grantor and the grantee. This is the first instance of the "–or" and "–ee" suffix discussed in this textbook. As a general rule, the "–or" gives the document and "–ee" receives it. The prefix (grant) indicates what document is being given or received. For example, since the word grant means to give by deed, when using it as a prefix for "–or" as in grantor, it refers to the person who gives the deed. The grantee is the person who receives the deed, *See Figure 12*.

      a. **Grantor**: A person who grants title via a deed is called the grantor. The grantor is typically the owner or seller of the property. As will be seen, there are special requirements for a grantor's execution, i.e., signing and delivery of a deed, to make sure that the conveyance is valid and in recordable form.

      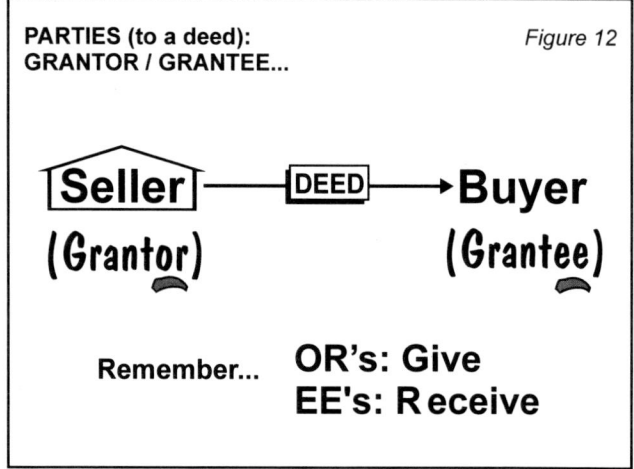

      b. **Grantee**: A person to whom the grant is made is known as the grantee. The grantee is typically the buyer of the property. Since the grantee merely receives the deed, his requirements are less stringent than those of the grantor. There are additional requirements if the parties wish to have the deed be in recordable form.

   2. **Deeds are not assignable**: Once a deed is signed by the grantor and delivered to the grantee, it evidences the transfer of title, but only to the grantee (or grantees) as the individual(s) named in the deed. As a result, this particular deed cannot be subsequently assigned, meaning transferred or given, to a third person and be a valid conveyance of title to that person. Instead, a new deed would have to drafted by the transferring party, naming the new recipient as grantee, and then delivered to the grantee. Assignment of documents and contracts is discussed further in Chapter 12.

   3. **Establishing validity**: There are numerous requirements for a deed to constitute a proper transfer of title. Since property ownership rights are so important, these requirements may generally not be waived. A deed can leave no doubt whatsoever as to what is being conveyed, who is conveying, and to whom it is being conveyed.

      a. ▶ **When title passes**: A deed must meet certain mechanical requirements for validity including (1) execution by the grantor and (2) delivery to the grantee. Title actually passes upon delivery of the deed. Additional requirements exist for a deed to be in proper legal form. They are explained in the next subsection.

      b. ▶ **Specific requirements for proper legal form**: The specific requirements for a deed to be in proper legal form center around things such as proper identification of the parties and the property, naming of consideration, words of conveyance, and any exceptions or exclusions from the conveyance.

         (1) **Grantor**: The grantor must be properly identified by name on the deed. This avoids misidentification and confusion. It is also a good idea to make sure that the spelling of the grantor's name parallels what was on the deed when he originally received title as the grantee.

            (a) **Legal capacity**: The grantor must have legal capacity at the time of the conveyance. This means he is of sound mind and legal age. One is deemed to have legal capacity to enter into a contract or conveyance if he is capable of understanding the nature and consequences of his acts.

               i) **Voidable conveyance**: Capacity is important since a deed issued by a grantor who lacks capacity is voidable. This means that the conveyance may be invalidated if it can be demonstrated that the grantor was a minor or had a mental disability at the time of the conveyance.

Chapter 5: Deeds and Title Transfers

(b) **Concurrent ownership**: If the property is concurrently owned, meaning jointly, all grantors must join in the conveyance by executing the deed. This is the only way to insure that full title has been conveyed to the grantee. Failure to include all grantors leaves potential clouds on the title. As discussed in Chapter 7, there are different forms of ownership in which multiple owners can convey their interests at different times and using separate deeds.

(2) **Grantee**: The requirement regarding the grantee's name is not as stringent because the grantor is the one who is releasing a legal claim to the property. This does not mean, however, that the person who prepares the deed can be lax about including the name of the grantee.

(a) **Must be named**: At the very least, the grantee's name must appear on the face of the deed with sufficient certainty. When looking at the chain of title, it must be clear who the conveying party is as well as to whom the conveyance is made. The grantee does not sign the deed, however.

(3) **Recital of consideration**: The deed should recite, meaning spell out or specify, the exact amount of consideration that was given by the grantee to the grantor in exchange for the deed. In most cases, the consideration is the price paid for the property. In simple terms, consideration is defined as something of value that one party to a contract or instrument gives to another as an inducement to enter into the agreement.

(a) **Need not be shown**: The actual dollar amount of consideration does not have to appear on the face of the deed as long as the nature of the consideration is indicated. For example, the phrase "for one hundred dollars and other valuable consideration" is acceptable. The deed should at least indicate that the transfer was made in exchange for valuable consideration as opposed to good consideration.

(b) **Good versus valuable consideration**: Consideration falls into one of two categories; either good consideration or valuable consideration. Valuable consideration includes money and goods or services that have a monetary value. Good consideration, on the other hand, has no dollar value and is often informally called "love and affection." Consideration is discussed in more detail in Chapter 12.

(4) **Words of conveyance**: A deed contains specific words of conveyance. These words set forth the quantity and quality of the property interest being conveyed by the deed. Also known as the granting clause, this section sets forth the extent to which the grantor intends to convey the described property. Words such as grants, releases, gives, conveys and warrants, quitclaims, and bargains and sells are commonly used in granting clauses.

(5) **Accurate legal description**: Although a formal legal description is best, at a minimum, the deed must sufficiently describe the property to enable a court to figure out what is being conveyed. Without a proper description, the deed is considered to be void. A void document has no legal effect whatsoever.

(6) **Deed reservations and exceptions**: Deeds sometimes contain reservations and exceptions. These clauses are used by the grantor to withdraw or hold back a portion of the land from the conveyance. Although the terms exception and reservation are often used interchangeably, there is a technical difference.

(a) **Exception**: A deed exception withdraws a portion of a property from the total amount being conveyed. It identifies an interest the grantor owned, but never intended to convey. For example, a grantor conveys a 10 acre parcel of land "except the mineral rights" to the property. In this case, the grantee does not take title to the mineral rights.

(b) **Reservation clause**: A reservation clause creates some right that had not previously existed, and reserves it for the grantor after conveyance. For example, a grantor sells one of two adjoining lots he owns in a wooded area. He creates an easement on the sale property to make it easier for him to access a back road.

A deed reservation does not affect the actual description or amount of the property being conveyed. This means that the grantee does take title to the land encumbered by the easement. Contrast this with the deed exception in which the grantee does not take title to the mineral rights.

(7) ▶ **Deed restrictions**: A deed restriction is a provision in a deed by which the grantor can limit or prohibit certain uses of a property by the grantee. They are frequently placed in deeds that convey title to a series of neighboring properties to enhance the value of the entire development. Examples might include limits on building height, architecture, or density. A deed restriction may also take the form of a restrictive covenant.

    (a) ▶ **Creation of a Homeowners' Association (HOA) through CC&Rs**: A homeowners association, or HOA for short, includes property owners who serve as the governing body for enforcing the rules pertaining to the properties within the subdivision. It is generally created (and recorded) by the developer in a written document referred to as a Declaration of Covenants, Conditions and Restrictions, or CC&Rs for short. By purchasing a home within the subdivision, the new owner is bound by the document, becomes a member, and pays any required dues. An HOA is typically a Michigan Nonprofit Corporation. Contrast this with a condominium owners association discussed in Chapters 7 and 21.

    (b) **"Subject to" clause**: A "subject to" clause is a form of deed restriction that sets forth the existing encumbrances to which the conveyed title is subject. This clause is important, especially in the case of a warranty deed, since the grantor guarantees that the title will be free of all encumbrances except those mentioned in this section of the deed.

    (c) **Racially restrictive covenant**: A racially restrictive covenant is a device that was historically placed in deeds to bar certain classes of individuals from purchasing the properties. For example, a group of non-minority owners agrees to place covenants in their deeds prohibiting future owners from selling and conveying title to a minority buyer. Since such clauses prevent the transfer to title to a person based on race (or any other named protected class) and are discriminatory, illegal, and unenforceable.

(8) **Execution**: To execute a document means to sign it. Execution of a deed verifies that all grantors have voluntarily agreed to convey their interest to the grantee. A deed is invalid if it contains a forged signature of the grantor or if the grantor's signature has been obtained by improper means including duress, menace, and undue influence.

    (a) **Signature by grantor's representative**: A grantor may use an attorney-in-fact to execute a deed in the grantor's absence. The authorization is given when the grantor gives a power of attorney to a designated person who acts as the grantor's attorney-in-fact. As noted in Chapter 2, a real estate licensee should avoid serving as an attorney-in-fact for a client due to increased liability and possible exclusion from errors and omissions insurance.

    (b) **Illiterate grantor**: An illiterate grantor can execute a deed by placing an authenticating mark on the deed's signature line. Since a signature signifies a party's intent to convey the property, an alternative mark can serve the same purpose. As discussed later in this chapter, the mark must be notarized for the deed to be in recordable form. This holds true for all grantor signatures.

        i) **Execution using a foreign language**: A grantor who does not write or sign his name using the English language, may sign his name in another language. If the deed is to be recorded, the register of deeds may require that the English version of the name be typed or printed beneath the signature along with notarizing.

        ii) **Use of fingerprint as proper mark**: According to Act 266 of 2005, if a grantor is unable to write, his proper mark may include a classifiable fingerprint made with ink or another substance. Accordingly, a person with a disability who is unable to write can legally execute a document. A licensee should not advise the person of his legal rights with regard to an alternative mark, instead the person should be referred to legal counsel.

    (c) **Grantee**: As noted, the requirements surrounding the grantee's name appearing on a deed are less stringent. Although the grantee's name must appear, he is not actually required to execute it. This is due to the fact that grantor is one who is conveying title, not the grantee.

    (d) **Electronic signatures**: Digital or electronic signatures have become common in the marketplace. Michigan's Uniform Electronic Transactions Act defines an electronic signature as an electronic sound, symbol, or process attached to or logically associated with a record and executed or adopted by a person with the intent to sign the record. As long as the parties to an agreement consent in writing to its electronic formation, and the text can be visually displayed, any electronic signature will be fully enforceable. See Chapter 12 for further information.

      i) **Recordation of electronic documents**: Michigan's Attorney General has indicated that a register of deeds is not required to, but may, accept and record documents affecting title that are in electronic format and bearing electronic signatures. If recorded, an electronic document provides the same level of constructive notice that any other recorded document provides.

(9) ▸ **Delivery**: As previously mentioned, the act or process of delivery is necessary for a deed to be a valid conveyance of title. Delivery makes the grantor's intention to convey title visible and it must occur during the lifetime of the grantor. This is why a land contract buyer, i.e., vendee, often requires the seller, i.e., vendor, to place the deed in escrow at the closing. The specific reason for this practice is explained in Chapter 16.

    (a) **Acceptance**: Sometimes delivery is referred to as delivery and acceptance. As long as the deed has been delivered by the grantor, the act of acceptance is not critical since it is generally assumed to be part of a proper delivery. Acceptance can become important if the grantee rejects the delivery by refusing to take the deed.

    (b) **Deed takes effect on delivery**: A deed takes effect on its actual delivery to the grantee. The only exception to this is a Sheriff's Deed issued in connection with a foreclosure. At the actual foreclosure sale, the court official signs and delivers the Sheriff's Deed to the high bidder. It does not actually convey title to the foreclosed property until the passage of a redemption period during which the homeowner has the opportunity to pay the debt and reclaim his property from the foreclosure process. See Chapter 16 for further details on mortgage foreclosure.

c. ▸ **Statutory requirements for recording (and importance of)**: A document is recorded to serve legal notice to the world of its existence. The order in which documents are recorded is also important. In the event that multiple claimants or interests are involved in a single property, the order of recording establishes their priority of claim. For example, a property owner obtains three loans at different times, all of which include liens on the property as security. In the event of judicial foreclosure, debts are paid in the order of recording.

Recordation is not, however, a prerequisite of validity. For a document to be in recordable form, there are more requirements compared to the basic requirements for it to simply be valid. The following list is a sample of Michigan's recording requirements for a deed.

(1) **Name of the grantor**: The name of the grantor must be printed, typed, or stamped beneath his original signature.

(2) **Discrepancy in names**: There can be no serious discrepancy between the name of each person as printed, typed, or stamped beneath his signature and the name as recited in the acknowledgment of the deed. Courts may, however, be willing to allow minor discrepancies to exist according to certain rules.

(3) **Acknowledgment**: The grantor must acknowledge the execution of the deed in front of a notary public, judge, or clerk of a court of record within the state. The requirement of acknowledgement is discussed later in this chapter and is commonly known as notarizing.

(4) **Grantee's name and address must appear**: This is the address to which the deed will be returned after recording. If the grantee since moved, the grantee should notify the appropriate register of deeds (which is determined by the county in which the property is located).

(5) **Drafting party**: The name and business address of the person who prepared the deed must appear on the deed. In the event of any discrepancy, the drafting party can be contacted.

(6) **Recording fees**: Documents are recorded at the county register of deeds. Effective 2016, recording fees for nearly every county in Michigan was changed to $30 per document regardless of page count. This fee is typically paid by the person seeking recordation. This fee is separate from the transfer tax.

(7) ▸ **Payment of the real estate transfer tax**: When a person records an instrument conveying title to property such as a deed, transfer taxes are charged to the seller-grantor. Transfer taxes are based on

the consideration recited on the deed, i.e., the purchase price. They are paid at the time of recording to the register of deeds in the county where the property is located.

    (a) **Two transfer taxes**: There are two real estate transfer taxes levied on the recordation of a deed; one by the county and a separate tax by the state. The person recording the deed issues one check payable to the county register of deeds and the county then disburses the appropriate portion to the state. The county transfer tax was formerly called revenue stamps since payment was actually reflected by stamps affixed to the recorded document.

        i) ▸ **County transfer tax rate**: The county transfer tax is 55 cents ($0.55) for each $500 or fraction thereof of the total consideration, i.e., price paid, recited on the face of the deed.

        ii) ▸ **State transfer tax rate**: The additional state real estate transfer tax is levied at the rate of $3.75 for each $500 or fraction of $500 of the total consideration paid for the property.

        iii) **No federal transfer tax**: There is no federal transfer tax. Generally, federal taxes only come into play with a real estate transaction if a sale results in a qualifying capital gain. Capital gains are a form of unearned income that may be subject to federal income taxation. Capital gains taxation is discussed further in Chapter 15.

        iv) **Concealed purchase price on deed**: In the event a grantee wants to conceal the actual dollar amount paid for the property on the face of the deed, a Real Estate Transfer Tax Valuation Affidavit must be prepared and submitted with the deed for recording. It lists the actual amount paid. The deed must at least indicate that the property was transferred for valuable consideration with a statement such as "... for $100 and other valuable consideration." The local assessor's office is able to rely on the affidavit to verify the property's value for purposes of future assessments.

    (b) ▸ **Transfer tax example**: If you are asked on the real estate licensing examination to calculate the total amount of transfer tax due when a deed is recorded, add $0.55 (for the county tax) and $3.75 (for the state tax) for a total of $4.30 for each $500, or fraction of $500, of consideration on the deed. Some find it easier to calculate the total transfer tax as a multiple of $1,000 of value. In such case, the tax would be $8.60 per $1,000.

Using this latter approach, assume that a property sells for $187,250. First, round the price up to the nearest fraction of $500. In this case, the basis for taxation is 187.5 ($1,000s). Next, multiply this number by the combined tax rate of $8.60. The formula looks like the following: 187.5 × $8.60 = $1,612.50 due in total transfer taxes.

    (c) **State transfer tax exemption**: A seller is exempt from payment of the state real estate transfer tax providing three conditions are met at the time of sale: (1) the seller must have occupied the property as a principal residence and claimed a principal residence exemption, (2) the property's state equalized value (SEV) for the calendar year of the sale must be equal to or less than its SEV for the calendar year in which the seller originally acquired the property, and (3) the property cannot have been sold for an amount greater than the true cash value (TCV) for the year of the transfer. The TCV is typically double the amount of the SEV.

In other words, the property must not have increased in value over the period of time the seller owned the property and he cannot have sold it for a profit. A seller who claims the exemption, but who fails to meet all three conditions above can be assessed a penalty equal to 20% of the state transfer tax in addition to the actual tax due under the Act. There is no similar exemption for the county transfer tax.

4. **Deed contents**: The contents of a deed are divided into three primary sections: (1) the premises clause, (2) the habendum clause, and (3) the testimonium clause.

    a. **The premises clause**: The premises clause contains the general introductory information about the property transaction and its parties. It also contains the date of the deed.

        (1) **Date**: The date on the deed typically refers to when it was drafted. It is possible for a deed to be drafted on one day, executed by the grantor and notarized on another day, delivered to the grantee on a different day, and finally recorded on a subsequent day. This is why most experts do not consider a deed without a date to be void. There will be a place near the bottom of the deed for the notary to enter the date the grantor's signature was acknowledged.

Chapter 5: Deeds and Title Transfers

(2) **Importance of the date of recording**: The date a deed is recorded is arguably the most important date, because it actually can establish the priority of claim in the chain of title should a problem with multiple claimants arise.

(3) **Other contents**: The remainder of the premises clause includes the names and addresses of the grantor and grantee, consideration, granting clause, legal description, and any reservations or restrictions that may exist.

b. **The habendum clause**: The habendum clause of a deed operates as a supplement to any specific words of conveyance contained in the premises clause. It normally begins with the words "TO HAVE AND TO HOLD." The covenants and warranties of title typically follow the habendum clause and define the quality of the deed; for example, whether the warranties cover the full chain of title or are special in that they only cover a limited period of time.

c. **The testimonium clause**: The testimonium clause of a deed contains the grantor's execution, i.e., signature, which must also be acknowledged before a notary public for the deed to be in recordable form.

(1) **Acknowledgment–notarizing**: The process of acknowledgment involves a formal declaration by a party (e.g., grantor of a deed) who signs an instrument (e.g., deed) in front of an authorized official (e.g., notary public) acknowledging that the signing is a free and voluntary act. Acknowledgment is also known as notarizing. Notarizing protects against forgeries and other similar acts of property fraud.

(2) **Attestation–witnessing**: Attestation is the act of witnessing the execution of a deed or other document. As of 2002, witnessing is no longer required on deeds or land contracts in Michigan. Notarizing, however, continues to be required for deeds to be in recordable form.

B. ▶ **Types of deeds**: There are several different types of deeds that may be used to convey title. It is especially important for buyers to understand their differences because some deeds convey full warranties whereas others convey no warranties. The terms of the purchase agreement generally set forth the type of deed the seller is required to convey to the buyer at the closing.

1. ▶ **Warranty deed**: A warranty deed is the most popular deed for the conveyance of residential property. This is due to the fact that the grantor guarantees, meaning warrants, that the title is good and marketable. These guarantees essentially cover the full history of the chain of title. Of particular importance to grantees is the grantor's obligation to cure any problems that may affect the grantee's interest in the future. The warranty deed is also known as a general warranty deed.

a. ▶ **Marketable title**: A title which is marketable is free from encumbrances and reasonable doubt as to its validity. It is clear of any defect that could diminish the quality or quantity of the conveyed interest. As a result, the title is considered to be saleable to a future buyer.

(1) **Enforceable in court**: While no title is technically perfect, a marketable title is sufficiently devoid of problems that a court can compel a buyer-grantee to accept it in spite of any objections he may have over minor issues.

(2) **Example**: A buyer enters into a purchase agreement with a seller and, before the scheduled closing, learns that a common utility easement exists on the property. The buyer refuses to close and take title claiming that the title is not marketable. A court will not likely recognize the buyer's claim based on the fact that certain issues including utility, cable, and road easements are so commonplace that they are not considered to be title defects.

(3) ▶ **Marketable title versus insurable title**: An insurable title is one that can be subject to a title defect. Nevertheless, a title insurance company may still be willing to insure against the defect. There is one potential problem for a buyer who receives insurable title rather than marketable title, however. When the buyer goes to sell the property later, the next buyer's insurance company may not be willing to insure over the title defect. Therefore, obtaining marketable title is preferable.

b. **Grantee has legal recourse**: Assume that a true title defect arises resulting in the grantee receiving less than what was represented in a warranty deed. The grantee can sue the grantor for breach of covenant and may be entitled to damages or to have the defect cured by the grantor. A covenant is a written promise (as is a warranty) in a contract or a deed.

c. **Covenants of title**: As discussed, a warranty deed contains multiple warranties that provide the greatest protection of any type of deed. This makes it the most desirable deed from the grantee's perspective.

If the purchase agreement is silent about the type of deed the grantor must give the grantee, the law presumes the parties intended to convey title via a warranty deed.

    (1) **Covenant of seisin and right to convey**: Through this covenant, the grantor guarantees that (1) he is the owner of the property, (2) the exact quantity and quality of the interest stated in the deed is accurate, and (3) he has the right to convey title to the property. The word seisin is an old feudal term for having both possession and title. The feudal system is briefly discussed from a historical perspective in Chapter 6.

    (2) **Covenant against encumbrances**: Through the covenant against encumbrances, the grantor represents to the grantee that the property is free from all encumbrances such as mortgages, liens, and easements except those expressly mentioned in the deed. This is not a guarantee that there are no encumbrances, only that no unstated or undisclosed encumbrances exist.

    (3) **Covenants of quiet enjoyment and warranty**: This covenant is a promise that no superior interest exists that can interfere with grantee's quiet enjoyment of possession. The grantee's possession will be defended against all claims by third parties that were in existence at the time of the immediate conveyance. This even extends to interests that might surface from the actions of any of the prior owners in the entire chain of title.

        (a) **Meaning of quiet title**: The term quiet title refers to an ownership interest in which the grantee is free from the risk of being legally or physically ousted from the property. It has nothing to do with freedom from noise or other physical nuisances.

        (b) **Importance of title insurance to the grantor**: A grantor may be concerned about guaranteeing the entire chain of title for as long as the grantee and the grantee's heirs own the sale property. This is especially true since the grantor would not necessarily be aware of what a former owner did years ago to create the problem. This promise is easily honored by the grantor purchasing title insurance for the grantee. Title insurance is discussed further in Chapter 8.

    d. **Doctrine of after-acquired title**: A grantor in a warranty deed promises that he will make whatever future conveyance may be necessary so the grantee will have the full title interest described in the deed. For example, a deed purports to convey 5 acres, but the grantor only owns 3 acres. If the grantor is subsequently able to obtain title to the remaining 2 acres, they automatically pass to the grantee. Title to the after-acquired 3 acres automatically passes by operation of law to the grantee.

2. ▶ **Special warranty deed**: A special warranty deed differs from a general warranty deed in that the guarantees only cover the period of time the grantor held title. In other words, the grantor only promises to guarantee and defend the title against defects or claims that might have arisen since he originally acquired the title. The grantor warrants that he, or anyone claiming under him, has not encumbered the title. No warranties are extended to problems that may have been created by an earlier owner in the chain of title. A special warranty deed is also known as a Covenant Deed or C Deed. It is illegal under Michigan law, however, to actually label a document purporting to convey title as a Limited Warranty Deed.

    a. **Similar to a general warranty deed in all other respects**: The warranties conveyed in a special warranty deed are similar to those in a general warranty deed with the difference that they only cover problems that arose during the time the grantor held title. This means that the actions of prior owners in the chain of title are not covered.

    b. ▶ **Application**: A special warranty deed is most commonly given by a grantor who acts as an interim owner; for example a trustee, corporation, asset manager, estate representative, or a bank-owned property transfer.

3. **Bargain and sale deed**: A bargain and sale deed is a type of deed that sets forth the consideration paid by the grantee and then conveys whatever interest the grantor has in the property at the time of conveyance, without any warranty or guarantee. Although the grantor makes no promises, it is generally implied that he can convey legal possession and a substantial title interest in the property.

    a. **Offers little protection**: Since no warranties are offered, a bargain and sale deed affords almost no protection to the grantee. Consequently, the grantee would have little recourse if a defect is found to exist. When a grantor will only convey title via a deed that lacks substantial warranties, the grantee can ask the grantor to provide title insurance or the grantee can purchase his own title policy. At the very least, a prospective grantee of a bargain and sale deed should conduct a preliminary title search to ascertain whether or not there are any clouds or detectable problems.

Chapter 5: Deeds and Title Transfers

4. ▶ **Quitclaim deed**: A quitclaim deed is used to convey an interest in a property by releasing or quitting the grantor's claim to it without guarantee. The deed passes whatever interest the grantor may have in the property, if any, at the time of the conveyance. It is important for the grantee to realize that the grantor only promises to convey the interest he actually has, but does not warrant that he has an interest.

   a. **Offers the least protection**: From the grantee's perspective, a quitclaim deed provides the least protection of any deed due to the total lack of warranties or other promises. If the grantor has an interest, it is conveyed. If he does not, no fraud has been committed.

   b. ▶ **Used to clear clouds on the title**: A quitclaim deed does serve a useful purpose. It is used to clear clouds on the title which are uncertain or doubtful claims. It is also used in divorce situations when a husband, for example, transfers his interest in the joint, marital estate to his wife as part of the settlement. The deed may also be used (1) for property transfers that occur between family members, (2) in business transactions, and (3) when property is conveyed into a trust.

   c. **Differs from a bargain and sale deed**: A quitclaim deed is not the same as a bargain and sale deed. In the case of a quitclaim deed, it merely releases any interest in the property without suggestion or implication that the grantor owns or has the right to convey.

5. **Lady Bird Deed**: A Lady Bird Deed, also known as an "enhanced life estate deed," is a type of conveyance in which the grantor conveys his property to what is known as a contingent grantee and reserves to himself a life estate in the property. Contingent means that the grantees must wait for the grantor to die to gain ownership of the property. It is primarily used as an estate planning tool because the property automatically passes to the grantee on the grantor's eventual death without having to go through a probate court. Lady Bird language can be included in a warranty deed or quitclaim deed to create this type of property transfer.

   A key feature of a Lady Bird Deed is that the grantor reserves the absolute right to sell, mortgage, lease, or otherwise profit from the use of the property during his lifetime without needing the permission of the grantees. The grantor can also cancel the grantees future interest by conveying the property to someone else. As discussed in Chapter 6, the owner of an ordinary life estate does not have the right to sell or mortgage the property so as to deprive the holders of any remainder interest of their rights on the owner's death. The origin of the name flows from a story that former President Lyndon B. Johnson used the instrument to deed his property in this manner to his wife, "Lady Bird" Johnson.

IV. **Involuntary transfers of title**: An involuntary conveyance is one that takes place without the property owner's consent. It can result from things such as adverse possession, a suit to quiet title, accession, eminent domain, escheat, and foreclosure.

   A. **Adverse possession**: An action for adverse possession arises when someone other than the true owner possesses certain land for a statutory period of time, and does so in a way that is considered to be adverse (meaning contrary) to the fact that anyone else but him holds title. It often occurs with unimproved land in which the true owner cannot be located or appears to have abandoned it. After adversely possessing the property for a minimum period of time, a court action is initiated by the claimant seeking a court order to transfer legal title to him. For this to occur, certain elements must be established. Adverse possession is also known as "title by prescription."

   1. **Physical requirement**: An adverse possessor must meet and prove certain physical requirements before a court will award him the title. The nature of the claimant's possession is important since someone else who may actually own the property is on the verge of losing it.

      a. **Elements of possession**: Possession must be actual, exclusive, open, visible, notorious, continuous, and hostile to the idea that anyone other than the adverse possessor has a rightful claim to the property. In one sense, the possessor is living there in defiance of the rights of the true owner.

         (1) **Establishing possession–Residential property**: In the case of residential property, actual possession is required along with the payment of property taxes. Other beneficial evidence can be found if the possessor improved the property and used it as his legal address.

         (2) **Acts not supporting a claim**: To protect the rights of the actual owner, the following actions will not result in the loss of title through adverse possession: mistaken possession; non-exclusive possession; or possession transferred by consent or permission such as that which is granted through a lease.

2. **Statutory period**: Not only must possession be open and notorious, it must also be continuous for the full statutory period of time which is fifteen years under Michigan law for real property.

   a. **Tacking**: It is possible for different adverse possessors to join partial periods of possession in order to meet the full statutory requirement. There must, however, be an unbroken and successive chain of possession from one possessor to the next. The last claimant in possession is entitled to file the claim for the entire title in his name.

B. ▶ **Suit to quiet title**: A suit to quiet title is a court action that establishes title in a particular person. It bars any other claimant from asserting his own independent claim. The action is also used to remove a title defect or cloud on the title. The term is derived from the fact that the court quiets all dissenting claimants in favor of one.

C. **Accession**: Under the legal doctrine of accession, the owner of a property acquires title to all that his property produces. This includes crops, timber, and discovered minerals. It also creates an ownership right to everything that is attached to the owner's property, either naturally, artificially, by intention, or by mistake.

   1. **Additions to improvements**: When a property is improved, the owner acquires an automatic ownership right to all fixtures or enhancements that are added to an existing structure. It is important for tenants under residential leases to be aware of this fact.

   2. **Application to leases**: Unless agreed to otherwise with the landlord in writing, if a tenant adds an improvement to the leased property during the term of the lease, it becomes the property of the landlord. For example, if a tenant adds a wood deck structure to the back of a leased home, the deck is deemed to become part of the real property owned by the landlord.

D. ▶ **Eminent domain**: Under eminent domain, federal, state, and local governments have the right to take private property for public use. This makes it an involuntary form of title transfer. Since property ownership is a constitutionally-protected right in this country, its taking must meet certain criteria such as the payment of just compensation to the owner for the loss. The precise details of how eminent domain works are discussed in Chapter 11.

E. ▶ **Escheat and unclaimed property**: Escheat is the process by which the property of another transfers to the state for the lack of any person who is rightfully entitled to inherit it. For example, a real property owner dies without leaving a will, i.e., intestate, and has no heirs who are legally entitled to inherit his property. The property escheats, meaning reverts, to the state.

   In Michigan, the state serves as the legal custodian of the property, but is not considered to be the owner of it. Accordingly, property that escheats to the state is a form of unclaimed property. In Michigan, unclaimed property is handled by the Unclaimed Property Division of the Michigan Department of Treasury. Refer also to Chapter 12 for the discussion pertaining to earnest money deposits as unclaimed property.

F. **Foreclosure**: Since foreclosure is an involuntary loss of title to the lender, it is included in this list. Foreclosure is a legal process which is initiated by a lender when the owner defaults by ceasing to make his scheduled mortgage payments. A foreclosure is different from a short sale. In a short sale, the owner voluntarily sells his property for an amount lower than the balance due on the mortgage, and attempts to obtain a cancellation or forgiveness of the deficiency from the lender. The foreclosure process is discussed further in Chapter 16.

V. **Title transfer of a decedent's estate**: When a real property owner dies, a statute known as the Probate Code is used to determine how the real estate must be transferred. Title to real property passes at the time of the owner's death either to (1) his heirs at law through a process known as descent, or (2) those heirs named in a will through a devise clause.

A. **General terminology**: The law that governs a decedent's estate is beyond the scope of a real estate licensing course. However, since the disposition of real property is frequently involved when an individual dies, a licensee should have a general understanding of the terms associated with the process. These terms are introduced in this section using a series of questions. Note how some of the terms have multiple meanings and other terms share a similar meaning.

   1. **Question 1**: "Who has died and what property was left?"

      a. **Decedent**: The term decedent refers to a person who has died, whether he has died with or without leaving a will.

   2. **Question 2**: "Did the decedent die with instructions as to the disposal of his property such as a will?"

Chapter 5: Deeds and Title Transfers

a. **Will**: A will is a legal instrument that a person uses to predetermine how his real and personal property should be disposed and the estate settled. The difference between a will and a deed is that a will takes effect upon the death of the decedent whereas a deed takes effect upon its delivery during the lifetime of the grantor.

   (1) **Testate**: Technically speaking, a testate is a person who has prepared a will. The term is also used to refer to a person who has died having left a will.

   (a) **Testator**: The term testator can refer to a person who has authored a will or to a person who died leaving one. Testator is also a gender-specific term used to describe a male who authored a will.

   (b) **Testatrix**: Similar to the gender-specific use of the term testator, a testatrix is a female who authored a will.

b. **Devise**: When used as a noun, a devise is a gift of real or personal property that is made through a will. Used as a verb, the term devise means to dispose of real or personal property through a will.

   (1) **Devisor**: A person who gifts his property through a will is known as a devisor. The term can also be used to refer to the maker of a will.

   (2) **Devisee**: A devisee, on the other hand, is the person to whom the real property is given through the will of a devisor. Devisees are typically the heirs of the devisor or other persons designated to receive the testamentary, meaning will-based, gift.

3. **Question 3**: "If no will exists, what do the laws in the jurisdiction require for succession, meaning passage, of the decedent's estate?"

   a. **Descent**: The term descent refers to the succession of property ownership by inheritance or by law.

   b. **Intestate**: To die without leaving a will is to die intestate.

4. **Question 4**: "Who is responsible for managing or disposing of the decedent's estate?"

   a. **Administrator**: An administrator is a person appointed by a probate court to take charge of the assets and liabilities of a decedent. A male who performs this function is called an administrator while a female is called an administratrix.

   b. **Executor**: An executor is a person named or appointed by the author of a will to carry out the directions and requests of the will. He or she fulfills the orders listed in the devise clause.

   c. **Personal representative**: A personal representative is a person under Michigan law who can fulfill the role of either administrator or executor. Personal representative is the term most frequently used today.

B. **Probate**: The term probate refers to the legal procedure used to prove whether a will is valid or not. It is also used to describe the legal process by which a decedent's estate is administered when no will exists. The probate court is one of three trial courts in the State of Michigan. It exists in most counties and has supervision over the probating of wills, administration of estates and trusts of deceased persons by personal representatives, and guardianships and conservatorships for persons with mental or developmental disabilities.

   1. **Guardianship**: A guardian under Michigan law is a person who is given the legal responsibility for another person's physical well-being. Guardians handle needs such as housing, necessities including food and clothing, and medical care. A guardianship can also be established to see to the well-being of a child or a person with a disability. A testamentary guardianship is one requested in the will of a parent for the care of a minor child or adult child with a disability.

   2. **Conservatorship**: A conservator, on the other hand, is an individual who is appointed by the probate court to manage the property or affairs of an individual who the court has determined is unable to care for himself. This protection may be warranted when a person has a disability, is incapacitated, or has an age-related infirmity.

C. **Will substitute**: Will substitutes are common legal devices through which an individual can avoid having his property go through the probate process. Typically, will substitutes involve property held in a form of joint ownership with a survivorship element. When the decedent dies, the subject property automatically passes to the surviving co-owner(s) without their having to be named in a will or being an heir. Common examples of will substitutes include property held as joint tenants, joint bank accounts, certain trusts, life insurance policies, and Lady Bird Deeds.

What two words are more powerful than "I can't"?
Answer: "I can."

DIAGNOSTIC PRACTICE QUESTIONS – CHAPTER 5

IMPORTANT STUDY TIP!

Step 1: Carefully review the information located in this chapter.

Step 2: Take the following Diagnostic Practice Questions. Review any question you answered incorrectly by researching the topic in this textbook. If you are still uncertain as to why the question is answered as it is, consult your program provider.

NOTE ON CHAPTER PRACTICE QUESTIONS

The following questions are representative of the type encountered on the Michigan real estate licensing examination. While some of these questions may be similar in nature and style, there is no way of predicting the exact wording of a question that will appear on the exam. Spending time memorizing these questions is, therefore, not recommended.

These questions are designed to help you determine how well you comprehend the material in this chapter. They are also intended to help you develop problem solving skills and to become comfortable with question formats.

Do not attempt to answer these questions until you have attended the lecture corresponding to this chapter and spent the appropriate time studying the material.

1. The right that a grantee acquires to reconvey his property in the future, will it, mortgage it, or otherwise encumber it is best known as:
   A. The bundle of rights.
   B. A legal estoppel.
   C. The right to assignment.
   D. Livery of seisin.

2. Barbara purchased a residential property that was in the process of being foreclosed. She intends to fix it and then resell it for a substantial profit. She is concerned that a shrewd buyer may go to the public records see the price she paid for the property on the deed and then use it to negotiate a lower price. Since Barbara wants to protect her interest in the newly-acquired property, what can she do to try and hide the purchase price?
   A. Leave the actual price paid off of the deed providing she discloses the nature of the consideration in its place.
   B. Refrain from recording the deed.
   C. Direct that the transfer tax not be posted anywhere on the deed.
   D. There is no way to hide the purchase price when recording a deed exists.

3. All EXCEPT which of the following statements regarding the execution of a deed are true?
   A. All of the grantees who are listed on a deed must sign any subsequent deed which is drafted to convey the property to a new purchaser.
   B. The exact form of name and spelling which is used to list the grantees on a deed must be used when conveying the property in the future.
   C. A grantor who is illiterate is limited in terms of who the property can be transferred to due to diminished capacity.
   D. A grantor who is out of the country during a closing may authorize an attorney-in-fact to actually sign the document for him in his absence.

4. A seller of a residential property was marketing his property at an advertised price of $185,000. An interested purchaser offered $175,000 and, after intense negotiations, the parties agreed on a price of $179,000. Shortly after the closing, the purchaser recorded his new interest in the property. How much is the transfer tax?
   A. $769.70
   B. $1505.00
   C. $1539.40
   D. $1591.00

5. Which of the following situations would likely constitute a valid claim of unmarketable title?
   A. The fact that a purchaser may have paid 10% more than market value for his property.
   B. A purchaser who suddenly realizes that the purchase agreement does not call for a title insurance policy.
   C. A utility right of way that prevents the owner from constructing a shed on the back 15 feet of his lot

D. An undisclosed 5% interest conveyed to a sister-in-law by a prior grantor.

6. Which of the following statements about a deed is true?
   A. A deed must be recorded before it is considered to be valid.
   B. The grantor's signature does not have to be witnessed for the deed to be valid.
   C. Marketability of the title is established by the date on a deed.
   D. The grantee's name must appear under the signature line.

7. Which of the following types of deed would create the greatest potential risk for the grantor?
   A. A trustee's deed.
   B. A quitclaim deed.
   C. A special warranty deed.
   D. A general warranty deed.

8. A declaration made by a person to a qualified official that he freely and voluntarily executed a deed or other instrument is called an:
   A. Acknowledgment.
   B. Execution.
   C. Authorization.
   D. Authentication.

9. A quitclaim deed is used to convey whatever interest may be held by the:
   A. Grantee.
   B. Mortgagee.
   C. Grantor.
   D. Lessee.

10. The gift of real property by will is commonly known as a:
    A. Donation.
    B. Conveyance.
    C. Devise.
    D. Covenant.

11. The term escheat most nearly means the:
    A. Claiming of a property by a buyer when there is no clear legal title.
    B. Right of the government to take private property for public use upon payment of just compensation.
    C. Right of an owner to reclaim property sold through foreclosure proceedings.
    D. Passing of title to the state when the property owner dies intestate and without heirs or descendants.

12. All EXCEPT which of the following statements are true about a title which is defined as marketable:
    A. A title that a purchaser is safe in assuming should be saleable in the future.
    B. A title which is sufficiently free of problems to enable a court to specifically enforce it.
    C. A title that a reasonable grantee would be willing to accept in the exercise of ordinary care.
    D. A title that is free of any and all types of encumbrances.

13. The term quieting a title most closely refers to which of the following:
    A. The deposit of a title with an escrow agent.
    B. A mortgagor's relinquishing a title after foreclosure.
    C. A title insurance company's search of a title.
    D. The removal of a cloud on the title by court action.

14. A covenant against encumbrances in a deed conveyance warrants against the existence of all the following EXCEPT:
    A. Mortgages against the land.
    B. Judgment liens against the land.
    C. Easements that adversely affect the land.
    D. Zoning ordinances that limit the use of the land.

15. All of the following statements concerning a deed that is dated on a Sunday and delivered on a weekday are true EXCEPT:
    A. It is valid.
    B. It can be recorded.
    C. It conveys title.
    D. It is unenforceable.

16. A deed must be acknowledged in order to:
    A. Record the deed.
    B. Obtain title insurance.
    C. Record mortgages and judgments.
    D. Make the transfer of ownership legal.

Chapter 6
Interests in Real Property

Determining the quality and quantity of ownership.

I. **Foreword**: In the last chapter we explored the process by which real property ownership is transferred from one person to another. This chapter continues the discussion of property ownership by examining how the extent of the estate being transferred by the grantor to the grantee is measured. The current system of property ownership in the United States originates from the old system of English land law known as feudalism.

  A. **Feudal system**: Feudalism is an archaic system of land law where all land is owned by a king who gives possession to regional lords in exchange for providing services to the kingdom. In the United States, feudalism has been abolished in favor of our present-day allodial system.

  1. **Allodial system**: Under our modern allodial system of land law, real property can be individually owned without being subject to any of the historical feudal duties or burdens. Private property ownership is one of the most cherished rights in our country.

  2. **Vestiges of the feudal system**: Interestingly, we see a vestige, meaning trace, of the feudal system with present day leases. A real property owner acting as a landlord can legally transfer the limited right of possession to a tenant while retaining his right to own the property. This is evidence that modern property law treats property rights (e.g., ownership by a landlord) and property interests (e.g., exclusive right to possession by a tenant) as separate from one another.

II. ▶ **Types of estates in land**: The term estate refers to the degree, quantity, nature, and extent of an interest in real or personal property. It is synonymous with the terms right, title, and interest. Estates are divided into freehold and leasehold categories.

  A. ▶ **Freehold**: A freehold estate is one in which ownership (as opposed to mere possession) is implied. It is also in the nature of a "fee" meaning that it is inheritable. A freehold interest must involve land and exist for an indeterminable period of time. Indeterminable means that the duration of ownership is measured either by the lifetime of the owner (as in the case of a life estate) or it is indefinitely inheritable (as with a fee estate). See Figure 13.

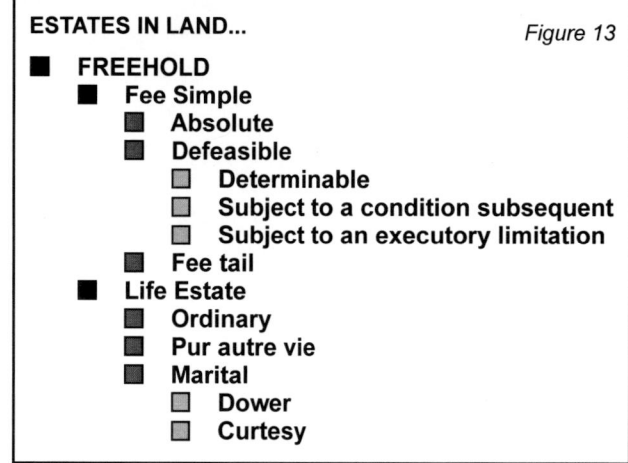

Figure 13

  1. ▶ **Fee simple**: In basic terms, "fee" and "fee simple" refer to a freehold interest in land that carries with it the right to possession and ownership. It is inheritable by the heirs of the owner. The interest can also be without condition or limitation or it can include a limitation depending on the wishes of the grantor.

    a. **Fee simple absolute**: A fee simple absolute interest is one created in a person, i.e., the grantee, and his heirs and assigns forever, without limitation or condition. It is the highest and most common form of ownership available under the law for residential property. The terms fee, fee simple, and fee simple absolute, although technically different, are often used interchangeably.

    b. **Fee simple defeasible**: A fee simple defeasible interest is one in which the grantor conveys his property with a condition, restriction, or other limitation as to how the grantee can use the property as the new owner. These conditions typically run with the land to future grantees. The seller-grantor is the one who places the condition on the title. These conditions or restrictions can vary widely. For example, a grantor owns a house on a four-acre lot located next to his church. He conveys the property to the grantee on the condition that the back portion of the lot remain available for church overflow parking during services.

2. ▶ **Life estate**: A life estate is an actual ownership interest in property with a duration that is measured by the lifetime of the new owner (known as the grantee or life tenant) or some third person. The estate is limited to the balance of the subject person's life. Upon the death of the life tenant or third person, the property either reverts back to the grantor or transfers to a different party named in the deed. *See Figure 14.*

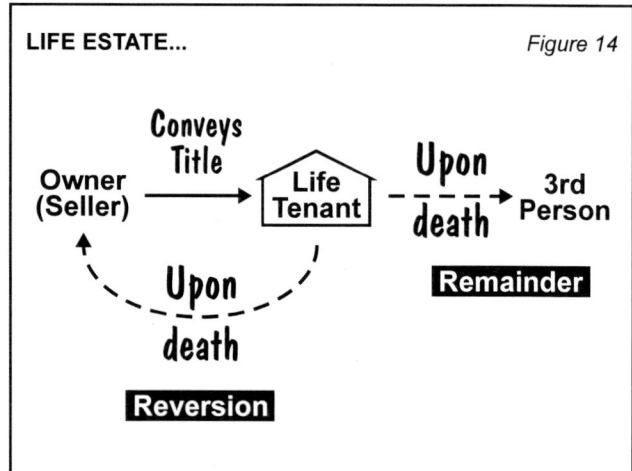

a. **Must create a future interest**: Due its nature, a life estate is not inheritable by the heirs of the life tenant. Upon the life tenant's death, the ownership changes to either a reversion or a remainder interest. In either case, the heirs of the life tenant have no claim to the property when the life tenant dies.

(1) **Reversion interest**: A reversion or reversionary interest is a future interest created when an estate reverts, meaning returns, to the original fee simple owner, i.e., the grantor. It arises from a life estate when the life tenant dies. If the grantor had previously died (or sold his reversion interest in the property), the grantor's heirs or assigns receive the reversion interest when the life tenant dies.

(2) **Remainder interest**: A remainder interest is another future interest similar to a reversion, but it is created in someone other than the grantor. The party named in the deed to whom property passes upon the life tenant's death is called a remainderman. Should the remainderman predecease the life tenant, the remainderman's heirs or assigns are entitled to the property rather than the grantor or grantor's heirs. For example, a husband in a second marriage owns property in his own name. He establishes that should he predecease his second wife, his property passes to her as a life estate while naming his children from his first marriage as remaindermen.

b. **Ordinary life estate versus life estate pur autre vie**: As noted, a life estate can be measured by the lifetime of a third party rather than the life tenant. This is called a life estate pur autre vie which means "for another's life."

(1) **Ordinary life estate (for the life of the grantee)**: As a review, under an ordinary life estate, the lifetime of the grantee is used as the measuring life for the estate. Thereafter, a reversionary or remainder interest is created depending on how the grantor created and conveyed the life estate.

(2) **Pur autre vie (for the life of another)**: In the case of a life estate pur autre vie, the grantor names a third party who is used as the measuring life. When this third person dies, the life estate terminates and passes to whatever future interest the grantor created, whether it is a reversion or a remainder interest. Technically, the life tenant as owner of the life estate could still be alive at the time of the third party's death.

For example, Grantor-Smith sells his cottage on a land contract to a 19 year old. The mother of the 19 year old, who is a close friend of Smith's, agrees to make the monthly payments so her daughter will have a place to live. Smith conveys the home via a life estate pur autre vie (with a reversion). The mother is established as the measuring life. When the mother dies, title to reverts back to Smith.

c. **Rights and responsibilities of life tenant**: It is important to remember that a life tenant is still considered to be an owner in spite of the fact that the interest is not inheritable. As an owner, the life tenant has certain responsibilities regarding the property. Failure to meet these obligations can impair the rights of those holding the reversion or remainder interest.

(1) **Maintenance**: The life tenant has a duty to maintain the property and make necessary repairs.

Chapter 6: Interests in Real Property

(2) **Property taxes**: The life tenant must pay all property taxes as they come due to prevent the property from being sold through a tax foreclosure.

(3) **Sale, mortgage, or lease of the life estate**: Although a life tenant can technically sell, mortgage, or lease the property during his lifetime, the sale, mortgage, or lease is automatically terminated upon the death of the life tenant, and either reverts back to the grantor or transfers to the remainderman. In other words, a life tenant cannot change the character of the life estate by simply selling the property. There is a concept in property law that states "he who hath not, cannot give." This means that someone cannot grant more power or rights than he himself has in property.

d. **Historical marital estates**: Dower is the historical law that protected a surviving widow whose deceased husband owned property in which she was not an owner. In Michigan, for example, a widow was entitled to a one-third interest in such property for the balance of her life. If the wife was named in the deed, dower generally did not come into play since she was a co-owner. Other states (but, not Michigan) also afforded a married man a similar interest in the property exclusively owned by his deceased wife known as curtesy. The Michigan legislature repealed dower rights effective in April, 2017.

3. ▶ **Land contract as a freehold interest**: We have examined fee simple and life estates as two forms of freehold interests. Another form of freehold interest is created in the buyer of a property under a land contract. The seller of the property, who is called the vendor, may take a down payment and surrenders possession of the property to the buyer, who is called the vendee.

In a land contract, the seller-vendor retains the deed (which represents the legal title) as security for the repayment of the full amount due payment under the contract. Since the buyer-vendee is actually purchasing the property, he is deemed to hold an equitable title interest in the property and is treated as the owner. Land contracts are discussed in further detail in Chapter 16.

B. ▶ **Leaseholds**: A freehold interest in a property implies that the holder has ownership. Anything less than a freehold is considered to be a leasehold interest. A leasehold interest in a property implies that the holder has a mere possessory right. A rental agreement, or lease, is a type of leasehold interest. To draw a basic distinction between freehold and leasehold interests, think of a leasehold as a possessory interest with a fixed term or duration. Leases and leasehold rights are discussed further in Chapter 13.

III. ▶ **Encumbrances generally**: As an interest in real property, an encumbrance is any right that exists in a person other than the owner. Encumbrances include a claim, lien, charge or liability that is attached to and binding upon the real property. From the perspective of the property owner, an encumbrance potentially impairs the value of the affected land.

A. **Runs with the land**: Encumbrances usually pass with the title when transferred from one owner to another. This is one of the primary reasons why a buyer should have a title search conducted before purchasing a property. A lender will also conduct a title search before committing loan funds for the purchase of property. Title insurance companies commonly perform these searches as part of their services.

IV. ▶ **Easement**: An easement is another form of interest in a property. It creates a limited right to use or enjoy the property of another for a particular purpose. The principal right is that of ingress and egress, meaning the right to enter and exit the subject property, to accomplish the purpose of the easement. Easement rights are non-possessory and do not include the right to remove any part of the subject land.

A. **Creation of easements**: Easements are commonly created by contract or other form of agreement between the owner and holder of the use right. A deed can also be used to create easement rights. The exercise of eminent domain by a local unit of government can also create an easement, for example, as part of a road widening project.

B. **Types of easements**: There are several different easement types that vary based on the circumstances of the use. Some are created by the parties voluntarily while others are based on necessity.

1. **Easement appurtenant**: An easement appurtenant is based on two adjoining properties. One property contains the easement that benefits the neighboring property. Since an easement appurtenant benefits a tract of land rather than a particular person, it is said to "run with the land." This means that it passes with any subsequent conveyance to a future owner. *See Figure 15.*

a. **Dominant estate or tenement**: The property that benefits from the easement is known as the dominant estate. The owner of dominant estate, known as the dominant tenant, acquires the right to use the easement located on the adjoining property.

b. **Servient estate or tenement**: The servient estate contains and is burdened by the easement. The owner of this property, known as the servient tenant, must allow the owner of the dominant estate to pass over or use his land in accordance with the easement rights.

c. **Easement may result from a party wall**: An easement appurtenant may result from the construction of a party wall. A party wall is an actual wall built on the boundary line of two properties. The wall may provide common support for one building that spans two lots. Each owner acquires title to one-half the wall and an easement for its support in the other half.

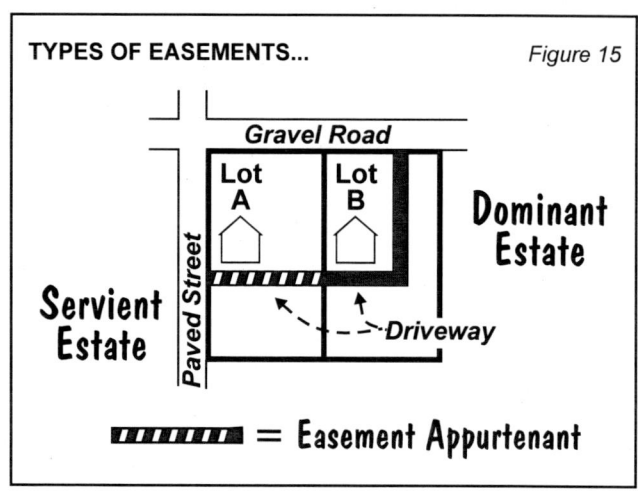

2. **Easement in gross**: An easement in gross creates a personal interest in the land of another. Since the benefit runs to a person rather than a neighboring tract of land, only a servient estate exists. Examples of easements in gross include (1) common access ways to power, telephone, and cable lines, (2) highway and railway easements, and (3) other public utilities.

3. **Easement by implication**: An easement by implication is one that is implied or presumed to exist by law even though the parties to a transaction may not have created it or reduced it to written form. Under certain circumstances, the law presumes the parties intended to include an easement. The rule of implication states that when the law gives anything to a person, that person receives by implication all that is necessary for its enjoyment.

Two lots that share a common driveway is one example of an easement by implication. Each owner receives, by implication, the right to use that portion of the driveway located on the other property. Since the easement is implied by law, it continues to exist even if the property is sold to a new owner. *See Figure 16.*

4. **Easement by necessity**: An easement by necessity is closely related to an easement by implication. The easement is considered a necessity to the use of the land and not just implied from the owner's prior use. The most common example is seen with two adjoining properties where one landlocks the other. A landlocked parcel is completely shut off from access to any public road. An easement must be granted from the road, across the servient tenant, to the landlocked (dominant) parcel. *See Figure 16.*

5. **Easement by prescription**: An easement by prescription results from the long-term enjoyment and uninterrupted use of a servient land by one who is not the owner. It is similar to adverse possession except that the use by the claimant only results in an easement being imposed on the property rather than ownership. The use must be adverse, open, and hostile. In legal terms, a "prescription" is the process of acquiring rights by asserting an uninterrupted use of something over a long period of time.

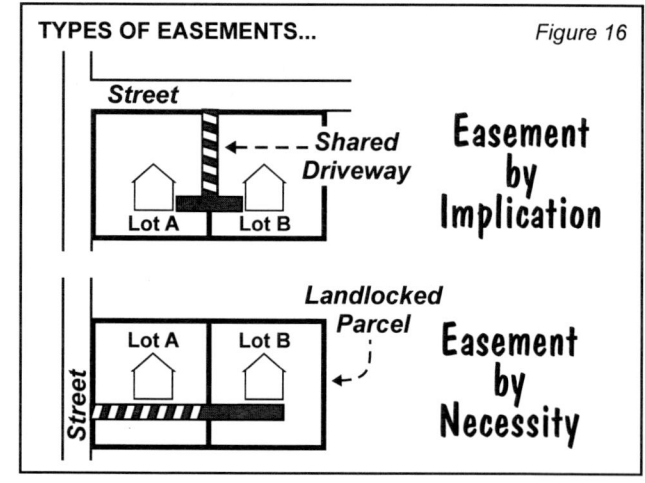

C. **Termination**: Easements may be terminated by (1) written release of the interest by the dominant tenant, (2) merger of the dominant and servient estate in one owner, (3) cessation of the necessity as in the case of an easement by necessity, or (4) non-use or timely interruption of the use by a person attempting to establish a prescriptive easement. A court may also order the termination of an easement.

V. **Other non-possessory interests**: There are several other interests that can affect real property that are non-possessory in nature. These interests include a license, encroachment, profit, and emblement.

Chapter 6: Interests in Real Property 101

A. ▶ **License**: In terms of property rights, a license is a personal privilege afforded to a person, called the licensee, to perform some act, or series of acts, on the land of another, called the licensor. A license does not afford the licensee any title, interest, or estate in the land. When an owner grants a license, it amounts to giving permission to use his land for a particular and limited use. Since it does not create an ownership interest in the property, the license does not run with the land to future owners.

License examples: A license is created when an owner gives permission to another to do things such as (1) hunt, fish, or swim on the licensor's property, (2) park an automobile on a municipal or private parking lot, or (3) construct a billboard on a property that borders a busy highway.

1. **Easement distinguished**: A license is not the equivalent of an easement since the license does not create a real property interest that runs to a person or parcel of land. The license merely acts as permission to enter a land for a certain, limited, and often one-time purpose.

2. **Bailment distinguished**: The doctrine of bailment is not generally considered to be part of real property law. Nevertheless, it is important to distinguish a license from a bailment. Legally, a bailment involves the delivery of personal property from one person, called the bailor, to another, called the bailee, in accordance with some form of a contract. The bailee must exercise due care of the property and return it to the bailor when the contract is fulfilled.

   With a license, the property owner who grants permission to the licensee is not liable for the actions of the licensee, nor is the owner of the land responsible for damage or loss of the licensee's property. For example, a public parking lot owner avoids a bailment by instead granting a license to customers to park their cars on the lot at the car owner's own risk. There is no bailment because the lot owner does not take possession of the cars and agree to care for them while they are parked.

B. ▶ **Encroachment**: An encroachment is any illegal intrusion that invades a highway, waterway, or the property of another. When a building, or some part of it, illegally extends beyond its lot line, it is deemed to have encroached on the adjoining property or street. Encroachments can affect the marketability of both the offending, meaning encroaching, property and the property burdened by the encroachment. An encroachment can also occur within the boundary of a lot. For example, a family room addition is constructed on the side of a house which inadvertently extends one foot into a side lot setback area.

1. **Detection of an encroachment**: Encroachments are detected by physically inspecting a property or by conducting a formal survey. Since a title search does not involve the physical inspection of a property, it is not used to discover an encroachment.

C. **Profit**: A profit is a right that one person exercises in the soil of another, accompanied with participation in the monetary profits derived from use of the soil. Profits are commonly granted by the property owner, for a fee, to outside companies that harvest timber by logging, mine minerals, drill for gas and oil, or excavate gravel. A profit differs from an easement since a profit includes the right to take something from the land encumbered by the profit.

D. **Emblements**: The term emblement specifically refers to an annually produced crop that results from the labor and industry of a tenant rather than appearing spontaneously by nature. Examples include planted vegetables, wheat, corn, and fruit. A tenant under a lease generally has the right to harvest, meaning take and carry away, emblements after the tenancy has ended because they resulted from the tenant's own labor. The lease should clearly state this right in the agreement to avoid any misunderstanding.

VI. ▶ **Liens**: A lien is a claim on the property of another for the payment of some debt, duty, or obligation. A lien gives the creditor a qualified right to force the sale of the debtor's property to satisfy the debt it secures. Since a lien runs with the title to the land when it is recorded, it can affect future owners and constitutes an encumbrance on the title. A mortgage is one of the most common lien types in existence today. *See Figure 17.*

A. ▶ **Senior versus junior liens**: Liens are often classified based on the order in which they arise. A senior lien is the first lien to attach to the property, and generally the first one that must be satisfied under judicial foreclosure. It has precedence over subsequent liens that are placed on the title. All liens that follow the senior lien are designated as junior or second liens.

B. **Parties to a lien**: The parties to a lien include the lienor and the lienee.

1. **Lienor**: A lienor is the holder of a lien right on the property of another. He owns the lien which is placed on the property of the debtor. A lender in a mortgage loan is a lienor. Do not confuse a lienor with a mortgagor, however, as the terms refer to two different individuals. As discussed in Chapter 16, a mortgagor is

a person who gives a mortgage contract to a lender which results in a lien being placed on the property.

2. **Lienee**: A lienee is the person whose property is subject to a lien. As with the previous discussion, it is important not to confuse the term lienee with mortgage. A mortgagee is a person or entity who receives a mortgage contract from a borrower which makes the mortgagee a lender.

C. ▶ **Types of lien**: While there are many different lien types, they are either considered to be general liens or specific liens.

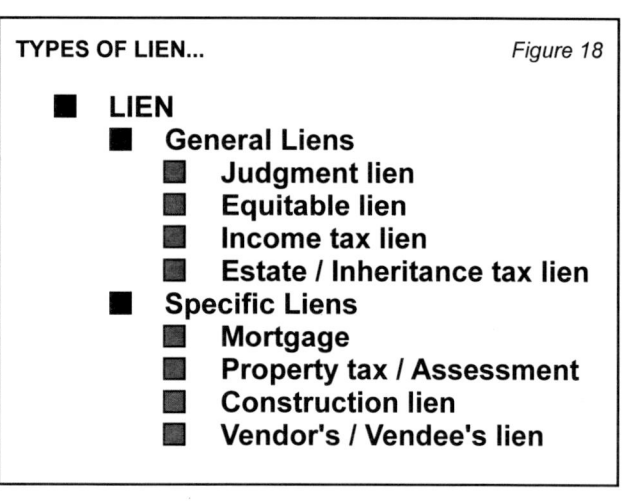

1. **General liens**: With some exceptions, a general lien attaches to all of the property of a particular person, including both personal and real property. Examples include judgment liens, equitable liens, income tax liens, and estate and inheritance liens. A general lien typically arises from the actions of a person rather than through consent or agreement. *See Figure 18.*

    a. **Judgment lien**: After rendering a verdict in a civil court case, the judge may order the non-prevailing party to pay a sum of money to the prevailing party. If the non-prevailing party cannot pay the money at that time, a judgment lien may be entered to assure that the money will be repaid. A judgment lien can be attached to both real and personal property.

2. **Specific liens**: A specific lien directly affects a particular property regardless of ownership. Examples include mortgages, property tax liens (but not income tax liens), construction liens, and vendor's or vendee's liens. A lien must be recorded, thereby serving legal notice, for it to affect a future grantee who was not a party to the transaction giving rise to the lien.

    For example, a grantee takes title to a property with a previously recorded mortgage on it. The lender can foreclose the lien on the property since the grantee took title with notice of its existence. This is another reason why it is critical for a prospective buyer to conduct a title search prior to acquiring title to a property.

    a. **Property taxes and special assessments**: The non-payment of property taxes, special assessments, and public utilities such as a water or sewer bill can result in an enforceable lien in favor of the local unit of government. Any of these fees left unpaid at the time of closing are deducted from the grantor-seller's proceeds from the sale so the grantee can take clear title.

    b. **Construction liens**: In Michigan, a contractor, subcontractor, materials supplier, and laborer have the legal right to place a lien on a property he builds or improves to secure payment for the value of the work performed and/or materials. While construction lien law can affect a property owner who builds, remodels, or otherwise rehabilitates a property, the subject is no longer tested on either the Michigan real estate broker's or salesperson's license examination.

D. ▶ **Lien priority**: Problems can occur for both owners and lien holders when a property is subject to multiple liens. This is especially true in markets when real estate values are decreasing over a sustained period of time. Since nearly all lien types are deemed to be of equal legal importance, the issue of priority and which lien gets satisfied first out of the sale proceeds usually comes down to timing. In other words, whichever lienholder gives first notice as to the existence of his lien is said to have priority over any other liens on the property.

1. **Order of recording determines priority of claim**: Under the most common rule, the order in which liens are recorded determines the priority in which they are repaid in the event of a foreclosure. The actual date

Chapter 6: Interests in Real Property 103

on which the lien arose may not necessarily be the deciding factor, however. If the funds from the foreclosure of the property are exhausted before all liens are satisfied, each remaining lienholder is left with a personal claim against the owner-debtor for his outstanding debt. This assumes that the owner executed a note or promise to pay along with agreeing to the lien being placed on his property.

2. **Subordination agreement**: A subordination agreement makes the claim of one lienholder subordinate or junior (meaning lower) to a subsequent lienholder's claim. Assume that "Lien 1" is recorded first as a senior lien and contains a subordination agreement. It is automatically moved to a secondary or junior position to "Lien 2."

    Example: Ms. Smith obtains a mortgage loan from First Bank to purchase a residential property. This represents "Lien 1." She later obtains a home equity line of credit (HELOC) from Second Bank which results in a junior lien being added to her title. This is "Lien 2." If Ms. Smith later refinances her mortgage with First Bank, a new mortgage is created that is in a junior position to the HELOC loan. First Bank will agree to issue the refinance loan only if Second Bank subordinates its HELOC lien to it.

    As a note, when an existing loan is refinanced, the refinance lender issues a new loan. The homeowner uses the proceeds to pay off and discharge the existing mortgage. This holds true even if the same lender issues the first and refinance loans because the new loan is almost always sold in the secondary market to a different investor. Lending concepts are discussed further in Chapter 16 and Chapter 17.

3. ▶ **Priority of a property tax lien**: The people of the State of Michigan are deemed to hold a valid lien on all land with delinquent taxes, including the right to enforce it as a preferred claim. Subject to certain exceptions, this claim supersedes mortgages and easements and can encumber mineral rights. Under federal law, a property tax lien is afforded "superpriority" status over an IRS lien. This priority status even applies to a lien resulting from nonpayment of a special assessment.

E. **Transfer of property subject to lien**: As discussed, if a prospective buyer receives notice that a lien exists on the subject property, he takes title subject to rights of the lienholder and the lien can be foreclosed. This is true even if the prospective buyer is not contractually bound to the debt. This became a significant issue for buyers of short sale properties in the early 2000s when the marketplace was flooded with these transactions. The short sale process is discussed in more detail in Chapter 16.

F. **Enforcement**: To be valid, a lien must be (1) created for a legal purpose, (2) applied equitably, meaning fairly, and (3) properly levied, meaning enforced.

1. **Sale of property to avoid foreclosure**: A homeowner-debtor who believes that his lender is ready to begin foreclosure may attempt to sell his property to avoid losing it. This is not recommended because (1) it does not erase the contractual debt, and (2) any buyer will take title subject to the lien. The following tools are generally available to lienholders to warn prospective buyers that the property is subject to a pending lawsuit or lien.

    a. **Lis pendens**: A lis pendens is a formal legal notice of a pending lawsuit. It is filed, meaning recorded, at the register of deeds to warn all persons, particularly future buyers, that the title to the property is in litigation and may be adversely affected by a judgement.

        (1) **Not a lien**: The lis pendens itself is not a lien. Rather, it is a notice that litigation is pending that could result in the sale of the property. Buyers should view it as a warning not to purchase the property until the matter is settled. If a buyer proceeds with the purchase, he is deemed to have received fair notice, and the property can be sold to satisfy the debt owing.

        (2) **Clouds the title**: A lis pendens clouds the title to a property on which it is recorded. As a result, legal counsel should be consulted before filing one. A person who is owed money often wonders if he can file a lien or lis pendens on the property held by his debtor. The law governing this matter is clear: If a creditor does not have a court-ordered, contractual, or statutorily-prescribed right to a lien on a property, he may not do so. If a lien or lis pendens is filed improperly or for malicious purposes, it could give rise to a slander of title action by the property owner.

        (3) **Slander of title**: A claim for slander of title arises when a person knowingly and maliciously publishes false statements that disparage a person's right in his property. This prevents a creditor or other person from filing an invalid lien or lis pendens for the purpose of causing the property owner harm. For example, a person cannot record a lis pendens merely to stall or stop a property sale and transfer from taking place. Penalties include all legal costs to clear the cloud, actual attorney fees, and damages. Depending on the filing party's intent, more serious penalties could flow.

(4) **Commercial Real Estate Broker's Lien Act**: Under Michigan law, a real estate broker can file a lien on real property for unpaid commercial real estate commissions and services. This lien right does not flow to a real estate salesperson or any one else working under the broker. No lien right exists for the following property types: Real estate zoned for single-family use where no structure is located; Real estate where four or fewer residential units are located; or Real estate on which more than four single-family residential units are located, if the units are conveyed on a unit-by-unit basis. Again, care must be exercised by a commercial real estate broker and legal counsel should be consulted to make sure all filings are done properly.

b. **Attachment**: An attachment is a court order that acts to legally seize a property and secure a creditor's claim after a judgment is entered in the creditor's favor. It, in essence, takes a property into court custody until the debt is satisfied. This prevents the debtor from attempting to sell his property or destroy it to avoid it being used to satisfy the debt.

DIAGNOSTIC PRACTICE QUESTIONS – CHAPTER 6

IMPORTANT STUDY TIP!

Step 1: Carefully review the information located in this chapter.

Step 2: Take the following Diagnostic Practice Questions. Review any question you answered incorrectly by researching the topic in this textbook. If you are still uncertain as to why the question is answered as it is, consult your program provider.

NOTE ON CHAPTER PRACTICE QUESTIONS

The following questions are representative of the type encountered on the Michigan real estate licensing examination. While some of these questions may be similar in nature and style, there is no way of predicting the exact wording of a question that will appear on the exam. Spending time memorizing these questions is, therefore, not recommended.

These questions are designed to help you determine how well you comprehend the material in this chapter. They are also intended to help you develop problem solving skills and to become comfortable with question formats.

Do not attempt to answer these questions until you have attended the lecture corresponding to this chapter and spent the appropriate time studying the material.

1. A property interest which is created for the specific purpose of limiting its duration to the remainder of a grantee's life is commonly known as a:
   A. Remainder interest.
   B. Life estate interest.
   C. Reversionary interest.
   D. Fee simple defeasible.

2. The grantee under a life estate has a duty to do which of the following during the term of ownership?
   A. Rebuild the property in the case of total loss due to an act of God.
   B. Turn over to the grantor all rents earned on leased portions of the property.
   C. Make repairs necessary to prevent losses resulting from permissive waste.
   D. All of the above.

3. Mr. Tee owns a 15 acre parcel of land upon which he resides. The only access to the road is from the north border of his property. The south end of his property has 400 feet of lake frontage on a large, secluded lake. A purchaser approaches Tee and asks if he would be willing to sell a portion of the property that fronts the lake. Tee is only willing to sell a 100 foot × 100 foot portion of the property at the south end. Which of the following statements is *true*?
   A. Tee must grant an easement by necessity.
   B. Tee must convey an irrevocable land lease.
   C. The purchaser would be able to claim a prescriptive easement upon taking possession of the property.
   D. There is no way Tee can sell such a portion.

4. Which of the following liens will likely be satisfied first in the event a property is subject to a foreclosure?
   A. A property tax lien.
   B. A credit card lien.
   C. A construction lien.
   D. A general lien.

5. Mrs. Beasley is a property owner who lives next to very difficult neighbors. The neighbors play their stereo loudly until late in the evening, their kids taunt Mrs. Beasley and their large dogs regularly soil her lawn. After talking to her ex-husband, a licensed attorney, Mrs. Beasley filed an "attention getting" lien on the neighbor's property. She plans on removing it as soon as they apologize. Which of the following statements is true?
   A. The lien can remain providing it is removed within one year from the date of filing.
   B. Mrs. Beasley is within her rights because she sought a legal opinion prior to filing the lien.
   C. The filing of the lien under the circumstances constitutes slander of title and must be removed.
   D. Mrs. Beasley has acted inappropriately unless it can be shown that her right to quiet enjoyment has been compromised.

6. All EXCEPT which of the following are qualities of a freehold interest?
   A. It is a form of ownership.
   B. It can be subject to a condition.

C. It may have a duration subject to a person's lifetime.
D. It lasts for a fixed term.

7. Ingress and egress are terms utilized most commonly in which of the following items:
   A. Encroachment.
   B. Escheat.
   C. Encumbrance.
   D. Easement.

8. Which of the following is characteristic of a fee estate?
   A. It cannot be inherited.
   B. It cannot be subdivided.
   C. Title to it cannot be split between two or more persons.
   D. It cannot be limited by conveyance to the heirs of the grantee.

9. The definition of encumbrances includes all of the following items EXCEPT:
   A. A mortgage.
   B. A deed.
   C. An easement.
   D. A judgment lien.

10. The right to use the land of another without the existence or necessity of an adjacent or dominant estate is most closely referred to as a(n):
    A. Easement in gross.
    B. Easement appurtenant.
    C. Prescriptive easement.
    D. Encroachment.

11. In which of the following interests does the benefit run with the land?
    A. License.
    B. Easement appurtenant.
    C. Easement in gross.
    D. Easement in net.

12. Which of the following is NOT true about a life estate?
    A. It may be sold to a third person.
    B. It is inheritable.
    C. It may be mortgaged.
    D. It may be leased.

13. Blackacre is a property with multiple liens attached to it. If one of the lien holders forecloses on its lien, which of the following best describes what happens to the remaining liens?
    A. If a junior lien is foreclosed, it is paid first, then the senior lien is paid before any others.
    B. Regardless of which lien is foreclosed, all liens will be typically paid in the order in which they arose.
    C. If an unrecorded federal tax lien is involved, it must be satisfied before payment of other liens.
    D. Regardless of which lien is foreclosed, all liens are typically satisfied according to the order of recording.

14. The highest form of ownership recognized by law is known as:
    A. Fee simple determinable.
    B. Fee tail.
    C. Fee simple absolute.
    D. Fee simple subject to a condition.

15. In the year 2009, Albert conveyed his property on Delta Lane to Bob for the balance of Bob's life. When Bob dies, the property is to transfer to Charley. Charley died in 2013 and was survived by both Albert and Bob. The following year Albert died. Upon Bob's death in 2015, what happens to Delta Lane?
    A. It reverts to the heirs of Albert.
    B. The remainder interest goes to the heirs of Bob.
    C. The remainder interest goes to the heirs of Charley.
    D. It escheats to the state.

16. Which of the following statements is false regarding a license that is held in the property of another?
    A. A license gives the licensee a limited right to possess the property of the licensor.
    B. A license can be issued to the licensee for purposes of hunting on the land of the licensor.
    C. A license does not create a real property interest in the property of the licensor.
    D. The granting party is not responsible for the actions of the licensee.

Chapter 7
Forms of Ownership

Determining who owns and how they hold title.

I. **Foreword**: Property rights have evolved over the course of history to the point where private individuals can now hold title as a sole owner or in association with other co-owners. Ownership of real property is likewise possible by business entities such as corporations or by a third party, in trust, for the benefit of another. The bundle of rights associated with property ownership can also be separated as a landlord does when he conveys exclusive possession via a lease to a tenant and retains legal title to the leased property. With all the options and variables that exist today, it is important to be able to determine exactly who owns a particular property and exactly how the person holds title. This is the subject of this chapter.

    A. **Licensees must understand ownership forms**: Real estate licensees must have a general working knowledge of the various forms of ownership. Determining the identity and nature of property owners affects how documents such as listing agreements, purchase agreements, and deeds are prepared. As we have already learned, licensees must not use what they know about property ownership principles to answer legal questions or provide legal advice.

    B. **Licensees must not give ownership advice**: Licensees must exercise care when answering specific ownership questions. It is generally considered permissible for a licensee to answer basic questions relating to ownership and the preparation of an offer to purchase. No specific legal interpretation should be provided by the licensee, however. For example, two buyer clients ask their buyer's agent what the best form of property ownership is when making an offer on a commercial building. A specific recommendation by the licensee likely amounts to the unauthorized practice of law.

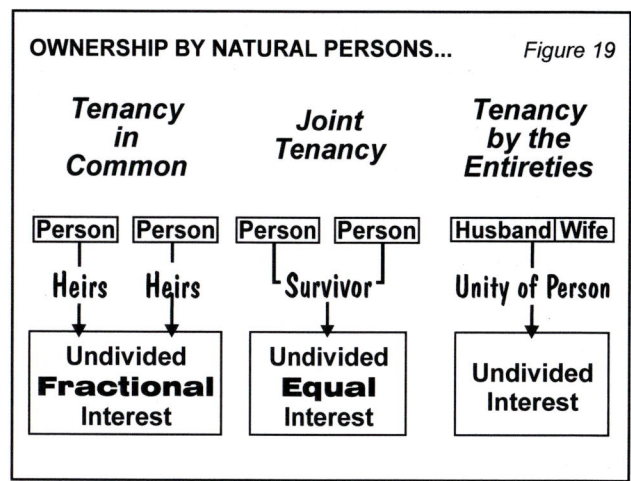

II. ▶ **Ownership by natural persons** [*Most Common*]: This section looks at the different forms of ownership for individuals rather than business entities. *See Figure 19.*

    A. ▶ **Ownership in severalty** ["*severed*"]: Ownership in severalty is created when title to real or personal property is held by one owner, without any other person joining him in his ownership. The word severalty refers to "sever" rather than "several" as in one owner severed from others.

    B. **Co-ownership**: It is possible for individuals to co-own and hold either equal or differing degrees of interest in the same property. The term co-ownership is synonymous with concurrent ownership. Determining who owns what under a concurrent form of ownership can be complex because there can be varying title interests arising from the same deed.

        1. **One deed may contain several titles**: The terms title and deed each have a different meaning. Recall from previous discussion that the term title is synonymous with ownership and the term deed refers to the document that conveys title. Viewing a title as separate from the deed allows for different ownership configurations under a concurrent ownership situation. For example, four co-owners are named in one deed and legally hold four separate titles. The four owners could also share one title equally. It is also possible that each co-owner's interest could have been conveyed via separate deeds. This will become clearer in the following sections.

2. ► **Tenancy in common**: A tenancy in common is a concurrent form of ownership, meaning two or more persons own the same property at the same time, where each person is deemed to hold a separate, undivided title interest in the same deed. Their interests are also deemed to be undivided and fractional. While the ownership interests may coincidentally be equal, they do not have to be under a tenancy in common as they would under a joint tenancy.

    a. **Meaning of fractional**: A fractional ownership interest is one that is divided into shares. Each co-owner holds a separate part of the legal title. This should not be confused with a timeshare, however. In a timeshare, the interest is traditionally associated with the title to a specific unit, and the rights are limited to a specific calendar unit of time.

    b. **Rights of the parties**: The rights each party in a tenancy in common hold are important, especially when it comes to the sale or mortgaging of an interest by one of the co-owners. It is also important to understand what happens to the interest of one of the co-owners when he dies.

        (1) **Undivided use**: Each tenant in common holds an undivided interest with an undivided use of the entire property. This means that all owners have the right to use the entire property unless they agree to lease it to one of them on an exclusive basis. The concept of undivided ownership is also called unity of possession.

        (2) **Other rights**: As a general rule, tenants in common are legally able to mortgage or transfer their particular property interest to a third party without the consent of the remaining co-owners. The third-party buyer receives only that interest the selling tenant in common held. Remember that a grantor can only convey whatever he held in the property at the time of conveyance, and no more.

    c. **When a co-owner dies, his heirs are protected**: Upon the death of one tenant in common, his specific interest passes to his personal heirs or devisees. This is a key characteristic of a tenancy in common. There is no automatic right of survivorship. One way a surviving tenant in common could take the decedent's interest is if the surviving tenant in common is a natural heir or named in the decedent's will.

        Example: Two sisters own a property as tenants in common. One sister dies and the surviving sister receives the deceased sister's interest. The surviving sister does so by virtue of inheritance, not because she is the surviving co-owner. As we will see, the outcome is different under a joint tenancy.

    d. **Statutory presumption when a deed is silent**: If two or more non-married individuals acquire an interest in a property, and the deed is silent as to the form of ownership (meaning that the deed does not mention it) a tenancy in common is legally presumed to exist. The law assumes that the co-owners intended to protect their families, heirs, or devisees.

3. ► **Joint tenancy**: A joint tenancy is a concurrent form of ownership in which two or more persons own a single estate in land on a completely equal basis. Creating multiple interests in a single title which are equal in all respects distinguishes the joint tenancy from all other forms of concurrent ownership. This equality of ownership is measured by what is referred to as the four unities.

    a. **Creating the estate**: To establish a joint tenancy, the unities of Time, Title, Interest, and Possession must be present. If any unity is missing or interrupted, there is no joint tenancy. It is possible to create a joint tenancy and then see part of it change to a tenancy in common. This occurs if one of the unities is subsequently broken. For example, one joint tenant co-owner sells his interest to a new buyer who was not part of the original conveyance.

        (1) **Unity of time**: According to the unity of time, all co-owners must have obtained title at the same time. This requires them to obtain their joint interests in the same moment and in the same conveying instrument or deed.

        (2) **Unity of title**: Under the unity of title, all joint tenants are deemed to share the same title to the property. Note how this differs from a tenancy in common where the owners are deemed to hold separate title interests in the same property.

        (3) **Unity of interest**: The unity of interest states that all joint tenants acquire the same share or percentage of ownership. This percent changes as the number of co-owners increases or decreases. For example, two co-owners each have 50%, three have 33⅓%, four have 25%, and so on.

        (4) **Unity of possession**: With the unity of possession, each joint tenant has the full right to possess, use, and enjoy the entire property. The unity of possession also exists in a tenancy in common.

Chapter 7: Forms of Ownership

b. **Death of co-owner, right of survivorship**: The distinguishing characteristic of a joint tenancy is the right of survivorship upon the death of a co-owner. When one joint tenant dies, his interest is extinguished and automatically passes to the remaining joint tenants who share it equally. Heirs and surviving family members who are not part of the joint tenancy have no rights. The deceased joint tenant's interest does not pass through probate either.

c. **Creditor's rights**: If one joint tenant individually signs a mortgage in exchange for a loan, he does not automatically obligate the other joint tenants who did not co-sign it. Even if a lender is willing to give a loan under such circumstances (which is unlikely), the lien only attaches to the signing owner's interest in the property. If the obligated joint tenant defaults, the lender can attempt to foreclose which could have the effect of severing the joint tenancy, but only for the defaulting joint tenant.

d. **Rights of co-owners**: The rights of the remaining joint tenants becomes an issue if one of them attempts to sell his specific interest. At common law, a joint tenant who desired to sell his interest to a third party could not do so without the permission of each of the joint tenants. This strict rule has given way to one which is more relaxed.

   (1) **Modern courts**: Modern courts in Michigan may not require the consent of all joint tenants before any one of them sells his individual interest. The buyer, however, may be held by the court to be a tenant in common with the other owners who remain joint tenants to one another. This is due to the fact that the unities of time and title do not exist between the buyer and the remaining joint tenants.

   (2) **Michigan joint tenancy hybrid**: Michigan recognizes two forms of joint tenancy; a traditional joint tenancy and a hybrid form labeled a "Joint Tenancy with Full Right of Survivorship." In this hybrid, the survivorship aspect cannot be severed by the sale of one joint tenant's interest. While the joint tenant with full rights of survivorship may sell his interest to a new buyer, the sale does not terminate the survivorship aspect with regard to the remaining joint tenants.

   In a complex Michigan court decision, one joint tenant with full right of survivorship was allowed to sell his individual interest without the consent of the other joint tenants. However, when the selling joint tenant eventually died, his buyer's interest passed back to the remaining joint tenants. The buyer, in essence, acquired a life estate pur autre vie.

e. **Drafting language must be clear**: Since there is a statutory presumption in favor of a tenancy in common, a deed attempting to establish a joint tenancy should include language such as "to 'A' and 'B' as joint tenants and not as tenants in common." In the case of the hybrid joint tenancy, the deed should clearly state that it is a joint tenancy with full right of survivorship.

   (1) **Need for legal advice**: A layperson should never attempt to draft a deed establishing a joint tenancy without the assistance of legal counsel. The language in the deed must be precisely worded. If not, unintended outcomes could result.

   (2) **Licensee must not advise**: A licensee must not provide this level of advice since it could easily be viewed as the exercise of legal discretion and profound legal knowledge and, therefore, constitute the unauthorized practice of law.

4. ▶ **Tenancy by the entireties**: A tenancy by the entireties is another concurrent form of ownership which is reserved exclusively for a married couple. It is still possible, however, for a husband and wife to own property as tenants in common or as joint tenants providing the deed is clear as to this intent.

   a. **Unity of person**: An entireties estate contains the four unities of a joint tenancy along with the addition of unity of person. Under this unity, the property is owned by the husband and the wife as a whole. Viewed essentially as one person, the spouses must join in any mortgage execution or conveyance of their mutual property interest.

   b. **Termination of the estate by divorce**: Since divorce severs the unity of person in property ownership, it also ends an entireties estate. Michigan is known as an equitable distribution state and not a community property state. If the couple cannot arrive at a mutually agreeable property division, the court will equitably distribute the marital assets.

5. ~~Community property~~: Only 9 states, mostly located in the western United States, are community property states. Under community property law, the husband and wife are treated as each having an undivided one-half interest in all property commonly acquired and owned. Most community property states allow for a

spouse to hold property separately if it was acquired prior to marriage, by inheritance, or pursuant to a prenuptial agreement. Both husband and wife must join in the conveyance of any community property.

III. ▶ **Trust ownership**: The law of trusts can be highly complex and requires the assistance of legal counsel and an expert in financial matters. This section provides a brief overview of trust ownership of real property. Trust ownership is a legal arrangement by which the subject property is transferred to a third party (called the trustee) who controls it for the benefit of another person (called the beneficiary). *See also Figure 31*, Chapter 16. This topic is listed in the PSI Outline as only tested on the broker's license examination.

    A. **Parties**: There are three parties involved in a trust. They include the trustee, the beneficiary, and the trustor. The process of creating a trust is typically handled by an attorney who prepares a deed that conveys the subject property to the name of the trust.

        1. **Trustor**: The trustor is the person who creates the trust and transfers legal title to the property to the trustee.

        2. **Trustee**: The trustee is the person who holds title to the property for the beneficiary and acts according to the trustor's instructions.

        3. **Beneficiary**: The beneficiary is the individual for whom the trust has been created. This person "benefits" from the trust.

    B. **Reasons for placing property in a trust**: Most individuals who place property in a trust do so to avoid the expenses and delays of the probate process when a property owner dies. Since transfers to a trust are often part of an estate planning process, property owners have traditionally tended to be older. As the benefits of a trust are becoming more widely known, younger individuals are establishing them. Trusts allow the property owner to condition how the property is distributed upon death, control taxes to some degree, and protect the property from creditors and litigation to some extent.

IV. ▶ **Ownership by business entities**: Modern property law permits indirect ownership by individuals through business organizations such as partnerships, corporations, and syndications.

    A. **General partnership**: By definition, a partnership is an association of two or more persons to carry on, as co-owners, a business for profit. Title to real property can be issued directly in the name of both general partnerships and limited partnerships. The partners all share equally in the management responsibilities as well as any profits and losses of the partnership. Advantages include the ease with which a partnership can be formed as compared to a corporation. Tax filings may also be easier since income and losses essentially pass-through to the partners individually.

        1. **Partnership disadvantages**: One of the primary drawbacks of a partnership is the joint and several liability that exists for each partner. Any individual general partner can be held personally accountable for the entire debts of the partnership, and personally liable for the actions of any other partner. Under joint and several liability, members of a group can be held individually or mutually responsible for the action of the group or its members. This is why legal partnerships are not generally favored.

        2. **Tenancy in partnership**: A tenancy in partnership is a form of property co-ownership in which the parties are business partners. Each partner has equal rights to possess the property for purposes of furthering the partnership goals. Upon the death of a tenant in partnership, the deceased partner's interest transfers to the surviving partner or partners. This survivorship feature is similar to a joint tenancy.

        3. **Limited partnership**: A limited partnership is a business association with one or more general partners. All other partners are designated as limited partners who (1) contribute capital to the partnership, (2) do not manage the affairs of the partnership, and (3) are typically only personally liable to the extent of their individual capital investment.

    B. **Corporations**: A corporation is an artificial person created under state law for the purpose of carrying on a business, including owning real property. As a legal entity, a corporation is separate and distinct from the individuals, called shareholders, who own it. By default, a corporation is generally considered to be "C" or full corporation. The organizers may also elect to establish an S-Corporation. The "S" refers to Small Business Corporation. An "S" Corporation generally passes its taxable income or loss directly through to the shareholders while a "C" type corporation pays taxes on the corporate income directly.

        1. **Advantages and disadvantages**: Since a corporation is viewed as a person, its owners are shielded to a certain degree from personal liability. Personal liability is generally limited to the extent of an owner's investment in the company's stock. Disadvantages include the effort needed to create the corporation, satisfy its ongoing documentation requirements, and fulfill its IRS obligations.

Chapter 7: Forms of Ownership

2. **Professional service corporation**: A professional service corporation is a corporation owned exclusively by people who have been legally authorized to provide professional services under Michigan law such as doctors, attorneys, and real estate brokers. The professional service corporation may be formed by one or more licensed persons to render professional services. In Michigan, a professional service corporation is organized under Michigan's Professional Service Corporation Act.

   a. **Liability concerns for a professional services corporation**: Care must be exercised when forming a professional services corporation because the principals, i.e., the individuals who control and direct the company, can be held personally responsible for wrongful acts of misconduct committed in the delivery of professional services by anyone in the professional services corporation. Similarly, the principals may also be held personally responsible for the entire debts of the business entity.

C. **Limited Liability Company (LLC) as an alternative**: In 1993, Michigan authorized another form of business organization known as a limited liability company or LLC for short. One or more persons can form an LLC. It is an attractive alternative to a traditional corporation for many reasons including (1) active participation is allowed in the management of the company with limited personal liability, and (2) income of the company is taxed only to the individual members rather than the company and the members. A PLLC is a Professional Limited Liability Company that operates like an LLC, but for licensed professionals such as doctors and attorneys.

D. **Broker licensed as a business entity**: Michigan real estate license law allows a broker's license to be issued to the name of a business entity such as a traditional corporation, professional corporation, limited liability company, or partnership. When this occurs there must be at least one natural person (such as a partner or corporate officer) licensed to the company who can carry out the daily responsibilities of a broker. This person is specifically licensed as a principal associate broker. The type of business entity that a brokerage firm chooses is up to the principals of the company.

V. ▶ **Special forms of (common interest) ownership**: Cooperatives and condominiums represent multiple ownership arrangements that are in widespread use. Real estate licensees can be involved in the listing and sale of both types of interest, although condominiums are far more prevalent than cooperatives. As discussed below, licensees must exercise special care when selling an interest in a cooperative. *See Figure 20.*

A. ▶ **Cooperatives**: A cooperative is a form of ownership in which a corporation or land trust is organized to hold title to a multiple-unit dwelling complex. Individual units are then leased to shareholders in the corporation. The person who occupies a unit is actually a stockholder in the corporation rather than an individual property owner. The stockholders have a voice in the management of the corporation as well as control of the property. A cooperative may also be referred to as a housing cooperative.

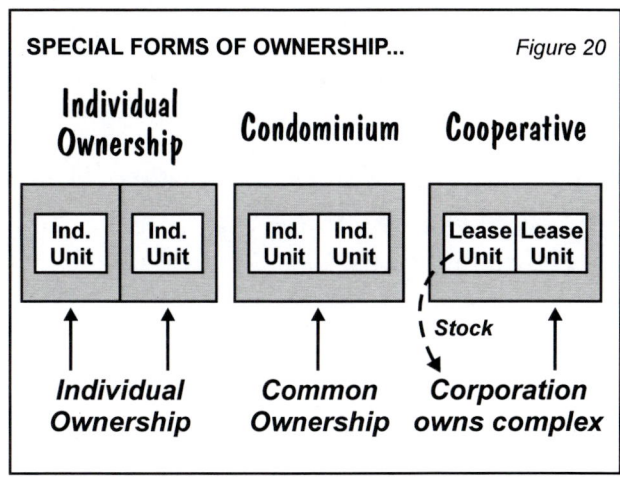

   1. **Elements of a cooperative**: A person who purchases stock with the anticipation of occupying a unit receives a proprietary lease that entitles him to possession of a particular unit. It is important to note that a proprietary lease in a cooperative is different from a traditional lease between a landlord and a tenant.

      a. **Proprietary lease**: Under a proprietary lease, the stockholder acquires the exclusive right to occupy a unit in the building owned by the corporation. The term proprietary implies that a type of ownership interest has been created.

      b. **Monthly cooperative assessment**: The corporation passes on the expenses of ownership to the stockholders in the form of a monthly assessment. These expenses include the mortgage principal and interest, property taxes, insurance, and maintenance. The assessment is paid in lieu of ordinary rent.

      c. **Potential to gain equity**: The ownership of stock in a cooperative creates a type of lease arrangement that has the potential to gain equity. Since stock is purchased as a condition to leasing a unit, its value can increase during possession. The lease itself is not capable of building equity.

d. **Disadvantages**: If enough owners fail to pay their individual monthly assessments, the corporation may default on its mortgage and/or property tax payments. A cumulative delinquency can result in the foreclosure of the property and the loss of all owners' rights.

When an owner elects to move out of the cooperative and sell his stock, some cooperatives have a right of first refusal price at which the stock must be sold back to the corporation. In such case, if the value of the stock has grown over the period of residency, the corporation realizes the profit rather than the owner. Before purchasing an interest in a housing cooperative, a prospective resident should have all documents reviewed by legal counsel.

2. **Securities law and other considerations for licensees**: A person who holds an interest in a cooperative for use as his residence may be able to sell to a buyer without registering the sale under securities law. The sale of stock by a real estate licensee, however, has the potential to trigger securities law. Therefore, the licensee's broker should check with legal counsel before representing a party in the purchase or sale of a unit in a cooperative.

   a. **Federal law**: Under federal law, the purchase and sale of shares in a cooperative corporation for the purpose of making money from the efforts of the corporation in renting the units likely triggers federal securities law. When stock is acquired by a "buyer" for the sole purpose of leasing a unit in which to reside, the shares are not treated as securities.

   b. **State law**: In Michigan, the initial offering of shares in a cooperative project falls under the definition of securities and is subject to the registration requirements of the Michigan Securities Act. Refer to Chapter 15 for further information.

B. ▶ **Condominium**: A condominium is an estate in real property consisting of a separate fee simple ownership in an individual unit that is located in a multiple-unit building or development. In addition to the unit, all owners have an undivided interest in the entire development. A condominium can also be characterized as a system of separate ownerships of individual units in a multiple-unit building or collection of buildings.

1. **History**: Some form of state-enabling legislation was needed to make condominium ownership a reality. The problem was how to survey and convey a lot that essentially consists of an air space or cube of air within a multiple-unit building. These original statutes were often referred to as Horizontal Property Acts. Michigan's current Act authorizing the development of condominiums is the Michigan Condominium Act. This important Act is discussed further in Chapter 21.

2. **Building uses can vary**: In addition to residential applications, non-residential uses can be created as condominiums. Examples include commercial, industrial, and mixed-land uses. Marina condominiums or dockominiums have also been authorized under Michigan law. Condominiums also vary in construction and architecture, from high-rise buildings and townhouses to site condominiums.

3. **Site condominium**: A site condominium is an actual condominium development. It is constructed to emulate the look and appeal of a neighborhood consisting of single-family, detached units constructed on separate, individually-owned lots. In a site condominium, the "individual lot" on which each structure is built qualifies as a limited common element. Common and limited common elements are jointly owned by all condominium owners.

4. **Creation of a condominium development**: The appropriate city, village, township, or county must be notified of an individual's intent to develop a condominium. The local unit of government is contacted to determine who or what entity must be notified along with what information and documents will be needed. If the township, for example, does not administer its own zoning ordinance pertaining to condominiums, the county may handle it.

   Generally, the appropriate county road and drain commissions must be notified and, possibly, the Michigan Department of Environmental Quality as well. To formally create the condominium complex, the developer prepares and records a master deed along with a set of bylaws and a condominium subdivision plan attached to it. An attorney who is experienced in the creation of condominium developments should also be consulted.

5. **Elements of a condominium**: According to state law, a condominium must contain certain elements. These elements distinguish it from a traditional form of ownership.

   a. **Deeds**: In a condominium, two different deed types are conveyed. They include the deed to the specific unit and the master deed to the entire development.

Chapter 7: Forms of Ownership

(1) **Master deed:** The master deed is the actual document that formally establishes the condominium. It describes the individual units along with the common elements, and authorizes the creation of an association of condominium co-owners. Common elements are divided into two categories–common elements and limited common elements.

    (a) **Common elements:** Condominium ownership is split into an individual ownership of a unit, coupled with co-ownership of all common areas. These common areas are known as the common elements. They consist of all areas outside and between each individual unit. Common elements are jointly owned on a pro rata, meaning prorated, basis with all other condominium owners. The percentage of ownership is usually based on the value of a particular unit as compared to the total cost of the entire development. *Roads, sidewalks, pools*

    Examples of common elements include the physical land on which all buildings are constructed, sidewalks and roads, parking areas, clubhouse, as well as any swimming pool, tennis courts, or other recreational amenities.

    (b) **Limited common elements:** A limited common element is a type of common element where the use is restricted to a particular unit owner or subgroup of unit owners. It is placed under the exclusive control of this designated owner or owners.

    Examples of limited common elements include garage stalls, carports, and other designated parking bays; porches, patios, and balconies; and the internal common walls separating the individual units.

(2) **Unit deed:** Along with a master deed, each owner receives a unit deed. The unit deed conveys the individual fee simple ownership to the owner's individual unit. It usually takes the form of a general warranty deed. The individual unit to which the unit deed conveys title may be referred to as an air lot. This lot consists of the space from the paint of one wall to the paint of the other wall and everything between.

    (a) **Exclusive control and rights:** The area comprising the individual unit is under the exclusive possession and control of the condominium owner. Since condominiums are individually financed, taxed, and maintained, any subsequent sale is at the independent discretion of the owner (as is the case with any traditional real estate ownership).

    (b) **Default:** If one condominium owner defaults on his mortgage payment, only his unit is affected by any resulting foreclosure. This is in contrast with a housing cooperative in which the collective default of enough residents can affect all residents. Even in a condominium, however, if multiple unit owners default on the payment of their monthly maintenance fees, this can affect the development as it struggles to meet its expenses.

b. **Bylaws:** Condominium bylaws are the regulations, ordinances, and rules adopted by an association or corporation for governing its internal operations. Condominium bylaws specify how the condominium project will be developed and administered.

    (1) ▶ **Condominium association and its responsibilities:** The association of condominium co-owners, also known as the condominium owners association, is a group consisting of all individual unit owners. It is responsible for the management or management decisions of the condominium development. Voting rights in the affairs of the association are determined on a basis which is similar to the determination of the percentage of common area ownership by each unit owner. The association of condominium owners renders decisions on issues that affect the entire complex such as the operating budget, expenditures, property management services, and insurance. Contrast this with a Homeowners Association (HOA) discussed in Chapter 5.

    (2) **Maintenance fee and issues:** Condominium owners must pay for the costs of maintaining the development. A monthly fee known as a maintenance fee or association fee is assessed each owner to cover his portion of the condominium maintenance and administration. If this fee is not paid on a timely basis, a lien may be placed on the individual unit and eventually foreclosed by the association. Before buying a previously-owned condominium, the buyer should find out whether maintenance fees have been paid or a delinquency exists. Further, some lender's include the maintenance fee in the monthly principal, interest, taxes, and insurance escrow when a loan is obtained to finance a condominium.

(3) **Insurance**: Since each condominium owner is jointly liable for negligence relating to the condition and maintenance of the common areas, the association will purchase liability insurance. Individuals should also maintain their own insurance coverage on their units for similar perils.

6. **Condominium conversions**: A condominium conversion is a multi-unit housing complex or development that began as a traditional lease-based apartment dwelling. The conversion arises when the use of the apartment building changes from rental to ownership. Michigan Condominium Act rules pertaining to condominium conversions are discussed in Chapter 21.

7. **Timeshare condominium**: Timeshares represent a form of condominium ownership. Ownership of each unit is fragmented into 52, one-week time intervals, typically in the form of a tenancy in common. A potential owner may purchase as many intervals as he wishes. A timeshare is sometimes referred to as "vacation ownership." Timeshare ownership, like fractional ownership, represents a way for individuals to attain the beneficial use of real property while sharing the expenses and maintenance associated with its ownership.

    a. **Fractional ownership**: The terms "fractional ownership" and "interval ownership" are used in the industry to describe a form of joint property ownership that is similar to a timeshare. As noted, a true timeshare creates up to 52 owners per unit–one for each week of the year. A fractional ownership arrangement significantly reduces the number of owners. While there are no specific limits, the number could be less than ten to a dozen or slightly more.

    The limited number of fractional owners means that each one will be able to enjoy several weeks of the property as opposed to just one. Each fractional owner acquires an interest as a tenant in common, for example, in a shared title to the property. The owners have the right to use the property for specified periods of time known as intervals. Expenses and management of the entire development are also shared.

8. **Michigan-specific condominium laws**: For more technical information pertaining to Michigan condominium law, read the summary of the Condominium Act in Chapter 21. The Act also references timeshares (but not fractional ownership).

Judgement is the justification the ego uses for its decision not to forgive.

DIAGNOSTIC PRACTICE QUESTIONS – CHAPTER 7

IMPORTANT STUDY TIP!

Step 1: Carefully review the information located in this chapter.

Step 2: Take the following Diagnostic Practice Questions. Review any question you answered incorrectly by researching the topic in this textbook. If you are still uncertain as to why the question is answered as it is, consult your program provider.

NOTE ON CHAPTER PRACTICE QUESTIONS

The following questions are representative of the type encountered on the Michigan real estate licensing examination. While some of these questions may be similar in nature and style, there is no way of predicting the exact wording of a question that will appear on the exam. Spending time memorizing these questions is, therefore, not recommended.

These questions are designed to help you determine how well you comprehend the material in this chapter. They are also intended to help you develop problem solving skills and to become comfortable with question formats.

Do not attempt to answer these questions until you have attended the lecture corresponding to this chapter and spent the appropriate time studying the material.

1. Which of the following features does NOT apply to an entireties estate?
   A. The estate is primarily designed to promote the interests of the family.
   B. Upon the death of one of the spouses, his or her interest automatically goes to their heirs rather than the surviving spouse.
   C. Upon a subsequent divorce, the court can destroy the entireties estate and partition the property.
   D. Both spouses are deemed to own the interest in the property together as a whole rather than equal undivided interests.

2. Phyllis acquires an interest in a townhouse condominium from Samuel. She loves her new purchase and wishes to make certain changes. Of the following, which one would Phyllis most likely need prior approval from the association before doing?
   A. Changing the color of the carpet on all three levels of her unit.
   B. Adding a free-standing cabinet at the back of her garage stall to store garden tools.
   C. Trimming the bushes under her back window which are blocking the view of her patio garden.
   D. Removing the exterior shutters and repainting them with a more muted, earth-tone color.

3. As a form of ownership, a partnership is generally considered to be less desirable than other forms of ownership. This is due to which one of the following features?

   A. A partnership is subject to a form of double taxation.
   B. One partner can be held personally responsible for the entire debts of the other partners.
   C. A partnership can only last for a certain period of time and must be terminated regardless of its level of success at the time.
   D. Investors are required who can play a significant role in the decisions of the general partners.

4. Archie and Veronica, a young couple, are engaged to be married and looking to buy their first home. They stop by the office of JTW Real Estate Company. Since the wedding will not occur until several months after the closing, they discuss what form of ownership would be best. Veronica wants to protect her daughter from a previous marriage in the event she dies. Archie is equally concerned about his two children from his previous marriage. What should Taylor, the broker, advise?
   A. To form a joint tenancy with full rights of survivorship.
   B. To consult with a CPA. and then create a real estate investment trust.
   C. To draft a will in conjunction with a tenancy in common prior to purchasing any property.
   D. To consult with an attorney before purchasing any property.

5. A man and woman marry and then purchase a parcel of land, in part with the gift money from their wedding. Which form of ownership is assumed to exist

between them if no other form of ownership is specified on the deed?
   A. Tenancy in common.
   B. Joint tenancy.
   C. Tenancy by the entireties. *assumed by marriage*
   D. Tenancy in partnership.

6. Ron, Jill, and Montana own property as joint tenants with full rights of survivorship. Montana decides to sell his interest to Dorothy. Which of the following is true if Ron and Jill do not approve of the sale?
   A. Dorothy may purchase Montana's interest, but it will terminate in the event of Montana's death.
   B. Montana will not be able to convey his interest to Dorothy.
   C. Dorothy may purchase Montana's interest and will be treated as being a tenant in common.
   D. Dorothy will acquire Montana's interest and become a full joint tenant with Ron and Jill.

7. Ownership in severalty refers to:
   A. Individual ownership.
   B. Co-ownership.
   C. Ownership by the entireties.
   D. Ownership in common.

8. Which statement concerning joint tenancy is most true?
   A. In the event of death, a co-owner's interest goes to his heirs.
   B. No right of survivorship exists.
   C. Each co-owner holds separate title interests.
   D. In the event of death, a co-owner's interest goes to the remaining co-owners.

9. Which of the following is true of a condominium?
   A. It is a legal form of property ownership.
   B. It provides unit owners with proprietary leases.
   C. Each owner holds a pro rata ownership interest in his unit.
   D. The master deed must be recorded after a unit is sold.

10. In which of the following are the owners/occupants in a building considered to be stockholders of a corporation that owns the building?
    A. A cooperative apartment house.
    B. A condominium building.
    C. A timeshare.
    D. Section 8 housing.

11. Two sisters, Margie and Debbie, inherit real property from their grandmother with a right of survivorship, further stipulating that one-third of the property is to go to Debbie and two-thirds to Margie. Which of the following statements is most accurate?
    A. Margie and Debbie are joint tenants in the property.
    B. The sisters hold the property by the entireties.
    C. Debbie may not mortgage her interest in the property without Margie's consent.
    D. The sisters are tenants in common.

12. Under common law, which of the following unities differentiates a joint tenancy from tenancy by the entirety?
    A. Interest.
    B. Person.
    C. Possession.
    D. Time.

13. The person in a trust who holds the property for the benefit of another is known as the:
    A. Settlor.
    B. Trustor.
    C. Beneficiary.
    D. Trustee.

14. Four individuals are interested in starting a company and playing active roles, but do not wish to necessarily become liable on a personal level for the actions of the others. Which of the following types of business arrangements should they consider?
    A. A corporation.
    B. A limited partnership. *LLC*
    C. A partnership.
    D. A real estate investment trust.

15. Sam and Carla have decided to become married. Sam is worried, however, because he owns a restaurant and lounge with his best friend Cliff. His concern is that if anything happens to him, Carla will have a claim to the property. He would rather provide for her with a large insurance policy and permit Cliff to own and operate the business on his own. Which form of ownership would most likely permit Sam to meet his desires?
    A. Ownership in severalty.
    B. Tenancy in common.
    C. Joint tenancy.
    D. Tenancy by the entireties.

16. All EXCEPT which of the following forms of ownership can be held jointly by a husband and a wife:
    A. Tenancy in common.
    B. Joint tenancy.
    C. Tenancy by the entireties.
    D. Ownership in severalty.

Chapter 8
Title Verification

Title Search

Researching and confirming the state of the title.

Clear and Marketable

I. **Foreword**: Any person who desires to purchase real property, or any financial institution that is considering lending money for the purchase of real property, needs to conduct a preliminary title search to determine if the property is subject to any title defects that could impair its future interest. As discussed in the previous chapters, a recorded interest in a title which is held by a third party constitutes an encumbrance. Many encumbrances run with the land and are binding on future buyers. Title verification is the process of ascertaining what these interests may be so an intelligent purchase or lending decision can be made. Researching, confirming, and assuring the title is the subject of this chapter.

   A. ▶ **Title search**: A title search involves a thorough examination of the public records to determine whether or not the title is good, meaning free of significant defects. Questions to be addressed include: (1) Is the title marketable, meaning salable?; (2) Are there any unpaid taxes, unpaid municipal utility bills, existing mortgages, or other liens of record that must be satisfied?; and (3) Are there any other interests in the public records such as deed restrictions or easements that pose an encumbrance significant enough to affect the marketability of the title?

   B. **Public records–Register of Deeds**: The public records consist of a document storage and retrieval system that is established in every city, county, and state. These records are maintained for the purpose of protecting owners and potential buyers. In Michigan, real property records are maintained by the county recorder's office or Register of Deeds. These records are open to the public for inspection.

II. **Title verification**: When a seller signs a purchase agreement, especially in the case where title will be conveyed via a general warranty deed, he promises to convey clear title to the buyer in exchange for the buyer's promise to pay the agreed upon purchase price. The first step in the title verification process is to look at the chain of title.

   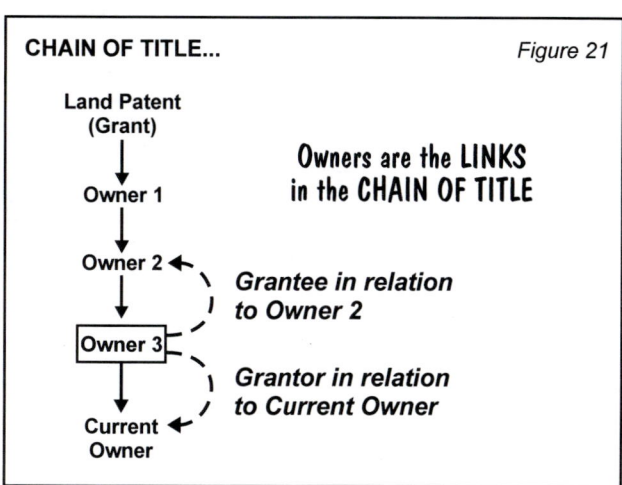

   A. ▶ **Chain of title**: The chain of title is the record of property ownership succession from the first owner to the most recent. A title examiner, title company representative, or buyer's attorney can determine the quality of the current seller's title by examining the quality of title that each preceding owner received (as the grantee) from his seller-grantor. See Figure 21.

      1. **Title examiner**: A title examiner is the individual responsible for inspection of the public records and assembling the chain of title on a property. Having gathered all available data on the property, the title examiner reviews it and prepares a report on the findings. A good title examiner not only possesses the skill to prepare a title abstract, but also understands the insurance side of the business.

      2. **Land patent**: A land patent is a grant of property made by the federal or state government to one or more individuals. In the United States, all private ownership of land ultimately stems from some form of land patent. A land patent is also known as a land grant.

PRD - Public Records Display

B. **Determining priorities**: When multiple claims exists on a single property such as liens, the issue of which creditor gets paid first is critical. This is especially true when the collective value of the liens exceeds the fair market value of the property. The massive number of short sales in the 2000s reflected this very issue.

The common-law rule for resolving multiple, and potentially conflicting, property claims was "First in time, First in right." In other words, the first interest to arise in time was satisfied before the others. Chronology, meaning time order, was the determining factor. Today, priority is determined by a rule based on which person gives first notice. Typically, this is the person who first records his interest in the public records. The public records are the most reliable source for determining the priority of multiple claims to a property.

C. **Recording**: An interest in a property is recorded by making an official and permanent entry in a specific book, file, or other register maintained by the local unit of government. Property records are maintained in the Register of Deeds in the county where the property is located. This recording system serves legal notice to the world of an interest in a property.

1. **Notice defined**: Notice is one of the most important characteristics of our legal system. As a basic concept, notice is information that a party either knows, should have known, or is legally charged with knowing. In real property law, notice is either actual, meaning gathered as a result of observation, or constructive, meaning legally imputed or charged. There is another form of notice that may be applied known as implied notice.

    a. **Actual notice**: Actual notice is that information which one has been directly given or has personally learned from direct contact. It includes facts actually communicated to and known by a person. Actual notice is synonymous with knowledge. For example, a landlord who is selling a residential property tells the prospective buyer that the buyer will not be able to take immediate possession because an existing tenant has a valid lease through the end of the year. The buyer has actual notice of the lease and takes title subject to it as the new landlord.

    ex: By Mail

    b. **Constructive notice**: Constructive notice is information the law imputes to a person, meaning charges him with knowing, even though the person may not actually be aware of the facts. The word constructive in this sense means to construe or interpret. When a person is charged with constructive notice of a fact, he is treated as if he knew it and cannot deny being aware of its existence. Although not common, constructive notice may also be referred to as record notice.

        (1) **Recording as constructive notice**: Recording is the most common, reliable, and efficient way in which constructive notice is given. When a document such as a deed is recorded, the world is served legal notice as to the existence of the recorded interest.

        (2) **Duty to inspect records**: Since buyers and lenders are charged with legal notice of all recorded claims, they must inspect the public records in advance of obtaining their future interest in a property to ascertain if any other prior interests exist. Some of the problems that a title examiner will search for include liens, judgments, gaps in the chain of title, recorded encumbrances, and deeds with incorrect information.

    Assumed

    c. **Implied notice (inquiry notice):** Implied or inquiry notice is another type of notice that can protect a claimant's interest in a property. It is similar to constructive notice in that the law implies or charges a person with knowledge of certain facts that would have led a reasonable person to make an inquiry under similar circumstances. It differs from constructive notice in that it is only based on facts and circumstances actually in existence that a party knew or should have known.

    Using the facts from the prior lease example discussed in connection with actual notice, assume that the prospective buyer was actually told that someone other than the seller has exclusive possession of the property, but was not informed that it was a tenant under a valid lease. One could argue that the buyer has a duty to make an inquiry to determine what rights, if any, the person in possession has before purchasing the property.

2. **Marketable Record Title Act**: Michigan's Marketable Record Title Act is a statute that allows an owner or prospective buyer to ignore certain title interests that are statutorily deemed to have little or no validity. For this to happen, the current chain of title must be unbroken from a period beginning with the present, back at least 40 years. The Act limits the scope of search necessary to verify title to land and eliminates concern over stale and abandoned claims that precede the 40 year period. (The marketable title period is reduced to 20 years for certain mineral rights interests.)

Chapter 8: Title Verification

D. **The Register of Deeds–methods of recording**: The Clerk of the Register of Deeds is the person whose responsibility it is to oversee the recordation of instruments. The Register of Deeds may or may not be under the direct jurisdiction of the County Clerk's Office.

1. **The mechanics of recording**: A document is recorded by delivering it to the Register of Deeds. A clerk's assistant collects a recording fee and notes the acceptance of the document in an entry book. The document is stamped with a liber, page, and other registration or identifying number and a copy is retained as a permanent record. The day, hour, and minute of recording is also noted. The assistant then affixes the official seal of the Register of Deeds on the document by making a legible impression and returns it to the owner of the document.

    In the past, all documents were recorded and indexed by hand. The liber referred to the specific book and the page number referred to the page in the book where the document could be located. Today, even though all information is stored and retrieved electronically, documents are still identified using liber and page numbers.

2. **Indexing recorded instruments**: Recorded documents are indexed. An index is a sequential arrangement of material or information. The two most common indices (i.e., the plural form of index) are the grantor-grantee index which is mandatory in Michigan and a tract index.

    a. **Grantor-Grantee index**: The grantor-grantee index is a master index which is alphabetized by the last names of grantors and grantees. It includes the date of transfer and a cross-reference to the specific book where a copy of the recorded document can be located. Ownership information can be found by researching the last name of a grantor or a grantee. [Buyer & Seller]

    b. **Tract index**: Under a separate tract index, all recorded transactions are entered for each parcel which may make it easier to trace the chain of title. A tract index is helpful since a property search can be conducted when the searching party only has a valid address, property description, or Sidwell number (see Chapter 10 for definition of Sidwell number). [Property ID # and/or address]

E. ~~Torrens system~~: The Torrens system is a method of assuring the quality of title through a title registration procedure that is similar to the United States system of automobile registration. It is only used on a limited basis in a small number of states, excluding Michigan.

III. **Forms of title assurance**: There are two primary tools that can be used to give an interested party assurance of the quality of a title. These include abstracts and title insurance. Today, title insurance is relied on exclusively by property owners. Many community historical societies collect older abstracts because of the detailed history they contain.

   A. ▶ **Abstract of title**: An abstract is a condensed and chronological history of a title to real estate. It is a record summary of all transactions, conveyances, and encumbrances that affect the subject property. It also includes a brief legal description and other maps, plats, or aids for physically locating the property.

   Since an abstract does not disclose a physical problem such as an encroachment, it cannot be used as a substitute for a survey. Further, an abstract is not a form of insurance nor does it contain any other promise of marketability. This is why an opinion of title is necessary.

   1. **Opinion of title**: A prospective buyer who is interested in discovering whether any title defects exist must take the abstract to an attorney who can review it. The attorney renders what is referred to as an opinion of title. As with the abstract itself, the opinion is not deemed to be an insurance policy against problems.

   B. ▶ **Title insurance and what it covers**: Title insurance is purchased by any individual who wants an actual policy that insures the marketability of the title to property. It insures against title defects. The insured who is named in the policy can recover losses from the title insurance company if the title turns out to be defective for any of several stated reasons. The form of title insurance most commonly used in Michigan is the American Land Title Association or ALTA Owner's Policy. [Potential Claims] [Paid for by seller the Title Policy]

   1. **Practical considerations**: In most purchase agreements, the buyer requires the seller to obtain and pay for a title insurance policy that names the buyer as the beneficiary. The cost of the insurance is paid as a one-time premium at the transaction closing.

      a. **Why seller pays for it**: A seller often wonders why he is asked to pay for a policy that protects the buyer as the new owner. In reality, a title policy indirectly affords protection to the seller. As discussed in Chapter 5, when a seller gives a warranty deed to a buyer, the seller agrees to defend the buyer's right to quiet enjoyment of possession against the claims of third parties. By purchasing the title policy for the buyer, the seller can relax knowing that any covered claim will be handled.

b. **Primary types of title insurance**: There are two primary categories of title insurance. One is purchased by the seller to protect the buyer. The other is purchased by the buyer to protect his lender when a mortgage loan is obtained. *See Figure 22.*

Purchased By Seller

(1) **Owner's policy**: The owner's policy is the most common form of title insurance. A seller provides it to a buyer guaranteeing that the title will be defended or reimbursed against losses. The policy coverage is based on the value, meaning sale price, of the property at the time of sale. An owner's policy is also known as a fee title policy. It is important not to confuse an owner's title insurance policy with a homeowner's insurance policy which protects the physical structure against various perils.

TYPES OF TITLE INSURANCE...	Owner's Policy	Mortgagee's Policy
Who pays	Seller (Grantor)	Buyer (Mort'or)
Beneficiary	Buyer (Grantee)	Lender (Mort'ee)
Policy amount	Based on the sale price at time of closing.	Based on the amount of the mortgage.
Policy term	For the life of the Grantee and heirs as long as property is held.	Until the mortgage is repaid and discharged.

Figure 22

Purchased By Buyer

(2) **Mortgagee's policy**: Another form of title insurance known as a mortgagee's policy is generally required by a lender when it loans money for the purchase of real estate which is used as the collateral to secure the loan. The buyer-mortgagor purchases it and names the lender-mortgagee as the policy beneficiary. If a title defect surfaces while the lender still has a lien interest in the property, the lender is protected. This interest is limited to the balance owing at any given time because the lender is only entitled to repayment of its loan.

2. **The commitment to insure**: Upon application for a title policy, a commitment or preliminary binder is issued. This evidences a title insurance company's willingness to insure the property subject to certain requirements that have to be met. This binder or promise to insure generally remains good for 45 to 90 days. The commitment also summarizes any known defects and exceptions to coverage.

3. **Sections of an ALTA Owner's Policy of Title Insurance**: ALTA is an acronym from the American Land Title Association. It is a national trade association that represents the interests of title insurance companies as well as abstract of title companies. ALTA assists in the development of standard title insurance forms that are used nationwide. The five sections of a typical ALTA policy of title insurance include:
   — Insuring Clause: This indicates what risks are actually covered in the policy.
   — Exclusions: This section lists any general interests or claims that are excluded, meaning not covered in any policy (see explanation below).
   — Schedule A: This section identifies the details of the property and transaction such as the names of the proposed insured parties, amount of coverage, legal description of the insured property, and effective date of the commitment.
   — Schedule B.
   Section I: This section sets forth any conditions to be met before the policy is issued such as (1) conveyance of the property at the closing, (2) recording of any deeds, mortgages, or liens, and (3) payment of outstanding property taxes.
   Section II: This section includes any further, often more specific, exceptions from coverage (see explanation below).
   — Conditions and stipulations: This section describes things such as the length of coverage and includes basic requirements for the owner such as what to do in the event of a claim.

   a. **Coverage**: Title insurance coverage is extended to defects that may affect the validity of the buyer's title, but could not be found even with a careful and meticulous search of the public records. Covered risks typically encompass: (1) Title to the interest described in Schedule A being vested in the grantee other than as stated in the deed; (2) Unmarketability of title; (3) Defects, liens, or encumbrances affecting the title; and (4) Challenges to the owner's right to access his property.

   b. **Exclusions**: Certain general issues can arise with any property over which a title company will not insure. These issues are stated in the exclusions section. As seen in the following examples, exclusions include both claimed property interests and activities that impact the marketability of the title:

Chapter 8: Title Verification

(1) A government exercise of police power including building and zoning ordinance changes, subdivision regulations, and environmental protection regulations.

(2) Losses due to condemnation through the exercise of eminent domain.

(3) Losses resulting from defect, lien, or encumbrance either created by, allowed by, or agreed to by the owner (or not known to the insurance company due to a failure to record it as of the date of the policy).

(4) Other technical claims involving bankruptcy transfers, fraudulent conveyances, and failure to record in a timely fashion.

c. **Conditions and stipulations**: Conditions of coverage are included in the policy. For example, the buyer as new owner is assured that the policy will continue in force for as long as he and his heirs retain title or an interest in the land. Coverage terminates if the property is sold to a new buyer. Stipulation is another word that means condition or requirement.

(1) **Notice requirement**: A condition is also imposed that requires the owner to notify the title company if a problem arises. If the insurance company pays the claim, the subrogation rights of the insurance company (stated in the conditions and stipulations section) are triggered.

(2) **Subrogation clause**: Subrogation is the substitution of one person in the place of another with regard to a lawful claim. If a title insurance company pays a claim on behalf of the insured, the subrogation clause allows the company to "step into the shoes" of the insured and sue the negligent party who caused the damages. The title company, in essence, switches legal places with the insured to recover the amount of damages it paid to the insured.

[margin note: A 3rd party has liability]

d. **Schedule B exceptions**: Schedule B, Section II lists any standard and specific policy exceptions from coverage. As with exclusions, the insurance company will not defend against an exception if it arises. Distinguishing between exclusions and exceptions can be confusing. While exclusions are general to all policies, exceptions tend to be more specific to a particular property or regional group of properties. In addition to the common "standard exceptions" listed below, the policy may also include "specific exceptions" that are added by the underwriter at the time the policy is issued:

(1) **Boundary discrepancies**: Issues involving boundary disputes, encroachments, overlapping improvements, and other setback violations are not covered.

(2) **Facts discoverable by survey or inquiry**: The policy does not protect against a claim of adverse possession.

(3) **Unrecorded interests**: Easements, liens, and encumbrances not shown in the public records are not covered.

(4) **Unrecorded liens**: An unrecorded construction lien, or right to a lien for services, labor, or material furnished to a property are not covered. This also includes unrecorded tax liens and special assessments.

4. **Issuance of a policy without exceptions**: A title insurance policy can be issued "without standard exceptions." This means that Schedule B, Section II exceptions are struck from the policy and will be covered. An extra cost may be assessed along with additional requirements. For example, removal of Schedule B exceptions 1, 2, and 3 (listed above) may require that a detailed ALTA survey with surveyor's certificate be provided along with an affidavit signed by the seller that every known potential cloud or defect was disclosed.

Removal of exception 4 would require the seller to sign an affidavit that if any improvements, materials, or labor has been provided to the land or improvements within the last 90 days, they have been paid in full. All supporting documentation required under Michigan's lien act must also be provided to the title company.

5. **Marked-up title policy (i.e., commitment)**. [margin note: Date's back to day of closing]

a. **Purpose**: A title insurance commitment is a promise to issue a final title insurance policy. The commitment is typically delivered to the insured (i.e., buyer-grantee) at or before the closing. The final policy is sent to the insured a few weeks after the closing. Traditionally, a title policy becomes effective on the date the deed is recorded by the register of deeds. The time between the transaction closing and the recordation of the deed is referred to as the "gap." When a title commitment is marked-up, the title agent alters it to indicate that the actual coverage afforded in the final policy begins immediately at the closing.

[margin note: Gap time]

b. **How the policy is marked-up**: At the closing, the title agent verifies that all of the policy requirements have been met, and that the seller has completed and signed an Owner Affidavit. The seller uses the affidavit to assure the title company that, among other things, no additional parties are legally in possession of the premises, nobody has been hired to perform any physical work on the property within the last 90 days (or, if so, that the contractor has been paid and/or lien removed), and that no bankruptcy actions have been filed.

Once verified, the title agent makes written notations on the commitment, by hand or computer, indicating that: the requirements for insurance have been satisfied; the buyer is the fee title holder; the standard exceptions have been removed; the lien resulting from the buyer-grantee's new mortgage (if applicable) has been added; and, that the coverage in the title commitment matches the coverage to be afforded in the final policy. As part of the insuring process, the public records will have been searched through the date of the issuance of the commitment.

c. **Alternative to a marked-up policy**: As an alternative to a marked-up policy, some title companies will issue a final policy at the closing. The process is nearly identical to the one described for a marked-up policy.

Developing productive habits is actually easier
than perpetuating unproductive ones.

DIAGNOSTIC PRACTICE QUESTIONS – CHAPTER 8

IMPORTANT STUDY TIP!

Step 1: Carefully review the information located in this chapter.

Step 2: Take the following Diagnostic Practice Questions. Review any question you answered incorrectly by researching the topic in this textbook. If you are still uncertain as to why the question is answered as it is, consult your program provider.

NOTE ON CHAPTER PRACTICE QUESTIONS

The following questions are representative of the type encountered on the Michigan real estate licensing examination. While some of these questions may be similar in nature and style, there is no way of predicting the exact wording of a question that will appear on the exam. Spending time memorizing these questions is, therefore, not recommended.

These questions are designed to help you determine how well you comprehend the material in this chapter. They are also intended to help you develop problem solving skills and to become comfortable with question formats.

Do not attempt to answer these questions until you have attended the lecture corresponding to this chapter and spent the appropriate time studying the material.

1. A buyer has just completed the closing of his new residence at the offices of the local title insurance company. Included with the numerous documents the buyer received was a title insurance policy. The buyer is wondering whether or not he should also record the deed he received. Should he do so?
   A. Yes, because the title policy does not protect the marketability of the title.
   B. No, because the title insurance policy provides all the protection an owner generally needs under modern property law.
   C. Yes, because recording establishes a priority of claim for the owner in the event a problem arises later.
   D. No, because the buyer paid cash for the property.

2. Which of the following is most likely to be covered under an owner's title insurance policy?
   A. A title which is subsequently determined to be unmarketable.
   B. An error in the surveying of the lot resulting in a loss of 3½ feet along one border.
   C. A construction lien which arose from improvements the seller made to the property to ready it for sale.
   D. An easement appurtenant granted by the prior owner to a neighbor who never recorded it or actually used it.

3. A purchase agreement executed between a buyer and a seller calls for the seller to provide an abstract of title to the purchaser as a form of title assurance. Upon receipt of the abstract the purchaser should do which of the following?
   A. Have it reviewed by an attorney to make certain no undisclosed or unrecorded claims exist.
   B. Have it reviewed by an attorney to make sure the chain of title is unbroken.
   C. Contact the abstractor to issue an opinion of title.
   D. Contact the Register of Deeds to issue an opinion of title.

4. Tiny Title Insurance Company issued a policy thirty years earlier on a property. A long-lost heir of a prior grantee in the chain of title now claims to own 75% of the property due to a fraud committed years ago. Must Tiny Title pay the heir?
   A. No, because the heir's claims are considered to be stale under Michigan's Marketable Title Act.
   B. No, because the heir is claiming in excess of 50% of the property's value.
   C. Yes, because this is one of the covered risks and the purchasing owner still holds title.
   D. Yes, because the owner is alive and a title policy covers all risks as long as the purchasing owner is alive.

5. Which of the following forms of title registration would a Michigan purchaser LEAST likely utilize?
   A. Torrens System.
   B. Grantor-Grantee Indexing.
   C. Tract Index.
   D. Recording System.

6. A buyer negotiates a purchase agreement, the terms of which require the seller to provide the buyer with a marked-up title policy. Which of the following statements best applies?
   A. Coverage includes all standard exceptions.
   B. Coverage will begin within 30 days of the closing.
   C. Coverage extends to marks made on the deed striking out the listed warranties.
   D. Coverage is retroactive to the date of the commitment rather than the date of the closing.

7. Title insurance provides what kind of protection under an owner's policy?
   A. Indemnification for all defects which arise after the date of the policy.
   B. Costs of defending a lawsuit brought about because of alleged defects in the title insured by the policy.
   C. A guarantee that the title is perfect coupled with a duty to pay in the event the title turns out to be less than perfect.
   D. Costs of defending title that is tied to the existing value of the property at the time the defect is detected.

8. All EXCEPT which of the following are common sections in a standard title insurance policy:
   A. General and special exceptions such as adverse possession and unrecorded easements.
   B. An escalation clause in case the value of the property increases over time.
   C. Exclusions against items such as zoning changes and condemnation losses.
   D. Subrogation clause in the event a loss is sustained by the title company.

9. A chain of title is formed by:
   A. A succession of owners who record their interests in the public records.
   B. The register of deeds when owners fail to record their interests in a property.
   C. The linking of subsequent title insurance policies to make sure that there is no break in coverage from owner to owner.
   D. The public recording of interests under the Torrens System.

10. John is given title to Blackacre from Ed. John does not record his interest in the deed but tells Jay that he just purchased Blackacre. Jay convinces Ed to convey another title to Blackacre to him and immediately records the deed. Under Michigan law, who is the rightful owner of Blackacre?
    A. Jay because he was the first to record.
    B. John because he was the first to acquire title.
    C. Ed because the title reverts back to him.
    D. John because he served notice on Jay before Jay acquired his interest in the property.

11. Which of the following statements is true under the Marketable Title Act:
    A. All titles must be marketable or else the seller will agree to pay for any defect that surfaces.
    B. Holders of certain unrecorded interests in a property must wait at least 40 years before they can bring a suit to quiet title in their name.
    C. A prospective purchaser can ignore certain title interests that date back at least 40 years from the date of purchase.
    D. If a title remains marketable for at least 40 years, title insurance will not be required.

12. The duty to insure that a title is marketable rests with which of the following individuals?
    A. The seller if a warranty deed is required in the purchase agreement.
    B. The attorney who issues the title policy.
    C. The broker involved in the real estate transaction.
    D. The purchaser in all cases.

13. All EXCEPT which of the following statements is true of an abstract of title?
    A. It contains a history of all recorded transactions made on a certain piece of real estate.
    B. It requires an independent assessment to determine whether or not the title is reasonably clear.
    C. It does not guarantee clear title.
    D. It insures title once an opinion is obtained.

14. All of the following statements regarding recording are true EXCEPT:
    A. A document must be recorded to be valid.
    B. Recording protects the owner against subsequent adverse claimants.
    C. A buyer who purchases without inspecting the public records is charged with notice of a recorded interest.
    D. Recording serves constructive notice to the world of the existence of a property claim.

15. Title insurance provides what kind of protection in a mortgagee's policy?
    A. Reimbursement to the holder of the owner's policy in the event the owner defaults on his mortgage.
    B. The amount of unpaid principal owed to a lender in case of a total loss from a pre-existing title defect.
    C. Any defects in title which result in loss of the owner's equity.
    D. The difference in value between the mortgage balance and the market value of the property.

Chapter 8: Title Verification

16. Which of the following statements regarding a mortgagee's policy is true?
    A. It is typically purchased by the mortgagee as a condition to obtaining a loan.
    B. It is designed to protect the mortgagor in the event of loss of title.
    C. Since it does not act to insure title, an opinion must be rendered by an attorney.
    D. It is purchased in the amount of the mortgage loan.

Courage is the recognition that fear is an illusion whose only source of power is the attention we give it.

Chapter 9
Real Estate Settlement Procedures

Preparing and orchestrating the closing.

handwritten margin notes: TRID — 3 day rule to the buyer * includes saturdays * no federal holiday

---

I. **Foreword**: A real estate transaction is concluded through a process called the settlement or closing. Settlement service providers (as defined later in this chapter) are relied on to assist the buyer and seller in preparing the necessary paperwork and fulfilling the necessary steps to bring the transaction to a successful end. As a settlement service provider, a real estate licensee must have a clear understanding of how this process works. This allows the licensee to explain the steps to his client or customer. State license law also places certain closing responsibilities on listing real estate brokers.

At the settlement meeting, also called the closing, the seller executes the deed promised in the purchase agreement and delivers it to the buyer. In exchange, the buyer gives the seller the promised purchase price. Since the purchase agreement contains the negotiated terms for the transaction, it serves as one of the key documents used to prepare the settlement package. Numerous disclosures and forms are involved in the closing process.

II. ▶ **TILA-RESPA Integrated Disclosure Rule (TRID Rule)**: The Consumer Financial Protection Bureau (CFPB), working as directed by the Dodd-Frank Wall Street Reform and Consumer Protection Act (Dodd-Frank Act), created a sweeping new rule that impacted consumer mortgage loans and closings. This Rule integrates, meaning to combine and replace, certain aspects of the separate mortgage disclosures that were formerly required under the federal Truth In Lending Act (TILA) and the Real Estate Settlement Procedures Act (RESPA). The TRID Rule became effective for qualifying loans on October 3, 2015. The CFPB, Dodd-Frank Act, TILA, and RESPA are all discussed in further detail in Chapter 17.

handwritten note: RESPA — Federal backed loans

  A. **History and rationale**: The research conducted in the years following the mortgage crisis uncovered that consumers (i.e., borrowers) of risky and subprime mortgage products did not fully understand the changes, especially to payment amount, that could occur over the term of their loans. The mortgage disclosures required prior to the TRID Rule were mandated by two separate Acts, i.e., TILA and RESPA. According to the CFPB, the overlapping nature of these disclosures was often confusing to consumers. Further, many lenders and settlement agents such as title companies believed the old disclosures were difficult to explain to consumers.

   1. **"Know Before You Owe"**: The new streamlined TRID Rule disclosures and timing requirements are designed to help consumers better understand the terms and true costs of the loan product they will be contractually bound to over the course of many years. Having enhanced information at the earliest stages of the lending process also allows consumers to comparison shop before making a commitment to any one particular lender. Early receipt of information also reduces the chance of being "surprised" at the closing table by unexpected loan terms or payment changes. This is why the new TRID Rule disclosures are also referred to as "Know Before You Owe" forms.

   handwritten note: Good Faith Estimate

   2. **TILA and RESPA are still in effect**: While some aspects of the closing disclosures and forms independently required by TILA and RESPA have been merged under the TRID Rule for certain mortgage loans, both Acts are still in effect. As noted later in this chapter, the former TILA and RESPA disclosures and forms are still used in non-TRID Rule loan transactions.

  B. **Transactions to which the TRID Rule applies**: The TRID Rule applies to nearly all closed-end consumer mortgage loans that are secured by real property. As noted in Chapter 17, a closed-end mortgage is one in which the entire loan amount is disbursed to the consumer (i.e., borrower) at the closing and no additional loan sums may be obtained during the term of the loan. "Consumer mortgage loan" means that the loan funds are primarily used for personal, family, or household purposes. The TRID Rule also specifies the exact nature of forms that must be used, when it must be used, and the timing for its delivery to the consumer.

handwritten note: TRID — not w/ cash transactions. Loans only

1. **Covered transactions**: The definition of a closed-end consumer transaction secured by real property includes: Home purchases; Refinancing; New construction loans (excluding home improvement and remodeling financing); Vacant land loans; Loans secured by 25 or more acres; and Credit extended to certain trusts for tax or estate planning purposes. An investment property transaction is covered by the TRID Rule if the loan transaction is primarily for a consumer purpose (e.g., an investor refinances a rental property for a cash-out to use for a strictly personal purpose).

2. **Transaction exceptions**: The TRID Rule does not apply to: Home equity lines of credit (HELOCS); Reverse mortgages; or Chattel-dwelling loans including mobile homes or dwellings that are not attached to land. An investment property transaction is also not covered by the TRID Rule if the transaction is primarily for a business purpose (e.g., an investor borrows money to purchase a rental property strictly as a business opportunity). A lender who issues five or fewer mortgages in one year is not a creditor and, therefore, is not covered by the Rule. Cash transactions and other seller-financed transactions such as those involving land contract sales are also not covered by the TRID Rule (providing the seller has not engaged in more than five such transactions in one year).

C. **The new forms–The Loan Estimate and The Closing Disclosure**: These two new TRID Rule forms provide key information and have specific timing requirements that must be understood and followed. Note that the new TRID Rule forms are only mandated for the covered transactions noted in this discussion. The former, separate TILA and RESPA forms are still used in non-covered, i.e., exempt, loan transactions.

1. **Who prepares and provides the forms**: The primary responsibility for providing both TRID Rule forms lies with the lender and not any settlement agent (such as a title company) who may be assisting with the closing process. As a result, nearly all lenders are electing to handle all aspects of form preparation and delivery. A real estate licensee who is involved in the transaction (whether as a seller's agent or buyer's agent) should make sure that the lender, or title company who is handling the closing for the licensee, receives all necessary transaction information in a timely fashion so the TRID Rule forms can be completed within the required deadlines.

    For purposes of the timing requirements of both forms, a business day may include a Saturday if the particular lending institution is open to the public on that day for carrying out substantially all of its business functions. Sundays and legal public holidays are never treated as business days.

2. **The Loan Estimate (LE)**: The first of the two key TRID Rule forms is called the Loan Estimate, or LE for short.

    a. **Contents**: The LE is a three-page form that provides the consumer (i.e., prospective borrower) with good-faith estimates of credit costs and loan transaction terms. It includes general information, loan terms, projected payments, and costs at closing. For TRID Rule loan transactions, the LE integrates and replaces the formerly-required Good Faith Estimate (GFE) required under RESPA and formerly-required initial Truth In Lending disclosure required under TILA. The lender is required to honor the terms and costs in the LE for ten (10) business days.

    b. **Timing**: The lender (i.e., creditor) must deliver the LE to the consumer (or place it in the mail) no later than three (3) business days after the consumer completes an application for a covered mortgage loan. Further, the LE must be delivered to the consumer at least seven (7) days before loan consummation (as described in the next section). The lender has the option of asking the consumer to sign and date the form to confirm receipt.

    c. **Information booklet**: A lender must also give the consumer a special information booklet prepared by the CFPB titled, "Your home loan toolkit, A step-by-step guide." It must be provided at the time of loan application or within three (3) business days thereafter. This booklet replaces the former consumer booklet required under RESPA that explained settlement costs.

    d. **Other issues**:

        (1) A mortgage application and LE are not treated as a commitment by the lender and consumer to enter into a loan. This allows the consumer to request LEs from multiple lenders for purposes of comparison shopping different mortgage loan products.

        (2) The consumer must actually express his "intent to proceed" with a particular application for the lender to move forward with processing the application. If a lender does not hear from the consumer within ten (10) business days, the application will most likely be closed out.

Chapter 9: Real Estate Settlement Procedures

(3) A lender may only charge a fee to obtain the consumer's credit report prior to providing the LE, but no other costs. Accordingly, formal pre-approvals at this point in the process are not possible for mortgage loans that are subject to the TRID Rule. Some lenders issue a conditional pre-approval by having the applicant complete the loan application, but without identifying a specific property.

3. **The Closing Disclosure (CD):** The second of the two key TRID Rule forms is called the Closing Disclosure, or CD for short. The lender provides the CD to the consumer within the required time. The lender may also contract with a settlement or closing agent (such as a title company) to provide it on the lender's behalf. The closing agent may not, however, provide a copy of the CD to any real estate licensee who represents or works with a party to the transaction. If the licensee wishes to review the CD in advance of the closing to make sure the purchase price, commission amount, or other charges are correctly reflected, the licensee must obtain a copy from the consumer.

    a. **Contents**: The CD is a five-page form that reflects the actual terms and costs of the mortgage loan transaction for the consumer. If these terms or costs change prior to the loan documents being signed at the closing table, the lender must provide a corrected disclosure. This can trigger a new timing requirement. For TRID Rule loan transactions, the CD integrates and replaces the formerly-required HUD-1 closing statement under RESPA and the formerly-required final Truth In Lending disclosure required under TILA. The CD also contains the license number and contact information for the lender, mortgage broker (if involved), and all real estate brokers who are involved in the transaction.

    b. **Timing**: The lender (i.e., creditor) must deliver the CD to the consumer at least three (3) business days before consummation of the loan by the consumer. Consummation occurs when the consumer signs the loan documents (i.e., mortgage and note) and becomes contractually obligated to the lender. While consummation generally occurs at the actual scheduled settlement (i.e., closing), it may occur on a different day. This timing requirement gives the consumer a relaxed opportunity to review the final costs rather than seeing them for the first time at the closing table. The consumer may be required by the lender to sign and date the CD to confirm receipt.

D. **Accuracy of costs and tolerances**: As noted, costs stated in the Loan Estimate must be made in good faith. Good faith is determined by examining whether the amount of any cost increased in the Closing Disclosure.

1. **Zero tolerance**: Generally, if a closing cost charged in the CD exceeds the cost for the service estimated in the LE, the lender cannot charge the difference and must honor the figure in the LE. This is known as zero tolerance. The actual cost imposed by the CD can be less, however. *No higher than expected costs*

2. **10% cumulative tolerance**: Certain charges may increase subject to a 10% tolerance. In other words, the total of the costs disclosed in the CD may be higher providing it is within 10% of the charges disclosed in the LE. These charges are limited to: Recording fees; Charges for third-party services where the charge is not paid to the lender and the consumer shops for the service and selects a provider from the lender's written list of providers.

3. **No tolerance limits**: A lender may charge more on the CD without any tolerance limitation for: Prepaid interest; Property insurance premiums; Property tax escrows (which may also be referred to as impounds); Required services the lender allows the consumer to shop for where the consumer selects a provider <u>not</u> on the lender's written list of providers; and Services paid to a third-party provider that are not required by the lender. The estimated charge on the LE must have been based on the best information reasonably available to the lender at the time the LE was provided.

E. **Corrected Closing Disclosure may trigger a new three-day waiting period**: As previously noted, a lender may correct the information provided on the CD prior to the loan consummation. Depending on the nature of the correction, it may trigger a new three (3) business day waiting period.

1. **Significant changes**: A significant change or correction to the CD will require the preparation and delivery of a new CD and a new three (3) day waiting period. These changes include:

    a. An increase in the Annual Percentage Rate (APR) that is greater than 1/8% on a fixed rate mortgage or greater than 1/4% on a mortgage with irregular payments or periods such as an adjustable rate mortgage (ARM).

    b. The actual loan product being obtained changes (e.g., the consumer applies for a fixed rate mortgage and then changes it to an adjustable rate mortgage before the closing).

    c. A prepayment penalty is added by the lender.

2. **Less significant changes**: Other changes to the information on the CD will require the lender to provide a corrected CD, but will not mandate a new three (3) day waiting period. Examples of these changes include:

   a. Unexpected discoveries on a pre-closing walk-through of a property such a broken refrigerator or missing stove, even if the seller is required to issue a financial credit to the buyer to cover the problem.

   b. Changes to payments made at the closing resulting from adjustments to real estate commissions, prorations of taxes and utilities, and amounts required to be paid into escrow, for example.

   c. Typographical errors discovered at the closing table.

F. **Impact on real estate licensees**: The TRID Rule does not impose specific requirements on real estate licensees. However, since most residential real estate closings involve closed-end consumer mortgage loans, licensees must be aware of the new forms and timing requirements. Further, clients and customers should understand that mortgage loan closings subject to the TRID Rule take time to process and cannot be rushed. Lenders and title companies (acting as closing agents) are noticing that the TRID Rule is resulting in a beneficial reduction in consumer confusion and "surprises" at the closing table.

III. **Settlement/Closing in general**: Closings of real estate transactions that are not covered by the TRID Rule are likely to be handled by using the traditional forms and procedures employed prior to the rule's imposition in October, 2015. These forms and procedures are described in this section.

   A. ▶ **The closing statement**: A closing statement, also known as a settlement statement, is a written analysis and itemization of the amounts either owed by or due to the buyer and seller. As we will see, license law requires a broker to furnish, or cause to be furnished, a closing statement to the parties to a real estate transaction. The broker is also required to sign the statement. The state-mandated broker's closing statement is not, however, the only closing statement that may be used in connection with a real estate transaction.

      1. ▶ **Form HUD-1 Settlement Statement**: The HUD-1 is a federal closing statement that discloses the actual charges and adjustments to be given to the parties in the transaction. Prior to imposition of the TRID Rule, the Real Estate Settlement Procedures Act (RESPA) required the use of a HUD-1 Settlement Statement for any transaction that involved a federally-related mortgage loan. Today, the HUD-1 may be used for non-TRID Rule transactions involving cash sales, land contracts, and business-related (commercial) properties. A copy of a HUD-1 is located in the Appendix at the back of this textbook.

      2. **Broker's closing statement**: Brokers, especially listing brokers, must continue providing a broker's closing statement to their clients even in transactions that fall within the TRID Rule. Even though the listing broker bears legal responsibility, he often relies on a title company to prepare the statement to make sure no inconsistencies exist between the TRID Rule forms and the broker's closing statement. Closing statement requirements under Michigan license law are covered in Chapters 19 and 20.

   B. **Factors that affect the closing**: How a particular transaction is actually closed can vary based on (1) the region of the country or state where the transaction is closed, (2) the type of financing involved, (3) who prepares the closing package, and (4) who conducts the actual closing meeting.

      1. ▶ **Preparation of the closing package (and the closing agent)**: The closing agent, who may also be referred to as an escrow agent, is the person or entity who actually prepares non-TRID Rule closing statements. As noted, title insurance companies frequently fulfill this function, so the individuals who handle everything work for the title company. In other geographic regions, a real estate broker or an attorney may handle the entire non-TRID Rule closing process from preparation of all documents through conducting the closing meeting.

   C. **Preliminary considerations**: The seller must understand, in advance, what his net proceeds will be after deduction of all expenses. In a time of fluctuating and recovering property values, this has become more important than ever. Calculation of the seller's net proceeds determines whether the seller leaves the closing table with an equity check in hand or has to write a check to his lender to cover a mortgage deficiency (if the debt is greater than the property's market value). Similarly, the buyer must know exactly how much money to bring to the closing, if any, to cover the difference between the earnest money deposit check and the purchase price as well as any prepaid expenses.

   D. **Escrows, escrow closings, and split closings**: By definition, the word escrow refers to a legal document or money delivered by a person to a neutral third party to be held until the occurrence of some event or contingency. Escrows are commonly established in connection with real estate transactions. In some parts of the

Chapter 9: Real Estate Settlement Procedures

country, transactions are closed in escrow on behalf of the buyer and seller rather than using brokers, lenders, title companies, or attorneys.

1. **Escrow closings in Michigan**: While not common, a title company may close in escrow under certain circumstances when both parties are not able to attend the same closing. For example, a seller needs to delay a scheduled closing date to cure a recently discovered defect. The title company agrees to prepare and then hold the closing documents and funds in escrow pending fulfillment of the conditions causing the delay.

2. **Split closing**: A split closing is one in which the seller and buyer each select separate title companies. The two title companies work together to coordinate the necessary steps to close the transaction. One company represents and closes the seller's side of the transaction. This company typically issues the owner's title policy which is ordered by the seller. The other company represents and closes the buyer's side. This company issues the mortgagee's title policy for the buyer's lender.

   Split closings have potential advantages and disadvantages. For example, a licensee who represents a client, and is more familiar with a particular title company, may be able to better facilitate his client's interests. This often holds true in the sale of foreclosed, bank-owned properties, where the bank wants a particular title company to be used for the owner's policy and the buyer seeks independent representation by his own title representative to issue the mortgagee's policy. Split closings do require more coordination. Since two title companies are involved, the closing may or may not involve slightly increased fees, and may slightly add to the time needed to close the transaction.

IV. **Settlement procedures** [Closing procedures]: This section provides a basic overview of the licensee's role and time frame for assisting with the closing of a standard real estate transaction, without complications or unusual circumstances. It is important to remember that no two transactions are exactly alike. Therefore, the suggested time frames listed below can vary. For example, a short sale can add several weeks to the closing process depending on the number of loans with liens on the property that need to be settled. A TRID Rule loan may also take additional time.

Assume for this discussion that a seller is working with a listing broker and the buyer is working with a selling broker. For purposes of this discussion, the role each broker plays in the settlement process is independently discussed. In practice, the brokers simultaneously fulfill their respective functions.

A. **Role of the Selling Broker (the broker and salesperson who work with the buyer).**

   1. **Days 1 through 7**: During the first week following execution of a purchase agreement, the main objective of the selling broker is to make sure that no unfulfilled contract contingencies exist and the buyer applies for a mortgage loan on a timely basis with a reputable and licensed loan officer.

      a. ▸ **Surrender of deposit and purchase agreement**: The selling salesperson will immediately give the company's copy of the signed offer to purchase and the earnest money deposit check to the salesperson's broker. The broker depends on his affiliated licensees to make sure that the company transaction file contains all required documents and notations since the broker is ultimately responsible. Ultimately, the broker has 2 banking days from the time the broker receives notice that the purchase agreement is signed by the buyer and the seller to deposit the earnest money check in the broker's trust account. See Chapters 19 and 20 for further details on earnest money deposit requirements.

      b. **Satisfaction of contingencies**: The purchase agreement will probably contain separate contingency clauses for obtaining a loan and a home inspection. The buyer's promise to purchase is not enforceable until both contingencies are either satisfied or waived by the buyer. The satisfaction or waiver of contingency clauses should be noted in the file and promptly communicated to the listing broker. Contingency clauses are discussed further in Chapter 12.

      c. **Loan application assistance**: The selling broker will typically help the buyer shop for a lender by recommending one or more licensed loan officers. The selling broker may also recommend one or more home inspectors. Ultimately, the decision regarding which lender or home inspector to use is exclusively that of the buyer. Licensees often recommend multiple professionals to their clients and customers rather than just one to avoid the appearance of an endorsement. Some brokers and their attorneys believe this insulates the broker from potential liability. There is no law that requires multiple recommendations, so each broker should set his own policy on the matter.

   2. **Days 8 through 45**: During the next several weeks, the selling broker will await the approval from the lender on the buyer's loan application.

a. **Maintain contact with the buyer**: It is recommended that the broker keep in touch with the buyer at least once per week during this phase of the settlement process. This gives the broker an opportunity to keep the buyer apprised of the settlement status and answer any questions the buyer may have.

b. **Appraisal scheduling**: Approximately two weeks after the loan application is completed, the selling broker should check to see if the lender's appraisal has been scheduled. This is important at this stage because of the time constraints included in most purchase agreements. The terms of the purchase agreement generally require the buyer to make his loan application and obtain approval within a certain time. There may also be a requirement that the transaction close within a certain time frame.

c. **Deliver the title commitment to the buyer**: The listing broker usually orders the title policy commitment which arrives in the form of what the industry calls a preliminary binder. Copies are forwarded to the selling broker who gives one to the buyer. If a split closing is used, the selling broker is responsible for communicating with the desired title company that will provide the mortgagee's policy.

B. **Role of the Listing Broker** (the broker and salesperson who works with the seller).

1. **Days 1 through 7**: During the first week following execution of a purchase agreement, the listing broker usually has more to do than does the selling broker. To make certain that nothing is missed, the listing broker should use a transaction processing checklist.

   a. **Begin preparation of the closing statements**: Recall that license law requires a broker to furnish or cause to be furnished a complete and detailed closing statement. Either the listing broker or the selling broker may handle this, however, the final responsibility rests with the listing broker. Most brokers "cause" the closing statement to be furnished by ordering it through the title insurance company of their choice. When this occurs, the broker remains ultimately responsible for the contents and accuracy of the closing statements.

   b. ▶ **Coordinate the home inspection**: If the buyer makes his purchase offer contingent on a satisfactory home inspection, it must be arranged within the time frame specified in the purchase agreement. While the selling broker coordinates this with the buyer, the listing broker can follow up to make sure that it gets done. The home inspector will require that all mechanical and appliance systems in the home are turned on and/or running if possible. Examples include electricity, plumbing, furnace, air conditioner (if the weather is sufficiently warm), hot water heater, tub pumps, attic fans, dishwasher, and kitchen disposal. The listing broker can convey this need to the seller.

      (1) **Buyer attendance at home inspection**: It is generally thought to be a good idea for the buyer to attend the home inspection. It provides an excellent opportunity for the buyer to learn about the property and its systems and to ask any questions while the expert inspector is present. Many inspectors prefer that the buyer be present.

      (2) **Licensee attendance at home inspection**: Whether a listing licensee or selling licensee should attending a home inspection is a matter of internal policy for each broker. The listing licensee may wish to attend solely for purposes of providing access to the property and to make sure the property is properly secured after the inspection has concluded. A buyer's agent may wish to be present to merely support his buyer-client.

      If either licensee attends, he or she must not provide advice, actively participate in the inspection or questioning process, or attempt to serve in a consulting capacity. All inspection-related questions by a buyer should be directed to the inspector. Further, a licensee should not provide keys or lockbox combinations to home inspectors without proper authorization and identification.

   c. **Monitor contingencies**: While most purchase agreement contingencies relate to conditions specific to the buyer, it is possible for the seller to include his own contingency clause. This frequently occurs in the context of a short sale. For example, the seller conditions his acceptance of the offer to purchase on receipt of a satisfactory short sale approval letter from his lender. Another seller may include an attorney review contingency. The listing agent should monitor the process to make sure that any seller contingencies are satisfied or waived in a timely fashion. The transaction file should be noted accordingly and the selling broker informed of the status.

   d. **Order title insurance**: After all contingencies have been satisfied or waived, the listing broker orders the title policy.

Chapter 9: Real Estate Settlement Procedures

e. **Order mortgage payoff letters**: The seller must pay the balance on all ex<!--cut-->ing any home equity lines of credit, so all liens can be removed from the <!--cut--> convey marketable title to the buyer.

f. ▶ **Check for municipal (city) certification and inspection requirement**<!--cut--> comply with municipal and/or county certification and inspection requir<!--cut--> not close without first obtaining the appropriate certification or permit. Ci<!--cut--> inspection codes are designed to make sure that minimum standards are m<!--cut--> habitability, zoning, fire safety, and smoke and carbon monoxide detection.

Additional inspection requirements may exist for rental properties located within the municipality. If the property is not connected to city water or sewer systems, both well and septic certifications will be required by the county. Well and septic system evaluations can be performed either by the county health department or a private evaluator who is registered with the county.

g. ▶ **Coordinate termite or other pest inspections**: Termite or other pest inspections may be required depending on the type of financing (such as FHA and VA) or local code. If so, the listing agent should make sure that they are obtained and/or coordinate them with the selling broker as warranted. With regard to a VA loan, termite inspections are required on existing properties if they are located in an area where the probability of termite infestation is "very heavy" or "moderate to heavy" according to the Termite Infestation Probability Map published in the International Residential Code. The only part of Michigan that is located in the "moderate to heavy" zone is the southern base of the lower peninsula.

C. ▶ **Handling expenses**: Real estate licensees are expected to review the expenses for which the buyer and the seller are responsible at the closing. The listing and selling brokers can use the forms, figures, and worksheets provided in the closing package prepared by the title company to review with their respective clients or customers. Each licensee should receive the state-mandated settlement statement as well as the appropriate TRID forms if the loan is federally-related. The following expenses are typically encountered in connection with a real estate closing. For purposes of the real estate license exam, be prepared for a question asking you to calculate the buyer's funds needed at closing.

1. Commissions (seller pays listing agent; possibly buyer pays buyer's agent).
2. Title insurance (seller pays fee title policy; buyer pays mortgagee's policy).
3. County transfer tax, state transfer tax, and other recording fees (seller typically pays).
4. Tax and insurance reserves or escrow if required by the lender (buyer typically pays).
5. Mortgage-related expenses (buyer typically pays).
6. Attorney's fees and other closing costs (either/both parties can pay).

D. **Debits and Credits**: Closing statements must itemize all debits and credits for each party to the transaction. A <u>debit</u> is any amount of money which is entered on a closing statement as a charge or cost assessed to a party. A <u>credit</u> is any amount of money which is prepaid or for which a party must be reimbursed. In simple terms, a debit is a "payable" and a credit is a "receivable." Often, a debit for one party is a credit for the other. For example, the purchase price is a debit for the buyer and a credit for the seller.

E. **Settlement documents**: There are a number of different documents that come into play at a real estate closing. Which ones are needed depend on factors such as the nature of the particular transaction, the type of property which is involved, the type of conveying documents that are used, and the type of financing that may be involved.

1. **Documents relating to sale**: The key document that relates to the actual sale of the property is the purchase agreement. Less frequently, a sale may be triggered via the exercise of a previously-issued option agreement by a seller-optionor to a buyer-optionee. Options are discussed in Chapter 12.

2. **Documents related to transfer of ownership**: While the purchase agreement sets forth the terms and conditions of the sale, a separate set of documents are used to actually transfer ownership. These documents include the following (which are all discussed in other chapters of this textbook).

a. **Deed**: A deed is used by the seller to convey the full title interest to the buyer.

b. **Land Contract**: A land contract is used to convey an ownership interest to the buyer (referred to as equitable title) in a seller-financed transaction in which the seller retains the deed (referred to as legal title) pending final payment years later.

Bill of Sale: When personal property is included in a real estate transaction, the seller must prepare a bill of sale to convey ownership of it to the buyer. This is needed because the deed does not transfer title to any personal property, only the real property.

3. **Documents related to financing**: When a real estate purchase takes place, several more documents come into play as noted below. The information in this section is provided merely as an overview. Further detail is available in other chapters.

    a. **Note**: The lender on a financed sale requires the buyer-borrower to sign a contract, referred to as a note, that personally obligates the buyer-borrower to repay the full amount of the debt. The loan terms typically require the buyer-borrower to make monthly payments for the term of the loan.

    b. **Mortgage**: In addition to a note, the lender on a financed sale also requires collateral. The mortgage serves this purpose by creating a contractual lien on the property. If the buyer defaults on the payments, the terms of the mortgage may allow the lender to force the sale of the property and satisfy the balance owing.

    c. **Deed of Trust**: A deed of trust is a document used to secure the financing of real estate in which the borrower conditionally conveys title to a trustee who holds title for the lender pending repayment. It is a less common alternative to a traditional mortgage and note.

    d. ▶ **Private Mortgage Insurance Policy (PMI)**: Private mortgage insurance is a form of insurance that a lender requires when it is asked to loan more than 80% of the appraised value of the subject property. For example, a buyer has 10% to put down on a house. The lender agrees to increase the amount of the loan to 90%. The PMI company insures the lender against the risk of default for the additional 10%. The lender assumes the default risk for the first 80% of the loan.

    e. ▶ **Transfer of Tax, Insurance Escrows**: When a buyer finances the purchase price of a property, the lender will likely require that property taxes, insurance, and possibly association fees (in the case of a financed condominium) be prepaid into an escrow account. Each month thereafter, 1/12 of the upcoming year's expenses are deposited into the escrow so they can be paid by the lender on the due date. When the property is sold at some later date, any excess funds in the escrow are credited to the seller. If the buyer intends to pay the taxes and insurance separately, he will have to show proof of payment at the closing.

    f. **Estoppel Certificate**: The buyer-borrower may be asked to execute an estoppel certificate attesting to a certain set of facts.

4. **Miscellaneous documents**: Other documents come into play at a real estate closing. This section merely lists these documents for purposes of awareness. Some of these documents are discussed in this chapter, others are discussed elsewhere in this textbook.

    a. Settlement Statements including the broker's closing statement required under license law and the Form HUD-1 Settlement Statement if the transaction is federally-related.

    b. Truth-in-Lending Disclosures.

    c. Appraisal Reports.

    d. Notice of Payment of Taxes and/or Utilities.

    e. Assignment of Lease, Security Deposit, and/or Tenant's Estoppel Certificate (if the property is subject to a valid lease).

    f. Waivers or Release of Prior Liens and/or Subordination Agreements.

    g. Survey Reports.

    h. Inspection reports and certifications such as well, septic, pest, and/or environmental.

    i. Title Insurance Policy.

    j. Homeowner's Policy.

    k. Flood Insurance.

    l. Certificates of Occupancy.

m. IRS filing requirements including Form 1099-S (for reporting of proceeds from a real estate transaction), Form 8300 (for reporting the receipt of more than $10,000 in cash), and Foreign Investment in Real Property Tax Act or FIRPTA affidavit (for reporting proceeds resulting from the sale of a U.S. real property interest by a foreign seller). FIRPTA is discussed in Chapter 15.

V. **Prorations**: When a parcel of real estate is sold, the closing usually takes place during the middle of a tax year rather than on the due date of a tax bill. Tax obligations will generally have been paid by the seller in advance. Less frequently, taxes are due and payable by the buyer at the end of the billing period. This is known as payment in arrears. Further discussion and calculation examples can be found in Chapter 22

  A. **Proration defined**: Proration is the process used to divide and then allocate a share of a financial obligation to the seller and the buyer. The exact amount of a proration depends on the calendar date the transaction is closed in relation to the due date of the obligation. *See Figure 23.*

   1. **Look to local custom**: The guidelines by which financial obligations are prorated vary from one jurisdiction to another. Most often, local custom or the negotiated terms of the purchase agreement determine how the proration is to be calculated. The municipal, county, or township treasurer's office can be contacted for exact amounts and due dates of taxes. While title insurance companies and lending institutions process most closing documents, the broker is still responsible for the calculations and should double-check all figures for accuracy.

   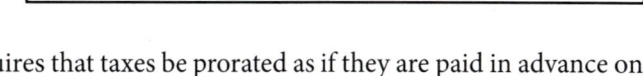

   2. **Purchase agreement controls**: It is best if the actual method of proration is specified in the purchase agreement to avoid confusion. If the purchase agreement is silent, Michigan law requires that taxes be prorated as if they are paid in advance on a due-date basis with the buyer being responsible for the day of the closing.

  B. **Considerations for prorating property taxes**: There are several considerations for the proration of property taxes of which licensees must be aware such as: (1) Property taxes are levied by different governmental units or taxing districts including county, school, city, village, or township; (2) Individual taxing districts may operate on different fiscal years which require individual proration of each tax; and (3) Various taxes may be combined into one or two annual tax bills which are prorated on either a due date basis (meaning when the bill is received) or on a fiscal year basis (meaning when the tax district closes out its financial books). Additional information on property taxes is located in Chapter 15.

   1. **Tax day and Levy date**: Confusion often exists as to the meaning of the terms tax day and levy date. This section clarifies the difference, including the reason for the assessment of certain taxes on a summer and/or winter bill. Study this material in conjunction with the generation discussion of real property taxes in Chapter 15.

      a. **Winter versus summer taxes**: Property taxes in Michigan may be collected in the summer and/or the winter. Townships traditionally collected their property taxes on the winter bill. From a historical perspective, this gave their mostly agricultural residents an opportunity to complete the fall harvest.

      Most cities today now collect property taxes in a summer levy. As of July 2007, all of the county general property tax is collected in the summer tax levy. School taxes may be levied on the summer bill or split equally between the summer and winter tax bills.

      b. **Tax day–used to determine assessed value**: For purposes of real property taxation, tax day is December 31. The local property assessor determines the assessed value of all property each year using the condition of the property as of December 31 of the previous year. For example, the condition of the property on December 31, 2017 is used to determine the 2018 assessed value which is then used to calculate the 2018 property tax bills.

      c. **Levy date–taxes become due and payable**: Property taxes are not actually levied, meaning collected, and do not actually become due and payable until the following December 1 when the tax bills are mailed. Charter cities and villages may provide for a different day. Otherwise, December 1 is the traditional date on which the lien arises. If the property is sold and closed prior to the levy or lien date, the seller and buyer will prorate the taxes as a shared obligation. In those jurisdictions authorized to levy a Summer tax, July 1 is the date when taxes are deemed due and payable.

2. **Payment in advance versus in arrears**: Taxes and other bills may be due and payable either in advance or in arrears. Knowing which method is used is important since closing expenses can be significantly affected.

   a. **In advance**: If taxes are due in advance, the owner is asked to pay for government services which will be received in the future. Since the seller has prepaid the taxes for these services, he is entitled to a credit from the buyer on the closing statement.

   Tax prorations in advance are listed on the TRID Closing Disclosure under "Summaries of Transactions." See line items below "K. Due from Borrower at Closing." Refer to the sample Closing Disclosure in the Appendix.

   b. **In arrears**: If taxes are paid in arrears, the owner is asked to pay for government services that have already been received. Since the seller has used or benefitted from part of the services without paying for them, he must credit that portion to the buyer on the closing statement. Interest on a mortgage is another example of a payment that is made in arrears. See Chapter 16 for further details on mortgage payments.

   Tax prorations in arrears are listed on the TRID Closing Disclosure under "Summaries of Transactions." See line items under "L. Paid Already by or on Behalf of Borrower at Closing." Refer to the sample Closing Disclosure in the Appendix.

3. **Responsibility for the day of closing**: For purposes of prorating closing costs, the seller has traditionally been treated as the owner of the property on the actual day of closing. Accordingly, the seller was charged for the daily cost of all prorations including taxes and insurance on that day. In some jurisdictions, the buyer may be charged for the daily cost of taxes and insurance on the day of closing. As noted earlier, Michigan law indicates that in the absence of an agreement to the contrary, the buyer is responsible for the day of the closing.

4. **Treatment on the Michigan real estate examination**: When addressing proration questions on the licensing examination, use a 360-day year, 30-day month unless directed to do otherwise in the question. If the exam question asks you to prorate based on a 365-day calendar year (which is possible), make sure to note which calendar months are involved. Then, adjust for the exact number of days in those months whether they be 30 days, 31 days, or 28 days as in the case of February. As it relates to which party is responsible for the actual day of closing, read the question to see if it specifies who should be assessed. If the question does not indicate which party, assume that the buyer is charged. This means that the buyer will be assessed the prorated costs beginning with and including the day of closing (assuming that taxes are paid in advance).

C. ▶ **Calculation steps**: Follow these simple steps when calculating proration questions on the salesperson's or broker's state examination.

   1. **Step one**: Determine what item is being prorated. For example, does it involve taxes, insurance, or some other prorated fee? The type of fee may provide a clue as to its billing term. Typically, taxes will be for a year or other 12-month period. It is important to read proration examination questions carefully. While not likely, it is possible to be given a multi-year item to prorate such as a 3-year insurance policy purchased by the seller.

   2. **Step two**: Determine if the prorated item was due and payable in advance. If so, make sure to verify that the seller actually prepaid the item as billed. If not, the seller may be in default and will owe the buyer for the time it became due to the day of closing. Penalties and interest may also be due.

   3. **Step three**: Next, determine if the prorated item is an accrued item, meaning due and payable in arrears. If so, the seller will owe the buyer for the beginning of the billing period to the day of closing. Any individual prorated item will either be charged in advance or in arrears, but not both.

   4. **Step four**: Determine what calculation process is required. See the discussion under "Treatment on the Michigan real estate examination," above.

   5. **Step five**: Mathematically calculate the proration and then select the appropriate answer on the examination.

Chapter 9: Real Estate Settlement Procedures 137

VI. ▶ **Real Estate Settlement Procedures Act (RESPA; Regulation X)**: The Real Estate Settlement Procedures Act was enacted by Congress in 1974 to safeguard consumers who apply for federally-related mortgage loans from overpaying for settlement costs. RESPA was actually implemented by the Department of Housing and Urban Development (HUD) through what is known as Regulation X. RESPA is currently administered, supervised, and enforced by the Consumer Financial Protection Bureau (CFPB) pursuant to the Dodd-Frank Wall Street Reform and Consumer Protection Act.

RESPA requires lenders to provide consumers with certain information regarding the nature and amount of settlement costs. Potential borrowers can compare various lenders' fees and make better-informed decisions about the closing process and costs prior to obtaining a loan. The Act does not limit the actual amount of finance costs a lender may charge, it merely requires their full and timely disclosure.

A. **Application and exemptions**: The disclosure requirements of RESPA only apply to federally-related mortgages. Therefore, depending on the nature of the financing in a real estate transaction, the Act may or may not apply. Even if a particular loan is exempt from RESPA requirements, other regulatory laws may come into play.

1. **Mortgage loan defined broadly**: A mortgage loan is defined under RESPA as any loan secured by a first or subordinate lien on residential real property designed for occupancy by 1–4 families. Individual units in condominiums and cooperatives as well as refinancing loans are also covered. A loan is federally-related if the lender participates with the federal government through the FDIC, FHA, VA, HUD, Ginnie Mae, or if the loan will be immediately sold to Fannie Mae, Freddie Mac, or other similar government-sponsored enterprise that participates in the secondary mortgage market.

2. **Exemptions**: Various loan transactions are either not covered by RESPA or are exempt from coverage. For example, loans involving properties with more than one-to-four units are not covered. It is important to note that a loan which is exempt under RESPA may still have to comply with the TRID Rule disclosure requirements. The following list contains an overview of transactions or loan circumstances which are either not covered or are exempt from coverage under RESPA:

    a. A loan on property of 25 acres or more.

    b. Loans extended purely for business, commercial, or agricultural purposes.

    c. Temporary or interim financing such as construction loans (however, if the loan is rolled into a long-term mortgage financed by a federally-related lender, i.e., an end loan, it is covered by RESPA).

    d. Any construction loan with a term of two years or more is covered by RESPA, unless it is made to a bona fide contractor (bridge loans are not covered).

    e. A loan secured by vacant or unimproved property (where no loan proceeds are used to construct a one-to-four family residential structure).

    f. The assumption of an existing loan by a buyer where prior lender approval is not required.

    g. A conversion of a loan to different terms which are consistent with provisions of the original mortgage (as long as a new note is not required).

    h. A transfer of a loan obligation in the secondary market (but, certain mortgage servicing requirements still apply).

    i. Transactions that are fully financed by a private seller such as a purchase money mortgage or land contract (however, if the purchase money mortgage or land contract is funded in whole or in part by the proceeds of a loan made by a lender or other entity subject to RESPA, the purchase money mortgage or land contract is deemed to be a federally-related mortgage loan and falls under RESPA).

    j. Certain loans, such as reverse mortgages, are granted partial exemptions from the disclosure requirements of the TRID Rule. However, loans that are not subject to the TRID Rule (such as reverse mortgages) continue to be subject to RESPA's Good Faith Estimate, the HUD-1 settlement statement, and other TILA disclosures.

3. **Settlement services**: The following items qualify as settlement services which are subject to RESPA regulations. It is important to note that real estate brokerage services do fall under RESPA.

    a. Title searches, examinations, and insurance.

    b. Legal services.

    c. Preparation of closing documents.

d. Property surveying.

e. Credit reporting.

f. Appraisal services.

g. Pest, fungus (i.e., mold), and property inspectors.

h. Home warranty services.

i. Hazard insurance.

j. Real estate brokerage services.

k. Loan origination, application, processing and underwriting (as they apply to federally-related loans).

4. **Settlement service providers**: The Dodd-Frank Act defines a settlement service provider as "any person that provides a material service to a covered person in connection with the offering or provision by such covered person of a consumer financial product or service." This technical definition essentially covers individuals and companies that provide settlement services such as those listed in the previous section. Title insurance companies, attorneys, surveyors, appraisers, inspectors, home warranty companies, hazard insurance companies, and real estate licensees are all potential settlement service providers.

B. **Requirements**: A lender must meet all RESPA information and disclosure requirements. RESPA disclosures are all time-critical.

1. **Disclosures required at the time of loan application**.

    a. **Information booklet**: For non-TRID loans, the borrower must receive the same special information booklet that is required for mortgage loan transactions covered by the TRID Rule. As a reminder, the booklet is prepared by the CFPB and is titled, "Your home loan toolkit, A step-by-step guide."

    b. **Good Faith Estimate of settlement costs**: For certain non-TRID loans (e.g., reverse mortgage), the lender must provide the borrower with a standardized Good Faith Estimate (GFE) of the anticipated settlement costs and interest rate related terms. The GFE facilitates shopping among settlement service providers. The estimated costs in the GFE and the actual costs at settlement (listed on the HUD-1) have to be within certain tolerances or a refund of the difference may be due the consumer. Further, to facilitate the shopping of third-party settlement services, the lender's loan originator must provide the borrower with a written list of settlement service providers when the GFE is provided. For loans covered by the TRID Rule, this information is incorporated in the Loan Estimate form.

    c. **Mortgage Servicing Disclosure Statement**: The mortgage servicing disclosure statement informs the borrower if the lender intends to retain and service the loan itself or transfer it to another lender for third-party servicing. It also tells the borrower how any complaints can be resolved.

    Mortgage servicing consists of the administration of a loan, typically from the time the funds are disbursed to the borrower at the closing until the final payment is made. Functions of a servicer include payment recordkeeping, collection and disbursement of payments to the holder of the note (sometimes referred to as the investor), payment of escrowed property taxes and insurance when they come due, and initial handling of any delinquencies.

2. **Disclosures required prior to the closing**.

    a. **Affiliated Business Arrangement (AfBA) Disclosure**: RESPA also regulates fee splitting and referral fee payments between affiliated businesses that provide settlement services. The Act contains specific requirements including (1) disclosure of the relationship, (2) loan applicants cannot be required to use any particular settlement service provider, and (3) compensation received by one affiliated business must be limited to a mere return on the ownership interest in the other affiliated business. As far as affiliated business disclosures are concerned, a lender is generally required to give the prospective borrower the names, addresses, and telephone numbers of any designated settlement service providers.

        (1) **Affiliated business arrangement defined**: An affiliated business arrangement rises when one person who is in a position to refer settlement services has an affiliated relationship or direct ownership interest (of more than 1%) in the business of another settlement service provider to whom the person refers business (or influences the selection of that provider by a borrower). For example, a buyer's agent of ABC Realty recommends that her buyer-client apply for a loan with ABC Realty's

Chapter 9: Real Estate Settlement Procedures

mortgage company or use ABC Realty's title insurance company (both of which are owned by the broker of ABC Realty).

(a) **Requirements for affiliated business arrangement**: When a qualifying AfBA exists, the following are required.

   i) The relationship must be fully disclosed;

   ii) The consumer, i.e., borrower, must be free to obtain the services from the provider of his choice (a lender can, however, require that a specific provider be used if it relates to a credit reporting agency, appraiser, or attorney);

   iii) A list of typical fees charged by the affiliated provider must be disclosed; and

   iv) No fees (such as referral fees or kickbacks) can exchanged between providers for the sole purpose of referring business.

(b) **Timing of disclosure**: The referring entity must give the disclosure to the consumer no later than the time of each referral or, if the lender requires a particular settlement service provider, at the time of the loan application.

[Handwritten margin note: RESPA Violation — referrals are legal]

(2) **Kickbacks, fee-splitting, and unearned fees**: Generally speaking, settlement service providers may not split fees or give or receive a kickback solely for the referral of business. This prevents lenders from increasing loan costs simply to pay these unearned fees. For example, if lenders were allowed to pay referral fees to real estate licensees, the lenders would likely add the fees to the overall cost consumers pay for loans.

[Handwritten note above (2): Anything of Value]

Fees may be shared between settlement service providers as long as they are paid in direct proportion to a service actually provided. Such fees are deemed to have been legitimately earned. Fees paid merely for a referral are considered to be unearned and are illegal.

(a) **Payments not constituting an illegal kickback**: The following payments are permissible in connection with a qualifying loan without constituting a RESPA violation. In other words, they do not fall under the illegal kickback or unearned fee restrictions.

   i) Payments to an attorney for services rendered.

   ii) Lender paid fees to employees and agents for loan origination, processing, or funding services.

   iii) Fees paid by a title company to its agents for services performed in issuing a title policy.

   iv) Real estate brokers may (1) make payments pursuant to compensation and cooperation arrangements with other participants in a Multiple Listing Service, (2) pay standard real estate referral fees to other brokers for referring brokerage business, and (3) pay commissions to their affiliated licensees. Such payments do have to comply with other real estate license law and rule provisions.

   v) A settlement service provider can pay for normal promotional and educational activities that are not conditioned on the referral of business. As examples, (1) a title insurance company could sponsor a real estate company's education offering at which it advertises its title services; (2) a representative from a lending institution could take a real estate broker out to dinner to discuss using the lender's loan programs; or (3) a hazard insurance company could purchase an advertisement on a real estate agent's website.

   Any such expense must be commensurate with the reasonable cost of the good or service provided to the real estate licensee. This means that a lender, for example, could not offset a real estate broker's ordinary cost of doing business as a "thank you" for referring business. Compare these permissible examples to the ones in the section that follows.

[Handwritten margin note: Referral fee's between agents OK]

(b) **Impermissible payment examples**: The following examples would likely constitute a RESPA violation as either an illegal kickback or an unearned fee. Notice how the payment exceeds the market value of the good or service. Each example is followed by a permissible expense in parentheses.

Example 1: A mortgage lender hires and pays for an expensive speaker to conduct a company-wide program for a large real estate brokerage operation. The lender also purchases an expensive lunch. The licensees can participate for free. The lender does not attend the program to advertise his services during breaks or provide promotional materials for distribution to students. (The lender might be able to sponsor a reasonable portion of the cost in exchange for the opportunity to personally advertise his services on breaks and after class without violating RESPA. Also, no RESPA violation occurs when a broker pays for the entire class for his own affiliated licensees.)

Example 2: A title company signs a long-term lease on an expensive color copy machine and has it delivered to a client-broker's office for general use by the real estate licensees. Title company representatives are rarely in the office to use the copier. (A title company with a satellite office located in a broker's branch office could share the expense of a reasonably-priced copier. The payments must be in direct proportion to the actual use of the copier by its title officers when they are in the broker's office.)

Example 3: A real estate attorney pays the entire cost of a joint advertising campaign that features his legal services along with those of the client-broker. The attorney does this to encourage the broker's licensees to send referrals to his law firm. (The attorney could pay for his portion of the joint advertising campaign, however.)

Example 4: A lender hires a technology expert to develop a dynamic new website for a broker who routinely refers business to the lender. The lender pays the entire $7,500 cost for the website's development. The lender includes a link to its website on the broker's new site. (Providing the broker paid for his own website development, the lender could pay the broker a reasonable pay-per-click advertising fee for the advertising link.)

(3) **Computer Loan Origination services (CLO)**: A Computer Loan Origination service is an online service that assists consumers in finding a lender, selecting a mortgage product, originating a mortgage, or choosing among other settlement service providers and products. A CLO allows a real estate broker to access information relating to available mortgage loans from remote locations such as the broker's office. Some sophisticated CLO programs also allow the broker to pre-qualify the borrower, take the loan application, and transmit the information to the lender for processing.

(a) **Payment for services**: RESPA does not prohibit any payment by a borrower for CLO services as long as the fee is reported on the Good Faith Estimate and the HUD-1. If the payment for CLO services is made by another settlement service provider, the payment must bear a reasonable relationship to actual services provided by the CLO. This is nearly identical to the referral fee and kickback limitations described earlier in this section.

(b) **Practical reality**: With the passage of the Secure and Fair Enforcement for Mortgage Licensing Act (S.A.F.E. Act) of 2008 by Congress, and Michigan's subsequent passage of the Mortgage Loan Originator Licensing Act in 2009, any form of loan origination, computerized or otherwise, must be handled by a person who holds a state-issued loan originators license (or falls within one of the exemptions). These Acts are explained in Chapter 17. Many websites operate for the sole purpose of offering paid advertisements for lenders and mortgage brokers, but these Internet-based companies cannot and do not originate loans.

3. **Disclosures required at the closing**.

   a. **Form HUD-1 Settlement Statement**: In the case of a non-TRID transaction, a final copy of a fully-completed HUD-1 Settlement Statement must be provided at or before the closing that shows the actual charges assessed each party. The form is generally completed by the person or entity who prepares the settlement package and conducts the actual settlement. In cases where there is no settlement meeting, the HUD-1 is mailed to the consumer. For loans covered by the TRID Rule, this information is incorporated in the Closing Disclosure form.

   b. ▶ **Escrow Account Operation and Disclosures**: A lender typically requires a borrower [Buyers] to establish an escrow account into which future taxes and insurance premiums will be paid during the term of the loan. This protects the lender in the event the borrower defaults on the mortgage payments. The foreclosure process can take a year or so to complete during which property taxes and insurance premiums still have to be paid. The escrow is designed to ensure that sufficient funds will be available for the lender to continue making these payments.

At the settlement, or within the next 45 days, the person servicing the loan must give the borrower an initial escrow account statement. It shows (1) all payments that are expected to be deposited into the escrow account, and (2) all of the disbursements which are expected to be made from the escrow account during the year ahead. This may also be referred to as the Initial Escrow Statement.

4. **Disclosures required after the closing:**.

   a. **Annual Escrow Loan Statement**: The Annual Escrow Loan Statement summarizes all escrow account deposits and payments made during the past year (also known as servicer's twelve month computation year). It also places the borrower on notice if there are any surpluses or shortages and how they can be refunded or paid.

   b. **Servicing Transfer Statement**: A Servicing Transfer Statement is required if the loan servicing rights are sold or assigned to a new loan servicer. The loan servicer must notify the borrower 15 days before the effective date of the loan transfer. The notice must also include the name and address of the new servicer, any toll-free telephone numbers, and the date the new servicer will begin accepting payments.

5. **Other consumer protections**.

   a. **Seller-required title insurance**: The seller of a property is prohibited from requiring a buyer to use a particular title insurance company. The buyer may sue a seller who violates this provision. Accordingly, a listing salesperson should not counsel his seller-client to reject an offer by a buyer who does not agree to use the title insurance company owned by the listing salesperson's broker. The listing salesperson can suggest that the seller use the broker's title company and schedule a split closing if the buyer wishes to use a different title company for the mortgagee's policy. The seller could offer to pay for the mortgagee's title policy, and if the buyer agrees, the seller can use the title company of his choice.

   b. **Limitations on advance escrow deposits**: A lender may not require a borrower to excessively pad his escrow account. Only 1/12th of the total estimated mortgage principal, interest, taxes, and insurance can be required as an advance monthly escrow (in addition to a small cushion not to exceed 1/6th of the estimated total annual payments from the account). If the purchase involves a condominium, for example, the lender may also require the monthly condominium association/maintenance fees be escrowed as well.

C. **Remedies and penalties**: By statute, RESPA provides for remedies as well as penalties in the event of a violation.

   1. **Qualified Written Request (QWR)**: A consumer can initiate a complaint action against his loan servicer by initiating what RESPA refers to as a Qualified Written Request process, or QWR for short. A QWR consists of a form letter sent by the borrower to the customer service department of the lender setting forth the borrower's concerns. The servicer has 5 days to acknowledge the QWR and 30 days to respond. The response time can be extended an additional 15 days upon giving the borrower proper notice.

   2. **Penalties**: A lender who violates RESPA provisions may face stiff penalties of up to $10,000 and/or one year in prison. Violators of the provisions relating to kickbacks, referral fees, and unearned fees are subject to criminal and civil penalties. In a criminal case, a settlement service provider may be fined up to $10,000 and imprisoned for up to one year.

   In a private lawsuit filed within one year, a settlement service provider who violates the provisions relating to kickbacks, referral fees, and unearned fees may be liable for an amount equal to three times the amount of the charge paid for the service. The tripling of damages is known as treble damages. HUD, a State Attorney General, or State insurance commissioner may bring an injunctive action to enforce RESPA violations within 3 years. Other damage provisions exist for a settlement service provider who fails to properly respond to a valid Qualified Written Request.

*Life is a series of challenges and you have two choices . . .
get ahead or get a helmet.*

DIAGNOSTIC PRACTICE QUESTIONS – CHAPTER 9

IMPORTANT STUDY TIP!

Step 1: Carefully review the information located in this chapter.

Step 2: Take the following Diagnostic Practice Questions. Review any question you answered incorrectly by researching the topic in this textbook. If you are still uncertain as to why the question is answered as it is, consult your program provider.

NOTE ON CHAPTER PRACTICE QUESTIONS

The following questions are representative of the type encountered on the Michigan real estate licensing examination. While some of these questions may be similar in nature and style, there is no way of predicting the exact wording of a question that will appear on the exam. Spending time memorizing these questions is, therefore, not recommended.

These questions are designed to help you determine how well you comprehend the material in this chapter. They are also intended to help you develop problem solving skills and to become comfortable with question formats.

Do not attempt to answer these questions until you have attended the lecture corresponding to this chapter and spent the appropriate time studying the material.

1. The process whereby a real estate transaction is concluded with the seller conveying title and the buyer paying for the property is generally referred to as which of the following?
    A. Informal conference.
    B. Mediation.
    C. Escrow.
    D. Settlement.

2. Which of the following persons would NOT likely be called upon to prepare a closing statement for a residential real estate transaction?
    A. The lending institution representative.
    B. The attorney acting on behalf of the seller.
    C. The listing broker.
    D. The title insurance company.

3. Broker Able of ABC Realty has a listing. Broker Xavier of XYZ Realty is working with a buyer who makes a full price and terms offer to purchase the listing. In preparation for the closing, which of the following is NOT a function that broker ABLE would be called upon to perform?
    A. Check for any city certification requirements that might apply to the listed property.
    B. Place the order for the title insurance commitment.
    C. Order the mortgage payoff letter.
    D. Assist the purchaser in selecting a suitable lender and applying for the loan.

4. Lori, a listing broker is preparing a settlement statement on behalf of her client, the seller. The closing is scheduled for January 15 and the quarterly water bill (for the first three months of the year) is paid in arrears and due April 1. Which of the following statements most correctly reflects how it should be treated on the closing statement?
    A. The purchaser is entitled to a credit of ½ month from the seller.
    B. The seller must prepay the bill prior to the closing and seek a credit for 30 days' estimated use.
    C. The seller is entitled to a credit of 2½ months from the buyer.
    D. As a municipal service, water bills are handled privately and not included on the closing statement.

5. A purchaser of a property makes a loan application at Benevolent Bank. Since the bank refers its customers to Artesian Appraisal Company, the purchaser is recommended by Benevolent's loan officer to call his friend at Artesian Appraisal. Which of the following statements is true regarding the referral to Artesian Appraisal?
    A. Benevolent Bank can collect an undisclosed referral fee from Artesian Appraisal providing the amount does not exceed a $25.00 threshold.
    B. Designated settlement service providers must file for a solicitor's license with the state before making such a referral.
    C. Benevolent Bank can only make a recommendation that the purchaser contact Artesian Ap-

praisal, but cannot require that he go there for appraisal services.
D. Benevolent Bank may make the recommendation without further disclosure requirements.

6. Amir is a licensed salesperson working as a buyer's representative. The buyer-client is nervous about the home inspection and asks Amir to attend. Which of the following statements is most accurate?
   A. Amir should conduct a thorough search of the property as a back-up in case the inspector missed anything.
   B. Amir may attend for purposes of providing access to the property, but should not participate.
   C. Amir may meet the buyer-client at the property, but may not enter the premises with the buyer and inspector.
   D. Amir may not attend the inspection under any circumstances.

7. Common purchaser credits on a closing statement include all of the following EXCEPT:
   A. The listing broker's commission.
   B. A water bill if it is assessed in arrears.
   C. An earnest money deposit.
   D. A tenant's security deposit in the case of a sale subject to an existing lease.

8. The property taxes on a seller's property are billed on January 1 and are due in advance. If the property is sold on October 15, which of the following statements is true regarding the property taxes?
   A. The seller will be credited 9 months, 14 days.
   B. The actual proration period is 2 months, 17 days.
   C. The taxes are due in arrears.
   D. Property taxes are exempt due to the principal residence exemption.

9. Something of value deposited with a disinterested person by whom it is to be delivered to the promisee on fulfillment of some condition is called:
   A. a covenant.
   B. a deed of trust.
   C. a bond.
   D. an escrow.

10. A lien can be placed on a property and subsequently foreclosed for failing to pay all EXCEPT which of the following items:
    A. A property tax.
    B. A water bill.
    C. A special assessment.
    D. A natural gas bill.

11. Under RESPA, which of the following items cannot be required:
    A. Mandatory delivery of the booklet titled "Settlement Costs and You."
    B. Mandatory Use of the HUD Form 1 closing statement.
    C. Mandatory use of certain settlement service providers
    D. Mandatory providing of good-faith estimates and anticipated closing costs.

12. RESPA regulations apply to all EXCEPT which of the following types of mortgage loans:
    A. Loans insured by the Federal Housing Administration.
    B. Loans issued by lenders associated with the Federal Deposit Insurance Corporation.
    C. Loans designed to be purchased by the Federal Home Loan Mortgage Corporation.
    D. Loans originated by a federally-related lender for apartment buildings.

13. A seller purchased a two-year hazard insurance policy for $800 on May 20, 2014. If the property is sold and the closing takes place on June 5, 2015, approximately how much must the buyer credit the seller when prorating on a calendar year basis?
    A. $383
    B. $427
    C. $417
    D. $361

14. All EXCEPT which of the following documents would a buyer or seller be likely to encounter at a real estate closing:
    A. HUD-1 settlement statement.
    B. A deed.
    C. Seller's past utility bills.
    D. A purchase agreement.

15. An escrow agent acts on behalf of whom?
    A. The buyer only providing a buyer's agent has been hired.
    B. The seller only regardless of circumstances.
    C. The lender only if the transaction is federally-related.
    D. All parties to the transaction.

16. RESPA covers which of the following:
    A. Construction loans.
    B. All residential real estate loans.
    C. Federally-related mortgage loans.
    D. Loans by state-chartered lenders.

Chapter 10
Legal Descriptions

Determining and describing the exact location of property.

I. **Foreword**: Nearly every contract or document that involves real property includes a reference to a specific parcel or parcels of land. The word parcel refers to a lot or plot of land; typically one that is created by subdividing a larger plot. According to the doctrine of heterogeneity (discussed in Chapter 1), no two parcels of real estate are identical. With so many contracts referencing so many different properties, there is a critical need for precise and accurate legal descriptions. It is important to be able to legally describe, locate, and identify one parcel from another. This chapter covers legal descriptions and how they are determined.

   A. ▶ **Survey**: A survey, or boundary survey as it may be called, is the most accurate way to define and describe the precise boundaries of a parcel of real property. It involves a process of measuring land by ascertaining its boundaries, directions, corners, and dimensions. The object is to formally establish the extent of a property's perimeter. The locations of existing improvements such as buildings and other structures, easements, setbacks, and encroachments are indicated along with the boundaries.

      The word survey can be used either as a noun (when referring to the actual survey report) or a verb (when referring to the process of measuring and describing the boundaries). A survey should not be confused with a property inspection. A property inspection is limited to an examination and reporting of the physical condition of any structures that are located on land. There are several types of surveys depending on the need of the person hiring the surveyor.

      1. **Types of survey**: When an individual thinks of a survey, it is usually a boundary survey (as described in the previous section). A boundary survey may also be referred to as a lot survey or stake survey.

          a. **ALTA survey**: An ALTA survey is a property or boundary survey that has been prepared and certified that it is in compliance with strict standards adopted by the American Land Title Association and the American Congress on Surveying and Mapping. Many title companies and lenders will require an ALTA survey before issuing a policy or a loan on a commercial building. Since an ALTA survey can be expensive and time-consuming to complete, they are required mostly on commercial properties.

          b. **Mortgage survey**: When a property is purchased using financing, the lender will require that a mortgage survey be conducted. As discussed in Chapter 16, a buyer-borrower who obtains a loan will be required to give the lender a lien on the property as security against default. A mortgage survey is a simplified or more basic version of a full boundary survey. It verifies the borders and structures located on the property for the lender and indicates if the property is affected by any encroachments. It does not, however, estimate the value of the property which is the function of a licensed appraiser.

      2. **Surveyor**: A surveyor is a person who undertakes the process of surveying properties using the special equipment necessary to take exact measurements. Professional surveyors must be proficient in complex mathematical principles, physical sciences, and techniques of measuring acquired by professional education and practical experience. They must also have a thorough command of property law and know how to use modern tools including electronic distance measurement stations, digital levels, and global positioning systems. A person who holds himself out as a professional surveyor must be licensed in Michigan.

II. ▶ **Legal description defined**: A formal and fully detailed legal description is no longer a legal requirement in contracts and conveying instruments. Instead, all that is needed is a description which is deemed to be legally sufficient. The Statute of Frauds, which governs the enforceability of certain contracts such as those that transfer an interest in land, requires that a legally sufficient description be included (see Chapter 12 for further details on the Statute of Frauds). This chapter explores some of the historical and current methods used to formally describe property.

A. **Sufficient legal description**: A legally sufficient description is one in which enough information is provided to enable a competent person such as a surveyor or civil engineer to locate and identify the land with certainty. All legal documents that sell, transfer, or otherwise affect an interest in land must contain at least a legally sufficient description of the property.

B. **Street address**: A street address is nearly always used in conjunction with a more formal method of property description. Street address is also referred to the common address. By itself, a street address is not a legal description or even one that is legally sufficient for purposes of conveying property.

III. ▶ **Specific property description methods and their usage**: The description methods covered in this section include Metes and Bounds, Monuments, U.S. Government Survey System, Lot and Block, and Sidwell Numbers. Each method has its own benefits and limitations.

A. **Metes and bounds**: Metes and bounds is an accurate method of describing property. It specifies the precise measurements, directions, and shape of the lot boundaries. The process involves measuring boundaries from a known point of beginning using distances and directions. It is one of the first systems used in this country dating back to the original Thirteen Colonies. It was brought here from England. See Figure 24.

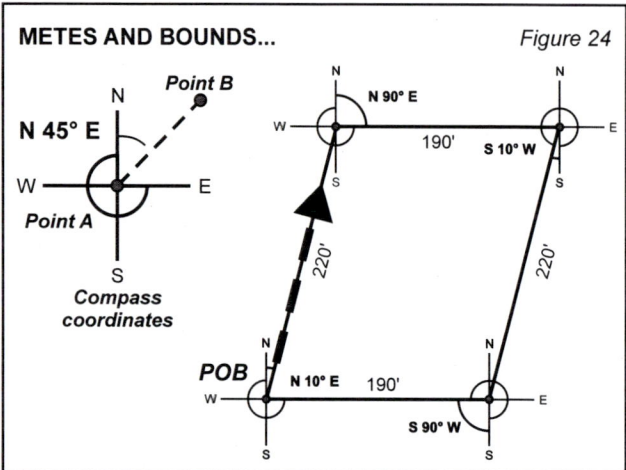

1. **Used when precision is needed**: While metes and bounds is a common method for describing property, it is particularly appropriate where precision is desired such as in subdivided areas with smaller lots as well as lots that are irregularly-shaped.

2. **Point of beginning (POB)**: The POB is the starting point from which the entire property boundary is traced. The tracing process must be conducted with a degree of accuracy that brings the surveyor back to a point that completely encloses the lot. The POB is typically referenced by a monument or benchmark.

    a. **Monument**: A monument is any natural or artificial object that contains a physical mark or indication of location. Monuments are sometimes used to signify the lines and boundaries of a survey. For example, trees, large boulders, water boundaries, wooden stakes, pipes, fences, and even rock piles have been historically used as monuments.

    b. **Property pins as monuments**: Property pins are often used to mark the corners of a property that is being surveyed. A property pin may consist of a two-to-three foot long piece of steel rebar with a diameter of approximately 1/2 inch. The surveyor drives the rebar into the ground at the exact property corner and places a plastic cap on top that may contain customized information. These steel bars can be easily located at some future date by using a metal detector. The term rebar comes from the fact that they are primarily used as reinforcing bars for concrete. A benchmark is another type of boundary marker.

    c. **Benchmark**: A benchmark is a specific point on land with a marked position that is known to a high degree of accuracy. In surveying, the benchmark is typically placed on a fixed object with an indication of the elevation of the topography along with other surveying information. The most common form of benchmark is a metal disk that a government surveyor embeds in the ground, often in the center of a concrete highway.

3. **Locating property with metes and bounds**: Once the monument, benchmark, or other point of beginning is located, the distance and direction are accurately measured to the nearest corner of the subject property. Refer again to *Figure 24*.

    a. **Compass coordinates**: A surveyor uses a compass to determine the direction of each boundary line and then moves from one corner to the next in either a clockwise or counter-clockwise direction.

    b. **Take readings from each corner**: The same steps used to determine bearing, meaning direction, and measurements are then repeated for each corner until the entire lot is fully enclosed by the description.

Chapter 10: Legal Descriptions 147

4. **Process overview**: To help understand how a metes and bounds description works, review the following steps. As you do this, refer to *Figure 24*.

    a. Visualize a compass superimposed over a selected corner of the parcel.

    b. Determine the precise direction to the next corner in terms of degrees on the compass.

    c. Measure the distance between the two corners in feet and inches.

    d. Repeat the process for each corner.

5. **Curved boundaries**: Curved boundaries can present a challenge for a metes and bounds description. When necessary, geometry principles and geometric terms are used to describe curves in a property description. Curved boundaries frequently appear when properties are located on a cul-de-sac.

    a. **Cul-de-sac**: A cul-de-sac is a street or other passageway with only one means of egress. It typically takes the form of a short street that ends in a dead end, court, or traffic turn-around.

B. **Monuments property description**: The monuments property description method is similar to metes and bounds with one significant difference. It relies nearly exclusively on monuments to mark the starting point and all boundaries rather than precise compass directions and measured distances (as would be accomplished using metes and bounds). A monuments description traces the lot's boundaries by referencing one monument to the next. As a result, all distances and directions are considered approximate. *See Figure 25*.

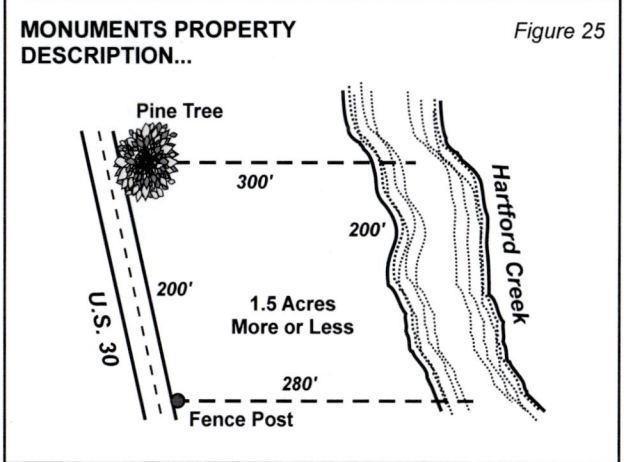

1. **Used in rural setting**: This relaxed property description method is more appropriate for use in large acreage, rural settings where precision is not essential. It is also common in older property descriptions. Many monuments descriptions date back 100 years or more.

2. **Practical problem**: Since monuments descriptions are generally older, the markers used as benchmarks tend to be less permanent. This may make them difficult, if not impossible, to locate today.

C. **U.S. Government survey system**: The U.S. Government Survey system is a property description method that dates back to 1785. The method was created as part of the Land Ordinance of 1785 when the Continental Congress decided to pay the American Revolution War debt by selling off the unmapped territory west of the original states. The method is based on an imaginary grid placed over the majority of what is now the United States (including Michigan). It is also historically known as the Rectangular Survey System.

Today, the U.S. Government Survey system is referred to as the Public Land Survey System or PLSS for short. Individual lots are referenced by their specific location within the grid. The key to understanding how this system works is found in learning what the various reference points and markers are called. As you learn about it, refer to *Figure 26*.

1. **Principal meridian and baseline**: The U.S. Government Survey System utilizes a principal meridian and a base line located within a state such as Michigan. A meridian is a north-south line such as a line of longitude. A base line is an east-west line such as a line of latitude.

    To remember which line runs north-south, think of the word "long" in longitude; for example, the word long implies a North-South direction. When is comes to latitude, think of the word "lay;" the word lay implies an east-west direction. A grid is created from the principal meridian and baseline. This grid forms a checkerboard-like pattern of perpendicular intersecting lines.

    a. **Range lines, township lines, and townships**: Range lines (running north-south) are located every 6 miles east and west of, and parallel to, the principal meridian. Township lines (running east-west) are located every 6 miles north and south of, and parallel to, the base line. The checkerboard pattern is formed as these range lines and township lines intersect with one another to form 6 mile-by-6 mile areas called townships.

b. **Location of specific range and township lines**: As seen in *Figure 26*, range and township lines are assigned numbers based on their proximity, meaning closeness, to the point where the principal meridian and base line intersect. For example, the township with numbered sections in the figure is located at R3E (meaning range 3 east), T2N (meaning township or tier 2 north). The order may be reversed with the Township line reference listed before the Range line reference.

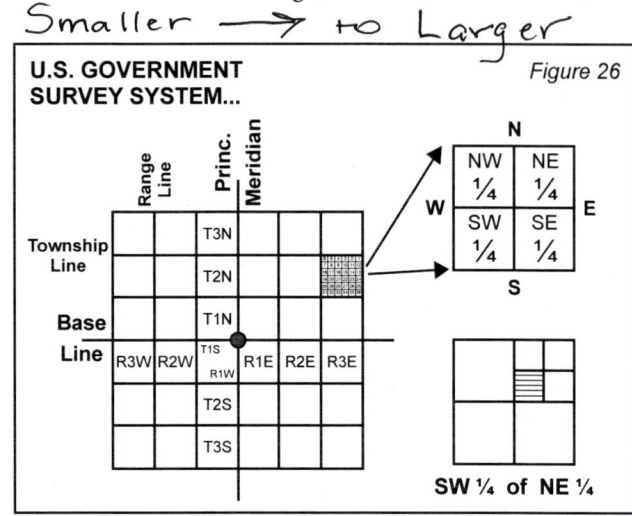

Figure 26

c. **Townships and sections**: By definition, a township is a measurement of land that is subdivided into 36 square miles. Each one square mile area is called a section. A section is, therefore, one mile on each side and contains 640 acres. You should memorize this number to answer any simple math question related to this method of property description. It is also important to note that there are 43,560 square feet in one acre of land.

  (1) **Fractional divisions**: A particular parcel of land can be located using the information learned so far. The parcel will typically be described as a fractional portion of a specific numbered section. As an illustration, a given parcel may be described as the North 1/2 of the Northwest 1/4 of the Northeast 1/4 of the Southeast 1/4 of Section 14.

  (2) **Reading and interpreting fractional divisions**: To determine the location and dimensions of a parcel, read the description from right to left. This begins with the largest division and works down to the final and smallest fractional portion.

  Returning to *Figure 26*, use the following directions to describe the shaded lot (located in the lower right corner of the figure):
  – Start with the location of Section 14 which is one square mile;
  – Locate the Northeast 1/4;
  – Within this quarter section, locate the Southwest 1/4.

  (3) **Calculating acreage**: Since a given fractional portion of a section is the same no matter where it is located within the section, the only consideration is the size of the portion. Continuing with the above example:
  – Delete the compass references to the Northeast 1/4 of the Southwest 1/4 of Section 14 so you only have the fractions; for example 1/4 × 1/4
  – Multiply the fractions 1/4 × 1/4 so you have 1/16 of a section (when multiplying fractions, first multiply the top numbers or numerators, then multiply the bottom numbers or denominators);
  – Divide as follows, 640 acres/section ÷ 16 = 40 acres.

2. **Plat maps/Plat books**: Plat books have been created by a number of different sources as part of the Public Land Survey System (i.e., the Government Survey System). They show county land ownership patterns and may be referred to as plat maps. It is important to note that plat maps are not considered to be legally accurate representations of ownership interests in land since they are based on the last deed recorded at the time the map was prepared.

A plat map must not be confused with a formally-prepared recorded subdivision plat pursuant to the Land Division Act of Michigan. A subdivision plat must be filed when qualifying acreage is subdivided. It must also contain accurate descriptions of all information on the plat. See Chapter 21 for further details.

D. **Lot and block**: The lot and block method of property description is convenient because it relies on, and makes reference to, a previously recorded subdivision plat. When a subdivision plat is recorded, a permanent record is created which is open to the public. Specific reference can then be made in a contract or deed to a particular lot within this plat. See *Figure 27*.

  1. **Plat**: A formal plat is a scaled down representation of a subdivision which is comparable to a subdivision "blueprint." When a tract of land is platted, it is divided into smaller parcels called lots. Each lot is assigned

Chapter 10: Legal Descriptions

a specific number. Plats also provide other information such as property boundaries (sometimes explained by way of rectangular survey or metes and bounds), easements, and streets or roads.

E. **Sidwell permanent parcel numbering system**: Sidwell numbers are commonly used in conjunction with individual property descriptions. A Sidwell number is also known as a parcel identification number or tax identification number. A county register of deeds may require that a Sidwell number be applied to a document, such as a deed, that is presented for recording. While Sidwell numbers are commonly found on real estate contracts, they must not be exclusively used as a substitute for a proper legal description.

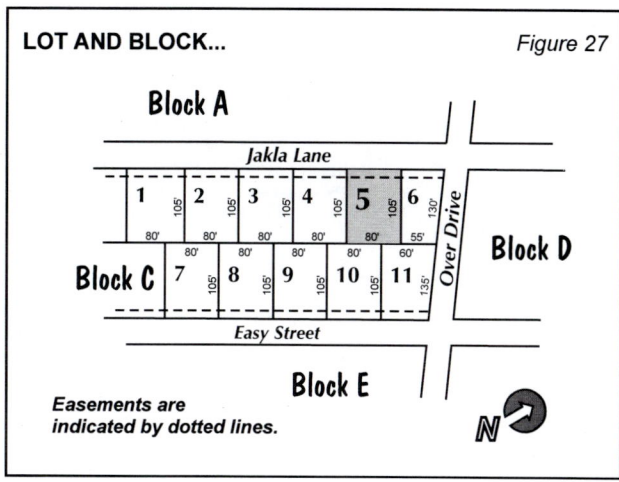

1. **History**: The Sidwell company was formed in 1927 as a mapping company. Sidwell maps have been used for years by multiple listing services and various local units of government to quickly identify lots within subdivided land.

2. **Sidwell number**: A Sidwell number is considered to be reliable because no two lots have exactly the same number. Sidwell numbers are used by municipalities to reference properties in the assessing and taxing process.

    a. **Components of a Sidwell number**: Assume for example that the Sidwell number for a specific parcel of real estate is 08-15-122-035. These numbers are broken into the following components.

    (1) **Township number–08**: Reading the Sidwell number from left-to-right, the first two digits represent the survey township number.

    (2) **Section number–15**: The next two digits represent the specific section number within which the parcel is located (see U.S. Government Survey System for information on the numbering system for sections).

    (3) **Block number–122**: The next three digits describe the quarter-section within which the lot is located (in the specific numbered section of the township). In urban areas with multiple blocks, the last two of the three digits refers to a specific block (see Lot and Block description).

    (4) **Parcel number–035**: The last three digits identify the specific parcel within the designated block.

Time is the only investment that provides no refunds. Spend it wisely.

DIAGNOSTIC PRACTICE QUESTIONS – CHAPTER 10

IMPORTANT STUDY TIP!

Step 1: Carefully review the information located in this chapter.

Step 2: Take the following Diagnostic Practice Questions. Review any question you answered incorrectly by researching the topic in this textbook. If you are still uncertain as to why the question is answered as it is, consult your program provider.

NOTE ON CHAPTER PRACTICE QUESTIONS

The following questions are representative of the type encountered on the Michigan real estate licensing examination. While some of these questions may be similar in nature and style, there is no way of predicting the exact wording of a question that will appear on the exam. Spending time memorizing these questions is, therefore, not recommended.

These questions are designed to help you determine how well you comprehend the material in this chapter. They are also intended to help you develop problem solving skills and to become comfortable with question formats.

Do not attempt to answer these questions until you have attended the lecture corresponding to this chapter and spent the appropriate time studying the material.

1. A survey is primarily used to determine all of the following characteristics EXCEPT:
   A. Boundary distances.
   B. Title defects.
   C. Perimeter dimensions.
   D. Building locations.

2. Which of the following types of property description utilizes a formal point of beginning or POB and precisely traces the boundary lines until the lot is actually enclosed?
   A. U.S. Government Survey System.
   B. Metes and Bounds System.
   C. Monuments Property Description.
   D. Lot and Block Method.

3. A specifically-numbered section of land will commonly be used as a key component of which of the following property description methods?
   A. Metes and Bounds System.
   B. Lot and Block Method.
   C. Monuments Property Description.
   D. U.S. Government Survey System.

4. Which of the following would typically NOT be referenced on a subdivision plat?
   A. An easement in gross.
   B. A county road.
   C. An encroachment.
   D. The boundary of a lot.

5. All of the following statements regarding townships is correct EXCEPT:
   A. 1 township = 640 acres
   B. 1 township = 6 miles square.
   C. 1 township = 36 square miles
   D. 1 township = 36 sections

6. A Sidwell number refers to:
   A. A type of appraisal technique used in FHA-financed properties.
   B. A well inspection certification number issued by a city inspector.
   C. A lot identification number frequently used in conjunction with legal descriptions.
   D. The number of allowable splits of a parent parcel under the Land Division Act.

7. Which of the following characteristics applies to a monuments property description:
   A. It avoids the use of items such as trees, stakes, and boulders to reference property lines due to their destructibility.
   B. Directions are traced from monument to monument until the lot is enclosed.
   C. It is best suited to properties located in densely-populated, urban settings.
   D. It is only available for rural properties consisting of 10 or more acres.

NOTE: Questions 8 through 10 refer to Section 5 of Beezer County as represented in the figure on the next page. Refer to this figure when answering these questions.

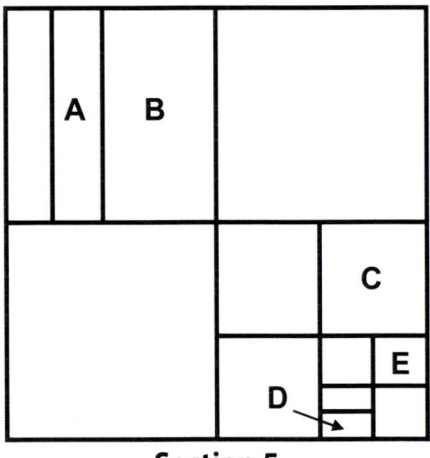

Section 5

8. The description of the lot designated as "C" would reads as follows:
   A. SE ¼ of NE ¼ of Section 5.
   B. NE ½ of SE ¼ of Section 5.
   C. NE ¼ of SE ¼ of Section 5.
   D. S ¼ of NE ¼ of Section 5.

9. How many acres are there in the lot represented as "B" in Section 5?
   A. 80 Acres.
   B. 40 Acres.
   C. 20 Acres.
   D. 10 Acres.

10. Which of the lots represented in Section 5 has the following property description: E ½ of W ½ of NW ¼.
    A. "C"
    B. "D"
    C. "A"
    D. "B"

11. The layout of an owner's lot is highly irregular with many different sides. Which type of property description method is the owner most likely to see on his survey?
    A. Lot and block method.
    B. Metes and bounds method.
    C. Monuments method.
    D. U.S. Government survey system.

12. A particular method of property description cites a subdivision map that references individual lots by number, including other identifying characteristics. A record of the map is then made with the register of deeds or county recorder's office. This method of description is most commonly known as the:
    A. Lot and block method.
    B. Metes and bounds method.
    C. Monuments method.
    D. U.S. Government survey system.

13. At a minimum, all legal documents involving the sale or transfer of an interest in land must contain which of the following:
    A. Common address.
    B. Legally sufficient description.
    C. Reference to a recorded plat.
    D. Metes and bounds description.

14. A perfectly square-shaped lot consisting of four sections equals which of the following:
    A. Four square miles.
    B. 320 acres.
    C. Four miles square.
    D. A township.

15. Broker Mateo tells a buyer interested in a residential property that the home is located in a cul-de-sac. This home is well-suited to the buyer if he is looking for what type of property:
    A. A property located on a street that is accessible from two different directions.
    B. A property that is subject to a high degree of automobile traffic.
    C. A property that is likely to have a higher degree of privacy.
    D. A property that is directly across from a commercially-zoned area.

16. The N 1/2 of NW 1/4 of SW 1/4 of a section contains how many acres?
    A. 10
    B. 20
    C. 30
    D. 40

Eminent Domain   5th Amendment

Chapter 11
Land Use Controls & Real Estate Development

How government affects private ownership.

I. **Foreword**: Michigan land use regulations are designed to assure the consistent development of land throughout all participating units of government from the local level up to the state. Other forms of land use controls regulate things such as population density, permissible land uses, and building restrictions. Land use controls emanate from the police power that every state has to pass or enact certain regulations.

   A. ▶ **Police power, ordinances, and municipal codes**: Police power is the right that each state has pursuant to the Tenth Amendment of U.S. Constitution to pass laws designed to promote the health, safety, and welfare of its citizens. This power is then delegated, meaning shared and entrusted, to local units of government such as counties and cities. Using this power, these smaller units of government are able to enact and enforce ordinances dealing with local concerns such as zoning, building codes, subdivision regulations, and administration of environmental concerns such as wetlands.

   An ordinance, by definition, is an order or decree that has the effect of law, but only within the borders of the issuing municipality such as a city. A municipal code is a body of such local ordinances passed by the municipality. By comparison, a law is a legislative decree that applies to the entire state without regard to municipal border. The term municipality refers to a political unit, such as a city, town, or village, that has been incorporated for purposes of local self-government.

   B. **Planning**: Municipal planning is the systematic and formal process of developing land within a local unit of government. The primary goal of planning is to determine and then set forth the best method for utilizing the land within the municipality. This is important due to the different number of land uses that may exist within a municipality. Planning considerations also take into consideration schools, transportation, utilities, recreation, and nuisance regulations.

   1. **Planning commission**: A planning commission or planning board is created for the purpose of making planning recommendations. Commission members are often appointed by the local unit of government and may also have authority over the approval of land uses proposed in site plans. A site plan is a detailed and graphic representation of how a building site is proposed to be developed. Prior to issuing a building permit, municipalities typically require the filing of a site plan for review by local officials.

   2. ▶ **Master plan**: The goals and recommendations made by the planning commission are eventually incorporated into a comprehensive plan called a master plan. Long-range population and economic prospects for the community are balanced against current housing, industry, and recreation needs. Once completed, police power devices such as zoning are used to put the master plan into effect and legally enforce it.

II. ▶ **Eminent domain**: Eminent domain is the power a state, municipality, or other authorized government entity has to take private property for public use. Since eminent domain is based on the Fifth Amendment of the U.S. Constitution, when private property is taken for public use, the owner must be paid a fair and just compensation. The Fifth Amendment dates back to 1791 and guarantees that no person shall be deprived of property without due process of law and that private property shall not be taken for public use without just compensation.

   If a municipality determines that private property must be acquired to fulfill a necessary government objective such as widening a main road, it will first conduct an appraisal and make a good faith, written offer to purchase the property for what it believes the fair market value to be. There is no guarantee, however, that the private property owner will agree to the amount of the offer or even the sale. Ultimately, the property can be forcibly taken through the process of condemnation.

Fair market value

A. ▶ **Condemnation**: Eminent domain is exercised through condemnation which is a legal proceeding used to obtain title to a subject property. In Michigan, condemnation is handled according to the requirements of the Michigan Uniform Condemnation Procedures Act and the Michigan Constitution.

   1. **Calculating just compensation**: The owner is legally entitled to the fair market value of the property as of the date of the taking. Both the government and the owner will present evidence and expert appraiser witnesses to testify as to what they believe the fair market value to be. The jury ultimately decides the exact amount of compensation. In cases where only part of a property is taken, the value of the remaining property may actually be enhanced; for example, a strip of a commercially-zoned property is taken to widen a road which causes an increase in the volume of commercial traffic brought to the area.

B. **Public use versus public benefit**: In the 1980s, the "public use" aspect of eminent domain was broadly interpreted by the federal courts to allow municipalities to take private property and then transfer it to private groups and corporations who promised to redevelop the area thereby creating a "public benefit." This represented an attempt to force the sale of private property to advance economic development in partnership with private enterprise.

   1. **Michigan Supreme Court case–a historical view**: In 2004, the Michigan Supreme Court limited this wider interpretation. The case outlined three instances or tests in which condemnation actions involving the taking of private property for public use would be permissible. They included: (1) Public necessity, (2) Accountability to the public, and (3) Public concern. According to this new interpretation, property could only be taken as follows.

      a. When the transfer involved a public necessity; for example, construction of a highway project.

      b. When the property was being condemned for a private party who remained accountable to the public in its use; for example, construction of an oil pipeline which is regulated by the state.

      c. When the property was taken to serve a public concern such as condemnation of blighted property for urban renewal by private developers.

   2. **Amendment to the Michigan Constitution–current law**: In 2006, state voters amended the Michigan Constitution and the Michigan legislature passed additional legislation to further clarify the conditions under which the government can currently exercise eminent domain. They include the following:

      a. The government may not take private property and transfer it to a private individual or business exclusively for economic development or increasing tax revenue.

      b. When private property is taken for public use, the individual must be paid at least 125% of the property's fair market value.

      c. When property is transferred to a private individual or business, it must involve an extreme public necessity, public accountability, or public concern (see previous section for examples).

      d. If the private property is taken due to concern over blight, the government is held to a higher standard of proof to demonstrate that the taking constitutes a public use.

C. **Inverse condemnation**: When a land use regulation negatively impacts a property's use or value, the owner may claim that the regulation amounts to a taking thereby entitling him to just compensation. The taking in such case is said to be indirect or the inverse of a direct condemnation action. For example, a wetlands ordinance prohibits any building on 95% of a large lot purchased by a developer. The owner offers to purchase additional adjacent acreage for purposes of relocating the wetland, but the municipality denies the request. The owner brings a legal action arguing that the regulation is so restrictive that he is denied any reasonable use of his property.

This example also points out why buyers of vacant land should exercise an appropriate level of pre-purchase due diligence to determine if the intended use of a property will be permitted. The buyer can hire an attorney who understands the land development process to draft an offer to purchase with a comprehensive developer's contingency clause. The concept of purchaser due diligence and feasibility will be explored further in connection with zoning and subdividing.

III. ▶ **Zoning**.

   A. **Zoning defined**: As a police power device, zoning is a process that involves the division of a local municipality (such as a city or town) into districts or zones where the actual use of the land is regulated by ordinance. Along with use regulations, zoning can prescribe things such as minimum lot and building sizes, building height,

Chapter 11: Land Use Controls & Real Estate Development

noise level, construction of billboards, and the right to house certain animals. As long as the zone is reasonable and non-discriminatory, meaning non-exclusionary, it will generally be enforceable. Zoning is the most common form of land use regulation. Local units of government often use zoning to regulate wetlands in a manner consistent with state and federal laws (as discussed later in this chapter).

1. **Use zoning**: Under use zoning, a municipality is divided into categories such as (1) residential, (2) commercial, (3) industrial, and (4) agricultural. Any one of these districts may be further divided into subcategories such as light and heavy industrial. Subcategories are common in density zoning.

2. **Density zoning**: Density zoning consists of common restrictions that primarily regulate the number of dwellings that may be constructed per acre or minimum lot sizes per dwelling. These regulations are designed to maintain a uniform and attractive appearance of properties within a municipality. For example, a city creates a residential use zone to control density and further divides it into three subcategories: (1) Detached, single family dwellings; (2) One-to-four-unit residential structures; and (3) Apartment dwellings.

3. **Setback requirements**: A setback requirement is a common ordinance that regulates how closely a building can be located to the front or side lot lines, for example. Setbacks provide for safety, fire alleys, proper drainage, an unimpeded access to utilities, and uniform neighborhood appearance. For example, one side yard setback establishes that no dwelling can be closer than 4 feet to a side property line. It further requires a combined distance of 14 feet between two dwellings. So, if one house is 4 feet from the side boundary, the neighboring property can be no closer than 10 feet (which creates 14 feet of distance).

   It is possible for a building to be constructed within the boundaries of a property, but still be deemed an encroachment. This occurs if a portion of a building such as an eave (i.e., the outer edge of the roof) extends beyond the setback. A setback may also be referred to as a building line.

4. **Buffer zone**: A master plan may call for buffer zones. A buffer zone is a designated district or area that separates two other districts with more widely differing zones. The intent is to make the two inconsistent uses blend more easily with one another. Examples: (1) A recreational park is developed to separate a residential district from a commercial district; and (2) A shopping district is established between a residential district and a manufacturing district. *"green space"*

5. **Exclusionary zoning**: An exclusionary zone is any restriction or regulation that makes it difficult for certain social or low-income groups to locate within a community. If no legitimate justification can be advanced by the municipality for a particular zoning ordinance, it can be struck down by a court as exclusionary, and therefore, illegal. For example, no government ordinance may be imposed specifically to exclude mobile home developments. Other zoning ordinances that completely exclude low-income housing from being developed have also been successfully challenged. *[not allowed]*

6. **Airport zoning**: Local zoning departments in Michigan are responsible for implementing airport zoning pursuant to the Airport Zoning Act of 1950. Airport zoning has the same force and effect as more traditional zoning tools. This special zoning typically controls the area surrounding an airport for up to 10 miles and overlaps or overlays other zoning ordinances. The use of property located in the vicinity of local airports, along with the height of structures and natural objects, are restricted. The objective is to prevent the establishment of airport hazards, and to provide for the safety of airport users and individuals who live and work in the area.

B. **Zoning administration**: In 2006, the Michigan Zoning Enabling Act was enacted to transfer common powers and responsibilities to local units of government, e.g., county, township and city/village, for the purpose of zoning land. Having uniform provisions and hearings procedures helps to lower zoning administration costs to government and businesses alike.

   1. **Permitted use variations**: Whenever the government regulates how private citizens can use their property, certain unintended hardships can result. For example, a new zoning ordinance could affect properties that were in existence prior to the imposition of the zone. Special treatment of these nonconforming uses can be provided through variances, special use permits, and in some jurisdictions, spot zoning.

      a. **Nonconforming use**: A land use that was in existence before implementation of a zoning change, and which does not conform to the new zone, is called a nonconforming use. It operates like a type of "grandfather" provision. Such pre-existing uses are technically a violation of the new ordinance. Providing the prior use was valid to start with, the owner may be able to continue with the nonconforming use. Zoning principles are designed to create uniformity within geographic areas. Nevertheless, principles of individual fairness also come into play when a municipality grants permission to the owner to retain the nonconforming use.

b. **Variance**: By definition, a variance is a form of permission [*an exemption*] that an owner seeks to use a property in a way that varies from an existing zone. A variance may also be sought for dimensional or use deviations without there having been any pre-existing, nonconforming use. The party requesting the variance must show that there is a unique and localized physical hardship that can only be overcome by varying how the zoning ordinance is applied to the individual's property, and that the variance will still be consistent with the existing zone.

Since a variance is not granted to a particular owner, it runs with the land and passes with ownership unless the new owner intends to make any substantial changes to the use. Once a variance is granted, it is administered similarly to a nonconforming use.

c. **Special use permits**: Most ordinances list certain uses that are excepted from local zoning requirements such as hospitals, churches, private schools, and clubs. The planning commission understands that these beneficial uses will be needed so they are actually regulated in advance through a zoning ordinance that allows for a case-by-case application.

(1) **Based on public benefit rather than hardship**: A special use permit is issued on the basis of a public benefit analysis whereas a variance is decided as a matter of individual hardship. State-licensed family day care homes and group day care homes have been ruled proper residential uses that are entitled to special use permits.

d. **Spot zoning**: A spot zone is a specific change in the zoning of a small area to a use that is inconsistent with the master plan for the region. Since a spot zone change generally benefits only one or very few properties and their owners, it is disfavored in many jurisdictions. Contrary to popular belief, spot zoning is not in and of itself illegal in Michigan. Instead, the practice is closely scrutinized by Michigan courts to make sure that the basis for the separately-zoned area was pursuant to a master plan and not done so arbitrarily.

2. **Zoning challenges–Zoning Board of Appeals**: Authority for handling zoning challenges rests with the local Zoning Board of Appeals or ZBA. The ZBA also hears requests for changes due to building permits, variances, and special use permits. With regard to the constitutional validity of a zoning ordinance, a court will ask questions such as: (1) Is the zoning classification reasonable? (2) Does it bear a relationship to public health, safety, and welfare?, and (3) Does it exclude otherwise legitimate uses of an owner's land?

3. **Purchase of development property subject to zoning change**: There are times when a developer-buyer may be interested in purchasing a property, but only if he can obtain some form of zoning change, special permit, or approval from the municipality. Depending on what the buyer is seeking, the process can take up to several months and the outcome is not guaranteed. Seeking municipal approval often requires the buyer to obtain numerous impact studies. In addition to the investment of time, the process can be expensive. As a result, the buyer should make his offer contingent (meaning conditional) on the approval.

a. **Option agreement**: From the seller's perspective, he may not want to tie the property to such a long contingency period only to learn the prospective buyer cannot obtain the approval. To balance these concerns, the parties can enter into an option-style agreement. The buyer will have the time he needs to seek the approvals without having to obligate himself to a purchase if his request is ultimately denied. For the option to be enforceable, the buyer must pay valuable consideration to the seller. This compensates the seller for the time the property is off the market.

b. **Recommend legal counsel**: Development-based options tend to be highly complex agreements, with multiple contingencies. Therefore, a real estate license should make sure that his client or customer seeks the assistance of legal counsel when drafting or accepting such an offer. From the seller's perspective, he may wish to condition his acceptance of an option on receiving copies of all impact studies paid for by the buyer. See Chapter 12 for further discussion of option agreements and contract law.

C. **Modern zoning techniques**: Various zoning devices have been created to grant developers more flexibility in how they arrange land uses within a municipality. These techniques include cluster zoning, planned unit developments, and contract zoning.

1. **Cluster zoning**: Lots within a traditional zoning scheme are generally subject to minimum size restrictions. In cluster zoning, the size of lots and required frontage can be reduced if the overall density of the development does not exceed the master plan. The homes are actually clustered instead of being uniformly spread

Chapter 11: Land Use Controls & Real Estate Development

out, thus leaving more area available for recreation areas, parks, and schools. Michigan requires municipalities to include open space preservation provisions such as cluster zoning in their zoning ordinances.

2. **Planned unit development (PUD)**: A planned unit development is a flexible development and regulatory device that permits a developer to meet overall density and land use goals without being bound by strictly-enforced zoning requirements. It is typically applied at the time a project is approved and consists of a mixed-use plan of commercial, industrial, and residential uses, for example. It is similar to a cluster zone, but differs in that multiple uses are incorporated into the PUD. This zoning technique helps developers to lower costs for consumers and ultimately lower maintenance costs for the municipality.

   One type of PUD might involve specific parcels of property that are zoned for planned unit development. Another type could involve a floating PUD zone that can be located on particular parcels at the request of the property owners. A floating PUD operates like an overlay district which does not appear on the zoning map until the application is actually approved.

3. **Contract zoning**: Contract zoning involves an agreement by a municipality to grant a zoning request on condition that the developer or property owner agrees to do certain things like dedicate some of the property back to the municipality or protect the environment in some specific way. This "contract" between the government and the property owner is legal in Michigan as long as the required conditions are reasonable.

IV. **Regulations that affect new and existing structures**: There are a number of municipal regulations that can affect new construction as well as the structural remodeling of existing structures. For example, before an owner commences a new building project or substantial remodeling, one or more permits will be required by the local building department. New construction may also trigger the need for a sewage disposal permit. Other similar regulations can be enforced against existing properties such as resale inspections (including well and septic), rental property registrations, and vacant property registrations.

   A. ▶ **Building code**: A building code is a form of land use control that establishes standards for new construction and remodeling. These codes are designed to protect the public by making sure that minimum safe standards for design, construction, and materials are met. Other building codes may be imposed to regulate use, occupancy, or appearance. Code standards also exist for electrical, mechanical, i.e., heating and air conditioning, plumbing, and energy efficiency. Building codes are also referred to as construction codes.

   1. **State-wide in nature**: The 2009 Michigan Residential Code establishes state-wide standards for new residential construction. It is enforced on a municipal level by local building code officials. The officials review all building plans and then inspect the project during various stages of the construction process.

   2. **Building permit**: Before a building or remodeling project can commence, an owner or his builder must apply for (also called "pulling") a permit with the local building department. A number of different inspections are generally required to make certain that the builder follows all applicable construction codes. The permit puts the municipality on notice of the project. Failure to obtain the necessary permits can result in financial penalties and a cease and desist order issued on any further construction. It is also important to check the property deed, master deed, and/or subdivision regulations for any other restrictions pertaining to construction or remodeling.

   3. **Certificate of use and occupancy (C of O)**: Upon final inspection of the project, and prior to the owner actually occupying it (meaning taking possession), a certificate of use and occupancy or C of O must be issued. It confirms that all construction was performed in accordance with the building permit, building codes, and other applicable ordinances.

   4. **Fire safety in residential construction**: The Construction Code Act and Housing Law of Michigan were amended in 2004 to include requirements pertaining to fire safety and the installation of smoke detectors in both single- and multiple-family dwellings.

   B. **Sewage disposal permits**: If the lot upon which an owner seeks to construct a new residential dwelling is not connected to the municipal sewer system, a septic system is required. It is an efficient, self-contained, underground waste water treatment system designed to dispose of household waste. The two major components of a septic system include a holding tank and a drain field. Before a septic system can be designed, a percolation test must be conducted on the site. A sewage disposal permit issued by the county health department is also required.

   1. **Percolation test**: A percolation test is used to determine if a sufficient depth of drainable soil exists to absorb the liquid from a septic system. It involves digging a hole, usually with an excavating device such as a backhoe, to a depth where ground water is present. A percolation test is also known as perk test or

perc test. If a perk test reveals a high water table, for example, special foundation and/or engineered septic system installation requirements may be imposed.

C. **Resale inspections**: Many municipalities now require that a resale inspection be conducted of any residential property within its jurisdiction prior to the sale and transfer from the owner to the new buyer. These inspections are exclusively used to verify that the property minimally complies with local health and safety codes such as building, electrical, plumbing, and heating. County inspections may also be required if the property is served by a well and septic system. Buyers must be aware that these inspections are not intended to serve as a substitute for a private inspection.

 1. **Real estate agent involvement**: An ordinance may attempt to make real estate licensees liable if they sell a house in violation of city certification and inspection requirements. In such cases, care must be exercised to make sure that all permits and clearances have been obtained prior to closing. Penalties include misdemeanor violations involving a $500 fine and up to 90 days in jail.

D. **Rental property registrations**: Local units of government often pass ordinances that require the registration of rental properties located within their respective jurisdictions. These ordinances are designed to assure citizens that all residential rental structures are properly maintained, sanitary, and safe for tenant-occupants. Registration requirements apply to residential rental structures and units located within the municipality. Properties must be registered with the city and receive a rental certification. Similar inspection requirements may also be in force for commercial lease structures.

E. **Vacant property registrations**: Vacant property registrations are designed to make certain that vacant properties located within the municipality are properly maintained. This is accomplished, in part, by requiring the designation of a person who agrees to be responsible for maintenance of the properties. Vacant property registrations prevent property deterioration and neighborhood blight, ensure that properties remain secured, and protect property values. Some registration forms provide spaces for the name of a real estate broker, company address, and telephone number. A real estate licensee should not obligate his real estate company on the form without the authority of his broker.

V. **Land preservation regulations**: Various regulations have been enacted on the federal and state levels to preserve certain areas and uses of land. Examples include wetlands regulations, open space preservation acts, and historic preservation regulations.

A. **Michigan environmental protection agencies**: There are two separate agencies in Michigan whose functions are to oversee and manage the state's environment. The first of these agencies is the Department of Natural Resources or DNR. The other agency is the Michigan Department of Environment, Great Lakes, and Energy or EGLE.

 1. **Department of Natural Resources (DNR)**: According to the DNR mission statement, "The Michigan Department of Natural Resources is committed to the conservation, protection, management, use and enjoyment of the state's natural resources for current and future generations." The DNR is responsible for habitat and wildlife management including: fisheries; wildlife; parks and recreation; and forest, mineral and fire management.

 2. **Department of Environment, Great Lakes, and Energy (EGLE)**: The mission of the Department of Environment, Great Lakes, and Energy is to protect Michigan's environment and public health by managing air, water, land, and energy resources. EGLE was created by executive order of the Governor in 2019. The order reorganized the former agency, the Michigan Department of Environmental Quality (MDEQ), into EGLE. As part of the reorganization, the Office of Climate and Energy was created and the Office of the Great Lakes was moved from DNR to EGLE. Other changes included:

    a. the creation of an Interagency Environmental Justice Response Team to assist in developing and implementing a statewide environmental justice plan;

    b. the new position of Environmental Justice Public Advocate to investigate complaints and concerns relating to environmental justice in Michigan; and,

    c. the office of Clean Water Public Advocate to investigate complaints and concerns relating to drinking water quality.

B. **Various wetlands regulations**: The power to regulate wetlands ultimately comes from federal law. Michigan also has enacted its own wetlands regulation. Finally, property owners, including developers, may encounter the regulation of wetlands on a local level. The goal of a wetlands regulation is to protect the environment without unnecessarily stifling building and development, which is not always easy to balance.

1. **Federal regulation–Clean Water Act**: Wetlands regulation in the various states stems from Section 404 of the federal government's Clean Water Act (CWA). The CWA regulates the discharge of dredged or fill material into the navigable waters of the United States.

    a. **Navigable waters defined**: Navigable waters is broadly defined as that which is subject to the ebb and flow of the tides and are used to transport interstate or foreign commerce, including tributaries to navigable waters, interstate wetlands, wetlands which could affect interstate commerce, and wetlands adjacent to other waters of the United States.

    b. **EPA and U.S. Army Corps of Engineers**: Federal jurisdiction over wetlands is jointly administered by the Environmental Protection Agency (EPA) and the U.S. Army Corps of Engineers. The Corps handles daily administration and permit review, while the EPA provides program oversight. For historical purposes, the U.S. Army Corps of Engineers was founded in 1775 by George Washington. In 1802, it was established as, and remains today, a separate, but permanent branch of the U.S. Army. The Corps contributes to both military and civilian construction and works projects in the U.S. and around the world. With approximately 37,000 civilians and soldiers, it provides military and civilian engineering services to more than 130 countries worldwide including the U.S.

2. ▶ **State regulation–Wetlands Protection (Part 303 of NREPA)**: Michigan's wetlands regulation was formerly known as the Goemaere-Anderson Wetland Protection Act. It was repealed and recodified (meaning statutorily rearranged) as Part 303, Wetlands Protection, of the Natural Resources and Environmental Protection Act (NREPA). In the 1980s, Michigan entered into separate agreements with the EPA and the U.S. Army Corps of Engineers through which Michigan was given authority to administer state wetlands protection laws in a manner consistent with federal law (i.e., the Clean Water Act). Interestingly, Michigan is only one of two states that administer their own wetlands regulation at the state level.

(Note: Refer to Chapter 1 for additional information on water-related rights, including ownership of bottomland and the definition of ordinary high water mark. Refer to Chapter 21 for information pertaining to NREPA and its Michigan-specific environmental protection provisions.)

    a. **Definition of a wetland**: Michigan's wetlands regulation is designed to provide for the preservation, management, protection, and use of wetlands and to regulate the permits required to alter wetlands. There are numerous and critical ecological benefits of wetlands. Under Michigan law, a wetland is defined as land which is characterized by the presence of water at a frequency and duration that supports wetland vegetation or aquatic life and is commonly referred to as a bog, swamp, or marsh and is either:

        (1) contiguous to the Great Lakes, an inland lake or pond, or a river or stream;

        (2) more than 5 acres in size (and not contiguous to the Great lakes, an inland lake or pond, or a river or stream); or

        (3) 5 acres or less (and is not contiguous to the Great lakes, an inland lake or pond, or a river or stream) and EGLE determines, and has notified the owner, that protection is essential to preserve the natural resources.

        Contiguous means there is direct physical contact with interflowing surface or ground water. Also, wetlands are frequently located above the ordinary high water mark of an inland lake or stream.

    b. **Permit requirements**: According to Michigan wetlands protection legislation, no person may build or otherwise develop a designated protected area without first obtaining a permit from the Michigan Department of Environment, Great Lakes, and Energy (EGLE). EGLE is the state's permitting authority for wetlands. The permit must be in the public interest, necessary to realize the benefits derived from the activity, and the activity must be lawful. The applicant must also show that the activity is dependent on being located in a wetland or that a feasible alternative does not exist.

        (1) ▶ **Mitigation**: EGLE can require that an environmental assessment be conducted before a permit is issued. The developer may also have to mitigate damages to an existing wetland by creating a substituted wetland. For example, if one wetland must be taken to develop a new subdivision, the EGLE permit may be conditioned on the developer reserving other open land to establish a replacement wetland.

(2) **Inverse condemnation**: If a permit to develop a wetland is denied, the property owner may seek judicial relief by claiming the denial constitutes an act of inverse condemnation. If successful, the owner may be entitled to: compensation for lost value; have his property purchased by the municipality; or receive an order that requires the EGLE to modify its denial.

(3) **Wetland inventories**: EGLE creates inventories of wetlands on a county-by-county basis.

    c. **Prohibited acts**: A person cannot do the following within a wetland without first obtaining a permit–Deposit or permit the placing of fill material; Dredge, remove, or permit the removal of soil or minerals; Construct, operate, or maintain any use or development; or Drain surface water.

    d. **No permit required**: A person may engage in the following activities without first obtaining a permit–Recreational uses such as fishing, trapping, hunting, swimming, boating, and hiking; Agricultural uses such as grazing of animals and certain farming activities including lumbering and ranching; and, Maintenance and improvement of public streets, highways, and roads.

    e. **Penalties**: As a civil action, the Attorney General may seek an injunction for a wetlands violation. The court may impose a $10,000 fine for each day of violation. A violator may be ordered to restore the wetland to near original condition. Under criminal law, a first violation is a misdemeanor subject to a $2,500 fine. A wilful/reckless violator is subject to between $2,500 and $25,000 per day of violation and/or 1 year imprisonment. A subsequent violation is a felony punishable by $50,000 per day and/or 2 years imprisonment.

  3. **Local regulation–zoning**: Michigan law allows local units of government to regulate wetlands in a manner that is consistent with state law. Some local units of government include wetlands protection in their local zoning ordinances. Other local units pass separate ordinances. A local ordinance may be stricter than state law, but not more permissive. If a stricter ordinance is passed, the local unit of government is subject to the same owner-based challenges as are available through EGLE.

C. **Historic preservation**: Certain buildings, structures, sites, or districts are of such historic significance that they are protected against destruction or significant modification without approval of a local historic preservation commission. The National Historic Preservation Act creates a national register of historic places whose owners are entitled to receive grants, loans, and tax advantages for the preservation of qualified properties.

VI. **Private land use controls**: There are a number of private land use controls that can also impact land development. Some of the most common include deed restrictions and covenants. A legal deed restriction is a type of private land-use regulation because it operates like a contract between the grantor (who imposes the restriction) and the grantee (who is bound by it). See Chapter 5 for further information on deed restrictions.

VII. **Real estate development**: When real estate is subdivided, a tract of land is parceled or divided into two or more smaller lots. The financial goal of a developer is to create as many buildable sites as possible. Depending on the type of community being created, the developer may also construct the infrastructure which refers to the interconnected structural elements of a development such as roads, sewers, power grids, public and private utilities, and telecommunication lines. After completion of the infrastructure, homes are constructed on the subdivided land for eventual sale to consumers. Some developers limit their activities to subdividing and installation of infrastructure, and then sell the newly-created lots to builders who construct homes for consumers.

  A. ▶ **Subdivision control**: Similar to building codes, subdivision regulations are imposed on private developers to provide for: the orderly layout of land; adequate streets and drainage; and suitable building sites. See Chapter 21 for details on Michigan's Land Division Act. If the developer creates the streets, they are typically dedicated to the government who then assumes the long-term maintenance of these areas.

    1. **Dedication**: A dedication is the process by which an owner's private property is granted to the government for public use. Dedication is a voluntary transfer of land. Compare this to the forced taking that occurs with condemnation and the exercise of eminent domain. A developer may dedicate areas to be used as schools and parks.

    2. **Donation, Donor and Donee**: A donation is a gift of property from the donor, i.e., gifting party, to the donee, i.e., recipient. Legally speaking, the term donation is generally not used in connection with a dedication of land. However, should the terms donor or donee appear in an examination question about a dedication, consider the donor to be the developer and the donee to be the municipality.

  B. ▶ **Subdivision planning**: Once a developer selects a suitable parcel of land to purchase for possible development, its highest and best use is analyzed, and research is conducted to ascertain zoning compliance and whether or not there are any wetlands or environmental issues that could impact the intended use of the parcel. This may also be referred to as a feasibility study.

1. **Platting**: The actual process of subdividing land begins with the preparation of a plat. As discussed, a plat is analogous to a subdivision "blueprint." It shows the subdivision layout, including lot lines, on a topographic map. A topographic map is a flat, two-dimensional map of an area that provides a three-dimensional view. This is accomplished by using contour lines to show how the elevation changes on the surface of the land.

    Plats also indicate things such as drainage and floodplain areas. Several different county and municipal officials or agencies review the plat to make sure that all statutes, ordinances, and municipal codes will be met with regard to the development. See Chapters 10 and 21 for more information.

    a. **Preliminary plat process**: Under most state land development statutes, plats must be recorded and filed with various state, county, and municipal agencies such as the road commission, drain commission, and utility companies that serve the area. Once preliminary plat approvals are obtained from applicable agencies, the developer submits copies of the approved plat to the local unit of government that ultimately exercises control over the subdivision. After review, the plat is formally surveyed and then recorded. This begins the final stage in the process before the actual modification of the raw land can begin.

    b. ▶ **Floodplain and floodway**: Issues arise when land is developed in a designated floodplain area. A floodplain is any land area that is susceptible to being inundated by flood waters from any source. The 100-year floodplain, also referred to as a 100-year base flood, is any land adjacent to a river, lake, or stream that will be inundated by water during a flood, which has at least a 1% chance of occurring in any given year.

    As a general rule, construction and fill may be permitted in the portions of the floodplain that are not in a floodway provided local ordinance and building standards are met. A floodway is the channel of a river or stream which is reasonably required to carry and discharge a flood. New residential construction is specifically prohibited in floodways. See Chapter 15 for further information.

    c. **Final stages**: After all preliminary legal requirements have been met, the developer can begin working on the land modifications including installation of the subdivision infrastructure. Lastly, construction of the actual homes begins. At the appropriate time in the process, the developer formulates and initiates a marketing program to attract potential buyers.

C. **Site condominiums**: A site condominium is a residential development that physically looks like a traditional subdivision of separate, single-family homes constructed on separate lots. In reality, it is developed as a condominium form of ownership. See Chapter 7 for further information on site condominiums.

VIII. **Regulation of land sales**: The phrase "land sales" as used in this section refers to the sale of lots within a development across state lines through the use of a common promotional plan. Property can be developed in one state, and then sold to buyers who are residents of other states. This is relatively commonplace with the sale of timeshare properties. The geographic distance between the in-state buyer and the out-of-state developer (or promoter) who is selling the land creates an opportunity for fraud. The following federal law was enacted to address this concern.

A. **The Interstate Land Sales Full Disclosure Act**: This federal law was passed by the U.S. Congress in 1968 to protect the public from fraud resulting from the sale or leasing of land on an interstate basis. It accomplishes this goal by (1) requiring registration with the Department of Housing and Urban Development (HUD) of qualifying subdivisions sold under a common promotional plan, (2) mandating that buyers of qualifying land receive a property report prior to purchase, and (3) imposing several antifraud provisions. Under the Dodd-Frank Wall Street Reform and Consumer Protection Act, administration of the Interstate Land Sales Full Disclosure Act was transferred from HUD to the Consumer Financial Protection Bureau (CFPB) on July 21, 2011.

1. **Requirements**: The Interstate Land Sales Full Disclosure Act applies to the interstate sale or lease of non-exempt lots in developments consisting of 25 or more lots that are sold or leased under a common promotional plan. Along with the property report that must be provided to prospective buyers, the developer or out-state promoter must submit full particulars of the development to the CFPB. Annual reports must be filed as well.

2. **Qualifying properties**: If the development contains 100 or more lots, the development must be fully registered with the CFPB. Along with registration, the antifraud provisions of the Act apply. If the development contains 25–99 lots which are sold under a common promotional plan, only the antifraud provisions of the Act apply and federal registration is not required.

3. **Exempt properties**: A partial list of the exemptions under the Act include: Developments with fewer than 25 lots; Sales of improved lots (meaning with fully habitable buildings); Government sales; Cemetery lots; Sales to builders; Industrial or commercial developments; and Mobile homes.

B. **Michigan Land Sales Act repealed**: For years, Michigan had its own Act that governed out-of-state land sales known as the Michigan Land Sales Act. The Act was repealed in 2010 due to the lack of reported Michigan violations and the existence of the federal Interstate Land Sales Full Disclosure Act which affords consumers essentially the same protection. Federal law now exclusively guides the sale of qualifying lots which are located in other states and sold within Michigan.

IX. **Environmental regulations**: Real estate development is subject to several state and federal environmental-based laws. These regulations not only play a critical role in the development process, but also have the potential to affect the purchase or sale of land on which dwellings exist. Therefore, pre-purchase inquiries and inspections are warranted, especially when buying unimproved, i.e., vacant, land for future development. A real estate professional can alert a prospective buyer with whom he is working of this need.

A. **Environmental regulation issues**: Some of the more important environmental statutes are designed to protect the quality of land, air, and water. These laws are comprehensive and carry heavy penalties for violations.

1. ▶ **Importance to land owners–cleanup**: From a financial perspective, responsibility for environmental contamination cleanup costs is a great concern for property owners and potential purchasers. In some cases, the government can compel a private party to bear some of the cleanup costs. The first issue is to determine who the potentially liable parties may be.

    a. ▶ **Liable parties**: A land owner can be held liable for some or all of the costs incurred by the government in cleaning up a contaminated site. This is why potential buyers should attempt to determine whether the land contains any hidden environmental problems prior to purchasing. Other persons who may be brought into an action include lending institutions, landlords, tenants, and sellers.

    b. **Innocent purchaser defense**: A purchaser of a contaminated site can attempt to escape some liability provided that, prior to the purchase, all appropriate inquiries were made into the previous ownership and uses of the property. The court may take into account the knowledge and experience of the purchaser, whether the problem was obvious, and the ability to detect the contamination through an appropriate inspection. This type of inspection is referred to as an environmental site assessment.

        (1) ▶ **Environmental site assessment**: An environmental site assessment is a multi-tiered investigation to determine the existence of environmental hazards on a property. It is typically handled in three phases: (1) An investigation into the history of the property and surrounding areas including past uses; (2) Soil boring and groundwater sampling if the past uses indicate the potential for contamination; and (3) Cleanup if necessary based on the sampling. An environmental site assessment is generally not warranted on a single-family residential property in an area that has been zoned and used for residential purposes. A buyer should still consider having a private inspection conducted.

        (2) ▶ **Environmental hazards**: There are a number of environmental hazards that may be uncovered when inspecting a structure, the soil, and/or surrounding land. Examples include mold, urea formaldehyde, asbestos, radon, leaking underground storage tanks, polychlorinated biphenyls and related chemical compounds, petroleum distillates, groundwater contamination, and hazardous waste dumping and spills. Each one of these has the potential to cause harm to humans, property, and the environment and, therefore, must be discovered and remediated to the extent possible.

        (3) ▶ **Environmental impact statement/report**: An environmental impact statement, also known as an environmental impact report, is required under federal law for federally-funded projects that have the potential to significantly affect the quality of the human environment such as highways and bridges. The report examines things such as visual impact, effect on waterways and wetlands, land use and zoning, farmlands, and noise.

2. **Use of "as is" clauses**: One of the questions that a seller may wonder when a property is sold is whether or not liability can be avoided for environmental problems by including an "as is" clause in the purchase agreement. While the seller cannot totally escape liability, the clause may be useful in transferring liability among potentially responsible parties. "As is" clauses are part of the standard boilerplate found in nearly all contracts for the sale or transfer of an interest in land.

The term boilerplate refers to standardized and uniform language that is inserted in contracts. These standardized terms are intended to have a uniform meaning regardless of the contract in which they are inserted. Boilerplate may also called the "fine print" of the contract. For further information on contracts, see Chapter 12.

3. ▶ **Brownfields, Greenfields, and restrictions on sale**: The term brownfield refers to any environmentally-contaminated property that is abandoned or underutilized. These properties are, most often, commercial and industrial in nature and located in core urban areas. Developers tend to shun these areas due to the potential for huge cleanup costs, legal entanglements, and health concerns for the buyers to whom the developed lots will eventually be sold.

    As a general rule, the sale or development of contaminated property is prohibited. However, various statutes have been enacted to encourage the cleanup and redevelopment of brownfields through development incentives, tax credits, and tax abatements. By comparison, a greenfield is any undeveloped area where there are fewer environmental obstacles to development.

4. **Clandestine "meth" labs and the environment**: Methamphetamine, also known as meth, crystal, speed, and ice, is a highly addictive, illegal drug that is classified as a powerful stimulant. Side effects range from nervousness to brain damage and death. It is considered to be a controlled substance under both state and federal law and its private manufacture, sale, use, and possession are all strictly prohibited. Michigan law classifies it as a Schedule I Substance which is the most serious drug classification.

    a. **Manufacturing produces toxic waste**: Meth is manufactured from common household chemicals through a volatile manufacturing process that produces highly toxic waste. It is produced most frequently in clandestine or undercover laboratories that may be located anywhere in urban or rural areas. It becomes a real estate-related problem because the toxic manufacturing by-products pollute dwellings, soil, municipal waste systems, and surrounding water supplies. Problems for the owners of leased dwellings arise when their tenants secretly use the leased premises as clandestine labs. Similar problems exist for the owners of motels, especially in rural areas.

    b. **Decontamination and remediation**: There are a number of different approaches that can be used to deal with a property that had been used as a meth lab: (1) Physical on-site inspection; (2) Decontamination; and (3) Post decontamination verification and preparation of a closure report. This process can be lengthy and expensive.

    c. ▶ **Disclosure issues for owners and licensees**.

        (1) **Owner issues**: Sellers who suspect or become aware that their property is or has been used as a meth lab must proceed with physical caution and legal prudence. The first concern involves human health, safety, and welfare. Thereafter, the legal issues must be handled appropriately. Note the following:

            a) Never enter a building suspected of being used in connection with drug lab activities. Identification and decontamination must be left to trained professionals. There is also a personal safety issue if the perpetrators are still on the premises.

            b) No one should occupy the dwelling until it, and the surrounding structures and land, have been properly decontaminated. The potential liability for landlords is significant as future tenants could become sick and children are especially susceptible to residual toxins.

            c) Indicators of past clandestine lab activities include: Strong odor of chemicals; Numerous containers of household and farm-related chemicals; Chemical drums in the yard; Fortification bars on doors and windows; High incidence of chemical stains and burns in toilets, drains, and on floor coverings; and Complaints from neighbors.

        (2) **Licensee issues**: While there does not appear to be any specific disclosure directive for real estate licensees, existing laws regarding property condition disclosure and fiduciary duties should be followed.

            a) **Real estate risk management**: Consider applying similar suggestions to those listed later in this chapter under the heading "Mold risk management guidelines." Licensees should never hold themselves out as experts on the subject of meth lab inspection or safety. Follow basic safety considerations and immediately refer the seller to his attorney.

b) **Threats to safety**: Concerns over immediate threats to health and safety should be referred to the appropriate law enforcement agency and/or fire department.

c) **License law and stigmatized property**: A stigmatized property is one that has been psychologically impacted by an actual or suspected event that had no material effect on the property or its improvements. Examples include locations of murders, suicides, and certain illegal activities. Even though there is no physical defect with the property, some buyers shy away from them.

According to Michigan license law, Section 2518(b), an action shall not be brought against a licensee for failing to disclose that a property was or was suspected to have been the site of an occurrence prohibited by law which had no material effect on the condition of the property. The fact that drugs were used or sold on a property does not, in and of itself, rise to the level of a property defect. If a meth lab was located on the premises, it would likely constitute a property defect due to high potential for environmental contamination.

(3) **Other state resources**: Further information can be found at the Michigan Department of Community Health website. To report suspicious activity, the Michigan State Police can be contacted by calling 1-866-METH-TIP.

B. ▶ **Lead-paint disclosure requirements–target housing**: Lead has long been recognized as a harmful environmental pollutant. Most homes built prior to 1960 contain paint that was heavily leaded, and homes built as recently as 1978 have the potential to contain lead in paint that was commonly used. The primary health problems occur either when (1) the paint is improperly removed through open sanding, for example, and the particles are inhaled or ingested, or (2) deteriorating paint chips are ingested by children. Lead adversely affects all bodily systems.

To warn consumers of lead dangers, federal law requires sellers or landlords of residential housing constructed prior to 1978–generally referred to as target housing–to disclose the presence of known lead-based paint in their properties. Lead-based paint was banned in residential dwellings in 1978. This law is regulated by the federal Environmental Protection Agency (EPA). Three questions are posed in this textbook to help the reader understand the lead-paint issue from a real estate licensee's perspective.

1. **What type of property is covered?**: Disclosure requirements apply to residential properties constructed prior to 1978. Exempt property includes (1) zero-bedroom housing, (2) short-term rentals, (3) housing reserved exclusively for the elderly, (4) housing sold through foreclosure, and (5) housing certified to be lead-free.

2. **What does the Act require?**: While sellers are not actually required to test for lead on behalf of buyer, sellers (or landlords) must observe the following:

    a. Disclose known lead-based paint hazards and provide inspection reports if they are available;

    b. Give purchasers and tenants a federal pamphlet titled "Protect Your Family From Lead in Your Home;"

    c. Permit purchasers a 10-day period within which to conduct a lead-based paint inspection at their own expense if desired (the number of days to conduct the inspection can be changed by mutual consent of the parties); and

    d. Include language in the purchase agreement or lease ensuring that disclosure and notification takes place.

3. **Are real estate licensees liable under the Act?**: A listing agent must make seller-clients aware of their disclosure obligations including ensuring that sellers give purchasers the 10-day opportunity to conduct an inspection if desired and that purchase agreements and lease contracts contain proper disclosure language.

    a. **Buyer's agent is not responsible for seller compliance**: Joint regulations between HUD and the EPA attempted to make a buyer's agent (unless compensated solely by the buyer and not from the listing agent through the MLS offer of compensation on a cooperative transaction) responsible for ensuring that the seller complies with the Act. Subsequent court cases have, however, ruled that no such responsibility exists.

    b. **Buyer's agent may have fiduciary duty to buyer**: The previously mentioned cases left the possibility open for a buyer-client to bring an action against a buyer's agent for a breach of fiduciary duty if the buyer-client is not informed about his rights under the Act.

(1) A vigilant buyer's agent will ensure that his buyer-client understands what he is entitled to from the seller as it pertains to lead disclosure. This would apply even if the buyer's agent receives his compensation directly from the buyer and not from the listing agent through the MLS offer of compensation on a cooperative transaction.

(2) Similarly, even though a transaction coordinator owes no fiduciary duties, he may still wish to make a buyer-customer aware of the Act if the real estate documents and forms do not.

    c. **Michigan's Lead Safe Housing Registry**: Michigan's Lead Safe Housing Registry is an information resource for the public on housing in which lead-based paint has either been abated or interim controls have been applied. The registry covers residential, multi-family properties, and child-occupied facilities such as day care centers and preschools.

        (1) ▶ **Lead-free versus lead-safe**: Confusion often arises over the difference between the terms lead-free and lead-safe. Lead-free means that the lead has been abated and all hazards have been removed from the property. Abatement refers to the process of removing all lead hazards. A property is deemed to be lead-safe if interim controls have been applied. Interim controls include temporary containment and encapsulation such as painting over the hazard.

        (2) **Registration requirements**: If the qualifying property has been abated or interim controls have been applied, the owner <u>must</u> register the property. The owner of a qualifying property <u>may</u> register the property if it is certified as not containing a hazard meaning that lead-based paint was never applied to the property or it was built on or after January 1, 1978.

    4. **Lead-based paint remediation/abatement contractor**: Any person performing lead-based paint remediation in the State of Michigan must be certified by the Michigan Department of Community Health, Healthy Homes Section (HHS). Certified lead abatement workers and supervisors must be employed by a certified Lead Abatement Contractor. The requirements for these certifications are available online.

C. **Radon as an environmental issue:** After cigarette smoking, radon is the second leading cause of lung cancer. It is a radioactive gas that is estimated to cause approximately 20,000 deaths per year. Radon cannot be seen, detected by odor, or tasted which makes it a serious potential problem for homeowners and dwellers who are not aware of its existence. Radon is found throughout the U.S. including Michigan. The EPA website has further information on the subject at <epa.gov/radon>.

    1. **Source of radon contamination**: Radon emanates from the natural decay of uranium that is found in soil. It moves up through the ground to the air above and into homes through cracks and other holes in the foundation. The radon becomes trapped and concentrated in the home where it is then inhaled by the occupants. Radon can be tested by using a simple passive testing kit that is available through most county health departments at low to no charge to residents of the county.

    2. **Disclosure requirements**: A seller who is aware that radon is present in a sale property must disclose it to potential buyers. Failure to do so could result in an action for intentional misrepresentation, i.e., fraud. Michigan's "Seller's Disclosure Statement" requires disclosure of known environmental problems to all potential buyers of qualifying residential properties.

        On the actual disclosure statement, this is found at "Question 10. Environmental Problems: Are you aware of any substances, materials, or products that may be an environmental hazard such as, but not limited to, asbestos, radon gas, formaldehyde, lead-based paint, fuel or chemical storage tanks and contaminated soil on the property." Buyers in communities where radon levels are known to be high often make offers to purchase existing homes subject to an acceptable radon level test in addition to a traditional home inspection.

    3. ▶ **Radon mitigation–ventilate**: There are a number of different radon reduction systems that can be used to reduce or mitigate radon levels in a home. These ventilation systems vary depending on the type of foundation in the home. Local code in some communities requires at least a passive radon control system be installed in new residential construction. A properly installed passive system is designed to keep radon gas from entering the structure. An active system relies on a continuous foundation suction and roof venting pipe coupled with an exhaust fan.

D. ▶ **Toxic mold as an environmental/legal issue:** Mold is a recognized, legitimate concern for many homeowners. If the property is being offered for sale, prospective buyers will also want to know if it is present in the structure. While mold spores are everywhere and do not necessarily cause health problems, it can proliferate to such a level that it becomes a recognized property defect. When this occurs, and the seller is aware of the problem, it must be disclosed to prospective buyers on the seller disclosure form.

For a mold problem to accelerate to the extent that property damage and health concerns arise, certain conditions are needed including oxygen, moisture, and organic material on which the mold can feed. Although oxygen and organic materials cannot be eliminated in living environments, moisture can easily be controlled by the home owners. Unfortunately, some older building techniques resulted in serious mold issues for home owners.

1. **Synthetic stucco (EIFS) and mold**: EIFS stands for Exterior Insulation and Finish System and is generically referred to as synthetic stucco. The potential problem with an EIFS system is that it can trap moisture inside the wall system, whether from water migrating as vapor from the home's interior or water penetrating roof joints or door and window frame openings.

    There was a considerable amount of litigation around the country involving home exteriors that were constructed using synthetic stucco. Around 1997, builders began using a new, drainable system to eliminate trapped water and resulting mold within the exterior wall. While most of the EIFS-constructed homes are located in southern climates, there are some located in Michigan. EIFS is more common in commercial buildings in Michigan.

2. ▶ **Mold risk management guidelines for licensees**: Regardless of the nature of the mold problem in a dwelling, certain precautions should be heeded. Note the following basic risk management guidelines for real estate licensees on the potentially sensitive issue of mold:

    a. **Do not attempt to become an authority**: Do not hold yourself out to customers and clients as being an expert on mold assessment or remediation. Instead, direct questions to a competent inspector or remediation expert.

    b. **"As Is" and Inspection clauses**: Standard "as is" and inspection contingency clauses will not insulate a seller or his listing agent from liability if either one perpetrates a fraud on an unsuspecting buyer. A seller should consult with his attorney before deciding to remain silent about any suspected mold problem in the sale property. The fact that the seller may be selling at below market value is no excuse for not disclosing a known mold issue.

    c. **Property inspections**: A buyer should condition his offer to purchase on the performance of a qualified property inspection. If mold (or EIFS problem) is uncovered or suspected, the buyer should hire the appropriate expert in mold inspection and remediation. The inspector should also be qualified to examine an EIFS system.

    d. **Property inspection disclaimers**: Property inspectors typically use forms that contain a disclaimer limiting the extent of an inspector's financial liability to the return of the cost of the inspection. As long as the disclaimer is contractual in nature, the language is clear and unambiguous, and the buyer is not forced or otherwise tricked into signing the inspection contract, courts appear likely to uphold them. Buyers should carefully read all inspection agreements.

    e. **Hold harmless/Indemnification language**: Listing brokers commonly protect themselves by including indemnification language in their listing agreements. These clauses require the seller to indemnify and hold the broker and his affiliated licensees harmless from certain instances of liability. The hold harmless clause protects an innocent broker who is named by a buyer-plaintiff in a lawsuit against the broker's seller-client for alleged misrepresentations.

    f. **Service provision agreements**: Listing and buyer's agency agreements use language that specifically defines the services that are to be performed by the broker and affiliated licensees. A well-drafted agency agreement also contains language that limits what the broker is expected to do. For example, a buyer's agency agreement might state that the broker is not acting as an environmental expert, structural or mechanical engineer, or home inspector.

E. **Asbestos as an environmental concern**: Asbestos is naturally occurring mineral fiber that occurs in rock and soils. It is mined and then processed into fibers which can be combined with other agents to form building materials. Asbestos was widely used in various construction applications due to its strength, fire resistance, and insulating properties. Unfortunately, it is also highly toxic and a known cause of various cancers, including lung cancer.

Materials that contain asbestos are characterized as either friable or non-friable. Friable asbestos-containing materials can be disturbed, damaged, or crumbled by hand with a resulting release of airborne asbestos fibers. Non-friable asbestos-containing materials cannot be easily crumbled and the fibers are, essentially, "locked" in place. Depending on the materials used in construction, their current condition, and how accessible they are to the building occupants, encapsulation (i.e., surrounding and sealing to prevent the release of fibers) may be preferable to actual removal. Asbestos abatement refers to either encapsulation or removal.

Asbestos can be found in older homes in floor tiles, roofing materials, furnaces, and plumbing systems. If a seller is aware of asbestos in a residential structure, it should be disclosed in the seller disclosure statement. In Michigan, asbestos-related work such as abatement can only be performed by an accredited contractor who has completed the required training course. It should never be attempted by a property owner.

F. **Vermiculite insulation and asbestos concerns**: Vermiculite is a naturally occurring mineral that expands into a light, accordion-like structure when it is heated. Since vermiculite is odorless and fire-resistant, it was thought to be a good material for insulating attics and was used mostly in retrofit applications, meaning added to existing structures, rather than in new construction.

 1. **Vermiculite as an environmental concern**: In the 1970s, it was discovered that the vermiculite originating from the largest U.S. mine in Libby, Montana, also contained especially high levels of a naturally occurring asbestos due to a deposit of asbestos also being located there. The vermiculite currently being mined at other facilities is thought to be safe.

 2. **Vermiculite as a real estate issue**: Existing laws regarding property condition disclosure and fiduciary duties should be heeded just as they would for any environmental issue.

    a. **Seller's concerns**: Sellers are not currently required to have insulation tested. Michigan's Seller's Disclosure Statement, however, asks if "any substance, materials or product that may be an environmental hazard" is present in the home. If a seller knows that vermiculite insulation is present, it is best to disclose it to prospective buyers (subject to a legal opinion from an attorney).

    b. **Buyer's concerns**: A buyer should condition his offer to purchase on a property inspection and hire a competent inspector to conduct it. If the seller has disclosed the presence of vermiculite insulation, or the inspector discovers it, the buyer may wish to seek further testing. Remember that not all vermiculite insulation is believed to contain asbestos particles.

    c. ▶ **Licensee's concerns**: Real estate licensees should first check with their broker before providing information or recommendations to buyers or sellers on any environmental concern. Questions should be referred to the appropriate expert.

If joy and peace are your goals, then remove your attention from fear.
Only you get to decide what you think about throughout the day.

DIAGNOSTIC PRACTICE QUESTIONS – CHAPTER 11

IMPORTANT STUDY TIP!

Step 1: Carefully review the information located in this chapter.

Step 2: Take the following Diagnostic Practice Questions. Review any question you answered incorrectly by researching the topic in this textbook. If you are still uncertain as to why the question is answered as it is, consult your program provider.

NOTE ON CHAPTER PRACTICE QUESTIONS

The following questions are representative of the type encountered on the Michigan real estate licensing examination. While some of these questions may be similar in nature and style, there is no way of predicting the exact wording of a question that will appear on the exam. Spending time memorizing these questions is, therefore, not recommended.

These questions are designed to help you determine how well you comprehend the material in this chapter. They are also intended to help you develop problem solving skills and to become comfortable with question formats.

Do not attempt to answer these questions until you have attended the lecture corresponding to this chapter and spent the appropriate time studying the material.

1. Building codes, zoning ordinances, and subdivision regulations may be created and imposed by a local municipality with the full force of the law by what authority?
   A. Executive power granted by the federal government.
   B. Police power granted to the state government.
   C. Administrative power delegated by the federal government.
   D. Administrative power delegated by the state government.

2. The amount of just compensation awarded a homeowner for the loss of property due to government seizure is based upon which of the following?
   A. The original purchase price adjusted for estimated inflation.
   B. The lowest price for similar properties in the neighborhood which have sold in the past 3 months.
   C. The fair market value of similar properties located in a non-conforming neighborhood.
   D. The fair market value of the property at the time of the taking.

3. A zoning restriction within a particular township states that: "Residential lots must be at least 1.5 acres; One-story dwellings must be at least 2,200 square feet in size; Two-story dwellings must be at least 2,900 square feet in size; and Multi-family dwellings are prohibited." A developer who wishes to construct low-income housing is refused a building permit and seeks to strike down the restriction because it is:
   A. A racially restrictive covenant.
   B. Exclusionary zoning.
   C. A fair housing violation.
   D. Inverse condemnation.

4. A developer acquired a large parcel of vacant land for the purpose of creating approximately 150 lots. To make the lots attractive to buyers, the developer wants to create commercial use areas conveniently located near the residential lots and to preserve as much open space as possible. The best form of zoning to accomplish this would be which of the following?
   A. Cluster zoning.
   B. A floating zone.
   C. A planned unit development.
   D. High-density zoning.

5. The buyer of a lot in a rural portion of a county wishes to construct a residential home. Since there are no municipal water or sewer hook-ups immediately available, which of the following will the owner initially be required to do?
   A. Pay to have the closest sewer line brought to the property boundary.
   B. Arrange for an outside contractor to construct an above-ground, engineered septic system.
   C. Pay for a survey to make certain no wells are within 200 feet of any proposed septic field.
   D. Apply for a sewage disposal permit and conduct a percolation test.

6. A property is listed on Michigan's Lead Safe Registry as "lead-free." This means that the property:
   A. Is free of all lead hazards and is safe for occupancy by children.
   B. May not be inhabited by children until all surfaces have been re-painted by an EPA-certified professional.
   C. Is subject to interim lead controls such as encapsulation.
   D. Has been inspected by local building code officials and certified as being built prior to 1978.

7. Which of the following statements applies to the process of eminent domain?
   A. It is exercised when a private developer issues a condemnation order to clear out a public area for development.
   B. It can be exercised only when there is an award of fair compensation to the owner whose property rights are lost.
   C. It only occurs when government land is taken for a public use and benefit.
   D. The power to take land emanates from a private agreement between two or more land owners.

8. A nonconforming use is a (an):
   A. Illegal use under a zoning ordinance and must be removed.
   B. Pre-existing use under a zoning ordinance that would otherwise be illegal.
   C. Variance.
   D. Use that is incompatible with the surrounding use pattern.

9. As used in connection with real estate, which of the following most accurately describes a variance?
   A. An exception to a zoning regulation.
   B. A court order prohibiting certain land uses.
   C. A reversionary interest in a life estate.
   D. A nullification of an easement.

10. Which of the following statements about building codes is true?
    A. They have been fully standardized throughout the United States.
    B. They establish value standards for the appraisal of new construction.
    C. They establish minimum standards in design, structural systems, and construction materials.
    D. They are enforced by the U.S. Army Corps of Engineers.

11. A property owner is told by the municipal building department that he must leave a 6 foot strip between his lot and his neighbor's property. From which of the following does this order most likely stem:
    A. A zoning regulation.
    B. A density requirement.
    C. A variance.
    D. A setback.

12. An assessment of taxes on real property according to its value is known as which of the following?
    A. Appraisal.
    B. Ad valorem.
    C. Replacement cost.
    D. Accretion.

13. Tax levies on specific property owners to pay for street improvements are called:
    A. Revenue enhancement fees.
    B. General property taxes.
    C. Special excise taxes.
    D. Special assessments.

14. A plat is best defined as a:
    A. Legal device used to record the subdivision of land.
    B. Process whereby variances to required development standards may be obtained.
    C. Diagram showing how structures are to be placed on a lot.
    D. Surveying instrument used in determining angles.

15. A special requirement that a residential property be subject to a local government inspection in connection with a private sale is referred to as:
    A. A seller disclosure statement.
    B. A survey certification.
    C. A city certification requirement.
    D. An architect's seal.

16. Relief from a zoning ordinance by showing a unique hardship to the land from the imposition of the regulation is called:
    A. A variance.
    B. An encumbrance.
    C. A nonconforming use.
    D. A public easement.

Chapter 12
Contract Law

The purchase agreement & selling phase.

I. **Foreword**: Contract law is a branch of civil law that governs agreements formed between two or more parties, the interpretation of their rights under that agreement, and how those rights can be enforced. It creates guidelines through which contracting parties can establish and define their relationships with confidence. Contract law is usually enforced through state laws.

The process of reducing an agreement to written form allows the parties to capture their individual understandings and expectations in a manner than fosters confidence. It also allows a court, arbitrator, or mediator to resolve any disputes in a manner that best reflects the true intent of the parties. Consistent with the "Notice" in the beginning of this textbook, any sample contract language in this chapter is provided merely for purposes of education.

   A. ▶ **Importance of contract law to licensees**: Every real estate transaction involves one or more agreements between the parties. Contract law, like agency law, guides the functions of real estate licensees and the operations of brokerage firms. This is why licensees are expected to have a reasonably strong foundation of knowledge in contract law. Contract law also happens to be a favorite topic for real estate students and practitioners alike.

   1. ▶ **Contract defined**: A contract is an agreement between two or more persons to do or refrain from doing something. The basis of the agreement is a promise or set of promises that are exchanged between the parties. If one party fails to fulfill his promise, contract law provides remedies to the other, non-breaching party.

   2. **Examples of real estate contracts**: A number of contract possibilities exist within a real estate transaction. Here are some examples: (1) A service provision agreement is used by a listing agent and a buyer's agent to represent their client; (2) A purchase agreement or option contract is entered into to by a buyer and seller to bring about a purchase and sale; (3) A mortgage and note, or a land contract, may be executed to finance the sale of real estate; and (4) A lease contract is entered into by a landlord and a tenant when land is leased, and a property management agreement is executed between a property manager and his landlord-client.

   B. ▶ **Electronic transactions**: The digital age has created new opportunities for contracting parties to exchange ideas, conduct negotiations, and create binding and enforceable agreements via the Internet. In the year 2000, the Michigan legislature passed Public Act 305 known as the Uniform Electronic Transactions Act (UETA). The Act authorizes and sets forth the terms and conditions under which information and signatures can be transmitted, received, and stored by electronic means.

   1. **Meaning of electronic**: According to the Act, the word "electronic" means relating to technology having electrical, digital, wireless, optical, electromagnetic, or similar capabilities. This includes email, facsimile, and other related technologies through which digital content can be dispatched, meaning sent. An electronic contract is referred to in the Act as an electronic record. The easiest way to visualize an electronic contract is to picture the information that is written on a paper contract, and then see it formatted as an email message or a PDF (portable document format) attachment to an email.

   2. **Meaning of electronic signature**: Under UETA, an "electronic signature" can include any electronic sound, symbol, or process attached to or logically associated with a contract and executed or adopted by a person with the intent to sign the contract. In simple terms, an electronic signature is any electronic indication that a party adopts to show his intent to be bound by the terms of an electronic contract. It is a good idea for the parties to indicate in their agreement what constitutes an electronic signature.

As an example, the terms of an electronic contract call for the parties to "sign" it by typing their name in all capital letters, followed by the word SIGNATURE in all capital letters and parenthesis, on the signature line of the electronic contract. This leaves no doubt that each party intends to agree to its terms; for example, "MARY T. SMITH (SIGNATURE)." Today, real estate professionals tend to rely one of the Internet-based services through which offers, acceptances, counteroffers, and associated documents such as disclosures can be uploaded. The service then forwards the documents to the contracting parties and their licensees for electronic signing and communication.

3. **Other requirements**: The parties to an electronic contract must agree to conduct their transaction by electronic means. This is easily accomplished by including language in the electronic contract to this effect. Another requirement of many contracts is that they be in writing (rather than oral) to be enforceable. This is known as the statute of frauds and is discussed later in this chapter. An electronic contract does satisfy this requirement for a writing. Accordingly, it is enforceable in a court of law to the same extent as a contract written on paper.

4. **A note about text messaging**: Text messaging, also known as Short Messaging Service (SMS), is widely used by nearly everyone for electronically delivering messages to one another. Daily text messages in the U.S. alone measure in the billions. Michigan law has yet to recognize text messages as the legal equivalent of a written contract for purposes of satisfying the statute of frauds (which requires real estate contracts to be in writing to be enforceable). Therefore, licensees should not use text messages to attempt to establish the terms or conditions of an offer, acceptance, counteroffer, or delivery of same. Instead, they should rely on actual written contracts or their email or facsimile counterparts.

C. ▶ **Purchase agreement**: The purchase agreement is the key real estate contract used by a property owner to sell his ownership rights to a buyer. For purposes of this chapter and ease of understanding, the purchase agreement is used as the sample contract to explore the elements of basic contract law.

1. **Offeror**: In a traditional real estate purchase and sale, a buyer first decides what property he would like to acquire. If the property is being offered for sale by a seller, the buyer then writes what is referred to as an offer to purchase. The offer sets forth the buyer's proposed terms and conditions of sale and is delivered to the seller for his consideration. The buyer is referred to as the offeror. Recall that the party with the "– or" ending gives the document and the party with the "– ee" ending receives the document.

2. **Offeree**: Since the seller receives the buyer's offer to purchase, he is referred to as the offeree. Once the seller unconditionally accepts the terms of the offer by signing it (and this acceptance is communicated back to the buyer), the offer becomes a purchase agreement. It is important to keep in mind, however, that many different outcomes are possible in a real estate negotiation. For example, the seller can reject the buyer's offer or make his own counteroffer. These possibilities are discussed later in this chapter.

D. ▶ **The role of real estate licensees**: Real estate licensees must never engage in the unauthorized practice of law while assisting the buyer and/or seller in the preparation of a purchase agreement. While this sounds easy to avoid, the line between what a real estate licensee can and cannot do can be confusing, especially for new licensees. If in doubt, a licensee should first check with his broker before providing any questionable advice.

In some states, a licensed attorney must be involved in certain aspects of a real estate contract such as drafting additional language or creating conditions. This is not the case in Michigan. Real estate licensees in this state can directly assist buyers and sellers in the formation of a purchase agreement with some important limitations.

1. **Act as scriveners**: Michigan real estate licensees should not draft a contract affecting the rights of others from a blank sheet of paper, hold themselves out to consumers as being able to draft contracts, or charge a separate fee exclusively for the drafting of legal documents. Licensees can, however, assist buyers and sellers in filling in blank spaces on pre-printed forms, including addenda. This process is similar to the function of a scrivener. A scrivener is a person who prepares a document for another, setting forth the terms and conditions as requested by the other person, without giving any legal advice in the process.

A licensee can certainly answer questions to help the parties better understand the basic elements of the contract being prepared. However, no advice should be provided that would constitute a legal conclusion as to a buyer's or seller's best legal outcome. Instead, the buyer or seller must be directed to an attorney. See Chapter 3 for further information pertaining to what constitutes the unauthorized practice of law.

2. **Pre-printed forms and addenda**: Instead of drafting agreements from scratch, real estate licensees almost universally use pre-printed contracts, forms, and addenda. These pre-printed instruments have typically been drafted, thoroughly reviewed, and evaluated by an attorney.

Chapter 12: Contract Law

a. ▶ **Addendum defined**: An addendum is a form which is attached to an existing agreement to add new or special terms, instructions, conditions, or lists (such as an itemized list of personal property to be included with the sale). Care must be exercised when preparing an addendum since its terms actually become part of the primary contract.

In practice, an addendum is most often another pre-printed form that is written on a separate piece of paper with its own title. It also contains a clause that incorporates itself into the purchase agreement. An addendum must be signed by all parties to the primary contract. The plural of addendum is addenda.

b. ▶ **Amendment defined**: An amendment is a form or other writing that actually changes the terms or conditions of an existing contract according to the mutual agreement of the parties. Consequently, an amendment can be viewed as a modification to the primary contract. The best way to learn the difference is to remember that an <u>add</u>endum "adds" to a contract and an a<u>mend</u>ment "mends" or changes a contract.

c. **Boilerplate language**: Most pre-printed contracts contain basic terms and clauses that are so common to a particular type of transaction that they rarely change. These routine details, terms, clauses, conditions, and provisions are often called the fine print of the contract. Boilerplate is another slang term used for this standardized language.

E. ▶ **Bilateral versus unilateral contract**: A contract can be grouped into one of two major categories based on the nature of its promises and any requested manner of acceptance. The prefix "bi" versus "uni" indicates whether the contract contains "two" (as in the case of bi) promises that are being exchanged by the parties or "one" (as in the case of uni) promise given by only one of the parties. The following definitions assume that there are only two contracting parties. In reality, a bilateral or unilateral contract can have multiple parties.

1. **Bilateral contract**: A bilateral contract is one in which two parties enter into mutual obligations by exchanging their individual promises. In other words, each party gives his promise in return for a promise from the other party. A bilateral contract is binding the moment the agreement is created even though the promises may not actually be performed until some time later. A purchase agreement is the key bilateral agreement used in a real estate transaction.

Example: Buyer Ms. Green makes an offer to purchase the property of seller Mr. Black. Ms. Green drafts an offer to purchase in which she promises to pay a set price in exchange for Mr. Black's promise to deliver marketable title. Mr. Black accepts the offer and delivers a fully signed copy of the agreement to Ms. Green. The contract is bilateral in nature since two promises are being exchanged. The promises are immediately binding even though the price will not be paid and the titled conveyed until the closing weeks later.

2. **Unilateral contract**: A unilateral contract is one in which only the offeror makes a promise without expecting any return promise. Instead, the promise is given in exchange for a requested performance by the offeree. Since there is only one promise, the offeree does not have to perform anything. A unilateral agreement can be viewed as a promise which is given in exchange for an anticipated performance. Neither party is bound until the promisee accepts the contract by actually performing.

Example: (While the following is not a real estate-specific example, it is helpful for understanding the nature of a unilateral contract.) Mr. Smith offers to pay Ms. Jones $100 if Ms. Jones will walk across the Mackinaw Bridge on Labor Day carrying a sign advertising Mr. Smith's business. Since this is a unilateral contract, Ms. Jones is not obligated to cross the bridge on Labor Day with the sign. Mr. Smith is bound by his promise to pay the money, but only if the offer to pay is accepted by Ms. Jones actually crossing the bridge. In a real estate context, an option contract is the most common unilateral contract. Option contracts are discussed later in this chapter.

II. ▶ **Contract formation**: To form a valid and legally binding contract, certain basic elements must be present. They include (1) offer, (2) acceptance, and (3) consideration. See Figure 28.

A. ▶ **Offer**: An offer is a manifestation, meaning expression, of a party's willingness to enter into a contractual bargain. It represents a proposal to either do or refrain (i.e., forbear) from doing something. The offeror is in complete control of the terms and conditions of his offer. Likewise, the offeree will be in complete control of the decision to accept or reject the offer. For an offer to lead to a legally enforceable contract, other aspects must also be present.

1. **Intent**: The language of the offer must indicate the offeror's present intent to be bound by its terms. If the offer language is vague or merely expresses the offeror's desire, no contract can be formed from it. When

an offeror expresses mere desire, for example, "I would like to purchase...," the promise is said to be illusory and cannot serve as the basis for a contract. If the offeror's intent to be bound is clear, the offer creates a power of acceptance in the offeree.

2. **Definite terms**: An offer must also be sufficiently definite as to its material terms so that any required promises or performances are reasonably certain. The offer should clearly identify (1) the names of the parties, (2) the property, (3) the price, and (4) all pertinent terms and conditions. The statute of frauds, discussed later in this chapter, mandates that these elements be present in the final contract for it to be enforceable in a court of law.

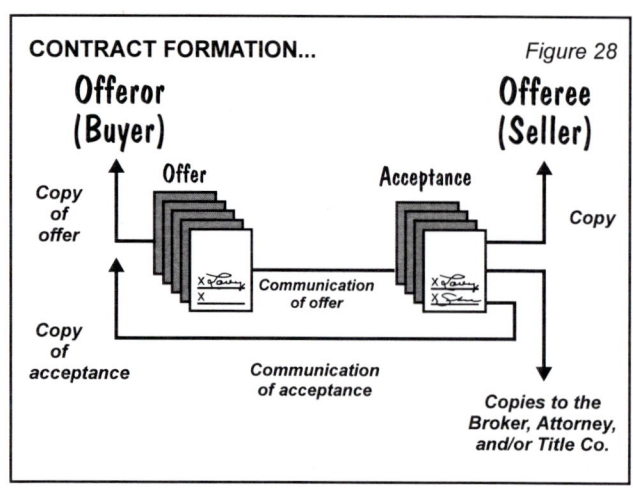

3. ▶ **Communication of an offer (and acceptance)**: Once the offeror drafts his offer, it must be formally communicated to the offeree. Communication in this context means delivered. Typically, the method of communication used by the offeror to deliver his offer serves as an invitation for the offeree to communicate the acceptance back to the offeror in the same manner. The language of the offer may also control or limit how the acceptance can be communicated back to the offeror. In the absence of a specified form of delivery, any reasonable method is acceptable.

Traditionally, offers and acceptances were made by personal delivery to the parties or their agents (excluding unlicensed assistants) or through postal mail. The computer age has added more secure electronic means of communication including facsimile, email, and online transaction management services such as instanet solutions® and dotloop® (that add enhanced security for protecting the personal information of clients). Michigan law requires the prior agreement of the parties when using electronic forms and signatures. Currently, telephone calls and SMS (text) messaging are not acceptable forms of communication due to the lack of a formal writing.

4. **Offer containing dual price terms**: In a competitive seller's market, multiple buyers often find themselves vying for the same property. For example, to gain a price advantage, "Buyer A" submits an offer to a seller for a certain price (such as $225,000) with a condition stating that, if the buyer's offer is not the highest, he will increase it to $1,000 over the highest competing offer on submission of written proof of the higher offer. So, if "Buyer B" submits his offer for $228,500 and the seller accepts Buyer "A's" offer based on the condition, "Buyer A" will have succeeded in obtaining a binding purchase agreement on the seller's property for $229,500 ($228,500 + $1,000).

While this practice is probably legal, there are several potential problems that can arise if the offer is not carefully drafted. For instance, will a court find the price is certain enough, meaning not vague, to create a binding power of acceptance in the seller? What if "Buyer B's" offer contained other financial terms not in "Buyer A's" offer? Are the additional terms automatically incorporated into "Buyer A's" offer? How long does "Buyer A's" offer to pay the extra $1,000 remain in force? How will "Buyer A" know that the higher offer he is attempting to match is bona fide? In other words, what if the seller asks his friend to make a high bogus offer to obtain an even higher offer from "Buyer A?" For these reasons, a licensee should consider referring a buyer who wants to make such an offer to the buyer's attorney for assistance.

B. ▶ **Acceptance**: A contract is not actually formed until the offer is accepted by the offeree. By definition, acceptance is the voluntary expression by an offeree that he agrees to be bound by the exact terms and conditions stated in the offer. Acceptance must be in a timely fashion meaning that offers legally expire after the passage of a reasonable amount of time. If the offer is time-dated by its terms, it expires on the day and time described. What constitutes "reasonable" is determined by the courts after looking at the nature of the agreement, who the parties are and how they have dealt with each other in the past, the subject matter of the contract, and what is customary in the trade or industry for similar types of agreements.

1. **Acceptance must be unconditional**: A contract acceptance must be unequivocal and unconditional. This means that the terms in the offer are agreed to exactly as they are written, without any modification

Chapter 12: Contract Law

whatsoever. If the offeree attempts to change any of the terms before accepting the offer, no matter how minor, the change legally operates as a rejection of the entire offer. The change is called a counteroffer.

2. ▶ **Counteroffer**: A counteroffer arises when an offeree makes any change to the terms or conditions of an offer which is then signed by the offeree and communicated back to the offeror. The offeree is proposing a new offer which operates as an implied-by-law rejection of the original offer. This is why a counteroffer is treated like a rejection or cancellation of the original offer.

    a. **Parties change position**: A counteroffer changes the original position of the contracting parties. In other words, the offeree becomes the offeror of the new or counter offer. The offeror has a couple of options available once his offer is countered.

    b. **Options available to parties**: Since a counteroffer is a rejection of the original offer, the original offeror, typically the buyer, returns to his pre-offer position with no obligations. He can shop for another property as if no offer had been made. The offeror can also accept the counteroffer thereby creating a contract according to the new, countered terms. Additionally, the original offeror can propose yet another offer, meaning he can counter the counteroffer.

    c. **Multiple counteroffers**: Some contract negotiations include multiple counteroffers between the same two negotiating parties as then go back and forth searching for terms which are mutually agreeable. Real estate licensees must exercise care in these types of negotiations to make sure that the final counterproposal is signed or initialled by both parties. This is the only way to make sure that the negotiations ultimately result in a legally enforceable contract. If there have been multiple counteroffers, it may be preferable to prepare a new, clean-looking contract with the final terms.

3. ▶ **Communication–when the contract becomes binding**: Just as the offeror (typically the buyer) must communicate or deliver his offer to the offeree (typically the seller), so too must the offeree communicate his acceptance back to the offeror. Communication of the acceptance is the exact moment the offer becomes a binding and enforceable contract between the parties. This timing is critical because an offeror can generally revoke his offer at any time prior to communication of the acceptance. Refer to the previous paragraph titled, "Communication of an offer (and acceptance)" for acceptable methods of communication.

    a. **Communication through agents**: Under the law of agency, communication of an offer or acceptance may be made to a seller's agent or a buyer's agent. Recall from the agency discussion in Chapters 2 and 3 that when notice is served on an agent, it is also considered to be served on the agent's client. For example, a seller unconditionally accepts a buyer's offer. The seller's listing agent delivers the acceptance to the buyer's agent. Communication of the acceptance has now occurred and the contract is enforceable even though the buyer-client has yet to actually see the acceptance. If the buyer is working with a subagent (whose fiduciary duty is to the seller rather than the buyer), communication is not complete until the acceptance is actually delivered directly to the buyer.

    b. **Mutual assent and meeting of the minds**: The phrases "mutual assent" and "meeting of the minds" are often used by people when discussing the formation of a contract. It is important to understand what these phrases actually mean from a legal perspective. Mutual assent is required to form a contract. When mutual assent occurs, each party understands the terms and conditions of the agreement exactly as the other party does, and each is willing to fully comply with these terms. In other words, the offer has been made and communicated to the offeree who has agreed to its terms and communicated his acceptance back to the offeror.

    The expression "meeting of the minds" is a less specific phrase that may also be used to refer to the point at which a contract is formed. Saying the parties have a meeting of the minds does not, however, necessarily indicate that mutual assent has taken place. The phrase is sometimes used to indicate that the offeror and offeree have agreed in concept to certain terms and conditions, but still need to reduce them to a written agreement.

    c. **Acknowledgment of acceptance–bottom lining the agreement**: It is now understood that communication of the acceptance determines the exact point when a contract is formed. To prove that the offeror has received a fully signed copy, most contracts have a line at the bottom of the agreement for the offeror to sign or acknowledge that he has received the signed acceptance. This is called "bottom lining the contract." Technically, bottom lining is not required to form a contract. See Chapter 20, Rule 307, for further information on a licensee's duties regarding delivery and acceptance of offers.

C. ▶ **Consideration**: Along with offer and acceptance, consideration is another of the essential elements of a contract. It is the price paid or inducement given by a promisee in exchange for a promise received from a promisor. Consideration is what actually binds the promisor to his promise. When a promisor makes a promise to give or do something, the promisee must give something of value in exchange for the promise to be binding in a court of law. This "bargained for exchange" is an important part of consideration.

If a promise is not supported by a return consideration, the promisor has made a gift rather than a contractual promise. A promise to make a gift is generally revocable any time before it is actually given. A contractual promise, on the other hand, is binding even though it almost always involves something to be delivered in the future. The easiest way to understand the legal concept of consideration is to look at how it operates in a purchase agreement.

1. **Consideration in a purchase agreement**: A purchase agreement is bilateral in nature because it contains an exchange of two promises. Each promise serves as the consideration for the other. While this may sound confusing at first, it is necessary to the enforceability of each promise in the purchase agreement.

    a. **Buyer as promisor**: One of the promises in a purchase agreement is made by the buyer to pay the purchase price to the seller. This promise is not scheduled to be fulfilled until the closing of the transaction at which time the buyer (as the promisor) pays the purchase price to the seller (as the promisee). If the buyer defaults and refuses to honor his promise, the seller can seek enforcement because the seller gave consideration in exchange for the buyer's promise.

    b. **Seller as promisor**: The other promise in the purchase agreement is made by the seller to convey marketable title to the buyer. This promise is also not scheduled to be fulfilled until the closing of the transaction at which time the seller (as the promisor) delivers the deed to the buyer (as the promisee). If the seller defaults and refuses to honor his promise, the buyer can seek enforcement because he gave consideration to the seller in exchange. In both cases, notice how the promise of one party serves as the consideration for the promise of the other party.

2. **Valuable versus good consideration**: The consideration given by a promisee in a contract must be valuable in nature for the promisor's promise to be considered binding. Valuable consideration includes anything that has monetary value including money, goods, or services. Good consideration, on the other hand, is founded on a sense of natural duty or moral obligation.

    Good consideration does not have a definite dollar value. Good consideration is sometimes referred to as "love and affection." Once a court determines that the consideration is adequate, meaning that it is valuable rather than good, it rarely looks to see if it is sufficient, meaning high enough in value. Courts recognize that a promisor may wish to give a promisee a good financial deal.

D. ▶ **Duration of an offer–when it terminates**: An offer remains open until it is (1) revoked by the offeror, (2) accepted by the offeree, or (3) a reasonable period of time has lapsed. The time the offeree has to consider the offer can also be limited by the terms of the offer itself. For example, the offer may contain a provision similar to the following: "This offer shall expire on _____ [date] at _____ [time] and be of no further force or effect." This is known as a time-dated offer. Keep in mind that an offer does not need to be time-dated by law since the buyer-offeror can revoke it at any time before communication of the acceptance.

1. **Revocation–action by the offeror**: Revocation is defined as the repeal or withdraw of some right, power, or authority that has been previously granted. It may also be called a rescission as in "the buyer rescinded his offer." As discussed, an offer can be revoked by the offeror any time prior to communication of the acceptance by the offeree. There are circumstances, however, when an offeree may want the offeror to leave an offer irrevocably open for a defined period of time. Irrevocable means not able to be revoked, canceled, or made invalid.

    a. **The irrevocable offer**: An irrevocable offer is one that the offeror promises to keep open for a stated time (which could be measured in hours, days, weeks, or months). In essence, the offeror promises not to revoke his offer for the stated period. This gives the offeree time to decide whether to accept or reject the offer. Recall from the earlier discussion, however, that all promises must be supported by valuable consideration to be enforceable.

        (1) **An irrevocable offer must be supported by consideration**: For an offer to be considered legally irrevocable, the offeree must pay a separate consideration. When this occurs, an option contract has been created. The offeror in this context is known as the optionor and the offeree is known as the optionee. An irrevocable offer might contain language similar to the following: "In exchange

for $_____ and other valuable consideration, this offer shall remain open during a period of time beginning on _____ [date] and lasting until _____ [date] at _____ [time]." Since consideration is involved, the offeror must keep the offer open as promised.

Note: The irrevocable offer described in this section is rarely, if ever, encountered in the practice of real estate. It is mentioned here to help the reader better understand the concept of an irrevocable offer. A more likely scenario involves a real estate option contract.

(2) ▶ **The real estate "option contract"**: A traditional option contract in real estate arises when a prospective buyer-optionee acquires the right or opportunity to purchase a seller-optionor's property without actually being bound to its purchase. The seller contractually options his property to the buyer using a unilateral contract in which the seller promises to sell, but the buyer does not promise to purchase the property.

(a) **Short definition for examination review**: An option is a contract in which a seller-optionor gives a buyer-optionee the exclusive right to purchase his home, during a specified period of time, for a predetermined price and terms. An option contract is unilateral because the seller-optionor promises to sell without asking for a return promise to purchase from the buyer-optionee.

Providing the buyer-optionee pays valuable consideration (in exchange for the optionor's promise not to revoke his offer for the stated time), the option is irrevocable. An option cannot be supported by good consideration.

(b) **Exercising the option**: The optionee has the right to exercise the option at any time during the period by accepting the offer to sell thereby agreeing to purchase the property. The option then becomes a bilateral purchase agreement which culminates in the closing of the transaction. Some buyers who speculate in land acquire options in properties they believe will become more valuable over time. The buyer-optionee can exercise the option himself or sell and assign the option right to a new buyer.

(3) **An option is structured like a purchase agreement**: An option contract has the same structure as a standard purchase agreement because it potentially leads to the sale of real property.

2. **Rejection–action by the offeree**: An offer also terminates when it is rejected by the offeree. A rejection is a refusal to accept an offer. Remember from the earlier discussion that a counteroffer is another form of rejection.

3. **Operation of law**: In the absence of any action by either the offeror or the offeree, an offer terminates after the passage of a reasonable period of time. This generally applies if the offer is silent, meaning no time is specified as to when it will lapse. Other factors that cause an offeree's power of acceptance to end include the lapse of a time-dated offer, and possibly, the death of either party. It is important to distinguish between a death that occurs before acceptance (while the offer is still open) and one that occurs after an enforceable contract has been formed. For example, if a seller dies after accepting a buyer's offer to purchase, the purchase agreement may be binding on the seller's heirs who can be legally compelled to convey title to the buyer at the closing.

4. ▶ **Time is of the essence clause**: As a general rule, if a contract does not state a time, date, or other deadline for performance, a material breach has not necessarily occurred merely because one party's performance is slightly delayed. In those instances when dates and times for performance are critical, the parties can include a deadline along with a "time is of the essence" clause. The clause is found in most real estate contracts. A "time is of the essence" clause lets the parties know that all obligations must be performed within any stated deadlines.

Even when a deadline and a "time is of the essence" clause are included in a contract, a court may still give the breaching party extra time to perform. A court may also disregard a contract deadline if it is felt that the deadline is unfair, unrealistic, or that the parties really never intended that their contract be terminated over the missed deadline. While this can create some uncertainty, it is still a good practice to include deadlines and "time is of the essence" clause when deadlines are essential to a party's expectations. An interested party should also consult with an attorney who is skilled in contract drafting.

III. ▶ **Contract validity**. The goal of a contract is to create legally enforceable promises. A contract that is valid has force or strength and is enforceable in a court of law. The contract contains all necessary elements and formalities, so it exists in the eyes of the law and is binding on the parties.

A. ▸ **Void contract**: A void contract, on the other hand, does not exist in the eyes of the law. It is not binding nor is it enforceable. The parties can, in fact, ignore a void agreement. It is still important, however, that no contract be ignored without first consulting with an attorney. Further, a real estate licensee should never counsel a client or customer to ignore a contract.

B. ▸ **Voidable contract**: A voidable contract is one which is valid, but due to special circumstances, one of the parties may elect to avoid it or ratify it. Ratification is defined later in this Chapter. Examples of a voidable contract include one entered into by a minor or a contract in which one party has been induced to enter into it via misrepresentation. Such contracts are voidable at the option of the minor or the innocent party in the case of misrepresentation. Since a voidable contract can be enforced by one of the parties, it is not considered to be void.

C. ▸ **Unenforceable contract**: A contract which is unenforceable has no legal effect in a court of law. In other words, a court cannot compel a breaching party to honor his promise. The two most common examples of unenforceable contracts include (1) an oral contract which was required by the statute of frauds to be in writing, and (2) a contract which a party attempts to enforce after a statute of limitations has expired. If a contract is unenforceable, it is not necessarily void since the parties can mutually agree to honor its promises.

   1. **Statute of limitations**: A statute of limitations is a law or series of laws enacted by a legislature that establish maximum time periods during which certain actions can be brought to enforce rights. Statutes of limitations cover various areas such as breach of contract, personal injury, and injury to property. In the case of a breach of contract in Michigan, a legal action must commence within 6 years from the date of the breach or default. The doctrine of laches is similar, but not identical, to a statute of limitations.

      a. **Laches defined**: Sometimes there is no specific statute that governs the time within which a legal action must be brought. In such cases, the doctrine of laches can be applied in an attempt to bar a stale claim. This is based on principles of equity or fairness rather than a statute. Laches is used as a defense when the plaintiff failed or neglected to assert an otherwise valid right or claim in a timely fashion. It prevents a plaintiff from waiting until the "eleventh hour" to assert his rights, when such a delay deprives the defendant of time to remedy the claimed problem.

      b. **Laches example**: Harry Homeowner and his neighbor Sarah have a strained relationship. Sarah hired a swimming pool contractor to install a large, in-ground pool. Due to contractor error, the pool is located six inches beyond the side lot setback requirement. Harry is aware of the encroachment before excavation begins, but waits until the pool is completed and filled to raise the issue in court. It is possible that Harry's claim may be barred by the defense of laches.

   2. **Statute of frauds**: Certain contracts must be in writing to be enforceable according to the statute of frauds. This important contract law is discussed later in this chapter.

IV. ▸ **Contract essentials**: Up to this point, we have examined the basics of contract formation. In practice, there are other equally important aspects that affect contract validity and enforceability. Beyond offer, acceptance, and consideration, other requirements include legal capacity of the parties, lawful subject matter, reality of consent, and proper legal form.

   A. **Legal capacity**: All parties to a contract must have legal capacity. This means the ability to incur legal liability. Certain persons such as minors and the mentally incompetent are protected from their own inability to understand the nature and consequences of contractual obligations.

      1. **Infant (minor)**: The word infant is the legal name for a minor. A minor is any person under the age of legal competence. In most states including Michigan, majority is attained once the infant reaches 18 years of age. When a minor, for example, enters into a contract, it is deemed voidable at the minor's option. An exception to this rule exists, however. Contracts entered into by minors for necessities such as food, clothing, lodging, and possibly real estate or real estate financing may be enforceable against the minor.

      2. **Mental incompetence**: A party to a contract is considered to be incompetent when he is legally unable to understand the nature and consequences of the contract or transaction. This can result from any medically-recognized mental or cognitive disorder. The contract is voidable at the option of either the person with the mental disability or his guardian.

         A question sometimes arises regarding an intoxicated person's right to invalidate a contract that was entered into under the influence of alcohol or drugs. Voluntary intoxication may not necessarily be a defense since a person is expected to take responsibility for his actions. The defense of capacity might be available if the intoxicated person was so inebriated that he could not understand what he was doing, and the non-intoxicated person knew or had reason to know of the other party's state of mind and took advantage of it.

3. **Avoiding or ratifying the contract**: A minor or innocent party in a contract involving misrepresentation can elect to either avoid (meaning to make void) or ratify his contract. To ratify means to adopt or agree to uphold the terms of the contract. When a voidable contract is ratified, both parties are bound to it. A person who is mentally incompetent, however, may not be able to ratify due to his inability to understand the consequences of his contractual assent.

B. **Subject of contract must be lawful**: The subject matter of a contract must be for a legal purpose. Obviously, a court will not enforce a contract for the commission of a crime or any contract that perpetuates a misrepresentation or other grossly inappropriate outcome. The subject matter of a contract is also known as the object of the contract. If the object of a contract is unlawful, the entire contract is void and neither party may attempt to enforce it.

1. **Specific examples of illegal contracts**: Illegal contracts include (1) Contracts involving the commission of a crime such a contract to pay a gambling debt; (2) Commercial bribery agreements; (3) Contracts that violate licensing requirements such as a listing agreement entered into by an unlicensed broker or by a licensed salesperson who holds himself out to be a broker; (4) A contract to perpetrate a mortgage fraud; and (5) Contracts with excessive forfeiture and penalty provisions.

C. **Reality of consent**: Reality of consent looks at how freely and voluntarily a contracting party entered into an agreement. Consent must not have been coerced by the use of force or gained through trickery such as misrepresentation. The usual remedy for a problem involving consent is to treat the entire contract as voidable at the option of the innocent party. The decision by the innocent party to avoid or ratify the contract will be binding on the wrongdoer. If the contract involves an illegality, it is treated as void from the start.

1. ▶ **Misrepresentation—generally**: Misrepresentation is an assertion, by words or conduct, that are not in accord with the facts. When one party to a contract misrepresents a material fact, two different deals have, in essence, been created. One deal is based on the misrepresented or untrue facts. The other deal is based on the true facts. This distinction is important because an innocent party cannot be contractually bound to facts that are not true. Note the example in the following paragraph.

   [margin note: Fraud]

   Assume for purposes of illustration that a seller tells a prospective buyer that his basement never leaked during the 18 years he owned the home. In reality, the basement occasionally leaks during heavy rainstorms. The seller saying the basement does not leak represents the untrue facts. The true facts are the buyer is purchasing a house in need of expensive repair. If the misrepresentation is discovered before the closing, the buyer may be able to terminate the contract. If the closing has already occurred, the seller will be likely liable for damages equal to the cost of the repair.

   a. **Types of misrepresentation**: Several different types of misrepresentation exist under Michigan law including (1) Intentional misrepresentation; (2) Innocent misrepresentation, and (3) Nondisclosure or Silent fraud.

      (1) ▶ **Intentional misrepresentation (fraud)**: Intentional misrepresentation is also known as fraud. To find that an intentional misrepresentation has occurred, certain elements must be established. They include (1) a material representation, (2) that is false, (3) known to be false or recklessly made without regard to truth, (4) with the intent that it be relied on by the innocent party, (5) who actually relied on the statement, and (6) suffered damages as a result. When these elements are present, the law protects the innocent party and allows for damages that can vary based on the loss suffered by the innocent party.

      (2) ▶ **Innocent misrepresentation**: With an innocent misrepresentation, the wrongdoer did not actually know his statement was false at the time it was made. A claim is allowed in a court providing the innocent party detrimentally relied on the false representation and suffered an injury that resulted in a benefit to the wrongdoer.

      Applying the facts from the example about the leaking basement, assume the seller is a landlord who is selling a home that was previously occupied by a tenant. The landlord honestly does not know the basement leaks. When the prospective buyer previews the home and asks about the condition of the basement, the seller makes an affirmative statement that it does not leak. If the buyer purchases the property, the seller will have benefitted from the sale and may be held liable for innocent misrepresentation.

(3) ▶ **Silent fraud**: Under Michigan's silent fraud rule, a buyer may recover for a seller's failure to reveal certain material defects. Accordingly, a seller has a duty to disclose all known material defects that are not readily discoverable by a buyer. In the case of a residential property, Michigan requires a seller to complete a Seller's Disclosure Statement that describes the known condition of nearly every component of the property. The statement is so complete that it basically leaves little opportunity for a silent fraud to occur.

[handwritten margin note: Lie by ommission]

b. **Caveat emptor**: Caveat emptor is a Latin phrase that means "Let the buyer beware." It is a legal doctrine or principle that places a duty on a buyer to examine and judge for himself all property that he is about to purchase. According to the rule, a buyer assumes the risk of all patent, meaning obvious, defects that would be evident from making a reasonable inspection. The rule does not apply, however, to defects that are latent, meaning hidden.

There has been a long-evolving trend in the law to shift away from caveat emptor and toward a requirement for sellers to inform buyers about all defects known to the seller whether they are obvious or not. This is especially true when applied to residential real estate transactions and seller disclosure laws. As a legal principle, caveat emptor still applies to some degree in many other property transactions.

(1) ▶ **Caveat emptor, modern seller disclosure laws, and inspections**: As noted, Michigan law requires sellers of most residential properties to disclose known property defects to all prospective buyers before a binding purchase agreement is executed. Nevertheless, a buyer should not rely on the Seller's Disclosure Statement as a substitute for an independent property inspection that is conducted by a competent inspector. A seller honestly may not be aware of certain hidden defects in the property.

(2) ▶ **Pre-purchase due diligence**: This phrase "due diligence" is often voiced by real estate and legal professionals. It is a principle that states a buyer has a caveat emptor-like responsibility to inspect and investigate a property prior to its purchase. Some courts are somewhat less sympathetic toward a buyer who misses a defect that a reasonable inspection would have uncovered. This assumes the seller was honestly unaware of the defect. Due diligence or due care refers to the conduct a reasonable person would exercise in the particular situation.

c. **"As is" clause**: Nearly all purchase agreements include an "as is" clause. The clause is an acknowledgement by the buyer that he is purchasing the property as it is and is accepting it in its present condition. Consistent with caveat emptor, the clause is intended to shift the burden of pre-purchase inspection for obvious defects to the buyer. An "as is" clause does not, however, eliminate a seller's duty to disclose known, hidden defects to an unsuspecting buyer. Silent fraud rules and seller disclosure requirements for residential properties still apply.

2. **Improper use of force**: The other action that can give rise to a reality of consent claim involves the use of force to compel a person to do something against his will. The two primary categories are duress and menace. Another category involves undue influence. Such acts typically render a contract voidable at the option of the innocent party.

a. **Duress**: In the context of a contract, duress is the illegal use of threat or coercion to induce an innocent person to enter into bargain. The innocent person is forced to do something he would not otherwise have done. Duress can arise from threats of violence, imprisonment, a wrongful taking and keeping of one's property, or to commit other improper acts. Duress can be used to terminate a contract since it was not entered into voluntarily. In other words, there was no reality of consent.

b. **Menace**: An act of menace occurs when a wrongdoer threatens to engage in an act of duress against another. Since it deprives the innocent person of his own free will, it can be used as a defense against a claim to enforce a contract. This is similar to duress.

c. **Undue influence**: Undue influence is another form of pressure and persuasion that falls short of duress, but is so strong that it overpowers the innocent person's free will and induces him to enter a contract that he might not otherwise have entered into. For example, a nephew and his wife vigorously pressure an older and ailing aunt into signing a purchase agreement to her large home. They trick her into believing it is the only way she can afford to stay in a convalescent home while she recovers from a fall. The purchase price is a fraction of the true value of the home. As a result, the purchase agreement is voidable.

D. **Proper legal form**: A contract must be in proper legal form to be enforceable. After contract negotiations have concluded and a contract has been signed, a party may realize that some of the terms do not appear in the contract exactly as they were discussed. Or, possibly a negotiated term was omitted altogether.

As long as both parties agree to the final terms as they appear in the contract, there is no problem. Sometimes, however, one party later decides not to honor the signed contract based on a changed or omitted term. The statute of frauds and the parol evidence rule, both of which are governed by state law, were created to deal with issues such as this.

1. **Statute of frauds**: The statute of frauds is a law that requires certain classes of contracts to be in writing to be enforceable by a court. The law dates back to a 1677 English law that was passed to prevent individuals from attempting to show or prove through the use of perjury and fraud that a contract or agreement exists when in fact it does not. It prevents a person from lying about the terms of an alleged agreement. A court will not enforce agreements that fall within the statute unless they are in written form. The writing may also be called a memorandum.

    a. **Sufficient memorandum**: Not only must certain contracts be in writing, but the writing, document, or memorandum itself must contain the essential elements of the agreement. The statute of frauds does not actually require a full, detailed contract; only that it constitutes a sufficient memorandum. By definition, a memorandum is a written note or brief summary of something. Memorandum literally means to be remembered. The minimum essentials are sometimes referred to as the "Four P's."

        (1) **Parties**: The name of each contracting party must be included in the writing. Further, any party who is charged with an obligation must sign the contract.

        (2) **Property**: The subject matter of the contract must be described. In a real estate transaction, this would take the form of a legally sufficient property description (see Chapter 10).

        (3) **Price**: Either the purchase price must be stated or the agreement must indicate the type of consideration involved, for example, valuable as opposed to good.

        (4) **Pertinent terms**: The writing must also contain the pertinent or essential terms of the agreement.

    b. **Contracts covered by the statute of frauds**: The following contracts are said to fall within the statute of frauds. This means that they must be in writing (and contain the necessary elements to qualify as a sufficient memorandum) to be enforceable.

        (1) **Contracts for the sale or transfer of an interest in land**: Contracts for the sale or transfer of an interest in land include purchase agreements, land contracts, option agreements, assignment of a land contract vendor's interest, and an agreement to execute a mortgage.

        (2) **Contracts for more than one year**: Contracts which by their nature cannot be performed within one year must be in writing to be enforceable. This means that an oral, i.e. verbal, lease agreement for one year or less is enforceable. A multi-year lease, on the other hand, must be in writing to be enforceable.

        (3) **Contracts for the sale of goods**: Generally, a contract for the sale of goods, such as personal property, that exceeds $500 in value must be in writing to be enforceable.

        (4) **Contracts to pay a commission**: Listing agreements, buyer agency contracts, and landlord or tenant representation agreements which involve a promise to pay a commission for the sale, purchase, or lease of real estate must be in writing and signed by the party promising to pay the commission to be enforceable.

    c. **Governs enforceability**: A key aspect of the statute of frauds is that it only governs the enforceability of executory contracts rather than their validity. In other words, the statute does not automatically render an oral contract void. Similarly, the statute cannot be used to reverse a contract (whether oral or written) that has been fully executed. As noted below, the word executed can have one meaning within the statute of frauds and another meaning when it is used to describe the signing of a contract.

        (1) ▶ **Executory agreement**: An executory contract is one in which the promises or obligations in the agreement have yet to be performed by either one or both of the parties. For example, a fully signed purchase agreement that is pending (meaning waiting for) the closing is executory since the buyer has yet to give the purchase price and the seller has yet to convey marketable title. Assume that both parties attend the closing and the buyer is prepared to give the purchase price, but the

seller refuses to convey title believing the price is too low. The agreement is still executory since one obligation remains unfulfilled.

  (2) ▸ **Executed agreement:** An executed contract is one in which the obligations are fully performed by all parties. Once a contract is executed, it cannot be undone (absent evidence of a misrepresentation, illegality, or mutual mistake about the object of the contract).

2. **Parol evidence rule**: The parol evidence rule is another rule that guides contract creation and enforcement. It bars, meaning prevents, a party from attempting to introduce what is called extrinsic evidence in a court of law for the purpose of "adding to" or "contradicting" what is in an existing written agreement. Extrinsic evidence can take the form of oral testimony by a party to explain to a judge what an ambiguous provision was supposed to mean. It could also include the introduction into evidence of preliminary notes, writings, or draft versions of the agreement to show that something was omitted that should not have been. Parol literally means oral or verbal.

   In simple terms, a party to a written contract cannot attempt to escape it by telling a judge that the agreement was really intended to mean something other than what it actually states. The law expects a person to read and understand a contract before he signs it. Parol evidence may be allowed by a judge, however, if it is the only way to show that an agreement was procured, meaning obtained, through fraud or misrepresentation, for example.

   a. **Integration and merger clauses**: The parol evidence rule applies to contracts that are total integrations. This means the contract is the final and complete expression of the party's agreement. Nothing is left open for later interpretation. Modern purchase agreements typically contain an integration clause to confirm this fact. These contracts usually contain a merger clause as well. This clause states that all prior and contemporaneous agreements and understandings are merged into the final written contract and have no force or effect. Contemporaneous means occurring at the same time.

   b. **Sample integration and merger clause**: "The parties hereby agree that this is the entire agreement between the parties and that there are no other written or oral understandings. The parties further agree that this agreement supersedes any and all prior agreements, understandings, or representations made by the parties or their agents whether oral or in writing."

V. **Contract performance, discharge, and breach**: Once a contract has been created and signed by everyone, one of the parties may have difficulty fulfilling his promise due to a problem that is out of his control. Many of these problems are so common that they can be anticipated and managed through contract contingency clauses.

 A. ▸ **Contract conditions (contingencies) generally**: A contract condition is typically a stated event (often drafted as part of a specific contract clause) that must occur before a party's promise is treated as binding and legally enforceable. The promise is said to be contingent on the event occurring (or possibly failing to occur). In this context, contingent means dependent.

  For example, a buyer wishes to make an offer on a seller's property, but is concerned that his credit score may not be high enough for him to qualify for an affordable loan. To protect himself, the buyer makes his offer contingent on obtaining a loan approval letter from his lender. The promise to purchase is not enforceable unless the buyer obtains the necessary loan.

  1. **Protects the parties**: A contingency clause is not required by law, but operates like a "safety net" by preventing a party from being bound to a contract he cannot legitimately honor. The party must, however, act in good faith and not deliberately use the contingency clause to simply get out of the contract.

  2. **Classification of conditions**: There are a number of different conditions that can form the basis of a contingency clause. For example, one clause may state that a condition must occur before a party's obligation becomes enforceable. Another type of clause can release a party from an already enforceable obligation. Other obligations are treated as concurrent conditions of one another.

   a. **Condition precedent**: Since "pre" means before, a condition <u>precedent</u> is one that must occur before a contractual promise is considered binding and enforceable. In other words, the condition precedes the enforceability of the promise. The promisor is not obligated until the condition occurs. A party can also waive a condition by indicating that he is willing to proceed even though the condition has not been met. To waive is to relinquish or give up a legal right.

    Examples: Notice in each of the following examples how the buyer is able to condition his obligation to purchase on the fulfillment of the condition named in the clause. If the condition fails or cannot be met (without any wrongdoing or bad faith on the part of the buyer), the buyer is released from the agreement. The parties to a contract must carefully read any contingency clauses since they are not all worded identically.

(1) ▶ **Financing contingency clause**: In a standard financing contingency, the buyer conditions his promise to purchase on being able to obtain a satisfactory mortgage loan. The buyer is not obligated to purchase unless the loan is approved. If not, the buyer is released from the agreement and can seek the return of any earnest money deposit he might have made. The language in the agreement generally controls and should specify the loan type and details the buyer is willing to accept.

(2) ▶ **Home inspection contingency clause**: With a home inspection contingency, the buyer conditions his promise to purchase on having a competent home inspector verify that the physical condition of the home is acceptable. The buyer is technically not obligated to purchase until he receives a satisfactory inspection report. Some inspection contingencies place the purchase agreement "on hold" until the buyer indicates his intent to proceed to a closing. Other clauses presume that the buyer intends to proceed if he does not voice his intent to be released due to an unfavorable inspection report.

(3) ▶ **Attorney review clause in a purchase agreement**: An attorney review clause allows a party to condition his obligation on an attorney review and approval of the agreement. If the attorney does not approve the contract, the party who included the contingency is not bound to it.

b. **Condition subsequent**: A condition subsequent extinguishes, meaning terminates, an already enforceable obligation if the stated event occurs. For example, a purchase agreement states that the seller will deliver possession of the property to the buyer in substantially the same condition as it was at the time of entering into the contract. If the property is destroyed or otherwise damaged by fire or other casualty prior to the closing, the buyer's obligation to take title to the impaired property is extinguished. Some of these clauses further require the seller to surrender possession to the home at the closing in a condition that is broom-clean and free of debris and/or personal property.

As discussed later in this chapter under equitable conversion, buyers are also protected by Michigan's Uniform Vendor and Purchaser Risk Act. Under this law, the risk of loss due to property damage remains on a seller until either title or possession to the property is transferred to the buyer.

c. **Condition concurrent**: When conditions are treated as concurrent, they are dependent on one another and the parties typically exchange their performances at the same time. For example, the buyer's obligation to pay the purchase price and the seller's obligation to convey clear title in a purchase agreement are fulfilled simultaneously at the closing. The non-performance of an obligation by one party may excuse the other party from performing his. Concurrent means occurring at the same time.

B. **Equitable conversion**: Deeds are generally viewed as containing both a legal title interest and an equitable title interest. Equitable title refers to the actual ownership interest conveyed by the deed. Legal title refers to the deed itself. Equitable conversion is a common law doctrine that is based on these principles.

Under equitable conversion, the buyer of real estate becomes the equitable owner of the property immediately on the creation of a fully binding purchase agreement (even though the closing will not take place until some later time). As we will see, common law principles are based on notions of fairness. Since real property is unique, it is felt that the default by a seller who refuses to convey title may leave a buyer who wants or needs the property without a satisfactory remedy.

1. **History**: From a purely historical perspective, when a seller refused to convey title after signing a purchase agreement, the buyer's remedy was often limited to monetary damages for the seller's breach of contract. Since the seller still had title, specific performance may not have been available to the buyer. The buyer did not yet have a property interest that a court of equity could protect. Equitable conversion was created to protect the buyer in such circumstances. By immediately transferring equitable title to the property on execution of a purchase agreement, the buyer has a property interest and specific performance can be obtained as a remedy. Equitable conversion does, however, carry the potential for certain consequences.

2. **Risk of loss**: Since the buyer becomes the equitable, or true, owner of the property before the closing, a problem can arise if the structure is damaged or destroyed. Technically, the buyer could be compelled to take title to a property with a value that has been significantly diminished. To avoid such a harsh result for an innocent buyer, protections were devised both contractually and statutorily.

a. **Contingency clause (contractual solution)**: Years ago, attorneys recognized the potential problem triggered by equitable conversion. Purchase agreements were drafted with contingency clauses that shifted the risk of loss from the buyer back to the seller. If the property is damaged or destroyed during the gap between the signing of the purchase agreement and the closing, the buyer's obligation under the purchase agreement is extinguished. This contingency is based on a condition subsequent, namely, the damage or destruction of the property. Unfortunately, not all buyers had access to these purchase agreements and the Michigan Legislature created a more universal solution.

b. **Uniform Vendor and Purchaser Risk Act (statutory solution)**: Some states such as Michigan enacted statutes in the 1970s to shift the risk created through equitable conversion. Michigan's law is called the Uniform Vendor and Purchaser Risk Act. It presumes that all contracts for the "purchase and sale of realty" place the risk of loss on the seller providing he retains title and remains in possession of the property pending the closing. The parties are also free to specify otherwise in writing.

A buyer who wishes to begin moving his personal effects into a vacant home or make renovations before the closing must be careful since these acts could constitute taking possession as defined in the Uniform Vendor and Purchaser Risk Act. When a buyer takes legal possession, he potentially becomes responsible for any property damages. The buyer should at least check with his attorney and insurance agent before doing anything to or with a property prior to the closing. See also Chapter 13 and the section titled "Seller retains possession" for further information on issues that arise from a "days possession" clause in a purchase agreement.

3. **Application to land contract sales**: Equitable conversion is also applied to land contract sales in which the seller finances the purchase price through an installment contract, but retains legal title pending final payment by the buyer. When the land contract is executed at the closing, the buyer acquires equitable title to the property. When the final payment is made, the seller delivers the deed to the buyer. This merges the equitable title with the legal title in the buyer. Land contracts are discussed further in Chapter 16.

C. **Transfer of contract rights to third persons**: Contract rights can be transferred by one of the original contracting parties to a third person. To accomplish this, a legal mechanism is needed. The two most common of these include (1) an assignment and (2) a delegation. As a general rule, contract rights are assigned and contract duties are delegated.

Everyone must agree.

Technically, a "right" in a contract is the legally enforceable claim that one party has against the other party. For example, the seller of real estate has a legal right to collect the agreed upon purchase price from the buyer. Technically, a "duty" in a contract is something that one person owes to the other person. For example, a landlord in a lease agreement owes a legal duty to his tenant to provide a habitable, meaning livable, dwelling. In practice, many people often apply very similar definitions of both terms.

1. ▶ **Assignment**: An assignment is the transfer of contract rights. When a contract is assigned, only the remaining balance of the rights are transferred. In other words, an assignment of an existing contract does not re-start the terms from the beginning. While most contract rights are freely assignable by the parties, recall from Chapter 5 that a deed is not assignable. Instead, the party desiring to transfer his ownership rights in the property, i.e., the grantor, must create a new deed and deliver it to the grantee.

   a. **Parties to an assignment**: The transferring or assigning party is called the assignor. He is the one who gives or transfers the balance of the contract rights to the third person. The party who receives the transferred rights in the contract is called the assignee.

   b. ▶ **Responsibilities and novation**: Since an assignment involves the transfer of an existing contract, the transferring party-assignor is liable for the obligations remaining in the contract. These obligations can be released through the granting of a novation. A novation is an agreement to substitute a new obligated party (i.e., the assignee) for one of the original contract parties (i.e., the assignor). See Chapter 16, mortgage assumption, for an illustration of how contract assignment and novations arise in the context of a mortgage.

   c. **Assignment of a real estate contract**: Contract rights are generally considered to be freely assignable. Consequently, both the seller and the buyer can assign their individual rights in a purchase agreement to a third party. Assignment rights are typically set forth in an assignment clause.

   d. **Limitations on assignment**: One party to a contract may, however, attempt to limit any future assignment by the other party by including a non-assignment clause. This clause may also be called a non-alienation clause. In a real estate context, to alienate means to transfer rights in a property to another.

Most courts do not favor clauses that restrict or restrain a person's right to transfer his rights in a contract unless some legitimate reason can be shown.

Lease example: A non-assignment clause is placed in a lease by the landlord. Notice how it does not actually prevent the assignment, but rather, requires the tenant to seek the prior permission of the landlord. This protects the landlord from a tenant attempting to assign the lease to a financially unqualified third party. Sample: "Landlord expressly prohibits the assignment, subleasing, or sharing of premises without the prior written notice and written authorization of the Landlord. Authorization is at the sole and exclusive discretion of the Landlord."

2. **Delegation**: In a delegation, a contracting party appoints a third person to perform the contracting party's duty, obligation, or task as set forth in the agreement. For example, in a listing agreement, the listing broker delegates the fiduciary duties he owes to his seller-client to another broker who is acting as a subagent. This commonly occurs in multiple listing arrangements.

D. ▶ **Discharge of contracts**: There are several actions that can cause the discharge of contractual obligations. When discharged, the agreement between the parties is fully extinguished and they are released from all further obligations. The actions of the parties can cause a contract to be discharged and so can operation of law.

1. **Acts of the parties**: The actions of the parties that can lead to a discharge of the contract include performance, rescission, mutual release, and modification.

   a. ▶ **Performance**: When the parties to a contract completely fulfill what they promised to do (or refrain from doing), their agreement is deemed performed and they are released from any further obligation. This is the preferred method of discharging a contract because the expectation of each party has been completely fulfilled. In a listing agreement, this occurs when the broker locates a suitable buyer for the seller and the seller pays the commission to the broker at the closing.

   b. **Rescission**: The word rescind means to take back or cancel. When a rescission occurs, the contract is legally cancelled and each party is returned to the position he was in before the contract was signed (as if it had never existed).

      (1) **Triggering factors**: Rescission can occur by mutual agreement. It can also occur by judicial order when one of the parties is in breach, there is a mistake, or a party was induced to enter into the contract by fraud. When a triggering event arises, rescission is a form of relief sought by the innocent party.

      (2) **Mistake**: A mistake is any belief of a contracting party that does not correspond to the facts. If the mistake involves the material facts or subject matter of the contract, one or both of the contracting parties may seek judicial relief. The parties can also be mistaken as to the legal effect of their contract, but this usually does not usually lead to rescission. In other words, the mistake must be one of fact rather than law. It is also important to know whether the mistake is unilateral or mutual.

         (a) **Unilateral versus mutual mistake**: A unilateral mistake is one made by only one party to the contract. The other party was not aware of the mistake nor attempted to take advantage of it. A mutual mistake, on the other hand, is one made or shared by both parties.

         (b) **Contract enforceability and reformation**: The law involving the enforceability of a contract with a mistake can be very complex and depends on the facts of each case. As a general rule, a contract can be rescinded if there is a mutual mistake of fact, or a unilateral mistake that was induced by fraud. Rescission is not granted if one party simply claims he misunderstood the purchase agreement or did not realize the property's true market value when he made or accepted his offer.

         In the case of a mutual mistake, a court could also reform the agreement so it meets the true expectations of the parties. Reformation is a judicial correction or "rewriting" of the facts of an agreement. A court will not reform a contract without convincing evidence that the right exists. Courts do not enter into these actions lightly.

         (c) **Mistake example**: A seller owns two adjoining vacant lots. A buyer makes an offer to purchase "Lot 1" and the seller accepts it. Due to a clerical error in the offer that neither party recognized, the contract contains the legal description of "Lot 2." The mistake will be grounds for rescission of the agreement because it is a mutual mistake of fact. The court could also reform the contract by changing the legal description so it reflects that of "Lot 1" since that was the intent of the parties.

c. **Release (mutual)**: A contract is formed from the mutual assent of the two parties. The parties can also mutually agree to terminate their agreement. If a contract is required to be in writing, a mutual release should also be in writing. An attempt by one party to unilaterally release himself from his contractual obligation constitutes a breach of contract. The most common mutual release in real estate is triggered when a buyer's financing contingency cannot be met, the parties sign a mutual release, and the buyer's earnest money deposit is returned.

d. **Modification**: A modification of a contract is a change to one or more of its essential terms. This may only occur with the mutual consent of all parties. The modification becomes a "substituted agreement" and acts to discharge and replace the original agreement. Do not confuse a modification with a counteroffer. With a counteroffer, the offeree attempts to change the terms of a written offer. Recall that this has the effect of rejecting the offer.

e. **Death of a party to the contract**: As a general rule, the death of a party to a contract does not automatically discharge or terminate the contract. Instead, the contract remains binding on the decedent's heirs, personal representatives, or any successor in interest. For example, a seller-vendor sells his property to a buyer-vendee on land contract terms. The seller-vendor dies during the term of the land contract which remains in force and binding on the seller-vendor's heirs. As a side note, if a contract is for personal services such as a listing agreement, it may terminate if the broker dies. Refer to Chapter 3 for further details.

2. **Operation of law–merger**: Certain events such as merger act to legally discharge a contract. Merger occurs when contracting parties enter into a subsequent agreement that is superior to, supersedes, and replaces the prior agreement. For example, a purchase agreement merges into the deed at the closing. Another example occurs when a landlord and tenant enter into a lease-option. If the tenant elects to exercise the option during the term of the lease and purchase the property, the lease is discharged by merging into the deed at the closing.

E. ▶ **Breach of contract**: A breach of contract occurs when one party fails to perform any of his promises without having a legal excuse. When one party breaches a contract, the other party is generally excused from his performance and may be able to sue for damages. A breaching party is said to be in default.

1. **Default**: As a noun, a default is a failure to perform either a legal or a contractual duty. For example, "The parties to a note have failed to make their required payments for three months are in default." The word default can also be used as a verb such as, "The parties to the note default when they miss a payment."

2. ▶ **Contract remedies**: When a breach of contract occurs, the non-breaching party has several options. The nature of remedies often depends on the actual terms of the contract. These remedies can include damages and equitable remedies.

a. **Damages**: In the event of default, the non-defaulting party may usually seek monetary damages. These money damages are awarded by a court if the contract calls for them or if the court believes that justice can only be served by awarding them. There are many different kinds of damages available to an innocent party. This chapter discusses the basic categories of actual, punitive, and liquidated damages.

(1) **Actual damages**: Actual damages represent a form of compensation awarded to an injured party for his real, provable, out-of-pocket losses. They do not include any amount imposed by a court as punishment or to merely vindicate an innocent party when no actual loss can be proved. Actual damages may also be referred to as compensatory or general damages.

(2) **Punitive damages**: Punitive damages are awarded by a court to punish the wrongdoer for his behavior and possibly to set an example for others. Some breaches are considered by a court to be so serious that actual damages are not sufficient to cover the innocent party's loss. While the parties to a contract may generally set forth actual damages in their agreement, only a court can impose punitive damages.

(3) **Liquidated damages**: Liquidated damages are those which the parties to a written contract set forth in their agreement, typically in the form of a dollar amount, in the event one of them defaults. The most common form of liquidated damages is the earnest money deposit provision in a purchase agreement (e.g., the buyer backs out of the contract and refuses to purchase the property).

Chapter 12: Contract Law

(4) ▶ **Earnest money deposit (EMD):** When a buyer executes an offer to purchase, he customarily pays a sum of money to the seller known as an earnest money deposit or EMD. It is used to demonstrate the buyer's good faith and intent to perform the terms of the offer. The earnest money deposit may also be called good faith money, although this phrase is rarely used in practice. It is important to note that no EMD is required by law to make a purchase agreement binding. The EMD clause is merely a liquidated damage provision.

[margin note: Can be 3-5000. Both parties must agree to return]

(a) **Amount of EMD:** The amount of EMD is often a point of discussion in a real estate transaction. Although the exact amount can be negotiated between the parties, the buyer usually determines what he is willing to provide. It is common to see deposit checks issued in the range of 1% to 3% of the sale price. The amount cannot be so large, however, as to constitute a punitive damage which, as noted earlier, cannot be negotiated by the parties to a contract.

   i) **EMD concerns:** Although it may be in the seller's best interest to seek a large deposit, the opposite is usually true for the buyer. For instance, a buyer may not want to pay more than a nominal amount over concern about getting his money back if the transaction cannot close through no fault of his own.

   ii) **Damages covered by the EMD:** There are two damages that a seller possibly suffers when a buyer rescinds an offer in bad faith. First, when the buyer's offer was accepted, the seller removed his property from the market. If the buyer rescinds after several weeks or months, the seller may have lost the advantage of a stronger seller's market and be forced to take a lower price with the next buyer. Second, there are costs involved in having to re-market the home. While these are primarily borne by the listing broker, it represents a potential inconvenience for the seller as well.

[margin note: 24 hours must be deposited]

(b) **Retaining the deposit pending closing:** State license law controls how EMD payments are to be held by a real estate broker. Chapters 19 and 20 discuss these requirements in detail. This section provides an overview of what happens. Upon preparing an offer to purchase, the buyer typically issues the EMD check for an amount he is most comfortable offering. The broker must deposit the funds in a special trust account within two banking days after he receives notice that the offer has been accepted by all parties (meaning both buyer and seller).

   i) **Retained by broker who receives the deposit:** The check is commonly made payable to the selling or cooperating broker with whom the buyer is working. The agency status of the selling broker does not matter when it comes to license law EMD requirements.

   ii) **Retained by third party:** The buyer and seller may also opt that the EMD check be made payable to a third party escrowee such as a title company, lender, or attorney instead of the broker. This practice is authorized under license law providing the licensee who receives the check delivers it to the title company or other named escrowee within the required deadline. In the case of a short sale, the seller's lender may also require that the EMD check be made directly payable to and retained by the listing broker rather than the selling broker.

(c) **How the EMD is ultimately applied:** If no problems arise in the performance of each party's promises, the EMD is generally credited on the closing statement to the down payment owed by the buyer. In the case of a purchase agreement default, the disposition of the deposit depends on who is the defaulting party.

   i) **Disbursement:** As discussed in Chapter 20, Michigan Administrate Rules control the disbursement of EMD funds by a broker. Funds can only be disbursed according to the terms of the purchase agreement. If there are any changes to these terms, the buyer and seller must sign a mutual agreement before the broker can disburse the funds according to the modified terms.

   For example, before the closing, the buyer requests a partial refund of the EMD from the retaining buyer's broker to cover an unexpected financial emergency. Before the broker can disburse the funds, the seller would have to agree to it in writing. If a lender is involved, it must be notified since the partial refund causes a change to the information on the mortgage application.

ii) **Buyer defaults**: If the buyer defaults by not completing the purchase as promised, the funds theoretically should be disbursed from the retaining broker's trust account to the seller according to the terms of the forfeiture provision in the purchase agreement. Brokers should not, however, disburse the funds without the buyer and the seller signing a mutual release form. If the buyer refuses to sign the release, the seller may have to sue for the deposit in a court of law. While real estate license law and rules do not require the use of a mutual release in this situation, it is a good risk management practice for brokers to observe.

iii) **Seller defaults**: If the buyer is prepared to close on time, but the seller does anything contrary to the purchase agreement, the buyer is entitled to a full refund of his deposit. Again, no check should ever be disbursed by a broker without a mutual release signed by the buyer and the seller. Failure to do so could result in the broker facing a legal action (meaning lawsuit) by the non-receiving party for wrongful disbursement.

iv) **Both parties claim the deposit–interpleader**: It is possible that the transaction may not close as anticipated and both parties claim entitlement to the deposit. The broker who holds the deposit cannot wrongfully disburse it. To resolve the conflict, the broker can file an action with a court of law for a legal determination of entitlement. The money is placed in court custody and a judge makes the decision. This is known as an interpleader. The broker often bears the cost of this legal action.

v) **EMD as unclaimed property**: EMD checks retained by a broker that are unclaimed by the buyer or the seller must eventually be surrendered to the Michigan Department of Treasury pursuant to the Michigan Uniform Unclaimed Property Act. Any escrow account is considered to be unclaimed after a dormancy, meaning inactivity, period of three years (from the date of the last contact with a party). The State has strict filing deadlines that must be followed, so a broker should consult legal counsel to make sure that he complies with the annual deadlines and uses the property form.

(d) **Promissory note in lieu of funds**: Instead of issuing a check for the EMD, a buyer may want to execute promissory language in the offer to purchase that the EMD will be paid to the seller only if and when the buyer defaults. This is a promissory note which operates like a contract (the note) within a contract (the purchase agreement). While legal, the note does not afford the seller a ready source of funds and may not truly evidence the buyer's sincerity to the satisfaction of the seller. Further, the seller may encounter collection issues if the buyer claims that he was not legally in default when he backed out of the contract.

For the reasons mentioned, a promissory note to pay an EMD may not be attractive to the seller. In a strong seller's market where buyers face multiple, competing offers, each buyer wants to make his individual offer as attractive as possible to the seller. A competitive, higher EMD check may accomplish this goal.

(e) **Conditional payment**: To avoid having to secure a mutual release from the seller if a contingency cannot be satisfied, some buyers elect to wait to actually issue the EMD check until after a satisfactory inspection report has been received and/or receiving their mortgage approval. The wisdom of doing so again depends on whether the transaction is being negotiated in a seller's market or buyer's market.

(f) **Nonrefundable deposit**: There is no legal requirement that an EMD actually be refundable to the buyer if the seller does anything contrary to the purchase agreement before the closing. Although uncommon in residential sales, a buyer can make a non-refundable payment to the seller. Similar to an option, the buyer pays the seller to keep the property off the market for a specified period of time.

i) **Contracting parties should check with legal counsel**: If a non-refundable deposit is requested by a party to a purchase agreement, a licensee should recommend that the party first consult with legal counsel on the matter.

ii) **Broker should check with legal counsel**: If an EMD-like payment is truly non-refundable to the buyer regardless of the circumstances, it is not considered to be earnest money and does not have to be placed in the broker's trust account. In such case, a broker should first check with his company attorney to verify that the money can be immediately given to the seller rather than being retained in the broker's trust account pending the closing.

b. **Equitable remedies**: Money damages are the first contract remedy we explored. Equitable remedies represent another. They are awarded by a court based on principles of justice and fairness, meaning equity, rather than strict rules of law. Equitable actions include specific performance, injunctive relief, rescission, and reformation of a contract. Historically, separate courts heard cases at equity (for equitable relief) and at law (for money damages). Now, the same court can hear cases in which the parties seek either equitable relief or damages.

  (1) **Specific performance**: Specific performance is a court award in which a breaching party is compelled to perform specifically what he agreed to in a contract. For example, a defaulting seller under a purchase agreement may be ordered to convey title to his property. The action may also be referred to as a decree of specific performance. It is limited to certain contracts like real estate in which the subject matter is unique and money damages are deemed inadequate.

  (2) **Injunction**: An injunction is a court order that (1) prohibits a person from doing a specified act, (2) restrains a person from continuing some act, or (3) forbids a person from accomplishing a threatened act. An injunction might be sought, for example, when a creditor is concerned that the debtor may try to sell his real property to avoid a lien being placed on it.

c. ▶ **Arbitration–an alternative to a lawsuit**: Arbitration is a type of alternative dispute resolution in which the contracting parties are given an opportunity to present their evidence to a neutral third person, or panel of persons, who have the power to render a decision which is final and binding on the disputing parties.

  (1) **Arbitration advantages**: Arbitration has several advantages over litigation. They include (1) a speedy hearing, (2) less money to initiate and conduct the hearing, (3) hearings are conducted at or near the parties' location, (4) the hearing is informal and more relaxed, and (5) the process is less intimidating. Some legal and real estate experts feel that a disadvantage can also exist for clients, such as giving up rights that might be available if the dispute is litigated in a court of law. If a client asks his licensee about the advantages or disadvantages of arbitration or mediation, the licensee should refer the client to the client's attorney.

  (2) **Mediation contrasted**: Mediation is another form of alternative dispute resolution in which a mediator meets with the parties and acts as a facilitator so the parties can resolve the issue themselves. While the mediator may suggest how best to resolve the problem, he has no power to impose a binding settlement. In contrast, an arbitrator conducts a hearing and evaluates the relative strength of each party's claim after which he renders a binding decision.

  (3) **Arbitration under Michigan law**: Michigan law strongly favors arbitrations. Michigan courts will uphold the decision of an arbitrator and not rehear the matter unless either party was not afforded due process during the arbitration process.

    (a) **Due process defined**: Due process is the constitutional requirement that all parties to a hearing be given (1) fair notice of the hearing including all charges, (2) an opportunity to prepare an adequate defense, and (3) a hearing conducted by an impartial tribunal. A tribunal is a forum or place where justice is administered including a court.

    (b) **Parties are free to decide**: Some purchase agreements include a clause that allows the parties to specify in advance if they want to arbitrate, mediate, or litigate a dispute. In Michigan, the parties to a contract can decide what they want to do at the time of entering into the contract, or leave the question open and decide later if a dispute arises. A real estate licensee should never offer advice on whether litigation or alternative dispute resolution is in a buyer's or a seller's best interest. Instead, the parties should be referred to an attorney to address the question.

All experience is preceded by thought. Let positive thoughts pave the way for positive outcomes. This is understood and practiced by all happy people.

DIAGNOSTIC PRACTICE QUESTIONS – CHAPTER 12

IMPORTANT STUDY TIP!

Step 1: Carefully review the information located in this chapter.

Step 2: Take the following Diagnostic Practice Questions. Review any question you answered incorrectly by researching the topic in this textbook. If you are still uncertain as to why the question is answered as it is, consult your program provider.

NOTE ON CHAPTER PRACTICE QUESTIONS

The following questions are representative of the type encountered on the Michigan real estate licensing examination. While some of these questions may be similar in nature and style, there is no way of predicting the exact wording of a question that will appear on the exam. Spending time memorizing these questions is, therefore, not recommended.

These questions are designed to help you determine how well you comprehend the material in this chapter. They are also intended to help you develop problem solving skills and to become comfortable with question formats.

Do not attempt to answer these questions until you have attended the lecture corresponding to this chapter and spent the appropriate time studying the material.

1. Which of the following statements is NOT accurate regarding real estate licensees and purchase agreements?
   A. A real estate licensee must use a pre-printed form that was drafted by an attorney, subject to the attorney's final approval once the agreement is signed by the buyer and seller.
   B. While not a recommended practice, a knowledgeable real estate licensee may draft a binding purchase agreement from a blank sheet of paper.
   C. A real estate licensee may fill in the blanks on a pre-printed real estate purchase agreement form which will be binding according to the filled-in terms.
   D. A purchase agreement may be supplemented with various addenda which, when attached to the contract, will have the same legal force and affect.

2. At the request of Penelope Purchaser, homeowner Richard Chaz gives her a written offer to sell his home for an agreed upon price. Penelope has up to three months to decide if she would like to actually complete the purchase and close the transaction, but is under no such obligation to do so. In exchange, she pays Richard $2,500 for this right. This agreement is:
   A. Binding on Penelope since she is obligated to perform.
   B. Binding on Richard because of the $2,500 consideration.
   C. Bilateral in nature because of the bargained for exchange of duties.
   D. Not binding because the transaction involves the sale or transfer of an interest in land.

3. Sandra, a broker working with a buyer as a subagent, prepared an offer to purchase on a property listed with another broker. Sandra called the listing agent to present the offer but was told to drop the offer off at the lister's office and it would be presented later that evening. The lister told Sandra that he would send her a text message with the results immediately after meeting with the seller. At 10:00 p.m. that same evening, the listing broker called Sandra and said, "Congratulations, the seller accepted your buyer's offer as is." Before Sandra could pick up the signed offer, the buyer called her to revoke it. Does a binding contract exist?
   A. Yes, because the listing agent properly communicated the acceptance to Sandra.
   B. Yes, because a telephone call constitutes sufficient acceptance of a signed offer to purchase.
   C. No, because the revocation occurred before the acceptance was communicated to the buyer.
   D. No, because Sandra has not been given a durable power of attorney from the buyer.

4. A seller is offering her residential property for sale. The prior winter, a small amount of water worked its way into the basement at the bottom of the foundation wall. The seller was told by a local contractor that it was "one of those freak things that happened once and probably will cause no further problems." Which one of the following statements is true?

A. If the seller neglects to disclose the leak to a buyer, the seller has committed a fraud.
B. The seller is under no duty to disclose the leak to a buyer due to caveat emptor.
C. If the seller is acting in good faith, and relies on the contractor's statement, the seller is under no duty to disclosure the incident to a buyer.
D. If the purchase agreement contains an "as is" clause, the seller may remain quiet about the leak.

5. A prospective buyer makes an offer on a property and includes the following provision at the seller's request, "This offer will remain open and cannot be revoked for 5 days from the date of receipt by the seller." Three days later, the buyer sees a new listing that he finds more to his liking. The buyer immediately contacts the seller to withdraw his prior offer. Upon hearing from the buyer, the seller refuses to release him from the 5 day provision. Which of the following statements best describes the buyer's options?
   A. The buyer may not withdraw the offer because the seller has a binding promise to leave the offer open for 5 days.
   B. The buyer may not withdraw the offer according to the statute of frauds.
   C. The buyer may withdraw the offer due to the mandatory 3-day cooling off period.
   D. The buyer may withdraw the offer since there was no consideration exchanged to bind him to the 5 day period.

6. A salesperson receives an earnest money deposit designated in the purchase agreement as being "nonrefundable." Which of the following is true?
   A. The deposit must be placed in the broker's trust account since the law does not recognize a nonrefundable deposit.
   B. A nonrefundable deposit can only be used in connection with a commercial property transaction.
   C. The salesperson must retain the earnest money because it may need to be refunded at any point in the transaction.
   D. The earnest money does not have to be deposited in the broker's trust account, but must be surrendered to the broker for handling.

7. A contract where a promise is exchanged for a return promise is referred to as what type of contract?
   A. Executory contract.
   B. Unilateral contract.
   C. Express contract.
   D. Bilateral contract.

8. Deeds and sales agreements must be in writing to satisfy the requirement of:
   A. Michigan License Law.
   B. The Statute of Frauds.
   C. Uniform Commercial Code.
   D. The Parol Evidence Rule.

9. If the phrase "time is of the essence" is inserted in a real estate sales contract, which of the following is most correct in regard to the contract?
   A. A reasonable time is presumed for the performance of all obligations in the contract.
   B. All performances will be rendered as soon as possible.
   C. All performances will occur within the time periods specified in the contract.
   D. All performances must be rendered no later than thirty days of acceptance.

10. Which of the following is not likely to qualify as an excuse for nonperformance of a contract?
    A. Destruction of subject matter.
    B. Fraud.
    C. Unilateral mistake.
    D. Misrepresentation.

11. The term contractual ability means which of the following?
    A. The parties to the contract are competent to enter into an enforceable agreement.
    B. The contract is drawn up by a person legally qualified to do so.
    C. The agreement contemplates a purpose that is legally permissible.
    D. The contract contains all the clauses and covenants necessary to be valid.

12. The written transfer of the balance of an interest in a bond, mortgage, lease, or other contract is most commonly known as:
    A. A divestiture.
    B. A dedication.
    C. An exculpation.
    D. An assignment.

13. A seller has his attorney draft a purchase agreement that he will insist a buyer use to make an offer on his home. At the attorney's recommendation, a standard "as is" clause is included. Which of the following effects may the clause have on the transaction?
    A. The clause shifts the burden of repair to the buyer in the event a previously unknown defect arises.
    B. The clause encourages a buyer to purchase the home since it acts as a warranty against problems by the seller.
    C. The clause shields the seller from having to disclose all defects in the property.
    D. The clause is mandated by Michigan's seller property condition disclosure law.

14. All EXCEPT which of the following statements regarding an option is true?
    A. It is in the nature of a contract.
    B. It must be written to be enforceable.
    C. It must be supported by consideration to be enforceable.
    D. The transaction must be reviewed by each party's attorney.

15. The buyer's agent in a cooperative transaction delivers an offer made by his client on another broker's listing. After the listing broker presents the offer to the seller, the listing broker calls the buyer's agent to say that a meeting of minds has been reached. What does this most likely mean?
    A. All the elements of a contract have been satisfied.
    B. An offer and an acceptance have been reached.
    C. The contract is clear to close.
    D. A counteroffer is being made.

16. A person who has secured the right to purchase a property at a fixed price for a designated period of time and has paid a consideration for this privilege would own:
    A. A lease.
    B. An agreement to purchase.
    C. An option.
    D. An assignment of interest.

17. The requirement of legality of object for a contract means that:
    A. The title to all property that is the subject matter of a contract must be free of legal encumbrance.
    B. An agreement expressed in a contract must be stated in legally correct terms.
    C. A contract is unenforceable if its purpose is not legally permissible.
    D. A contract is legally untenable unless both buyer and seller have agreed upon the same object.

18. If a property owner gives an interested party a properly executed option with December 31 as the fixed expiration date, and the property owner dies before that date, which of the following is true?
    A. The option immediately becomes void.
    B. The option remains enforceable.
    C. The option remains in effect only if the property owner dies intestate.
    D. The option remains valid but must be exercised within a statutory period.

19. The cancellation or reversal of a contract by a court which treats the contract as if it never arose is referred to as:
    A. Estoppel.
    B. Specific performance.
    C. Rescission.
    D. Arbitration.

20. In order for a purchase agreement to be valid as a contract, which of the following is absolutely required:
    A. Witnesses.
    B. Date of closing.
    C. Acknowledgment.
    D. Execution.

21. A buyer wants to purchase a particular property before another buyer makes an offer on it; however, he does not have sufficient cash reserves in his bank and will need to obtain financing. Which of the following should the buyer do?
    A. Ask the seller to permit a 72 hour contingency clause to be included in the contract to provide sufficient time for a loan application to be made.
    B. Include a contingency clause in the offer to purchase with the approval of the loan being a condition precedent to the enforceability of the contract.
    C. Place a clause in the offer conditioning the purchase on receipt of a pre-qualification from a reputable lending institution.
    D. Look for a less expensive home since no seller will take their home off the market long enough for a lender to approve a buyer's loan application.

*Never cast anything off the dock at night that you don't
want washed up on the shore in the morning.*

Chapter 13
Leases

How a landlord-tenant relationship is created and maintained.

I. **Foreword**: Leasing plays a critical role in housing. For those who are not financially ready or able to purchase a house, or for those who choose not to invest in a residential dwelling, leasing allows them to fulfill their housing needs. Leasing also serves an equally important role in commerce. Many, if not most, businesses in the United States enter into commercial lease arrangements rather than purchasing a building to use as a business facility.

A lease creates a landlord-tenant relationship whether the leased property is used for residential or commercial purposes. While there are many similarities between residential and commercial lease arrangements, the law can vary greatly. The focus of this chapter is primarily on residential leasing. Most of the statutes governing landlord-tenant relationships deal exclusively with residential leases. Commercial leases are generally governed by principles of contract law including statutes and common law, and most importantly, the written lease contract between the landlord and the tenant.

A. **Basic terminology**: As discussed in Chapter 6, the allodial system of property law allows a property owner to separate his exclusive right to possession of a property and transfer it to another person. In doing so, the property owner becomes a landlord and the person to whom exclusive possession is conveyed through a lease becomes the tenant. The ability of a property owner to convey possession to a third party while retaining ownership is the legal foundation upon which the modern landlord-tenant relationship is based. This section explores the basic terminology used in leasing.

 1. ▶ **Lease, rent definitions**: A lease is an agreement by which the owner of a property conveys exclusive occupancy of his real property, or exclusive possession of his personal property, to another person. The owner gives up the right to possess, use, and enjoy his property in exchange for valuable consideration which is called rent. Recall that the parties to most contracts, including leases, are assigned specific names based on the –or and –ee endings. The word "rent" can be used as a noun (i.e., the actual money paid to lease a property) or a verb (i.e., to lease a property to another).

    a. **Parties to a lease–lessor and lessee**: Recall that the party with –or ending is the one who gives and the one with the –ee ending receives. Since the landlord gives the lease rights, he is the lessor and the tenant is the lessee. Using lessor and lessee or the common names landlord and tenant are both acceptable.

    b. **Reversion**: The term of a lease can be established for a predetermined and set period of time or it can be left open. Regardless of its length, a lease contains an implied understanding that it is not a permanent conveyance. This even holds true in the case of a 99-year lease. Possession reverts back to the landlord at the end of the lease. This is called a reversionary interest. If the lessor dies during the term of the lease, the lessor's heirs receive the reversion and stand in the position of the landlord.

    Note: Historically, a 99-year lease was the longest period for which a property could be leased. These leases are not used much today, except in the case of a few historic buildings and land sites such as museums which are owned by the government and leased to private enterprises.

    c. **Demise**: The technical term for a transfer of possession through a lease is demise. It implies two promises: (1) That the landlord-lessor has the legal right to lease the premises; and (2) That the tenant-lessee will receive quiet enjoyment of the leased premises. Do not confuse the term demise with devise which is a gift or transfer of property via a will.

        (1) **Meaning of quiet enjoyment**: Quiet enjoyment is a right that accompanies possession to a leased premises. It is a promise by the landlord to the tenant that the tenant will be able to enjoy the premises during the term of the lease in peace and without disturbance or interference. The phrase

has nothing to do with sound or other noise. Rather, it is an assurance that possession will not be interrupted by the conflicting claim of another.

2. **Leasehold (non-freehold)**: Chapter 6 also discussed freehold versus leasehold interests. A leasehold is a type of ownership right or interest in property that is limited to mere possession, without including any title interest in the possessed land. It is created by virtue of a lease. Since the tenant holds a leasehold estate in the leased premises, the landlord retains his freehold or ownership interest. Ownership is limited, however, since the landlord cannot take possession of the premises during the term of the lease.

B. **Lease distinguished from other interests**: What distinguishes a lease from other interests such as easements, licenses, or hotel guest rights is the fuller extent of rights that a tenant receives. Most of these other interests are either non-possessory or possessory for a highly limited term as with a hotel guest. Separate innkeeper's laws govern short-term housing options such as inns, hotels, and public lodging houses rather than landlord-tenant laws.

C. **Practical applications for licensees**: Licensees frequently encounter landlord-tenant transactions in the practice of real estate. For example, real estate licensees often work with investment property buyers who rent their properties to tenants. As another example, a seller-landlord may list his rental property with a broker to locate a new tenant. Further, some real estate brokers offer professional property management services in addition to traditional real estate services. Licensees must be familiar with lease arrangements so they can properly guide their clients.

The subprime mortgage crisis of the 2000s created thousands of new rental relationships as homeowners lost their homes to foreclosure and needed to establish new residences in rental units. Another source of leases during the economic downturn came from sellers whose home values dropped. Rather than taking a large loss with a sale, many of these sellers listed their properties with a broker to locate a suitable tenant. These were often called list-to-lease relationships.

1. **Licensing requirements to represent landlords and tenants**: Michigan real estate license law requires that anyone "who leases or offers or rents or offers for rent real estate or the improvements on the real estate for others, as a whole or partial vocation" must be licensed as a real estate broker. A licensed real estate salesperson, essentially, can perform the same functions, but must be licensed under and acting for his broker when doing so. To recap, a real estate license is required to represent a landlord-client who is searching for a tenant or a tenant-client who is searching for a property to lease. These licensing requirements are discussed more thoroughly in Chapter 19 in connection with Article 25 of the Occupational Code.

2. **Seller retains possession after closing**: Nearly all purchase agreements have a section dealing with possession of the property by the seller after the closing. These clauses set forth a period of time such as 30, 60, or 90 days, for the seller to remain in the property after the closing if he so chooses. The seller may need extra time to secure a new residence and/or move out of the sale property.

   a. **Not treated as a leasehold**: Under Michigan law, when a seller elects to retain possession after the closing, a landlord-tenant relationship is not created. The buyer does not become a landlord. Instead, the seller's possession merely fulfills a term of the purchase agreement.

   b. **Funding**: Since the buyer becomes the title holder at the closing, he is entitled to compensation for any time the seller remains in possession. A per diem, meaning per day, fee is negotiated in the purchase agreement which approximates the cost of ownership in terms of mortgage principal and interest, taxes, and insurance. Some contracts call for 1½ times this amount and that the full per diem for the "days possession" be escrowed with a designated escrow agent. If the seller moves out sooner, the unused portion of the escrow is refunded to him.

   c. **Insurance viewpoint**: While Michigan courts may characterize the relationship between the buyer and seller as the fulfillment of the "days possession" clause in the purchase agreement, insurance companies may view it from the perspective of a landlord-tenant in the event of a casualty loss. The seller should check with his insurance agent to make sure he is covered in terms of his personal belongings and premises liability. The buyer should alert his insurance company that the seller will continue to occupy the property for a limited time.

   d. **Seller's failure to vacate**: If the seller fails to vacate in a timely fashion after the possession period ends, the buyer must evict the seller by filing a demand for possession in the district court. If there is no "days possession" clause in the purchase agreement and the seller remains in possession after the closing, the buyer may be able to recover the fair rental value of the property plus costs in a district court.

Chapter 13: Leases

3. **Sale subject to a lease**: A property which is subject to an existing residential lease may be sold by the landlord. The effect of the sale on the tenant's rights is discussed in a later section titled, "Transfer of the lessor's interest."

II. **Lease essentials and standard provisions**: A lease must contain the essentials of a valid contract. Many of the same contract essentials discussed in Chapter 12 apply equally to lease agreements. With the exception of a lease for 1 year or less, all lease agreements must be in writing to be enforceable. Due to the importance of the rights conveyed, even a 1 year lease should be in writing to protect both parties.

   A. **Lease essentials**: A lease agreement should contain the following essentials: (1) Offer and acceptance; (2) Consideration; (3) Contractual capacity of the parties; (4) Object of the contract is legal; (5) Term of the lease; and (6) Execution of the agreement. Contract essentials are discussed further in Chapter 12.

   1. **Offer and acceptance**: To form a contract, there must be an offer and an acceptance. The landlord offers or "lets" his right to possess the property to the lessee. The tenant "takes" the offer and accepts it in exchange for his promise to pay the rent. This is why a lease may also be called an agreement to let and take. In the law of conveyancing, the word let means to lease a property.

   2. **Consideration must be exchanged**: For an offeror's promise in a contract to be enforceable, the offeree must give consideration in exchange for it. Since a lease is bilateral in nature, each party makes a promise to the other. The landlord promises to convey exclusive possession of the property for the stated term. The consideration given by the tenant is the promise to pay the rent. This promise binds the landlord to his promise. Conversely, the tenant's promise to pay the rent is supported by consideration given by the landlord (which is his promise to convey exclusive possession).

   3. **Parties must have contractual capacity**: The parties to a lease agreement must have contractual capacity. This means they are of sound mind; i.e., capable of understanding the nature and consequences of the lease agreement, and of legal age. If either party lacks capacity, the lease is voidable by the innocent party.

   4. **Object of the contract must be legal**: The subject of the lease contract must be for a lawful purpose. For example, if a landlord knowingly leases a property to a tenant to warehouse stolen property, the lease is void. Landlords frequently include a provision in their leases that restrict the premises to a particular use, thereby excluding other legal and all illegal uses. This is especially true in commercial leases.

   5. **Lease term**: Depending on the nature of a written lease arrangement, its length or term is specified in the contract. This is not mandatory in all leases, however, since a lease without a stated termination date is acceptable as either a periodic tenancy or an estate at will.

   6. **Execution of lease**: According to the statute of frauds, a written lease contract must be signed by any party who is charged with an obligation in the agreement. In the case of a lease, the landlord is charged with conveying possession and quiet enjoyment to the lessee. If the tenant does not sign the lease and takes possession of the property, the lease is generally held to be valid. Most lease agreements, however, do require the lessee to sign the contract. This is a sound practice since the tenant is obligated to pay the rent. Recall that the statute of frauds applies to leases that cannot be performed within 1 year.

   B. **Miscellaneous provisions**: Modern lease agreements are embodied in detailed contracts. There are a number of important issues that landlords especially want to make sure are covered. They include things such as the security deposit; cleaning fees; whether pets are allowed and, if so, is a pet fee required; is smoking permitted in the unit; use of controlled substances on the premises; the required domestic violence provision; and whether assignment or subletting of the property permitted. There are numerous other issues that a landlord may wish to address including things such as peaceful use of the property; premises liability; parking; landlord inspection rights; and how damages and repairs to the property are handled.

   1. **Security deposit**: Nearly all residential and commercial lease contracts require the lessee to pay a security deposit. Security deposits in residential leases are fully regulated by a 1972 Michigan statute titled, "Landlord And Tenant Relationships." This important Act is discussed in Chapter 21.

   2. **Cleaning fees**: A landlord cannot use funds held as a security deposit to defray the ordinary cost of cleaning the premises after a tenant vacates. They can be used to repair damages caused by the tenant. A landlord may include a separate provision in his lease requiring the tenant to pay an up-front cleaning fee providing it is reasonable in amount and is not refundable (even if the tenant cleans the premises himself). As discussed in Chapter 21, any amount collected at the time of leasing which is potentially refundable at the end of the lease qualifies as a security deposit. This makes it subject to the 1½ month's rent limit.

3. **Pets or other animals**: Domestic animals that live in a leased premises have the potential to be destructive to the dwelling. As a result, a landlord can legally restrict or prohibit pets altogether in the dwelling. If a landlord is willing to permit a domestic pet to occupy the dwelling, the landlord should add a Pet Clause to the lease or use a separate Pet Addendum. This provision can limit things such as the size, weight, type, and/or number of permitted animals. The clause will also set forth the tenant's responsibility for damages and personal liability.

   a. **Pet fees**: A landlord can charge a reasonable, non-refundable pet fee to cover damages caused by the pet. If the fee is refundable, it is treated as part of the security deposit and falls under the 1½ month's rent limit. This is similar to how a refundable cleaning fee is treated.

   b. **Service animals and assistance animals**: A "no pets" policy must be waived by a landlord in the case of a service animal or assistance animal for a tenant who has a disability. This is based on the fact that such animals are not considered to be pets. As a general rule, a tenant who makes a request for a service animal or assistance animal must have a disability-related need for one. Refer to Chapter 18 for further discussion on assistance and service animals.

4. **Smoking**: A landlord may legally include a non-smoking provision in a lease. A question often arises whether this general prohibition can also be applied to the smoking of medical marijuana on the premises. This question is discussed at the end of this chapter in a special section.

5. **Use of controlled substances**: A landlord should include a clause in his lease that prohibits the use of controlled substances on the property. Various criminal forfeiture laws can impact the property if the landlord is aware of any on-site use or distribution of controlled substances. Additional serious environmental problems can arise from the production of some controlled substances. See the section covering clandestine meth labs in Chapter 11. The forfeiture problem is discussed at the end of this chapter as it pertains to medical marijuana.

6. **Assignment and subletting**: Some tenants wish to relocate to another property before the expiration of their leases. Since a tenant is contractually obligated to the full lease term, he may attempt to find another tenant to take possession, pay the landlord, and finish out the lease. This occurs either through an assignment or a sublease. In either case, the tenant remains liable to the landlord for the original lease covenants, including the promise to pay rent, unless specifically released by the landlord.

   a. **Assignment versus sublease**: An assignment involves the transfer of the entire balance of lease rights by the tenant-assignor to the new tenant-assignee. If anything less than the full interest is transferred, a sublease has been created. A sublease can also occur if the tenant leases a portion of the leased premises to a third party. It operates like a lease within a lease. In either case, if the assignee defaults, the landlord can pursue the original tenant for the rent.

      (1) **Example–assignment**: A tenant signs a 1-year residential lease and takes possession on February 1st. On April 1st, the tenant's job is suddenly relocated to another state. The tenant's brother-in-law is willing to assume the lease for the 10 months remaining.

      (2) **Examples–sublease**: In one example, a commercial tenant who has completed year 1 of a 5-year lease, subleases years 2 and 3 to a third party. The original tenant resumes the lease for years 4 and 5. In another example, a commercial tenant leases 5,000 square feet and then down-sizes his business. The tenant-assignor subleases 1,200 of the 5,000 square feet to an attorney-assignee who needs the space for an office. The sublease ends when the original lease ends.

   b. **Nonassignment clause**: A lease is generally held to be fully assignable unless there is a lease provision to the contrary such as a nonassignment clause. Many landlords carefully screen the credit-worthiness of their tenants to reduce the possibility of default. A landlord might want to restrict assignments over concern that the tenant could assign the lease to a third party who has questionable credit. Nonassignment clauses, especially in residential leases, can be upheld for good cause. This would include an assignee who has a poor credit history.

   c. **Sale or transfer of the lessor's title interest**: As a general rule, if a landlord sells his leased property during the lease term, the lease is not automatically terminated and the buyer becomes the new landlord. From the tenant's perspective, the lease continues and the tenant vacates on the regularly-scheduled end date. If the landlord wants the lease to terminate in the event of a sale, he must reserve the right by including a sales clause in the lease agreement.

Chapter 13: Leases

        Sales clauses in leases are not common since few tenants are willing to invest the time and money relocating to a new residence or commercial building knowing that the landlord could sell the property and terminate the lease.

    7. ▸ **Lease-option**: A buyer who cannot afford to purchase a property due to poor credit or lack of a down payment may request that the owner lease the property to him with an option to purchase the property during the term of the lease. The transaction is referred to as a lease-option. In a variation of this situation, the landlord does not want to commit to selling his property using a lease-option. The landlord is willing, however, to give the tenant the right to match any offer the landlord receives if the landlord sells during the lease term.

        a. **Right to renew**: A right to renew clause is a flexible lease provision that allows the original lease term to be extended for an additional period of time. The clause may also be called an option to renew. For example, a 10-year lease with a 5-year option to renew may be treated by the tenant as a 15-year lease. The decision to renew is binding on the landlord if the tenant elects to take advantage of the option. The tenant does not have to exercise the renewal.

        b. ▸ **Option to purchase**: In a written lease with an option to purchase, the landlord gives the tenant an irrevocable and unconditional offer to purchase the leased property during the term of the lease or other stated period of time. To be enforceable, the option must be definite as to the time within which the option may be exercised as well as the price to be paid. Other option requirements must also be met including a statement that valuable consideration has been given by the tenant to the landlord. If the tenant is a holdover after expiration of the lease and has not exercised the option to purchase, it expires.

           (1) **Sale of property to someone other than the tenant**: If the landlord sells the property during the term of the lease-option to someone other than the tenant-optionee, the option runs with the land and is binding on the buyer (who becomes the new landlord). This holds especially true if the lease-option was recorded. In other words, the tenant keeps his option rights and can exercise them against the buyer.

           (2) **Not a right of first refusal**: As will be seen, an option to purchase can be confused with a right of first refusal. This is why careful drafting of leases is very important. A real estate licensee who is working with a landlord-client or tenant-client who wants to draft a lease-option should refer the client to his attorney. *[handwritten: tenant has option to make first offer]*

        c. ▸ **Right of first refusal**: A right of first refusal is a lease provision that gives a tenant the right to match an offer if the landlord sells during the lease term. It differs from a lease-option because it is conditioned on the landlord's mere willingness to sell without containing a binding promise to do so. If the landlord markets the property for sale during the term of the lease and receives an offer, the tenant is given the right to match it. This is why the landlord must condition the acceptance of the buyer's offer on the tenant's non-exercise of the right of first refusal.

           (1) **Conditional option**: A right of first refusal is also known as a conditional option since the landlord is not absolutely obligated to sell the property to the tenant during the term of the lease. The distinction may be found in the use of the word "first" in the lease clause. A clause labeled "first option" would be treated as a first refusal rather than an option.

III. **Legal implications of relationship**: There are multiple implications for the parties to a lease. In the case of a landlord, he must make sure that the property is leased and maintained in a habitable condition. The landlord is responsible for certain defects in the leased premises as well as defects and safety in the common areas of a multi-unit building. Tenants have their own responsibilities such as placing the landlord on notice for covered repairs and keeping the property in a sanitary condition. This section assumes that the parties have entered into a residential lease.

    A. **Condition of the premises**: At common law, caveat emptor was strictly applied to the landlord-tenant relationship meaning that the tenant took the premises in an "as is" condition regardless of the living conditions. Around the 1960s, legislatures began imposing statutory duties on residential landlords to provide a habitable premises, even if the negotiated lease did not so require them. These are known as implied warranties.

        1. **Implied warranty of habitability**: In the case of a residential lease, an implied warranty is one which the legislature presumes a landlord intended to include in his lease. This warranty requires the landlord to keep the rental property and all common areas (1) fit for the use intended by the parties, (2) in reasonable repair during the term of the lease, and (3) in compliance with applicable health and safety laws. Implied

warranties do not flow to commercial leases. Instead, the commercial tenant must negotiate whatever he wants into the lease agreement.

A residential landlord cannot attempt to waive or modify his duty to keep the premises habitable. If the landlord can show that a problem resulted from damage or neglect of the tenant, the landlord may be relieved of the duty to repair. Nevertheless, it may make sense for the landlord to repair the problem to prevent any further damages and then seek monetary damages in a court of law.

2. **Repair and maintenance issues**: Repair and maintenance issues generally fall into one of three categories. These categories include: major repairs; emergency repairs; and routine repairs and maintenance.

   a. **Latent defects versus patent defects**: Before assigning responsibility for repairs, a distinction must be drawn between defects that are patent, meaning obvious, and those which are latent, meaning hidden, from the tenant's view or knowledge. As a general rule, if a defect is latent, responsibility for repairs and liability for injuries shifts to the landlord.

      (1) **Major and emergency repairs**: A number of foreseeable problems relating to structural, mechanical, and appliance systems can arise during a lease. Repairs for these systems in residential leases are generally the responsibility of the landlord. This is due, in part, to the implied warranty of habitability.

      A major repair is one that has the potential to affect the quality of the living environment. An emergency repair can affect the living environment, but also poses an immediate threat to the health or safety of the occupants. Emergencies require prompt action by the landlord and include things such as natural gas leaks, floods and water infiltration, and heating and cooling system failures.

      The tenant must give the landlord notice and a reasonable time within which to make any major or emergency repairs. Reasonable will be determined by the severity of the problem, whether it represents a health or safety hazard to the occupants, and/or has the potential to cause escalating damage to the dwelling or the personal property of the tenant.

      (2) **Routine repairs and maintenance**: Routine repairs and maintenance include things like burned out light bulbs, dripping faucets, and carpet soils. The tenant is expected to keep the premises in a safe and sanitary condition. If the lease calls for the landlord to handle routine repairs and maintenance, the tenant must give the landlord notice and a reasonable time within which to make the repairs. If the tenant fails to notify the landlord or negligently makes the repair himself, he alone may be liable for injuries suffered by anyone in his household, including invited guests.

      Many lease agreements prohibit the tenant from personally making or arranging for an outside contractor to make repairs. Instead, the landlord reserves the right to do so to make sure that all repairs are done correctly (by the appropriate licensed contractor, if necessary). Depending on the lease and nature of the repair, the landlord may reserve the right to invoice the tenant for the cost. The lease may also give the landlord the right to periodically enter the premises to check for routine maintenance issues such as smoke detectors, leaking plumbing fixtures, and furnace filters.

   b. **Withholding rent**: Tenants often believe that they can withhold payment of the regularly scheduled rent if a landlord fails to make a requested repair. Unfortunately, it is not always that simple and a tenant should contact an attorney before doing so. In some cases, withholding rent can be viewed as a breach of contract by the tenant. If the problem renders the premises uninhabitable, the tenant may be released from the duty to pay rent as long as he surrenders possession to the landlord.

   If the tenant does not wish to relocate, the tenant's attorney may recommend that the tenant personally make the repair if absolutely necessary to protect the tenant's property, place the rent in an escrow account to show good faith, and serve written notice on the landlord. A real estate licensee should never suggest this course of action to a landlord or tenant with whom the licensee is working.

B. **Areas under the landlord's possession and control**: A landlord is generally responsible for (1) areas under his exclusive control including common areas such as hallways, stairs, entrance ways, parking areas, and recreation facilities; (2) areas that he has agreed in the lease to repair; and (3) equipment he owns, but reserves for the use of his tenants such as laundry machines and dryers.

C. **Improvements to premises**: Since a residential tenant takes a leased premises "as is," subject to the warranty of habitability, his only responsibility upon expiration is to return the property in the same condition minus

Chapter 13: Leases

normal wear and tear. Tenants, especially those who rent a single-family residential property, sometimes make improvements to the property during the lease. The parties to the lease should decide how to handle the added value to the structure (which may already be addressed in the lease agreement).

1. **Accession**: Under the doctrine of accession, all that is added to a property by nature or industry becomes part of the owner-landlord's property. Therefore, when a tenant improves a leased premises by adding things like fixtures, the items become part of the leased fee and ownership to them reverts to the landlord at the end of the lease. A landlord can prevent challenges over such items by including a clause to this effect in the lease.

2. ▶ **Trade fixtures**: Recall from Chapter 1 that trade fixtures are treated as the personal property of the tenant. In a commercial lease, the tenant will be allowed, and sometimes required, to remove all trade fixtures on expiration. In doing so, the tenant must restore the property to its original condition and repair any damages caused by their removal.

IV. ▶ **Types of leasehold estates**: There are many different types of leasehold arrangements that a landlord and tenant can create. Some arrangements are more suitable for commercial leases as opposed to residential leases. This section lists the more common types of leasehold estates and how they operate. For purposes of discussion, the expressions "estate" and "tenancy" are synonymous; for example, estate for years and tenancy for years. *See Figure 29.*

A. ▶ **Estate for years**: Estate for years refers to any lease that is created for a definite, fixed period of time. The length does not matter as long as the term is fixed for a given period of time in the terms of the lease. This is the most common type of leasehold. *[No notice needed to vacate]*

   1. **Termination**: Many leasehold types require the tenant to give the landlord notice if he wants to terminate the lease and vacate. In the case of an estate for years, the tenant does not have to give notice. The lease simply ends by natural expiration. There is a possibility, however, that the tenant does not vacate as required. When this occurs, the tenant is considered to be a holdover.

   2. **Holdover**: If a tenant becomes a holdover after the expiration of an estate for years, the landlord has a couple of options. It is best for the landlord to carefully weigh which option is best before pursuing one. An attorney can help with the selection process since legal actions dealing with residential landlord-tenant issues are typically handled in the local district court. If the dollar amount involved in a longer term lease exceeds $25,000, the circuit court is the proper jurisdiction.

   > **TYPES OF LEASEHOLD ESTATES...** *Figure 29*
   >
   > ■ **FREEHOLD** (ownership)
   > ■ **LEASEHOLD** (possessory)
   >   ▪ Estate for Years
   >   ▪ Estate at Will
   >   ▪ Periodic Tenancy
   >   ▪ Estate at Sufferance

   a. **Lessor options**: In the case of a holdover tenant, a lessor may elect to (1) treat the tenant as a trespasser and have him legally dispossessed, (2) renew the tenancy based on the fact that the tenant chose to remain in possession, or (3) convert the estate for years to a month-to-month or periodic tenancy providing the original lease called for monthly or periodic rental payments. *[month to month]*

   b. **Acceptance of rent after the lease expires**: A holdover tenant may continue to pay his rent on a timely basis. Landlords should be careful since the acceptance of rent after expiration may constitute a lease renewal. To avoid this, the landlord can include a lease provision stating that acceptance of money after a lease expires does not operate to extend or renew the lease.

B. ▶ **Estate at will**: An estate or tenancy at will is any lease in which a tenant is given implied consent to occupy a premises. It lasts for an indefinite period of time. As long as the tenant continues to occupy the property in an appropriate manner, the landlord may allow the tenancy to continue. The estate is terminable at the will or desire of either party. Historically, a tenancy at will arose when an owner allowed a party to move in and occupy his home, often without requiring compensation. *[Indefinite "99 Years"]*

   1. **Termination**: All that is required to terminate a tenancy at will is sufficient notice given by either party. In the case of a residential estate at will, 30 days advance notice is generally sufficient. Legal counsel should be consulted before attempting to terminate a tenancy at will.

[You must give notice to vacate]

[Handwritten at top: Freehold –]

2. **Examples**: An owner moves to a new home and allows a family member to occupy the old home until such time as the owner determines what he want to do with it. In another example, a tenant urgently needs to relocate to a new residence. The landlord allows the tenant to move in with the understanding that a written lease will be drafted at the earliest convenience of the parties. Care should always be exercised before allowing anyone to take possession of a premises without first having a written agreement.

C. ▶ **Estate from period-to-period**: An estate from period-to-period is similar to an estate at will in that it lasts for an indefinite or uncertain period of time. It differs in that the tenant acquires possession based on an actual agreement, i.e., a written lease, rather than implied consent. Rent payments can be made on a monthly, yearly, or other time-period basis. The agreement may be referred to as a month-to-month or year-to-year lease. It is also known as a periodic tenancy. Since the intent of the parties is to continue the lease arrangement indefinitely, it automatically renews from period-to-period until notice of termination is given.

[Margin note: Month to Month]

1. **Termination**: To terminate a periodic tenancy, either party simply needs to give sufficient notice to the other. The amount of advance notice may be determined by the rental period, but is typically a minimum of 30 days. Care should be exercised when a period is calculated on anything longer than a monthly basis. In such case it is best to first consult with legal counsel.

D. ▶ **Estate at sufferance**: An estate at sufferance arises after a tenant comes into lawful possession of a premises, meaning with the permission of the landlord, and then fails to vacate it after expiration. It is also known as a tenancy at sufferance. The landlord can enter a demand for possession with the district court to evict the tenant. The landlord can also attempt to hold the tenant over which converts the original leasehold to a periodic tenancy. If the landlord does nothing to dispossess or hold the tenant over, the tenant's continued occupancy is termed a tenancy at sufferance.

1. **Distinguished from trespass**: A trespass is the unlawful entry on the land of another. Technically, an estate at sufferance is not a trespass because the tenant acquired possession by way of the landlord's permission and agreement. Under Michigan law, a peaceful entry with a forceful stay is grounds for eviction.

V. ▶ **Specific types of leases**: There are many different types of specific lease agreements. The most variation is seen in commercial lease applications where flexibility is often critical. As a tip for learning lease types for the real estate examination, notice how most leases vary based on how the rent is calculated. Lease terms can also be tailored to meet other tenant needs.

A. ▶ **Gross lease**: In a gross lease, the tenant pays a set amount of rent from which the landlord then pays the major expenses associated with ownership of the property. These expenses typically include the property taxes, insurance, maintenance, and some utilities such as water. The word gross means consisting of some total before deductions. In the case of a gross lease, the tenant pays the total needed by the landlord to both cover his expenses and to make a profit. The gross lease is the most common type used in residential applications and is also known as a fixed gross lease.

[Margin note: – landlord pays mortgage – property taxes etc]

B. ▶ **Net lease**: With a net lease, the landlord calculates the rent on the basis of desired profit, but does not factor in expenses. Instead, the lessee is expected to pay expenses such as property taxes, insurance, maintenance, and most if not all utilities. In this sense, the landlord charges a rent amount that reflects what he wants for a net profit and then requires the tenant pay the expenses directly. The only major expense that the landlord continues to pay is the debt service on the property which is the mortgage principal and interest. A net lease is common in commercial properties. *[Handwritten: * does not includ mortgage]*

[Margin note: Tenant pays property taxes]

C. ▶ **Percentage lease**: A percentage lease allows the landlord to charge a fixed minimum rent along with a percentage of the lessee's gross business profits or gross sales. This type of lease is better suited to a tenant who has a new business that needs time to become financially established. Normally, a prime location carries a higher rental rate. To help the tenant, the landlord starts the lease at a lower base rent along with a fixed percent of the tenant's total business earnings. As earnings increase, so does the rent. A percentage lease is more likely to be used in shopping centers and similar commercial applications.

1. **Recapture clause**: While income potential may look promising for a start-up business, the possibility exists that the business could fail to reach expectations. To protect the landlord against this possibility, a percentage lease may include a recapture clause. The clause allows the landlord to prematurely terminate the lease and dispossess the tenant if gross sales do not reach a predetermined benchmark or level.

D. **Variable rent lease arrangements**: Since commercial leases are commonly long-term in nature, the landlord may wish to include one or more rent adjustment mechanisms. A landlord cannot increase the rent in a lease

Chapter 13: Leases 203

without the contractual right to do so. These variable adjustment mechanisms are found in graduated leases, index leases, and reappraisal leases.

1. **Graduated lease**: A graduated lease is one in which periodic rent adjustments are tied to the mere passage of time. The word graduated means progressive. Other lease types can also include a graduated rent clause.

2. **Index lease**: In an index lease, the rental rate is tied to an economic indicator such as the Consumer Price Index (CPI). As economic conditions fluctuate, the index changes and the rent rate can be adjusted accordingly. The CPI is a good index since it reflects changes in the prices of goods and services for consumers. When the rent rate is tied to an index, it can increase as the index is adjusted upward, but rarely decreases if the index is adjusted downward.

3. **Reappraisal lease**: A reappraisal lease is one in which the rent is tied to the appraised value of the building being leased. This lease is well suited to a landlord who constructs a building on the outskirts of an urban area. To attract new businesses, the landlord decreases the rent to a lower rate. As the area develops and the building becomes more valuable, the landlord increases the rent to reflect the increase in value. Periodic rent adjustments are typically tied to a percentage of the current appraised value or assessed value of the building.

E. ▶ **Ground lease**: A ground lease involves either the leasing of vacant land or the leasing of land excluding any existing buildings. The lease is generally net in nature and involves forestry, farming, and other agricultural uses. A tenant who enters into a ground lease for forestry or agricultural purposes should include a provision that allows the profits and emblements to be harvested. See Chapter 6 for the definitions of profits and emblements.

F. **Section 8 Housing**: The Department of Housing and Urban Development (HUD) manages several programs which are designed to help lower-income families obtain a decent place to live. These programs stem from Section 8 of the United States Housing Act of 1937. Some Section 8 programs target privately-owned housing where HUD helps apartment owners offer reduced rent rates to low-income tenants. Other public housing programs are established to provide affordable apartments for low-income families, the elderly, and persons with disabilities. An important Section 8 program provides for Housing Choice Vouchers that allow tenants to locate their own place to live and then use the voucher to pay for all or part of the rent.

G. ▶ **Rentable square feet versus usable square feet**: When commercial space is offered for lease, especially office space, the landlord or property manager typically lists the available space using the phrase "rentable square footage" or "rentable building area" rather than usable square footage. This distinction is important for tenants.

1. **Rentable square footage**: Rentable square footage includes the actual space the tenant will occupy along with a prorata share of all common areas. Prospective commercial tenants generally only look at the actual floor space they intend to occupy. From the landlord's perspective, all tenants in the building benefit from common area features. These include: lobbies and hallways; community restrooms, conference and meeting spaces, kitchens, cafeterias, and storage spaces; security stations; and possibly protected parking areas.

2. **Usable square footage**: Usable square footage is typically a smaller number compared to rentable square footage. This is due to the fact that usable square footage only includes the specific floor space to be occupied by the tenant. It also includes any floor space designated for the exclusive use of the tenant such as private restrooms, kitchenettes, storage, unit hallways, etc.

VI. **Termination of lease rights**: Lease rights are similar to other contract rights. Termination may result from the actions of the parties including performance and expiration, giving proper notice, merger, and abandonment of the premises. Rights may also be terminated by operation of law including condemnation of the leased premises, some bankruptcy actions, and destruction of the premises.

A. **Performance and expiration**: The most common and preferred way for a lease to end is through complete performance by the tenant. Upon expiration, the responsibilities of both the landlord and the tenant end except those relating to unpaid or back rent, unpaid utility bills, or damage to the structure resulting from the actions of the tenant.

B. **Notice**: As noted in earlier discussion, when a leasehold automatically renews from period-to-period or continues at will, it can be terminated by either the landlord or the tenant serving proper notice on the other party. Typically, 30-day advance notice is required. This time is shortened by statute if a notice to quit is given by the landlord to the tenant for non-payment of rent, use of a controlled substance on the premises, or threats of physical violence by the tenant. These factors are explained later in this chapter.

C. **Merger**: Recall from Chapter 12 that a prior, inferior contract can merge into a subsequent and superior contract that covers the same subject matter. Assume for this example that a tenant purchases the leased premises prior to the expiration of the lease. The tenant's possessory interest in the lease merges into the ownership interest acquired through the purchase. In other words, the lease merges into the deed at the closing of the sale and is no longer in effect.

D. **Abandonment of the premises**: Abandonment of a lease is a unilateral action by a tenant who stops paying rent and vacates the premises before expiration of the lease. As a basic rule, abandonment does not terminate the lease. The tenant remains liable for the balance of the rent as it comes due. This is based on the concept that a tenant can enter into a lease for a dwelling and then choose to live elsewhere. As long as the lease remains in effect, the tenant has the exclusive right to possess the premises and owes the rent.

If a tenant legally abandons the leased premises, the landlord has the option of treating the abandonment as a surrender of possession. When the landlord accepts the surrender, it operates as an agreement to terminate the lease. The tenant is no longer liable for any future rent. The landlord can also attempt to re-let (meaning re-rent) the premises to a new tenant.

1. **Surrender (and acceptance)**: A surrender differs from an abandonment in that a surrender is a mutual agreement by the parties to terminate the lease prior to expiration. When a tenant surrenders a lease, he relinquishes possession and the landlord agrees to accept it. This is why a surrender is also called a surrender and acceptance. Mere abandonment, even if the landlord accepts the keys, is not enough to constitute a surrender. There must be some form of agreement between the parties to terminate the lease. An acceptance of the tenant's surrender would likely be construed by a court if the landlord accepts the keys from the abandoning tenant and assumes control of the unit by cleaning and preparing it for a new tenant.

2. **Duty to mitigate damages**: Under Michigan common law, when a tenant abandons a premises, even if the abandonment is wrongful, the landlord has a duty to mitigate the tenant's damages. To mitigate means to reduce. If the tenant abandons the premises, the landlord cannot simply wait for each month's rent to come due and then sue for it. A landlord must, instead, use reasonable efforts to locate a new tenant who is willing to rent the abandoned premises.

   Without delay, the landlord should place a "for rent" sign on the premises, possibly place an advertisement in a local newspaper or online, and perform the normal cleaning, maintenance, and preparation of the premises for a new tenant. The abandoning tenant is responsible for any rent that accrues until a new tenant is located. Once the new tenant is secured, the rent is used to offset the balance of the rent the abandoning tenant owes. If the new lease is for a lower rent, the abandoning tenant is liable for the difference. Michigan's Truth in Renting Act prevents a landlord from using a lease that releases the landlord from his duty to mitigate damages (see Chapter 21 for further information).

E. **Operation of law**: Events that can cause a lease to end by operation of law include (1) the condemnation of the property, (2) destruction of the premises, and (3) some outcomes in a bankruptcy action. When it comes to the bankruptcy of a commercial landlord, the tenant should monitor the process with the help of his attorney since the landlord may be given an opportunity to either assume or reject any existing leases.

F. **Breach of a lease covenant and forfeiture**: At common law, a forfeiture clause in a lease gave the landlord the right to terminate the lease upon the default of any specific lease covenant by the tenant. Some landlords have attempted to use arguably oppressive forfeiture clauses as a legal hammer to terminate a lease and all of the tenant's rights. Courts tend to view such forfeiture clauses with suspicion and interpret them in favor of the tenant as the non-drafting party. As discussed below, residential lease laws in Michigan do allow a landlord to serve a notice to quit on a breaching tenant under certain circumstances.

G. **Eviction**: Nearly all lease-related statutes are designed to protect residential tenants against unscrupulous landlords. Fortunately, the majority of residential landlords are responsible individuals. However, to make sure that all residential tenants are treated fairly, statutes have been enacted and court rulings have been handed down to make sure a tenant's rights in an eviction procedure are equitably and uniformly applied.

1. **Eviction defined**: As a legal concept, eviction is any act by the landlord which is intended to dispossess a tenant of his rights under a lease. These acts can result from the landlord re-entering the premises without the lawful right to do so, or from the landlord physically ejecting the tenant. Eviction can also occur by process of law. To summarize, eviction includes the lawful process a landlord uses to dispossess a tenant, as well as improper actions by the landlord to remove a non-defaulting tenant.

Chapter 13: Leaves

legal w/ sheriff

a. **Actual eviction**: Actual eviction is the form of eviction that occurs when a landlord physically dispossesses his tenant from all or a substantial portion of the premises. It can also result from any demand by a landlord that his tenant vacate the premises. When a landlord serves a notice to quit on a tenant, an actual eviction has commenced.

b. **Constructive eviction**: Constructive eviction, on the other hand, occurs when a landlord commits some act, or fails to act when necessary, thereby rendering the premises unfit for the intended occupancy. Recall that the word constructive means construed or implied by the law. Examples include a landlord who fails to pay for utilities that are called for in the lease, or a landlord who refuses to repair a leaking roof that was damaged by a recent storm.

   (1) **Tenant relinquishes possession**: In the case of a constructive eviction, the tenant may be able to surrender possession within a reasonable time, but not merely to withhold the rent. If the tenant remains on the premises, he may be deemed to have waived the condition. Even in such case, however, the condition cannot be so severe that it affects habitability or safety since a residential tenant is always protected by the statutory implied warranty of habitability.

c. **Retaliatory eviction**: A retaliatory eviction is any eviction brought by a landlord in an attempt to strike back at a tenant who has done something to anger the landlord. The eviction in such circumstances is considered to be improper and may be illegal. For example, a tenant whose landlord fails to repair a broken furnace in the winter files a complaint with the city for an ordinance violation. The landlord evicts the tenant for filing the complaint. Other cases involve tenants who were evicted for reporting civil rights violations by their landlords. Retaliatory eviction is illegal in Michigan for residential leases. If it happens in a commercial lease, it may represent a breach of contract by the landlord.

H. **Summary proceedings and the right of reentry**: Since a landlord conveys exclusive possession, he does not have the right to reenter the leased premises without a provision in the lease to do so. A landlord may reserve the right to reenter the premises for purposes of maintenance and repair and to protect the property in the case of emergencies. Michigan law provides several circumstances in which a landlord may legally enter a premises to regain possession. These circumstances are found in the Summary Proceedings Act.

1. **Summary proceedings**: A summary proceeding is a prompt and simple court action that does not involve a jury. Michigan's summary proceedings statute allows a landlord to recover possession of a leased premises based on certain conditions. The statute makes it easier for landlords who are dealing with defaulting tenants by providing for a speedy trial. An action is filed by a landlord in the local district or municipal court. Before a landlord can dispossess a tenant, the tenant is entitled to notice. In some cases, the tenant is given an opportunity to cure or remedy the problem.

2. ▶ **Demand for possession/Notice to quit defined**: The "demand for possession" *(violated terms)* and "notice to quit" *(notice to move)* are types of forms used in eviction. While the terms are often used interchangeably (including on the real estate exam), there is a difference based on the situation or event that triggers the eviction. For example, a demand for possession is used when a breach of a lease term has occurred such as non-payment of rent or use of controlled substances on the leased premises. The notice to quit is used in situations in which a landlord wants the tenant to move out at a natural point in the tenancy; for example, at the end of a particular month in a periodic tenancy.

   The landlord officially serves the form on the tenant. It must be in writing, addressed to the tenant, include the address or brief description of the premises, the reason for the demand, and time to take remedial action. The form can be personally delivered, sent by first-class mail, or sent electronically, via email, to the tenant. (Before using email, the landlord must have written permission and send a test email to which the tenant responds for verification purposes.) The notice to quit does not require the tenant to move out within the stated time, although the tenant may voluntarily do so. It merely places the tenant on notice that a legal action will commence in district court to regain possession at the end of the notice period.

   a. **Violation of a lease provision–30 day notice to quit**: If a tenant violates a lease provision, and the lease specifies that the lease may be terminated in the event of a breach, the landlord can serve the tenant with a 30 day notice to quit. This time period is consistent with the minimum notice a landlord must give a non-defaulting tenant in the case of a periodic tenancy or for a holdover tenant. For example, a lease contains a "no pets" clause and a tenant obtains a dog as a pet without seeking permission from the landlord. The tenant fails to re-home the dog upon written demand by the landlord and the landlord serves the tenant with a 30 day notice to quit.

b. **Nonpayment of rent–7 day notice to quit**: A 7-day notice to quit may be filed by a landlord on a tenant for nonpayment of rent. If the lease contains a valid forfeiture clause for nonpayment of rent, the proper authority is allowed to terminate the lease and re-enter the premises upon issuance of a writ of eviction by the court. An eviction action includes a hearing before the district court judge and a jury trial if the tenant requests one. The entire process can take from approximately 4 weeks to 8 weeks, so the landlord needs to be patient.

   (1) **Removal of tenant's property**: Upon gaining the legal right to retake possession, the landlord should never touch or remove the personal belongings of the tenant without a Sheriff present to conduct the process. The landlord should also take photographs before removing property and after properly removing it to avoid a claim by the tenant of conversion, meaning theft. The lease may also call for the landlord to store the defaulting tenant's personal belongings in a suitable storage facility for a short term such as 30 days.

   (2) **Landlord's acceptance of rent during the 7 day period**: While not all courts may rule the same way, if a landlord accepts any rental payments during the 7 day period, it may constitute a waiver by the landlord of the right to continue with the eviction action. To avoid this result, a landlord should consult with legal counsel before accepting rent after serving a notice to quit.

c. **Use of controlled substances on premises–24 hour notice to quit**: Providing there is a lease provision to this effect, a lease may be terminated if a tenant, member of the tenant's household, or a person under the tenant's control uses, possesses, manufactures, or delivers controlled substances, i.e., illegal drugs, on the premises. The landlord can bring a summary proceeding action to recover possession if the tenant fails to vacate within 24 hours after being served a demand for possession for a controlled substance violation.

   (1) **Police report must be filed**: A formal police report must first be filed alleging that the person has unlawfully manufactured, delivered, or possessed a controlled substance on the property. Originally, the landlord must have been the person who filed the report. The landlord can now rely on a police report that has been filed by any other party such as a neighbor or occupant of another rental unit.

d. **Injury to premises**: A 7 day notice to quit may be issued by a landlord within 90 days of discovering that a tenant has willfully or negligently caused a serious and continuing health hazard on the leased premises or caused extensive and continuing physical injury to the premises. The tenant may substantially restore or repair the premises to avoid eviction. As noted in Chapter 16 (in the discussion pertaining to foreclosure), this can result in a termination of the statutory redemption period for an owner whose mortgage has been foreclosed.

e. **Causing or threatening physical injury to an individual**: A 7 day notice to quit may be issued by a landlord if a tenant, a member of the tenant's household, or a person under the tenant's control causes or threatens physical injury to an individual. The police department must first be notified that the tenant has caused or threatened such physical injury. This provision does not apply if the injured or threatened person is the tenant or a member of the tenant's household, or if the eviction would result in a violation of federal housing regulations. Michigan law has a separate provision that protects tenants who are victims of domestic violence. It is discussed later in this chapter.

3. **Self-help and Michigan's anti-lockout law**: At common law, a landlord had the right of self-help to use reasonable force to personally remove a defaulting tenant. Today, this is no longer true. A landlord's right to re-enter a leased premises is limited to the Summary Proceedings Act. Michigan law also contains an anti-lockout provision to further protect tenants from wrongful ejection.

I. **Death of landlord**: The death of the landlord automatically terminates a tenancy at will, for example, due to the personal nature of the tenancy. Other written lease types continue if the landlord dies. When a landlord dies, his heirs or devisees typically inherit the property and the lease continues according to its terms. The tenant pays the rent to the estate or the landlord's heirs. If the heirs attempt to evict the tenant, they may be liable for breach of contract and damages under Michigan landlord-tenant laws.

J. **Foreclosure and short sale of a leased property**: Questions can arise if a property which is subject to a valid lease is foreclosed. For example, does the foreclosure of the property cancel the lease, or does the tenant retain possession until the lease expires in spite of the fact that title to the property has transferred to the lender? Also, does the foreclosure of the property relieve the tenant of his contractual duty to pay rent?

Chapter 13: Leases

1. **State law**: Michigan law does not allow a tenant to stop paying rent even if the landlord is in jeopardy of losing the property to a mortgage, tax, or association lien foreclosure. If a foreclosure is initiated, the landlord is considered to have breached the lease. However, until the landlord's rights in the property are actually terminated, the tenant is obligated to pay rent. This is due to the fact that the landlord has the ability to cure the default. The landlord can redeem the property up to the last day of the statutory redemption period. Foreclosure rights are discussed in more detail in Chapter 16. In the case of unpaid association fees, the tenant may be able to pay them to keep the property from being foreclosed and then deduct the amount from the rent due the landlord.

2. **Short sale of a leased property**: When a landlord attempts the short sale of a property which is subject to an existing lease, the tenant's rights may be affected. Ordinarily, the terms of a lease control whether or not it terminates if the property is sold during the lease term. The fact that a short sale is being attempted should not change these terms. The "short" aspect of the sale is strictly a matter between the seller-landlord and his lender which is separate from the lease agreement. Whoever acquires ownership of the property from the landlord as a result of a short sale stands in the same legal position as would any other buyer, and the lease likely continues depending on its terms.

K. **Domestic violence and duty to pay rent**: According to P.A. 199, effective October 5, 2010, a landlord must release a tenant from rental payment obligations when the tenant submits a written notice, by certified mail, together with the required documentation that the tenant has a reasonable apprehension of present danger to the tenant or his or her child due to domestic violence, sexual assault, or stalking. Proponents of this law note that victims of domestic violence are often vulnerable to repeat violations and must relocate to evade their abusers.

   1. **Required documents**: There are several forms of acceptable documentation that a tenant can provide to assert his or her reasonable apprehension. These forms generally include a provision that the alleged or actual abuser is not to have contact with the tenant or the tenant's child. The specific forms of notice include the following:

      a. **PPO**: A valid Personal Protection Order or Foreign Protection Order.

      b. **Probation**: A Probation Order, Conditional Release Order, or Parole Order.

      c. **Police report**: A written police report may be used if it resulted in the filing of charges by the prosecuting attorney having jurisdiction over the matter.

      d. **Third party report**: A report may be submitted to the landlord in the form of an affidavit that is verified by a qualified third party such as a licensed health professional, social worker, or clergy member.

   2. **Release from rent**: Upon submission of the written notice and corresponding documentation, the tenant must be released from any further obligation to pay rent. The release does not apply to prepaid amounts such as the first and last months' rent nor does it prevent a landlord from withholding security deposits in compliance with Michigan law.

   3. **Required notice of tenant's rights**: All residential tenants must receive notice of their rights under this Act.

      a. **Notice in the lease agreement**: A rental agreement may contain a provision stating "A tenant who has a reasonable apprehension of present danger to him or her or his or her child from domestic violence, sexual assault, or stalking may have special statutory rights to seek a release of rental obligation under MCL 554.601b."

      b. **Alternate notice**: If a rental agreement does not contain the above-stated provision, a landlord must either post a written notice in a visible place in his or her office or deliver a separate written notice to the tenant when the rental agreement is signed.

L. **Use of marijuana on a leased premises**: The Michigan Medical Marihuana Act (MMMA) of 2009 and the Michigan Regulation and Taxation of Marihuana Act approved by Michigan voters in 2018 are raising numerous questions for landlords. Many of these questions involve a landlord's right to restrict or prohibit the smoking or other use of medical or recreational marijuana on a leased premises (note that Michigan laws use the spelling "marihuana"). Other questions involve a tenant's right to request a reasonable accommodation under civil rights laws thereby enabling the tenant to use medically-prescribed marijuana based on a claim that his disability justifies its use. In other words, does a landlord violate a tenant's civil rights for failing to permit the smoking or growing of medical marijuana on the leased premises.

Marijuana use and cultivation (i.e., growing) laws continue to evolve through new state laws, statutory amendments of existing laws, court cases, Attorney General Opinions, and U.S. Justice Department opinions. As a result, any landlord, tenant, or property manager who is confronted with questions pertaining to marijuana (whether for medical or recreational use) should first consult legal counsel for an opinion. Further, a real estate licensee should not attempt to provide any level of guidance or advice on the issue.

1. **Marijuana use in Michigan**: Under Michigan's medical marijuana law, seriously ill individuals are allowed to use marijuana for its pain or symptom-relieving effects. Even though medical marijuana was still considered to be illegal when the MMMA was enacted in 2009, patients possessing a registry identification card were protected from prosecution under state law. With the approval of the Michigan Regulation and Taxation of Marijuana Act in 2018, all persons who are at least 21 years of age may now possess up to 2.5 ounces of marijuana and grow up to 12 plants for personal use in non-public places.

2. **A landlord may prohibit smoking and cultivation on a premises**: Public Act 546, effective April of 2017, gives a landlord the right to prohibit the smoking and/or cultivation of marijuana anywhere on a leased premises. This prohibition must be included in the written lease. It also appears that this prohibition applies to patient- or caregiver-tenants under the MMMA providing the lease clause clearly spells this out.

3. **Prohibiting the use of medical marijuana does not violate civil rights**: An Attorney General opinion in 2011 indicated that Michigan's Elliott-Larsen Civil Rights Act and Persons with Disabilities Civil Rights Act do not prohibit a property owner, i.e., landlord, from adopting a policy declining to rent, lease, or provide an accommodation to a person who engages in the medical use of marijuana on the premises. P.A. 546 appears to strengthen this opinion. To be on the safe side, however, if a tenant requests a reasonable accommodation to smoke or otherwise use medical marijuana in a leased premises under Michigan civil rights law, the landlord should consult legal counsel prior to denying the request.

4. **Local ordinances may not preempt state law**: A 2014 Michigan Supreme Court case held that local municipalities may not enact local ordinances (such as zoning ordinances) that attempt to preempt, meaning take away, marijuana rights afforded under state law.

5. **Forfeiture of property under federal law**: Under federal law, marijuana is illegal whether for medical or recreational use. Some legal experts, therefore, suggest that a landlord should never authorize a tenant to smoke, use, or grow even medical marijuana on a leased premises due to the forfeiture provisions of the federal Controlled Substances Act. The Act allows for the forfeiture of real property owned by the landlord that is used in the commission of a violation under federal law. Such violation could also result in the tenant forfeiting his leasehold interest and any personal property or money deemed to have been used in connection with the violation.

    a. **Safe harbor**: Federal law creates a safe harbor for a landlord to the extent that the violation was committed "without the knowledge or consent of the landlord." This safe harbor protection could potentially be lost if a tenant-patient asks the landlord for permission to smoke or grow medical marijuana on the premises. If the landlord consents, he may not be able to later defend the forfeiture on the basis that he was not aware of the illegal activity.

    b. **New concerns for landlords**: Previously, the Department of Justice of the United States (DOJ) was not challenging laws passed in states legalizing medical marijuana or recreational use by adults. In 2018, the DOJ reversed its policy of noninterference with state law. While a landlord may believe most tenants will not violate existing laws, if a tenant does, the landlord could potentially lose his property.

6. **Potential title insurance and lender issues**: Many lenders and title insurance companies are reluctant to provide their services and close on transactions for properties intended to be used for cultivating and/or selling marijuana. While the reasons for doing so are beyond the scope of this textbook, real estate professionals should be aware of the potential for this problem to arise in a particular transaction.

7. **Working with buyers and sellers who list or purchase properties involving the marijuana industry**: If a real estate licensee is asked by a seller or purchaser to assist in the listing or acquisition of a property that will be used in the marijuana business, the licensee should first contact his broker to determine what the company's policy is on the matter. Assuming the broker approves the listing or sale, the client or customer should be immediately advised to contact an attorney who is competent in marijuana law who can advise the client or customer. Since state and federal laws are currently inconsistent as to rights, responsibilities, and/or potential liability, great care must be exercised.

DIAGNOSTIC PRACTICE QUESTIONS – CHAPTER 13

IMPORTANT STUDY TIP!

Step 1: Carefully review the information located in this chapter.

Step 2: Take the following Diagnostic Practice Questions. Review any question you answered incorrectly by researching the topic in this textbook. If you are still uncertain as to why the question is answered as it is, consult your program provider.

NOTE ON CHAPTER PRACTICE QUESTIONS

The following questions are representative of the type encountered on the Michigan real estate licensing examination. While some of these questions may be similar in nature and style, there is no way of predicting the exact wording of a question that will appear on the exam. Spending time memorizing these questions is, therefore, not recommended.

These questions are designed to help you determine how well you comprehend the material in this chapter. They are also intended to help you develop problem solving skills and to become comfortable with question formats.

Do not attempt to answer these questions until you have attended the lecture corresponding to this chapter and spent the appropriate time studying the material.

1. A group of 4 biology students from the local university sign a lease agreement to rent a cottage near a nature preserve. Since they are conducting research for 1 semester, the term of the lease is only for 16 weeks. This lease is an example of a:
   A. Tenancy for years.
   B. Periodic tenancy.
   C. Tenancy at will.
   D. Tenancy at sufferance.

2. Lynda Lessee entered into a 5 year lease in a retail strip center to open a specialty children's clothing store. Two years later, her daughter and son-in-law surprised Lynda with a granddaughter so Lynda decided to move to Nashville to be near them. She sold her business to her sister Mary and the landlord agreed to allow Mary to continue the lease. This transfer of rights is called a(n):
   A. Subrogation.
   B. Sublease.
   C. Assignment.
   D. Sublet.

3. Under Michigan law, a landlord is expected to keep a residential leased premises in reasonable repair according to the:
   A. Implied warranty of fitness for a particular use.
   B. Implied warranty of habitability.
   C. Implied agency that exists between a landlord and his tenants.
   D. Implied warranty of good workman-like quality.

4. A prospective tenant is starting a new computer-related business. Although the tenant does not have much working capital, his likelihood for success is high due to the nature of the business. As a result, the landlord proposes to establish a lower base rent and then charge a small percentage of the tenant's gross receipts. This type of lease is best described as:
   A. A gross lease.
   B. A percentage lease.
   C. A net lease.
   D. A reappraisal lease.

5. Upon the expiration of a 1 year lease, all of the following obligations survive EXCEPT:
   A. Past due rent.
   B. Damages to the premises.
   C. Overdue utility bills.
   D. Common area maintenance.

6. A landlord of a multi-unit residential apartment building is told by a neighboring tenant that another tenant is using his unit as an illegal methamphetamine lab. All of the following statements are true EXCEPT:
   A. The lease must have a provision dealing with eviction under such circumstances.
   B. The landlord can bring a summary proceeding if the tenant fails to vacate within 24 hours after being served a notice to quit.
   C. The tenant can be evicted, but only if he is the person directly responsible for manufacturing the illegal drugs.

D. A police report must be filed with the local authorities before evicting the tenant.

7. When the lessor under an existing written lease dies, how is the agreement between the parties affected?
   A. The lease is void.
   B. The lease is immediately terminated.
   C. Most leases can be terminated, but only by the lessor's estate.
   D. Most leases are generally not affected.

8. The conveyance of an estate by lease is called a:
   A. Devise.
   B. Demise.
   C. Decree.
   D. Dedication.

9. Terrance Tenant lives in a multi-unit residential building and finds that the living conditions become unacceptable due to rodent infestation. Upon reporting it to the landlord, he tells Terrance, "It's not my problem since they are in your apartment." All EXCEPT which of the following statements accurately describes the tenant's rights?
   A. The tenant may treat the landlord's response and inaction as an act of constructive eviction.
   B. The tenant may vacate the premises and stop paying rent under the circumstances.
   C. The landlord has violated his implied warranty of habitability in the leased premises.
   D. The landlord is within his rights to refuse the request because a lease conveys exclusive possession.

10. Using the facts from question 9 above, another tenant in the building reports the landlord to the county health department based on the rodent infestation. The landlord, who is cited and fined, demands that the reporting tenant leave the building. The landlord has committed a:
    A. Retaliatory eviction.
    B. Distraint.
    C. Constructive eviction.
    D. Summary proceeding.

11. A net lease ordinarily does not require payment by the lessee for which of the following:
    A. Mortgage debt service.
    B. Property tax.
    C. Maintenance on the property.
    D. Insurance premiums.

12. To allow a property owner to benefit from the effects of changing price levels, which type of lease arrangement would a property manager most likely favor for his client?

A. Long-term with rental set at middle of present-day range.
B. Long-term with rental set at the high end of present-day range.
C. Any length term with rental set at the high end of present-day range.
D. Any length term with an escalation clause.

13. After a one year lease expires, the tenant retains possession of the premises without informing the owner. The landlord may now treat the lease as:
    A. A tenancy for years.
    B. A tenancy at will.
    C. A tenancy from month to month.
    D. A tenancy at sufferance.

14. Which of the following is not ordinarily associated with a lessor-lessee relationship?
    A. A life estate.
    B. An estate at will.
    C. An estate for years.
    D. A demise.

15. The lowest estate in real property known to law is:
    A. A trespassory estate.
    B. A tenancy at sufferance.
    C. An estate for years.
    D. A tenancy at will.

16. Under which of the following circumstances is a lessee released from his or her obligation to pay rent?
    A. If he abandons the leased premises.
    B. If he believes that the payment of rent is conditioned on the lessor's performance of the lease.
    C. If he is constructively evicted from the leased premises.
    D. If the landlord has not responded to a request for a rent concession.

Chapter 14
Property Management *Brokers License*

Generating rental income and preserving an income property owner's investment.

I. **Foreword**: Property management is an area of real estate specialization that has grown due to the increase in urban development and multi-unit housing complexes. In recent years, many traditional real estate brokers have added property management to the services they offer. This has been partly in response to the increase in lease transactions resulting from the high number of foreclosures of the 2000s. Fluctuating property values have also played a role in this growth.

As an example, a property owner wants to sell his home, but is concerned that he will not be able to realize a suitable price for his home due to the decline in property values in his neighborhood. The owner instead elects to lease his home for a year to allow property values to recover. The owner "lists" his home with a real estate broker to locate a tenant (rather than a buyer). Since the owner may be a first-time landlord, it is natural that he would turn to his broker for help managing his new landlord-tenant relationship during the lease.

   A. **Who benefits from professional management**: Property managers assume the long-term operation and maintenance responsibilities for the owners of commercial structures, multi-unit residential developments, and single-family dwellings in various locations. The following property types are especially well-suited to professional management: office buildings; retail shopping centers; warehouses; manufacturing facilities; hotels and resorts; parking garages; multi-family apartments; condominium associations; homeowner's associations; manufactured (i.e., mobile) home communities; and vacation properties and timeshare communities.

   B. **Property management defined**: Property management is a real estate service through which an income-property owner hires a professional to administer, control, and/or oversee the operation of his property for the purpose of fulfilling one or more key goals. Many states, such as Michigan, require property managers to be licensed.

   C. **Property manager defined**: A property manager is the professional who is hired by the income property owner to: (1) Generate income through renting of the owner's property; (2) Preserve the value of the investment by making sure that the property is properly maintained; and (3) Manage the relationships the landlord has with his tenants. A broker does not act in the capacity of a property manager when he merely "lists" a client's home or building for the purpose of locating a tenant. Property management services only come into play when that same owner hires the broker to perform the services described above.

      1. ▶ **License law definition**: According to Michigan real estate license law, property management is the leasing or renting, or the offering to lease or rent, of real property of others for a fee, commission, compensation, or other valuable consideration pursuant to a property management employment contract.

      2. **Property manager licensure requirements**: As first introduced in Chapter 13, the Michigan license law definition of a real estate broker includes one who leases or offers to lease real estate for others. Therefore, property management services can only be provided by a licensed real estate broker. There is no separate property manager's license. No license is required, however, if a property owner self-manages property he owns regardless of the number of properties involved. Refer to Chapter 19, Article 25, for further discussion about real estate license law and property manager licensing requirements.

         A property management employment contract must exist between the broker and the owner of the managed property. A salesperson may not manage property for others in his individual capacity. When a real estate salesperson provides property management services, it is only as an agent for the broker under whom the salesperson is licensed. As discussed in Chapter 20, the administrative rules for the practice of real estate allow a real estate salesperson to self-manage any property that he personally owns.

II. **Scope of management services**: Although maintaining friendly landlord-tenant relations is an important goal of a property manager, other more critical objectives exist including generating income from property rentals and preserving the value of the owner's investment in the property. Property management encompasses a potentially wide range of services. Full-time professional property managers typically offer all or most of the services discussed in this section based on the needs and desires of the client.

   A. **Generating income**: A property manager seeks the highest net operating income over the economic life of his clients' properties. One way to accomplish this is by reducing both vacancy rates and/or excessive operating expenses. As discussed in Chapter 4, the value of an income property such as a multi-unit office building is measured in terms of its ability to attract and retain qualified, paying tenants. An income property will be of little value to its owner if the vacancy rate remains at a high level year-after-year.

   B. **Preserving the investment**: A property manager is expected to preserve the value of an income property by making sure that it is properly maintained in a cost-efficient manner. The manager will be responsible for hiring individuals such as contractors to handle repairs and capital improvements, landscaping professionals to maintain the grounds, and custodial help to keep the common areas clean and functional. Most of these services are provided by outside contractors. Custodial workers can either be directly employed by the building owner or hired and managed by an outside contractor. The property manager will often negotiate the contracts and oversee the work to make sure it is completed properly and on time.

   C. **Agency status of a property manager**: Since a property manager is hired to manage a broad range of activities, he usually acts in the capacity of a general agent for the owner-client. Along with specific management duties, the property manager owes each of the fiduciary duties discussed in Chapter 2. They include things such as loyalty, notice of material facts, care, obedience, and accounting.

   D. **Ascertaining compliance with existing laws**: A property manager is expected to be aware of and conform all management activities to existing laws including: the Truth in Renting Act which governs residential lease contracts; the Landlord Tenant Relationships Act which governs security deposits in residential lease applications; as well as local, state, and federal fair housing laws. Many municipalities also have ordinances that affect leasehold properties. A municipality can issue an expensive citation for violations of its codes. Chapter 13 discusses some of these rental property ordinances.

   1. **Environmental hazards**: A knowledgeable manager can alert his owner-client if a tenant's proposed use of a leased premises is potentially risky from an environmental perspective. A working knowledge of basic environmental hazards posed by various uses will be helpful to a property manager who handles certain commercial properties. For example, dry cleaners, gas stations and automotive service stations, and many manufacturing facilitates use or generate hazardous by-products.

III. **Types of managers**: Just as property management can involve different types of properties, the nature of property management services can vary based on the type of property being managed. Notice the difference between a building manager, resident manager, and the type of services commonly provided by real estate brokers who offer property management services.

   A. **Building manager**: A building manager is an individual who offers property management services that are limited to one particular building rather than many different properties. A building manager may be employed by a property management company and then assigned to a particular client's building. A building manager can also be directly hired by a building owner as an employee who earns compensation on an hourly or salaried basis.

   B. **Resident manager**: A resident manager typically acts as an on-site representative of a property management company that manages a large apartment complex. These complexes often consist of several hundred units. He is called a resident manager because he lives in a designated unit at the complex that is often attached or adjacent to the rental office. One or more resident managers may be hired per residential complex.

   C. **Services offered by real estate brokerage firms**: As noted, a real estate broker has the statutory authority to offer the full range of property management services to commercial and residential income property owners. Traditional real estate brokers have historically been reluctant to offer property management services over concern about enhanced liability. This concern is justified to some degree because professional property management is a complex undertaking that requires special knowledge and experience.

   In recent years, some of these traditional brokers changed their position to allow their affiliated licensees to offer full property management services including locating tenants, collecting rent during the term of the lease, arranging for maintenance on the properties, receiving calls from tenants on behalf of the landlord, and assisting with basic eviction procedures. Other brokers only permitted their affiliated licensees to enter into listing agreements with a landlord-client to locate a qualified tenant, or a tenant-client to locate a suitable lease property.

1. **Liability concerns**: Real estate salespersons or associate brokers should never attempt to offer any form of property management services without authorization from their broker. The broker should make sure that his errors and omissions policy and general liability policy covers property management services. While many of these insurance policies do provide coverage for a broker, it may be limited.

    For example, one errors and omissions policy may cover property management as long as the revenue generated from the practice does not exceed a certain percent of total company revenue. Another insurance policy may allow the practice providing it is limited to residential properties. Once these thresholds are crossed, additional coverage must be purchased.

2. **Company policy should be modified**: Once a decision has been made to offer property management services, the broker should include an authorization in his company policy manual. As will be seen in the chapter discussing Michigan real estate administrative rules, a broker must supervise all work of affiliated licensees and provide written operating policies and procedures. These policies are a crucial part of the broker's risk management strategy since they set forth and limit what affiliated licensees can do on behalf of the broker.

IV. **Functions of a property manager**: Along with the functions mentioned so far, there are many other tasks that a property manager may be asked to perform for a client. These services include management planning, preparing budgets and accounting, handling tenant relations, monitoring maintenance and repairs, and maintaining adequate insurance.

   A. **Management planning and evaluation of the rental market**: Property management is best handled according to a written property management plan. The management plan is prepared by the property manager and sets forth the course of action for how the property will be managed. It is based on an assessment of the owner's needs and desires relative to his property. As part of the plan, the property manager evaluates the rental market for the owner including factors such as vacancy rates, special business needs, economic conditions and trends, and unemployment rates.

   B. ▶ **The management agreement**: In Michigan, property management services must be delivered pursuant to what is referred to in license law as a "property management employment contract." It is defined as a written agreement, entered into between a real estate broker and client, concerning the real estate broker's employment as a property manager for the client. It sets forth (1) the real estate broker's duties, responsibilities, and activities as a property manager and (2) limits as to what the manager can do on behalf of the owner.

      1. **Essentials:** The management agreement must be in writing and include the names of the parties to the contract and a description of the property to be managed.

      2. **Term:** The term or length of the contract is set forth. When the agreement expires, the property manager is no longer authorized to represent the owner.

      3. **Authority**: The contract establishes the responsibilities of the manager as well as the extent of his authority. In other words, it specifies the types of agreements to which the manager can bind the owner or negotiate on his behalf.

      4. **Reporting requirements and owner's financial statement**: The agreement specifies the types of reports the manager will provide to the owner. These reports relate to building operations and finances and typically include a monthly statement of income and expenses. Periodic profit and loss statements are then compiled using this data.

         a. **Budgeting:** A budget is a formal statement of the financial position of a business or other enterprise. A property management budget begins with an estimate of anticipated revenues and expenses that are likely to be encountered. The property manager is responsible for preparing the operating budget and making adjustments as needed based on actual income and expenses. Subsequent budgets are fine-tuned based on the actual numbers gathered from previous years.

         b. ▶ **Property management (trust) account**: License law requires a property manager to maintain a property management account. This account is different and separate from a broker's real estate trust account. A property management account is defined as an interest-bearing or non-interest bearing account, or other instrument, that is used in the operation of property management. The "interest-bearing" and "instrument" aspects of a property manger's account are the primary differences from a standard real estate broker's trust account into which earnest money deposits are placed.

Examples of instruments include certificates of deposit, money market accounts, mutual funds, bonds, or treasury securities (which are all interest-bearing). The property management account should clearly specify the nature of the account as well as who acquires the rights to any earned interest.

5. **Management fee**: The agreement will also set forth the property manager's compensation for services rendered. It is commonly calculated as a percentage of monthly gross operating income. Additional fee arrangements can involve a flat rate or commission fee based on leasing volume. Some fee structures include incentives for things such as low vacancy rates.

C. **Handling tenant relations**: A property manager understands that a successful income property ownership experience depends on the ability to maintain excellent landlord-tenant relations. It starts with attracting and selecting high quality tenants, and then continues with rent collection and maintaining a good working relationship between the owner and his tenants.

1. **Attraction and selection**: The process of attracting tenants for a residential property will vary from the techniques used to locate tenants for a commercial property. With both commercial and residential properties, advertising plays a key role. Online social media outlets and online classified advertising sites are being relied on with increasing frequency.

   In the case of residential properties, one of the most effective ways to attract tenants is to offer clean, properly maintained properties. Nobody wants to live in a home that looks unattractive. Commercial property managers may offer incentives to existing tenants for the referral of new tenants as well as rent concessions for new and existing tenants. They may also participate in a multiple listing service designed exclusively for commercial properties.

   a. **Rent concession**: A rent concession is an abatement or reduction in the normal rent which is advertised or stated in an existing lease. It is commonly offered as an inducement to get a new tenant to sign a lease, or to encourage an existing tenant who is considering relocating at the end of the lease to sign a new long-term lease.

   b. **Tenant selection**: While commercial property managers like to have a choice in who they rent to, this may not always be possible. Depending on the state of the local economy, the strength of the commercial rental market, and the competition among commercial buildings in the area, a property manager may have to settle for a less-than-ideal tenant.

      (1) **Showing the property**: As part of the showing process, the property manager will demonstrate the property to prospective tenants. The manager will present the property in the most favorable light possible pointing out material facts and features that may be of interest. It may be necessary to discuss and negotiate any tenant-required building improvements or build-outs at this time.

      It should be noted that Michigan law does not require income property owners to provide a seller disclosure statement to prospective tenants. Since hidden defects are typically the responsibility of the landlord, it may be prudent to disclose any property conditions that could impair the tenant's use of the property. The manager may also recommend to the owner that defects be repaired prior to making the property available for lease.

      (2) **Qualifying tenants**: Regardless of the state of the economy, all tenants should be screened for basic credit worthiness. A tenant with a bad credit history is more likely to default than one with a good credit history. More information on obtaining credit reports is discussed later in the chapter.

      Each tenant's business should also be evaluated in advance to determine its credit standing as well as the nature of the business it conducts. This is especially important in retail environments where a landlord may have promised one tenant that his will be the only type of business in the mall or strip center. For example, no tenant in a retail strip center wants to compete with other tenants who offer the same type of product or service.

   c. **Establishing rent rates**: Property managers also assist their owner-clients in establishing an appropriate rental rate. Factors to weigh include the strength of the existing rental market including competing properties, what they are charging, average vacancy rates in the marketplace, and local economic trends. For example, if a community is becoming known as an emerging area for certain businesses, a landlord might be able to charge a higher rent rate.

d. **Negotiate lease agreements**: Professional property managers are skilled negotiators. They negotiate maintenance agreements with contractors, employee contracts, agreements with on site managers, possibly purchase agreements on new land acquisitions, and most importantly, lease agreements with tenants. Commercial lease agreements tend to be complex documents with many different types of clauses. These clauses are designed to protect the landlord against certain issues that can arise during a long-term lease.

2. **Rent collection**: If all prospective tenants have been properly qualified, rent collection should be an automatic process of receiving on-time payments. The property manager maintains a monthly record-keeping system, prepares regular financial reports, and makes adjustments for the next year's budget. Rent collection can, however, be a challenging process when dealing with tenants whose businesses are struggling due to poor business practices or a slow economy. Property managers must be prepared to deal with such tenants in a firm and uniform manner. A thorough understanding of the eviction process is also important.

3. **Maintain owner-tenant relationships**: Even though a property manager is hired by and works directly for the building owner, he often tries to act as a neutral buffer between the owner and his tenants. Tenants can talk to the property manager and voice opinions that they might not be comfortable discussing directly with the owner. Conversely, the property manager can raise the owner's concerns in a manner that might be better tolerated coming from the manager rather than the owner.

    a. **Negotiate tenant conflicts**: Whenever a group of individuals inhabits a multi-unit building or residential dwelling, periodic conflicts can arise. Not only does a property manager act as a third-party intermediary in handling tenant complaints against the owner, he also addresses disputes between existing tenants. If these disputes are not appropriately handled, the landlord can end up losing both tenants, especially if they are near the end of their respective leases.

D. **Handling maintenance and repairs**: Preserving the value of an owner's investment is accomplished by keeping the property properly maintained and arranging for repairs when they are needed. The property manager must also be prepared to explain to a commercial tenant why a particular repair is the tenant's responsibility, and to make sure that it gets done to avoid further damage to the property. Even though the tenant signed the commercial lease and should be aware of his responsibilities, it does not mean that he will gladly acknowledge the duty to pay for the repair. In the case of residential leases (where repairs may be the landlord's responsibility), the property manager must follow all laws and lease terms when entering a unit to make a repair.

E. **Miscellaneous issues**: This section reviews insurance needs and the Fair Credit Reporting Act. The Act must be understood since property managers are often called on to obtain and review the credit reports of prospective tenants on behalf of the owner-client.

   1. **Maintaining adequate insurance**: Both the building owner and the property manager have important insurance needs. An annual insurance check up is a good risk management practice.

      a. **Protection for the property owner**: A property manager should make sure that the owner-client has the appropriate insurance and periodically review the policies to make sure that the coverage is adequate. The need for landlord-based insurance is tremendous to cover perils such as physical damage to the structure from fire, weather, or vandalism. Other perils needing coverage include: personal injuries suffered on the premises (especially the common areas) by tenants and their employees, customers, and invitees; injuries suffered by workers on the property; and possible loss of rental income.

      b. **Protection for the manager**: The manager should also make sure that he has adequate business insurance to cover his property management business. This includes professional liability insurance to cover legal actions involving wrongful eviction or unfounded allegations of a fair housing violation. It is also important to have a general liability policy to cover claims that may be filed against the property manager involving injuries and loss of property.

   2. **The Fair Credit Reporting Act**: The Fair Credit Reporting Act (FCRA), which is only briefly summarized in this section, imposes duties on credit reporting agencies and users of credit reports to make certain an individual's credit file is accurate and not misused. The Act applies to consumer credit and residential lease applications. In order for a landlord to obtain a copy of a prospective or existing tenant's credit report, the applicant or tenant must provide written authorization. The landlord can access the report without first obtaining permission if the landlord can demonstrate that he has a "legitimate business need" for the information.

The following appears to qualify as a legitimate business need: (1) the landlord is obtaining the report in connection with a lease application that is initiated by the applicant, i.e., prospective tenant; (2) the landlord is screening the credit of an existing tenant who owes him past due rent; or (3) the landlord is screening the credit of an existing tenant to determine whether or not to renew the lease. These restrictions apply equally to a property manager who is acting as the agent of the owner-landlord.

   a. **Permission is advised**: Although prior consent to obtain a credit report may not be required if a legitimate business need exists, it is wise to include a clause in the tenant application authorizing the landlord or his agent to obtain a copy of the applicant's credit report. The applicant should also sign the authorization. A similar clause should also be included in the lease that a report can be obtained under the circumstances listed above.

   b. **Adverse actions based on credit report**: After reviewing the credit information, a property owner or manager may elect not to lease a unit, or may change the terms in favor of the owner to reflect any perceived risk from leasing to a tenant with questionable credit. In such case, the tenant or applicant is entitled to a notice of the adverse action, information pertaining to the credit reporting agency that furnished the report, and notice that a free copy of the report can be obtained.

   c. **Tenant concerns about accessing his credit report**: Many prospective tenants with good credit are concerned that a landlord's accessing of the prospective tenant's credit report may impact the score by lowering it. A property manager acting on behalf of a landlord should not give specific advice to a prospective tenant or make an affirmative statement that the score will not be negatively affected. However, as noted below, the score is generally not affected in this circumstance.

      (1) **Hard inquiries**: By definition, a hard credit score inquiry is one the consumer personally initiates by filling out a credit application. A high number of hard inquiries can negatively affect a credit score. They remain on a credit report for two years, but are only used in calculating the credit score for a one-year period. Multiple inquiries in any 14-day period, however, only count as a single inquiry thereby allowing mortgage or auto loan shopping without affecting the score.

      (2) **Soft inquiries**: Soft inquiries result from (1) requests by a consumer for a copy of his credit report or credit-score, (2) requests by existing creditors for purposes of review only, (3) requests by creditors to determine pre-approved credit offers, (4) employment offer credit reviews, and (5) landlord screening of prospective tenants. Soft inquiries are only shown on a personal report requested by consumers and do not appear on reports requested by potential creditors. Therefore, if coded correctly on the report, soft inquiries do not negatively affect a credit score.

***Avoid the trap of . . . "I'll wait until (fill in the date) to accomplish my goals.
It's a better day for me." That day never seems to arrive.***

Chapter 14: Property Management

DIAGNOSTIC PRACTICE QUESTIONS – CHAPTER 14

IMPORTANT STUDY TIP!

Step 1: Carefully review the information located in this chapter.

Step 2: Take the following Diagnostic Practice Questions. Review any question you answered incorrectly by researching the topic in this textbook. If you are still uncertain as to why the question is answered as it is, consult your program provider.

NOTE ON CHAPTER PRACTICE QUESTIONS

The following questions are representative of the type encountered on the Michigan real estate licensing examination. While some of these questions may be similar in nature and style, there is no way of predicting the exact wording of a question that will appear on the exam. Spending time memorizing these questions is, therefore, not recommended.

These questions are designed to help you determine how well you comprehend the material in this chapter. They are also intended to help you develop problem solving skills and to become comfortable with question formats.

Do not attempt to answer these questions until you have attended the lecture corresponding to this chapter and spent the appropriate time studying the material.

1. A property manager typically acts on behalf of the owner of a commercial income property in what capacity?
   A. Universal agent.
   B. General agent.
   C. Special agent.
   D. Attorney-in-fact.

2. From a property manager's perspective all the following factors can affect his client's income EXCEPT:
   A. Fluctuations in property values.
   B. Vacancy rates.
   C. Operating expenses.
   D. Default rates on rent.

3. The owner of a retail shopping center who is concerned about tenant competition from neighboring commercial developments currently under construction might be best served by hiring:
   A. A commercial real estate sales agent.
   B. A property manager.
   C. An attorney specializing in commercial real estate transactions.
   D. A licensed personal assistant.

4. Melissa is a licensed real estate salesperson who has worked in the residential resale market for 2 years. Her brother Brian owns a single-family residential home that he would like to rent out. Brian asked Melissa if she would act as property manager on the property. May she do so?

   A. No, because the family relationship disqualifies her.
   B. No, because she does not have 3 years of relevant, related experience in the business.
   C. Yes, providing Brian and Melissa's broker enter into a property management employment contract.
   D. Yes, provided she first acquires a property management certification.

5. In the event that a dispute arises between a long-term tenant in an apartment building and the owner of the property, a recently-hired property manager for the property would most likely:
   A. Negotiate the dispute on behalf of the owner without regard to the tenant's demands.
   B. Not become engaged in the dispute since the tenant leased the premises prior to the property manager being hired.
   C. Recommend that the owner give in to the tenant to prevent the tenant from terminating his lease.
   D. Act as an intermediary to resolve the dispute in an objective manner.

6. A real estate licensee acting as a property manager for a large retail strip center has reason to believe that a proposed use by a prospective tenant may present a possible environmental issue. The property manager should:
   A. File a request for a "show cause" hearing with the Michigan Department of Environmental Quality.

B. Inform the client of the proposed use and allow the client to determine the best course of action.
C. Mail a notice to existing tenants to ascertain the number of potential complaints that may be filed.
D. Immediately schedule a Phase I environmental site assessment.

7. A professional property manager is most commonly compensated by a:
   A. straight salary.
   B. percentage of gross income.
   C. percentage of net income.
   D. percentage of potential income.

8. All EXCEPT which of the following individuals would require a real estate broker's license?
   A. A person who acts as a property manager for the owner of a large, commercial office building.
   B. A person manages a 200-unit residential apartment complex for a corporation.
   C. Managing a large retail shopping center for an investment group.
   D. A person who manages 75 single-family homes that he owns as an investor.

9. A broker who enters into a property management contract is considered to be a:
   A. fiduciary.
   B. lessor.
   C. trustee.
   D. surety.

10. In order to act as a property manager in Michigan, which of the following licenses is required:
    A. Mortgage broker's license.
    B. Real estate broker's license.
    C. Securities dealer's license.
    D. Property management license.

11. A person who provides property management services but whose activities are limited to one building is known as which of the following:
    A. A resident manager.
    B. A general property manager.
    C. A real estate broker.
    D. A building manager.

12. The typical functions performed by a property manager include all of the following EXCEPT:
    A. Acting as an attorney-in-fact.
    B. Preserving the value of the investment.
    C. Management planning.
    D. Generating rental income.

13. If a property manager recommends to an owner that he offer a rent concession, the manager has suggested that the owner:
    A. offer a lease-option program.
    B. offer a rent-for-services program.
    C. create a condominium conversion.
    D. reduce the advertised rent to attract new tenants.

14. All EXCEPT which of the following persons may benefit from professional property management services:
    A. The owner of a single-family residence.
    B. The purchaser of a single-family income property.
    C. An owner of a small commercial strip center.
    D. A buyer of an owner-occupied duplex.

15. By law, a property manager must maintain which of the following for his client?
    A. A confidential registry of information about each tenant's gender and race.
    B. A chronological list of the order in which each tenant signed a lease.
    C. A property management account.
    D. Credit card information about each tenant.

16. All EXCEPT which of the following would a property manager be expected to do?
    A. Manage each aspect of a client's personal and business financial affairs.
    B. Review a credit report of a potential tenant.
    C. Work with a builder to complete a build-out for a new tenant.
    D. Obtain the best rate for liability insurance for an office building.

Chapter 15
Financing Considerations of Ownership

Understanding the investment, taxation, and insurance aspects of ownership.

I. **Foreword**: Real estate satisfies the basic human need for shelter. As we have seen, real property can be owned and it can be leased. From a landlord's perspective, real estate serves as an investment tool. Whether the landlord owns residential or commercial property, the investment side of ownership means financial gains and losses are both possible. In the early 2000s, many individuals leapt into real estate investing without fully considering the possibility that they could actually lose money.

Real estate has the potential to perform well as an investment if careful research is conducted and attention is paid to the timing of acquisitions and sales. Most real estate licensees are not trained to serve as investment counselors and should not hold themselves out as such. Nevertheless, they should have a basic understanding of real estate investing, taxation issues, and insurance requirements. This includes knowing when to recommend that a client consult with an attorney, tax consultant, investment counselor, or commercial-industrial real estate specialist.

II. **Real estate as an investment**: An investment is something that is purchased with the intention that it will increase in value or generate income in the future. The saying "it takes money to make money" illustrates this principle since an initial sum of money must be used to purchase the asset which is hoped to grow in value or produce an income stream. For example, a residential house is purchased for $100,000 cash. Three years later, the owner sells it for $120,000. Simply stated, the investment of $100,000 generated a $20,000 profit for the owner. An asset is any resource that has an economic value.

   A. **Return "on" investment**: A return "on" an investment is the actual profit earned from an initial expenditure of money. Using the prior example, the owner did not make a $120,000 profit since he had to invest $100,000 initially to purchase the house as an asset. His return "on" the investment was $20,000. This represents the appreciation value of the asset. In another example, a bank loans money to a borrower to purchase a house. The monthly interest paid by the borrower is a return to the bank "on" its investment of the money it loaned.

   B. **Return "of" investment**: A return "of" an investment is the return, meaning recovery, of the actual amount paid by the investor. Returning to our example, the sale of the property for $120,000 included a return of the original $100,000 paid for the home. This is the return "of" the buyer's investment. In the case of the bank loan example, the payment of the monthly principal is the return "of" the bank's investment. When a property is sold that had been purchased using a bank loan, the recovery of the down payment is a return "of" the buyer-owner's investment.

   C. **Advantages and disadvantages**: As with any investment, there are advantages and disadvantages that must be carefully weighed. One of the biggest mistakes that novice or casual investors make is to purchase on pure emotion, gut feelings, or tips. This holds especially true when it comes to real estate investing. Careful research, which is also called pre-purchase due diligence, is the key to successful real estate investing.

   1. **Investing advantages**: There are distinct advantages to real estate investments. Appreciation of an asset that is held long-term can be significant. Investment real estate can also serve as an inflation hedge. For example, a landlord has a clause in his commercial lease that indexes the rent to the rate of inflation. As the inflation goes up, so does the rent. Real estate can also be used to diversify an investment portfolio. Finally, property owners have the ability to influence the performance of their real property assets by improving them with repairs and additions.

      a. **Appreciation defined**: Appreciation is the increase in the value of an asset over time. It is the most common form of return "on" a real estate investment for a property owner. Appreciation is also the primary form of return for owner-occupied real estate. Appreciation is almost always realized over longer rather than shorter periods of time. The only exception to this would be in a market that is experiencing dramatic increases in value. Investors who purchase in such markets must be careful, however, since these properties can also decrease in value quickly.

    (1) **Equity**: Another term often associated with appreciation is equity. It represents the difference between the market value of a property at a given point in time and its total indebtedness. Equity is the actual dollar amount of value that an owner has in his property. For example, a property has a fair market value of $235,000 and the balance owing on the mortgage loan is $95,000. The equity is represented as: $235,000 − $95,000 = $140,000.

    (2) **Release of equity through refinancing**: Equity can be released through refinancing. To illustrate this concept, assume that a property is purchased for $100,000 using a mortgage loan for $95,000 and a $5,000 down payment. The value of the property increases to $110,000 over time which means that the owner now has $15,000 in equity. The owner can release this appreciated value as cash by obtaining a home equity loan for $10,000. The original $5,000 down payment remains as equity in the property.

    An owner should exercise care and restraint when releasing equity in his property. Some owners refinance their homes to purchase depreciating assets such as boats and cars. For many homeowners their house is the only asset they own that gains equity. It might make more financial sense to save for the car (or separately finance it) and keep the money in the house.

  b. **Flipping**: In the 2000s, a large number of real estate investors used property flipping as an investment strategy to earn quick profits. A flip involves the purchase of a property with the intention that it be quickly resold for a profit thereby earning a return "on" the investment. The return was realized either in the form of property appreciation in a rapidly appreciating market, or from purchasing a run-down property at a low value and then making repairs and improvements to immediately increase its value.

    (1) **Legitimate investment tool**: When flipping is used as a legitimate investment tool, the buyer faces the normal risks associated with any investment such as price depreciation in a declining housing market. The buyer can also generate a profit. For example, a short-term investor purchases multiple properties and holds them for several months before flipping, meaning selling, them. If their values have increased sufficiently, the flip can be financially successful.

    (2) ▶ **Predatory application**: Property flipping is not, in and of itself, illegal. It has, unfortunately, been used as a predatory tool by some unscrupulous investors. An activity is predatory if its purpose is to improperly exploit others for personal gain. To exploit is to take unfair advantage of someone.

    For example, some investors were purchasing distressed properties in the 2000s with very low offers and then quickly reselling them at a considerable profit with artificially-inflated values established with help from unscrupulous local lenders, appraisers, and real estate licensees who acted as accomplices. Rarely were any repairs made on these properties and the only people who profited from these activities were the investors and those who were in collusion with them.

    (3) **HUD "anti-flipping" rule**: HUD regulations were enacted in 2003 to curb predatory flipping. Borrowers are prohibited from using FHA-insured loans to purchase a home from a seller who had purchased it himself within the previous 90 days. See Chapter 17 for further information.

  c. **Leverage**: Leveraging is the financing of an investment using only a small amount of one's own funds, commonly a down payment, with the balance of the purchase price consisting of borrowed funds. It is using someone else's money to enhance the borrower's money. Leverage allows an investor to purchase property without using a large amount of personal funds as would occur in a cash sale. Higher leverage does equate to higher risk for a lender, however, since more money is borrowed. The borrower pays interest charges and faces the risk of foreclosure if the loan is not repaid.

    Applying the figures from an earlier example, a $100,000 property is purchased with a $5,000 down payment coupled with a mortgage loan for $95,000. The value of the property thereafter increases to $110,000. The buyer only invested $5,000 of personal funds and used, i.e., leveraged, the bank's money to make an additional $10,000 of profit on the resale.

2. **Investing disadvantages**: Just as there are advantages to real estate investing, there are also disadvantages. They include (1) fluctuations in property values, (2) illiquidity, (3) the need for management expertise in the case of commercial or residential income property, (4) the need for outside advice, and (5) the high cost of purchasing and selling.

Chapter 15: Financing Considerations of Ownership

    a. **Liquid versus illiquid assets**: Liquidity is an expression of the degree to which an investment can be purchased and then sold without significantly affecting its value. The more liquid an asset is, the quicker the investor can sell and obtain a return "of" his investment. However, the return "on" a liquid asset tends to be much lower. When money is invested in an illiquid asset, meaning non-liquid, there are higher risks, but a greater potential for a return "on" the investment. Savings accounts are liquid and pay very low interest returns, whereas real property is illiquid and has the potential to earn a high return.

D. **Securities law–security defined**: In the financial markets, a security is an instrument or similar document that represents an ownership share in a company such as stocks and bonds. Common stocks are known as equity securities and bonds are known at debt securities. There are many different types of securities that are purchased and sold every day.

Securities are commonly traded on markets such as the New York Stock Exchange. There is also a bond market where participants can issue new debt or purchase and sell existing debt securities. Due to the high potential for fraud in buying and selling any paper evidence of ownership or indebtedness, special federal and state securities laws have been enacted. Note: The information in this section is provided as a simplified overview. Securities and securities laws tend to be highly complex and require specialized expertise.

1. **Federal Securities Act of 1933**: In 1933, Congress passed a comprehensive securities law. This important law was passed during the Great Depression to require that all securities sold to the public be registered with the U.S. Securities and Exchange Commission (which was established approximately one year after passage of the Act). The Act (1) requires that investors receive financial and other significant information concerning any securities being offered for public sale, and (2) prohibits deceit, misrepresentation, and other fraud in the sale of securities. Prior to the passage of the Act, the sale of securities was governed by state legislation. These state laws were known as Blue Sky Laws.

2. **Blue Sky Laws**: Blue Sky Laws are state statutes designed to provide regulation and supervision of securities offerings and sales within the respective states. They protect ordinary citizen-investors from giving money to fraudulent companies. The term is thought to have gained popularity when cited in a 1917 Supreme Court case upholding a state's power to regulate securities. The opinion essentially stated that these state laws are intended to prevent investment schemes which have no more value than so many feet of blue sky.

3. **Michigan Uniform Securities Act (2002)**: In 1964, the Michigan Uniform Securities Act was passed. It sets forth specific requirements for the offer and sale of securities in Michigan. It was replaced in 2009 with a revised law titled "Uniform Securities Act (2002)." All securities that are sold in Michigan, and the individuals who sell them or provide fee-based advice on which ones to purchase, must either be registered or exempted from registration. Various divisions of Michigan's Department of Licensing and Regulatory Affairs (LARA) oversee registration and enforcement.

4. **Potential application to real estate transactions**: Securities laws can be triggered by certain real estate investment activities. Real estate licensees should understand when the advertisement and sale of real estate interests potentially triggers the application of securities laws. The easiest way to accomplish this is to know the elements of an investment security.

    a. **Definition of an investment security**: A security interest consists of four basic elements: (1) an investment of money, (2) in a common enterprise, (3) with the expectation of profits, (4) that is derived solely from the efforts of others. Securitization involves the conversion of an asset into investment interests. Real estate securitization occurs when investment dollars are solicited from investors who seek a return from the distribution of cash flows generated from rental properties, for example.

    b. **Limits for licensees**: A licensed real estate broker (and his affiliated licensees) can list and sell real property and earn commissions without concern over securities laws. This holds true even if the property is intended to be used by a buyer for investment purposes. When that same real estate is securitized, the appropriate securities license is required to solicit the investment dollars. A person who sells securities is known as a securities dealer or securities broker. While a licensed securities broker can earn a fee for selling securities, he cannot legally compensate a real estate licensee for assisting in their sale.

        (1) **Example–no securities laws triggered**: In the first example, Buyer Smith purchases a commercial office building through Jones, a real estate broker who is acting as a buyer's agent. Smith then hires Broker Jones to act as a property manager. Broker Jones rents the units to tenants. The actions of Broker Jones and Buyer Smith do not fall under securities laws.

(2) **Example–securities laws triggered**: In the second example, Buyer Smith hires Broker Jones to advertise and solicit investment money from the public for investment in commercial real estate. The advertising holds out the potential for a high rate of return for the investors. Buyer Smith hires Broker Jones to act as the property manager. Buyer Smith pays the investors a portion of the profits earned from the leasing and sale of the commercial buildings.

5. **Application of securities laws to different property types**: This section examines whether shares held by residents in a housing cooperative, condominium, or securitized TIC are governed by securities law.

    a. **Housing cooperatives**: As discussed, an investor in a securities transaction parts with his money along with other investors in the hope of receiving a financial return derived from the efforts of others. This pure investment motive does not apply when a person purchases stock in a corporation for the sole purpose of obtaining a lease in a housing complex to use as his personal living quarters. Cooperatives, which are also called housing cooperatives, are defined in Chapter 7.

        (1) **Federal law**: The U.S. Supreme Court held that shares in a state-subsidized and supervised non-profit housing cooperative are not securities within the meaning of federal securities law.

        (2) **Michigan law and initial cooperative sales**: Under Michigan securities law, however, the initial sale of stock in a housing cooperative by a developer may be viewed as a security. Consequently, a developer should consult with legal counsel before selling stock in a new housing cooperative to determine if it would be best to register the offering or seek an order to exempt it under Michigan securities law.

        (3) **Resale by real estate licensees**: While not absolutely clear, both federal and Michigan securities laws do not appear to apply to the resale of an interest in a cooperative. Many cooperative bylaws set limits on resale prices and the amount of equity or ownership that members can build up, so they are not generally viewed as investment opportunities. Nevertheless, a real estate broker should check with legal counsel before proceeding with the resale of an interest in a housing cooperative.

    b. **Condominiums and other ownership interests**: Depending on how a real property interest is marketed, securities laws can be triggered. For example, an investment promoter markets several condominium units as "excellent investment opportunities." Each buyer is required to make his unit available for rent and to sign a mandatory management agreement under which both rental income and expenses are pooled with the profits and losses of other investors. The economic benefits to the investors are derived from the managerial efforts of the promoter who handles the rental of units to tenants. This offering likely requires prior registration under securities laws.

    c. **Sale of a business by a real estate licensee**: According to Michigan real estate license law, a real estate broker may negotiate the purchase or sale or exchange of a business, business opportunity, or the goodwill of an existing business for others. License law makes no distinction on how the business is organized, meaning whether it is a corporation, partnership, sole proprietorship, or LLC. Nevertheless, a distinction must be drawn between selling the assets of a business and selling the stock of a business.

    A broker can likely sell the assets of a business without possessing a securities license. If the sale includes the stock of the business, it appears that the real estate broker must also be a licensed securities broker (which is highly unlikely). A broker should consult legal counsel before selling any business that potentially also involves the sale and transfer of stock.

    d. **Securitized TICs**: "TIC" is an acronym for Tenants In Common and refers to an investment opportunity through which investors realize the ownership benefits of investment property without being burdened by its management responsibilities. It was originally created so investors could engage in simplified tax-deferred, like-kind exchanges.

        (1) **How a securitized TIC works**: A TIC promoter or sponsor solicits investment funds from unrelated individuals who will be engaged in the common enterprise of owning real estate for profit, but will not have to play an active role in its management. The sponsor retains an ownership interest in exchange for handling the day-to-day management responsibilities. A securitized TIC is subject to state and federal securities laws because the elements of a security are all present.

        (2) **Real estate law also applies**: Since securitized TICs involve the sale of real estate, state real estate license law also applies to the same extent it would for any traditional real estate transaction.

Chapter 15: Financing Considerations of Ownership   223

- (3) **Non-securitized TIC**: If a real estate licensee is working with a small, limited group of investors who are familiar with one another, and are working together to acquire and personally manage the property, a tenancy in common may be formed without triggering securities laws. The buyer-investors in this example should first consult with legal counsel to make sure that securities laws are not being triggered. Even though there is likely no problem for the real estate broker in listing or selling the property for the owners, he should double check with legal counsel before proceeding.

E. **Forms of investment property ownership**: Investment properties can be directly owned by one or more individuals or by business entities. Knowing which form is best for any particular investor often requires the advice of a qualified expert. Real estate licensees should not provide specialized professional advice that is outside of their field of competence. Instead, the client should be directed to the appropriate expert. Most commercial real estate specialists are qualified to provide business-oriented advice to their clients. No licensee should ever provide a legal opinion as to which form of ownership is best for a client.

1. **Direct ownership**: Direct ownership of investment property by individuals is the most common form of ownership. Investment properties can be held for either short-term or long-term purposes. Most investment properties, however, are held for their long-term appreciation potential as well as for generating a present-day cash flow. Cash flow refers to the stream of income or expenses that a business experiences over a period of time.

2. **Ownership by business entities**: Group investors can form one of many different business arrangements including corporations, partnerships, syndicates, and trusts. These business entities can then purchase and hold the investments. See Chapter 7 for more information on corporations and partnerships.

   a. **Syndicates**: A syndicate is a special group of business investors (and sometimes bankers) that is formed for the purpose of handling a large transaction that would be otherwise too complex to handle individually by the members of the syndicate. Syndicating allows the members to share their expertise, the cost of the project, risk, and any profits related to the purpose for which it was formed. The pooling of resources and sharing of risk is attractive to many real estate investors. A syndicate is typically formed for the limited purpose of a particular project rather than to exist as an on-going entity. Syndication potentially falls under securities laws.

   b. **Real Estate Investment Trust (REIT)**: A Real Estate Investment Trust or REIT is a financial device through which investors purchase shares in a trust that has been invested in real estate ventures. It operates like a mutual fund, but instead of investing in stocks as with a mutual fund, the REIT invests in real property assets. It qualifies as a security and is governed by securities laws.

      (1) **Types of REITs**: Equity REITs own properties and realize an investment return on rental income and appreciation when any property in the portfolio is sold. Mortgage REITs invest in mortgages and earn a return on the interest. A Hybrid REIT invests in both properties and mortgages.

      (2) **Advantages**: The advantages of a REIT include (1) it is a more liquid form of property ownership that has the potential to pay higher dividends, (2) the investor can participate in commercial property ownership without the responsibility of management, (3) simplified tax treatment, and (4) diversification of an investment portfolio.

      (3) **Disadvantages**: Since a REIT invests in real estate, it carries the same risks that any investor in real estate may experience. For example, real estate values can decline in a slow economy, occupancy rates can decrease in commercial structures thereby affecting cash flow, and rising interest rates affect the cost of loan funds for future real estate holdings in the REIT.

III. ▶ **Taxation**: Ownership of real property is subject to various forms of taxation. Along with the county and state transfer taxes that are due on the sale of real property interests, state and local taxes are assessed each year on the ownership of both residential and commercial real estate. Local property taxes are due whether or not the property is subject to a mortgage loan.

When an owner pays off his mortgage, he may be surprised to later find a large property tax bill in his mailbox. During the term of the mortgage, the owner's monthly payment included 1/12th of the property taxes which were paid into an escrow for the following year's tax bill. The lender forwarded the payment of the property taxes to the municipality on behalf of the owner.

A. **Tax defined**: A tax is a charge or monetary burden laid on an individual or his property to support the government. Taxes are imposed for the use and service of the government and its facilities, and as a means of generating revenue for public needs. Property taxes are typically used to pay for things such as police, fire, and paramedic services; local courts and sheriffs; and local government and community services.

B. ▶ **Property tax**: Along with income taxes, property taxes are a common form of revenue collection. Property taxes represent a fee levied, meaning charged, on the value of personal or real property that is owned by the taxpayer. Property taxes are based on a percentage of the value of the property at the time of the assessment. (Note: If you are preparing for the real estate broker's or salesperson's license examination, study this section in conjunction with the discussion on tax prorations in Chapter 9.)

1. **Ad valorem**: Real estate taxes are assessed on an ad valorem basis. This means they are charged in direct proportion to the value of the real estate being taxed. Ad valorem is Latin for "According To Value." The value of a property for tax purposes is determined through an assessment process which, essentially, is an appraisal. Real property taxes that are not paid in a timely manner can result in a specific lien being attached to the subject property and a subsequent foreclosure.

    a. **Assessed value (AV)**: The assessed value of a property is established by a taxing authority for purposes of calculating the amount of property taxes due. For each property, the combined value of the land and all improvements (which include the house and its capital improvements) is calculated. A capital improvement is anything (excluding ordinary repairs) that enhances the value of a property; for example, a new exterior deck or finished basement. The actual tax due is calculated by multiplying the tax rate by the assessed value as follows: Tax Rate × Assessed Value (SEV) = Tax Amount Due.

        (1) **Calculation**: The assessed value of a property is 50%, or half, of its true cash value (TCV). While the term true cash value is the legally appropriate term, for exam purposes it may be expressed as fair market value or simply market value.

        (2) **Challenges to assessed value**: A property owner may attempt to challenge the assessed value of his property by first contacting the assessor to see if a reduction is possible based on some factor the assessor may not have calculated properly. Next, the owner may appeal the assessed value at the next scheduled local board of review meeting. Thereafter, the owner will have to appeal it to the State Tax Tribunal. Changes are only based on evidence provided by the owner that the current assessment is not appropriate to the property.

        (3) **Board of review**: A Board of Review is appointed by each township to hear and decide challenges by property owners to their property assessments. The Board of Review is required to meet in March of each year. If there is additional business to conduct, the Board of Review also meets in July and December.

    b. **Tax day–used to determine assessed value**: Recall from Chapter 9 that December 31 is known as tax day. The local assessor determines the assessed value of a taxable property in the current year based on its condition as of December 31 of the previous year. The assessed value is then used to calculate the tax bills. For example, the condition of the property on December 31, 2017 is used to determine the 2018 assessed value of the property which is then used to calculate the 2018 property tax bills.

2. **Equalization and State Equalized Value (SEV)**: Equalization is the process by which property assessments are increased or decreased by the percentage necessary to make sure that all properties within the state are uniformly and fairly assessed. After the local assessor determines the assessed values of all properties within the city, township, or village, the county board of commissioners equalizes them by applying the necessary adjustment factors to make sure the local assessments are fair. The state tax commission then annually reviews, adjusts if necessary, and approves the state equalized valuation for each of the counties. As will be seen, the SEV serves as the initial basis for calculating property taxes upon taking ownership.

3. **Tax rate**: To determine the actual tax rate for properties within a municipality, the local unit of government calculates how much revenue is needed to fund all government services and then divides this number by the combined assessed values (SEVs) of all eligible residential and commercial properties within the municipality. The resulting number is the tax rate.

4. **Computation of owner's bill**: Once the applicable tax rate is determined for the municipality, each individual property owner's tax bill is calculated by multiplying the tax rate by the assessed or taxable value of the property (as discussed below). Tax rates are commonly expressed in terms of dollars of tax per $100 of assessed valuation or as a millage.

a. **Tax per $100 of assessed valuation**: When calculating taxes using this method, the rate is expressed as actual dollars of tax due for every $100 of assessed value of the property. For example, $2.80/$100 = .028 (hint: notice that the decimal moved two places to the left from 28 to .28).

b. **Millage**: One mill equals one-tenth of 1 cent or 1/1000th of a dollar (which is expressed as .001). This means that there is $1 of actual tax due for every $1,000 of assessed value. For example, 28 Mills = .028 (hint: notice that the decimal moved three places to the left from 28 to .028).

5. **Changes in taxable value–Proposal A**: From 1963 to 1994, all property taxes were strictly based on a residential or business property's SEV, which as discussed, was based on 50% of the property's fair market value. This meant that property tax bills went up in direct relation to increases in actual property values. The passage of Proposal A helped to slow down these tax increases by employing what is known as a capping mechanism. Proposal A also exempted homestead properties (now called principal residences) from payment of the local school taxes up to an 18 mill limit. Some of this lost tax revenue was offset or recaptured through an increase in the state's general sales tax from 4% to 6%.

   a. **Taxable (capped) value**: Under Proposal A, the annual basis for calculation of property tax was changed from the SEV to what became known as the taxable value of the property or TV. Changing the basis of calculation did not actually alter how property taxes were calculated. It did, however, significantly change how high property taxes can increase from one year to the next. The benefit of this cap is realized by residential as well as commercial property owners.

      (1) **How the cap works**: When a property is first acquired by a buyer, the SEV in the year following the sale is used as the initial (i.e., starting) taxable value for purposes of calculating that year's property taxes. For example, a buyer purchases a property (i.e., there is a transfer of ownership) in 2017. The buyer's 2018 tax bills are calculated based on the 2018 SEV. Thereafter, annual increases are capped at the lesser of an inflation rate multiplier (which is determined using the Consumer Price Index) or 5%.

      The actual number used for the Consumer Price Index (CPI) equals the percent of increase from one year to the next rather than the actual numerical increase. Over the past 10 years or so, the CPI inflation rate multiplier never exceeded 5%. While the SEV never caps and can change from one year to the next, annual taxes are calculated based on the capped taxable value.

      (2) **Taxable value cannot exceed assessed value**: The taxable value of a property cannot exceed its assessed value. This became important in the 2000s when property values were dropping significantly from the subprime mortgage collapse. For example, the market value of a property is $225,000, its assessed value is $112,500 (i.e., half), and the taxable value is $102,000. If the market value drops to $180,000 the next year, the assessed value also drops to $90,000 which is greater than the $102,000 taxable value. The owner is entitled to a lowering of the taxable value to the new assessed value.

      (3) **Property improvements can increase the Taxable Value**: If an owner makes improvements to his property, this can increase the taxable (i.e., capped) value by more than the rate of inflation or 5% since the property has been made more valuable. This will be reflected in the assessment which affects the following year's tax bill. Future increases in taxable value are then limited to the lesser of the inflation rate multiplier (CPI) or 5%.

   b. **Uncapping of taxable value (the "pop-up" tax)**: When a property is purchased by a buyer in a given year, property taxes are prorated based on the seller's existing (and likely lower) capped taxable value. As previously discussed, the taxable value of the property increases in the year following the sale to that year's SEV. This process is referred to as uncapping. The buyer's increase in taxes resulting from the uncapping of the seller's taxable value to the SEV in the year following the sale is also called a "pop-up" tax.

   The term "pop-up" probably should not be used since it can be misleading to buyers. Proposal A was passed to cap future increases in property taxes after purchasing a property–not to impose a surprise tax on a buyer. In other words, all property owner's capped taxable value started with the SEV in the year following the sale. As long as the new owner does not convey title to his property, taxes continue to be based on the lower, capped taxable value rather than the annual SEV. When the property is thereafter sold or title is transferred, the same process is used to uncap and recap for the next buyer.

c. **Uncapping exemptions**: The taxable value does not increase with transfers, including: from one spouse to the other spouse; from a decedent to a surviving spouse; some transfers to family members resulting from a life estate; some transfers of a residential property between a parent and child, blood relatives of a spouse, step-relationships, and adopted relationships; transfers through foreclosure, forfeiture, or a deed in lieu of a foreclosure; some transfers creating or terminating a joint tenancy; transfer of a qualified agricultural property; certain transfers to a trust (typically for estate planning purposes); and some business transfers. If a mortgagee, i.e., lender, takes a property back through foreclosure and does not sell the property within 1 year of the expiration of any applicable redemption period, property taxes are uncapped. Some of these transfers listed in this paragraph are exempt only if the use of the property remains residential.

d. **Property Transfer Affidavit**: When a buyer purchases real property, he must file a Property Transfer Affidavit with the local assessor within 45 days of the transfer (which is essentially the closing). It alerts the assessor that a transfer in ownership has taken place for purposes of uncapping the Taxable Value. If the buyer (as the new owner) fails to file the form, a penalty of $5.00 per day up to a maximum of $200 can be levied by the assessor. This penalty increases if the subject property is commercial rather than residential.

Failure to file the affidavit can lead to an additional problem for the new owner. If the property taxes are not uncapped and reset to the SEV, the new owner will not be paying the correct amount for his property taxes. When the error is subsequently discovered, even years later, the municipality can recalculate the taxes that should have been paid and bill the owner (plus penalties and interest). Finally, a real estate licensee should not take on responsibility of filing the affidavit for a client.

e. **How property taxes can increase in a declining market**: Proposal A only prevents taxes from increasing in a quickly-rising real estate market. It does not actually index taxes to property value. As a result, if the market value of a property declines, the taxable value is not automatically lowered with it. This means that market value can drop while the Taxable Value increases by the cap-limited amount. Recall from previous discussion, however, that the Taxable Value cannot exceed the assessed value.

f. **How a buyer estimates property taxes that have been capped**: There are a number of different financial considerations for a buyer who is deciding how much to offer on a sale property. The affordability of the mortgage payment ranks at or near the top of this list. As discussed in Chapter 16, the majority of loans are amortized and the monthly mortgage payment includes 1/12th of the annual property taxes. As a result, a licensee who is working with a prospective buyer needs a reliable way to estimate the buyer's new property taxes.

Property taxes cannot be estimated merely by looking at the seller's current tax bill. First, the buyer may offer more for the property than two times the seller's current SEV (which, while not immediately, could cause taxes to increase based on total sales in the area). Second, the seller's taxes have been capped and will be uncapped as a result of the sale to the buyer. The State of Michigan has an easy-to-use property tax estimator on its website to help individuals calculate the buyer's estimated new taxes. The best way to locate this website is to search online for "Michigan property tax estimator" using a top-ranked search engine.

g. **Land contract sales**: As discussed in Chapter 16, a land contract does not convey legal title to the subject property until the entire contract price is paid. For property tax purposes, however, the conveyance of the property is deemed to occur when equitable title is transferred along with the execution of the land at the closing. In other words, the land contract seller's capped taxable value is uncapped as a result of the land contract sale.

6. **Principal Residence Exemption (PRE)–Proposal A**: The Principal Residence Exemption, which also resulted from the passage of Proposal A, exempts the owner of a principal residence from payment of the tax levied by a local school district for school operating purposes up to a maximum of 18 mills. It is important to remember that the statute does not set forth an 18 mill reduction in property taxes. It only provides an exemption from local school taxes up to a maximum of 18 mills.

To qualify for a PRE, the owner must be a Michigan resident who owns and occupies the property as a principal residence. The PRE does not apply to commercial or other income properties. A property owner can only claim one principal residence at a time, therefore only one PRE. There is a conditional rescission, however, that may be available to an owner who is attempting to sell one home and purchase a new one at the same time (which is discussed, below).

a. **Principal residence defined**: A principal residence is the one place where an owner of a property has his true, fixed, and permanent home, to which whenever absent, he intends to return. Factors to be considered include where the taxpayer keeps his most important possessions, houses his family, votes, maintains club and lodge memberships, buys automobile licenses, maintains a mailing address and banking location, or operates a business in the area. While no single factor is controlling by itself, they are designed to prevent people from claiming multiple principal residences and exemptions in different taxing jurisdictions.

 (1) **Examples not considered to be a principal residence**: A PRE cannot be claimed for a second home, a cottage, rental property (including leases with option to purchase), commercial and industrial property, or property owned by a corporation regardless if a husband and wife establish and own the corporation. Spouses who own separate principal residences and file joint income tax returns may not claim a PRE on both properties.

 (2) **Application requirements and filing deadlines**: A principal residence owner who wants to exempt his property from the local school taxes must file a Principal Residence Exemption (PRE) Affidavit with the assessor on or before either June 1 or November 1 of the first year of the claim. Two deadlines were created because some municipalities assess all school taxes on the summer tax bill, some assess them entirely on the winter bill, and others split the school taxes between the summer bill and the winter bill.

 (a) **If the closing occurs before the filing deadline**: If the closing on the purchase of a principal residence occurs in time to meet the June 1 (or November 1, if applicable) deadline, no school taxes are due that year. The buyer must also rescind his PRE on the old home in a timely manner (as discussed later in this section).

 (b) **If the closing occurs after the filing deadline**: If the closing on the purchase of a principal residence occurs after the June 1 (or November 1, if applicable) deadline, school taxes are due that year. The buyer can file in time for next year's deadline and his taxes will be lowered at that time. This assumes that the property is purchased from an owner who does not qualify for the PRE and the property is billed at the non-homestead rate (as explained later in this section).

 (c) **If the taxes are split between the summer and the winter bills**: If school taxes are split with 9 mills on the summer bill and 9 mills on the winter bill, the owner will only be exempt from the full 18 mills if he meets the June 1 deadline. If a PRE exemption is filed in time for the November 1 deadline, then he will only be exempt from the 9 mill winter levy for that year. The full exemption is available in the following year and every year thereafter until the owner establishes a new principal residence elsewhere.

 (3) **Owner's responsibility to file (licensee should avoid)**: While title companies often assist with the preparation of closing documents, it is the owner's responsibility to make sure that the PRE Affidavit is filed with the assessor after the closing. The taxes calculated on the closing statement are based on the current status of the property. Figures can vary depending on whether the taxable status is listed as homestead or non-homestead.

 A real estate licensee should avoid filing a PRE Affidavit for a buyer since the buyer may not actually occupy the property by the filing deadline. This could lead to the buyer being assessed the difference between the homestead and non-homestead rate, plus penalties and interest. The buyer may then attempt to seek payment from the licensee who filed the form.

b. **Homestead versus non-homestead tax rate**: The phrase "homestead tax rate" is sometimes used to refer to the reduced taxes a principal residence owner pays when he qualifies for a PRE. In such case, the property tax bill does not include the school taxes. Conversely, the phrase "non-homestead tax rate" may be used when referring to the increased taxes an owner pays who does not qualify for a PRE. In other words, the property tax bill includes the school taxes.

c. **Rescission and denial of a PRE**: When one principal residence is sold and a new principal residence is purchased, the owner files a Request to Rescind Principal Residence Exemption form. The PRE is considered to be rescinded as of December 31 of that year. This allows the seller to file a PRE on the newly-acquired home. It must be filed by the seller within 90 days of no longer owning or occupying the property as a principal residence.

If a request for a PRE is denied, an informal conference can be requested with the Michigan Department of Treasury. Subsequent appeals are filed with the Michigan Tax Tribunal. Tax errors by the local unit of government such as misfiling of an application or mistakenly uncapping an assessment without a change in ownership are appealed to the local Board of Review. If the appeal is successful, the owner is entitled to a refund of any overpayment.

(1) **Conditional rescission**: Recall that a PRE can only be claimed on one property at a time. However, in a slow real estate market, an owner who wishes to purchase a new principal residence may not be able to quickly sell his old property. A conditional rescission allows the owner to simultaneously rescind the PRE on the sale property (and maintain its PRE or homestead tax rate) and file a new PRE on the purchase property.

(2) **Qualifying for a conditional rescission**: To qualify for a conditional rescission, the sale property (i.e., former principal residence) cannot be occupied for any purpose whatsoever, it must be continually marketed for sale (such as listing it with a real estate professional), it cannot be leased, and it must not be used for any business or commercial purpose. A conditional rescission must be renewed for each year it is claimed (up to a three-year limit).

7. ▶ **Special assessment**: A special assessment is a category of property tax that is limited to those properties that receive a specific benefit such as street repaving. Other improvements that give rise to special assessments include water and sewer lines, sidewalk improvements, and special street lighting. A property owner must treat a special assessment seriously since a lien is placed on his property for the full amount owing. The lien arises when the special assessment is adopted and entered on the tax roll.

   a. **Handling in a property sale**: A special assessment may be levied (i.e., charged) in full or, in the case of a township assessment, in annual installments. In the case of a sale, the seller is responsible for payment of the entire assessment which is not prorated on the closing statement. If an outstanding township assessment is payable in annual installments, the lien only attaches to the particular installment due at the time of the sale. If the purchase agreement calls for the seller to pay all liens of record, the buyer will be responsible for future installments. Since the purchase agreement may provide for other payment instructions, it must be carefully reviewed by the parties prior to execution.

8. **Foreclosure for non-payment of property taxes**: Properties with delinquent property taxes are subject to sale through a foreclosure process. Foreclosure can result from unpaid taxes, special assessments, and unpaid municipal service bills such as water and sewer. While not identical, the foreclosure and redemption process used to collect delinquent property taxes is similar to the system used for mortgage foreclosure.

   a. **Michigan tax reversion process**: Tax reversion refers to the process by which delinquent real estate property taxes are collected for non-payment. In 1999, the Michigan legislature simplified this process by vesting more control in the counties as opposed to the state. The process will now be briefly outlined for purposes of illustration.

   (1) **Forfeiture and foreclosure (tax sale)**: The 1999 change streamlined the entire process to approximately three years. A delinquent taxpayer should not, however, rely on having three years to avoid foreclosure due to the automatic forfeiture provision.

   (2) **Example time-line**: Assume for this example that a property owner failed to pay the winter tax bill issued on December 1, 2014.

      (a) February 14, 2015: The winter tax is considered to be delinquent and the collection process begins.

      (b) March 1, 2015: All taxes billed in 2014 become delinquent and are submitted to the county treasurer with additional interest and penalties accruing. A 4% administrative fee may be added along with interest at 1% per month. Additional fees are added and the interest rate on the outstanding delinquency increases as the process continues.

      (c) March 1, 2016 (statutorily prescribed as the second year following the year in which the unpaid tax bill was issued): The property is forfeited to the county treasurer and a certificate of forfeiture, which is similar to a lien, is recorded within 45 days thereafter. At this point in the process, forfeiture only allows the county to seek a judgment of foreclosure. It does not convey title to the property in the county.

Chapter 15: Financing Considerations of Ownership 229

(d) <u>May 1, 2016</u>: The county files a petition in Circuit Court to have the forfeited property foreclosed. Before the foreclosure takes place, anyone with an interest in the property is given notice and 2 opportunities to object–one at a show-cause hearing before the county and the other at the actual foreclosure hearing.

(e) <u>January, 2017</u>: A show cause hearing is held at which the taxpayer can appeal the foreclosure action.

(f) <u>March 1, 2017</u> (or no earlier than 30 days before this date): A foreclosure hearing is conducted in Circuit Court and a judgment of foreclosure is entered and signed by the judge.

(g) <u>March 31, 2017</u>: The opportunity for redemption expires. Absolute title to the foreclosed property vests in the county. Later that year, the county sells the tax foreclosed property at an auction to recover the back taxes, interest, and penalties.

(3) **Notice requirements**: Following forfeiture, the county must search the public records to identify anyone who may have an interest in the property. If an owner or interested party cannot be located or notified, a notice is published for three weeks in a county newspaper. A personal visit may also be made to the delinquent taxpayer.

(4) **Redemption**: Forfeited property may be redeemed at any time up to the March 31 date immediately following the entry of a judgment of foreclosure. To redeem, all delinquent taxes plus interest, penalties, and fees must be paid.

9. **Miscellaneous property tax items**: Property taxes are also potentially subject to, or benefit from, a Homestead Property Tax Credit, poverty exemption, tax abatement, Neighborhood Enterprise Zone, and a grandfathering in a Renaissance Zone.

   a. **Homestead Property Tax Credit**: Michigan's Homestead Property Tax Credit (HPTC) is designed to provide some relief from property taxes for senior citizens, persons with a disability including sight-impaired individuals, disabled veterans and their surviving spouses, as well as certain low-income individuals. The relief is provided in the form of a modest income tax credit to a qualified owner of a principal residence. This credit reduces the amount of income tax owed by a percent of the property tax paid. The HPTC is separate and distinct from the PRE.

      (1) **Qualifications**: To claim the HPTC, the homestead must be in Michigan, the claimant must be a resident for at least 6 months during the year, the taxable value of the home must not exceed $135,000, and total household resources must be $50,000 or less.

   b. **Poverty exemption**: Under a separate Michigan statute, the owner of a principal residence who meets the federal poverty threshold (as established by the U.S. Department of Health & Human Services) is exempt from payment of all local property taxes. The exemption must be filed with the local board of review each year it is claimed. Some municipalities limit the exemption to a maximum number of years such as three.

   c. **Tax abatement**: A tax abatement is a decrease in the actual amount of tax that a commercial property owner must pay. Abatements are frequently used by local governments to encourage location and expansion of business activities within the municipality.

   d. **Tax exemption**: Some properties are statutorily entitled to an exemption from real property taxation. A few examples of exempt properties include: Municipal, state, and federal property; Certain nonprofit housing for the elderly and disabled families; Houses of public worship and parsonages (i.e., housing in which the religious leader resides); Certain farmlands; Trust properties used for hospitals and other public health purposes; Principal residences of honorably discharged veterans who receive assistance from the VA for adaptive housing; and State-supported educational institutions.

   e. **Neighborhood Enterprise Zone (NEZ)**: Michigan's Neighborhood Enterprise Zone Act promotes investment and ownership of new residential construction and rehabilitation in areas the local community elects to designate as a NEZ. The community offers a tax abatement which reduces the taxes owed on properties for up to 15 years. An owner or developer of a proposed facility or rehabilitation in a NEZ must file an application for an NEZ certificate with the local unit of government. When an eligible property is sold, the certificate can be transferred to the new owner providing he continues to meet the NEZ requirements.

f. **Renaissance Zone**: Michigan Renaissance Zones were originally created to foster economic opportunities in Michigan, facilitate economic development, and to stimulate industrial, commercial, and residential improvements. Properties located within a designated renaissance zone received tax credits and exemptions from state and local taxes. As part of tax reform measures taken by the Michigan legislature, these exemptions were repealed for any renaissance zone designated after January 1, 2012. Residents in zones designated before this date retained their state tax exemptions.

C. **Federal income taxation and benefits of real estate ownership**: There are several different types of taxes levied in the United States on the federal, state, and local levels. We have previously examined property taxes. This section discusses federal income taxes and capital gains taxes. Income taxes are imposed on individuals, corporations, and other legal entities such as estates and trusts. To calculate personal income taxes, the applicable tax rate is multiplied by the individual's taxable income.

While licensees are viewed as general real estate advisors, tax questions should never be answered. Instead, the licensee should refer the customer or client to a competent tax expert such as a Certified Public Accountant (CPA), tax attorney, or other qualified tax expert. It is important to note that Federal income tax statutes and interpretations can be highly technical and complex. They are also subject to periodic modification by Congress, the Internal Revenue Service, and the tax courts.

1. ▶ **Income taxation basics**: Income taxation is based on taxable income. Taxable income is defined as the gross, meaning total, income from all sources, minus allowable deductions and exemptions. One of these sources includes ordinary income. Ordinary income is the income received from wages, salaries, commissions, and interest. Cash that is received for the use of real property is taxable as rental income. Expenses related to the renting of the property can generally be deducted from the rental income. Income from partnerships typically passes through to each partner individually. Finally, tax rates are set and periodically adjusted by Congress.

2. ▶ **Tax benefits of home ownership and reporting of real estate sales**: The government allows the deduction of certain expenses related to the purchase and ownership of homes. The information in this section is provided only as a basic overview. A tax expert should be consulted when filing a tax return.

   a. **Deductible expenses resulting from home ownership**: To deduct the expenses of owning a home, the taxpayer must file a Form 1040 and itemize his deductions on Schedule A (Form 1040). The following list includes some of the more common deductible expenses.

      (1) Loan acquisition costs such as origination fees and points (however, they cannot be fully deducted in the year they were paid, but must be deducted over the life of the loan).

      (2) Mortgage interest payments on first and second homes.

      (3) Mortgage interest payments on home equity loans secured by real estate.

      (4) Real property taxes paid in the year of the deduction.

      (5) Some charges related to refinancing such as mortgage interest, loan origination fees, and discount points.

   b. **Non-deductible expenses**: Non-deductible expenses include property insurance, utilities, most settlement costs, and down payments.

   c. **Reporting of a real estate sale**: In the case of a primary residence (i.e., main home), the owner does not have to report the sale on his tax return unless he (1) has a gain, meaning profit, and does not qualify for the exclusion, or (2) received Form 1099-S resulting, for example, from a short sale of the residence. Short sales are discussed in Chapter 16.

3. ▶ **Tax benefits of income property ownership**: The direct economic benefits of income property ownership include (1) the income received through tenant-paid rents, (2) having property expenses paid by commercial tenants under net leases, and (3) property appreciation. Some of the expenses paid by an owner-landlord can be used to offset or shelter the income he receives. Additionally, an income property owner may be able to take advantage of IRS depreciation.

   a. **Tax shelter**: A legal tax shelter is a tool used by a taxpayer to reduce his taxable income. For example, allowable rental property tax deductions can be subtracted from the owner's gross income. By lowering gross income, taxes get reduced. The most common form of tax shelter for the average taxpayer is a qualified retirement account such as an employer-sponsored 401(k) plan.

Chapter 15: Financing Considerations of Ownership

Attempts to "hide" income from the IRS, such as assigning part of one's income to a family member who is in a lower tax bracket or having income deposited into an undeclared bank account, are illegal tax shelters. Penalties can be rather stiff. Criminal prosecution and a prison sentence are also possible. Fortunately, there are several legal shelters that are available including tax deductions and tax credits.

(1) **Tax deduction**: A tax deduction is an amount of money that is subtracted from a taxpayer's gross income before calculating his actual taxable income. The amount remaining is called the adjusted gross income. The actual dollar savings to the taxpayer represents a percent of the deduction.

(2) **Tax credit**: A tax credit is a direct, dollar-for-dollar reduction of the actual tax due. It reduces taxes by the actual amount of the credit. As a review, a tax deduction is subtracted from gross income whereas the tax credit is subtracted from the actual taxes due.

(3) **Income property deductions**: Common tax deductions for income property owners include: (1) mortgage interest on any loans used to purchase or improve the property; (2) repairs that are necessary, ordinary, and reasonable in amount; (3) travel expenses related to rental activities; (4) expenses related to employees and independent contractors; (5) insurance costs; (6) casualty losses; and (7) expenses related to legal and other professional services including outside property management.

b. ▶ **IRS depreciation**: IRS depreciation is a method of recovering a portion of the cost of an income-producing property over its useful life. The IRS allows an income property owner to recover the cost of certain property types that are used for the production of income. IRS depreciation is one of the main advantages of owning income property. It can be highly complex and should be calculated by a qualified tax expert. IRS depreciation is also known as accelerated cost recovery. Technically, the term "IRS depreciation" is commonly used to mean depreciation allowable under the Internal Revenue Code.

(1) **Based on deterioration of structures**: Income-producing property is purchased to make money rather than lose it. The IRS is aware that, over time, buildings tend to lose their income-producing potential. As a result, the owner is given deductions for the loss in value resulting from wear and tear, deterioration, and obsolescence.

(2) **Applied to building, not the land**: IRS depreciation can only be taken on an income-producing building, not the land on which it was constructed.

(3) **Method of depreciation–MACRS**: A rental property must qualify for depreciation as follows: (1) the taxpayer owns the property; (2) uses it for income-producing purposes; (3) it has a determinable useful life; and (4) it is expected to last more than one year. Assuming it does, the owner will likely be required to use the Modified Accelerated Cost Recovery System or MACRS. This system allows for greater accelerated depreciation depending on certain circumstances.

c. ▶ **Section 1031 like-kind exchange**: According to the IRS, whenever a person sells a business or investment property, he generally has to pay a tax on any gain resulting from the sale. Section 1031 of the Internal Revenue Code provides an exception which allows the person to postpone (i.e., defer) paying tax on the gain if he reinvests the proceeds in a similar property as part of a qualifying like-kind exchange. Like-kind means both properties must be held for use in a trade or business or for investment.

Unless a real estate licensee is highly experienced in commercial property, he should not attempt to provide guidance on like-kind exchanges. Further, clients should be directed to consult with a competent financial expert and/or tax attorney prior to signing any document that purports to transact such an exchange.

4. **Self-employed individuals and income tax obligations**: Under federal tax law, a self-employed individual is one who carries on a trade or business as a sole proprietor or independent contractor. Since real estate licensees are almost always hired as independent contractors under Michigan license law, it is important that they understand their tax obligations. According to the Internal Revenue Service, a self-employed individual is required to file an annual return and pay estimated taxes on a quarterly basis.

In addition to income taxes, a self-employment tax must also be paid. This is a tax to cover the Social Security and Medicare taxes that would have been withheld by the employer had the licensee been working as an employee. Taxes are paid on the net profit earned from business activities. A licensee who is an independent contractor should consult with a qualified tax expert for advice on how to meet all federal, state, and possibly local income tax obligations.

D. ▸ **Capital gains taxation**: When a parcel of real property is sold, the equity (which includes the down payment and appreciated value) is cashed out to the owner in the form of a check. The money qualifies as income which is subject to special tax treatment. By definition, a capital gain is the profit an owner or investor realizes when a capital asset is sold at a price that is higher than its original purchase price. A capital asset is any useful or valuable thing that a business or individual holds for its ability to generate a profit. Common capital assets include land, buildings, and equipment.

1. **Calculation of capital gains and losses**: When a capital asset is sold or exchanged by the owner, the capital gain is the difference between the amount the owner sells it for (minus selling expenses) and the property's adjusted cost basis. Assume for the following discussion that a property owner purchased a property for $50,000 three years ago and sells it for $75,000 today. To assist in your understanding, review the following illustration and then read the three paragraphs that follow.

   Illustration:

Purchase price (basis)	$50,000
Selling price	$75,000
− Selling expenses (closing costs)	− $ 7,500
Amount realized	$67,500
− Adjusted basis	− $59,000
Capital gain	$ 8,500

   a. **Basis**: A property's basis is the initial cost or value assigned at the time of acquisition; in other words, the original purchase price. In the above example, the basis is $50,000.

   b. **Adjusted basis**: In simple terms, the adjusted basis is the purchase price plus amounts paid for capital improvements minus allowable losses. According to the IRS, capital improvements include (1) improvements that put a property in a better operating condition, (2) additions or new or replacement components, and (3) that which upgrades, modifies, or extends the useful life of a property. Examples include a room addition, garage addition, exterior deck, finished basement, and replacement windows. Repair expenses and routine maintenance do not qualify as capital improvements.

   Using the figures from the illustration: The owner added a new deck for $5,000 and several replacement windows that cost $4,000. The adjusted cost basis is $50,000 (basis) + $9,000 (all improvements) = $59,000.

   The capital gain is the amount realized from the sale minus the adjusted basis or $67,500 − $59,000 = $8,500. With capital gains taxation, notice how only the return "on" the owner's investment is taxed rather than the return "of" his investment.

   c. **Capital loss**: A capital loss occurs if the adjusted basis is higher than the amount realized from the recent sale. The loss may only be deducted on an investment property, not on property that is held for personal use such as a primary residence.

2. **Tax treatment of capital gains**: Income tax laws have traditionally treated capital gains differently than ordinary income by taxing them at a lower rate than the rate applicable to ordinary income. The rates have fluctuated over the years based on the economic climate of the country. While the rates reflected in this section are accurate as of the date it was written, a qualified financial expert must be consulted for the most accurate and up-to-date rates since they are subject to change.

   a. **Holding periods (long-term versus short-term)**: Capital gains are labeled long-term or short-term based on how long the taxpayer owned the property. If it is held for more than one-year, the gain (or loss) is treated as long-term. If it was held for only one year or less, the gain (or loss) is treated as short-term.

      (1) **Long-term capital gains**: When selling a capital asset that was held for longer than 12 months, the long-term capital gains rate is 15% (for single taxpayers earning $36,250-$400,000 and married couples earning $72,850-$450,000) or 20% (for income earners over these amounts). Earners in the lowest tax bracket pay 0%.

      (2) **Short-term capital gains**: When selling a capital asset which has been held for 12 months or less, the asset is taxed as ordinary income at the regular tax rate which ranges from 10% to 39.6%.

   b. **3.8% unearned income Medicare contribution tax**: An additional 3.8% tax is applied to single taxpayers who earn over $200,000 and couples who earn over $250,000. If this income threshold is reached, the capital gains tax rates increase by 3.8%.

Chapter 15: Financing Considerations of Ownership

3. **Excluding the gain–the universal exclusion**: A taxpayer may qualify under IRS rules for an exclusion of all or part of a capital gain on his main home which is also known as a principal residence. This may also be referred to as the IRS universal exclusion. Married homeowners filing a joint tax return may exclude up to $500,000 of capital gains. A single taxpayer filing a tax return in his individual capacity may exclude up to $250,000 of capital gains realized from the sale of his property.

   a. **Qualifying for the exclusion**: To qualify for the exclusion, the taxpayer(s) must meet the ownership test, use test, and not have excluded any gain from the sale of a main home during the 2-year period preceding the date of the immediate sale.

      (1) **Ownership test**: The home must have been owned for an aggregate (meaning, total) of at least 2 years out of 5 years immediately preceding the sale. The two years do not have to be consecutive. In the case of a married couple, at least one of the spouses must meet this ownership test.

      (2) **Use test**: All taxpayer(s), regardless of marital status, must have lived in the home as their main home for at least 2 years out of 5 years immediately preceding the sale.

   b. **The exclusion can be used more than once**: The deduction can be used more than once as long as the transaction qualifies under the rules discussed in this section.

   c. **Reduced exclusion and exceptions**: A taxpayer may be entitled to a reduced exclusion if he cannot meet the ownership or use tests based on a change in his place of employment, health reasons, or unforeseen circumstances such as the destruction of the home, condemnation, or divorce. There is an exception to the use test for individuals with a disability providing they are unable to care for themselves and have owned the home for 2 out of 5 years and have lived in the home for at least 1 year of the preceding 5 years.

   d. **IRS reporting requirements**: If all of the capital gain is excluded under the IRS rules, it does not have to be reported to the IRS on the taxpayer's tax return. The gain must be reported if it does not qualify for an exclusion, the taxpayer chooses not to exclude it, or it resulted from a debt forgiveness that was reported to the taxpayer on a Form 1099-S.

4. **Reporting real estate transactions (IRS 1099-S)**: We have just explored how capital gains taxes are due on the sale of certain property. When this occurs, the seller's proceeds must be reported to the IRS on Form 1099-S which is titled, "Proceeds From Real Estate Transactions." These reporting requirements apply to the sale or exchange of non-exempt real estate, including condominiums and cooperatives.

   a **Exceptions**: The following transactions do not have to be reported:

      (1) The sale or exchange of a principal residence for $250,000 or less ($500,000 or less for a married couple filing jointly). This is due to the universal exclusion from capital gains taxation. The seller must certify, however, that the gain is excludable from gross income; i.e., that the gain qualifies for long-term capital gains treatment.

      (2) The seller is a corporation, government unit, or international organization.

      (3) The transfer is a bequeath, gift, or refinancing not related to the acquisition of real estate.

      (4) The transfer is in satisfaction of a debt secured by the property; e.g., a foreclosure, deed in lieu of foreclosure, or an abandonment.

      (5) The transfer is for less than $600.

      (6) The transfer involves an off-site manufactured (i.e., mobile) home that is unrelated to the sale or exchange of real estate; in other words, the manufactured home is not affixed to a foundation as of the date of the closing.

   b. **Who must file**: The person who closes the transaction or is listed as the settlement agent on the HUD-1 statement must file Form 1099-S with the IRS. If no HUD-1 statement is used (or two or more settlement statements are used in the closing), the responsible party could be the buyer's attorney, seller's attorney, disbursing title company, or the mortgage lender, seller's broker, buyer's broker, or buyer. Legal counsel should be consulted with regard to the responsibility for filing the form.

E. **Foreign Investment in Real Property Tax Act (FIRPTA)**: The sale of a U.S. real property interest by a foreign seller is subject to special IRS withholding requirements under FIRPTA. The purpose of the Act is to assure collection of capital gains taxes from foreign sellers who might not otherwise be inclined to pay them if and when they are due. The buyer is required to withhold 15% of the total purchase price due the seller as a result of a sale and then transmit it to the IRS.

1. **Qualifying sales**: The withholding requirement is triggered by a sale. The term "sale" includes installment sales such as land contracts, qualifying real property exchanges, and foreclosures.

2. **Covered parties and responsibilities**: FIRPTA applies to nonresident foreign persons and certain business entities that sell a U.S. real property interest. The Act does not cover a sale by a U.S. citizen, resident alien with a valid green card, or a seller who meets the IRS "substantial presence test." Under this test, a person is considered to be a U.S. resident for tax purposes if he or she is physically present in the United States on at least 31 days during the current year, and 183 days during the 3-year period that includes the current year and the 2 years immediately before that.

   a. **Buyer's requirements**: To ensure compliance, a buyer should seek an affidavit of nonforeign status from the seller that includes the seller's name, home address, and Tax Identification Number (TIN). The TIN is typically the social security number if the seller is a U.S. citizen or a foreign worker with authorization to work in the U.S. A buyer can also rely on a Qualified Substitute to meet his obligations. A person who closes the transaction, including an attorney or title company, may serve as a Qualified Substitute. While a buyer's agent (but not a listing agent) can legally serve as a Qualified Substitute, real estate company policy may not allow for this practice.

      (1) **Buyer liability**: If a buyer does not withhold the 15%, the IRS can assess him the amount due plus interest and penalties. The assessment can also be imposed if the buyer does not obtain an affidavit of nonforeign status and the seller fails to pay the capital gains taxes due on the sale.

         (a) **Assuring compliance**: Even if a seller informs the buyer that he is not a foreign person, the buyer should still insist that an affidavit of nonforeign status be provided. If no exemption applies and the seller fails to provide his social security number to the buyer, the buyer must withhold 15% of the purchase price.

         (b) **Seller's receipt**: When a seller provides an affidavit of nonforeign status with all required information, the seller should protect himself by obtaining a receipt from the buyer acknowledging that it was provided.

      (2) **Notice of compliance in purchase agreement**: The purchase agreement should also include a clause or written acknowledgment that the parties are aware of and intend to comply with all FIRPTA requirements.

   b. **Potential application to licensees**: A real estate licensee who represents the buyer and/or seller as agent is potentially liable under FIRPTA if the licensee knows that an affidavit of nonforeign status provided by the seller is false. The penalty is the lesser of 15% of the sale price or the amount of commission received. A closing officer is not considered to be a real estate agent for purposes of this requirement.

      (1) **Enhanced liability for listing agents**: If the seller is a foreign corporation that provides a false affidavit of nonforeign status, the listing agent can be held liable even if the seller's agent had no actual knowledge that it was false. Consequently, a listing agent should consult legal counsel for assistance when representing a corporate seller that may be a foreign business entity.

      (2) **Buyer recommendation**: A real estate licensee who represents a nonresident foreign buyer of a U.S. real property interest may wish to recommend that the buyer apply for an Individual Taxpayer Identification Number (ITIN) since it will be needed when the buyer eventually resells the property. An ITIN is a specific form of taxpayer identification number issued by the IRS.

   c. **Exemptions**: A real property sale by a U.S. citizen, a resident alien with a valid green card, or a seller who meets the IRS "substantial presence test" are exempt from FIRPTA withholding and reporting requirements. Other exemptions under FIRPTA include:

      (1) A purchaser who acquires a property for use as a residence and the sale price does not exceed $300,000.

      (2) A purchaser who receives a "withholding certificate" from the seller which specifies that either no withholding, or a reduced amount, is required.

Chapter 15: Financing Considerations of Ownership 235

(3) A seller who provides the purchaser with a written notice that, according to the IRS, no recognition of any gain or loss on the sale is required. A purchaser should not, however, rely on a "nonrecognition provision" without first consulting legal counsel or a CPA to verify its accuracy.

(4) The amount realized by the seller on the sale is zero.

(5) The sale is of an interest in a qualifying domestic corporation or an interest in a domestic corporation that certifies no U.S. real property interest is involved. Again, a licensee should consult with legal counsel before relying on such a certification.

3. **Handling of withheld funds**: While the purchaser is primarily responsible for meeting FIRPTA's withholding and reporting requirements, compliance is generally managed by the lender or title company who handles the closing. IRS Form 8288 and Form 8288-A are used to report the withholding of the seller's proceeds as well as reporting and payment of the required amount to the IRS within 20 days of the closing.

IV. **Insurance**: Real estate ownership is either subject to or benefits from insurance coverage. An insurance policy is a contract where one party (the insurer), for an agreed upon fee, undertakes to compensate another party (the insured) for losses on a subject (such as property) that result from any number of specified perils or risks. The underwriter for the insurance company assesses whether or not to underwrite, meaning issue, the policy after evaluating the likelihood that the company might have pay out a loss under the circumstances. This evaluation also includes a determination of the cost of the policy.

A. **Classification of insurance**: Both property owners and business persons face risks that can have devastating financial consequences. A homeowner who faces the total loss of a structure and its content due to storm damage may never financially recover if he does not have a homeowner's policy that protects the structure and its contents. A broker faces similar challenges with respect to his real estate business.

1. **Property-related policies**: Common property-related policies include the homeowner's policy, homeowner's warranty policy, flood insurance, and renter's insurance.

   a. ▶ **Homeowner's policy**: A homeowner's policy is obtained by a residential property owner to insure against risks such as fire, lightning, windstorm, hail, freezing pipes, and theft. The owner's personal belongings may also be covered up to a certain limit. Separate endorsements or riders may be required for higher value items, special items, and water damage from drain backups and sump pump failures. Most homeowner's policies cover personal liability for slips and falls, dog bites, and injuries caused by the policy holder to others or their property.

   A lender who loans money on a residential structure will require that the borrower have adequate insurance on the property to protect the lender's financial interest resulting from the mortgage/lien. Homeowner's insurance may also be referred to as hazard insurance.

   b. ▶ **Homeowner's warranty policy (HOW)**: A homeowner's warranty policy, or HOW, offers limited protection to a new homeowner against certain defects in the structure or mechanical items, usually for a period of one year from the closing. It is a home protection plan that covers the repair or replacement of many of the home's major systems and appliances such as the plumbing and electrical system, furnace and air conditioner, refrigerator, dishwasher, washing machine and dryer, and possibly roof leaks. A seller (and sometimes a builder or real estate agent) may provide a policy to the buyer to encourage the buyer to make an offer, and for the seller's peace of mind in case the buyer experiences a problem in the first year of ownership.

   c. ▶ **Construction warranty contrasted**: Residential builder's license law does not require a builder to provide a construction warranty to a buyer of new construction. Nevertheless, Michigan courts impose two implied warranties: (1) Implied warranty of workmanship; and (2) Implied warranty of habitability. Accordingly, the builder must demonstrate the appropriate level of skill and competence expected of residential builders. The builder can also be held responsible for any problems that result from defective work.

   d. **National flood insurance program (NFIP)**: Flood insurance is a policy that covers direct loss to a homeowner's property and his possessions that is caused by flooding. The NFIP was established by Congress in 1968 to enable homeowners, business owners, and renters to purchase federally-backed flood insurance. If the property is financed, the cost of the insurance is added to the borrower's monthly mortgage payment.

(1) **FEMA administers program**: The Federal Emergency Management Agency (FEMA) administers the National Flood insurance Program.

(2) **Coverage requirements**: An owner who lives in a floodplain, which is also known as a Special Flood Hazard Area (SFHA), is required to purchase flood insurance if he obtains a loan from a federally-regulated or a federally-insured lender. The policy must be carried for the life of the loan. An owner who resides outside of the mapped area can also purchase flood insurance and may be eligible for a lower cost Preferred Risk Policy.

Recall from Chapter 11, that the 100-year floodplain, also referred to as the 100-year base flood, is any land adjacent to a river, lake, or stream that will be inundated by water during a flood, which has at least a 1% chance of occurring in any given year.

(3) **Floodplain mapping in Michigan**: The primary source of floodplain mapping information in Michigan is the Flood Insurance Rate Maps (FIRMs) which are developed by FEMA. Of the 1,776 cities, villages, and townships in Michigan, about 750 have floodplain maps that have been developed by FEMA. Community status books are available through FEMA that identify all communities participating in the NFIP or for which flood maps are available.

e. **Renter's insurance**: Renter's insurance is a policy that can be purchased by tenants to cover things like the tenant's personal property, liability for injuries suffered by the tenant's guests, and temporary living expenses if the leased unit is rendered uninhabitable by fire, for example. Renter's insurance does not cover the structure since that is the landlord's responsibility. A landlord may require that his tenant purchase insurance to cover damages to the unit caused by the tenant's direct actions or neglect.

2. **Broker's business-related policies**: Insurance is a significant component of a broker's risk management program. Every brokerage business faces a number of different risks that can result in a financial loss, whether it be from actual physical damage to the broker's business property or monetary damages assessed by a court of law for errors and omissions. Regardless of the policy, all insurance should be periodically reviewed to make sure that it is adequate based on the broker's current business practices.

   a. **General liability insurance**: A general liability insurance policy covers the broker's business from the cost of a claim made by, for example, slip and fall cases. This type of policy may also be referred to as commercial liability insurance.

   A broker should make sure that his liability policy: (1) extends beyond the real estate office to open houses and covers slips and falls, damage to the seller's property, and theft; and (2) covers negligence committed by affiliated licensees and company employees. Individual licensed salespersons and associate brokers should also consider purchasing their own liability insurance to cover personal acts of negligence.

   b. **Professional liability insurance–Errors and Omissions insurance**: This form of insurance is discussed at the end of Chapter 3.

   c. **Commercial property insurance**: Commercial property insurance is purchased to cover the risk of loss to the broker's building (assuming the broker owns it) and any of the broker's personal property that is used in conducting his business. This could include loss of contents such as files and other valuable papers as well as damage to an outdoor sign.

   d. **Worker's compensation insurance**: A Michigan employer must assure its employees that it can pay benefits to them if they are injured on the job. Worker's compensation insurance offers this level of security by providing benefits such as wage replacement, medical expenses, and rehabilitation expenses. Brokers should consult with legal and insurance experts to determine what level of coverage they may need.

   For example, independent contractors are exempt from coverage if they maintain a separate business, hold themselves out to the public as being able to render services directly, and employ other workers themselves. Since affiliated salespersons and associate brokers may not meet these tests, the broker should determine whether worker's compensation insurance should be purchased to cover them.

3. **Miscellaneous policies**: There are other insurance policies that a real estate professional may wish to consider acquiring such as a personal umbrella policy and/or home-based business insurance.

   a. **Personal umbrella policy**: A personal umbrella policy operates like an extension to existing policies that have liability coverage. For example, it would supplement the coverage provided under a homeowner's policy or a automobile policy. It is typically sold in increments of $1 million of coverage and covers losses if and when the liability coverage on the primary policy is completely exhausted. Insurance experts often recommend an umbrella policy for clients who have children, dogs, have a swimming pool or trampoline, own rental properties, hunt, own a recreational vehicle, or coach youth sports.

b. **Home-based business insurance**: In-home business policies typically protect business property and provide general liability coverage. If the policy-holder's home is damaged to the extent that his business is temporarily shut down, a home-based business policy would cover any lost income and other on-going expenses such as payroll for a limited period of time. As with all policies, coverage is provided up to a set dollar amount and extends only to named perils.

*A real estate professional adds great value to the lives of others.
A real estate professional is important to the health of the U.S. economy.*

You can feel proud of the important work you are about to do.

DIAGNOSTIC PRACTICE QUESTIONS – CHAPTER 15

IMPORTANT STUDY TIP!

Step 1: Carefully review the information located in this chapter.

Step 2: Take the following Diagnostic Practice Questions. Review any question you answered incorrectly by researching the topic in this textbook. If you are still uncertain as to why the question is answered as it is, consult your program provider.

NOTE ON CHAPTER PRACTICE QUESTIONS

The following questions are representative of the type encountered on the Michigan real estate licensing examination. While some of these questions may be similar in nature and style, there is no way of predicting the exact wording of a question that will appear on the exam. Spending time memorizing these questions is, therefore, not recommended.

These questions are designed to help you determine how well you comprehend the material in this chapter. They are also intended to help you develop problem solving skills and to become comfortable with question formats.

Do not attempt to answer these questions until you have attended the lecture corresponding to this chapter and spent the appropriate time studying the material.

1. Terry and her husband Rick desire to acquire their first commercial investment property. They are particularly interested in the ability to generate rental income to offset mortgage and tax expenses. Since Terry and Rick are new to the commercial real estate market, they consult with real estate licensee, Kathy to assist them. Kathy should recommend all of the following EXCEPT:
   A. Consult with an attorney to review all sale contracts.
   B. Structure the title as a Joint Tenancy because the transaction involves commercial property.
   C. Consult with a CPA to review income reporting requirements and deductions.
   D. Conduct an extra thorough property inspection to reduce the risk of environmental liability.

2. Which of the following properties is LEAST likely to be exempt from ad valorem taxation?
   A. A local community hospital.
   B. A church operating out of a unit in a retail strip center.
   C. A private driving school.
   D. A state campground.

3. A special assessment is a category of:
   A. Property tax.
   B. Income tax.
   C. Estate tax.
   D. Inheritance tax.

4. A cautious seller of a residential property is particularly worried that a buyer may discover a problem with the physical condition of the dwelling and sue him after the sale. At the listing agent's recommendation, the seller accurately and fully completed a Seller Disclosure Statement. What else can the real estate agent recommend to the seller to reduce his concern?
   A. Increase the amount of title insurance coverage.
   B. Recommend that the seller take his property off of the market.
   C. Attach a hold harmless clause as an addendum to the purchase agreement.
   D. Provide a Home Warranty policy to the buyer.

5. Which of the following is true regarding a tax shelter?
   A. An owner-occupied residential dwelling is a form of shelter since the profit realized through appreciation is not taxable.
   B. A tax shelter is used to reduce the actual amount of tax owing as a result of owning certain property types.
   C. Sheltered income does not have to be reported to the IRS providing the property owner files in a timely manner.
   D. A REIT is the most common form of tax shelter.

6. The Homeowner's Principal Residence Exemption applies to all of the following EXCEPT?
   A. A shareholder in a cooperative.
   B. A condominium held as a single-family residence.
   C. A residential property held as a second home.
   D. Residence being purchased on a land contract.

7. In property taxation, millage refers to which of the following:
   A. One mill equals 1/10 of a dollar.
   B. Millage is a tax rate expression or method of calculating the tax due on a property.
   C. Millage means that all property owners within a community pay the same amount of tax.
   D. All of the above.

8. Blue-sky laws are primarily designed to protect which of the following:
   A. Corporate purchasers of real property interests in real estate investment trusts.
   B. The sellers of investment interests in cooperatives.
   C. Employees of the Securities and Exchange Commission.
   D. Purchasers of securities offerings from fraudulent companies.

9. All EXCEPT which of the following accurately describes a tax abatement:
   A. It represents a reduction in the actual amount of tax a property owner is required to pay.
   B. It is frequently used as a form of inducement to attract new businesses to a community.
   C. It is a principal residence exemption.
   D. It is frequently offered by municipalities.

10. A street in a residential development is repaved. How will the cost of the improvement most likely be handled?
    A. The city will pay the bill out of its general tax fund since all property owners are taxed, in part, for such improvements.
    B. The owners who live on the street will be issued a special assessment based on the benefits received.
    C. The county road commission will be issued a bill to be satisfied with state highway funds.
    D. A special bond will be issued to the property owners who live on the street.

11. A homeowner's insurance policy is used to protect homeowners from which of the following:
    A. Protection against loss of title due to certain defects or unrecorded claims.
    B. Physical risks of loss due to perils such as fire, weather, and accidents.
    C. Water damages caused to properties located in flood zones.
    D. Intentional acts of destruction caused by a homeowner with financial difficulties.

12. Mary, a 68 year-old woman, owns a large and expensive residential property in which she has resided for 7 years. She married a 66 year-old man who had taken advantage of his capital gains exclusion during his first marriage several years earlier. Within 2 months of her new husband moving into Mary's house, she wants to sell her property and exclude the payment of capital gains. What are Mary's rights?
    A. Mary is entitled to a one-time exclusion of the statutory amount because she is over the required age.
    B. Mary qualifies since at least one spouse met the eligibility tests of ownership and occupancy.
    C. Mary is entitled to the exclusion provided she depreciates the property on her tax return.
    D. Mary qualifies for a $250,000 exclusion providing she and her new husband files a joint tax return.

13. All of the following statements refer to property taxes EXCEPT:
    A. Local assessors always appraise property on an identical and equal basis.
    B. Collection of unpaid property taxes may be enforced by means of a lien.
    C. Certain property types are exempt from property taxes.
    D. Property taxes are assessed on an ad valorem basis.

14. The assessed value of a property includes the value of which of the following:
    A. The buildings and improvements excluding the raw land.
    B. Only the value of the land as if it had not been improved.
    C. The present worth of the land and all improvements.
    D. The present worth of the whole property multiplied by the state equalized value.

15. The capital gain on a property is defined as which of the following:
    A. The amount of a refund to which a tax-paying homeowner is ordinarily entitled.
    B. The combined value of property improvements which is entitled to special tax treatment.
    C. The difference between like-kind property in a tax-deferred exchange.
    D. The profit realized on the sale of property attributable primarily to appreciation.

16. Which of the following claims may have priority over all the others?
    A. Judgments against the previous owner.
    B. Judgments against the present owner.
    C. Delinquent real estate taxes.
    D. A first mortgage.

Chapter 16
Financing Instruments

Understanding the nature of debt and security.

I. **Foreword**: For most individuals, the purchase and sale of real property is the single largest financial transaction of their lives. A buyer with the appropriate financial resources can certainly purchase a property for cash. When this happens, the transaction will close quickly which is appreciated by everyone. Most buyers, however, require a loan from a lender to purchase their homes. While financing is a separate industry itself, it represents a critical part of nearly all real estate transactions. This is why licensees must have a thorough understanding of how the process works.

   A. **Security for the debt**: When the purchase of real estate is financed by a lender (such as a bank), the lender typically allows the buyer to take title to the property at the closing. This is significant because the lender's money was used to accomplish this. Once a deed is conveyed, no other party, even a lender, can arbitrarily take it back. As a result, the lender needs to secure the loan by requiring the buyer-borrower to give the lender a lien on the property in exchange for the loan. The lien creates a security interest in the property in favor of the lender who can bring a foreclosure action if the buyer-borrower defaults. The property serves as collateral for the loan.

      1. **Collateral**: The term collateral refers to property or other assets that a borrower pledges to a lender as security for the repayment or satisfaction of a debt. Since the amount of a real estate loan is typically higher than the cash resources of the buyer-borrower, the lender will require that the property be used as the collateral.

      2. **Pledge**: As a verb, to pledge is to transfer property to a creditor to be held as security for a debt or obligation. As a noun, the pledge is the actual property given as security.

      3. **Security alternatives**: There are a number of different security options available to finance the purchase of real property. These include: (1) traditional mortgage-backed loans obtained through regulated lending institutions or private investors; (2) deeds of trust; and (3) seller-backed financing such as land contracts and purchase money mortgages.

   B. **Role of the real estate agent**: Although lending institutions and their loan originators typically manage most of the financing aspects of a real estate transaction, real estate licensees should possess a thorough understanding of the process. This allows them to make sure the needs of their clients are being properly met. Licensees may also be relied on by buyers and sellers to answer basic financing questions.

II. ▶ **Mortgage defined**: A mortgage is a written debt instrument by which a property owner pledges his real property as collateral to secure a loan. It creates a contractual lien on the property. The lien gives the lender the ability to sell the property in the event the borrower defaults. The mortgage gives the lender a legal interest in the borrower's property. As a general information point, the word "instrument" refers to a written document.

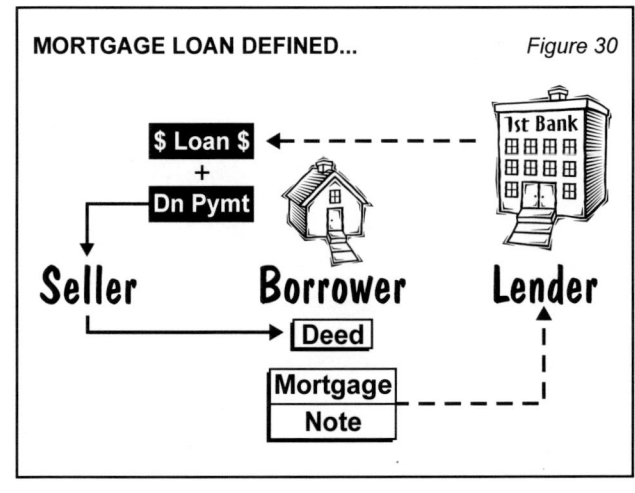

Figure 30

Without the mortgage, the lender would not have the legal ability to force the borrower's property for sale as part of a foreclosure proceeding. In some states, the issuance of a mortgage conveys conditional title to the lender. This "title" interest is cancelled or defeated when the debt is repaid. *See Figure 30.*

A. **Parties to a mortgage**: The parties to a mortgage include the mortgagor and the mortgagee.

Mortgagor: The mortgagor is the one who gives the mortgage, i.e., lien right, to the lender in exchange for the purchase money loan funds. He may also be referred to as the borrower or debtor. Recall that the party whose name ends with "–or" is said to give the document. People often mistake a mortgage for the actual loan funds since the phrase "mortgage loan" is sometimes used in practice. In reality, the mortgage is the contractual lien which is given in exchange for the loan.

Mortgagee: The mortgagee is the party who receives and holds the mortgage as security. The mortgagee is typically the lender or creditor. It provides the loan funds used to purchase the property in exchange for a lien right in the borrower's property. Recall that the party whose name ends with "–ee" is said to receive the document.

1. **Mortgagee as title holder versus secured party**: Depending on the laws of a particular state, a mortgage can secure a loan in one of two ways. Which way depends on whether the state is a title theory state or lien theory state.

    a. ▶ **Title theory**: In a title theory state, the transfer of a mortgage from the borrower-mortgagor to the lender-mortgagee operates to convey conditional title. If the mortgagor defaults, the mortgagee becomes the new owner. If the loan is repaid as agreed, full title is restored in the mortgagor as a result of a defeasance clause that is part of the mortgage terms. Mortgages historically operated under a title theory.

        (1) **Defeasance clause**: In a title theory state, the defeasance clause contains the specific language that revests title in the mortgagor when all terms and conditions of the loan have been met. The primary condition is repayment of the loan as agreed. Think of it as defeating the conveyance aspect of the mortgage.

    b. ▶ **Lien theory**: In a lien theory state such as Michigan, the mortgage merely gives the lender a lien right in the purchase property without conveying any ownership interest. Under this more modern approach, the lender does not need a title interest since the lien gives it an opportunity to force the sale of the property through foreclosure to recover whatever balance is due.

B. **The standard mortgage**: In practice, a mortgage is actually a document package involving two separate instruments that act together–the mortgage and the promissory note. The mortgage creates the lien and the note contains the promise to pay the debt.

1. **Recourse versus nonrecourse debt**: A mortgage alone is considered to be non-recourse in nature while the note is recourse in nature.

    a. **Nonrecourse debt**: With nonrecourse debt, the debtor is not personally liable for repayment of the actual debt. Armed with only a mortgage, a lender can foreclose on the lien and force the sale of the property. If the sale price at the foreclosure (i.e., sheriff's) sale exceeds the debt owing, the lender will recover its money. If the sale price is less than the debt, the lender cannot sue the borrower personally for the deficiency since the mortgage itself lacks a promise to pay the debt.

    b. **Recourse debt**: When a note is executed along with a mortgage, the lender can legally pursue any deficiency. This makes the debt recourse in nature. As discussed later in this chapter, the mortgagee-lender initiates a foreclosure action and the court gives it a judgement for the full debt owing. The property is ordered sold at a sheriff's sale to offset this debt. If the sale price is less than the debt owing, the mortgagee-lender can use its judgment to pursue the deficiency against the borrower personally. The default also constitutes a breach of contract since the promise to pay in the note was not fulfilled.

2. ▶ **Mortgage–technical aspects**: This section explores several specific requirements of the mortgage document. The technical aspects of the note are explored in a separate section that follows.

    a. **Only the mortgagor's interest is pledged**: A borrower who pledges his property as security for a debt is only able to mortgage the rights he actually has in the property. For example, a fee simple owner can mortgage his entire fee simple interest in the property. Similarly, a married couple who owns their property under a tenancy by the entireties can jointly mortgage their combined interest. A tenant in common, on the other hand, who has a one-quarter interest in a property can only mortgage his specific interest. If the lender forecloses, only the tenant in common's one-quarter ownership interest can be sold without affecting the other remaining owners' interest.

    b. **Writing**: Mortgages in Michigan fall within the statute of frauds and, therefore, must be in writing to be enforceable in a court of law. If an oral mortgage were granted a lender in exchange for a loan, the lender would not be able to enforce the lien if the borrower defaulted. See Chapter 12 for further information on the statute of frauds.

c. **Capacity**: The parties to the mortgage, especially the mortgagors, must be clearly identified and have contractual capacity. Legal capacity is another contract law principle that applies to mortgage agreements. A person who is mentally incompetent is protected. For example, if he pledges his property as security and is found to be incapable of understanding the nature and consequences of doing so, the mortgage is voidable.

d. **Language that secures the debt**: The mortgage must contain specific language through which the mortgagor voluntarily pledges his property as security for the loan. Without this, the lender does not acquire a lien on the property and cannot commence a foreclosure action if the mortgagor defaults. The mortgage also incorporates the terms of the note by reference.

   (1) **Incorporation by reference clause**: An incorporation by reference clause links two separate documents into one enforceable agreement. The referencing or primary document describes a second document, and by doing so, brings the terms of the second document into the terms of the primary document. The two documents are both treated and enforceable as one document. For example, the mortgage incorporates by reference the terms of the note and vice versa.

e. **Extent of the mortgaged interest**: The full extent of the interest being pledged must be specified in the mortgage. The clause describes the exact extent of the lien interest obtained by the lender. It would set forth, for example, that the lien exists in the entire fee interest of a single owner (as opposed to a partial interest in a property that is jointly owned).

f. **Sufficient description**: As with all contracts, the mortgage must contain a sufficient legal description of the mortgaged property.

g. **Execution**: The mortgagor is required to formally execute, meaning sign, the mortgage to show his intent to allow a contractual lien to be placed on the property.

   (1) **When all parties do not sign**: In cases where a property is jointly held and all owners do not execute the mortgage, only those who do sign have contractually agreed to the lien rights being established in the property. For example, assume that two buyers, "A" and "B," purchase property using a bank loan. Party "A" is the only one who executes the mortgage and the note. If a default occurs, the lender can only foreclose on "A's interest since "B" did not agree to the lien.

   The above example is provided for purposes of illustration only. In reality, a lender is not likely to issue a mortgage loan on a property in which it does not acquire a lien on the entire estate. Another example involving joint tenant owners can be found in Chapter 7 under the heading "Creditor's rights."

h. **Description of the mortgagor's responsibilities**: The parties to a mortgage acquire several responsibilities. Along with repayment of the debt, the mortgagor is required to pay property taxes, keep the property insured against damage or loss, and the property must be properly maintained.

   (1) **Debt repayment**: The debt must be repaid in strict compliance with the terms expressed in the note. At a minimum, this payment includes principal, interest, and late charges. Failure to pay constitutes a default since it represents a breach of the promise to pay contained in the note.

   (2) **Taxes**: All property taxes must be paid when due. Failure to pay the property taxes can result in a tax foreclosure. This obviously impairs the lender's lien interest in the property. As discussed later in this chapter, lenders of residential mortgage loans generally include a portion of the property taxes in the monthly mortgage payments to prevent this from happening.

   (3) **Insurance**: The lender requires the mortgagor to carry a hazard insurance policy that covers the structure in the event of physical damage. The hazard insurance policy names the mortgagee as an additional insured on the policy. The mortgagor must also purchase a form of title insurance known as a mortgagee's policy. This protects the lender's interest against title defects if the lender becomes the new owner through foreclosure. See Chapter 8 for further discussion on the mortgagee's title policy. Failure by the homeowner to maintain adequate insurance can result in the lender imposing what is known as force-placed insurance (which can be expensive for the homeowner).

   (4) **Property maintenance**: The mortgage agreement requires the mortgagor to protect the lender's investment in the property by maintaining the property and making necessary repairs when the

need to do so arises. The lender determines how much money it is willing to risk on a mortgage loan by appraising the value of the property as part of the loan origination process. The mortgagor must maintain this value throughout the life of the loan.

i. ▶ **Acceleration of the debt**: An acceleration clause allows the lender to accelerate the entire unpaid principal balance and declare it immediately due upon the occurrence of some event or circumstance. This event is typically a breach of a mortgage term or provision. For example, if the mortgagor fails to make his mortgage payment as agreed, the lender can accelerate the debt and foreclose. Acceleration most commonly results from nonpayment of the debt.

   (1) **Protects the lender-mortgagee**: Acceleration cannot occur unless there is a clause in the mortgage that authorizes it. This is important since nearly all loan contracts permit the borrower-mortgagor to make monthly payments over the life of the loan. If a default occurs and there is no acceleration clause in the mortgage, the mortgagor can only be forced to resume the payment schedule and satisfy any back payments.

   When an acceleration clause is included in the mortgage, it becomes one of the terms. Upon default, it gives the lender the right to immediately demand the payment of the entire unpaid balance. As a result, the lender does not have to wait and sue for each future payment as it comes due. The original monthly payment schedule is, in essence, collapsed into one lump sum.

   (2) **Triggering events**: Nonpayment of a mortgage installment is the most common event that triggers acceleration. Other events include the failure to properly maintain hazard insurance or to keep the property maintained. Failing to pay property taxes and hazard insurance–if these payments are not already budgeted in the mortgage payment–can also trigger an acceleration. Finally, selling the property without paying off the mortgage balance can result in the lender accelerating the debt.

   From a timing perspective, a lender may not initiate acceleration until the second or third month after a payment has been missed. It is generally in the best financial interests of a lender to give the mortgagor some time to get back on track with his payment schedule. As discussed later in this chapter, foreclosure is an extensive and time-consuming procedure for a lender.

   (a) ▶ **Due-on-sale clause**: A due-on-sale clause is a type of acceleration clause that can be enforced if the mortgagor sells or transfers an interest in the property without paying off the balance. This is important to a lender because the original loan funds were committed to the mortgagor based on his particular creditworthiness. If the mortgagor later attempts to sell the property to a new buyer who is not as creditworthy, the lender can prevent the sale by accelerating or calling in the debt.

   A due-on-sale clause also gives the lender an opportunity to research the new buyer's credit and approve the assumption as is or with an adjustment in the mortgage terms. Assumptions are discussed in more detail later in this chapter. Additionally, in the case of a federally-related mortgage, the due-on-sale clause is triggered if the property is leased for a period longer than 3 years or the property is leased with a lease-option.

   (b) **Michigan's Due-On-Sale Clause Act**: All due-on-sale clauses were made legal and enforceable in the United States with the passage of the federal Garn-St. Germain Depository Institutions Act of 1982. In 1984, the Michigan Legislature enacted similar legislation. While state law does not preempt (meaning overrule) federal law, it contains a provision that is important to Michigan real estate licensees.

   (c) **Real estate licensee liability**: Under Michigan law, a person who is licensed to do business in Michigan (such as a real estate licensee), who knowingly advises a seller (who is a mortgagor) not to notify a lender of a sale, or who knowingly aids or assists a person in evading the Act is subject to a $5,000 fine and loss of license. Evading the Act occurs when a mortgagor whose property is subject to a mortgage with a due-on-sale clause sells without notifying his lender. A licensee must not recommend or knowingly participate in such a transaction.

   (d) ▶ **Alienation clause**: An alienation clause is a related provision that forbids a mortgagor from transferring the property without the lender-mortgagee's consent. It is also known as a non-assumption clause. Legally speaking, any clause that outright forbids an owner from transferring his property is generally held to be invalid.

Chapter 16: Financing Instruments   245

An alienation is a "voluntary" transfer of a property from one person to another (as opposed to a involuntary transfer by operation of law). When a person transfers his property, he alienates himself from any future rights. By contrast, a due-on-sale clause does not attempt to stop the mortgagor from selling, it merely says that if he does, the lender can accelerate the debt. This is why a due-on-sale is generally enforceable.

j. ▶ **Release or satisfaction of mortgage**: The mortgage remains in force for as long as the debt is unpaid. When the final payment is made, the mortgagor has the right to have the lien removed. This is accomplished by the lender recording a release in the public records known as a satisfaction of mortgage. When a future title search is conducted, the lien appears in the records followed by the release showing that the property is free and clear of the encumbrance.

3. ▶ **Note–definition and technical aspects**: A note is an instrument, meaning a written legal document, that contains an absolute promise to pay a definite sum of money to a specified party. In terms of a mortgage loan, the note is a personal contract between the borrower and the lender that can lead to a breach of contract claim if the debt is not paid in strict compliance with its terms.

   a. **Evidences the debt**: Since the note contains a promise to pay, it serves as the contractual evidence that the debt exists. The borrower acknowledges this debt by promising to pay it. The promise-to-pay aspect of the note is what distinguishes it from the mortgage (lien).

   b. **Negotiable instrument defined**: A negotiable instrument is a legal document that contains a promise to pay a sum certain to a specific person. These instruments can be transferred, sold, or assigned from one individual to another. Notes and checks are common examples. The practice of selling notes that are backed by mortgages on real property is common in the secondary mortgage market.

   When a mortgagee sells an existing mortgage to a third party investor in the secondary mortgage market, for example, the third party generally requires the following: (1) confirmation of the balance due and terms of the mortgage and note; (2) that there are no defaults; and (3) an acknowledgment by the mortgagor that the balance is now payable to the third party. An estoppel certificate can be used for this purpose.

   (1) **Estoppel certificate**: An estoppel certificate is a signed statement given by a party for the benefit of another, certifying that a statement of facts is correct as of the date the statement is issued. For example, when the mortgage funds are issued at the closing, the lender may require the mortgagor to sign an estoppel certificate that certifies he is of legal age. If an underage mortgagor lies about his age thereby committing a fraud, he will have no defense should he later attempt to avoid the note based on his status as a minor.

   (2) **Certificate of no defense**: An estoppel is also known as a certificate of no defense. It legally bars any future defense to the matter asserted in the certificate. In other words, the signatory, i.e., the party who signs the estoppel certificate, establishes the validity of the facts at the time of execution and cannot later claim they are or were not true.

   (3) **Other applications**: When an investment buyer purchases a rental property which is subject to an existing lease, and the buyer intends to rely on the income from the lease, the tenant may be asked to validate its enforceability by executing an estoppel certificate. A lender may also require a tenant's estoppel certificate be executed if a loan is secured by a leased property. Estoppel certificates may also come into play in refinancing transactions and the sale of existing loans to investors.

   c. **Parties to the note**: The parties to a note are referred to as the obligor and the obligee.

   (1) **Obligor**: The obligor is the party who gives the note and thereby obligates himself to repayment under its terms. Simply stated, the obligor is the borrower (who is also the mortgagor under the mortgage). This person must be clearly named in the note.

   (2) **Obligee**: The obligee is the party who receives the note and the one to whom the obligor must make the payments. In simple terms, the obligee is the lender (who is also the mortgagee under the mortgage).

   d. **Obligor must sign**: A lender will generally require all parties who have an interest in a mortgaged property to sign the note. This is important since only those who physically sign the note are legally obligated to repay the debt.

Example: A single man purchases a home using a mortgage loan and gets married the following year. The husband then defaults on the mortgage payments. The lender can foreclose on the marital home because of its prior recorded lien right under the mortgage. If there is a deficiency, meaning the price realized at the sheriff's sale was less than the total debt owing, the lender can only sue the husband on the basis of the note because he is the only person who signed it. The wife is not personally liable under the note since she did not sign it.

e. ▶ **Interest and principal defined**: The note contains the terms of interest which the lender charges for making the loan. Interest is defined as compensation the debtor pays for the use of the lender's money over time. It can be viewed as a form of "rent" charged for the use of money. It is also the lender's reward for taking the risk that the loan may not be repaid. Interest charges are typically expressed as an annual percentage rate.

The principal is the amount borrowed. It can also be viewed as the outstanding amount of the loan which is due at any point in time. The basic components of a loan payment include the principal and interest. While this appears simple, the actual calculation of a loan payment can be complex.

(1) **Payments in advance versus arrears**: Payments under a loan contract can be due either in advance or in arrears. This is typically specified in the terms of the contract.

(a) **Advance**: An advance payment is that which is due at the beginning of a payment period. For example, rent that a tenant owes a landlord on a lease is typically due and payable in advance. In other words, the rent paid on January 1st covers the use of the premises during the month of January. Insurance is another example of a payment which is usually due in advance of coverage. In the case of real estate taxes, they may be paid either in advance or in arrears. See Chapter 9 for further details on the proration of property taxes.

(b) **Arrears**: Payments which are due at the end of a payment period are said to be paid in arrears. Although a mortgage payment may be due on the 1st of the month, it is not considered to be a payment made entirely in advance due to the interest component. It is illegal to charge interest in advance.

Example: Assume that a $600 mortgage payment which is due and payable on October 1st includes $500 in interest and $100 in principal. Further, the principal balance remaining after the September 1st payment is $100,000. The $500 October 1st interest payment is made in arrears because it was based on the September balance. The $100 principal portion of the payment made on October 1st is deducted that same day leaving a new balance of $99,900 for October. Thereafter, the November interest payment will be based on the $99,900 October balance, and so forth. Since the principal payment is applied on the first of each month, it is said that the principal is paid in advance.

(2) **Simple versus compound interest**: There are two basic ways that interest can be calculated. Since one method, called compounding, yields a higher return for the lender, it is more common. Smaller, short-term consumer loans are more likely to be based on simple interest than are long-term mortgage loans which are almost exclusively based on compound interest calculations.

(a) **Simple interest**: Simple interest is calculated as a straight percent of the principal (loan) balance and treated as separate from the principal. To calculate the monthly interest, first calculate the annual interest based on the principal balance in a given month, and then divide it by twelve. In other words, simple interest is calculated solely as a percent of the principal balance. See Chapter 22 for specific real estate math examples involving simple interest calculations.

(b) **Compound interest**: Compound interest is a challenging concept to explain. Technically, it is interest computed on the principal balance in a given month <u>and</u> on the interest the loan has already earned. When interest is compounded, it merges with the principal and becomes part of the base on which future interest is calculated. Even though it is not the case, many debtors feel as if they are "paying interest on interest."

For purposes of calculating compound interest on a real estate math question, the interest is first calculated and then subtracted from the total monthly payment. The remaining amount is applied to principal reduction. Subtracting the dollar amount of interest from the monthly payment before applying the balance to the principal results in less money paying down the

Chapter 16: Financing Instruments

loan. The best way to learn how this works is to refer to Chapter 22 and study the real estate math examples involving compound interest calculations.

f. ▶ **Amortization**: By definition, amortization is the repayment of a loan or other debt over a period of time. Most mortgage loans are fully amortized which results in the borrower making the same monthly payment over the entire life of the loan. Amortization is a way of budgeting the loan payments. The word amortize is derived from the Latin words "ad" meaning "to" and "mort" which means "death." To amortize, therefore, is to bring the debt to death or retirement.

The following factors are important to an amortized loan: (1) Principal; (2) Annual interest rate; (3) Length of loan; and (4) Monthly payment. If any of three of these factors are known, the fourth can be calculated. Amortization is discussed further in Chapter 17.

(1) **Amortization schedule (table)**: An amortization schedule is a complete and detailed list or table that sets forth the monthly principal and interest payment that is due on a loan amount (excluding monthly property tax or insurance costs). The schedule shows how the monthly payment changes with different interest rates and loan terms. Even though the monthly payment remains the same over the full term of a fully amortized loan, the portion of each payment that is applied to interest is highest at the beginning of the loan and gradually decreases each month as the principal balance is repaid. This occurs when interest is compounded. Math examples of this can be reviewed in Chapter 22. *See sample schedule.*

Sample Amortization Schedule

Rate%	15 yr	20 yr	30 yr
3.00	$6.91	$5.55	$4.22
3.50	$7.15	$5.80	$4.49
4.00	$7.40	$6.06	$4.77
4.50	$7.65	$6.33	$5.07
5.00	$7.91	$6.60	$5.37
5.50	$8.17	$6.88	$5.68
6.00	$8.44	$7.16	$6.00
6.50	$8.77	$7.51	$6.39
7.00	$8.89	$7.75	$6.65

Dollar amounts are indicated per $1,000 of principal

Today, loan officers rely on amortization calculators to make loan calculations rather than referring to schedules. Nevertheless, amortization schedules are useful to show buyer-clients how a change in the rate of interest or loan term can affect the monthly payment. Many schedules (like the schedule provided in this section) express the payment as dollars per thousand dollars of loan. Others show interest options in 1/4% increments and provide additional term options.

Use the amortization schedule to calculate the following sample questions:

Sample question 1: A buyer purchases a home for $147,200 with a 10% down payment. What is the monthly payment if the buyer is approved for a 30 year loan at 3.5% interest?

Calculate the loan: $147,200 purchase × 90% loan to value ratio = $132,480 loan amount

Calculate the loan payment using the amortization schedule: At 30 years, 3.5% interest, the payment is $4.49 per $1,000 of loan.
    $132,480 loan = 132.48 thousands
    132.48 × $4.49 (per $1,000 of loan) = $594.83 per month (principal and interest)

Sample question 2: A well-qualified couple purchases a home for $148,000 and makes application for a zero-down mortgage loan. The couple wants to know how much their monthly payment will increase if they take advantage of the better interest rate on a 15 year loan at 3% versus a 30 year loan at 4.5%. What does the loan officer tell the couple?

Determine the difference in payment (per thousand):
    15 year loan at 3.00% $6.91
    30 year loan at 4.50%   −$5.07
                                  $1.84 more per month per $1,000 of loan

Determine the actual increase in monthly payment based on the purchase price:
    $148,000 loan = 148 thousands
    148 × $1.84 (per $1,000 of loan) = $272.32 per month more (principal and interest)

g. ▶ **Points**: As used in financing, a point is a one-time fee that is collected by a lending institution at the time a loan is originated and closed. One point equals one percent of the principal amount and is typically paid by the borrower (although who pays the charge is sometimes negotiated). Points may also be referred to as discount points.

- (1) ▶ **Application and determination of points**: Points are sometimes charged to offset the differential between market interest rates and a lower rate offered by a lender. Each point increases the effective yield or return on the loan for the lender by ⅛ of 1% over the full term. This means that for each ⅛ percent difference between the two interest rates, 1 point would need to be charged (2 points for ¼ percent; 4 points for ½ percent, etc.).

- (2) ▶ **Discount points**: Points may also be assessed when an existing loan is sold by one lender to another lender or investor. The purchasing investor reduces the amount it pays by a given number of points. This is a common practice when a secondary market participant purchases one or more loans that have been originated and closed by a local lender.

    ▶ **Example**: Assume that the balance on an previously originated loan is $100,000. Several more years' worth of payments are remaining under the note. The originating lender sells the loan to an investor on a 15 point discount. This means that the investor will pay 85% or $85,000 for the right to collect the $100,000 balance on the loan. The originating lender is willing to sell the loan at the discount since it already collected more in interest in the early years of the loan than it will lose on the sale of the loan. The originating lender will also cash out the loan so it can apply the funds to new investments.

h. **Terms of repayment**: Along with interest charges, all financing terms must be specified in the note. The terms generally include how the loan is to be repaid including the maturity or due date, number of payments, applicable grace period, late charges, and to whom the payment must be made. To fully appreciate and understand all aspects of a note, it is best to refer to an actual note agreement.

i. **Maturity date**: The maturity date is the precise date on which the final payment is due and payable. When all terms have been fully satisfied as agreed, the loan is said to have matured.

j. **Default**: Legally, default is a failure to perform a legal or contractual duty. A default can result from a party failing to do something required in a contract (such as not making timely payments) or doing something he was not supposed to do (such as willfully damaging a property). With a standard mortgage, the documents specify the duties owed by the mortgagor as well as the consequences that can result from failing to meet these duties. As will be seen in the section discussing mortgage foreclosure later in this chapter, a lender must follow certain requirements when collecting the debt. These requirements are based on various state statutes as well as the terms and conditions of the mortgage and note itself.

Mortgagors often wonder exactly when their mortgage is in default for non-payment of a monthly installment. This question may or may not be directly addressed in the contract. For example, the due date of payments will be set forth, but the contract may not provide a specific date on which the lender will act on a missed payment. Many lenders do not consider their loan to be in default until 30 days has lapsed since the due date of a payment. Also, preliminary collection proceedings usually do not begin until any applicable grace period has lapsed.

- (1) **Grace period–a forbearance**: A grace period is a clause included in most notes whereby the lender agrees to wait a certain period of time before enforcing its rights to collect the debt. A typical grace period is 10–15 days from the actual due date. A grace period is legally known as a forbearance. To forebear means to agree to refrain from doing something.

- (2) **Other acts that can trigger default**: As discussed previously in the section on the responsibilities of the mortgagor, non-payment of property taxes, failure to keep the property insured, or failure to properly maintain the property can trigger default. This ultimately depends on the language in the mortgage and/or note.

4. **Assignment generally**: As discussed in Chapter 12, an assignment is the transfer of the balance of an interest in a contract. When a note is assigned, all existing rights, responsibilities, and remedies are transferred from the assignor to the assignee.

Examples: Depending on the terms of the note, either the mortgagee (lender) or original mortgagor (borrower) can assign its specific rights and interests in the note. As an example, Lender X sells one or more of its mortgages and assigns the notes to Investor Y who is a participant in the secondary mortgage market. In another example, a mortgagor desires to sell his mortgaged property to a new buyer who is willing to

Chapter 16: Financing Instruments

continue making the mortgagor's payments under his existing mortgage loan. In this instance, the mortgagor assigns his mortgage to the new buyer who assumes responsibility for the balance of the payments.

a. **Certificate of reduction of mortgage–the payoff letter**: When a note is sold, the purchaser may request a formal statement from the selling lender (meaning the original mortgagee) to determine the exact amount of unpaid principal. Payoff letters may also be requested by a real estate licensee to determine the balance due on an existing mortgage when listing a seller's home. This allows the licensee to roughly estimate what the seller's net proceeds will be from the sale of the property.

b. ▸ **Sale "subject to" versus "assumption" of mortgage**: When a mortgagor sells his property to a new buyer without paying off the loan, the buyer may acquire the property either subject to the mortgage or the buyer will assume the mortgage. A buyer who purchases a property that is subject to an existing debt must take care since the property remains encumbered by the lender's previously-recorded mortgage (lien). This lien is superior to and takes priority over the buyer's interest as will be seen in the following discussion.

   (1) ▸ **Subject to mortgage**: When a buyer takes title subject to the mortgage, no formal acknowledgment of the existing debt under the note takes place. The buyer continues to make the payments to the original lender. If the buyer defaults, the lender can foreclose on the mortgage. When a property is foreclosed there is no guarantee that the sale price of the property will be sufficient to satisfy the balance owning on the mortgage. In some cases there may be a surplus and in other cases there may be a deficiency.

   (a) **Foreclosure deficiency**: In the case of a sale subject to the mortgage, the buyer does not assume or share liability under the note. Instead, the original mortgagor-seller remains personally liable since he agreed to pay the full amount in the original note (which was assigned to the buyer). If the foreclosure sale price is less than the balance owing on the debt, the lender can sue only the original mortgagor for breach of contract. This is why no lender today would likely permit the sale of a property subject to the mortgage.

   (b) **Foreclosure surplus**: If the foreclosure sale price is greater than the debt balance, a surplus exists. In such case, the surplus is returned to the new mortgagor because it represents his equity in the property. The original mortgagor is entitled to nothing since his equity was cashed out at the time of the sale to the buyer.

   (2) ▸ **Assumption**: When the mortgage is assumed, the new buyer pays a sum of money that equals the seller's equity and agrees to pay the seller's existing debt balance. In other words, the buyer contractually agrees to become personally liable for the debt. Since this is an assignment of the original mortgage rather than a mortgage payoff, the seller remains liable. This is a risky proposition for the seller since the new buyer may default at some future time.

   (a) **Buyer defaults**: If the buyer defaults in an assumption, the property is sold and the buyer is held primarily liable for any deficiency. If the buyer is uncollectible, the mortgagee may look to the seller as the original mortgagor. This does not hold true if the lender granted the seller a novation at the time of the sale.

   (b) **Novation**: A novation is the substitution of one debtor for another debtor where the debt remains the same, but the original debtor's obligations under the note are extinguished. The lender formally releases the original mortgagor from any further liability under the note. If a deficiency exists, the new buyer is the only one who is liable and can be pursued for a deficiency judgment.

   (c) **Simple assumption versus formal assumption**: A simple assumption is one that may occur without having to seek the lender's prior approval of the new buyer. Before mortgages routinely contained due-on-sale clauses, they were also freely transferable without the lender's permission. FHA loans originated before 1986 and VA loans originated before 1988 may be assumed without the approval of the FHA or VA. Most of the loans discussed in this paragraph have long since matured or been repaid.

   In a formal assumption, the lender's approval of the new buyer's creditworthiness must be obtained prior to the sale and assumption taking place. The assumption of an FHA loan after the 1986 cutoff date is called a "creditworthiness assumption process." If a lender approves the new buyer and allows the assumption of the mortgage, the seller-mortgagor is usually granted a novation and released from any further obligation under the note. A buyer assuming a VA loan must also be creditworthy.

5. **Priority issues**: The discussion so far assumes that the lender recorded its mortgage immediately after obtaining the mortgagor's signature on it. The lender records the mortgage by physically delivering it to the county register of deeds. The recording of the mortgage protects the lender's security interest in the property by establishing a priority of claim in the event the property is sold without the lender's knowledge and consent or pay off.

III. **Miscellaneous issues affecting mortgages**: The mortgage industry faced many changes and challenges during the past two decades. The widely-used MERS system is one such example. Another example is the MARS Rule that was created by the Federal Trade Commission in an effort to combat mortgage fraud. While the acronyms MERS and MARS sound alike, they are quite different.

A. **Mortgage Electronic Registration System (MERS)**: The Mortgage Electronic Registration System, or MERS for short, was created in 1993 by several large mortgage lenders. It streamlined the mortgage process by replacing traditional paper forms with electronic commerce. MERS is technically not a mortgage lender or servicer, but rather a holding entity. Mortgage originators, servicers, warehouse lenders, wholesale lenders, retail lenders, document custodians, settlement agents, title companies, insurers, investors, county recorders, and consumers all use the system. MERS became an important tool when the financing industry increasingly engaged in the sale and resale of notes during the 1990s and 2000s.

1. **MERS becomes the mortgagee of record**: MERS acts as a nominee in the county land records for investor-lenders and servicers. A nominee is a person or entity into whose name liens against real property can be transferred, but who is not actually the owner of the property. Under the MERS system, a mortgage (referring to only the lien and not the note) is registered with MERS which then serves as the mortgagee. Its position as mortgagee does not change regardless of how many times the note is sold or traded.

   The MERS system protects investors in future assignments of the note. To accomplish this, the mortgage and the note are split. MERS holds the mortgage and the note is held by the lender or current investor. MERS is approved by Fannie Mae, Freddie Mac, Ginnie Mae, and all of the major Wall Street rating agencies to serve as the original mortgagee.

2. **Foreclosure of a MERS loan**: In the event that a foreclosure becomes necessary on a MERS loan, MERS is authorized by the member lenders to initiate and carry out the foreclosure proceedings on their behalf. In other words, MERS acts as the actual foreclosing mortgagee. Numerous Michigan court cases challenged MERS' ability to act in such capacity. These cases culminated in a Michigan Supreme Court decision ruling that a lender can contract with a third party such as MERS to hold the mortgage, and then authorize MERS to foreclose on it. A MERS mortgage is legal and fully enforceable.

B. **Mortgage Assistance Relief Services (MARS) Rule**: MARS is an acronym that stands for Mortgage Assistance Relief Services. The Federal Trade Commission (FTC) issued the MARS rule to protect homeowners from fraudulent mortgage rescue companies that preyed on distraught and unsuspecting homeowners who were facing the foreclosure of their homes. The MARS Rule became effective on January 31, 2011.

1. **Rule overview**: The MARS Rule targets bogus mortgage relief companies that charge a fee in exchange for false claims that they can negotiate with a consumer's mortgage lender or servicer to obtain specific mortgage relief. The Rule does not apply to a real estate licensee who provides traditional real estate services (such as listing and selling) that do not involve mortgage assistance relief services. Under the Rule, a real estate licensee can provide mortgage assistance relief services as long as he abides by all strict MARS Rule requirements.

   In the 2000s, many traditional real estate licensees were actively involved in the listing and selling of properties subject to short sale approvals by the sellers' lenders. Since a short sale qualifies as a mortgage assistance relief service, this presented a challenge to these licensees. To address this concern, the FTC issued an exception to the Rule for a real estate licensee who assists in the negotiation of a short sale that is part of the listing and sale of the property. This exception is discussed later in this section.

2. **MARS service defined**: A mortgage assistance relief service is any service, plan, or program, offered to consumers in exchange for consideration that: (1) assists in negotiating a loan modification that reduces the interest, principal, payments, or fees; (2) stops, prevents, or postpones a foreclosure or repossession; or (3) obtains other types of foreclosure relief. As noted, this definition does not include a real estate licensee who merely assists a homeowner in the listing and sale of his property to a buyer.

Chapter 16: Financing Instruments 251

3. **Requirements**: There are four basic facets or requirements of the MARS Rule along with specific disclosure requirements. A real estate licensee who provides actual mortgage assistance relief services beyond merely assisting in the short sale of a property, must abide by all Rule requirements.

   a. **No up front fee**: A company or individual, known as a MARS provider, who offers to help a consumer get his loan modified, or sells the consumer other types of mortgage assistance relief services, may not charge an up-front fee for the service or product.

   b. **Fee must be linked to actual success**: When MARS services are provided, the fee may not be collected by the MARS provider until the consumer has signed a written agreement with the lender that spells out the relief actually obtained by the provider.

   c. **Notice of right to reject**: When the MARS provider presents a consumer with the relief from the lender, it must inform the consumer, in writing, that the consumer can reject the lender's offer without obligation; and if the consumer accepts the relief, what is the total fee due the MARS provider.

   d. **Change must be documented**: Before the consumer agrees to accept the mortgage relief from the lender, the MARS provider must also give the consumer a written notice from the lender or servicer showing how the relief will change the terms of the consumer's loan.

   e. **Disclosures**: Generally, disclosures must be clear, concise, and prominently displayed in the written offerings of a MARS provider. A disclosure of information is required before a homeowner signs any agreement for services. If the provider advises a consumer not to pay his mortgage, the negative consequences that could result must also be disclosed. Further, the provider must warn a customer that failure to pay his mortgage could result in the loss of his home or cause damage to his credit rating.

4. **Short sale exception for real estate licensees**: On July 15, 2011, the FTC announced that it would refrain from enforcing most provisions of its MARS Rule against a real estate professional who assists a consumer in obtaining a short sale from the consumer's lender or servicer. This means that real estate licensees acting in their licensed capacity do not need to comply with the Rule's requirements including the required disclosures, advance fee ban, and recordkeeping requirements. This only applies to real estate brokers (and real estate salespersons under the broker's direction and control) who are:

   a. Licensed and maintain good standing pursuant to any applicable state law requirements;

   b. In compliance with state laws governing the practices of real estate professionals; and,

   c. Assisting or attempting to assist a homeowner in negotiating, obtaining, or arranging a short sale of a dwelling in the course of securing the sale of the homeowner's home.

5. **Penalties for Violation of the Rule**: A MARS provider who violates the MARS Rule is liable for a civil penalty up to an inflation-adjusted $16,000 for each violation or, in the event of continued violations, up to $11,000 for each day that the individual fails to comply.

IV. ▶ **Deed of trust**: A deed of trust is a security instrument through which legal title to financed property is conveyed to a trustee to secure the repayment of the loan. It operates similarly to a mortgage with the only difference that title is held by a trustee rather than a lien being held by a lender. Although not common in Michigan, they appear to be acceptable under state law. See Figure 31.

   A. **Creates a three-party relationship**: A mortgage is a two-party relationship between the mortgagor and the mortgagee. By contrast, a deed of trust is a three-party relationship with a trustor, a trustee, and a beneficiary.

      1. **Trustor**: The trustor is the borrower. He gives the deed of trust to the trustee as security for the repayment of the debt. The deed of trust, in essence, replaces a traditional mortgage-lien.

      2. **Trustee**: The trustee is the party who receives the deed of trust and holds it in trust. Common examples of trustees include public officers, attorneys, lenders, and title insurance companies.

3. **Beneficiary**: The lender, as the holder of the note, is the beneficiary of the trust. The trustee acts on behalf of the beneficiary.

B. **Default**: If a trustor-borrower does not repay the debt, the trustee may either conduct a trustee's sale or seek the foreclosure of the property for the lender.

V. ▶ **Land contract**: A land contract is another method that can be used to finance the sale of real property. It is an agreement, typically between a buyer and a seller, for the sale of land that calls for a down payment to be paid to the seller at the closing with the balance of the purchase price paid in subsequent installments. While a land contract may appear to be a simple agreement, it contains several sophisticated clauses and terms that should be thoroughly understood by the parties. A land contract may also be referred to as "contract for the purchase and sale of land," "contract for a deed," or "installment land contract."

A. **Parties to a land contract**: The formal labels for the parties to a land contract are vendor and vendee.

1. **Vendor**: The vendor is the seller in a land contract because he gives the equitable title and land contract rights to the buyer. Vendor is also a universal term that refers to one who sells or transfers property. For purposes of the Michigan real estate examination, vendor will most likely be used when referring to a land contract seller.

2. **Vendee**: The vendee is the buyer in a land contract because he receives the equitable title and land contract rights. The term vendee also universally refers to one who buys or receives property. For purposes of the Michigan real estate examination, vendee will most likely be used when referring to a land contract buyer.

B. **Seller finances**: In a land contract, the seller-vendor personally finances the sale of his own property as opposed to the buyer-vendee obtaining a loan from a lender such as a bank. To assure himself that he will be repaid by the buyer, the seller retains the deed (referred to as legal title) until the buyer makes the final installment payment. The holding of the deed by the seller is what distinguishes a land contract from a mortgage. Recall from Chapter 9 that a land contract which is fully financed by the seller does not fall within the requirements of RESPA.

C. **No separate security instrument**: There is no need for a lien, mortgage, or other security pledge with a land contract because the seller does not immediately convey full legal title to the buyer.

D. **Equitable conversion generally**: Chapter 12 introduced equitable conversion as a common law doctrine, meaning legal principle, that legally separates the ownership of a property (known as the equitable title) from the deed (which is referred to as the legal title). Regardless of the type of financing, the moment a buyer and seller execute a purchase agreement which is binding and enforceable, the equitable title interest immediately passes or converts from the seller to the buyer. In a traditional real estate transaction, equitable title is held by the buyer from the time the purchase agreement becomes binding until the closing. When the deed is conveyed, equitable title merges with the legal title and becomes one.

1. **Legal versus equitable title in a land contract**: In a land contract, the vendee maintains the position as the equitable title holder after the closing until the final payment is made months or years later.

    a. **Legal title–vendor's interest**: The vendor is not the true owner of the property during the land contract. He merely holds the deed in trust for the vendee. The vendor does, however, have a right to payment of the full purchase price and to receive assurances that the vendee is honoring his other obligations under the land contract.

    b. **Equitable title–vendee's interest**: In the case of a land contract, equitable title is held by the buyer for the entire term of the agreement. This makes the buyer-vendee the true owner of the property even though legal title will not merge until the last payment is made and the deed is conveyed by the seller-vendor. If the property is used as the buyer-vendee's principal residence during the term of the land contract, he can even file a principal residence (PRE) exemption affidavit to reduce his property taxes. See Chapter 15 for further information on the PRE.

E. **Technical requirements of a land contract**: Each clause in a land contract should be read and understood by the parties before signing the document. The best advisor for specific legal questions is an attorney. This section reviews a few of the more important clauses and requirements.

1. **Statute of frauds and land contracts**: As discussed in Chapter 12, the Statute of Frauds requires that all contracts involving the sale or transfer of an interest in land such as a land contract must be in writing to be enforceable. Accordingly, no oral land contract is enforceable in a court of law. The written memorandum (meaning agreement) must also set forth the names of the parties, the price or consideration paid, a

sufficient property description, and all pertinent terms of the agreement. Finally, it must be signed by all parties.

2. **Credit terms**: Since a land contract is a form of financing, the agreement must contain a definite statement of all terms of credit. This includes items such as an acknowledgement of the entire debt owing, the interest rate and method of calculation (whether simple or compound), the monthly payment, the payment due date, grace period, and any late fees or other penalties.

   a. **Land contract addendum**: When a buyer makes an offer with land contract financing through a real estate broker, a special form is sometimes used called a Land Contract Addendum. These forms should not be confused with the actual land contract itself. A Land Contract Addendum is designed to incorporate additional offer terms not usually found in a standard form purchase agreement. These terms may include the buyer's desired interest rate and payment schedule along with a statement of how the buyer would like to handle taxes and insurance during the land contract. If the offer (with attached addendum) is accepted by the seller, these terms will be incorporated into the actual land contract that is signed at the closing.

3. **Statement of vendee responsibilities**: Even though the seller-vendor holds legal title in trust for the buyer-vendee who owns the property, the vendee still owes certain duties to the vendor to protect the property from losing value. If the vendee defaults and the property is forfeited back to the vendor, the property value cannot be impaired through neglect. Along with proper maintenance, the vendee is also generally required to pay all real estate taxes and maintain adequate hazard insurance on the property during the entire term of the land contract. The hazard policy will name the vendor as an additional insured.

F. **Deed in escrow (in trust)**: When a land contract is created, the buyer-vendee is aware that the deed will not be delivered until several years or decades later. The grantor may die during this time thereby creating a potential legal issue for the vendee involving probate or a quiet title action when he makes his final payment. Recall from the discussion pertaining to the delivery of a deed in Chapter 5 that a deed must be delivered during the lifetime of the grantor to be a valid conveyance of title. To make it easier for the vendee to obtain legal title when the contract matures, the vendee should have the vendor place the deed in a trust or escrow at the time of entering into the land contract.

Assuming the vendor has died prior to maturity, when the vendee makes the final payment to the vendor's estate or heirs, notice is given to the trustee or escrow manager who then delivers the deed to the vendee. The delivery out of the trust relates back to the date when the vendor placed it in the trust as part of the closing. The vendor was, obviously, alive at that time. This should avoid any unexpected probate issues.

G. **Land contract default and collection remedies**: Any seller who is considering an offer with land contract financing should carefully think about what is involved in enforcing the land contract if the vendee defaults. There are two possible remedies and both have advantages and disadvantages. These remedies include land contract forfeiture and foreclosure. Once a remedy is legally started, the seller-vendor cannot change his mind and pursue the other remedy. This is known as an election of remedies.

1. **Land contract foreclosure**: A land contract can be foreclosed in a manner similar to judicial foreclosure of a mortgage. The land contract must contain a remedy clause informing the buyer-vendee that the land contract can be foreclosed, which is coupled with an acceleration clause. The acceleration clause allows the vendor to demand the full unpaid principal balance be paid upon default. The process begins when the seller-vendor's attorney files a formal lawsuit in a circuit court.

   a. **90-day waiting period**: Once the lawsuit is filed, there is a mandatory 90-day waiting period before the property can be sold. This is an equitable redemption period that gives the vendee time to avoid foreclosure by paying the past due amount.

   b. **Notice period**: At the end of the 90-day period there is an additional 4 week period for advertising the sale in the local legal news. This provides legal notice to anyone else who may have an interest in the property that he may wish to appear at the sale and submit a bid to protect his interest.

   c. **Vendor's judgment, auction sale, and redemption**: If the vendee is still in default after the appropriate waiting and notice periods have passed, the court enters a judgment ordering the accelerated balance to be paid. If the vendee cannot pay it, an auction sale is conducted and the property is sold to the high bidder. The vendee has the right to a sale of the property to offset, meaning satisfy, the debt. This sale is commonly referred to as a sheriff's sale.

Upon conclusion of the sale, a deed is issued which is commonly referred to as a sheriff's deed. Before title vests in the high bidder, however, the vendee is given a 6 month statutory redemption period within which to pay the bid price plus expenses to redeem the property from the foreclosure. If the property is redeemed, the sheriff's deed is no longer effective.

    d. **Bid price surplus and deficiency**: At the sheriff's sale, the vendor is expected to at least bid the lesser of the debt or the fair market value of the property. If anyone else enters a higher bid, the bid price is given to the vendor up to the balance owing on the land contract plus certain expenses. Any sale price surplus is returned to the vendee. If there is a deficiency, the vendor can pursue it against the vendee based on the previously issued judgment.

    e. **Advantages and disadvantages of land contract foreclosure**: While an attorney should be consulted to properly ascertain whether foreclosure or forfeiture is best from the vendor's perspective, foreclosure may be warranted if the payments on the land contract are higher than the fair rental value of the property. In a forfeiture action, the vendee may attempt to recover this difference. Since a foreclosure is a lengthy process, time and legal fees may sway vendors to consider forfeiture as an alternative.

2. **Land contract forfeiture**: As a legal principle, forfeiture is the loss or relinquishment of money or property without compensation as a consequence for engaging in some wrongful act. In a land contract, forfeiture is a remedy that a seller-vendor can pursue to get his property back if the vendee defaults. It avoids having to initiate a foreclosure. The vendor declares the land contract null and void which acts to terminate it. The vendee forfeits his equitable title and the right to a return of any payments made to date. These payments, in essence, are "written off" as payments made in lieu of rent.

    a. **District court action**: A forfeiture action is handled in a local district court rather than a county circuit court. The process is guided by Michigan's summary proceedings act. A notice to quit is given by the vendor to the vendee and a writ for possession is entered by the court in favor of the vendor. This is similar to the process used by a landlord to evict a defaulting tenant in a lease.

    b. **Right to redeem**: Before possession is restored in the vendor, the vendee is given a statutory right to cure the default and redeem the property from the forfeiture action. If 50% or more of the land contract price has been paid by the vendor, this redemption period is 6 months in length. If less than 50% of the contract price has been paid, the redemption period is shortened to 90 days (i.e., 3 months).

    c. **No acceleration of debt allowed**: There is no acceleration of debt allowed in a forfeiture action. Therefore, all the vendee has to do to cure his default is to bring the contract current. He does this by paying whatever back payments were due as of the date the forfeiture action was filed. From a vendee's perspective, this is financially less burdensome compared to a foreclosure. This creates a potential challenge for the vendor, however. For example, if the vendee fails to make his monthly payments during the actual redemption period, the vendor may have to file an additional forfeiture action to collect these newly-missed payments.

    d. **Advantages and disadvantages of land contract forfeiture**: The primary advantage of forfeiture over foreclosure is the reduced time and expense involved in the process. One key disadvantage for the vendor is the fact that multiple defaults can lead to multiple forfeiture actions having to be filed.

3. **Writ of restitution**: In the context of real property law, a writ is a court order directing a sheriff or other judicial officer to do that which is commanded in the writ. Restitution is a remedy that restores legal possession of real property to a vendor in the case of a land contract or landlord in the case of a lease. If the land contract is not redeemed in a forfeiture action, the sheriff goes to the property and physically removes the vendee and his possessions. A writ of restitution is also referred to as a judgment for possession.

H. **Land contract versus conventional financing**: There are several advantages and disadvantages of land contract financing versus traditional mortgage financing.

  1. **History**: Land contracts tend to be relied on more during and shortly after economic downturns. This is due to a tightening of conventional financial markets during such periods. For example, when the subprime mortgage crisis of the 2000s started to wind down, underwriting requirements become more stringent. Most lenders imposed a mandatory waiting period of 2 to 5 or more years to obtain a new loan for home buyers who previously suffered a short sale, foreclosure, or bankruptcy. If such a buyer has a sufficient down payment with a good job position and income stream, a seller may be willing to accept the buyer as a credit risk and sell to him on a land contract.

2. **Advantages**: From a buyer-vendee's perspective, a land contract represents an excellent source of financing when (1) conventional mortgage money is unavailable, (2) the vendee does not qualify for conventional financing, or (3) the buyer lacks the full down payment required by a lender.

   The primary advantage to the seller-vendor is the collection of interest over the life of the contract. With an interest rate cap of 11% under Michigan usury laws, this can represent a significant amount of money over the course of a long-term land contract. Further, some sellers only agree to sell on a land contract at a premium sale price. For example, Seller X is willing to sell to Buyer Y on a land contract because Buyer Y's low credit standing disqualifies him for a conventional loan. Seller X increases the sale price by several thousand dollars to offset the risk he takes in financing Buyer Y.

3. **Disadvantages**: The primary land contract disadvantage to a buyer-vendee is the higher potential cost of interest as compared to conventional bank financing. A seller-vendor bears a potentially higher risk of default when selling to a vendee who lacks a sufficient down payment and/or has an unstable credit history. Recall that land contract default and collection can be challenging for a vendor.

4. **Vendor due diligence**: A vendor who is thinking about selling on a land contract should explore a couple of issues to protect himself. Foremost, the vendor should consult with legal counsel before signing a binding purchase agreement involving land contract financing. Legal counsel may recommend that the seller review issues such as: (1) obtaining a credit report from the prospective buyer coupled with a few days to review it; (2) using a land contract form provided by the vendor's attorney; (3) fully understanding what will be involved if the vendee defaults; and (4) setting up payment collection and processing of the monthly payments through a servicing entity such as a local lender. A seller-vendor on a land contract must also be careful if he still owes a balance on an underlying mortgage. The sale to a buyer-vendee will trigger the seller-vendor's due-on-sale clause in his mortgage.

5. **Vendee due diligence**: A vendee who is thinking about purchasing on a land contract should also explore some things to protect himself. The vendee should first consult with his own attorney. The attorney may wish to condition the vendee's offer on the seller's agreement to use his own form. Further, the attorney will likely recommend things such as: (1) having the deed placed in escrow at the closing; (2) recording the land contract (or memorandum of land contract); and (3) if the property will be used as the vendee's principal residence, filing the Principal Residence Exemption Affidavit.

   The vendee's attorney may also recommend that the purchase agreement require the vendor to prepay the county and state transfer tax. Transfer taxes are normally paid when the deed is conveyed. In the case of a land contract, this may not occur for several years or decades. The likelihood of the vendor remembering this financial responsibility and willingly paying it is probably low.

VI. ▶ **Mortgage foreclosure**: Foreclosure is the procedure through which mortgaged property is sold if the borrower-mortgagor defaults in satisfying the debt or in meeting any other contractual obligation. The sale proceeds are used to satisfy the outstanding debt owed to the lender-mortgagee. The lender has a right to force the sale of the property under the terms of the mortgage which give the lender a contractual and consensual lien. After studying the discussion on mortgage foreclosure, it may be helpful to return to the section titled "Liens" in Chapter 6 as a review.

During the subprime mortgage crisis, many lenders opted to pursue remedies that stopped short of an actual foreclosure of the property. They included taking a deed in lieu of foreclosure and agreeing to a short sale. Short sales were commonly used when the mortgage balance was greater than the salable value of the property that secured the debt. A typical short sale involves the voluntary sale of a property by the mortgagor coupled with a contractual settlement, forgiveness, or cancellation of any remaining mortgage deficiency. A deed in lieu involves a voluntary conveyance of the property by the mortgagor to the mortgagee. Both of these processes are discussed in further detail later in this chapter.

   A. **Methods of foreclosure**: Foreclosure is the legal process that a lender uses to terminate the rights of its borrower-mortgagor when a contractual default occurs. There are four basic methods that can be used in the United States for the foreclosure of a mortgage, but only two are routinely used in Michigan. These include judicial foreclosure and foreclosure by advertisement. If the mortgagor stops making payments, the lender must first decide if it is going to declare a default and trigger the appropriate provisions contained in the mortgage and note documents. If it does, the next issue becomes which form of foreclosure to pursue against the mortgagor.

      1. **Strict foreclosure**: A strict foreclosure perfects absolute title in the lender-mortgagee as opposed to merely giving the lender a power of sale to force the sale of the property. When used as a verb, to "perfect"

something means to complete or finish it so it is without any defects. A court determines the amount of the mortgage debt and then orders the mortgagor to pay it within a certain period of time. If the mortgagor defaults in making this payment, title is vested in the mortgagee and the mortgagor's rights and equity of redemption are forever barred. Since the mortgagor has no redemption rights, this form of foreclosure will likely not be allowed in Michigan.

2. **Judicial foreclosure**: Judicial foreclosure is a type of foreclosure action that is supervised by a circuit court judge. The lender files a complaint in the county circuit court where the property is located. This is a type of lawsuit. All lenders in Michigan are statutorily authorized to foreclose their mortgages by judicial action.

   a. **Preliminary notices and money judgment**: Before filing the complaint, the lender will provide the mortgagor with notice of default and intent to accelerate the debt. Once the lender proves to the court that the debt exists in the mortgagor by producing the required documentation, the judge will enter a money judgement in favor of the lender for the accelerated balance on the note. The mortgagor is entitled to have the property sold to offset this debt. The sale takes place at the courthouse where the judgment was entered and is handled by the county clerk.

   b. **Preliminary waiting period and sale**: Before the property is actually ordered sold by the court in a judicial foreclosure, there is a mandatory 6-month waiting period followed by a 6-week publication period. This preliminary waiting period is like an equitable redemption or equity of redemption period. The publication period consists of notices posted in multiple public places within the city or township where the property is located. The mortgagor can stay, meaning stop, the sale from taking place by bringing to the court the accelerated principal balance plus accrued interest and costs. If this does not occur, the actual foreclosure sale will be conducted as an auction with the property going to the highest bidder.

   c. **Determination of the sale price**: Although a lender is not required to bid at the sheriff's sale, it typically protects its interest by entering a bid that is no higher than the debt owing, and as we will see, should not be significantly less than the fair market value of the property. If the lender (or any other third party) enters a bid that is well below fair market value, the court can protect the mortgagor by treating the bid price as if it were equal to the fair market value. This is called the upset price. The high bidder does not actually have to pay the increased amount. Instead, the upset price merely has the effect of limiting the amount of any resulting deficiency judgment. The following example illustrates how this works.

   Example: Assume a mortgagor owes $150,000 on his mortgage and the fair market value of his property is $130,000. At the sheriff's sale, the lender enters a low winning bid of $50,000 and then seeks a $100,000 deficiency judgment. In fairness to the mortgagor, the lender should have bid the fair market value of $130,000 and sought a $20,000 deficiency judgment. By establishing the upset price at $130,000, the court limits the deficiency to the appropriate amount.

   d. **Handling of a surplus**: The lender's interest in the property is limited to the debt balance plus costs. If the sale price exceeds this total amount, the excess funds can be obtained by the mortgagor since it represents the mortgagor's equity in the property. Costs typically include property taxes paid by the lender and property insurance premiums paid to keep the policy in force through the statutory redemption period.

   e. **Handling of a deficiency**: As previously discussed, if the sale price does not completely satisfy the principal balance plus allowable costs, a deficiency exists. Since the lender has already been issued a judgment by the court, the lender can use it to recover the deficiency. The deficiency becomes a personal debt against the mortgagor. There are various legal tools that the lender can use to collect it.

   f. **Disadvantage and advantages**: Judicial foreclosure can be time-consuming, taking up to one year or more from the default until the mortgagor is evicted from the premises if he fails to voluntarily vacate. This can translate into more expense for the lender to execute. Advantages include: (1) the ability for the lender to be awarded reasonable attorney's fees if the mortgage provided for them; (2) having a receiver appointed for the property if warranted; and (3) the ability of the court to more easily resolve priority disputes if there are multiple lenders.

3. **Foreclosure by advertisement (nonjudicial foreclosure)**: Foreclosure by advertisement is another type of foreclosure that a regulated lender can use. It is statutory in nature and allows the lender to bypass the need to first file a lawsuit for a money judgment. Great care must be exercised by the lender since a failure to

Chapter 16: Financing Instruments

fulfill all requirements can give the mortgagor a defense to the foreclosure action. One of the requirements is that the mortgage was properly recorded. If the lender assigned the mortgage to another investor (which is a common practice), the assignment must also have been recorded.

   a. **Power of sale clause**: In order to foreclose by advertisement, the mortgage (including the corresponding note) must meet certain requirements, most notably, that it contain a valid power of sale clause. It must also contain provisions relating to what constitutes a default along with a description of its consequences such as acceleration of the debt and payment of certain allowable costs.

   b. **Specific notice requirements**: A notice that the property will be foreclosed by sale must be published at least one time per week for four consecutive weeks in a newspaper that is published in county where the property is located. State law sets the requirements for the contents of this notice. The "Notices" section of the county legal news is commonly used for this purpose. Upon expiration of the required notice period, a sheriff's sale takes place.

4. **Sheriff's sale**: The lender is able to schedule the sheriff's sale directly which takes place at the circuit courthouse for the county in which the property is situated. It is conducted as an auction-type sale, commonly by a sheriff or deputy sheriff, in the same manner as a judicial foreclosure. The sheriff's sale actually extinguishes the mortgage contract and gives the mortgagor's rights in the property to the purchaser. If a third party is the high bidder, he must deposit cash or a cash equivalent for the property with a court. If the lender is the high or only bidder, no cash payment is required.

   a. **Sheriff's deed**: Once the high bidder is determined, the presiding sheriff immediately issues and delivers a sheriff's deed to the purchaser. To avoid any delay with the start of the mortgagor's redemption period, the deed should be recorded with the county register of deeds no later than 20 days after the sale. Although the sheriff's deed is signed and delivered, it is not an effective conveyance of title until expiration of the statutory redemption period.

   b. **Effect on other liens**: The sheriff's deed will extinguish any junior lien (but, not the note). Junior liens are those created and recorded after the mortgage (i.e., lien) being foreclosed. The sheriff's deed has no effect on a senior lien which remains valid. Any surplus or deficiency is handled in the same manner as previously discussed.

B. ▶ **Redemption**: A defaulting mortgagor has a statutory right to redeem his property after the sheriff's sale. This allows him to save the property and resume an ownership position completely clear of the mortgage and note. If the property is redeemed, the register of deeds makes the appropriate entry in the public records and destroys the sheriff's deed. The property may be redeemed by the mortgagor or the mortgagor's heirs. *See Figure 32.*

   1. **Requirements to redeem**: To redeem, the mortgagor must pay the amount bid at the sale plus the interest assessed from the time of sale (at the rate stated in the mortgage) and other administrative costs. Any amount due a senior lienholder may be added to the redemption amount. Condominium or homeowner association assessments may also be added as well as necessary property taxes or insurance paid by the purchaser at the sale. The sheriff's deed should have a "redemption affidavit" attached to it which includes the calculation of the redemption price and provides contact information for the purchaser or the purchaser's representative.

   2. **Forms of redemption**: There are two forms of redemption recognized by law–equitable redemption and statutory redemption. The difference is based on when each period begins and ends as well as what is required by the mortgagor to fulfill it. To redeem is to buy back or repurchase. Redemption allows the mortgagor to either stop the foreclosure process prior to the actual scheduled sheriff's sale by paying all past due amounts or to purchase the property from the high bidder after the sheriff's sale has been conducted.

      a. **Equitable redemption**: The equitable redemption is, essentially, the period of time from the default to a moment before

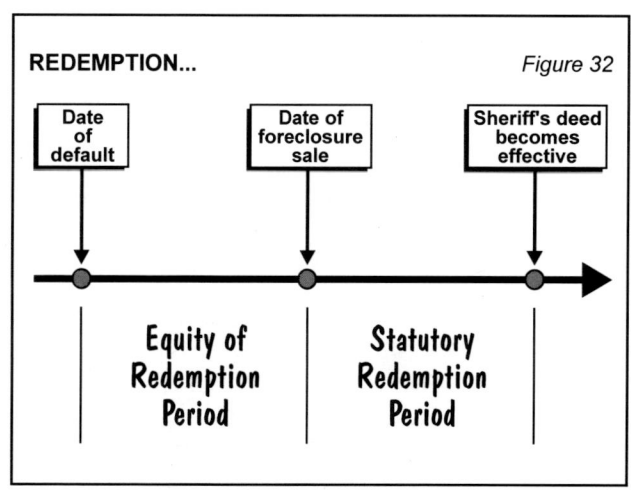

Figure 32

the foreclosure sale is conducted. During this time, the mortgagor can save the property from impending foreclosure. If the lender has not yet accelerated the debt, the mortgagor can bring the mortgage current by paying the back payments plus late fees and other contractual penalties. If it has been accelerated, the mortgagor may have to pay the full balance due under the mortgage unless he can negotiate the payment of back payments only (which is relatively common). This period is also known as the equity of redemption period.

   (1) **Period begins**: The period begins upon default and runs up to the actual sheriff's sale. If the property is redeemed in accordance with either the terms of the mortgage or an agreement with the lender, the sheriff's sale is cancelled.

   (2) **Length of period**: The length of the equity of redemption period varies depending on the lender's internal policy for handling pre-foreclosure collection. Up to 5 months is common.

   b. **Statutory redemption**: Statutory redemption is the legal right a mortgagor has to free the property from the foreclosure sale and void the sheriff's deed by paying the amount bid at the sale plus costs. The period begins with the date of the sheriff's sale and runs for a statutorily-prescribed period of time that varies according to the form of foreclosure used and the type of property that is foreclosed.

   (1) **6 months**: For commercial or industrial property, or multifamily residential property in excess of 4 units.

   (2) **6 months**: For residential property (defined as 4 units or less) where the mortgage balance is more than 2/3 of the original indebtedness. Note: If the mortgage balance at the time of the foreclosure sale is 1/3 or less of the original indebtedness, a 1 year redemption is applied.

   (3) **1 month**: For residential property which is abandoned. Note: Abandonment is presumed providing the lender (1) personally inspected the premises to make sure it appears to be abandoned, (2) both posted a notice on the premises and sent a copy via certified mail to the last known address of the mortgagor stating that the property is considered to be abandoned, and (3) has not, within 15 days of giving notice, received a written return notice from the mortgagor or person claiming under the mortgagor that the premises is not abandoned.

   (4) **1 year**: For property used for agricultural purposes.

   (5) **1 year**: All other instances of foreclosure not listed previously.

C. **Mortgagor's right of possession and limitations resulting from waste**: The mortgagor is allowed to remain in full possession of the property during the entire foreclosure proceedings. This includes the full time allotted for statutory redemption. In most cases, mortgagors take reasonably good care of the property in spite of the fact that they are in the process of losing it to the bank. Some mortgagors, whether out of apathy or anger, either fail to properly maintain the property during this process or wilfully destroy it.

During the mortgage crisis of the 2000s many foreclosed homeowners took their frustrations out on their properties by causing extensive damages during the redemption period. Some of these owners actually stripped their homes of kitchen cabinets, light fixtures, plumbing fixtures, flooring, copper pipe, and mechanical systems. This problem became so widespread that the Michigan legislature enacted a law to protect lenders (which is discussed later in this section).

1. **Appointment of receiver**: Prior to the enactment of the statute just referenced, in extreme cases where a property was deteriorating, the lender's only remedy was to petition the court to appoint a receiver to intervene and protect the property from waste. The receiver became obligated to preserve the property for the benefit of everyone including the mortgagor and the lender. A receiver is a third party who acts as an officer of the court to fulfill his appointed mission. The lender may be ordered by the court to pay the receiver's fees since it is benefitting from the receivership.

2. **Waste**: Legally speaking, waste is any abuse or destructive use of a property by one who is in lawful possession that results in unreasonable and substantial injury to the property. There are two basic types of waste–permissive waste and voluntary waste.

   a. **Permissive waste**: Permissive waste includes deferred maintenance or neglect of a property. To defer means to put off, delay, or postpone something to another time. It usually results from an owner's failure to make necessary repairs in a timely fashion. With some defaulting mortgagors, there is no intent to injure the property. However, due to their difficult financial circumstances, they lack the necessary funds to make repairs or adequately maintain the property.

Chapter 16: Financing Instruments

      b. **Voluntary waste**: Voluntary waste involves active destruction of the property beyond what could be argued resulted from ordinary wear and tear. There is a component of willfulness and intent to destroy. Voluntary waste can result in the appointment of a receiver to manage the property through the balance of the foreclosure process. The redemption period is typically not terminated as a result.

  3. **Damage can result in termination of redemption**: Michigan law was amended in 2013 to allow the purchaser at the foreclosure sale, typically the lender, to extinguish the redemption period and gain full title to the property regardless if redemption time remains. After the sale and periodically throughout the redemption period, the high bidder may also inspect the exterior and interior of the property for damage. If the mortgagor refuses to allow the inspection, or if damage is imminent or has obviously occurred, the high bidder may send the owner a 7 day notice to quit, and commence summary proceedings in district court to seek possession. This process is discussed further in Chapter 13. Here is a list of qualifying damages:

      a. The failure to comply with local ordinances regarding property maintenance.

      b. An exterior condition that presents a significant risk to the security of the property or significant risk of criminal activity occurring on the property.

      c. Stripped plumbing, electrical wiring, siding, or other metal materials.

      d. Missing or destroyed structural aspects or fixtures, including, but not limited to, a furnace, water heater, air-conditioning unit, countertop, cabinetry, flooring, wall, ceiling, roofing, toilet, or any other fixtures.

      e Deterioration below, or being in imminent danger of deteriorating below, community standards for public safety and sanitation that are established by statute or local ordinance.

      f. Causing a serious and continuing health hazard to exist on the premises, or causing extensive and continuing physical injury to the premises.

VII. **Avoidance of and alternatives to mortgage foreclosure**: Foreclosure is not the only remedy available to a homeowner who cannot continue making his mortgage payments in a timely fashion. With loan refinancing or loan modification, foreclosure can be avoided and the homeowner will continue living in his home with a more affordable payment. If refinancing or a loan modification cannot be obtained, the homeowner may attempt a foreclosure alternative such as requesting a deed in lieu of foreclosure or a short sale. While bankruptcy is technically not a foreclosure alternative, it is discussed in this section since many homeowners opted for this form of financial relief in the 2000s.

  A. **Refinance defined**: Refinancing involves the issuance of a new, more affordable, loan for the purpose of replacing an existing loan that cannot be repaid. The new loan generally has a lower interest rate, lower monthly payments, and/or a longer term. When the new loan is obtained, the proceeds are used to pay off the existing loan.

    A satisfaction of mortgage is recorded showing the existing loan as repaid and the lien removed from the title. Even if the refinance loan is obtained from the same lender that is servicing the existing loan, the investor who actually funds the loan will nearly always be different. The abbreviation "refi" loan is sometimes used in the industry to refer to a refinancing loan.

  B. **Loan modification**: As the words "loan modification" suggest, the terms and conditions of an existing loan are modified or changed to make the loan more affordable. It is typically offered to a mortgagor who cannot make his mortgage payments based on the current amortization schedule. Common loan modifications include lowering the interest rate or extending the length of the loan to reduce the amount of each monthly payment.

    Generally, the modified loan will be fully amortized regardless of the terms of the existing loan. For example, an existing interest-only loan will be modified to a fixed rate, fully amortized loan. As a comparison, a modification is a change to an existing loan which remains in force. Refinancing involves the creation of a new loan with the payoff of the existing loan.

    1. **Forbearance**: A loan forbearance is another form of loan modification. To forbear means to refrain from doing something that a person has a legal right to do. In terms of a mortgage loan, a forbearance is a written agreement by the lender that it will temporarily suspend the enforcement of the loan. The lender may agree to a reduction or total suspension of payments for a set period of time (rarely more than 12 months). A lender can also forbear by agreeing to halt a foreclosure proceeding for 90 days, for example, so the parties have time to negotiate a long-term mortgage modification or refinancing.

Since a forbearance is not a forgiveness, the mortgagor is required to pay all past due amounts plus interest at the end of the period. The arrearage may be due in a lump sum or higher mortgage payments for a given number of months. To qualify, the mortgagor must typically have a demonstrated financial hardship and not be more than 3–12 months behind depending on the program.

C. **Deed in lieu of foreclosure**: A deed in lieu of foreclosure is another remedy that a lender can use to remedy a mortgage default. The mortgagor voluntarily conveys the property title to the mortgagee in lieu (meaning instead) of being foreclosed. A separate consideration is required to make the conveyance to the lender binding. For example, in exchange for the title to the property, the lender agrees to release any deficiency if the debt is greater than the market value of the property. It is important for the mortgagor to understand, however, that the consideration does not have to be a release of deficiency. This is why a owner-mortgagor is strongly advised to seek legal counsel before issuing a deed in lieu.

   1. **Preliminary requirement**: The lender may require that the mortgagor first attempt to sell the property for at least 90 days to see if the deed in lieu process can be avoided. Often, the mortgagor is asked to actually list the property for sale with a real estate professional.

   2. **Disadvantages**: There are a couple of problems that can arise with a deed in lieu of foreclosure. First, the mortgagor gives up the right to any potential surplus if the property is worth more than the balance owing plus costs. It is also difficult to negotiate a deed in lieu if there are other junior liens on the property such as a second mortgage, home equity line of credit, unpaid taxes, unpaid association dues, construction liens, IRS liens, etc. Finally, as mentioned above, giving a deed in lieu to a lender does not automatically prevent the lender from suing the mortgagor for a deficiency if the property is worth less than the debt.

D. ▶ **Short sale:** The economy of the 2000s experienced a period of increased foreclosures and bankruptcies stemming from the subprime mortgage crisis. Decreasing home values coupled with multiple mortgage refinancing attempts, increasing reliance on second liens, subprime loans with high loan-to-value ratios, and predatory adjustable rate mortgages resulted in tens of thousands of distressed property transactions. Frequently, these properties were upside-down, meaning that the mortgage balance exceeded the fair market value of the property. These financially-strapped mortgagors could not sell their homes without facing huge deficiencies on the mortgage contract.

The short sale emerged during this time as an increasingly popular alternative to traditional foreclosure remedies. Mortgagors who could no longer afford their payments needed to sell and lenders were looking for ways to avoid taking the properties back into an already backlogged inventory. By the year 2013, as the real estate economy was well into recovery mode, the number of foreclosures and short sales dramatically decreased. Nevertheless, the market is still expected to face some short sales for a while longer. This is why real estate licensees should be familiar with the process and how it is carried out.

   1. **Short sale defined**: A short sale is a type of mortgage remedy that occurs when a property is sold for a fair market value that is insufficient to satisfy the entire outstanding balance due on the mortgage. The lender authorizes the sale, accepts the net sale proceeds (minus normal transaction costs), and releases the mortgagor from all or part of the deficiency. Negotiating a short sale is a complex task that must be fully approved by the lender-mortgagee.

   2. **Hardship is required**: In order for short sale relief to be provided, the mortgagor must be able to demonstrate a legitimate financial hardship. The information used as evidence of this inability to pay the monthly mortgage payment and deficiency is provided in a file commonly referred to as a hardship package. While a legitimate hardship probably exists in most short sale situations, the lender still to needs to verify it on behalf of the lender's investors whose money was loaned to the mortgagor. A lender is not going to forgive its debt for an otherwise financially healthy mortgagor. Examples of acceptable hardships may include things like loss of household income, serious medical issues, divorce, and unexpected job transfers.

      a. **Strategic default**: The fact that the mortgage balance is more than the fair market value does not, by itself, constitute a hardship. During the subprime mortgage crisis when home values were depressed, many homeowners purchased a new property at the lower prices, and then simply "walked away" from their mortgage on the old home. They assumed that the lender would foreclose it and not pursue the deficiency. This became known as a strategic default. As it turned out, this was not a good idea since the homeowner remained liable under the note for the statute of limitations.

      b. **Statute of limitations on debt collection**: The statute of limitations in Michigan for suing based on a breach of contract action is 6 years from the actual default. As a result, a lender (or collection agency to

Chapter 16: Financing Instruments   **261**

whom the debt is sold) can actively pursue collection for many years. If a mortgagor missed a payment on April 1, 2017, and the lender subsequently foreclosed by advertisement at a loss, the lender has until March 31, 2023 to initiate a legal action for the deficiency!

3. **Short sale process:** This subsection provides a brief overview of a short sale transaction in which a real estate licensee is providing assistance. It is important to know that a short sale has many variables, so the timeline of events can vary from one transaction to the next.

    a. **Aspects of a short sale**: The following steps are designed to show the types of things that must be done to conclude a successful short sale. They are not listed in any specific or necessary order.

        (1) **Property value is determined**: A determination of value is necessary if a homeowner is having difficulty paying his mortgage and believes that the market value is less than the total debt owing. The homeowner can either hire an appraiser to make this determination or, if the property is going to be listed for sale, the listing agent will prepare a comparative market analysis (CMA) that can be used to support the estimated value of the property. Some lenders refer to the CMA as a broker's price opinion or BPO. See Chapter 4 for further discussion on CMAs and BPOs.

        (2) **Total debt owing is calculated**: The total or aggregate outstanding debt affecting the property must be determined. This includes all second mortgages and home equity loans along with the primary mortgage. A short sale can be avoided if this total debt, plus costs of the real estate sale, is less than the property's estimated value. In a short sale, however, the market value is less than the total indebtedness.

        (3) **Selling costs are calculated**: A real estate licensee will typically estimate the closing costs and net sale proceeds for his seller-client. These costs are paid out of the gross sale proceeds.

        (4) **Lender is contacted**: The appropriate person or department at the lending institution is contacted to begin the process of determining the lender's willingness to negotiate a settlement of the deficiency. Often, it is the lender's Loss Mitigation Department that handles this.

            (a) **Provide additional information**: The lender will verify that the mortgagor is not going to profit from the sale as a result of the mortgage balance being reduced. Consequently, the lender will request information pertaining to: appraisals, CMAs, or BPOs already obtained; the current state of the neighborhood and local real estate market; the mortgagor's personal financial information and current credit position (i.e., can the outstanding debt be paid with funds from other sources); and copies of signed real estate contracts.

            (b) **Seek authority to negotiate**: A licensee should seek written authority from the mortgagor via the listing agreement or separate addendum before negotiating with the lender on the mortgagor's behalf. Negotiating a short sale goes beyond the normal authority granted in a typical listing agreement. Many brokers who list properties subject to a short sale approval refer the actual negotiation with the lender to an outside professional such as an attorney who specializes in short sale negotiations.

            (c) **Settlement possibilities**: In a best-case scenario for a mortgagor, the lender unconditionally releases him from the full amount of the deficiency. This may be referred to as a forgiveness, release, or cancellation of indebtedness. Some lenders require the mortgagor to make a financial contribution toward the deficiency based on the information provided in the hardship package.

                Example: A financially distressed mortgagor has a $150,000 mortgage balance on his home with a market value of $100,000. While the mortgagor has some cash reserves, it is not enough to pay off the resulting $50,000 deficiency. The lender may agree to a short sale providing the homeowner makes a cash contribution of $5,000 toward the deficiency at the closing. The leaves $45,000 of debt which is forgiven by the lender.

            (d) **Obtain a full discharge**: To conclude the short sale, the lender must discharge or release the mortgage-lien on the property. The short sale buyer will not take title to a property still clouded by the seller's original mortgage. The seller will also want to make sure that his lender fully discharges the note based on the agreement to forgive (meaning settle) the deficiency.

    b. **IRS issue**: The cancellation of debt granted in a short sale is a potentially taxable event. When money owed a lender is forgiven from repayment, the IRS views it as a form of unearned income to the mortgagor. A lender is required to file Form 1099 with the IRS to disclose the amount of the forgiveness. Unless the taxpayer meets the IRS insolvency exclusion, this income is treated as taxable income for the mortgagor in spite of the fact that the mortgagor did not actually receive any money at the closing.

From December 2007 through the end of 2016, federal law temporarily exempted this income from taxation to protect certain owners of principal residences who lost their homes in a short sale. Beginning in 2017, a CPA should be consulted to determine whether any forgiveness of debt discharged pursuant to a short sale in 2017 is taxable. Real estate licensees should not make any recommendations to clients or customers with regard to tax law or its consequences.

4. **Real estate licensee risk management considerations**: A licensee must exercise care if a seller asks what the best form of distressed property relief may be. The licensee should recommend that the seller consult with legal counsel. If a short sale is elected rather than foreclosure or a deed in lieu, the licensee must be equally careful when handling and/or negotiating it. In addition to avoiding the unauthorized practice of law, licensees should observe the following distressed property risk management considerations.

   a. **Do not make promissory statements**: A licensee should not make promissory statements about the likely success of a short sale or any other form of distressed property relief. There are far too many variables and uncertainties to make any predictions. A licensee can promise to work diligently to help the seller. The licensee cannot, however, promise what the lender will be willing to do.

   b. **Do not counsel the homeowner to stop making payments**: Some mortgagors believe that the best way to get a lender to agree to a short sale offer is to stop making their monthly payments. This is not only incorrect, but often causes other unintended problems. Only the homeowner's lender or attorney can offer counsel regarding mortgage payments.

   c. **Do not make improper disclosures of financial information**: Distressed property transactions involve highly sensitive personal and financial information such as social security number, loan account and credit card numbers, dates of birth, bank account numbers, and addresses and telephone numbers. These represent a gold mine to dishonest individuals and organized criminal enterprises that specialize in identity theft. No such information should ever be disclosed to a third party without following broker policy guidelines pertaining to privacy and data security.

   d. **Know the limits under the MARS Rule**: The Mortgage Assistance Relief Services Rule is discussed earlier in this chapter.

   e. **Be vigilant for potential mortgage fraud issues**: A licensee should not counsel a homeowner in a transaction involving an actual or suspected mortgage fraud scheme. A real estate salesperson should immediately refer the matter to his broker. A real estate broker should refer the seller to an attorney. If the broker suspects that he or one of his salespersons may be involved, the matter should be immediately referred to the broker's attorney. Mortgage fraud is discussed in Chapter 17.

   f. **Refer clients to appropriate experts**: Along with the recommendation that a homeowner contact an attorney for legal advice, tax and other financial questions should be referred to a financial expert such as the homeowner's CPA or a tax attorney.

E. **Bankruptcy actions**: Bankruptcy is a legal proceeding that a business entity or person who is unable to pay his outstanding debts can use to discharge or liquidate them. It is designed to afford the debtor what is referred to as a fresh start. While a bankruptcy action is not necessarily specific to real estate, its wide-ranging consequences can impact real property transactions and landlord-tenant relationships. Licensees occasionally have transactions that are affected by the filing of a bankruptcy action.

   1. **Exam preparation note**: Bankruptcy is not listed on the content outline as a topic that could appear on the salesperson's or broker's license examination.

   2. **Guided by federal law**: Bankruptcy actions fall under federal law which is divided into chapters that define the different types of filings. There are several different bankruptcy actions, the most common of which include:

      a. **Chapter 7**: The best known action is a Chapter 7 bankruptcy. Its purpose is to quickly, and in a relatively cost-efficient manner, discharge nearly all of an individual's debt. The Bankruptcy Abuse Prevention and Consumer Protection Act of 2005 places certain income limits or thresholds to qualify. Accordingly, households with higher incomes do not qualify under Chapter 7. Instead, they must seek other means of renegotiating debt with their creditors rather relying on the protection of a federal bankruptcy court. The 2005 Act also includes a counselling requirement that must be met by the debtor prior to filing for bankruptcy.

    b. **Chapter 11**: A Chapter 11 bankruptcy action is filed by corporations or other business entities. It can be a complex, time-consuming, and expensive process for a business. A business-debtor utilizes Chapter 11 to restructure its finances through a reorganization plan that must be pre-approved by the bankruptcy court. The goal of Chapter 11 is to allow a troubled business to reduce debt, thereby increasing profitability to the extent that it can remain in business. The business may also be required to sell some or all of its assets to repay its outstanding debt.

    c. **Chapter 13**: Chapter 13 is another form of bankruptcy primarily utilized by individuals. It is commonly known as reorganization bankruptcy. Debt is repaid through a specific plan that remains in place over a 3-to-5 year period. A Chapter 13 has more options and lacks the same income thresholds found in a Chapter 7 action. The Chapter 13 Plan can be very rigid for the debtor, however, who must live under the strict financial scrutiny of the bankruptcy court and trustee in bankruptcy for the length of the Plan.

3. **Common features of Chapter 7 and 13**: Regardless of whether a debtor files for Chapter 7 or Chapter 13 protection, two important things occur. A "bankruptcy estate" is created and a an "automatic stay" provision is triggered.

    a. **The bankruptcy estate and trustee in bankruptcy**: When a bankruptcy action is filed, a legal estate is created called the bankruptcy estate. It includes nearly everything the filing debtor owns, owes, and is owed. It is similar to a probate estate which is legally created when a person dies without leaving a proper will.

    The assets contained in the bankruptcy estate are administered and controlled by the bankruptcy court through an appointed person called a Bankruptcy Trustee or Trustee in Bankruptcy. Secured creditors (meaning ones that have a lien on the debtor's property) are afforded protection under the bankruptcy estate. Providing the creditor has a valid, existing lien such as a recorded mortgage, the property will not be liquidated to pay off other creditors.

    b. **Automatic stay and its effect on real estate**: In legal terms, to stay means to stop a judicial proceeding by court order. It operates like a suspension of an entire action or some portion of it. Immediately upon filing for bankruptcy, a stay arises automatically that bars all further collections by creditors and remains in effect for the duration of the bankruptcy action. A creditor cannot even place a collection telephone call to the debtor.

    From a real estate perspective, the automatic stay bars any foreclosure action including a sheriff's sale. However, a residential landlord who has been granted a judgement for possession before the filing of bankruptcy may continue with an eviction against a tenant-debtor. A landlord can also proceed with an eviction based on the illegal use of controlled substances on the property or endangerment of the leased premises.

4. **Other real estate issues in bankruptcy**: This section surveys a couple of potential real estate issues that can arise during a bankruptcy. Due to the complexity of such actions, a real estate licensee must never provide advice to a seller or buyer with regard to the impact of a bankruptcy. There are numerous attorneys specializing in bankruptcy who can be consulted.

    a. **Exempt property**: Bankruptcy law provides several personal and real property exemptions for individuals who file. Qualified individuals can protect certain property from being sold or liquidated to pay debts. One important exemption exists for a debtor's equity in his homestead (meaning principal residence). This exemption is of little value if there is no equity in the home, in which case, a lender may petition the bankruptcy court to lift the automatic stay so it can begin foreclosure.

    Rather than attempting to exempt real property, the debtor can actually surrender it to the Trustee. Unlike a short sale or a mortgage modification, surrender of mortgaged property in this circumstance requires no consent by the lender. However, a surrender only discharges the debtor-mortgagor's personal obligation under the note, but not the lien represented by the mortgage contract. The mortgage-lien can be removed by a foreclosure action, but this may not occur until the bankruptcy action is completed or the stay is lifted by the Trustee.

b. **Homestead exemption**: A debtor in bankruptcy can elect to use the exemptions available either under federal law or Michigan law. In Michigan, a single debtor or married debtors can protect the equity in a homestead in an amount not to exceed $30,000. If the debtor is 65 years of age or older or disabled, the amount increases. The federal homestead exemption is $22,975 for a single debtor which can be doubled (only under federal law) to $45,950 for married debtors who file jointly.

c. **Entireties estate exempt under bankruptcy**: Property held by a husband and wife as tenants by the entireties may be exempt from bankruptcy providing only one spouse files for bankruptcy and the husband and wife are not jointly liable for the debts.

d. **Chapter 13 lien stripping**: Lien stripping is a Chapter 13 process through which a second or third mortgage on a primary residence, for example, is converted from a classification of secured debt to unsecured debt. The mortgages obtained by the junior lien holders are literally "stripped" from the property with only the debt (as evidenced by the notes) remaining. Lien stripping is possible when the market value of the residence is less than the first mortgage.

Chapter 16: Financing Instruments

DIAGNOSTIC PRACTICE QUESTIONS – CHAPTER 16

IMPORTANT STUDY TIP!

Step 1: Carefully review the information located in this chapter.

Step 2: Take the following Diagnostic Practice Questions. Review any question you answered incorrectly by researching the topic in this textbook. If you are still uncertain as to why the question is answered as it is, consult your program provider.

NOTE ON CHAPTER PRACTICE QUESTIONS

The following questions are representative of the type encountered on the Michigan real estate licensing examination. While some of these questions may be similar in nature and style, there is no way of predicting the exact wording of a question that will appear on the exam. Spending time memorizing these questions is, therefore, not recommended.

These questions are designed to help you determine how well you comprehend the material in this chapter. They are also intended to help you develop problem solving skills and to become comfortable with question formats.

Do not attempt to answer these questions until you have attended the lecture corresponding to this chapter and spent the appropriate time studying the material.

1. The purchaser of a new home is making application for a mortgage loan and wishes to reduce the principal debt to the maximum extent possible with each monthly payment. What product would most likely accomplish this goal?
   A. Obtain a conventional loan, pay a slightly higher rate of interest, and reduce the mortgage term to 15 years.
   B. Obtain a conventional loan, pay a slightly lower rate of interest, and extend the mortgage term to 30 years.
   C. Obtain a term loan, pay a slightly higher rate of interest, and reduce the mortgage term to 15 years.
   D. Obtain a term loan, pay a slightly lower rate of interest, and extend the mortgage term to 30 years.

2. Which of the following statements about a note is true?
   A. A note always requires a mortgage to be valid.
   B. A note is a negotiable instrument that can be sold to an investor.
   C. The term of a note must be strictly adhered to.
   D. A note creates a lien on the real property subject to the debt.

3. If a loan involves more points in connection with a mortgage loan, this absolutely means that:
   A. the loan is a higher risk loan.
   B. a buydown has been entered into.
   C. the loan is going to be sold to the secondary mortgage market after the closing.
   D. higher closing costs will have to be paid.

4. A couple nearing retirement age is considering selling their property. They own their home free and clear. Since they already have considerable savings, they want to use the sale as another tool for sustaining themselves during retirement. Which of the following forms of sale would best accomplish this goal?
   A. A sale subject to a mortgage.
   B. A mortgage assignment.
   C. A sale and leaseback.
   D. A land contract sale.

5. A mortgagor on a 30 year mortgage with a principal balance of $85,000 has been regular with his payments. The mortgagor suddenly stops making his payments and the bank subsequently forecloses on the mortgage. The property had a market value of $140,000 but only brought $130,000 at the sale. Which of the following statements is true?
   A. The bank does not have to pay anything to the mortgagor because the owner has forfeited his rights.
   B. The bank does not have to pay anything to the mortgagor unless the mortgagor files for bankruptcy.
   C. The bank owes the mortgagor the entire surplus of $45,000.
   D. The bank owes the mortgagor $55,000 due to the fair market value of the property.

6. A seller approaches a licensed broker to list his home

and requests assistance in negotiating a short sale with the seller's lender. Which of the following statements is true?
   A. The broker should have written permission from the seller to contact the seller's lender.
   B. A real estate licensee is prohibited under license law from negotiating a short sale.
   C. A short sale should never be placed in an MLS due to the high likelihood of a lower commission.
   D. A lender may not reject a reasonable bid submitted, in good faith, by a licensed real estate broker.

7. When a borrower fully repays a loan, he should require the lender to issue which of the following:
   A. A partial release clause.
   B. A foreclosure release.
   C. A notice of lis pendens.
   D. A satisfaction of mortgage.

8. A lender of mortgage money is known as which of the following?
   A. The mortgagee.
   B. The vendee.
   C. The mortgagor.
   D. The vendor.

9. A written evidence of a promise to repay borrowed money is best known as:
   A. An abstract.
   B. An acknowledgment.
   C. A covenant.
   D. A note.

10. Which of the following describes a nonrecourse debt?
    A. The borrower has no recourse against the lender in the event the lender wishes to accelerate the debt.
    B. The borrower is entitled to stop payment at any time without risk of recourse by the lender.
    C. The lender may be entitled to sell the property but cannot sue the borrower in the event of a deficiency.
    D. The lender has no recourse in the event of default other than a personal suit against the borrower.

11. When a purchaser takes title to real property subject to an existing mortgage, which of the following persons can be held personally liable for the mortgage debt in the event of default?
    A. The seller.
    B. The purchaser.
    C. The lender.
    D. The taxing authority.

12. The clause in a loan agreement stipulating that if default occurs in an installment payment, the entire principal sum may be demanded is known as:
    A. A defeasance clause.
    B. An estoppel clause.
    C. A reversion clause.
    D. An acceleration clause.

13. Mr. Bennett wishes to purchase a home with the help of a loan from a savings and loan association. The purchase price is $40,000. The S & L is willing to make an 80% loan and will charge the seller three discount points. Mr. Bennett's attorney advises him that there will be an additional $1,000 in closing costs. Which of the following statements is correct?
    A. The down payment required is $9,000.
    B. The total amount of cash needed by Mr. Bennett to close is $8,960.
    C. The total amount of discount points charged to the seller is $960.
    D. Loan to value ratio has no effect on the calculation of points.

14. The maturity date on a loan refers to which of the following:
    A. The date when the borrower's right to obtain future advances expires.
    B. The date upon which the final payment on the loan is due.
    C. The closing date.
    D. The last date for payment of the accelerated debt in the event of foreclosure.

15. The seller under a land contract is known as which of the following:
    A. The vendee.
    B. The mortgagee.
    C. The lessor.
    D. The vendor.

16. All of the following statements apply to a deed of trust EXCEPT:
    A. A deed of trust operates similarly to a mortgage.
    B. In the event of default, a deed of trust may be foreclosed.
    C. A deed of trust involves the escrow of a deed for delivery at some later date.
    D. The deed of trust involves three parties: the trustor, trustee, and beneficiary.

17. Which of the following items are associated with a mortgage in a lien theory state?
    A. A defeasance clause is included.
    B. The mortgage creates an absolute conveyance of title.
    C. The contract gives the lender a lien right in the property of the borrower.
    D. Title automatically passes to the lender upon default.

18. A borrower under a conventional mortgage defaulted

Chapter 16: Financing Instruments   267

on his loan. At the foreclosure, the proceeds from the sale of the property were $2,000 less than the debt owing. How can the lender recover the shortfall?
A. The lender could bring an action for breach of the promise to pay contained in the mortgage contract.
B. The lender could sue for a deficiency judgment providing the lender holds a note signed by the borrower at the time of closing.
C. The lender could file a complaint with the Securities and Exchange Commission for fraud and seek damages.
D. There is no way to recover the shortfall since this is the risk any lender takes when entering into a mortgage loan.

19. Which of the following statements is accurate regarding a land contract?
A. A land contract is just another form of mortgage used when interest rates are high.
B. A land contract may be accelerated if the vendor elects judicial foreclosure.
C. A land contract is a form of seller financing in which a security device is given by the borrower in exchange for the deed.
D. The vendor under a land contract holds an equitable title interest.

20. Which of the following is true about a short sale?
A. A lender must agree to permit a short sale if the loan is federally-related.
B. A short sale is only permitted if the potential deficiency is greater than 10% of current fair market value.
C. A short sale may be permitted based on the severity of the mortgagor's financial hardship.
D. A short sale is the best form of mortgage relief in all cases where the lender approves it.

21. All EXCEPT which of the following represents a form of foreclosure available to a lender of a conventional mortgage loan:
A. Nonjudicial foreclosure.
B. Foreclosure by advertisement.
C. Judicial foreclosure.
D. Strict foreclosure.

*Financial success flows from the decision to stay focused.
Distractions cost more money than most are willing to admit.*

Chapter 17
Financing Options

Understanding loan types and sources of funds.

I. **Foreword**: When a buyer makes an offer to purchase a parcel of real estate and is not paying cash, the offer typically includes a financing contingency clause (see Chapter 12 for details regarding contingency clauses). Understanding that a buyer needs a mortgage loan is one thing. Knowing which product will best meet the buyer's financial needs is an entirely different matter. Buyers generally look to the real estate licensee with whom they are working for guidance on how to obtain the best mortgage loan product possible.

Real estate licensees must stay current with today's loan products and lending practices so they can provide preliminary information on sources of funds, types of loans, and loan options. This holds true even though the real estate licensee will refer the buyer to a loan officer who will recommend a specific loan product to the buyer. Once the appropriate lending source is located and the desired loan product is selected, the loan can be originated and the transaction can be closed.

A. **Economic conditions affect lending practices**: Economic conditions not only affect housing, but also strongly influence lending practices. Positive changes in the marketplace stimulate healthy competition between lenders who, in turn, innovate new products and programs. Negative economic conditions can lead to problems as witnessed when the marketplace was flooded with high-risk subprime mortgages.

1. ▶ **Subprime (non-conforming) loan defined**: A subprime loan is a type of mortgage that a home buyer with a low credit rating can obtain to purchase a home. It is said to be non-conforming because it generally does not meet the guidelines for sale in the secondary mortgage market. Normally, when a buyer has a low credit rating, a lender is less willing to give a conventional loan due to the increased risk of default. This risk is determined by evaluating criteria such as the buyer's credit score.

   Credit rating is important to conventional lenders as a predictor of a borrower's likelihood of repaying the loan without defaulting. A loan issued to a borrower with a FICO credit score lower than 640 typically is considered to be a subprime loan. (This number might vary between 600 and 640 depending on the lender.)

2. **Subprime loans can serve a legitimate purpose**: Subprime loans can serve the legitimate purpose of serving buyers who have a low credit rating, but are otherwise financially healthy. To offset the increased risk, a lender may be willing to give such a buyer a loan with a higher interest rate and/or base the loan on a lower loan-to-value ratio (which requires a larger down payment). Subprime loans, in and of themselves, are not necessarily problematic.

   For example, a lender that uses its own assets and reserves to issue and hold a subprime loan to maturity will likely adjust the loan terms to protect against the increased risk of default. The lender will also limit the number of high-risk, subprime loans that it originates to protect the assets of its depositors and investors. It is important to note that not all loans issued during the 1990s and 2000s were subprime in nature.

B. **Subprime mortgage crisis–overview**: This section contains a basic overview of some key factors that experts widely believe contributed to the mortgage crisis. Time and space do not permit a full exploration of the issue. As stated in the discussion relating to housing bubbles in Chapter 4, no specific position is being advanced in this textbook as to the precise cause or causes of the housing crisis. Instead, interested readers are encouraged to conduct their own research using multiple independent resources and to draw their own conclusions.

1. **Home prices rise**: Nearly every national housing index showed that U.S. home prices experienced strong and steady gains from the mid-1990s to the early 2000s. With so many buyer-borrowers being able to "get into the housing game" by obtaining subprime loans, inventory sharply decreased. Supply and demand

drove prices up to record levels in communities throughout the United States. Many of the subprime borrowers who purchased homes from sellers when prices were at their highest often made bids that exceeded an already high asking price. Many borrowers were also able to obtain mortgages for 100% of the appraised value of the home.

2. **Home prices do not go up forever**: Subprime loans back then were not thought to be as risky as they ultimately turned out to be. This was based on the mistaken belief that housing prices would continue to increase forever. If this were actually true, a default on a subprime loan would not be a problem because the home could be sold at tomorrow's higher price and the mortgage could be satisfied with the proceeds. As the competition for new borrowers increased, subprime loans were aggressively marketed to anyone who wanted to purchase or invest in real estate. This occurred in spite of the fact that many borrowers could not actually afford their loans on a long-term basis.

3. ▶ **Predatory loan products**: A predatory loan is one which is unfair, deceptive, or fraudulent. Some argue that any loan issued by a lender who knows the loan will ultimately be unaffordable is predatory. Some subprime loans were based on what can be characterized as financial gimmicks including low-to-no down payments, no need to verify income, virtually no reliance on credit history or scores, adjustable rate mortgages with quick and multiple rate increases, and excessively high debt-to-income ratios. In some instances, mortgage payments exceeded 50%-80% of the borrower's monthly income. Predatory loans dramatically increase the risk of default, foreclosure, and possibly bankruptcy.

4. **Mortgage-backed securities contribute**: A mortgage-backed security is a type of investment, the value of which is secured by a bundle or pool of separately-originated mortgage loans. Shares in these bundles are then sold to investors. The return on the investment comes from the timely payment of the mortgages in the pool. During the subprime years, mortgages were originated, packaged, sold, and resold on an escalating basis.

   As discussed earlier, when a lender originates a subprime loan to hold for the life of the loan, the lender tends to more carefully examine its risk. When that same lender knows it is going to quickly resell the loan to another investor, suddenly that concern about risk evaporates. This repackaging process triggered the proliferation of even riskier loans. Other problems stemmed from the purchase of credit default insurance by investors and the subsequent resale or swap of these insurance policies to underfunded investors. Government policies over the span of several administrations has also been raised by some experts as a contributing factor.

C. **Resulting legislation**: The subprime mortgage crisis resulted in the passage of several new federal and state laws. These laws included a federal tax relief act to help financially-strapped homeowners who face large short sale deficiencies; new federal and state licensing requirements for mortgage loan originators; and the Dodd-Frank Wall Street Reform and Consumer Protection Act (which is summarized later in this chapter).

II. ▶ **Conventional mortgage loans**: A conventional mortgage is a loan given to a buyer-borrower by a lender who, in exchange, is given a lien on the premises as collateral. Conventional mortgages are not government-insured by the Federal Housing Administration (FHA) or government-guaranteed by the Department of Veteran's Affairs (VA). This means that a conventional lender assumes the full risk of loss if the borrower defaults. To calculate the probability of default resulting from nonpayment, the lender obtains a credit report on the borrower or borrowers. The lender also orders an appraisal of the property to ascertain its market value. This is necessary because the sale price agreed to by the buyer and the seller in the purchase agreement does not always reflect the property's true market value.

   A. ▶ **Includes Fannie and Freddie (conforming) loans**: Conventional loans also include loans that are originated by a local lender and then sold in the secondary market to Fannie Mae (FNMA) or Freddie Mac (FHLMC). While Fannie and Freddie do not make loans directly, they do support the nation's housing finance system by purchasing what is referred to as conforming loans. These are loans that conform, meaning meet, Fannie and Freddie underwriting guidelines. Fannie and Freddie are explored in more detail later in this chapter.

   B. **Purchase money mortgage**: The technical and legally-correct term for a mortgage is "purchase money mortgage." However, if you ask a real estate licensee what a purchase money mortgage is, you might get a different answer. Depending on the transaction, they both could be correct.

      1. **Technical meaning**: In technical terms, a purchase money mortgage is any mortgage loan where the borrowed funds are used to purchase a parcel of real property; hence, the words "purchase money" in the

Chapter 17: Financing Options

name. In exchange, the property is pledged to secure the amount of the loan. All standard mortgage loans originated by institutional lenders are legally known as purchase money mortgages.

2. ▶ **Private financing by non-institutional lenders**: The term purchase money mortgage also describes a loan given by a private seller who acts as the lender. At the closing, the seller receives a down payment from the buyer, accepts a note or promise to pay the balance from the buyer, and conveys title to the property to the buyer-borrower. In exchange for the deed, the buyer gives the seller a lien on the property (which is the purchase money mortgage).

While this may appear identical to a land contract, it is not. A land contract is similar to a purchase money mortgage in that the seller receives a down payment and accepts a note or promise to pay the balance. It differs because the seller in a land contract retains title for the term of the contract instead of accepting a mortgage (lien). Land contracts are discussed at length later in this chapter.

C. ▶ **Loan-to-value ratio (LTV)**: The loan-to-value ratio is the numerical relationship between the actual amount borrowed and the appraised value of the property. To calculate it, take the loan amount and divide it by the lesser of the purchase price or appraised value of the property. Conventional lenders set caps or maximum amounts of a loan they are willing to issue.

The lender wants to make sure that the loan amount is lower than the market value of the property. If the borrower defaults and the lender has to foreclose to collect the balance, this gap (which is actually the down payment) reduces the possibility that a deficiency will remain following the sheriff's sale. Collection of a deficiency can be expensive, time-consuming, and uncertain for a lender.

1. **Typical conventional loan-to-value ratios**: The historic loan-to-value ratio on a conventional loan has been 80%. Since 2015, Fannie Mae and Freddie Mac conforming loans can be obtained for up to a 97% loan-to-value ratio. Once the loan-to-value ratio is established, the borrower knows how much of a down payment will be required. Using an 80% loan-to-value ratio, the borrower is responsible for a 20% down payment. The percent of down payment and the percent of the loan (represented by the loan-to-value ratio) should equal 100% of the purchase price.

    a. ▶ **Example**: Buyer X makes a full price offer to purchase a seller's home for $150,000 (which equals the appraised value of the property). Buyer X applies for a conventional loan and is approved for $135,000. The loan-to-value ratio is:
    $135,000 (loan amount) ÷ $150,000 (purchase price) = .9 × 100 = 90% loan-to-value ratio.
    Down payment: $150,000 (purchase price) − $135,000 (loan amount) = $15,000 (down payment).

    b. **The expression is a misnomer**: Even though the term loan-to-value ratio uses the word "ratio," this is actually a misnomer since the resulting number is a percentage of value rather than a true ratio.

2. ▶ **Down payment–initial equity**: A down payment is a cash contribution that a borrower makes at the closing of a loan transaction. The down payment is added to the dollar amount of the loan the buyer receives from the lender. These funds equal the purchase price and are given to the seller. The down payment is the personal investment made by the buyer and represents his initial equity in the property.

    a. **Appraised value versus sale price**: A lender bases its loan on the appraised value of the property rather than the actual sale price. This is why an independent appraisal is ordered for nearly every loan. If a seller is asking for a higher price than an appraisal will support, the buyer must make up the difference with an extra down payment. If the buyer does not have the additional down payment, the seller will have to lower the purchase price. While this may be frustrating for the parties to the transaction, a lender is not willing to risk a deficiency at a sheriff's sale due to an inflated sale price.

    b. **Equity cushion**: A down payment is an important risk management tool for a lender on a mortgage loan. Even the most secure borrower at the time of loan origination can unexpectedly fall on hard financial times. The down payment reduces the possibility of a foreclosure deficiency by creating a cushion of equity between the appraised value of the property and the loan balance. If a 10% down payment was made at the closing, the property would have to fall more than 10% in value which is unlikely. This also addresses why higher-risk borrowers are required to pay a higher down payment.

D. ▶ **Private mortgage insurance (PMI)**: Private mortgage insurance, or PMI for short, is an actual policy of insurance. It protects lenders who issue high loan-to-value ratio loans to buyers who cannot make a 20% down payment. If the borrower can put at least 20% down, the lender generally does not require the purchase of private mortgage insurance.

A PMI policy allows a lender to increase the loan-to-value ratio which decreases the down payment required by the buyer. What makes PMI attractive is the fact that the lender does not assume any risk for the extra loan amount it gives. One of the largest and best known PMI companies is MGIC, which is sometimes referred to in the industry as "Magic Mortgage." MGIC was formed in the 1950s as the Mortgage Guarantee Insurance Corporation.

1. **Conventional loan insurance program**: PMI can be a confusing concept for consumers since a mortgage loan with private mortgage insurance is sometimes referred to as a PMI loan. It is important to note, however, that a private mortgage insurance company is not a lender, nor does it originate loans itself. All lending is handled through a financial institution of the borrower's choice. The private mortgage insurance company merely agrees to insure the extra amount of the loan made to a buyer whose down payment was less than 20%.

2. **How the lender is protected–overview:** Private mortgage insurance is a somewhat complex form of insurance. As a result, this section merely provides an overview. Since coverage and rates change frequently, an expert loan specialist should be consulted in advance of obtaining any loan where the down payment will be less than 20%.

   a. **Policies vary**: A borrower must consider the monthly insurance cost when obtaining a PMI-insured loan. Further, private mortgage insurance coverage and policies can vary from one PMI company to the next. The borrower's credit history and score will impact the maximum loan-to-value ratio of the loan (which may be as high as 97%). For example, one PMI company may require a minimum credit score of 620 in order to qualify for a 97% loan-to-value ratio loan.

   b. **Coverage**: The coverage for the lender on a PMI loan is actually greater than the mere difference between 80% and the higher loan-to-value ratio with PMI. When a PMI policy is purchased, the coverage being assumed by the PMI company is established. If the coverage threshold is 25%, for example, the lender is protected for loses up to 25% of the original loan amount. In this instance, the value of the property at the sheriff's sale could drop to 75% of its original value and the PMI company will reimburse the lender for the entire deficiency.

   c. **Default**: If the borrower defaults while private mortgage insurance is in effect, the PMI company allows the lender to foreclose and then pays any loss resulting from a deficiency to the lender up to the amount of the coverage.

   Example: Borrower Smith wishes to purchase a new $100,000 principal residence. First Lender is willing to give Borrower Smith a 90% loan-to-value ratio loan with private mortgage insurance. First Lender's coverage threshold on the PMI policy is 25%. Borrower Smith defaults when the loan balance is $88,000 and the property is sold at a sheriff's sale for $79,000. The PMI company will reimburse the First Lender $9,000 for the loss. This represents the difference between the loan balance (i.e., $88,000) and the property's value which was established at the sheriff's sale (i.e., $79,000). The $9,000 payment is within the 25% threshold, so it is covered.

3. **Charge for service**: Since PMI is an insurance policy, a premium is charged the borrower at the closing. The actual amount of the monthly premium varies depending on the risk involved with the loan. For example, a borrower with an excellent credit score and 5% down payment may be required to pay approximately ½% of the loan which is divided by 12 and assessed each month until the PMI coverage is terminated. Depending on the loan type, there may be an additional upfront cost for mortgage insurance which is due at the closing.

4. **Termination of coverage**: Pursuant to the Homeowner's Protection Act of 1998, once the actual loan-to-value ratio drops below a certain level, the PMI coverage must be terminated and the annual premium no longer assessed. PMI coverage is canceled via one of two methods–borrower cancellation and automatic cancellation. The insurance is also cancelled any time the property is sold and the loan is fully repaid. On cancellation, the monthly mortgage payment decreases by the amount of the insurance cost which is typically a few dollars.

   a. **Borrower requested cancellation**: When the principal balance reaches 80% of the original value, the borrower may submit a written cancellation request to the lender, or whoever is servicing the loan, to cancel the PMI. The borrower must have a good payment history, the property value must not have dropped, and no subordinate liens with an outstanding balance can exist such as a home equity loan.

Chapter 17: Financing Options   273

(1) **Appreciated value is not mandated**: When a lender receives a cancellation request years after the closing, the property value may have appreciated. The lender is not required to use the present-day appreciated value when calculating the 80% loan-to-value ratio, but may do so. The borrower should check with the lender to determine if it will accept the appreciated value, and if so, whether an independent appraisal will be required to verify value.

b. **Automatic and final termination**: Automatic termination arises, and the lender must terminate coverage, when the borrower's loan balance reaches 78% of the original value of the home. If the borrower is behind on payments, PMI remains until shortly after the payments are brought current. Final termination arises at the midpoint of the loan's amortization schedule regardless of whether the 78% threshold has been reached; e.g., year 15 of a 30-year mortgage. Final termination has limited application.

E. **Loan risk grading and credit scoring**: There are many risks that a lender must weigh when considering whether or not to approve a prospective borrower for a mortgage loan. Property value fluctuation represents one of these risks. For example, a property could face a steep drop in value due to severe economic conditions. The property could also lose value due to damage resulting from a natural peril such as a lightning strike. The lender manages this second risk by requiring the mortgagor to purchase and maintain a hazard insurance policy until the loan is fully repaid.

Another area of risk emanates from the borrower's ability or willingness to make timely mortgage payments throughout the entire loan term. The lender ascertains this risk level by examining the loan applicant's credit as part of the approval process. A credit report and score must be provided to the lender as part of the approval and underwriting process.

1. **Credit report**: A credit report is a document that contains detailed information about an individual's credit history. It is obtained by the lender with the loan applicant's permission to determine the applicant's creditworthiness. The three major credit reporting agencies include Equifax, Experian, and TransUnion. A tri-merge report contains a summary of information from all three agencies, including all three scores and the composite tri-merge score.

   There are four sections in most credit reports. They include:
   – Identifying information (about the applicant);
   – Credit history of all accounts (which represents the actual historical substance of the report);
   – Public records information (such as bankruptcies, judgments, or tax liens); and
   – Inquiries (this is a list of all creditors and other parties who have requested a copy of the applicant's credit report).

2. **Credit score**: A credit score is a statistically derived number used to summarize the credit history and creditworthiness of a consumer. The score itself reflects the consumer's financial activities and credit behaviors during the preceding 24-month period. However, any negative information can remain in the actual report for up to 7 years. This includes late payments, foreclosures, and collections. A Chapter 7 Bankruptcy can remain for 10 years, and a government-backed student loan can remain indefinitely. Further information on qualifying for a loan is discussed later in the chapter.

   a. **FICO®**: The Fair Isaac Corporation, or FICO® for short, is the most widely-used and recognized credit reporting service. The score it provides for consumers is referred to as a FICO® Score. FICO® uses a special, proprietary algorithm (which is a set of mathematical steps) to calculate its score. Scores range from a low of 300 to a high of 850.

   b. **Different credit rating scores**: The various credit bureaus have different names for their credit scoring programs. FICO® Score, Pinnacle, and Empirica Score are all similar, but may use slightly different formulas known as algorithms for calculating credit scores. Some of these names merely refer to a newer version of the FICO® scoring system. VantageScore® is yet another competing scoring model.

3. **Loan grading**: Loan grading, also known as loan risk grading and loan scoring, is a system commonly used by lenders to assign a letter grade to loans on the basis of various risk factors. Phrases such as "A Paper," "B Paper," "C Paper" and "D Paper" are used to grade loans and their interest rates. "A Paper" loans qualify for the best terms. "D Paper" loans are higher risk, cost more for the borrower, and may be based exclusively on the borrower having substantial equity in the home.

   a. **Alt-A loan** : An Alt-A loan, short for alternative A-paper loan, is one given to a borrower with a good credit history, but due to factors such as a slightly lower credit score or less available loan documentation, does not fall within standard underwriting for A-paper or prime status. An Alt-A is not considered to be subprime, however.

F. **Mortgage options based on interest variations and repayment methods**: There are several mortgage variations, or aspects of a mortgage, that exist based on how the loan balance is repaid and how interest is charged. This section explores the term loan, amortized loan, fixed rate loan, adjustable rate loan, and a loan buy-down.

1. ▸ **Term (straight) loan**: A term loan is a type of short-term loan with a maturity date that generally does not exceed 10 years. Some lenders only required the borrower to make periodic interest payments with the entire principal balance due in one lump sum at the end of the loan term. The terms of a term loan can vary. Due to the short-term nature and interest-only aspect of a term loan, it is not used to finance real property acquisitions. Some lenders will issue term loans to businesses for the purpose of purchasing equipment or making capital improvements. It may also be referred to as a straight loan.

2. ▸ **Amortized loan**: In the context of a mortgage loan, amortization is the repayment of a financial obligation over a period of time in a series of periodic installments. The vast majority of mortgage loans today are amortized. Even though sophisticated financial software is used by lenders to assist in the preparation of the loan amortization schedule, real estate licensees should still understand the concept of amortization. Loans can be fully amortized or partially amortized. *See Figure 33.*

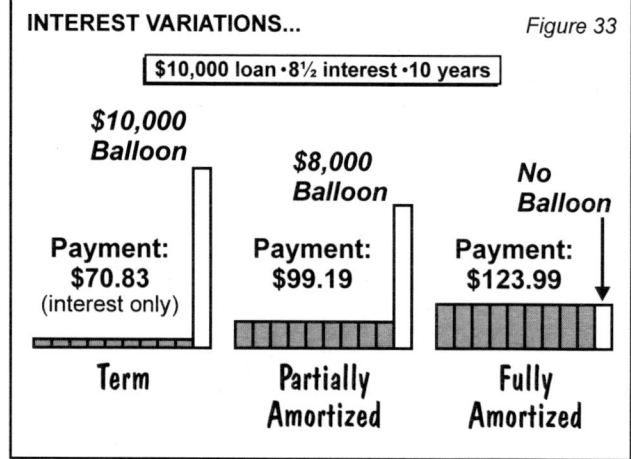

   a. ▸ **Fully amortized loan**: In a fully amortized loan, the monthly principal and interest payments remain the same throughout the life of the loan. The features of a fully amortized loan include:

   (1) A fixed monthly payment is calculated which includes 1/12th of the annual principal and interest costs. Payments are based on a schedule that indicates the monthly payment date, days in the month, payment number, interest rate, dollar amount of interest, dollar amount of principal, and the balance after application of the principal payment for the month.

   (2) The interest due is typically subtracted from the payment and the remaining portion of the payment is applied to reduction of the principal balance.

   (3) The amortization schedule is calculated so the amount of each principal and interest payment does not change during the loan and the full amount of the loan is reduced to zero dollars at the end of the loan term.

   b. ▸ **Partially amortized loan–balloon payment**: With a partially amortized loan, only a portion of the principal is amortized when the loan is originated. Consequently, the principal balance is not fully reduced to zero at maturity as it is with a fully amortized mortgage. Using the numbers in *Figure 33*, a $10,000 loan is given by a lender, but only $2,000 of it is actually amortized. The remaining principal is called a balloon payment which is payable at maturity. Interest payments are based on the full amount of the debt or $10,000. The goal of a partially amortized loan is to decrease the actual monthly payment to a more affordable level.

   (1) **Options at maturity**: If the mortgagor on a partially amortized loan cannot or does not wish to repay the balloon payment at maturity, he generally has a couple of options. First, the originating lender may be willing to refinance the balloon which requires the negotiation of a new loan (for $8,000 using the example). This may be a viable option since the mortgagor is now in a better equity position. If this is not possible, the mortgagor may seek a loan from a second lender to refinance the $8,000 and pay off the first lender.

   (2) **Balloon payment and potential risk**: Mortgages with balloon payments represent a risk since a large sum of money has to be paid at one time. Many defaults and foreclosures occurred during the subprime mortgage crisis due to short-term mortgage loans with relatively low monthly payments and high balloon payments that could not be paid off or refinanced. As a result of the Dodd-Frank

Wall Street Reform and Consumer Protection Act, a Qualified Mortgage can no longer include a balloon payment. In other words, the residential mortgage must be fully amortized. Dodd-Frank and allowable exemptions are explored later in the chapter.

   c. **Negative amortization**: Negative amortization occurs when the monthly payments on a loan are insufficient to even cover the monthly amount of interest due. The unpaid interest is added back to the principal balance which actually increases over time rather than getting paid down. Negative amortization can occur if the interest rate in an adjustable rate mortgage is increased without a corresponding increase in the monthly payment amount. Under Dodd-Frank, negative amortization is prohibited in a "Qualified Mortgage."

3. **Factors that can affect the monthly payment amount**: Several factors can cause a monthly payment to change in a fully or partially amortized loan. For example, if the loan has an adjustable interest rate (as discussed later in this chapter), the payment can change as the interest rate is changed. Also, if the mortgage budgets property tax payments and property insurance premiums into the payment, changes in assessed value or insurance costs can affect the payment.

4. ▶ **Budget mortgage–PITI (property tax and insurance escrows)**: As discussed in Chapters 9 and 15, lenders typically require a homeowner-mortgagor to prepay property taxes, property insurance premiums, and possibly association fees in the case of a financed condominium. The prepayment is deposited into an escrow account which is held by the lender or servicer. Each month, 1/12 of the following year's expenses related to these items is prepaid. This type of amortized mortgage is sometimes referred to as a budget mortgage. The combined monthly Principal, Interest, Tax, and Insurance escrow payment is referred to as PITI. If association fees are included in the payment, the acronym may be listed as PITIA.

   a. **Advantages for the mortgagor**: Property tax bills are usually measured in thousands of dollars. A budget mortgage payment allows the mortgagor to spread this obligation over equal monthly installments. As a result, no financial "surprise" arrives in the mail with a large summer property tax bill (which is usually the higher of the two tax bills).

   b. **Advantages for the lender**: A budget mortgage also provides a benefit to the lender, especially if it has to foreclose. As discussed in Chapter 6, a property tax lien will typically have priority over a recorded mortgage. With a budget mortgage, the lender holds approximately a one-year reserve with which to pay taxes and insurance. Since the foreclosure process can take up to a year or longer, the lender can proceed with foreclosure while having a reserve with which to pay some of the property taxes and insurance bills as they come due.

5. **Fixed rate mortgage**: A fixed rate mortgage is one in which the interest rate does not vary during the life of the loan. The lender establishes the rate it wants based on expectations for the money market during the term of the loan. As a general rule, a lender can charge whatever interest rate it wants as long as it remains within state legal caps known as usury laws. Usury is discussed in Chapter 21.

   Federal monetary policies and competition between lenders are two key factors that affect interest rates. Other factors include the credit standing of the borrower, type of loan, amount of down payment, and immediate and long-term economic outlook. Rates are also influenced by the salability of a loan if the lender knows it will be sold in the secondary mortgage market. In other words, the loan has to be attractive to possible investors.

6. ▶ **Adjustable rate mortgage (ARM)**: An adjustable rate mortgage, or ARM for short, is a loan in which the interest rate can be changed or adjusted by the lender during the loan term. Regardless of the loan type, when a lender extends a 30-year mortgage to a home buyer, it has to shield itself from the possibility of a future economic downturn. The lender of an adjustable rate mortgage is willing to originate the loan at a lower rate based on current economic conditions because it knows it can increase the rate in the future.

   Interest rates on an adjustable rate mortgage can go down as well as up. However, a decrease in the interest rates does not always mean that the monthly payments will be reduced. The loan clause that gives the lender the contractual right to increase the interest rate is sometimes referred to as an escalation clause. The borrower should understand what this clause states since it determines what can happen to the interest rate during the life of the loan.

   a. **Index and margin**: Adjustable rate mortgages are generally tied to a specific index that is described in the loan documents. How the various indexes actually work is complex. Therefore, this discussion merely mentions a few as examples. One of the most common indexes is the London Interbank Offered

Rate, or LIBOR for short. The following indexes are rarely used today, but include the Constant Maturity Treasury (CMT), the Cost of Funds Index (COFI), the 1-year T-Bill, and the Prime Rate.

The base interest rate on an adjustable rate mortgage is known as the margin. It does not change during the life of the loan. The index is used to calculate the additional amount of interest which can vary. For example, if the current interest rate on an ARM is 3.5%, the margin might be 2.5%, and the index 1%. Together, these numbers equal the 3.5% rate. If the index goes up by .25%, the new rate will be 3.75% (2.5% margin + 1.25% index).

    b. **Interest rate caps**: An ARM will also include interest rate limitations called caps which can vary based on the lender or the loan product. Caps represent an important protection for the borrower since they limit how high the rate can be adjusted. All adjustable rate mortgages represent some risk for a borrower since the payment can increase to a higher level than may be affordable at the time. While a low rate at origination may look attractive, it makes sense to consider the probability that rates and payments will increase. The two most common caps are the periodic cap and the lifetime cap.

        (1) **Periodic cap**: A periodic cap limits how high the <u>interest rate</u> can be adjusted from one adjustment period to the next. A 2% annual cap is common.

        (2) **Lifetime cap**: A lifetime cap limits how much the <u>interest rate</u> can increase during the life or term of the loan. A 5% cap is typical (which means the interest rate can increase an additional 5% over the initial rate).

        (3) **Payment cap**: A payment cap limits the actual <u>dollar amount</u> the borrower's loan payment can increase when an interest rate adjustment is made; e.g., 7.5% of what it was before the adjustment. Payment caps are not common since an interest rate adjustment will cause the monthly payment to increase, but if the payment amount is capped too low, a negative amortization can result.

    c. **Hybrid ARM**: Most ARMs include an introductory period during which the interest rate cannot adjust. For example, a 5/1 ARM indicates that the interest rate will be fixed for the first five years and can be adjusted one time per year thereafter (subject to other caps). It is called a hybrid ARM because the loan is at a fixed rate for the first five years and becomes adjustable thereafter. The Dodd-Frank Act now mandates that the interest rate on a Qualified Mortgage cannot change for the first five years of an adjustable rate mortgage. Other hybrids may have 3/1, 7/1, or 10/1 features.

7. **Buydown**: A buydown, also known as buying down the rate, is a financing tool with which the borrower makes a cash payment at the time of closing in exchange for a reduction in the interest rate. The name is derived from the fact that the borrower "buys" the interest rate "down" to a lower level. The rate may be lowered for only the initial years of the loan or it can be lowered for the entire term. Buydown fees are typically paid as points, meaning a percentage of the amount borrowed.

The lower interest rate means lower monthly payments. For example, purchasing one (1) point on a residential mortgage may cost $2,000 at the closing and lower the monthly payment by $30. The true financial benefit is measured over the life of a 30-year loan because the mortgagor realizes a net savings of $8,800 (360 months × $30 = $10,800 − $2,000 points = $8,800). Buydowns are not commonly used.

G. **Mortgage and other loan options based on prepayment variations**: A loan, including a mortgage loan, may be repaid prior to the scheduled maturity date. Another type of loan may assesses a monetary penalty if the borrower attempts to pays it off sooner.

    1. **Open loan**: An open loan allows the borrower to repay the loan more quickly than the amortization schedule requires. The borrower obviously is not allowed to miss payments as that would constitute a breach of contract and default. Another way to view an open loan is that it contains a prepayment privilege. Do not confuse an open loan with an open-end loan which is discussed later in the chapter.

    2. **Closed loan**: A closed loan can only be repaid in strict compliance with the amortization schedule. Technically, a lender cannot prevent a borrower from adding more principal to a payment or from paying off the entire principal balance prior to maturity. However, in a closed loan, the borrower is assessed a prepayment penalty if he does.

        a. ▶ **Prepayment penalty**: As stated, a prepayment penalty is a fine that a lender charges a borrower for making principal payments ahead of schedule. From the lender's perspective, it helps recover some of the unearned interest lost from the early principal payment.

Chapter 17: Financing Options

(1) **More common in commercial loans**: A commercial loan is one obtained by a business to fund capital expenditures. Smaller businesses especially need ready access to cash to meet their acquisition needs.

(2) **Limits under Michigan law**: Under Michigan law, a real estate mortgage loan or land contract may not: (1) include a prepayment penalty that exceeds 1% of the amount of the prepayment made within the first three years; (2) charge any prepayment penalty after year three of the loan; or (3) prohibit a prepayment altogether. This Michigan law applies to nearly all mortgage loans whether they are issued by state- or federally-chartered lending institutions.

b. **Closed-end loan**: A closed-end loan is one in which an initial sum of money is borrowed, and as the principal is repaid (and equity is established), no additional credit is considered available to re-borrow under the terms of the loan. Contrast a closed-end loan with an open-end loan discussed later in this chapter.

H. **Mortgages and other loan options based on flexible payment plans**: A number of different mortgage options are based on creating flexible payment plans for borrowers. Not all types are suitable for every buyer. Generally, the better the credit history and score the borrower has, the more options will be made available. These options include the Graduated Payment Mortgage, Growing Equity Mortgage, Renegotiable Rate Mortgage, and Reverse Mortgage.

1. **Graduated payment mortgage (GPM)**: A graduated payment mortgage, or GPM, is a fixed-rate mortgage that calls for reduced monthly payments during the initial years. This is accomplished by deferring (meaning postponing or putting off) some of the interest early in the loan and then adding it back to the principal for payment during later years. Over time, the monthly payment increases and exceeds what would have been due under a traditional fully amortized loan with level (meaning equal) payments. The mortgagor might experience annual increases in the amount of payment in the 7%-10% range.

    a. **Use**: While this loan type is relatively uncommon today, it was originally designed for a younger borrower with excellent income-earning potential. The loan allowed the borrower to purchase a home sooner since the mortgage payments started at a lower level. The loan is based on the principle that a borrower will be in a better position to handle the increasing payments as his income goes up over time. The Federal Housing Administration (FHA) has a GPM loan.

    b. **Risks**: There are certain risks to the parties to a GPM. Since the early payments often do not cover the interest cost, a negative amortization occurs. As a result, it likely does not meet the requirements for a Qualified Mortgage (discussed later in this chapter). Further, if the mortgagor's income does not rise as anticipated, the increasing payments can be a financial burden.

2. **Growing equity mortgage (GEM)**: A growing equity mortgage, or GEM, is a fixed-rate, long-term mortgage where the loan payments start out at a lower level and periodically increase according to a predetermined schedule. There is no negative amortization potential with a growing equity mortgage as there is with a graduated payment mortgage. With a GEM, the increase in payment is applied directly to the principal balance. A GEM operates like a series of scheduled prepayments without penalty. The Federal Housing Administration (FHA) has GEM loans.

    a. **Principal is reduced more quickly**: Since extra principal is paid with each scheduled increase, the loan is repaid more quickly than a fully amortized mortgage. This shortens the life of the loan which results in a significant savings in interest costs.

    b. **Expectation that borrower's income will increase**: As with any mortgage that includes interest or payment increases over time, the lender is making an assumption that the borrower's income will increase as time passes. If income does not increase, the borrower's inability to make the increased mortgage payment could trigger default and foreclosure by the lender.

3. **Renegotiable rate (rollover) mortgage (RRM)**: A renegotiable rate mortgage, or RRM, is a type of business loan in which the interest rate is periodically renegotiated, meaning refinanced. With each renegotiation, the balance (which is a type of balloon) rolls over to the next term. It operates as a series of short-term loans that are all secured by one long-term mortgage. The mortgage is typically 20–30 years in length with a refinancing opportunity for the lender every 3–5 years.

    To protect the borrower, the loan includes caps that limit how much the loan can change with each refinancing period. Caps relate to both interest rate and payment increases. There will also be a cap on the total allowable change over the life of the loan. It is similar in this manner to the adjustable rate mortgage discussed earlier in the chapter.

4. ▶ **Reverse mortgage**: A reverse mortgage is a loan tool that allows a homeowner to borrow money against the equity in his home and receive it in monthly installments or in a lump sum. In order to qualify, the borrower must be at least 62 years of age and own the home. There must also be sufficient equity in the home. The intent is to never repay the loan during the borrower's lifetime, instead satisfying the debt out of the borrower's estate upon death. If the borrower sells the property, the debt is satisfied out of the sale proceeds.

Advantages to a reverse mortgage include no monthly mortgage payment, only receipt of the monthly payment (i.e., annuity); no transfer of ownership at the time of origination; no requirement to repay the loan; and no tax liability on the funds obtained. The FHA reverse mortgage is known as a Home Equity Conversion Mortgage or HECM for short. Disadvantages include: potential higher loan costs; lower assets remaining for heirs; and it does not make financial sense if the borrower plans on moving in the near future.

I. **Mortgage and other loan options based on different property types**: Mortgage options can be based on the type of property that will secure the loan. Examples include the Blanket Loan, Construction Loan, Package Mortgage, and Chattel Mortgage. These loan products are typically portfolio in nature.

1. **Portfolio loan defined**: The term portfolio loan is any loan originated using a lender's in-house assets, with the intention that the lender will hold the loan in its portfolio rather than selling it to a private or secondary market investor. Since lending rules set by the secondary market do not apply to a portfolio loan, the lender has more flexibility in how its own funds can be used. For example, a good customer of a lender might be more likely to be approved for a jumbo loan if portfolio funds are used.

2. **Blanket mortgage**: A blanket mortgage is a loan that covers more than one parcel of property under a single security pledge. It is used by developers who borrow money to purchase a large tract of land for subdividing. The loan proceeds are used to make the initial purchase of raw land and to cover the costs of subdividing. As the lots are developed and sold to consumers, the individual parcels are released from the security.

   a. **Partial release clause**: A partial release clause is the provision in a blanket mortgage that individually releases each developed lot from the mortgage (lien). This is necessary because a buyer will not purchase a lot that is encumbered by a developer's lien. The partial release clause clears the lien from the title to the individual lot.

3. **Construction loan**: A construction loan, which may also be called a construction mortgage, is used to finance the construction of residential and commercial buildings. The length of a construction loan is typically measured in months rather than years. It is also known as interim financing.

   a. **Draws**: When a buyer purchases an existing home, there is something to which the mortgage (lien) can attach. With construction financing, the lender is advancing money for something that is not yet in existence. To protect itself against early default, the lender disburses the loan proceeds in stages or draws as the building proceeds. Construction mortgages also contain guidelines for monitoring the progress of the project to ensure that the funds are being used appropriately. Often third party companies are hired by the lender to monitor the construction schedule and submit tracking reports.

   b. **Interest considerations**: Due to the higher risk associated with a construction loan, the interest rate is generally variable and tied to the lender's prime rate plus a premium of one point or so. The prime rate is the commercial interest rate charged to its best customers who are also known as AAA customers.

   c. **End loan**: A consumer rather than a builder may also seek construction financing from a lender. This type of financing often includes two stages–the construction loan and an end or permanent loan. The end loan is typically a conventional, long-term mortgage that replaces the construction financing on completion of the project. Consumer construction loans are sometimes referred to construction-to-permanent financing.

4. **Package mortgage**: In theory, a package mortgage is a secured loan that is used to finance the purchase of a house along with appliances. In residential property, these items may include kitchen appliances and air conditioning, for example. Today, it is very difficult to obtain a mortgage to purchase a previously-owned home that includes additional loan funds for the borrower to purchase new appliances. If the buyer purchases new construction from a builder, the builder may supply the appliances as an incentive. So, the buyer only needs a traditional conventional mortgage.

Chapter 17: Financing Options

a. **Advantages**: Assuming that a package mortgage could be obtained, it would allow the borrower to finance the appliances over a longer period and at lower rates compared to credit card financing. It also avoids the need for two separate financing instruments.

b. **Sales concession as an alternative**: As an alternative, a buyer could make an offer to purchase a seller's home contingent on the seller adding or replacing appliances at the seller's expense. As a sales concession, the value of the concession will likely be deducted from the sales price when calculating the loan-to-value ratio (which is discussed later in the chapter).

5. **Chattel mortgage**: A chattel mortgage is an archaic (meaning old) security device that was used to finance personal property. They are not used today in favor of what are known as security agreements. A security agreement is a contract that gives a lender a lien-like interest in assets or other non-real estate property that is purchased with loan funds. Security agreements are governed by the Uniform Commercial Code (UCC). The UCC is beyond the reach of what a real estate licensee is expected to know.

J. **Mortgage and other loan options based on different applications**: Some mortgage or loan options are based on how the loan funds will be applied. Examples of loans used in specific circumstances include a Bridge Loan, Sale and Leaseback, Land Contract Mortgage, and Portfolio Loan.

1. ▶ **Bridge loan**: A bridge loan is any short-term loan that is issued as a form of temporary financing until a more permanent, long-term loan can be obtained. Also known as gap financing, it serves to bridge or cover the gap between a need for immediate financing and the approval of an end loan. For example, a person wants to purchase a new home, but has to sell the current home in which he is living. The seller lists his current property for sale and obtains a bridge loan to purchase the new home. The bridge loan will be repaid with the sale proceeds from the current (now former) home.

   a. **Importance of contingency clause**: When a buyer needs to obtain a bridge loan for a purpose such as one stated in the previous paragraph, the buyer should include it in the financing contingency clause of the offer to purchase. If the bridge cannot be obtained and the buyer cannot purchase the new home, he will be entitled to the return of his earnest money deposit.

   b. **Risks and terms**: A bridge loan is typically portfolio in nature and tends to carry a slightly higher interest rate because it is considered to be somewhat risky. The borrower is carrying two mortgage payments and there is no guarantee when, or if, the current home will be sold. The bridge loan term may only be for six months and is secured by the equity in the former home. If the former home does not sell and the borrower cannot continue making both payments, foreclosure could result.

2. **Sale and leaseback**: A sale and leaseback is a transaction that involves the simultaneous sale of a property which is then leased back to the seller. These transactions have historically been limited to commercial properties. The seller-grantor of the property immediately turns into a lessee. Likewise, the buyer-grantee becomes a lessor. If it involves commercial real estate, a net lease is commonly used.

   a. **Advantages**: From the seller's perspective, the sale can release much needed capital that would otherwise have remained tied up in real estate ownership. From the buyer's perspective, he receives a steady stream of rental income, appreciation gained from his new ownership investment, and possible tax benefits.

   b. **Residential property application**: While it is possible to conduct a sale and leaseback of a residential property, some financial experts recommend that it is too complex and risky to be transacted without the assistance of an attorney.

   Example: A financially-strapped homeowner cannot pay his mortgage and wishes to sell his home to an investor on the condition the investor immediately lease it back to the homeowner. The goal is to be free of the mortgage while retaining possession of the home. What frustrates many of these transactions is the fact that the mortgage balance is often too high in relation to the value of the home for the investor to make a profit. The investor is not interested in paying off the loan for the buyer as a favor. Or, even if the investor was willing to do so, the rent he would have to charge to make a profit makes the lease unaffordable.

3. **Mortgaging of an interest in a land contract**: As discussed in Chapter 16, a land contract is a form of seller financing that does not involve a lien, i.e., mortgage. An existing vendor-seller or vendee-buyer in a land contract may wish to use his individual financial interests in the property as security for a mortgage loan. The actual amount of the loan is limited to the extent of the interest the vendor or vendee holds in the property. Do not confuse the mortgaging of an interest in a land contract with a purchase money mortgage.

a. **Vendor obtains mortgage**: If the vendor seeks a mortgage, he will pledge his right to collect the balance due under the land contract as collateral for the loan. The vendor cannot obtain a loan pledging the vendee's equity as security, however. If the vendor defaults, the vendee simply makes his land contract payments to the vendor's mortgagee or high bidder at the foreclosure sale instead of the vendor. A potential vendee should always have a land contract reviewed by an attorney to see if it contains any provisions that allow the vendor to mortgage the vendor's interests, and if so, how the vendee would be protected.

b. **Vendee obtains mortgage**: If the vendee seeks a mortgage, he will use the equity he is building in the property, and his right to convey the property during the land contract, as collateral for the loan. If the vendee defaults, the mortgagee or high bidder at the foreclosure sale obtains the vendee's interest in the property. Providing the land contract was properly recorded, the vendor is entitled to the balance of the payments due.

K. **Mortgage and other loan options based on junior or second instruments**: Many homeowners have multiple loans on their properties. Each individual loan has a secured position in the property. Generally, a lender will not give a secured loan unless it will be protected by actual equity in the property. The problem for a junior mortgage is that all higher priority loans are paid first if a default occurs regardless of which mortgage is foreclosed. The lower the priority of the loan, the more likely it is there will be insufficient funds if the property is sold at a sheriff's sale.

1. **Junior mortgages, junior liens generally**: A junior mortgage is any loan originated after the first or senior loan on a property. The secured position it holds in the property is lower compared to the first mortgage. In practice, all mortgages that follow the first mortgage are designated as junior mortgages whether it is a second, third, or fourth mortgage.

    a. **Significance of a junior lien**: Recall that liens are satisfied out of the foreclosure sale proceeds based on their order of priority. The senior lien is satisfied first. If any sale proceeds remain in a judicial foreclosure, the junior liens may be satisfied in their order of priority (depending on the type of property being foreclosed). This order is generally determined by the order of recording–unless a prior mortgage is subject to a subordination agreement.

    b. **Subordination agreement**: A subordination agreement changes the priority of a senior lien to a junior position. The most common example involves the refinancing of a senior mortgage on a property that has a second mortgage on it. Since refinancing involves the creation of a new mortgage and note, the refinanced senior loan moves to a junior position relative to the second mortgage. The senior lender will require a subordination agreement from the junior lender before it agrees to the refinancing. A subordination agreement may also appear as a clause in a mortgage.

2. **Open-end mortgage**: An open-end mortgage includes a note that gives the mortgagor the contractual ability to obtain future advances of funds without re-writing the loan or having to re-qualify. Advances are made by the lender up to an established credit limit.

    a. ▶ **Home equity line of credit (HELOC)**: A home equity line of credit, or HELOC loan, is a common example of an open-end loan. The borrower-mortgagor receives a line of credit that is secured by the equity in his home. Although technically it is not a consumer credit card, a HELOC operates in a manner that is financially similar. A homeowner must be careful when he uses the equity in his home to pay off other debts such as credit cards and consumer loans. It only trades one bill for another, and potentially creates a bigger problem for the homeowner. Since a home equity line of credit is secured by a lien on real estate, default can lead to foreclosure. The same cannot be said for a default on a credit card bill.

    b. ▶ **Home equity loan**: In a true home equity loan, a sum of money is borrowed which is secured with a second mortgage on real property. As the home equity loan is repaid, no additional advances can be obtained by the borrower. Instead, the home equity loan must be fully repaid. Do not confuse a home equity loan with a HELOC loan. A home equity loan is generally a closed-end loan whereas a HELOC loan is open-end.

3. **Wraparound loan**: Technically, a wraparound loan is a tool used to obtain additional financing on a property that is already encumbered with an existing mortgage. The junior wraparound lender makes a loan to the homeowner and assumes the payments on the first mortgage. The first mortgage is not actually paid

off with the proceeds of the wraparound loan. The term is derived from the fact that the second loan, in essence, wraps around and makes the payments on the first mortgage.

    a. **Example**: A seller with a balance owing on a residential mortgage enters into an agreement to sell his home to a buyer who cannot qualify for his own mortgage loan due to credit problems. The buyer offers to pay $2,000 more for the home in exchange for the seller offering financing. The balance on the seller's existing mortgage is $80,000. The house sells for $150,000.

    The buyer gives the seller a $5,000 down payment and a note for $145,000 that is secured by a second mortgage on the property. The note is at a higher interest rate than the seller's existing first mortgage. The second mortgage wraps around the first and the seller continues to make payments on the first. The seller collects the interest differential on the first mortgage and the entire interest due on the second, wraparound mortgage.

    b. **Why this is a problem**: In theory, this may sound like a great idea to a buyer and seller. In practice, it will not work and they are rarely used. The seller's original mortgage will contain a due-on-sale clause that is triggered by the sale to the buyer. Since the buyer's ownership interest is subordinate to the seller's lender, the property can be foreclosed and the buyer will be ejected from the home.

4. **Alternatives based on lender participation**: A couple of loan types are based on the lender's participation in the loan. They include the participation mortgage and the shared appreciation mortgage.

    a. **Participation mortgages**: Depending on the lender, a participation mortgage may take on one of several meanings. In one example, the lender acquires an interest in the property being pledged as collateral. The lender not only charges interest on the loan, but receives a percent of any appreciation realized when the property is sold. In another example, the lender makes a loan on a large commercial rental property. In addition to principal and interest payments, the lender also receives a percent or participation fee in the rental income derived from the property.

    Sometimes multiple lenders participate in making a single loan on a large commercial project. This spreads out the risk so no one lender faces too high of a loss in the event the project fails. This type of loan may also be referred to as a syndicated loan.

    b. **Shared appreciation mortgage (SAM)**: With a shared appreciation mortgage, the lender agrees to originate a secured loan at a below-market interest rate in exchange for a guaranteed percentage of any gain realized through appreciation during a predetermined shared appreciation period or when the property is sold. In this sense, it can be viewed as a type of "participation" loan. The SAM was originally created when interest rates were extremely high. Shared appreciation mortgages are seldom used today.

L. **Michigan State Housing Development Authority (MSHDA) loan**: See Chapter 21 for details on this important loan option for first-time buyers and buyers of owner-occupied residential properties located in targeted economically-distressed areas.

III. **Government-backed loans**: Since the 1930s, the U.S. Government has played a significant role in furthering home ownership. Two agencies in particular, the Federal Housing Administration and the U.S. Department of Veteran's Affairs, have been at the forefront of these efforts. Individually, each agency assists qualified homebuyers by backing loans given to them by conventional lenders. FHA loans and VA loans are excellent options for thousands of buyers who might not otherwise be able to qualify for a home loan.

  A. ▶ **FHA Loan**: The Federal Housing Administration, which is also known as the FHA, was created in 1934 to insure mortgage loans originated by approved lenders throughout the U.S. It currently operates under the Department of Housing and Urban Development, or HUD for short. The FHA does not build homes, provide loan money directly, or insure the physical property that secures the debt. In the event of default, the loan is backed by the U.S. Government.

During the years before and after the Great Depression, home loans were based on short-term credit, large down payments were required, and they carried high interest rates. Lenders were highly cautious about making long-term home loans due to the high default rate during those years. The National Housing Act was passed in 1934 by Congress, in part, to stimulate lending through the creation of the FHA. This was accomplished by instituting an insurance program through which the lender can make a claim to the government for any loss that results from default.

    1. **Advantages**: There are several advantages to an FHA-insured loan for certain borrowers. For example, a borrower with a lower credit rating or a younger buyer might have an easier time qualifying. The down

payment on an FHA mortgage may also be lower compared to a conventional mortgage. Loan costs are often lower as well.

2. **Technical requirements**: An FHA loan must be structured according to specific federal guidelines even though it is originated by a local lending institution. Standards relate to borrower credit qualification, property type, and even construction. After taking the loan application, the lender submits it with all required documentation to the local HUD field office for review and approval.

   a, **Direct Endorsement**: Under FHA Direct Endorsement, an FHA-approved lender is authorized to consider single-family mortgage applications on an "in-house" basis without having to first submit it to the HUD Field Office. These approved lenders are able to underwrite for the FHA directly.

   b. **Loan insurance program**: As noted, an FHA loan is insured by the government against loss. This is why the reference to "government-insured" or "government-backed" is used in connection with FHA loans. The FHA works through approved lenders who originate loans that the FHA agrees to insure against loss resulting from default. As discussed later in this section, an insurance premium is paid by the borrower for this service.

   c. **The FHA appraisal**: Properties must be evaluated by an FHA Roster Appraiser. This means the appraiser has been approved and meets FHA standards. The amount of an FHA appraisal is critical to the buyer and seller because the loan-to-value ratio is based on the lesser of the appraised value or the sale price. If the purchase price exceeds the property's FHA-appraised value, the difference must be made up as additional cash down payment by the buyer or the seller must lower the purchase price.

      (1) **Appraisal requirements**: Appraisal guidelines for an FHA appraiser include the use of a specific appraisal form. The FHA wants to make sure that the appraisal reflects an accurate valuation that also takes property defects or deficiencies into consideration. This is the best way to protect HUD's interest in the loan as the underwriter of any lender losses.

      (2) **Repair requirements**: Certain deficiencies may be marked by the appraiser for repair. Since the government insures the loan, standards of fitness and repair must be met. FHA-required inspection and repairs must be made in addition to any city certification and inspection requirements that may apply. If a condition represents a risk to the health and safety of the occupants or affects the structural soundness of the property, repairs are mandated.

      A buyer cannot close an FHA-insured mortgage until all defects have been corrected. The seller may not want to personally pay for the repairs because it would reduce his anticipated profit from the sale. If the buyer pays for the repairs instead, the cost cannot be credited toward the statutory cash investment the buyer must make (which is discussed later) nor can it be financed.

      (3) **Notice requirement–Home inspection**: Buyers must be made aware that they should not rely on an FHA appraisal as a substitute for an independent home inspection. Buyers are entitled to a HUD/FHA form titled "For Your Protection: Get a Home Inspection." It is the lender's responsibility to provide this form in connection with an FHA mortgage application.

      A buyer must also receive a form titled, "Conditional Commitment, Direct Endorsement, Statement of Appraised Value." It again mentions the importance of home inspections and lists the loan commitment terms, estimated monthly loan expenses, and estimated value of the property.

   d. **Maximum loan amount**: Loan amount limits are established for FHA loans. They vary based on economic factors and the type of property whether it be single family, duplex, tri-plex, or four-plex. Borrowers may also see regional differences based on the state and county in which the property lies. In Michigan, the maximum FHA loan amount for 2020 is $331,760 for a single-family home (which is subject to change).

3. **Components relating to the FHA loan payment**: Since the government insures the lender against loan default, it limits the risk of default by controlling the maximum loan-to-value ratio. It also requires the borrower-mortgagor to pay a mortgage insurance premium for this service.

   a. **Maximum loan-to-value ratio**: The maximum loan-to-value ratio depends on the amount of closing costs borrowers pay in a given geographic area. Certain regions, including Michigan, are designated as "high cost" areas. This means they are considered to have high average closing costs compared to other regions of the country. The majority of states are designated as "high cost" areas.

Chapter 17: Financing Options 283

The actual loan-to-value ratio that a borrower can obtain on an FHA-insured loan is frequently adjusted. A financial expert such as a loan originator should be consulted for the current rate. Typically, FHA establishes a base loan-to-value ratio such as 96.5%. If the mortgage insurance fee is financed along with the loan amount, the loan-to-value ratio can increase to 98.25%, for example. Again, current figures must be obtained from a financial expert.

(1) **Statutory cash investment**: The maximum loan-to-value ratio assumes that the borrower has made a statutory cash investment or down payment of at least 3.5%. Closing costs cannot be counted toward this amount. Appropriately documented gifts from family members, however, can be counted. If the required cash investment cannot be made by the buyer, the offer to purchase may be withdrawn.

(2) **Financing of buyer-paid closing costs**: Closing costs paid by the borrower cannot be financed unless the loan involves refinancing and FHA loan-to-value ratio limits are not exceeded.

(3) **Meaning of CLTV**: Many HUD documents refer to CLTV limits. This stands for Combined Loan To Value ratio. It reflects the combined or total loan-to-value ratio when a property is subject to more than one loan. The CLTV manages the risk of default by considering the total debt a mortgagor carries on his property.

Example: A homeowner-mortgagor owns a home that is subject to a current FHA-insured loan plus a home equity loan. The homeowner wishes to refinance his existing FHA loan with a new FHA loan. The homeowner will be required to obtain a subordination agreement from the home equity lender. The refinancing lender must make sure the combined loans do not exceed the CLTV limit for the property.

b. **Mortgage insurance premium (MIP)**: To pay for the government insurance provided to the lender on an FHA loan, the borrower is charged a one-time, upfront mortgage insurance premium, which may be referred to as UFMIP, on the base loan amount. While fees and rates are subject to change, the upfront MIP is currently 1.75 percent (0.0175) regardless of the loan term or loan-to-value ratio. An annual renewal MIP is assessed in addition to the upfront MIP. It is calculated on the base loan amount as well.

(1) **May be financed**: The upfront MIP fee is typically added to the mortgage amount which means that it is financed by the purchaser. It can also be paid for with cash at the closing.

(2) **Annual renewal of MIP**: The annual renewal premium is calculated through what are called basis points or bps. One basis point = 0.01%. The annual mortgage insurance premium for a typical 30-year mortgage with a 3.5% down payment is 85 bps or 0.85% of the loan amount. Once the fee is calculated, it is divided by 12 to arrive at the monthly premium.

(3) **Cancelling the MIP**: There are two ways to eliminate payment of the annual MIP. The first way is for the borrower to refinance the loan with a new conventional loan. The other way occurs automatically when the loan to value ratio lowers to 78%. For this to happen, the borrower must have paid the annual MIP for at least 11 years. If the initial LTV exceeds 90%, the annual MIP remains for the life of the loan.

4. **Characteristics of an FHA-insured loan**: Other common characteristics of an FHA loan relate to interest rates, prepayment rights, other closing costs, and loan assumption.

a. **Interest rate**: Interest rates on an FHA-insured loan are not regulated by HUD or the FHA. It is up to the borrower to shop for the lowest rate he can find based on his credit history. Traditionally, FHA rates are slightly below conventional rates due to the fact that the loan is government-insured.

b. **Prepayment privilege**: All FHA loans are open and may be paid ahead of schedule. Of course, if payments are missed, the lender will commence collection efforts which can lead to a foreclosure in the same manner as any conventional loan.

c. **Other closing costs**: Other closing costs that may be included with an FHA loan include a loan origination fee, discount points, and seller-paid financing concessions.

(1) ▶ **One percent loan origination fee**: A one-percent loan origination fee may be charged at the lender's discretion for originating or issuing an FHA loan. This fee covers the administrative cost of issuing the mortgage. The buyer can attempt to negotiate with the seller to pay this fee, but the seller is under no obligation to do so.

(2) ▸ **Discount points**: A discount point or points represent a closing cost assessed by a lender to increase the yield on a particular loan by offsetting the difference between the lower FHA and the higher conventional interest rates. Recall that 1 point = 1% of the loan. Payment of points is negotiable between the buyer and seller. Points are covered in further detail in Chapter 16.

(3) **Seller-paid financing concessions**: The maximum amount of cash contribution that a seller can make to a buyer on an FHA loan is 6%. Concessions are discussed later in this chapter.

d. **Assumption of an FHA loan**: After originating an FHA loan, the borrower-mortgagor may sell the property prior to maturity and allow the new buyer to assume and agree to pay the FHA loan balance. The creditworthiness of the new buyer must first be reviewed and approved. If the original loan was closed after December 14, 1989, the assuming purchaser must occupy the home as his principal residence for the life of the loan. This means that an FHA loan cannot be assumed by an investor.

5. **Loan programs**: HUD's policy is to assist low- to moderate-income families (by lowering the initial costs normally associated with conventional loans) and to assist borrowers in under-served areas where loans have been difficult to obtain. Some of the primary FHA loan programs which are available will now be discussed. The word "Section" at the beginning of some loan titles refers to the specific statutory section of the National Housing Act that authorizes the Secretary of HUD to insure the particular loan.

   a. **Section 203(b) loan**: HUD's Section 203(b) loan is the most popular and abundant FHA-insured loan. It is used to finance the purchase of a one-to-four family residential property as well as home loan refinancing. The program is not available for an investor loan which means that the program is not available to an individual who is purchasing a rental property.

   b. **Section 203(k) loan**: HUD's Section 203(k) loan is used to finance the purchase of a single-family property where rehabilitation and repair costs are included in the loan amount. At origination, the borrower receives the amount of money necessary to purchase a property (or refinance a residence) along with funds to pay for the cost of repairs and improvements. The purchase offer should be contingent on the approval of an FHA Section 203(k) loan that covers all required repairs by the FHA or lender.

   c. **Section 234(c) loan**: HUD's Section 234(c) loan program insures loans for the purchase of a condominium unit. It is also useful for low- to moderate-income renters who might otherwise be displaced by a condominium conversion. In other respects, it is similar to a Section 203(b) loan.

   d. **Section 245(a) loan**: HUD's Section 245(a) loan program offers a graduated payment mortgage to assist a first-time buyer with low- to moderate-income, but whose income is expected to rise substantially in the next 5–10 years. Loans vary in the amount of monthly payment increases as well as the number of years over which the payments can increase. A Section 245(a) loan may be used to purchase or construct a residential, owner-occupied home.

   e. **Section 251 loan**: HUD's Section 251 loan is structured as an adjustable rate mortgage (ARM). The interest rate cannot increase more than 1 percent per year or more than 5 percent from the rate established at the time of origination. It is used in conjunction with Section 203(b), 203(k) and 234(c) loans.

   f. **Home Equity Conversion Mortgage (HECM)**: The Home Equity Conversion Mortgage, or HECM for short, represents HUD's reverse mortgage program. Homeowners 62 years of age or older can withdraw a portion of their home equity in the form of a monthly payment or annuity. The loan is not repaid until the borrower sells, moves, or dies. Due to the risk of reverse mortgages, applicants must attend and complete an approved counseling program. An annuity is a fixed sum of money that is paid to an individual, usually on a long-term basis. Annuities can be paid through a variety of financial instruments.

   g. **FHA Energy Efficient Mortgages (EEM)**: HUD's Energy Efficient Mortgage program, or EEM for short, enables a buyer to finance the cost of adding energy-efficient features to a new or existing home along with his FHA-insured mortgage. A borrower who meets Section 203(b) underwriting requirements can include the cost of the energy improvements providing the cost is less than the dollar value anticipated to be saved during the useful life of the home.

6. **HUD's 90 day (anti-flipping) Rule**: FHA loans are designed to help individuals obtain affordable mortgage loans on principal residences. FHA regulations have generally prohibited insuring a mortgage on a home that is purchased and owned for less than 90 days before the mortgagor resells the property. This 90-day ownership rule prevented short-term investors from using FHA resources to acquire properties and then flip, meaning quickly resell, them. This became known as HUD's "Anti-Flipping Rule." In 2010 through

Chapter 17: Financing Options   285

2014, the FHA waived enforcement of this rule (with certain restrictions) to help the struggling economy. The 90-day waiting period was reestablished in 2015 and is currently in effect.

7. ▶ **Down payment assistance programs**: Down payment assistance programs, also known as community redevelopment programs and down payment grants, offer affordable housing opportunities to qualified first-time home buyers and low- to moderate-income individuals. These programs provide assistance through grants, direct loans, and rental assistance.

   a. **HOME Investment Partnerships Program**: The HOME Investment Partnerships Program, or HOME for short, was created by Congress in the 1990s to provide formula grants, through HUD, to state and local governments. The HOME program also works in partnership with local nonprofit organizations. Funding is provided to increase affordable housing opportunities for low and very low-income individuals and can be used for construction, purchase, rehabilitation, or rental.

      (1) **Michigan participation**: Statewide and regional HOME programs are administered in Michigan through the Michigan State Housing Development Authority, or MSHDA for short (see Chapter 21), and Habitat for Humanity. The HUD website for homeownership assistance also lists numerous local resources that include participating cities and nonprofit organizations.

      (2) **American Dream Down-payment Initiative Act**: In 2003, a federal initiative was signed into law under the HOME program known as the American Dream Down-payment Initiative Act, or ADDI for short. This government program provides financial assistance for down payments, closing costs, and rehabilitation to eligible individuals. The funds are administered through local housing agencies that received HOME Investment Partnership funds from HUD.

   b. **No private down payment assistance with FHA loans**: In 2008, seller-funded down payment assistance programs were eliminated for any mortgage insured by the FHA. Thus, a borrower's down payment cannot be provided before, during, or after the sale by the seller, any other person or entity that financially benefits from the transaction, or any third party or entity that is reimbursed, directly or indirectly, by the seller or any other person or entity that financially benefits from the transaction.

B. ▶ **VA Loan**: A VA loan is one that can only be obtained by eligible service members, veterans, and their surviving spouses for the purchase or construction of a home. The loan is originated by a VA-approved lender and then guaranteed by the U.S. Department of Veteran Affairs. Except for rare direct loans made in isolated rural areas, the VA does not build homes, make loans, or insure the physical property. VA loans may be obtained for mobile homes and plots. VA stands for Veteran's Administration (even though the federal department is called the Department of Veteran Affairs).

   1. **Loan guarantee program**: A VA loan is government-guaranteed. Notice how this differs from FHA loans which are government-insured. This means that the eligible applicant does not have to pay a mortgage insurance premium. In the event of default on a VA loan, the lender is compensated for losses it sustains. The loan is considered to be high risk because it can be originated for 100% of the sale price or appraised value. Accordingly, VA is a "zero down" loan program.

   2. **Technical requirements**: This section explores what the lender must verify prior to issuing a VA-guaranteed loan including the loan applicant's eligibility and the value of the property.

      a. **Certificate of Eligibility**: Before a VA loan can be obtained from a lender of the applicant's choice, a Certificate of Eligibility, or COE, must be obtained from the VA. It verifies to the lender that the applicant is eligible for a VA-guaranteed loan, but not the actual loan amount that may be obtained. Basically, an applicant for a VA loan must be a veteran who has served for a minimum of 90 days during qualifying wartime or 181 days during peacetime. Those who are on active duty must have served for at least 90 days. Reservists and national guard members must have completed 6 years of service.

      b. **Restoring eligibility**: A veteran can use his eligibility to purchase a home and then have the eligibility restored to purchase a new home. The first VA loan must be fully paid, or the loan assumed by a qualified veteran, before this can happen.

      c. **VA appraisal/Certificate of Reasonable Value**: The purchase property is subject to a VA-approved appraisal which is similar to the appraisal required for an FHA loan. The lender must obtain a Certificate of Reasonable Value, or CRV, that states the property's current market value based on the appraisal. If the purchase price exceeds the CRV, the veteran may pay the difference as an extra down payment. This is common to most mortgage loans.

3. **Characteristics of a VA-guaranteed loan**: This section examines the maximum guarantee on a VA loan, the interest rate, prepayment options, whether a veteran can use his eligibility to purchase a rental property, and whether a VA loan is assumable by a non-veteran.

   a. **Maximum guarantee**: The VA does not limit how much a veteran can borrow to finance a home. Instead, it limits the liability the VA is willing to assume if a default occurs. This, in turn, affects how much a lender is willing to loan. While basic entitlement is $36,000, lenders typically are willing to loan four times this amount, which is $144,000, without requiring a down payment. The lending limit for a VA loan in Michigan is currently $484,350 (which is subject to change).

   b. **Interest rate**: The interest rate on a VA-guaranteed loan fluctuates and is negotiable. In this respect, it is similar to an FHA loan.

   c. **Prepayment privilege**: A VA loan must be open which means it can be repaid ahead of the amortization schedule. Any extra payment amount is applied to reduction of the principal balance. In this respect, it is similar to an FHA loan.

   d. **Closing costs resulting from VA-guaranteed loan**: A VA loan includes the typical closing costs associated with many conventional real estate loans. They include a loan origination fee, funding fee, and possibly points.

      (1) ▶ **Loan origination fee**: The lender may charge an optional loan origination fee not to exceed 1% of the loan. If the lender does so, it is prevented from assessing additional fees (other than allowable closing costs such as recording fees or hazard insurance).

      (2) **Funding fee**: A 2.15% funding fee may be charged for loans with a loan-to-value ratio of 96%-100%. If the veteran pays a higher down payment, the funding fee is reduced. This is due to the fact that there is less risk with a lower loan-to-value ratio.

      (3) **Points**: The lender may assess reasonable points as a closing cost or the borrower can pay them to buy-down the interest rate. The borrower, seller, and lender may negotiate the payment of points. Points are not usually financed into a VA loan.

   e. **No investor loans**: VA loans may be obtained for the purchase, construction, repair, or alteration of a house, condominium, or farm to be personally occupied by the veteran. The veteran's entitlement may not be used to purchase investor-owned, meaning rental property.

   f. **Assumption of a VA loan**: While a VA loan can only be originated by an eligible veteran or service member, the loan may be assumed by a non-veteran. Today, an assumption is allowed with the prior approval of the lender. If the assumption was previously approved, the veteran will be released from liability for any deficiency in the event the assuming buyer defaults. If lender approval was not obtained, and the mortgagor-veteran sells the property, the VA can enforce the due-on-sale clause contained in the mortgage terms and the veteran can be held liable for any resulting deficiency.

4. **VA-guaranteed ARM program**: A qualified veteran can obtain an adjustable rate mortgage under the VA program. The loan contains customary indexing of the rate and rate adjustment caps. A 5/1 VA ARM, for example, includes a maximum 1% annual interest rate adjustment and a 5% maximum increase over the life of the loan.

IV. **Financing concessions**: Some buyers believe they have the required down payment to purchase a seller's property. However, when they find out how much closing costs are, they suddenly realize that they lack sufficient cash to actually close the transaction. Rather than waiting to save the extra money needed to purchase the property, and risk another similar property not being on the market at the same price, the buyer may ask the seller to pay for some of the closing costs. Concessions, or contributions as they are sometimes called, are common in the purchase and sale of real estate. Real estate licensees should be familiar with the concept as it may become part of transaction negotiations.

   A. **Concession defined**: The subject of concessions can be confusing, even for a seasoned real estate professional. Part of this stems from the slightly varying definitions and explanations that are available. As an overview, a concession is a financial inducement offered by a seller (or a builder, developer, or real estate broker) to a buyer to entice the buyer to purchase the seller's property. Note: Do not confuse financing and sales concessions discussed in this section with a rent concession which is described in Chapter 14.

Chapter 17: Financing Options 287

1. **Fannie Mae (FNMA)**: Fannie May uses the term Independent Party Contributions, or IPC for short, when describing its policy on concessions. According to Fannie Mae, IPCs are either "financing concessions" or "sales concessions."

    a. **Financing concession**: A financing concession is a financial contribution that is made by the seller (or other interested party) that provides a benefit to the buyer-borrower. Financing concessions are subject to the limits set forth later in this discussion. Fees and closing costs that are customarily paid by the seller are not considered to be financing concessions.

    b. **Sales concession**: All other contributions paid by the seller or other interested party that do not qualify as financing concessions are considered to be sales concessions. Knowing the difference is important because sales concessions must be deducted from the sale price of a property before the loan amount is calculated based on the loan-to-value ratio. This is due to the fact that sales concessions are deemed to influence the purchase price that a buyer pays for a property. For example, a buyer may be willing to pay more for a property if the seller is willing to include items such as furniture or lawn equipment. These personal property items are not normally included in the purchase of a home.

2. **HUD (FHA)**: According to HUD, a seller concession is the payment of all or part of the buyer's cost by a seller or interested third party. Sales concessions are deemed to influence the price that a buyer pays for property and include items such as discount points, loan origination fees, interest rate buy-downs, closing cost assistance, monetary gifts, or personal property given to the buyer. HUD rules allow a seller to pay some concessions up to a set limit.

B. **Allowable versus non-allowable concessions**: A buyer and a seller are free to negotiate acceptable price and terms, including concessions. While concessions may be used to offset settlement costs normally paid by the buyer, they cannot be used to help the buyer fund his down payment or meet financial reserve requirements. Depending on the loan type, a lender may impose additional rules as to the nature and amount of any negotiated concession.

1. **Allowable concessions**: The following list includes common allowable concessions that may be paid by sellers (or other interested parties) on a buyer's behalf. Allowable means that the amount does not have to be deducted from the sale price (as an adjustment) before calculating the loan amount. Keep in mind that what is ultimately allowable can vary based on the lender, the type of loan, and the buyer's credit worthiness. Ultimately, even allowable concessions are subject to applicable limits.

    a. **Closing costs**: Allowable closing costs can include items such as discount points, origination fees, lender fees, homeowner association fees, transfer taxes, attorney fees, surveys, credit reports, and title insurance.

    b. **Prepaid items**: Common prepaid items include escrow setup, home insurance, and the interest due at the closing. (Note: The first mortgage payment is typically not due until the following month or two, even though the full amount of the loan is disbursed at the closing. This payment covers the interest due between the day of closing and the first payment.)

    c. **Tax prorations**: This category of allowable concession includes tax prorations that are paid to the seller. Recall that Michigan property taxes are generally paid in advance.

2. **Concessions that affect property value are non-allowable**: Down payments must be funded with the buyer's own verified funds. Assume, for example, that a buyer who lacks the necessary down payment to purchase a seller's house agrees with the seller to pay a higher price for a property. The seller "kicks back" the amount of the overpayment as a seller-paid concession which the buyer then uses as his down payment. From the lender's perspective, it is being asked to finance the down payment which it will not do.

    a. **Treatment of non-allowable concessions**: If a non-allowable concession is attempted such as raising the price of the house to "fund" the down payment, the lender will reduce the sale price by the dollar amount of the concession for purposes of calculating the loan-to-value ratio. The net effect is to put the buyer back in the same position of not having a sufficient down payment.

    b. **Include concessions in the offer**: A buyer who is seeking seller concessions as part of his offer should include the concession request in his offer to purchase. This helps protect the buyer's earnest money deposit in the event the lender will not allow the concession and the buyer must withdraw his offer. Licensees should refer buyers to a qualified loan officer for advice on structuring concessions. Also, parties who attempt to hide concessions from a lender are potentially engaging in illegal mortgage fraud.

3. **Concession limitations**: Both conventional and government-backed loans have specific rules regarding allowable concessions. Recall that an allowable concession does not have to be deducted from the sale price when calculating the loan amount. Notice in the following examples how the allowable contribution increases as the amount of down payment paid by the borrower also increases.

   a. **Conventional loans**: The following guidelines generally apply to conventional loans that conform to guidelines for purchase by Fannie Mae and Freddie Mac. These loans represent roughly 90% of all conventional loans written today. Other conventional loans such as jumbo loans and subprime loans may be subject to different limitations. Further, some lenders interpret certain seller paid costs to be concessions even though Fannie and Freddie might not classify them as such.

      (1) 2% of the lesser of the property's sale price or appraised value is allowed for a mortgage secured by an investment property.

      (2) 3% of the lesser of the property's sale price or appraised value is allowed for a mortgage secured by a principal residence or second home based on a loan-to-value ratio greater than 90% (meaning the down payment is less than 10%).

      (3) 6% of the lesser of the property's sale price or appraised value is allowed for a mortgage secured by a principal residence or second home based on a loan-to-value between 76% and 90% (meaning the down payment is between 24% and 10%).

      (4) 9% of the lesser of the property's sale price or appraised value is allowed for a mortgage secured by a principal residence or second home based on a loan-to-value that is equal to or less than 75% (meaning the down payment is 25% or more).

   b. **FHA loans**: Sellers can pay concessions of up to 6% of the property's sale price or appraised value. Contributions in excess of this limit are non-allowable and will be subtracted from the sale price before calculating the amount of the loan. This includes what are referred to as inducements to purchase (which are similar to sales concessions under Fannie Mae policy). Inducements to purchase include things such as decorating allowances, repair allowances, moving costs, and personal property items not normally included in the purchase of a property.

   c. **VA loans**: Sellers can pay all reasonable and customary closing costs, including discount points, without limit. The seller may also pay up to 4% of the purchase price toward certain other expenses.

4. **Cash down payment gifts from relatives**: Cash gifts given to buyer-borrowers from relatives are not considered to be concessions and may be applied to the down payment. A gift letter will be required that includes certain information such as the amount of the gift, the address of the subject property, the relationship of the "giver" of the gift to the buyer-borrower, and a statement that the money is, in fact, a gift and not a loan that must be repaid. The lender will likely have a specific process that must be followed for the money transfer to be accepted toward the down payment.

V. **Control of the financial market and sources of financing**: The financial markets of the United States are complex, intricate, resilient, and dependent on a wide range of interacting entities. Understanding the full scope of how this powerful "economic machine" works is beyond the scope of this textbook. There are, however, several aspects of which a real estate licensee should be aware. Licensees should also understand the difference between the primary and secondary mortgage markets since the majority of loans today are originated in the primary market and sold to a secondary market participant.

   A. **Federal Reserve System (FRS)**: The Federal Reserve System, or FRS for short, is the central bank of the United States. It serves as the banker for the U.S. Treasury. It was created by Congress in 1913 to make sure the U.S. monetary and financial system would be safe, flexible, and stable. The Federal Reserve System is also known as the Federal Reserve, Federal Reserve Bank, and "the Fed."

      1. **Responsibilities**: The Federal Reserve fulfills four primary areas of responsibility including:
         – Conducting monetary policy and influencing credit conditions in the economy to maintain price stability and high employment;
         – Supervising and regulating banks and other financial institutions to ensure the safety and soundness of the country's financial system and protecting the credit rights of consumers;
         – Maintaining the stability of the financial system by containing risk that may arise in the financial markets; and
         – Providing financial services to the U.S. Government, financial institutions, and foreign official institutions as well as operating and overseeing the nation's payment systems.

Chapter 17: Financing Options   289

2. **District and member banks**: Economic objectives of the Fed are accomplished through a Board of Governors located in Washington, D.C., along with 12 regional Federal Reserve Banks and their branches. Michigan is served by the Federal Reserve District Bank in Chicago, Illinois and a local branch in Detroit, Michigan.

3. **Control**: The Fed regulates the flow of money throughout the country by adjusting reserve requirements and discount rates.

    a. **Reserve requirements**: A reserve requirement is the actual dollar amount of money that a lender or other depository institution must hold back against its own debts. A lender's reserves are represented by currency deposits that are not loaned to borrowers. During recessions, a higher reserve requirement is usually required. This leaves less money available for lending which creates what is known as a tight money market.

    b. **Discount rates**: Member banks such as commercial banks are allowed to borrow money from the Federal District Reserve Bank to expand their local lending activities. The discount rate is the interest rate the district bank charges its member banks.

B. ▶ **Primary mortgage market**: The primary mortgage market is the source to which borrowers come directly to obtain a mortgage loan. A primary lender often originates a loan and then sells it to another investor. This investor could be another bank or a private investor who is in the position of a secondary mortgage market participant.

1. **Institutional participants**: Some of the more active participants in the primary market include mortgage banking companies, commercial banks, credit unions, savings and loan associations, mutual savings banks, and insurance companies. With the exception of mortgage banking companies and insurance companies, nearly all primary mortgage market participants are depository institutions. A depository is an institution or organization that accepts money deposits from its customers or members.

    a. **Mortgage banking companies**: A mortgage banker is a state-licensed individual or company whose purpose it is to originate and close mortgage loans. While a mortgage banker can hold and service the mortgage in its own portfolio, most loans are sold in the secondary mortgage market along with the servicing rights after the closing. Mortgage bankers earn their money by providing loan origination services.

        (1) **Warehouse lending source**: Mortgage bankers often use a revolving line of credit they have with a warehouse lender to fund the mortgage loans they originate. The actual loan funds the borrower receives to purchase the property come from this account. The note is used as collateral until the mortgage is sold in the secondary market, at which time the line of credit is repaid. Large commercial banks also provide warehouse lines of credit to mortgage bankers.

        (2) ▶ **Mortgage broker compared**: Do not confuse a mortgage banker with a mortgage broker. A mortgage broker is an individual who earns a commission as an agent for bringing a borrower and a lender together. The mortgage broker only serves as an intermediary and does not originate loans or directly supply financing capital. Mortgage brokers are typically paid a small percent of the loan, often by the borrower.

            (a) **Mortgage broker licensing requirements**: Michigan adopted the Mortgage Brokers, Lenders, and Servicers Licensing Act in 1987. Under this Act, a person cannot act as a mortgage broker, mortgage lender, or mortgage servicer in Michigan without first obtaining the appropriate license or registration. If a person is acting in the capacity of a loan officer as defined by Michigan's Mortgage Loan Originator Licensing Act (MLOLA), a separate loan originator's license must be obtained. MLOLA is a different law that is explored later in this chapter.

            (b) **Requirements**: A mortgage broker, lender, or servicer must obtain a license or registration from the state prior to engaging in one of the defined activities. A mortgage loan is any loan secured by a first mortgage on real property used (or improved to be used) as a dwelling for 4 or fewer families. The Act does not cover loans for unimproved (i.e., vacant) land and/or home improvement installment loans. It does contain a number of important requirements that must be understood by anyone who acts as a mortgage broker, mortgage lender, or mortgage servicer.

                i) **Mortgage broker**: A mortgage broker is an agent who acts, directly or indirectly, for (1) a prospective borrower who desires to locate a lender, or (2) another lender who wants to locate an interested borrower. As noted below, a real estate licensee is exempt from this definition.

    ii) **Mortgage lender**: A mortgage lender is a person who, directly or indirectly, lends the money on a mortgage loan.

    iii) **Mortgage servicer**: A mortgage servicer is one who, directly or indirectly, collects mortgage installment payments and keeps the required books for the mortgage lender for whom the servicer acts.

(c) **Exemptions**: There are several exemptions to the Mortgage Brokers, Lenders, and Servicers Licensing Act. Only those that might impact a real estate licensee are discussed.

    i) **Real estate licensee**: Licensed real estate brokers and salespersons are exempt from the Act providing no additional compensation is received beyond their customary commission on the sale or lease of real estate. A real estate broker may be licensed or registered as a mortgage broker, lender, or servicer for real estate sales in which the licensee is engaged. Once registered, the broker can receive additional compensation beyond his customary commission (subject to Michigan license law disclosure requirements–see Chapter 19).

    Note: Prior to serving in a dual capacity as a real estate broker and mortgage broker, lender, or servicer, the real estate broker should check with legal counsel to determine if any conflict of interest issues are raised and what specific recordkeeping and disclosure practices must be adopted pursuant to this Act.

    ii) **Land contract servicing**: A land contract servicer who services 75 or fewer land contracts (of which 10 or fewer require the collection of money for taxes or insurance) is exempt. This relieves a real estate broker who relies on land contract servicing functions for a significant percent of his business from having to obtain a mortgage servicers license.

b. **Commercial banks**: A commercial bank is a depository institution that provides one of the widest range of banking and lending services of any financial institution. Commercial banks provide both short- and long-term loans to individuals and businesses alike as well as credit card services. They also handle a wide variety of savings options including standard deposit accounts, checking accounts, and investment accounts. When people think of a traditional bank, it is usually a commercial bank that they have in mind.

  (1) **Assets**: In terms of asset strength, commercial banks have some of the largest asset pools of any lender. For comparison, it is estimated that commercial banks hold over 14 times more assets than credit unions. As a result, a commercial bank might be more willing than a small community bank to extend a loan on a complex commercial real estate project or a jumbo loan for a large residential property.

    (a) ▶ **Jumbo (non-conforming) loan**: A jumbo loan is one that exceeds the limits set for conforming conventional loans by Fannie Mae and Freddie Mac. As a result, it does not qualify for sale in the secondary mortgage market and is considered to be non-conforming. In Michigan, this is a loan that exceeds $417,000 (which is subject to change).

    (b) **Community bank**: A community bank is a smaller commercial bank that focuses its efforts on serving the banking needs of the local community in which it is located. Most of the deposits are obtained locally and many of their loans are extended to local businesses and residents. They tend to be privately owned and like to develop personal relationships with their customers.

  (2) **Real estate loans**: Historically, commercial banks did not play a significant role in issuing mortgage loans. That has changed with commercial banks regularly competing with mortgage banking companies for the home buyers' market.

c. **Credit unions**: A credit union is a not-for-profit financial cooperative that is owned by its members who are regarded as shareholders. Governance is typically handled by a board of directors who are also members. A credit union accepts deposits from members and uses them to make a number of different, competitive loans including home loans. Surplus income derived by the credit union is returned to members as dividends.

Chapter 17: Financing Options

   d. **Savings and loan associations (S&L)**: A savings and loan association, or S&L for short, is a depository institution that was originally created to allow members to deposit savings and obtain loans at more competitive rates. For years, savings and loan associations served as one of most important sources of long-term residential mortgage loans. They are also known as a thrift institutions. A thrift is any organization that is formed to further consumer savings.

   While the total number of savings and loan associations in existence has decreased since the S&L scandals of the 1980s, they still serve as a reliable source for long-term residential mortgages. They also make loans for refinancing as well as construction loans. Savings and loan associations tend to focus more on local lending needs.

   e. **Mutual savings banks**: A mutual savings bank is a depository institution that operates either like a savings and loan association or a commercial bank. Mutual banks, or mutuals as they may be called, were created to serve local communities and promote savings among their members. Mutuals that were chartered to act mostly like savings and loan associations focus more on promoting home ownership through their lending practices. Over 500 mutual banks are located in 44 states, but none in Michigan.

   f. **Insurance companies**: Insurance companies, especially life insurance companies, have served as a source of real estate loans for decades. Lending practices are generally limited to large, long-term loans for commercial and industrial properties. The insurance industry's lending contribution measures in the billions of dollars. Insurance companies often work through local intermediaries such as mortgage bankers and brokers.

   g. **Other primary sources**: Other primary sources include (1) individual and private investor groups, (2) foreign sources, and (3) pension funds.

2. ▶ **Procedural aspects of lending and loan application requirements**: Nearly all lending institutions that provide mortgage funding to individual borrowers follow a similar loan approval process. These steps include loan origination, processing, underwriting, closing, and servicing.

   a. **Loan origination and licensing requirements**: Loan origination is a process that begins with the completion of a loan application taken by a qualified individual such as a loan officer. This person is now required to be licensed under state law.

      (1) ▶ **Loan (mortgage) application**: When a purchaser applies for a mortgage loan, an application must be completed. The application requests detailed information such as type of mortgage and terms of loan, property information and purpose of loan, borrower information, employment information, monthly income and housing expense information, assets and liabilities, and purchase transaction details. A declarations section may also be included inquiring about citizenship and prior judgments, lawsuits, bankruptcies, foreclosures, delinquencies, and prior ownership interests.

      (2) **Licensing requirements–SAFE Act and MLOLA**: In direct response to rampant mortgage fraud that contributed to the subprime mortgage crisis, Congress passed the Safe and Fair Enforcement for Mortgage Licensing Act, also known as the SAFE Act, in 2008. The Act required individual states to establish licensing requirements for mortgage loan originators operating in the state.

      In 2009, Michigan passed the Mortgage Loan Originator Licensing Act of 2009, or MLOLA for short, to meet the requirements of the SAFE Act. Under MLOLA, an individual shall not engage in the business of a mortgage loan originator with regard to a residential dwelling (defined as consisting of 1–4 family housing units, including condominiums and cooperatives) without first obtaining and annually maintaining a mortgage loan originator's license.

         (a) **Originate/Originator defined**: To originate a loan means to (1) take a residential mortgage loan application, or (2) offer or negotiate the terms of a residential mortgage loan for a fee. A mortgage loan originator is, therefore, any individual who originates or negotiates residential mortgage loans for a fee.

         (b) **Real estate broker exemption**: Under MLOLA, a person who only performs real estate brokerage activities as a real estate licensee is exempt as long as the licensee is not offering financing or in any way employed or compensated by a lender, mortgage broker, or mortgage loan originator. As a result, a real estate broker should not accept any compensation from a lender for referring a buyer-loan applicant without checking with legal counsel. Any such referral could trigger MLOLA or RESPA (which is discussed later in this chapter).

(c) **Seller financing transactions**: According to Michigan's Department of Insurance and Financial Services (DIFS), the definition of a residential mortgage loan includes an installment sales contract (i.e., land contract). However, a loan originator's license is not required for certain seller-financed transactions in which a mortgage loan (or land contract) is offered or negotiated. These include the sale of an individual's residence, vacation home, inherited property, or sale to an immediate family member.

To qualify, the individual cannot be engaged in the business of mortgage loan origination. Based on the SAFE Act Final Rule, the DIFS will presume an individual to be so engaged if more than 3 transactions are originated in a calendar year. A real estate licensee may wish to recommend that a seller consult with legal counsel before listing or selling on a land contract.

(3) **Verifications**: Returning to our discussion about the procedural aspects of loan origination, the prospective borrower must supply certain information relating to his current financial position. To verify this information, the loan applicant will sign authorizations to release information about his bank account balance, employment history, current mortgage or rent payments, credit history and score, and information about any other outstanding loans.

(4) ▸ **Origination costs**: The borrower may be assessed costs to originate a loan including a loan origination fee as well as fees associated with the credit report, appraisal, and points.

(5) **Assemble documentation for processing**: After gathering all required documentation, it is assembled into a file and submitted to an expert whose job it is to process the loan application.

b. **Loan processing**: Loan processing involves the investigation and verification of the information supplied in the applicant's file. Since time is often an issue in real estate transactions, the processor will quickly order the credit report and appraisal. These items will be used to verify the creditworthiness of the applicant and the value of the purchase property. When the file is complete, it is sent to underwriting for approval or denial.

c. **Loan underwriting**: Loan underwriting is the process that a lender uses to determine if the risk associated with a loan application is within acceptable limits. The person who fulfills this function is called a loan underwriter. He makes the decision whether to approve or reject the mortgage application based on the criteria listed below.

(1) ▸ **Assess the applicant's ability to repay–qualifying buyers**: One significant area of risk for a lender is default by the borrower-buyer. To ascertain whether this is likely to occur, the underwriter will examine the credit report and credit score. The underwriter will also look at the applicant's income and limit the actual mortgage payment to a certain percent of gross monthly income using a debt-to-income ratio.

(a) ▸ **Debt-to-income ratios (DTI)**: For years, lenders applied a 28%/36% formula to qualify a loan applicant for a mortgage loan. The debt-to-income ratio may also be referred to as a buyer qualification ratio.

i) ▸ **28% formula**: The first number, 28%, represents the maximum percent of monthly gross income that can be applied to the PITI or PITIA mortgage payment. This assures the lender that adequate income remains for the borrower to fund essential living expenses without having to risk missing a mortgage payment.

▸ **Example**: $5,000 (gross income) x .28 (28%) = $1,400 (max. mortgage payment)

ii) ▸ **36% formula**: The second number, 36%, represents the maximum percent of monthly income a borrower can allocate to all financial obligations having 10 or more payment months remaining (including the mortgage payment). Under this formula, all monthly payments are added to make sure the aggregate monthly debt service (meaning the total of all payments due) does not exceed 36% of monthly income. As seen in the following example, if the borrower has a high number of consumer loans that drive the DTI over 36%, the mortgage amount must be lowered. With a 36% DTI, the lender knows that the borrower has 64% of gross monthly income remaining to cover normal costs of living and the occasional expensive auto repair.

▸ **Example**: $5,000 (gross income) x .36 (36%) = $1,800 (max. for all monthly payments)

Max. aggregate monthly debt allowed $1,800

Chapter 17: Financing Options

```
            -   Student loan payment/month      -   $  300
            -   Auto loan payment/month         -   $  400
                Max. remaining for mortgage payment   $1,100
```

(Note how the $1,400 number under the 28% formula reduces to $1,100 under the 36% formula after factoring in the other monthly payments.)

    iii) **Changes to DTI threshold**: Since the subprime crisis, lenders have been willing to adjust the 36% DTI upward to make it easier for borrowers to qualify for mortgage loans without losing protection. This upper limit was increased to 43% for Qualified Mortgages under the Dodd-Frank Wall Street Reform and Consumer Protection Act (which is summarized at the end of this chapter). Higher debt-to-income ratios–roughly in the 43% to 50% range–are possible for loans that are eligible to be purchased, insured, or guaranteed by agencies such as the FHA, the VA, Fannie Mae, or Freddie Mac (discussed later in this chapter).

(b) **Employment history**: The lender may also require the borrower to demonstrate at least two years of steady employment.

(c) ▶ **Changes to DTI prior to closing**: If a borrower incurs additional installment debt after completing the mortgage application, but prior to closing, it must be disclosed to the lender. Depending on the length of time between the mortgage application and the closing, the lender may order a "credit refresh report" to ascertain if this has occurred. This report is designed to uncover any new debt that may negatively impact the borrower's ability to qualify for the loan.

At the closing, the borrower signs a revised mortgage application in which the current balance of all outstanding liabilities (i.e., debts) is formally acknowledged. If, for example, the borrower purchased a new car on an installment basis the day before the closing, it would have to be disclosed to the lender. Failure to do so could constitute a mortgage fraud.

(2) **Assess the applicant's desire to comply**: Although a borrower might have the financial capability to repay a monthly mortgage debt, his credit report may indicate a slow-payment history on prior mortgages. An applicant who has not treated his past mortgage loans as important financial obligations to be paid in a timely fashion is not likely to do so in the present. Slow and late payments are reflected in a lower credit score as well.

(3) **Assess the property**: The underwriter examines the appraiser's report and makes an independent judgement as to the value of the property which is proposed to be used as collateral for the loan.

(4) **Issue a conditional approval**: Assuming that underwriting guidelines conform, the loan application is given a conditional approval. This is subject to actual receipt of all verifications, title assurances, inspection reports, insurance policies, etc. Some lenders or loan officers refer to buyers as pre-qualified or pre-approved. At one time, these terms carried some meaning, but currently they do not carry the same weight.

(a) **Pre-qualified buyer:** When a buyer is said to be pre-qualified, the lender has issued an opinion that the buyer can meet the loan qualification requirements based upon "unverified" information supplied by the buyer. The loan must still go through the full underwriting process for confirmation.

(b) **Pre-approved buyer:** When a buyer is said to be pre-approved, it technically means the lender has verified the information on the loan application and issued a loan commitment. Even in such cases, it is really conditional since most lenders reserve the right to deny the loan if any negative changes occur with the buyer's information or the property prior to the closing.

(5) **Underwriting overlays**: Individual lenders frequently use underwriting overlays when deciding whether or not to approve loan applications. An overlay is a set of lending criteria that is stricter than the guidelines used by the government agency or government sponsored enterprise that will eventually insure, guarantee, or purchase the loan from the lender. For example, FHA, VA, Fannie Mae, and Ginnie Mae have minimum underwriting guidelines that lenders must follow so the loan will conform to their respective guidelines. The lender that originates the loan may add its own guidelines, meaning apply its own overlay, if it does not feel these minimum standards are high enough.

d. **Loan closing/settlement**: The closing is the last step in the mortgage process. It typically consists of a scheduled meeting at which the buyer-mortgagor receives the loan funds to give to the seller in exchange for title to the purchase property. Closings often take place at the lender's site. Other locations include title insurance companies and real estate company offices. See Chapter 9 for further information on settlement procedures.

e. **Loan servicing**: The process of loan servicing involves: (1) collecting the mortgage payments; (2) maintaining property tax and insurance escrows; (3) payment of property taxes to the local government and hazard insurance premiums to the insurance carrier when due; (4) recordkeeping; and (5) handling delinquent accounts. When a loan is originated and then sold to an investor in the secondary mortgage market, the originating lender may be asked to continue its servicing and payment collection functions for a fee. Servicing fees may be a fraction of a percent of the unpaid mortgage balance which is paid on a monthly basis by the investor to the servicer.

3. **Review of typical mortgage timeline**: The functions listed below are fulfilled when a mortgage loan is obtained to purchase a residential property. They are listed in the approximate order they arise in practice. This timeline is oriented from the buyer/borrower's perspective.
   a. Pre-approval is obtained by the buyer (who works with a licensed loan officer).
   b. Loan application is taken and submitted (by the loan officer).
   c. Loan Estimate is delivered to the buyer (with the good faith estimates of loan costs).
   d. File goes to loan processing (to gather and verify all information for the underwriter).
   e. File goes to loan underwriting (for loan approval–with or without conditions–or denial).
   g. Final approval/Clear to close is issued (all requirements and/or conditions have been fulfilled).
   h. Closing Disclosure is delivered to the buyer (with an accurate accounting of all closing costs).
   i. Closing documents are sent to the title company.
   j. Three-day TRID waiting period runs (before the buyer can sign the loan documents).
   k. Closing is conducted (at which the purchaser signs all loan documents).
   l. Loan funds (meaning the lender releases the mortgage money to the title company).
   m. Loan documents are recorded.

C. ▶ **Secondary mortgage market**: The secondary mortgage market is a financial market comprising institutional and individual investors who purchase mortgage loans after they have been funded, meaning originated, by a lender in the primary market. Participants in the secondary mortgage market do not originate loans.

1. **Purpose and function**: When a primary lender gives a loan, that money is tied up until the loan is repaid. If the primary participant can sell the loan to a secondary market participant, the money is immediately replenished and a new loan can be originated. This keeps money flowing in the financial system.

   a. **Mortgage securitization**: As secondary participants, Fannie Mae and Freddie Mac purchase existing mortgages and hold them in their own portfolios. The purchased loans can also be packaged into what are known as mortgage-backed securities, or MBS for short, that are then sold to other investors. This is accomplished by pooling similar types of mortgages into groups (for example, fixed rate mortgage pools or adjustable rate mortgage pools). An investor receives a certificate representing his pro rata share of the principal and interest collected on the mortgages in the pool.

   b. **MBS difference from other investments**: Mortgage-backed securities are similar to other investments, but with one difference–they are protected by a lien on real estate. This is why some investors prefer them. In addition, Fannie and Freddie guarantee the timely payment of principal and interest on these loans which makes the investment more attractive.

2. **Government Sponsored Enterprise (GSE)**: A secondary participant such as Fannie Mae or Freddie Mac is often referred to as a Government Sponsored Enterprise, or GSE for short. A GSE is a privately held corporation created by Congress to enhance the flow of credit in the United States. GSEs also operate in various financial service arenas for the purpose of raising capital. As will be seen, Ginnie Mae is not a GSE because it is a government-owned corporation.

3. **Secondary mortgage market participants**: The secondary mortgage market participants explored in this section include Fannie Mae, Freddie Mac, Ginnie Mae, Rural Housing and Economic Development, and USDA Rural Development.

   a. **Federal National Mortgage Association (FNMA, Fannie Mae)**: The Federal National Mortgage Association, which is known as Fannie Mae, is the largest and most widely known secondary market investor. Since it operates in the secondary market, Fannie Mae does not make direct loans. In other words, Fannie Mae is not a loan originator.

   (1) **Loan limits for conforming loans**: Fannie Mae is regulated by the Federal Housing Finance Agency (FHFA) which sets loan limits that apply to what conventional mortgages can be sold to Fannie Mae. Loans that fall within these limits are called conforming loans. The general loan limit is currently $424,100 for a single-family dwelling located in Michigan (which is subject to change). The FHFA was created in 2008 during the subprime mortgage crisis to stabilize the economy by regulating aspects of the secondary mortgage market. This is accomplished through the agency's oversight of Fannie Mae, Freddie Mac, and the 12 federal home loan banks.

   (2) **Loan types**: Fannie Mae was organized by Congress in 1939 to purchase FHA-insured mortgages. Currently, Fannie Mae purchases a wide range of mortgage products with a wide range of mortgage terms from primary lenders. These loans include both fixed and adjustable rate conforming mortgages.

   b. **Federal Home Loan Mortgage Corporation (FHLMC, Freddie Mac)**: According to Freddie Mac, it was chartered by Congress in 1970 to keep money flowing to mortgage lenders in support of home ownership and rental housing. Like Fannie Mae, Freddie Mac does not originate loans. Freddie Mac, which is a Government Sponsored Enterprise, is regulated by the Federal Housing Finance Agency.

   (1) **Purchases conventional loans**: Freddie Mac primarily deals in the purchase of conventional conforming loans.

   (2) **Standardized forms**: Freddie Mac has a series of standardized forms and guidelines that all primary lenders are required to use if they intend to sell their loans to Freddie Mac.

   c. **Government National Mortgage Association (GNMA, Ginnie Mae)**: The Government National Mortgage Association, which is commonly referred to as Ginnie Mae, is a wholly owned government corporation established in 1968 within the Department of Housing and Urban Development (HUD). Therefore, it is not a Government Sponsored Enterprise.

   (1) **Purpose**: According to Ginnie Mae, it helps make affordable housing a reality for millions of low- and moderate-income households by channeling global capital into the nation's housing markets. It accomplishes this through a guarantee program that allows lenders to obtain a better price for the loans they originate and sell in the secondary mortgage market. While Ginnie Mae is considered to be a participant in the secondary mortgage market, it does not actually purchase mortgage loans.

   (2) **How the guarantee works**: Ginnie Mae provides a U.S. Government guarantee on government-backed loans that are originated by participants in the primary market which are then sold to the secondary market. Loan programs that Ginnie Mae guarantees include FHA, VA, USDA, and PIH (HUD's Office of Public and Indian Housing). Since these loans are guaranteed by Ginnie Mae, they are considered safer for investors. This, in turn, might allow the primary participant to sell the loans for a higher price.

   d. ▶ **Rural Housing and Economic Development (RHED)**: Rural Housing and Economic Development, or RHED, is an agency established within HUD to provide for rural building and housing support at the state and local levels. Competitive mortgage loans are made available to help low-income borrowers in eligible rural areas. Direct loans or guaranteed loans are available. The RHED also makes mortgage loans available for multi-family rental housing for moderate-, low-, and very-low-income families, the elderly, and persons with disabilities.

   e. ▶ **USDA Rural Development loans**: Under the United Stated Department of Agriculture's Rural Development Loan Assistance program, direct or guaranteed loans, grants, technical assistance, research, and educational materials are made available to residents and business owners in eligible rural areas. Under its guaranteed housing program, loans for modest housing can be obtained for up to 30 years. The interest rate on these loans is set by the lender, there is no required down payment, and the lender determines repayment feasibility using acceptable debt-to-income ratios.

VI. **Legislation affecting the financing industry**: The financing industry has always been subject to varying degrees of federal and state government regulation. These laws are primarily designed to prevent fraud, abuse, and predatory practices that have the potential to financially harm the consumers of loan products. The primary laws identified in this section include: Usury laws; Truth-in-Lending Act (Regulation Z); Home Ownership and Equity Protections

Act; Real Estate Settlement Procedures Act (Regulation X); Equal Credit Opportunity Act (Regulation B); and Dodd-Frank Wall Street Reform and Consumer Protection Act.

A. **Consumer Financial Protection Bureau (CFPB)**: The Consumer Protection Financial Bureau was created in 2011 as an independent federal agency to protect consumers by carrying out the various federal laws governing consumer financial transactions. It was created in response to the subprime mortgage crisis. The agency works to make all financial regulations as clear and streamlined as possible so consumers will be able to understand them on their own.

The CFPB was created by the Dodd-Frank Wall Street Reform and Consumer Protection Act of 2010. The rule-making authority that exists under many of the existing laws discussed in this section has been transferred to the CFPB. Many other changes are expected over the next couple of years as the agency assumes its intended role.

B. ▶ **Usury laws**: Usury is the practice of lending money and charging an unusually high or excessive amount of interest. Various laws have been enacted, primarily by state legislatures, that establish the maximum interest rate that borrowers of certain loans can be charged. A financing contract is deemed usurious, meaning illegal, if the interest rate charged by the lender exceeds what is allowed by state law. See Chapter 21 for a discussion of Michigan's usury law.

C. ▶ **Truth in Lending Act (Regulation Z, TILA)**: The Truth in Lending Act (TILA) was passed by Congress as title I of the Consumer Credit Protection Act. TILA was then implemented approximately 1 year later by Regulation Z. Regulation Z was adopted by the Board of Governors of the Federal Reserve System. Whether it is referred to as Regulation Z, Truth in Lending Act or TILA, this important federal law is designed to make sure that every customer who needs consumer credit is given meaningful information with respect to its terms and cost.

1. **Purpose**: The Truth in Lending Act protects consumers against inaccurate and unfair credit billing and credit card practices; provides consumers with rescission rights; provides for rate caps on certain adjustable rate loans secured by a dwelling; imposes limits on certain home equity lines of credit and closed-end home mortgages; and prohibits unfair or deceptive mortgage lending practices.

2. **Application**: Regulation Z applies to an individual or business that offers or extends credit providing: the credit is offered or extended to consumers; the credit is offered or extended on a regular basis; the credit is subject to a finance charge or is payable by a written agreement in more than four installments; and, the credit is primarily for personal, family, or household purposes.

    a. **Credit to which the Act applies**: TILA applies to the following credit transactions:

    (1) Credit that is extended for personal, family, or household uses in amounts of $50,000 or less. (This threshold is adjusted by any annual percentage change in the consumer price index which is also known as the CPI.)

    (2) All transactions secured by real property or a dwelling (regardless of loan amount). A dwelling is any residential structure containing one-to-four units, including condominiums, cooperatives, and mobile homes/manufactured housing that is used as a residence.

    (3) Refinancing transactions (where an existing obligation that was subject to Truth-in-Lending is satisfied and replaced by a new obligation undertaken by the same consumer).

    b. **Credit to which the Act does not apply**: Not all credit transactions fall within the requirements and limits of TILA. Some of these exempt transactions are noted below.

    (1) Credit extended for business, commercial, or agricultural purposes. (However, if a credit card is involved, the issuance of the card and liability for its unauthorized use is covered by TILA.)

    (2) Credit in excess of an annually adjusted threshold (that is not secured by real property or a dwelling).

    (3) Public utility credit, credit extended by a registered broker-dealer in securities or commodities accounts, home fuel budget plans, and student loan programs.

3. **Requirements**: Creditors must disclose to borrowers the true cost of obtaining credit. This information must be given in terms of actual percentages and total dollar amounts rather than attempting to hide costs with misleading statistics. The Act does not establish maximum or minimum interest rates or other charges, only the full disclosure of what the lender elects to charge.

a. **Specific disclosures**: Regulation Z requires disclosure in a timely fashion of costs related to the acquisition of credit; in other words, costs related to borrowing money.

   (1) **Charges included in the definition of finance charge**: A finance charge is a cost that a consumer of credit pays that is imposed by the creditor as a condition to the extension of credit. The following represents some examples of finance charges:

   (a) Interest and service charges.

   (b) Buyer-paid points. (Note that seller-paid points and other charges paid by a non-creditor seller on behalf of a buyer may not qualify as financing charges for purposes of TILA).

   (c) Loan fees, assumption fees, or finder's fees (including fees paid directly to a mortgage broker by a consumer).

   (d) Appraisal, investigation, and credit report fees.

   (e) Premiums for insurance or debt cancellation coverage when it is written in connection with a credit transaction.

   (2) **Charges excluded from the definition of finance charge**: Certain charges or fees do not fall under the definition of a finance charge. Therefore, they do not trigger the disclosure requirements of TILA. Note that some of these costs are related to the purchase of real property rather than the acquisition of credit; in other words, they are costs incidental to the purchase of property whether or not a loan is involved. Although some of the following closing costs are not covered under TILA, they may fall within the good faith estimate requirements of RESPA.

   (a) Application fees charged to all applicants whether or not credit is actually extended.

   (b) Fees charged for late payments, exceeding credit limits, delinquencies, and default.

   (c) Seller-paid points.

   (d) Real estate-related fees (providing the transaction is secured by real property) including fees for title examination, title insurance, and property survey; loan and other document (e.g., deed) preparation fees; notary and credit-report fees; appraisal and inspection fees if performed prior to closing. These fees must be actual fees and reasonable in amount.

   (e) Hazard insurance fees providing the consumer was informed he could obtain the insurance from the company of his choice.

b. **Annual Percentage Rate (APR)**: The true annual percentage rate or APR must be disclosed for nearly all consumer credit transactions including mortgage loans intended to finance the purchase of a dwelling. The APR is more than just the interest rate. It takes into consideration all relevant factors such as the total costs of credit (i.e., the financing charges) including transaction charges and premiums for credit guarantee insurance. A complex formula is used to calculate the APR, but simply stated, it is a measure of the cost of credit expressed as a yearly rate.

c. **Advertising regulations and triggering language**: Truth in Lending regulates qualifying advertisements of specific credit terms. Disclosures must be made in a clear and conspicuous manner. For example, if an advertisement states a rate of finance charge, it must be stated as an "annual percentage rate." Advertisements fall within the Act when specific credit terms are advertised.

All pertinent information must be disclosed if any specific trigger terms such as the following are included: Amount or percentage of any required down payment; Number of payments or period of repayment; Amount of any payment; Amount of any finance charge. Pertinent information also includes the terms of repayment (over the full term of the loan including balloon payment) and the annual percentage rate.

d. **Loan assumptions**: If a loan assumption actually qualifies as a new transaction, a new disclosure must be made to the consumer who assumes the loan. The disclosure figures are based on the loan balance being assumed.

e. **Meaning of the term creditor**: A creditor is one who regularly extends credit. This is further defined as one who offers consumer credit more than 25 times a year or more than five times a year where the transaction involves a dwelling as security.

f. **TILA appraisals for higher-priced mortgage loans**: Creditors must obtain full interior appraisals by a licensed appraiser for non-exempt, higher-priced mortgage loans. A second appraisal is required at the creditor's expense for certain properties held less than 180 days. Exemptions include Qualified Mortgages, reverse mortgages, bridge loans, construction loans, and certain manufactured homes.

g. **Other provisions**: If a consumer pays a fee directly to a loan originator in connection with a mortgage loan, the originator cannot receive an additional fee from anyone else connected to the transaction such as a mortgage broker. TILA also prohibits a loan originator from steering a consumer to a particular lender simply because the lender pays a higher fee. Creditors must also provide applicants with free copies of all appraisals developed in connections with all credit applications.

4. **Three-day right of rescission**: With consumer credit, the borrower has a cooling-off period which is a three-day right to rescind the financing transaction by notifying the lender. This does not apply to (1) first mortgages used to finance the purchase of a residential home, (2) loans to finance construction of a principal residence, or (3) loans to purchase investment properties. The right to rescind does apply if the dwelling is used as collateral for refinancing or obtaining a second mortgage.

5. **Penalties for noncompliance**: A lender can expose itself to significant penalties for not complying with the disclosure requirements of the Act. They include treble (meaning triple) damages for error resolution violations; $100 to $1,000 for individual actions; class action damages totalling $500,000 or more; and reasonable attorney's fees and court costs.

D. **Home Ownership and Equity Protections Act (HOEPA)**: The Home Ownership and Equity Protections Act, or HOEPA for short, was enacted in 1994 as an amendment to TILA. It was passed to address abusive practices that were occurring in refinancing transactions and (closed-end) home equity loans with high interest rates or high fees. A closed-end loan is one in which future advances are not permitted (as contrasted with the open-end line of credit). On high-cost mortgages, HOEPA requires special disclosure requirements, places restrictions on certain loan terms, and imposes consumer protections such as homeownership counseling. In addition to closed-end home equity loans, HOEPA also applies to refinances and home equity lines of credit which are referred to as HELOCs.

E. ▶ **Real Estate Settlement Procedures Act (Regulation X)**: RESPA requires disclosure of settlement costs before a closing occurs on a new first mortgage loan. It is also known as Regulation X. See Chapter 9 for details on this important federal law.

F. ▶ **Equal Credit Opportunity Act (Regulation B)**: The Equal Credit Opportunity Act, which was implemented by Regulation B, was originally enacted in 1974 to require financial institutions and other firms engaged in the extension of credit to make credit equally available to all creditworthy customers without regard to sex or marital status.

The Act was later amended and currently prohibits a creditor from discriminating against a credit applicant on the basis of: Race, Color, Religion, National origin, Sex, Marital status, or Age (providing the applicant has the capacity to contract); the fact that all or part of the applicant's income derives from any public assistance program; or the fact that the applicant has exercised any right under the Consumer Credit Protection Act in good faith.

1. **Notice**: Within 30 days of receipt of a complete application, a creditor must notify the applicant of any action taken on the applicant's request for credit regardless if the action is favorable or adverse.

2. **Adverse action**: If an adverse action is taken based on the application (such as a denial of credit), the consumer must receive written notice including the name and address of the creditor along with the nature of the action that was taken. The creditor must also either provide the applicant with the specific principal reason for the action taken or inform the applicant that he has the right within 60 days to request the reason.

3. **ECOA appraisals for loans secured by a first lien on a dwelling**: Dodd-Frank amendments to the Equal Credit Opportunity Act (ECOA) require creditors to provide applicants free copies of all appraisals written in connection with an application for a loan to be secured by a first mortgage on a dwelling. Notices of this right must also be provided to applicants.

G. **Dodd-Frank Wall Street Reform and Consumer Protection Act**: The Dodd-Frank Act was enacted by Congress in 2010 in response to the conditions that led to massive foreclosures and other severe problems in the financial industry. The Act is designed to prevent another similar financial crisis by curtailing excessive risk-taking and

Chapter 17: Financing Options								299

abusive financial practices. The Dodd-Frank Act is the most comprehensive finance-related legislation passed by Congress in years. It is expected to take several years to fully implement.

Dodd-Frank regulations principally target financial institutions through enforcement of several federal regulations. As previously noted, the Dodd-Frank Act established the Consumer Financial Protection Bureau (CFPB). In 2013, the CFPB issued final rules concerning mortgage markets pursuant to the requirements of Dodd-Frank. Some of the most significant changes affecting real estate lending became effective in January of 2014. These changes are summarized in a CFPB publication titled, "2013 CFPB Dodd-Frank Mortgage Rules Readiness Guide, Version 1.1." Many of the new rules are amendments to existing federal laws.

1. ▶ **Risky loan features–overview**: An important goal of the Dodd-Frank Act is to protect consumers from receiving risky mortgage loans. Such loans are more likely to end up in default due to what are known as toxic features. These include loans with: (1) Interest-only payments; (2) Zero down payment requirements, excluding VA loans; (3) Negative amortization; (4) Payment schedules exceeding 30 years; (5) Excessive upfront fees; and (6) Excessive debt-to-income ratios. The problems associated with these features are discussed throughout this chapter.

2. **What is a qualified mortgage (QM)**: The term qualified mortgage, or QM for short, applies to a residential mortgage in which it is presumed that the lender complied with certain Dodd-Frank requirements. One requirement is that the lender assessed the borrower's ability to repay the debt. The designation of QM is important to a lender because the law affords the lender some protection if a lawsuit is filed over the terms of the loan. This "safe harbor" protection is covered later in this discussion. There are three main categories of loans that fall under the definition of a Qualified Mortgage.

    a. **General category**: Any loan that meets certain product feature requirements and has a debt-to-income ratio of 43% or less is a QM. These mandatory features are discussed later in this section.

    b. **GSE-eligible category**: A loan that meets the product feature requirements and is eligible for purchase, guarantee, or insurance by a GSE, FHA, VA, or USDA is a QM regardless of debt-to-income ratio.

    c. **Small creditor category**: Loans made and held in portfolio by lenders who have less than $2 billion in assets and originate 500 or fewer first mortgages per year are QMs, as long as the lender has considered and verified the borrower's debt-to-income ratio. No specific debt-to-income ratio limit applies to this limited category.

3. **Ability-to-Repay and Qualified Mortgage Standards**: Regulation Z (that implements TILA) was amended by Dodd-Frank to prohibit a creditor such as a mortgage lender from making a residential mortgage loan without regard to the consumer's ability to repay it. Recall that thousands of subprime loans were given to individuals who later discovered they could not afford to repay them. To qualify as a QM, lenders are required to make a reasonable, good faith determination of a consumer's ability to repay the mortgage loan that is secured by a dwelling. They are also required to retain evidence of compliance for three years after a QM is consummated.

    a. **Ability to pay criteria**: Creditors must consider underwriting factors such as: current or expected income or assets; current employment status; monthly payment on the covered transaction or any simultaneous loan; monthly payment for mortgage-related obligations; current debt obligations, alimony, and child support; monthly debt-to-income ratio; and credit history.

    b. **Product features of a Qualified Mortgage**: A QM must have the following product features:

    (1) **Fee threshold**: Points and fees are less than or equal to 3% of the loan amount. Higher thresholds are allowed for loan amounts that are less than $100,000.

    (2) **No risky features such as balloon payments**: A Qualified Mortgage cannot contain risky features such as negative amortization, interest-only payments, or balloon payments.

    (a) **Small creditor exemption**: Balloon payments are allowed for loans originated until January 10, 2016 if other features of a Qualified Mortgage are met and the loan is held in a portfolio by a small creditor (meaning more than 50% of its mortgages were made in rural or underserved areas).

    (b) **Land contract exemption**: A balloon payment is also allowed under a "seller financing, one property exclusion." Under this limited exclusion, a balloon payment is permitted in a land contract. To qualify the seller: must be a person; must own the home; can only provide financing one time in any 12-month period; and cannot be a builder who constructed the home.

Further: the land contract cannot result in negative amortization; and if it contains an adjustable interest rate, it must have reasonable annual and lifetime limits on rate increases.

(3) **DTI threshold**: The debt-to-income ratio (DTI) cannot exceed 43% and the loan term must be 30 years or less.

c. **Non-Qualified Mortgage can still be valid**: The fact that a mortgage on a residential property is not considered to be a Qualified Mortgage does not mean it is necessarily illegal or voidable. To be an appropriate loan, the lender must still have made a reasonable, good-faith determination that the consumer has the ability to repay the loan based on customary underwriting criteria. The only risk is that a non-QM loan does not qualify for "safe harbor" protection under the law.

d. **Lender "safe harbor"**: If a lender makes a mortgage loan that is not a Qualified Mortgage, the consumer may seek to have the contract invalidated in a court if the loan is determined to be predatory or otherwise unfair to the consumer. If the loan meets the requirements of a Qualified Mortgage, the "safe harbor" provision protects the lender against such a legal action.

4. **Escrow requirements under TILA**: Regulation Z (TILA) originally required lenders to establish escrow accounts for one year on higher-priced mortgage loans secured by a first lien on a principal dwelling. Dodd-Frank extends this time to five years and creates a new exemption from the escrow requirement for small creditors (that make the majority of their loans in rural or underserved areas).

a. **Higher-priced mortgage loan defined**: As the term is used in Dodd-Frank, a higher-priced mortgage loan is one in which the annual percentage rate (APR) is 1.5% or more higher than the Average Prime Offer Rate (APOR). The APOR is an annual percentage rate that is based on average interest rates, fees, and other terms on mortgages offered to highly qualified borrowers.

5. **High-cost mortgage and homeownership counseling**: Dodd-Frank amends TILA and RESPA by requiring that consumers receive information about homeownership counseling providers.

6. **Mortgage servicing rules**: Dodd-Frank amended RESPA to require mortgage servicers to correct errors asserted by borrowers, to provide certain information that is requested by borrowers, and to protect borrowers in connection with force-placed insurance. With regard to delinquent borrowers, servicers must provide information about mortgage loss mitigation options, make sure that servicing personnel maintain continuity of contact with the borrower, and evaluate borrowers' applications for available loss mitigation options (such as a short sale or a deed in lieu).

TILA was further amended to address initial rate adjustment notices for adjustable rate mortgages, periodic statements for residential mortgage loans, prompt crediting of mortgage payments, and responses for requests for payoff amounts.

VII. ▶ **Mortgage fraud**: Mortgage fraud reached epidemic proportions in the 2000s. Individuals who participated in fraudulent behaviors included mortgage brokers, loan officers, appraisers, title insurance companies, buyers and sellers, investors, and real estate licensees. While mortgage fraud was rampant during this time, it is important to remember that the majority of real estate and real estate-related licensees, professionals, and service providers performed their jobs honesty, ethically, and with integrity. Unfortunately, it only takes a relatively small percentage of dishonest participants to cause significant harm to the marketplace.

A. **Mortgage fraud defined**: A mortgage fraud is the intentional misrepresentation of a material fact that is relied on by a lender to fund a loan. Any information that is required by a lender to enable the lender to decide whether or not to approve a mortgage loan is deemed to be material. A mortgage fraud might consist of incorrect or misleading information provided on a loan application. It could also consist of a deliberate omission of required information.

The key to a mortgage fraud is the intent to mislead a lender into providing a loan that would otherwise not have been extended had the true facts been known. Sometimes, multiple parties to a mortgage fraud conspire to obtain a loan for an unqualified buyer. Other times it might involve obtaining excessive loan proceeds for profit by providing false information to the lender. This can occur when a lender is tricked into extending a larger loan, often based on an illegally inflated appraisal report.

1. **Various schemes have been used**: To avoid becoming an unintended accomplice, real estate licensees should have a basic awareness of the different mortgage fraud schemes that have been perpetrated. An accomplice is one who joins with a primary offender in the commission of a crime, and thereby becomes

an offender himself. Notice in each of the following examples how the fraud induces the lender to fund a significantly higher risk loan.

  a. **The disappearing second mortgage**: In this fraudulent scheme, the buyer appears to borrow the money he needs for a down payment from the seller using a second mortgage. Without the lender's knowledge, the second mortgage is destroyed after the closing. With help from an accomplice loan officer, the second mortgage is not disclosed on the HUD-1. The buyer and seller inflate the purchase price with help from an accomplice appraiser. The buyer winds up receiving 100% financing as a result. This is a mortgage fraud because the lender unknowingly approves a loan for an inflated price and no equity in the property.

  b. **The silent second mortgage**: This fraudulent scheme is similar to the disappearing second mortgage. The buyer lacks the required down payment and borrows it from the seller using a second mortgage which is not disclosed to the lender. The second mortgage remains in existence, but is not recorded to avoid detection by the lender. The fraud occurs because the lender believes the borrower has personally funded the down payment.

  c. **The occupancy fraud**: To obtain a favorable interest rate and lower closing costs that are normally reserved for loans issued on owner-occupied residences, an investor-buyer falsely indicates that he intends to occupy the purchase property. After the closing, the property is "quietly" rented to a tenant or flipped for a quick profit. The fraud arises when the applicant intentionally deceives the lender about the occupancy.

  d. **Short sale fraud–Example 1**: A borrower-mortgagor requests a short sale approval from a lender based on a stated hardship. The lender approves the short sale and a full waiver of the deficiency due to the stated financial position. Unfortunately for the lender, the homeowner intentionally failed to disclose certain assets he owned to create the appearance of a more serious hardship. The fraud arises when the borrower-mortgagor withholds key information about his financial condition to induce the lender to approve a short sale and deficiency waiver that it might not have otherwise approved.

  e. **Short sale fraud–Example 2**: A homeowner-mortgagor sells his home on a short sale to a close relative without disclosing the personal nature of their relationship. The lender would not have approved the short sale because it was not an arms-length transaction. After conveying title to the relative and obtaining a release of the full deficiency from the lender, the mortgagor has his relative deed the property back. The relative never intended to own the property. Both the mortgagor and his relative are guilty of mortgage fraud for failing to disclose material information to the lender.

2. **Violations under state law**: Under Michigan law, a person who knowingly and with intent to defraud does any of the following is guilty of the crime of residential mortgage fraud:

  a. Makes a false statement or misrepresentation concerning a material fact, or deliberately conceals or fails to disclose a material fact during the mortgage lending process.

  b. Uses a false statement or misrepresentation made by another person concerning a material fact during the mortgage lending process.

  c. Receives or attempts to receive proceeds in connection with the mortgage lending process that the person knows resulted from a false statement or misrepresentation.

  d. Files with the register of deeds any document involved in the mortgage lending process that the person knows is a misrepresentation.

  e. Fails to disburse funds in accordance with the closing statement for the mortgage loan.

  f. Solicits, encourages, or coerces another person to commit a mortgage fraud.

3. ▶ **Cautions to clients regarding the financing process**: When a real estate licensee is working with a buyer who is seeking financing, the licensee should emphasize how important it is for the buyer to provide accurate and complete information throughout the process. This pertains to all applications, forms, verifications, and disclosures that the buyer will provide. Failure to do so could result in a denial of the loan application or, more seriously, a legal action being brought for mortgage fraud.

4. **What to do if confronted with a potential mortgage fraud**: A real estate licensee who suspects a possible mortgage fraud should follow a prudent course of action.

  a. Immediately alert the broker of any suspected problem.

- b. Document all aspects of the transaction and provide a copy to the broker.
- c. Do not proceed with the transaction until instructed to do so by the broker.
- d. Inform the client or customer of the potential problem and suggest that legal counsel be sought (a salesperson should obtain his broker's approval before doing so).
- e. A broker should consult with legal counsel for advice on how to proceed (which might include reporting the transaction to the proper authorities for investigation).

B. **Penalties for mortgage fraud**.
1. **Federal law**: The controlling federal statute creates a fine of one million dollars or imprisonment for a maximum of 30 years, or both.
2. **State law**: Fines under state law include a treble damage provision of three times the value of the property involved in the fraud. A violation is a felony punishable by imprisonment from 15 to 20 years and a fine ranging from $100,000 to $500,000. Additional punishment for real estate licensees may include those listed in real estate license law including revocation of a real estate license and a $10,000 civil fine for each violation.

*A challenge is life's tool for reminding us just how powerful we truly are.
Use the opportunity to prove this to yourself.*

Chapter 17: Financing Options

DIAGNOSTIC PRACTICE QUESTIONS – CHAPTER 17

IMPORTANT STUDY TIP!

Step 1: Carefully review the information located in this chapter.

Step 2: Take the following Diagnostic Practice Questions. Review any question you answered incorrectly by researching the topic in this textbook. If you are still uncertain as to why the question is answered as it is, consult your program provider.

NOTE ON CHAPTER PRACTICE QUESTIONS

The following questions are representative of the type encountered on the Michigan real estate licensing examination. While some of these questions may be similar in nature and style, there is no way of predicting the exact wording of a question that will appear on the exam. Spending time memorizing these questions is, therefore, not recommended.

These questions are designed to help you determine how well you comprehend the material in this chapter. They are also intended to help you develop problem solving skills and to become comfortable with question formats.

Do not attempt to answer these questions until you have attended the lecture corresponding to this chapter and spent the appropriate time studying the material.

1. The seller of a property is approached by a buyer who has questionable credit. In the past, the buyer has been turned down for loans based upon a poor payment history. Knowing that this will probably still be a problem for him, the buyer asks if the seller would be willing to finance the sale for him. Which of the following mortgage types could be used to finance this transaction?
   A. A purchase money mortgage.
   B. A conventional mortgage.
   C. A reverse mortgage.
   D. A graduated payment mortgage.

2. A purchaser needs to borrow $160,000 to purchase a $200,000 house. To keep the payments at an affordable level, the purchaser needs to amortize the payments over 30 years. Purchaser's lender is only willing to give the purchaser a 15 year loan. To keep the payments low over the 15 year term, the loan can be structured as a:
   A. term loan.
   B. fully amortized mortgage.
   C. growing equity mortgage.
   D. partially amortized mortgage.

3. The interest rate on a conventional loan is currently 7¼%. At that rate, the payments on the loan would be higher than the borrower wishes to pay. The lender is willing to reduce the rate to 6¼% providing the borrower pays 2 points at closing. The interest reduction is called a(n):
   A. aggregate cap.
   B. permanent buydown.
   C. adjustable rate.
   D. certificate of reduction.

4. Which of the following loans would most likely be used by a seller to buy a new home while awaiting the sale of her existing home?
   A. A sale and leaseback.
   B. A package mortgage.
   C. A bridge loan.
   D. A home equity line of credit.

5. All of the following are examples of information a borrower may be asked to supply a loan officer when applying for a mortgage loan EXCEPT:
   A. Current bank account balances and statements.
   B. Tax returns.
   C. Financial statements in the case of applicants who are self-employed.
   D. Social security entitlement statements.

6. A mortgage fraud is least likely to have occurred in which of the following circumstances?
   A. An appraisal comes in for a mortgage loan and is slightly higher than the average market values for the neighborhood.
   B. A loan officer requests that the purchaser execute two sets of documents, one of which is left blank.
   C. A closing agent recommends that the actual price paid for the property be omitted from the HUD-1 statement on a federally-related mortgage loan.
   D. A real estate agent's pre-qualification form indi-

cates that the purchaser cannot afford the property for which a mortgage loan was approved.

7. Which of the following loan types is MGIC most likely to insure?
   A. An FHA loan.
   B. A Veteran's Administration loan.
   C. A loan purchased by the FNMA.
   D. A conventional loan.

8. Which of the following terms do lenders use to describe the relative amount of money they will lend?
   A. Debt to equity ratio.
   B. Times interest earned.
   C. Loan to value ratio.
   D. Gross income multiplier.

9. Usury laws control which of the following?
   A. Maximum interest rates.
   B. Minimum interest rates.
   C. Length of time for loan repayment.
   D. Loan to value ratio.

10. Priorities of mortgages can be changed by a(n):
    A. Estoppel certificate.
    B. Release of mortgage.
    C. Subordination agreement.
    D. Collateral bond.

11. When personal property is used as a pledge for a mortgage, the kind of mortgage is called:
    A. An equitable mortgage.
    B. A conventional mortgage.
    C. A chattel mortgage.
    D. A package mortgage.

12. When a mortgage loan requires periodic payments which will not fully amortize the amount of the loan by the final payment date, the final payment is referred to as a(n):
    A. Release payment.
    B. Section payment.
    C. Balloon payment.
    D. Acceleration payment.

13. A mortgage that covers a number of parcels of real property and provides for the release of individual parcels as payments are made on the loan is called a(n):
    A. Blanket mortgage.
    B. Open-end mortgage.
    C. Limited reduction mortgage.
    D. Partially amortized mortgage.

14. All of the following statements are true regarding a Federal Housing Administration loan EXCEPT:
    A. The lender may charge a loan origination fee in addition to discount points.
    B. All FHA loans have a prepayment privilege.
    C. The monthly payment may include a contribution to a property tax escrow.
    D. An FHA loan cannot be assumed.

15. When a buyer makes an advance payment at the time of closing in exchange for a reduction in the interest rate during the first three years of the loan, it is called:
    A. A growing equity mortgage.
    B. A temporary buydown.
    C. A reverse annuity loan.
    D. A renegotiable rate period.

16. In conjunction with a VA loan, all of the following statements are true EXCEPT:
    A. A certificate of eligibility is required.
    B. A non-veteran may assume the loan and then rent the property to a tenant.
    C. A certificate of reasonable value is required.
    D. The loans are insured by the Veteran's Administration.

17. Which of the following lending sources is not a participant in the secondary mortgage market?
    A. The Federal National Mortgage Association.
    B. The Federal Savings and Loan Association.
    C. Government National Mortgage Association.
    D. The Federal Home Loan Mortgage Corporation.

18. As specified by the federal Truth-in-Lending Act, all the following are components of the annual percentage rate of a finance charge EXCEPT:
    A. Loan fees.
    B. Service charges.
    C. Points.
    D. Attorney's fee.

19. In a real estate advertisement that includes information on mortgage financing, which of the following is legally permissible, without further information being given?
    A. "Liberal terms available to qualified buyer."
    B. "Two thousand dollars down."
    C. "Monthly payment four hundred dollars."
    D. "Interest rate only 9%."

20. The federal Truth-in-Lending Act covers:
    A. Full disclosure of seller-paid points.
    B. Annual percentage rate and finance charges.
    C. All costs which are related to the purchase of a residential dwelling.
    D. Credit which is extended for a business loan.

21. The money for making Federal Housing Administration loans is provided by:
    A. Qualified lending institutions.

Chapter 17: Financing Options 305

B. Any government agency.
C. The Federal Housing Administration.
D. The Federal Deposit Insurance Corporation.

22. In a sale and leaseback transaction, all of the following are true EXCEPT:
    A. The grantor in the transaction immediately becomes the lessee.
    B. The transaction can provide potential tax advantages for either party.
    C. The transaction makes working capital available for the purchaser.
    D. The leasehold is typically structured in the form of a net lease.

23. An owner's agreement to personally finance the sale of a house for a buyer, wherein the buyer will receive title is known as a:
    A. Conventional loan.
    B. Land contact.
    C. Secured transaction.
    D. Purchase money mortgage.

24. All EXCEPT which of the following applies to a savings and loan association?
    A. It is local in nature.
    B. It engages in flexible lending practices.
    C. It is a source of long-term mortgage loans.
    D. It is the largest lender of real estate loans.

25. A method of obtaining additional financing on a property already encumbered by a mortgage is best known as a(n):
    A. A wraparound mortgage.
    B. A package mortgage.
    C. A reverse annuity mortgage.
    D. A participation mortgage.

26. A lending institution requires a down payment in conjunction with a conventional mortgage. All of the following statements regarding the down payment are true EXCEPT:
    A. It is an equity cushion.
    B. It typically is 20 percent of the loan amount.
    C. It protects the lender against a deficiency judgment.
    D. The amount can vary depending on the creditworthiness of the borrower.

A good teacher tells his students what to think. A great teacher shows her students how to think. Decide what kind of teacher you want to be.

Chapter 18
Fair Housing

The guarantee of equal access to housing opportunities.

I. **Foreword**: There are numerous laws, rules, ordinances, and ethical requirements that affect real estate. While they are all vital, those that further principles of fair housing rank at or near the top of the importance scale. Fair housing laws have been established at the federal, state, and local levels of government to guarantee citizens the equal right to housing opportunities regardless of their physical or cultural characteristics.

Certain classes or groups of individuals have statistically faced higher levels of unequal treatment compared to other members of the general population. To protect these groups, fair housing laws make this treatment illegal. This is why the groups are referred to as protected classes. While the terms civil rights and fair housing are often used interchangeably, there are technical differences.

A. **Civil rights defined**: The term civil rights refers to a broad category of rights that every citizen of the United States is guaranteed by the U.S. Constitution. These rights are also referred to as civil liberties and include equal protection under the law and freedom from discrimination. Technically, the U.S. Constitution protects the civil liberties of individuals from discrimination by the government or a government entity. The Supreme Court of the United States and many federal and state statutes have extended this protection by making it illegal for an individual to discriminate against another individual.

Example: A local municipality passes a city-wide rental ordinance that prohibits families with more than one child from leasing homes in a subdivision based solely on complaints from retired citizens who live there. If challenged in court, this ordinance is likely to be struck down as unconstitutional because it targets a protected class, i.e., families with children, and treats them less favorably than individuals and couples who do not have children or only have one child. (Note: As we will see, there are federal and state exemptions for senior citizen housing. However, this example does not qualify since it involves a discriminatory municipal ordinance.)

B. ▶ **Fair housing defined**: Fair housing assures individuals who fall within a legally-protected class that they will have fair and equal opportunities to lease or own housing. Think of it as the branch of civil rights laws that applies specifically to housing opportunities. Fair housing laws protect all real property interests including residential housing, vacant land on which residences will be constructed, financing opportunities, and real estate services. Even though the word "housing" is used in the term fair housing, protection is also afforded to buyers and tenants of commercial real estate.

Example: A large group of homeowners whose families have immigrated from the same country live in close proximity to one another. The homeowners all agree that if any one of them sells, it will only be to a person of the same nationality. The goal is to maintain the cultural appeal and harmony of the neighborhood. This agreement is discriminatory and cannot be honored without violating fair housing laws.

C. **Licensee's role**: Real estate licensees are expected to demonstrate a strong and unwavering commitment to fair housing principles and objectives. To this end, licensees must thoroughly understand all aspects of fair housing law. Licensees who are members of the National Association of REALTORS® are also bound to a strong Code of Ethics that contains important fair housing requirements.

A real estate licensee is expected to understand that no justification ever exists for a departure from fair housing principles and objectives. There is no excuse important enough, no rationalization logical enough, no explanation detailed enough, no apology sincere enough, or financial need large enough that can possibly supersede the protections afforded a customer or client under fair housing law.

II. ▶ **Protected classes**: A protected class is a defined group that the law seeks to protect. Fair housing violations have historically been based on the differences that humans notice or perceive in other humans. One group of humans treats another group differently, usually with disfavor, based on these differences.

In the evolution of fair housing laws, Congress was the first body to create classes and extend protection under federal law. State legislatures followed suit by passing statutes that created their own protected classes and levels of protection. Finally, a growing number of local municipalities have passed fair housing ordinances to protect housing opportunities within the community.

The list of federally-protected classes sets the floor or minimum protection that is afforded all citizens regardless of their state residency. A state legislature may increase fair housing protection by adding new classes, but it cannot diminish any protection that is provided under federal law. As an illustration, the Michigan Legislature added marital status and age to the list of state-protected classes (neither of which is protected under federal law). Michigan could not, however, elect to leave familial status out of state law since it is protected under federal law. The same is true for local fair housing ordinances. For example, sexual orientation could be added by the municipality, but no class protected under federal or state law can be omitted.

A. ▶ **Protected classes under federal law**: Federal law prohibits discrimination based on race, color, religion, national origin, sex, familial status, and handicap. For purposes of state law, the term "disability" has replaced "handicap" and "person with a disability" has replaced "handicapper." As discussed later, poverty is not a protected class and neither is occupation. *See Figure 34.*

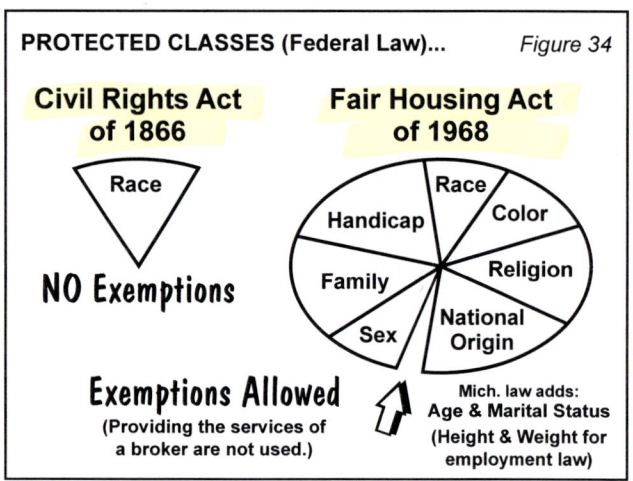

1. **Race**: A race is a group of persons who are related by common descent or heredity. It may also be viewed as a large body of persons who are customarily thought of as a unit because of common characteristics. The U.S. Supreme Court has extended the term race to all identifiable classes of persons, whether or not they can be scientifically classified as such. As discussed later in the chapter, racial discrimination is always prohibited despite exemptions that some federal or state laws may attempt to create.

2. **Color**: As a protected class, color involves the natural appearance or complexion of the skin of a particular people or race. Race and color are often confused because a race may share certain physical characteristics including skin color. Nevertheless, color is a characteristic that goes beyond race because there can be a variety of skin complexions within the same race. For example, a landlord cannot refuse to lease a property on the basis of the color of a prospective tenant's skin.

3. **Religion**: As a protected class, religion involves the belief or expression of a belief in a divine power which is worshiped by members of the religion. The term religion also includes a set of beliefs and practices concerning the nature and purpose of the universe. Since a religion is a specific system of beliefs, it is also thought to include atheism or the denial of the existence of a divine power. For example, the owner of an apartment building cannot refuse to rent to a prospective tenant on the basis of the prospective tenant's religion, the fact that the prospective tenant holds no religious beliefs, or that the prospective tenant's beliefs are different from the landlord's.

4. **National origin**: National origin refers to the country in which a person was born or the nation of one's ancestors. National origin discrimination arises when a party treats another differently or unequally on the basis of the person being from a particular country or part of the world. This also includes discrimination based on accent, ethnicity, appearance of ethnicity, or being married to or otherwise associated with a person on the basis of these qualities or characteristics.

5. **Sex**: Discrimination based on sex historically included gender-based discrimination and sexual harassment. It did not include discrimination based on sexual orientation or gender identity.

   a. **Federal protection for sexual orientation and gender identity**: In a groundbreaking 2020 decision based on federal employment law, the U.S. Supreme Court ruled that discrimination on the basis of

Chapter 18: Fair Housing 309

sexual orientation or gender identity is also discrimination based on sex. The protected class of sex has been part of the Fair Housing Act since 1974. This decision laid the foundation for even more important actions to follow.

In January, 2021, a Presidential Executive Order was issued to prevent and combat discrimination based on sexual orientation and gender identity at the federal level. As a direct result, in February of 2021, the U.S. Department of Housing and Urban Development (HUD) began administering and enforcing the Fair Housing Act to prohibit such discrimination (again, at the federal level).

  b. **Sexual harassment**: Sexual harassment involves unwelcome sexual advances, requests for sexual favors, or other verbal or physical conduct of a sexual nature where submission is a condition to obtaining employment, public accommodations, services, education, or housing. Sexual harassment also involves the creation of an intimidating, hostile, or offensive environment, or a substantial interference with an individual's employment, public accommodations, services, education, or housing. Sexual harassment constitutes discrimination and is illegal.

6. **Familial status**: The term familial status means of, or involving, a family. This classification of fair housing law protects adult families with children under the age of 18 years, providing they reside with a parent or an adult who has custody. Protection is also extended to families with children who reside with a designee under the written permission of the parent or custodial adult. Adults seeking permanent custody of a child and individuals who are pregnant are also protected. As a result, a person may not refuse to lease a property to a couple based on the fact that they have children living with them (unless the property qualifies for an exemption).

   a. ▶ **Adult only housing**: It is a violation of federal law to advertise a residential rental facility as "Adult Only." However, to accommodate the need and desire for senior citizen housing complexes, specific (and slightly differing) exemptions have been created under federal and state law. These are explored later in this chapter.

7. **Handicap (Disability)**: While federal fair housing law uses the term handicap, it is referred to as disability in this discussion. The term disability is also used in the Americans with Disabilities Act. An individual is considered to have a disability if he (1) has a physical or mental impairment that substantially limits one or more major life activities, (2) has a history or record of such impairment, or (3) is regarded as having such an impairment.

   a. **Meaning of impairment**: An impairment can result from a disease, injury, or functional disorder that is unrelated to an individual's ability to acquire, lease, or maintain property. For example, an individual who has difficulty reading due to a medically-recognized disorder such as macular degeneration has an impairment under the law and is entitled to protection. A person who has difficulty reading due to dropping out of school is not considered to have an impairment. Impairments are determined without regard to medication or adaptive devices used to reduce the impact of the impairment. So, a person who can walk without difficulty using an artificial limb is still afforded protection.

      (1) **Physical impairment**: A physical impairment under the law is any physiological disorder or condition, cosmetic disfigurement, or anatomical loss affecting one or more bodily systems. For example, a person with a communicable disease such as HIV/AIDS is considered to have a qualifying disability and is afforded protection.

      (2) **Mental impairment**: A mental impairment includes most mental or psychological disorders, an organic brain syndrome, emotional or mental illness, or specific learning disability. Organic brain syndrome is a general term used to describe decreased mental or cognitive function due to a medical disease.

      (3) **Not considered disabilities**: The term disability does not include physical characteristics such as eye color and left- or right-handedness. It also excludes a physical condition not resulting from a physiological disorder such as pregnancy. Personality traits and environmental, cultural, and economic disadvantages are not disabilities. Lack of education, having a prison record, or being a legal minor does not qualify. Likewise, an individual with a minor, non-chronic condition of short duration such as a sprain, broken arm, or the flu is generally not considered to have a disability.

      (4) **Meaning of "substantially limits"**: An individual is considered to be substantially limited if his disability renders him unable, or substantially limited in his ability, to perform an activity as

compared to an average individual of the general population. For example, blindness is a substantially limiting condition.

(5) **Meaning of "major life activities"**: Major life activities are those that an average individual can perform with little or no difficulty such as walking, speaking, breathing, seeing, hearing, learning, sitting, standing, lifting, reading, working, caring for oneself, and performing manual tasks.

b. **History of an impairment**: An individual is protected if he has a history of a disability or if he has been misdiagnosed as having a disability. For example, an individual with an illness that is either cured, controlled, or in remission, or an individual who has been mistakenly classified as having a learning disability, is considered to have a history of an impairment and is protected.

c. **Being regarded as having an impairment**: A person who does not have an impairment, but is treated as having one is entitled to protection.

Example 1: The owner of a small restaurant terminates the employment of a server because of a rumor being circulated by some of the customers that the server has HIV/AIDS. Under federal law, the server is a victim of discrimination even though subsequent testing revealed the server did not have the disease. That fact that the owner treated the server as having the disease was sufficient.

Example 2: A highly experienced and qualified technician at a popular health and beauty spa is the best qualified person for a pending opening in management. The technician does not receive the promotion because the owner believes the technician's prominent facial scar will disturb customers. The technician is likely a victim of discrimination.

B. ▶ **Protected classes under Michigan law**: Michigan civil rights and fair housing laws recognize the same classifications that federal law does with a few important differences. Recall that federal law sets the minimum protection that may be afforded an individual. Michigan raises this level of protection by adding the protected classifications of marital status and age.

1. **Sexual orientation and gender identity as protected classifications**: Sexual orientation and gender identity are not currently afforded status as a protected class under Michigan fair housing law. Nevertheless, many municipalities within Michigan have already addressed the issue. This is especially true with counties or cities in which a college or university is located.

    a. **Municipal ordinances may raise the bar**: Real estate licensees must remain vigilant for municipalities with civil rights or fair housing ordinances that prohibit discrimination on the basis of sexual orientation (or other similar classifications). As state law can raise the bar of protection, so too can a local unit of government through its municipal codes.

    (1) **Researching municipal ordinances**: Licensees who practice within any given community may be interested in learning more about local ordinances pertaining to civil rights, fair housing, and nondiscrimination. Many of these local ordinances can be accessed online at <www.municode.com>.

    (2) **Company policy considerations**: Along with the various laws, licensees must also make sure that their efforts conform to company policies and procedures on fair housing. Brokers should consider updating the fair housing section of their policy manuals on a regular basis and to mention the possibility of other protected classifications being added by municipal ordinances.

2. **Additional state classifications under state employment law**: For purposes of employment law, height and weight are included as protected classes under the definition of disability.

C. ▶ **Protected parties to a housing transaction under federal law**: Federal law extends fair housing protection to certain participants in a real estate transaction. These individuals include (1) persons acting as a buyer or lessee, (2) persons residing in, or intending to reside in, a dwelling after it is sold or leased, and (3) persons associated with a buyer or lessee. For example, a landlord threatens to evict a tenant because of the race of a frequent guest of the tenant. The landlord has committed a fair housing violation even though the direct target of the landlord's action was not the tenant.

III. **Prohibited acts**: Illegal discrimination is defined as the unfair treatment or denial of normal privileges to individuals because they belong to a protected class. Mere prejudice is not enough unless combined with some action against the protected person. Acts of discrimination can be shown through proof of intention or by circumstantial evidence. Lack of prejudice, however, does not conclusively establish the absence of discriminatory conduct. Finally, where there is a discriminatory impact as a result of a person's actions, discrimination will have occurred regardless of the person's intent.

Chapter 18: Fair Housing

A. **Blockbusting**: The attempt to induce a person, for profit, to sell or rent by making representations regarding the entry, or prospective entry, of a particular protected class of person or persons into the neighborhood is called blockbusting. It is also referred to as panic peddling and is considered to be as unethical as it is illegal under both federal and state law.

   Example: Broker X discovers that one of his salespersons sold a home in a particular neighborhood to a person who plans on establishing a group home. To boost listings in the area for himself, Broker X contacts surrounding neighbors and informs them of the plans to establish a group home, suggests that property values will be negatively affected, and offers to list and sell their homes before the group home becomes operational. Broker X has engaged in illegal blockbusting.

B. **Steering**: The directing, channeling, or diverting of a person into or away from an area based on his being, or not being, a member of a protected class is called steering. It could involve a real estate licensee who attempts to divert a buyer to an area where other members of the buyer's protected class reside. It could also arise if the licensee redirects a prospective buyer away from a desired area based on race, for example. Even if an agent believes that steering is desired by a buyer, it is still illegal.

   1. **Financial capability is not protected**: The only permissible factors for not showing properties include lack of financial qualification or an instruction from a seller that no showings can take place in his absence. When qualifying buyers, a licensee should always use company-approved forms and procedures. Further, it is important to maintain records of these efforts in the appropriate company file.

      Example 1: A listing seller who is concerned about the security of his personal belongings in the property instructs his listing agent that no showings take place while the seller is on vacation. If a buyer is told the property cannot be shown during this time, no fair housing violation has taken place because the seller excluded all showings rather than selective showings based on a protected classification.

      Example 2: Buyer Y, an African American, asks Broker X to see a home that is located in a predominantly white neighborhood. The buyer has excellent credit and is financially qualified to purchase the property. Broker X believes that Buyer Y would be more comfortable living in a different, but equally attractive neighborhood where other African Americans have purchased homes. Broker X only shows homes to the buyer in the other neighborhood. Broker X is guilty of illegal steering because he failed to show the requested home and then directed the buyer to different home, both solely based on the criteria of race. This holds true even if Broker X honestly believed that Buyer Y would have preferred the other home.

   2. **Handling buyer questions about neighborhoods**: Potential buyers often ask real estate licensees questions about neighborhoods and the people who reside there. For example, questions similar to the following are sometimes posed: "Is this a safe neighborhood?," "Are there any [named protected class] living in the area?," "Are there any playmates in the neighborhood for my children?," "How good are the schools?" Further complicating the issue is that many of these questions are posed by buyers for nondiscriminatory reasons. Licensees should not engage in any conversation or answer any question that involves a protected classification regardless of how benign (meaning not harmful) the question may appear.

      a. **Demographic data**: Municipalities often provide general community-based demographic information on their local websites and/or provide a link to the United States Census Bureau. Interested buyers can find information about total population and the composition of the population in terms of age distribution, race, national origin, gender, highest level of education completed, per capita income, number of households, along with information about local businesses. School information is generally available on the local school district's website. Many legal experts believe that this information should not be directly provided by real estate licensees.

      b. **Licensee's response**: A licensee must exercise great care if a customer or client requests demographic information or census-related data about an area. This is due to the fact that the intent of the person asking the question may not be known by the licensee. As a general rule, no question should be answered if it involves information pertaining to a protected class.

      One possible response for a licensee who is asked for general demographic information is to indicate that answering the question (or providing the information) is a potential violation of federal and state fair housing laws. Other experts suggest that a licensee can tell a customer or client who requests general demographic information to consult the website of the local municipality or school system to see what information may be available. Ultimately, each broker must decide (with help from legal counsel) which response is appropriate. Once this policy is set, all affiliated licensees must follow it without deviation.

C. ▶ **Redlining (and the Community Reinvestment Act)** [*re: Banks/Lenders*]: Redlining involves the refusal to make mortgage loans (or provide insurance coverage) for properties located in a specific area based on alleged deteriorating conditions. It also involves imposing more burdensome terms on loans based on the predominant protected class of the neighborhood's residents. The term is derived from the older practice of outlining the affected area on a map with a red pencil and then refusing to provide services there. Problems occur when financial services are denied based on the neighborhood in which a mortgage applicant's property is located rather than on the applicant's individual creditworthiness. The Community Reinvestment Act was enacted in 1977 to eliminate the practice of redlining thereby establishing an environment in which credit needs in low- and moderate-income neighborhoods can be met.

D. ▶ **Discriminatory advertising**: Advertising that states a preference for, or a limitation relating to, a protected classification is prohibited under all fair housing regulations without exception.

1. ▶ **Fair housing advertising–Equal Housing Opportunity Logo**: The advertising provisions of the federal Fair Housing Act establish guidelines for compliance as they relate to the sale, rental, or financing of residential real estate. Fair housing posters should be prominently displayed in real estate offices and HUD's Equal Housing Opportunity Logo should be incorporated into certain advertisements. Newspapers are also prohibited from publishing discriminatory advertising. An illustration of HUD's Equal Housing Opportunity Logo is located in this section. It may also be informally referred to as the fair housing logo. *See Figure.*

2. ▶ **Examples of discriminatory advertising**: The following statements and phrases can be interpreted as discriminatory, especially if an investigation discloses a pattern or practice of actual discrimination:

   a. A non-exempt apartment complex with a broad mixture of ages residing there wants to attract older, more financially secure renters and runs an ad that states: "Upscale Adult-only Leisure Living." (Note: This complex does not qualify as senior citizen housing.)

   b. A phrase in a display advertisement for a luxury condominium development states: "Isn't it time to move into an uncompromising community with neighbors who are just like you?"

   c. A sign in the window of a duplex being sold by the owner who resides in the other unit states: "Unit for rent. Single, white female only." (Note: As explained later in this chapter, while the owner of the duplex may qualify for an exemption, since the discrimination is based on race, no exemption applies.)

   d. A photograph of a multi-unit housing complex used in connection with advertisements only depicts human models of one race, and without any children.

3. **Licensee's responsibility**: Any time a real estate licensee is asked to engage in an act that constitutes illegal discrimination, the licensee must not participate. This holds true even if the client (or customer) is unaware that his request is illegal under federal, state, or local fair housing laws. It is the licensee's responsibility to know and understand all laws sufficiently to avoid a violation and to explain the laws to the client (or customer).

E. **Compliance programs**: Unfortunately, not all occurrences of discrimination are brought to the attention of the appropriate authorities. Since fair housing violations are considered to be a serious breach of the law, a variety of compliance-testing methods have been developed. Compliance-testing gauges how ready and willing a housing provider is to abide by fair housing principles. Under these programs, persons, companies, and their marketing programs can be subjected to a formal process called "testing."

1. **Testing**: Fair housing testing is a process used by a person who is known as a tester to ascertain whether a person, business, or housing complex is complying with existing laws. To gather information about a target housing provider's fair housing compliance, the tester typically poses as a potential purchaser or tenant. Housing service providers such as apartments, assisted living complexes, real estate licensees and brokerage companies, and builders are often targets.

The tester is a trained civil rights enforcer who generally works for a private or community-based fair housing advocacy group. Testing can also be conducted by government agencies. The goal is to search for differences in the level of service provided to minorities and other protected classes versus those provided to the general population.

- a. **How testing may be conducted**: One form of testing occurs when an individual tester targets a housing provider, asks predetermined questions, and generates a report of his experience. Other forms of testing use two testers who work in tandem. For example, a minority tester posing as a buyer with specific qualification criteria visits a real estate company and reports things like (1) the properties and geographic areas that were offered or shown to the buyer, (2) what price and terms were disclosed as being available, and (3) the level of service and courtesy that was afforded the tester.

  Next, a non-minority tester approaches the same target licensee or company using the same qualification criteria. After both testers gather their initial information, they compare notes to determine what, if any, differences in treatment were demonstrated. Further testing may be warranted to see if there is a pattern or practice of discrimination occurring, and to determine if the problem is limited to certain licensees or the entire sales staff.

- b. **Not entrapment**: Although testing has been criticized by some as a form of entrapment, the practice has been upheld by the courts as one of the only methods to catch violators. Entrapment occurs when an official of the government actually induces a person to commit a crime they might not have otherwise committed. Since a tester merely witnesses and reports actual acts of discrimination, the elements of entrapment are not present. Further, a tester does not have to identify himself as a tester if asked.

- c. **Concern for brokers**: Real estate brokers, especially those with large companies and multiple offices must exercise extra care to make sure they have a comprehensive fair housing company policy coupled with ongoing fair housing training. Testers may target different licensees at different branch offices of the same company. If each licensee provides the same high level of professional service and care, the tester will only be able to report full, company-wide compliance with the law.

2. **Affirmative marketing**: Affirmative marketing is a voluntary program whereby a real estate broker or brokers agree to engage in activities that increase community awareness of equal housing opportunities. The agreement also requires participating brokers to establish office policies and procedures that ensures there will be no denial of equal service. HUD also requires nondiscriminatory hiring of licensees and personnel.

F. **Burden of proof**: The complainant of an alleged fair housing violation bears the burden of proving that a violation has occurred. This means that the respondent will not be required to prove his innocence. The complainant does not need to show specific intent or guilty knowledge by the respondent, however. By definition, a complainant is a person who files a complaint that alleges wrongdoing and a respondent is the person against whom the complaint is lodged.

G. **Disparate impact doctrine**: The disparate impact doctrine is a legal principle that measures the impact of a discriminatory practice rather than the intent of the person who committed the discrimination. Finding a violation may be easier under this doctrine. Discrimination can be found if a restrictive practice has a statistically greater (and generally negative) effect on one classification versus the general population. Once the disparate impact is shown, the burden of proof shifts to the respondent to show that there is a valid, non-discriminatory reason for the statistical imbalance.

1. **Courteous disregard**: Courteous disregard is a form of passive-aggressive behavior, the effect of which is to ignore another. The "courteous" aspect of the behavior is designed to leave the impression of politeness and respect. The problem, however, arises when the member of a protected class is treated with "disregard." While not necessarily falling under the disparate impact doctrine, the concept of courteous disregard has the potential to unfairly impact members of a protected class. A pattern of unequal treatment often gives rise to serious fair housing violations.

IV. **History of civil rights**: The history of civil rights in the United States is an interesting story of human struggle and triumph. Since a full and detailed explanation is beyond the scope of this textbook, a brief chronicle will be provided. Emphasis is placed on particular events as they affected housing opportunities.

   A. **Post-Civil War amendments to the U.S. Constitution**: The Thirteenth, Fourteenth, and Fifteenth Amendments to the United States Constitution are referred to as the post-Civil War Amendments. The Thirteenth Amendment abolished slavery and involuntary servitude when it was ratified in 1865. The Fourteenth Amendment, ratified 3 years later in 1868, established an individual's dual citizenship between the United States and the various states. Among other things, it forbids a state from denying U.S. citizens the equal protection of federal laws.

The Fifteenth Amendment, which was ratified in 1870, guarantees all citizens the right to vote regardless of race, color, or prior servitude. Involuntary servitude occurs when a person is forced or compelled to work against his own will for the benefit of another person. The force is generally exerted through some form of threat.

B. **Racially restrictive covenants**: A racially restrictive covenant is a type of agreement or contractual promise between individuals, typically set in a deed or other conveyance document, whereby the purchaser either is restricted from or agrees not to sell, rent, or transfer the property to anyone who is part of a named protected class. It operates as a discriminatory deed restriction. For decades, private individuals used these covenants to maintain segregated communities by keeping persons of a certain race, national origin, or religion, for example, from purchasing or leasing property in their neighborhoods.

1. *Shelley v. Kraemer*: In 1948, the U.S. Supreme Court displayed a new and heightened concern for civil rights and racial equality with its landmark decision in *Shelley v. Kraemer*. Multiple state courts had been enforcing these covenants when individuals sold their properties to persons of a different race in violation of the covenants. *Shelley v. Kraemer* finally brought the debate over the enforceability of racially restrictive covenants by state courts to a national stage.

   The U.S. Supreme Court held that judicial enforcement of a racially restrictive covenant when a seller willingly chooses to sell to a person of a different race, for example, amounts to discrimination by the government. In the *Shelley* case, a private seller attempted to sell to a minority buyer despite the existence of a covenant that prohibited such a sale. The neighbors took the seller to a state court to have the covenant enforced and the sale to the minority buyer reversed.

   In the 1940s, there was only one federal law that prevented discrimination on the basis of race–the Civil Rights Act of 1866. The problem for victims of civil rights violations, however, is that the 1866 Act was interpreted as only preventing discrimination by the government, whether federal, state, or local. It was widely felt that the 1866 Act did not reach and prevent private individuals from discriminating. In the facts of the *Shelley* case, a state court enforced a private restrictive covenant. The U.S. Supreme Court said that the state court's enforcement of the covenant did, in fact, constitute government involvement which allowed it to overturn the state court's action.

2. **Post-Shelley application of racially restrictive covenants**: Even after the decision in *Shelley*, racially restrictive covenants continued to be included in purchase agreements and deeds. In 1972, the federal courts finally held that a deed or other document of conveyance could not be recorded by a register of deeds if it contained a racially restrictive covenant.

C. **Current constitutional interpretations**: An interesting turn of events occurred during the late 1960s. Socially, it was a turbulent time and racial equality was a major issue with which society was grappling. In 1968, Congress was deliberating over legislation of historic proportion which became known as the Fair Housing Act of 1968. This Act was passed to leave no doubt under federal law that private individuals cannot discriminate against other private individuals.

At the same time this legislative process was going on, the judicial branch of the federal government (through the U.S. Supreme Court) was hearing and ultimately deciding a case of equal significance in *Jones v. Mayer*. Even though Congress and the Supreme Court were acting independently of one another, they created a near simultaneous joint affirmation of civil rights in the United States. It is interesting to note that the *Jones v. Mayer* decision was handed down by the Supreme Court only 9 weeks after Congress passed the Fair Housing Act of 1968.

1. *Jones v. Mayer*: In 1968, the U.S. Supreme Court dramatically overturned a series of prior cases that made it difficult for lower courts to prevent private parties from engaging in acts of discrimination. The facts involved African American buyers, the Jones, who attempted to purchase a home from a real estate developer, the Alfred E. Mayer Co., but were refused based on the couple's race. Jones' attorneys argued in the lower federal court that the Civil Rights Act of 1866 gave all citizens the right to purchase property. The case against Mayer was dismissed with the judges concluding that the 1866 Act only applies to government action and does not reach private party conduct.

2. **Decision**: On appeal to the U.S. Supreme Court, the majority held that Congress did, in fact, have the power in 1866 to enact legislation to abolish what the Court referred to as "badges and incidents of slavery."

Chapter 18: Fair Housing 315

As a result, the Civil Rights Act of 1866 can, and does, prevent discrimination by private parties. This decision had far-reaching effects because the Civil Rights Act of 1866 Act does not have any allowable exemptions and the Fair Housing Act of 1968 Act does.

V. ▶ **Federal laws related to fair housing**: This section explores three pieces of federal legislation: (1) the Civil Rights Act of 1866, (2) the federal Fair Housing Act of 1968, and (3) the Americans with Disabilities Act. In spite of the fact that more than 100 years of social evolution separate the Civil Rights Act of 1866 and the Federal Fair Housing Act of 1968, both are considered good law today.

   A. ▶ **Civil Rights Act of 1866**: As noted earlier, the Civil Rights Act of 1866 was the first major piece of federal legislation dealing with civil rights and fair housing. The Thirteenth Amendment to the U.S. Constitution was ratified in December, 1865 to abolish slavery in the United States. Just four months later, Congress enacted the Civil Rights Act of 1866 to provide rights to the recently freed slaves including freedom from discrimination. The Thirteen Amendment is partially enforced through the 1866 Act.

   1. **Contract rights**: The language of the 1866 Act gave all citizens the same rights that white citizens had including the right to enter into and enforce contracts and the right to sue. It also required that all citizens be subject to identical treatment by the government.

   2. ▶ **Property rights**: Another provision of the 1866 Act states that all citizens of the United States shall have the same right, in every state and territory, as is enjoyed by white citizens thereof to inherit, purchase, lease, sell, hold, and convey real and personal property.

   3. ▶ **Covers race only**: Since the Act makes specific reference to white citizens, race is the only protected class covered by the law. It is also important to remember that the Act does not create any exemptions in its wording. Since *Jones v Mayer* ruled that the 1866 Act prevents individuals from discriminating on the basis of race, any race-based exemptions found in other federal or state civil rights laws are superseded and no longer applicable.

   B. ▶ **The Fair Housing Act of 1968**: The Fair Housing Act of 1968, which is technically called Title VIII of the Civil Rights Act of 1968, was the first comprehensive mandate for federal civil rights intended to prohibit nearly all forms of discrimination. The Act has been amended twice to expand the number of protected classifications. In 1974, as part of the Housing and Community Development Act, discrimination on the basis of sex was added. Later, the 1988 Fair Housing Amendments Act added familial status and physical or mental disability.

   1. ▶ **Purpose, application, and covered transactions**: As a matter of public policy, the Fair Housing Act of 1968 encourages equal opportunity in housing and requires that the law be construed generously to eliminate all traces of discrimination within the real estate industry. A person whose business involves residential real estate-related transactions is prohibited from discriminating on the basis of any federally-protected classification. The Act also applies to loan transactions secured by residential real estate and the sale or appraisal of residential real estate.

   2. **Prohibited conduct**: As with most civil rights and fair housing laws, specific language and terminology are used to prohibit certain actions or conduct. These are known as prohibitions. A prohibition is, therefore, a forbidden act. Viewed another way–that which a person is forbidden or prohibited from doing is a prohibition.

      a. ▶ **General prohibitions of the Fair Housing Act of 1968**: It is unlawful to perform certain actions, or to engage in certain conduct, with regard to another person on the basis of that person being in a federally-protected classification. Some of the following prohibitions may be subject to an exemptions under the 1968 Act.

         (1) **Sale or lease**: A person cannot discriminate by refusing to make available, sell, or rent a dwelling, or to refuse to negotiate with a person.

         (2) **Terms and conditions**: It is unlawful to discriminate against a person in the terms or conditions of a sale or rental of a dwelling, or in the provision of services or facilities in connection with a sale or rental.

         (3) **Advertising**: A person cannot make any statement, sign, or advertisement that indicates a preference, limitation, or discrimination.

         (4) **Representations of availability**: It is unlawful to discriminate by representing that a dwelling is not available for inspection, sale, or rental when such dwelling is available.

b. ▶ **Blockbusting**: The act of blockbusting is prohibited under the 1968 law. (Blockbusting was discussed earlier in the chapter).

c. ▶ **Access for persons with a disability**: It is unlawful to (1) refuse to allow the reasonable modification of a dwelling which is occupied or intended to be occupied by a person with a disability, (2) on the basis of the person's disability, (3) where the modification is necessary to afford the person full enjoyment of the premises, and (4) the modification is made at the expense of the person with a disability. The landlord may condition his permission to modify the premises on the tenant's agreement to restore the interior of the premises to its prior condition.

d. **Service animals and assistance animals in a leased premises**: Many landlords have strict "no pets" policies in their rental agreements. The purpose is to protect their rental properties since animals can cause expensive damages that the vacating tenants usually do not repair fully or properly. Nevertheless, public and private housing providers are required to modify these policies and practices if they deprive tenants with disabilities of their right to use and enjoy the leased premises. Two classes of animals are created by two different federal laws: "Service Animals" under the Americans with Disabilities Act (ADA) and "Assistance Animals" under the Fair Housing Act (FHA). Michigan law also addresses "Service Animals" in Public Acts 144 to 147 of 2015.

A service or assistance animal, such as a guide dog for the sight-impaired, is assumed to be essential to a tenant with a disability. For the tenant to be protected under the law, he must have a qualifying disability, the animal must serve a function that is directly related to the disability, and a reasonable request must be made by the tenant to have the service or assistance animal on the premises. Federal courts as well as Michigan state courts have upheld the right to a service/assistance animal for a tenant who has a qualifying disability.

(1) **ADA service animal**: As noted in the discussion of the Americans with Disabilities Act later in this chapter, the ADA only applies to public accommodations, including public entities such as universities and assisted living facilities that provide housing. The ADA uses the label "service animal." The language of the ADA limits a service animal to a dog that is individually trained to do work or perform tasks for the benefit of a person with a disability. This definition now also includes miniature horses as a result of a recent federal case and subsequent interpretation of the Department of Justice. Also, the ADA definition does not include a dog that merely provides emotional support.

Under the ADA rules, a public accommodation may not ask an individual if he has a disability, but may inquire if the service animal is required because of a disability and what work or tasks the animal has been trained to perform. Since the ADA and FHA rules differ, housing providers should check with legal counsel to see what rules apply. ADA guidelines are more strict than FHA rules in some respects. For example, FHA rules allow for emotional support animals.

(2) **FHA assistance animal**: For purposes of the federal Fair Housing Act (FHA), HUD rules define what qualifies as an assistance animal. Knowing the difference is important since the FHA applies to nearly all types of housing, including privately-owned and leased housing. The definition of assistance animal includes any animal that works, provides assistance, or performs tasks for the benefit of a person with a disability, or provides emotional support that alleviates one or more identified symptoms or effects of a person's disability. An assistance animal can be any type of animal and does not have to be specifically trained.

Under FHA rules, a landlord may ask about the tenant's disability and whether there is a need for the assistance animal. A HUD memo indicates that a housing provider may also ask the tenant to provide documentation of the need. The landlord may not, however, increase the monthly rent or assess the tenant a pet deposit on the basis of the assistance animal being on the premises. Assistance animals are sometimes referred to as emotional support animals. All landlords should consult with legal counsel when questions pertaining to assistance animals arise with tenants.

3. ▶ **Exemptions**: There are several important exemptions to the Fair Housing Act of 1968. An exemption applies to certain individuals in limited circumstances. Even though an individual may be exempt, he should not interpret his exemption as having permission to discriminate. Instead, exemptions operate as a release from certain prohibitions. In other words, the prohibitions of the federal Fair Housing Act of 1968 do not apply to one who is exempted. Owners and landlords should always consult with legal counsel prior to availing themselves of any exemption.

a. **Exemption for single family houses**: The prohibitions of the 1968 Act do not apply to a single family house sold or leased by a private individual. For this exemption to apply, four specific conditions must all be met:

   (1) Not more than three single family houses are owned by the private individual at any one time;

   (2) In the case of a sale by a private individual who does not reside in the house at the time of the sale, or was not the most recent resident of this house, the exemption will only apply to one sale within any 24-month period;

   (3) The sale or rental is made without the use of the facilities or services of a real estate broker, salesperson, or person in the business of selling or renting dwellings;

   (Note: The private individual cannot be in the business of selling or renting property (such as a property manager), a real estate licensee (including a broker, associate broker, or salesperson), and must not have used the services of a real estate licensee. The exemption does not, however, prohibit the private individual from using the services of an attorney, title company, or other professional who provides assistance that is necessary to transfer title.)

   (4) The private individual did not publish or mail any discriminatory advertisement or notice.

b. **Exemption for rooms in 1–4 family dwellings**: The prohibitions of the 1968 Act do not apply to rooms in dwellings containing living quarters occupied, or intended to be occupied, by no more than four families living independently of each other–if the owner occupies one of the living quarters as his residence. (Note: The four-family dwelling threshold under federal law differs from Michigan law in which the exemption is limited to a two-family dwelling. In either case, discriminatory advertising may not be used to attract a particular tenant.)

c. **Exemption for religious organizations**: A religious organization may give preference to, or limit the sale, rental, or occupancy of dwellings to persons of the same religion provided the religious organization does not operate the property for a commercial purpose and membership in the religion is not restricted on the basis of a protected classification.

d. **Exemption for private clubs**: A private club, which is not open to the public, may limit the occupancy of lodgings it owns to its members or give preference to its members provided the private club does not operate the property for a commercial purpose and the lodging is incidental to the primary purpose of the club. For example, a private hunting club owns five small cabins on a lake that it exclusively offers to members at a discount. Since members rarely rent the cabins, the club decides to offset their property tax and maintenance costs by renting them to the public. The exemption will no longer apply to the club since the cabins are now being operated for a commercial purpose.

e. ▶ **Exemption for senior citizen housing**: The prohibitions of the 1968 Act do not apply to certain housing facilities intended for older persons. Recall that familial status is one of the federally-protected classifications. Without this exemption, senior citizen and other qualified adult-only housing would be in violation of the law by excluding families with children. An exemption also exists for housing provided under a state or federal program designed and operated to assist elderly persons. There are two thresholds that determine if a senior complex is exempt under federal law:

   (1) **Persons 62 years old**: A housing complex is exempt if it is intended to be occupied solely by persons 62 years of age or older.

   (2) **Persons 55 years old**: A housing complex is also exempt if it: (1) provides housing for persons 55 years of age or older; (2) at least 80% of the units are occupied by at least one person 55 years of age or older; and (3) the housing facility or community publishes and adheres to policies that demonstrate its intent to qualify for the exemption.

f. **Threats to safety as an exemption**: A dwelling does not have to be made available to an individual whose tenancy would (1) threaten the health or safety of others, or (2) result in substantial physical damage to the property of others. Owners and landlords who intend to use this or any similar exemption should first check with legal counsel.

g. **Exemption based on financial qualification**: A person must be able to qualify to purchase or lease housing on the basis of financial, business, credit, or employment criteria. As a result, poverty is not a protected classification. No discrimination occurs if a prospective buyer or tenant is denied a sale or lease based on his true inability to financially qualify. It is important, especially for real estate licensees, to have a uniform method of qualifying prospects that includes documentation.

    h. **Number of occupants–housing ordinances**: The Fair Housing Act of 1968 Act does not affect the applicability of local, state, or federal restrictions regarding the maximum number of individuals who may occupy a dwelling (providing the occupancy restriction is reasonable). Therefore, a housing ordinance that limits the number of families or unrelated persons per dwelling is valid as long as the ordinance is reasonably related to the health, safety, and welfare of the community. An example of an impermissible ordinance would be one that requires all families who are living together to be related by blood or marriage.

4. **Enforcement**: A person who feels that he has been unlawfully discriminated against may either file a complaint with the Department of Housing and Urban Development (HUD) or can initiate a civil lawsuit in court. The office of the Attorney General may also be called on to process a complaint.

    a. **Enforcement under HUD**: When the Federal Fair Housing Act was amended in 1988, enforcement was strengthened by authorizing the Secretary of HUD to administer and enforce the law. HUD can investigate complaints, issue subpoenas, and compel production of records, documents, or other evidence. The Secretary of HUD may also enter into contracts and cooperative agreements with state and local governments as well as public and private nonprofit organizations to formulate or implement programs to prevent discriminatory housing practices.

        (1) **Penalties**: If an aggrieved party's case goes to an administrative hearing, HUD attorneys can litigate the case on the party's behalf. At the hearing, the Administrative Law Judge can order the respondent to: Compensate the complainant for actual damages (including humiliation and pain and suffering); Make the housing available to the complainant; Pay a penalty to the Federal Government not to exceed $16,000 for a first or second violation, and $65,000 if a third violation occurs within seven years; and reasonable attorney's fees and costs.

        (2) **Statute of limitations**: HUD enforcement requires a person to file his complaint with the Secretary of HUD within one year from the date the alleged discriminatory practice took place.

    b. **Civil action to enforce the Act**: An aggrieved party may also elect to enforce his rights by pursuing a civil action in a U.S. district court. The U.S. district court is the court of original jurisdiction or "entry-level" court for cases heard under federal law. There are two located in Michigan–one for the Eastern District and one for the Western District of the state.

        (1) **Remedies and damages**: A civil court may award the plaintiff actual and punitive damages and/or can grant a permanent or temporary injunction, restraining order, or other order. The court may, at its discretion, allow the prevailing party reasonable attorney's fees and court costs.

        (2) **Statute of limitations**: A person must begin a civil action not more than two years after the occurrence or the termination of an alleged discriminatory housing practice.

    c. **Enforcement by the Attorney General**: Upon referral by the Secretary of HUD, the Attorney General of the United States may commence a civil action for a discriminatory housing practice or breach of a conciliation agreement. A conciliation agreement is an attempt by a court to encourage the parties to reach a settlement in a friendly and non-adversarial manner before going to trial. If successful, a trial can be avoided.

        (1) **If a pattern or practice is found**: Whenever a person engages in a pattern or practice of discrimination, or where a group has been denied rights so as to raise an issue of general public importance, the Attorney General may begin a civil action in the appropriate U.S. District Court.

        (2) **Example of a pattern or practice of discrimination**: A local fair housing center conducted testing and a six-month investigation of Broker Z. It was found that Z's affiliated licensees routinely refused to list the homes of owners of a particular race, directed potential buyers to specific integrated neighborhoods based on their race, and used key words in advertising that suggested certain neighborhoods were exclusive, restricted, or preferential without any justifiable reason for doing so. Taken together, these actions were held to evidence a pattern or practice of discrimination by Broker Z and several of his affiliated licensees.

Chapter 18: Fair Housing — 1968 Fair Housing Act — 319

[Margin note: Harassment is a Violation for Fair Housing]

5. **Intimidation and violent interference:** The federal Fair Housing Act contains provisions that are designed to prevent intimidation and violent interference in the exercise of one's civil rights. It is a violation to engage in any of the following actions:

   a. Retaliate or discriminate against a person because he has opposed a discriminatory practice or because he has made a charge, testified, assisted, or participated in an investigation, proceeding, or hearing;

   b. Aid, abet, incite, compel, or coerce a person to engage in discrimination;

   c. Attempt to commit discrimination;

   d. Willfully interfere with the exercise of a power by the Civil Rights Commission;

   e. Willfully obstruct a person from complying with the Act;

   f. Coerce, intimidate, threaten, or interfere with a person in the exercise of his rights; or

   g. Coerce, intimidate, threaten, or interfere with a person because he has encouraged another person to exercise his rights.

6. ▶ **Relationship to the Civil Rights Act of 1866:** *[Margin note: Race only]* When Congress enacted the federal Fair Housing Act of 1968, it chose not to repeal the Civil Rights Act of 1866. This, coupled with the *Jones v Mayer* case discussed earlier, means that the exemptions under the 1968 Act are not available when discrimination is based on race. Recall from the discussion of the Civil Rights Act of 1866 that racial discrimination is prohibited without exemption.

   a. **Example:** The owner of a duplex resides in one unit and offers the other unit for lease. The owner refuses to lease to a particular applicant based on the applicant's race. The owner believes that he qualifies for an exemption under the federal Fair Housing Act of 1968. He does not because the refusal was based on race which is fully protected by the Civil Rights Act of 1866 (without exemption).

   b. **Effect on state law:** The federal Fair Housing Act of 1968 does not invalidate or limit a state law such as Michigan's Elliott-Larsen Civil Rights Act or any local law that protects the same or greater rights. Conversely, if a state or local law affords less rights to a person in a protected class, the federal Fair Housing Act will prevail.

[Margin note: 1976 ADA]

C. ▶ **Americans with Disabilities Act of 1990 (ADA):** *[Margin note: More w/ Brokers (public)]* The Americans with Disabilities Act of 1990 was enacted by Congress to provide a comprehensive national mandate for the elimination of discrimination against persons with disabilities. By invoking the sweep of Congressional authority, including the power to enforce the Fourteenth Amendment of the U.S. Constitution and to regulate commerce, the Act addresses the major areas of discrimination faced on a day-to-day basis by people with disabilities. The ADA has far-reaching provisions that deal with many aspects of life such as public transportation, communication, and new construction. Since the ADA is complex and contains many facets, the discussion of this material is limited to how it applies to employment and public accommodations.

   1. **The ADA amendments Act of 2008:** Since the passage of the ADA in 1990, the courts had interpreted the definition of disability so narrowly that it was difficult for a person with a verifiable disability to obtain protection. With the Amendments Act, Congress fixed the definition of disability to cover more individuals, and as a result, prevent more discrimination.

   2. **Purpose of the ADA:** Congressional findings have determined that discrimination against individuals with disabilities has been a serious problem that continues today. During hearings on the original Act, it was argued that society tends to segregate disabled individuals based on stereotypes that are not representative of the individual's true abilities. The ADA seeks to remedy this by prohibiting discrimination based on a disability.

      a. **Disability defined:** The definition of disability under the ADA essentially parallels the definition of handicap under the federal Fair Housing Act. An individual is considered to have a disability if he (1) has a physical or mental impairment that substantially limits one or more major life activities, (2) has a record (meaning history) of such impairment, or (3) is regarded as having such an impairment. Interestingly, under the employment provisions of the ADA, a person without a disability is afforded protection if they have a known association or relationship with another individual who has a disability.

      b. **Application to real estate licensees:** The ADA has direct application to real estate licensees in the areas of employment and public accommodations. In order to help enforce the Act, administrative rules have been created by both the Department of Justice and the Equal Employment Opportunity

Commission (EEOC). The EEOC interprets how the ADA applies to real estate brokers as both employers and businesspeople.

3. **Exclusions**: Certain individuals are not protected under the ADA and, therefore, are listed as exclusions. An exclusion is someone who is not considered to have a disability for purposes of the Act. Therefore, he is not entitled to protection.

   a. **Illegal use of drugs**: An individual who currently uses drugs illegally is not protected by the ADA. Illegal drug use includes the possession or distribution of drugs listed as unlawful under the Controlled Substances Act. The unauthorized use of prescription drugs also falls within the definition of controlled substances. Although it may be argued that a psychoactive substance abuse disorder resulting from the current illegal use of drugs is a disability, it is still not protected. However, former drug users who have been successfully rehabilitated are protected from discrimination based on their past drug addiction.

   b. **Sexual behavior**: Some sexual behaviors are not considered to be disabilities. Homosexuality and bisexuality are not, by definition, considered to be impairments or disabilities under the ADA. Sexual behavior disorders not resulting physical impairments are also specifically excluded.

   c. **Compulsions**: Persons with certain compulsive behaviors such as gambling, kleptomania, and pyromania are also excluded from protection under the ADA.

4. **Employment provisions**: As noted, the ADA applies to real estate brokers in their capacity as employers. The definition of employee includes an affiliated licensee who works on behalf of a broker.

   a. **Application–federal versus state law**: Federal employment provisions apply to all employers engaged in an industry affecting commerce who have 15 or more employees for each working day in each of 20 or more calendar weeks in the current or preceding calendar year. Under state law for Michigan (i.e., the Persons with Disabilities Civil Rights Act), the threshold is lowered to an employer who has "at least one employee."

   b. **Protection afforded**: A qualified individual with a disability cannot be discriminated against with regard to job application procedures or hiring, employee advancement, training, or discharge procedures. The phrase "qualified individual with a disability" means that the individual can perform the essential functions of the employment position with or without a reasonable accommodation.

   c. **Reasonable accommodation**: An employer must provide reasonable accommodations to allow an otherwise qualified individual with a disability to perform essential job functions. Existing facilities may also have to be made usable for individuals with disabilities. Reasonable accommodations may include job restructuring, elimination of nonessential job elements, or delegation or exchange of assignments provided that essential job functions do not need to be changed or new positions created.

   d. **Employer defenses**: A concern that some employers have regarding the ADA is the financial cost of compliance. To prevent undue hardships, regulated employers are afforded some defenses.

      (1) **Undue hardship**: An accommodation that would be costly or disruptive, or that would fundamentally alter the nature or operation of the business, constitutes an undue hardship and does not need to be made. Undue hardship is measured by the impact on the employer's resources rather than the salary of the person with a disability.

         (a) **Payment by employee**: Even where the cost of an accommodation is unduly burdensome to the employer, the accommodation can still be required if the employee with a disability is willing and arranges to pay a portion of the accommodation or otherwise arranges to provide for the accommodation himself.

         (b) **Alternative accommodation**: If one accommodation imposes an undue hardship and a different accommodation does not, the employer may still be required to make the different accommodation. To illustrate this point, assume that an accommodation is required to lower an existing wall-mounted drinking fountain for a wheelchair-bound employee. If this is determined to present an excessive cost, the employer may be able to purchase a separate, but equally functional, water dispenser for the employee.

      (2) **Threat to the safety of others**: An employer is not required to hire an individual or provide an accommodation where the individual or accommodation will create a direct threat to the health or safety of others. An employer may not simply assume that a threat exists which is why speculative

or remote risks are not enough. The employer must establish that substantial harm could occur in the workplace through objective and medically-supported methods.

    (3) **Hiring inquiries**: A prospective employer such as a real estate broker may not ask disability-related questions on an employment application or during an interview. Questions may be asked about the applicant's ability to perform specific job functions, however. If a medical issue is raised by the applicant, all information must be kept confidential.

5. **Public accommodations and services**: The provisions of the ADA apply to public accommodations and services operated by private entities whose operations affect commerce and fall within 12 categories.

    a. **Application**: The ADA is intended to prohibit discrimination on the basis of a disability in public accommodations. Public accommodations must meet the needs of persons with disabilities; for example, by removing barriers to access.

        (1) **Examples of public accommodations**: Public accommodations include (but are not limited to) nonresidential places of lodging such as hotels and motels; establishments serving food or drink; places of exhibition or entertainment; places of public gathering such as convention centers; service establishments including stores, banks, beauty shops, and health care providers; places of education; day care centers and senior citizen centers; and places of exercise. A commercial or sales facilities such as a real estate office also qualifies. If a real estate licensee uses a home office to transact business with customers and clients, that portion of the home used for business must be ADA compliant.

        (2) **Exemptions**: Private clubs, religious organizations, and entities controlled by religious organizations are exempt from the accommodation requirements of the ADA. The ADA typically uses the same definition and qualification standards for exemptions as are used under Federal Fair Housing law (discussed earlier in this chapter). The ADA also does not apply to strictly residential, privately-owned rental properties.

    b. **Reasonable accommodation guidelines**: A reasonable accommodation is defined as a change, exception, or adjustment to a rule, policy, practice, or service that may be necessary for a person with a disability to have an equal opportunity to use and enjoy public and common use spaces. Goods, services, and facilities must be provided in the most integrated setting appropriate to the needs of the individual. In other words, a person with a disability should not feel as if he is being separated or segregated.

        (1) ▶ **Architectural and communication barriers**: Where readily achievable, an owner or lessor must remove all architectural and communication barriers from existing facilities. If the removal of a barrier is not readily achievable, the goods, services, or facilities must be made available through alternative methods.

        Example: A small real estate company has a single sales office located in a two-story, converted residential structure. The conference room is located on the second floor which is only accessible by a wide staircase. A newly-hired licensee has a disability that prevents him from climbing stairs and installation of an elevator is not readily achievable. To comply with the ADA, the broker may have to install a commercial stair lift (if the cost is reasonable) or provide an alternate space on the first floor that serves the same purpose as the second floor conference room.

        (2) **Business policies**: The ADA requires that business policies and practices be changed where necessary to provide full and equal enjoyment of goods, services, and facilities to all members of society, including individuals with disabilities.

        (3) ▶ **New construction and remodeled building accessibility**: Newly-constructed buildings or those that are altered (meaning remodeled) must be built or altered in such a way that they are usable by individuals with disabilities.

            (a) **New construction**: New buildings constructed after 1976 must be usable by individuals with disabilities whether or not the buildings are to be open to the public (unless accessibility requirements are structurally impractical). Incorporating design requirements in new construction is the least expensive way to make a building accessible.

            (b) **Alteration of existing facilities**: Alterations of existing buildings must be completed so that the facility is usable by individuals with disabilities, including individuals in wheelchairs. In addition, the path of travel to the newly altered area must also be readily accessible (unless the cost for making the path accessible is disproportionate to the cost of the total alteration).

  (c) **Elevator installation**: Elevator installation is not required for facilities of less than 3 stories or less than 3,000 square feet per story. Facilities requiring elevator installation include shopping centers, shopping malls, and professional offices of health care providers.

 (4) **Questions for prospective tenants**: A provider of housing that qualifies as a public accommodation is generally prohibited from posing questions to prospective tenants about the existence of a disability, whether anyone who will be residing with them has a disability, or about the nature and severity of a disability. The provider may inquire if the prospective tenant qualifies for a unit made available on a priority basis to persons with a disability (if the question is asked of all applicants).

 (5) **Denial of reasonable accommodation**: A housing provider may deny a request for a reasonable accommodation if (1) the request is not made by or on behalf of a person with a disability, (2) there is no disability-related need for the requested accommodation, (3) it would result in an undue financial or administrative hardship on the housing provider, or (4) it would fundamentally alter the nature of the provider's business.

 c. **Retaliation and coercion**: The ADA prevents retaliation by a person against an individual who has opposed an unlawful practice, made a charge against, or who has assisted or participated in an investigation, proceeding, or hearing against the person. Likewise, no person can intimidate, threaten, or interfere with a person who is attempting to exercise his rights protected by the ADA.

 d. **Enforcement**: The Attorney General is required to investigate alleged violations of the ADA. A state is not immune from liability for a violation and is subject to the same remedies as those available against any other public or private entity. Alternative dispute resolution such as arbitration or mediation is encouraged.

 e. **Remedies and damages**: Available remedies under the ADA include jury trials, injunctive relief, and restraining orders. A court may order modification of existing policies and procedures, or that facilities be made accessible. Additionally, a court can forbid a discriminatory action such as the firing of an employee who has a disability by an employer who does not want to make a reasonable accommodation. Compensatory and punitive damages, court costs, attorney's fees, and expert witness fees may be recovered by a prevailing party.

 f. **Civil penalties**: A court may allow for civil penalties. Penalties for a public accommodation violation cannot exceed $50,000 for a first violation and $100,000 for any subsequent violation. The penalties for employment violations can range between $50,000 to $300,000 depending on how many employees the company has.

VI. ▶ **Fair housing in Michigan**: Congress passed a national legislative mandate that protects civil rights and fair housing. The Michigan Legislature passed its own state legislative mandate. Recall that federal law sets the minimum amount of protection afforded under the U.S. Constitution which is applicable to all states. Generally, states are free to increase the level of protection by adding additional classes and restrictions. Which law ultimately applies depends on whether the case is filed in a federal court or a state court, and on the precise nature of the discrimination.

 A. ▶ **Elliott-Larsen Civil Rights Act**: Michigan's Elliott-Larsen Civil Rights Act was signed into law in 1976 to prohibit certain types of discrimination in employment and housing. Only those provisions relating to housing and real estate are explored in this chapter.

  1. ▶ **Protected classifications**: Discriminatory practices based on race, color, religion, national origin, sex, familial status, age, or marital status are specifically prohibited under Michigan law. The classifications of height and weight are also protected, but only as they relate to employment opportunities. As with federal law, poverty and occupation are not protected classifications under state law.

  2. **Protected activities**: Elliott-Larsen provides equal opportunity to obtain employment, housing, and other real estate. It also provides for full and equal use of public accommodations, public services, and educational facilities. The Act preserves as confidential any misdemeanor arrest records that have not resulted in a conviction. Employers may inquire about convictions or pending felony charges, however.

  3. **Prohibitions**: Specific prohibitions are included in the Act that apply to housing, brokers' organizations, financing, and restrictive deed covenants. There are also provisions dealing with blockbusting, intimidation, and coercion.

Chapter 18: Fair Housing

a. ▶ **Prohibitions relating to housing**: A person participating in a real estate transaction, including a real estate broker or salesperson, cannot engage in any of the following acts on the basis of a protected classification. Many of these prohibitions are similar to those listed in the federal Fair Housing Act of 1968.

   (1) Refuse to engage in a real estate transaction with a person.

   (2) Discriminate against a person in the terms, conditions, or privileges of a real estate transaction or in the furnishing of facilities or services in connection with a real estate transaction.

   (3) Refuse to receive from a person or transmit to a person a bona fide offer to engage in a real estate transaction.

   (4) Refuse to negotiate with a person.

   (5) Represent that property is not available for inspection, sale, or lease when in fact it is so available; or knowingly fail to bring a property listing to a person's attention; or refuse to permit a person to inspect real property, or otherwise make unavailable or deny real property to a person.

   (6) Make, print, circulate, post, mail, or otherwise cause to be made or published a statement, advertisement, notice, or sign, or use a form of application for a real estate transaction, or make a record of inquiry in connection with a prospective real estate transaction, which indicates an intent to make a preference, limitation, specification, or discrimination with respect to a real estate transaction.

   (7) Offer, solicit, accept, use, or retain a real estate listing of real property with the understanding that a person may be discriminated against in a real estate transaction or in the furnishing of facilities or services in connection therewith.

   (8) Discriminate against a person in the brokering or appraising of real property.

b. ▶ **Prohibitions relating to brokers' organizations**: A person shall not be denied access to, or membership in, a multiple listing service or other real estate brokers' organization (such as a real estate trade association) on the basis of any protected classification.

c. ▶ **Prohibitions relating to financing**: Lenders may not discriminate against loan applicants. More specifically, a lender to whom an application is made for financing in connection with a real estate transaction or the construction, rehabilitation, repair, maintenance, or improvement of real property shall not discriminate against the applicant because of the applicant's being in a protected class. Nor can a lender make an inquiry or use an application form that indicates a preference, limitation, or discrimination as to the protected classification of the applicant or a person residing with the applicant.

d. ▶ **Prohibitions relating to restrictive covenants**: Restrictive covenants (including racially restrictive covenants) are prohibited under Michigan law. A person shall not insert in a written instrument a provision that is void under Elliott-Larsen nor honor such a provision in the chain of title. However, certain restrictions based on age and familial status may be permissible, including restrictions issued by religious organizations (providing they fall under the allowable exemptions discussed later).

e. ▶ **Prohibitions relating to blockbusting**: Michigan law provides an expanded explanation of blockbusting. A person shall not represent, for the purpose of inducing a real estate transaction from which the person may benefit financially, that a change has occurred, or may occur, in the composition of the owners or occupants in the area with regard to a protected classification. Nor shall a person represent that a change in composition may result in the lowering of property values, an increase in criminal or antisocial behavior, or a decline in the quality of schools in the area in which the real estate is located.

f. ▶ **Prohibitions relating to intimidation and coercion**: It shall be a separate violation to retaliate or discriminate against a person because he has opposed a practice in violation of this Act, or because he has made a charge, filed a complaint, testified, assisted, or participated in an investigation, proceeding, or hearing under the Act. It is also a violation to aid, abet, incite, compel, or coerce a person to engage in a violation of the Act.

4. ▶ **Exemptions**: There are several exemptions under Elliott-Larsen that especially apply to the classifications of age, familial status, and religious organizations. Again, it must be noted that the federal Civil Rights Act of 1866 supersedes any of these exemptions if race is involved.

   a. **Private clubs**: Elliott-Larsen does not apply to a private club which is not open to the public. However, if the private club is a place of public accommodation (or provides goods, services, facilities, privileges, advantages, or accommodations to another public accommodation), then the exemption does not apply and the club must comply. This is basically a parallel provision to the exemption in the federal Fair Housing Act of 1968 with some differences. For example, Elliott-Larsen adds a provision that a club may limit leagues for children (less than 18 years of age) to members of the same sex or age, if comparable and equally convenient access to the club's facilities is available to both sexes and the limitations are not used to evade the Act.

    b. **Lease of duplex in which family member resides**: The prohibitions do not apply to the lease of rooms in a single family dwelling, or to the lease of a dwelling in a building that contains housing accommodations for not more than 2 families living independently of each other, if the lessor or a member of his immediate family resides on the premises. Immediate family refers to a spouse, parent, child, or sibling. Compare this with the exemption under federal law for 1–4 family dwellings.

    c. **Sublease of a residence**: The prohibitions do not apply to the lease of a housing accommodation for not more than 12 months by the owner or lessor if it was occupied by him as his home for at least 3 months immediately preceding occupancy by the tenant and it is maintained as the owner's or lessor's legal residence.

    d. **Age and familial status–senior housing**: Another exemption exists for age and familial status as it relates to the sale or lease of senior citizen housing accommodations that meet the requirements of federal, state, or local housing programs for senior citizens, or accommodations otherwise intended, or operated for the purpose of providing housing for persons 50 years of age or older. (Compare this with the age thresholds under federal law of 62 and 55 years of age which was discussed earlier in this chapter).

    e. **Inquiries into marital status**: Requesting information on or inquiring into the marital status of an individual is not a violation of Elliott-Larsen when it in necessary for the preparation of a deed or other instrument of conveyance. Any other request for information about marital status would likely constitute a violation under Michigan, but not federal, fair housing law.

5. **The Civil Rights Commission**: Michigan's Civil Rights Commission was created by Michigan's 1963 Constitution to carry out its guarantees against discrimination. The Commission is a diverse body of individuals who are appointed by the Governor to four-year staggered terms. It meets on a monthly basis to set the policy or agenda for Michigan civil rights enforcement. While the Commission may investigate complaints, it generally does not. Instead, investigation and enforcement of complaints are handled by the Michigan Department of Civil Rights.

    a. **Michigan Department of Civil Rights**: The Michigan Department of Civil Rights was established two years after the Michigan Civil Rights Commission was created. The function of the Department is to provide staffing support for the important policies set by the Commission. The Department administers civil rights in the state by investigating complaint allegations, holding hearings if necessary, resolving discrimination complaints, and approving plans to correct past discriminatory practices.

    b. **State complaints must be filed within 180 days**: Complaints of unfair housing practices or other civil rights violations must be submitted within 180 days after the alleged practice occurred or was discovered. Compare this to the 1 year statute of limitations under federal law.

6. **Remedies and damages**: The Michigan Department of Civil Rights and the courts may issue injunctions. The state may revoke or suspend any licenses it has issued including a real estate license. Damages for injury may be obtained including payment to an injured party of the profits obtained for each violation, with court costs, attorney's fees, and expert witness fees. The respondent may also be required to pay a civil fine to the State if the unfair housing practice was committed in the course of the respondent's business of selling or renting housing. State law also allows an aggrieved party to file a complaint with any local commission on human relations established and maintained under local ordinance.

7. **Civil fines**: Civil fines may be issued in an amount related to the cost of enforcing Elliott-Larsen not to exceed $10,000 for the first violation, $25,000 for the second violation within 5 years, and $50,000 for 2 or more violations within 7 years.

8. **Plan relating to past discrimination**: A person may adopt and carry out a plan to eliminate the present effects of past discriminatory practices or to assure equal opportunity with respect to a protected classification under Michigan law if it is filed with the Commission.

B. ▶ **Persons with Disabilities Civil Rights Act (PWDCRA)**: Michigan's Persons With Disabilities Civil Rights Act of 1998 prohibits practices and policies that discriminate against individuals who have disabilities with reference to employment, public accommodation, public service, education, and housing. Real property includes a building, structure, mobile home or trailer park, leasehold, or interest in a condominium or a cooperative. The balance of this section discusses this comprehensive Act from the limited perspective of how it impacts housing and real estate practices.

1. **Application to housing**: The prohibitions set forth in the PWDCRA apply to a person, whether licensed or not, who sells, leases, or exchanges real estate, or who negotiates loans or mortgages.

    a. **Duty to make accommodations**: Under the Act, a landlord has a duty to make accommodations which are reasonably necessary for a person with a disability to enjoy the premises, unless it can be shown that doing so would constitute an undue hardship. Further, the person with a disability must be allowed to make reasonable modifications at his own expense (if the modifications are necessary to afford full enjoyment of the premises and do not impose an undue hardship). Similarly, a homeowner's association or management company must make reasonable accommodations in the rules, policies, and practices of occupancy, or in the services that it provides, when the accommodations are necessary to give the person with a disability an equal opportunity to use the property. Multifamily dwellings constructed after 1991 must also be readily accessible by persons with disabilities.

    b. **Rental units**: In the case of a rental unit, the lessor may require a lessee to restore the interior of the premises to the condition that existed before the modification, with reasonable wear and tear excepted. Some modifications may not have to be restored to their original condition such as a door opening that was enlarged to accommodate a person in a wheelchair.

    c. ▸ **Design and construction accessibility**: As it relates to the construction of multifamily dwellings: (1) dwellings must have an accessible route, (2) public and common portions must be readily accessible to and usable by persons with disabilities, (3) doors must allow passage into and within all premises and must be sufficiently wide to allow passage by persons with disabilities in wheelchairs, and (4) all premises must contain an accessible route into and through the dwelling, light switches and environmental controls must be in accessible locations, bathroom walls must be reinforced to allow for later installation of grab bars, and kitchens and bathrooms must allow for a person in a wheelchair to maneuver about the space (typically, a five foot radius of open floor space).

    State and local building codes and ordinances typically specify the exact dimensions which are necessary to meet these design and construction requirements. As a reminder, this only applies to multifamily dwellings. There are no specific requirements for the construction of 1–2 family dwellings (although codes and ordinances can be used as guidelines).

2. **Prohibitions**: The PWDCRA contains several prohibitions that relate to dwellings, broker's services, financing, and blockbusting.

    a. **Prohibitions relating to residential dwellings**: An owner or any other person engaging in a real estate transaction, including a real estate broker or salesperson, cannot discriminate on the basis of a disability of (1) a buyer or renter, (2) a person residing or intending to reside in a dwelling, or (3) any person associated with that buyer or renter. However, if a disability prevents an individual from properly maintaining the leased property, the lessor does not have to rent it to the individual. A landlord or property manager should not make a denial of this nature without first consulting with legal counsel to make sure that the prospective tenant's rights are not being inadvertently denied under the Act.

    The specific enumerated acts of discrimination listed in the PWDCRA essentially parallel those listed in the Elliott-Larsen Civil Rights Act. Please refer to the list titled "Prohibitions relating to housing" in the prior discussion of Elliott-Larsen.

    b. **Prohibitions relating to broker's organizations**: A person with a disability shall not be denied access to, or membership in a multiple listing service, real estate brokers' organization, or other service, organization, or facility relating to the business of selling or renting real property. Nor can a person with a disability be discriminated against in the terms or conditions of that access, membership, or participation.

    c. **Prohibitions relating to financing**: An individual shall not discriminate on the basis of disability in making or purchasing loans for acquiring, constructing, improving, repairing or maintaining real property, or in providing other financial assistance secured by or otherwise related to real property.

    d. **Prohibitions relating to blockbusting**: Blockbusting is prohibited under the PWDCRA. This is the same definition as the one used in Elliott-Larsen. Refer to the definition in that earlier discussion.

e. **Prohibitions relating to intimidation and coercion**: Among other things, it is a separate violation to retaliate or discriminate against a person because he has opposed a practice in violation of the Act, or has made a charge, testified, assisted or participated in an investigation, proceeding, or hearing. This includes coercing, intimidating, threatening, or interfering with a person in the exercise of his rights or because he has encouraged another person to exercise his rights.

3. **Exemptions**: There are several exemptions to the PWDCRA including ones related to the lease of rooms in an owner's residence, the creditworthiness of an applicant, and undue hardship to a landlord.

    a. **Owner residence**: The prohibitions of the Act do not apply to the lease of rooms in a single family dwelling, or to the lease of a dwelling in a building that contains housing accommodations for not more than two families living independently of each other, if the lessor or a member of his immediate family resides on the premises.

    b. **Creditworthiness**: An owner, lender, or his agent may require an applicant who seeks to buy, lease, or obtain financial assistance to supply information concerning the applicant's financial, business, or employment status, or other information designed solely to determine the applicant's creditworthiness, but not concerning disabilities in general.

    c. **Undue hardship**: As noted, a reasonable accommodation does not need to be made if the landlord can show that doing so would impose an undue economic hardship. Recall that a tenant with a disability can still pay for a modification. If he does so, the landlord's defense of hardship would no longer apply.

4. **Administration and affirmative action**: The Michigan Civil Rights Commission is empowered to administer the Persons With Disabilities Civil Rights Act. The Commission also encourages parties to adopt voluntary programs in regard to affirmative action to eliminate the effects of past discriminatory practices and to assure equal opportunity with respect to all persons with disabilities.

5. **Remedies and damages**: An injured party may obtain damages for injury or loss for each violation, including reasonable attorney's fees. He may also obtain an injunction in lieu of, or in addition to, damages. A person who asserts a civil action for failure to accommodate must have first notified the proper party (such as a landlord) of the need for an accommodation.

Luck is the residue of intention.
Make success your intention and create your own luck.

DIAGNOSTIC PRACTICE QUESTIONS – CHAPTER 18

IMPORTANT STUDY TIP!

Step 1: Carefully review the information located in this chapter.

Step 2: Take the following Diagnostic Practice Questions. Review any question you answered incorrectly by researching the topic in this textbook. If you are still uncertain as to why the question is answered as it is, consult your program provider.

NOTE ON CHAPTER PRACTICE QUESTIONS

The following questions are representative of the type encountered on the Michigan real estate licensing examination. While some of these questions may be similar in nature and style, there is no way of predicting the exact wording of a question that will appear on the exam. Spending time memorizing these questions is, therefore, not recommended.

These questions are designed to help you determine how well you comprehend the material in this chapter. They are also intended to help you develop problem solving skills and to become comfortable with question formats.

Do not attempt to answer these questions until you have attended the lecture corresponding to this chapter and spent the appropriate time studying the material.

1. A female worker in an automotive plant has bright green colored eyes and is teased by her co-workers, both male and female, about the color. She feels that she is being treated unfairly and files a civil rights action against the offending co-workers, the shift supervisor for not taking appropriate action, as well as the company owner. Which of the following statements describes the strength of her case?
   A. She is not likely to prevail because eye color does not constitute a protected classification.
   B. She is not likely to prevail because her actual claim should be for sexual harassment.
   C. She is likely to prevail because gender is involved and, therefore, entitles her to compensation.
   D. She is likely to prevail because the teasing amounts to a substantial impairment of her right to work.

2. Lawrence is the owner of a four-unit apartment building. He lives in one of the units and has one vacancy which is advertised in the local newspaper and a "For Lease" sign is posted in the window. The Mayfields, a married couple, contact Lawrence and inquire about one of the units. Lawrence is concerned because Mr. Mayfield is a minority and Mrs. Mayfield is not. While Lawrence feels they are a very nice couple, he refuses to lease to them feeling that his other tenants might leave. Has Lawrence violated any Federal fair housing laws and what is the most significant reason why or why not?
   A. No, because the building is four units or less and Lawrence resides in one of the units.
   B. No, because Lawrence faced an economic hardship and his decision was made in good faith.
   C. Yes, because the leasing decision was based upon the Mayfield's mixed marriage.
   D. Yes, because the property was advertised in the local newspaper and a "For Lease" sign was posted.

3. A method used to determine whether or not a broker is systematically violating the civil rights of minority prospects by posing as the very target of such discrimination is known as:
   A. Entrapment.
   B. Complaint enforcement.
   C. Testing.
   D. Affirmative action.

4. Ooshley Arms Apartments is located in Michigan and inhabited mostly by retired persons and couples who appreciate the fact that they do not have to contend with small children in their neighborhood. A recently-divorced mother of two young children would like to lease one of the units because the complex is close to her new job, but is refused by the resident manager. Is the refusal to lease by the resident manager permitted?
   A. Yes, providing the housing was operated for the purpose of providing housing accommodations for persons 50 years of age or older.
   B. Yes, providing the services of a real estate broker have not been employed and no discriminatory advertising was used.

    C. No, because the refusal was based upon family status which is a protected classification.
    D. No, because a resident manager is subject to the same fair housing laws as a real estate broker or salesperson.

5. Mary, who is confined to a wheelchair, has a friend at Alpine Realty who recommends that she apply for a position as a real estate salesperson. After interviewing Mary, the broker is worried that Mary's disability might pose a problem. Alpine Realty is operated out of an old, converted farm house with narrow hallways and three floors. The conference room and computers are located on the second floor. The broker declines Mary's request to join the firm. Was the refusal proper?
    A. Yes, because Mary is not a qualified individual with a disability under the legal definition.
    B. Yes, because Mary would not be able to reasonably accommodate the clients of Alpine Realty.
    C. No, because an employer cannot refuse to hire a disabled person under any circumstances.
    D. No, because the broker could have provided Mary reasonable accommodations such as first-floor amenities.

6. All EXCEPT which of the following are valid exemptions under the Federal Fair Housing Act of 1968?
    A. A private club that limits the leasing of units it owns to club members and their families.
    B. A deed to a single family residence that contains a racially restrictive covenant.
    C. A church that limits the rental of non-commercially operated cottages to its members.
    D. A single family residence owned by a person who offers it for sale by using a "By Owner" sign on the front lawn.

7. All of the following are protected classifications under the Elliott-Larsen Civil Rights Act of 1976 except::
    A. Sex.
    B. Age.
    C. Marital status.
    D. Occupation.

8. Richard Marten and Harriet Dooright are unmarried and have 3 children of their own. The couple entered the office of broker Hy Morales with their children to inquire about a particular listing. Hy commented on how well behaved the children were and then casually asked about the difference in Richard's and Harriet's last names. After hearing Harriet's honest reply, Hy refused to show the listing and asked the group to leave his office. Richard and Harriet would most likely have recourse under the:
    A. Elliott-Larsen Civil Rights Act of 1976.
    B. Civil Rights Act of 1866.
    C. Federal Fair Housing Act of 1968.
    D. Affirmative Marketing Program.

9. According to Michigan law, a person who believes she has been a victim of unfair housing practices may file a complaint with all of the following EXCEPT:
    A. Michigan Civil Rights Commission.
    B. Circuit court in a private lawsuit.
    C. Any local commission on human relations.
    D. U.S. District Court.

10. Which of the following situations would be covered by the Civil Rights Act of 1866 but possibly not the Federal Fair Housing Act of 1968?
    A. Homes sold by a part-time real estate salesperson.
    B. An owner of a ten-unit apartment house who lives in one of the units.
    C. An apartment building rented to the general public which is owned by a bona fide religious organization.
    D. A single-family residence sold by the owner without a broker or salesperson and without the use of discriminatory advertising.

11. Under which of the following circumstances may salespersons lawfully refuse to show a home to a minority prospect who has specifically asked to see it?
    A. When the owner has exercised his exemptions under the 1968 Fair Housing Law and designated his home as not available to certain minorities.
    B. When the agent sincerely believes that such a showing will cause panic in the neighborhood.
    C. When the owner is out of town and has instructed the agent that no showings may be made in his absence.
    D. A salesperson may never refuse to show a home to any prospective purchaser.

12. Which of the following court cases is most often cited as the modern authority for prohibiting discrimination on the part of private owners of property?
    A. Shelley v. Kraemer.
    B. Grutter v. Bollinger.
    C. Jones v. Mayer.
    D. Brown v. Board of Education.

13. A person who thinks that he has been unlawfully discriminated against under Title VIII of the Civil Rights Act of 1968 may file a complaint with the Department of Housing and Urban Development within which of the following:
    A. Sixty days from the alleged discriminatory practice.
    B. Ninety days from the alleged discriminatory practice.
    C. One hundred-eighty days from the alleged discriminatory practice.

Chapter 18: Fair Housing

   D. One year from the date of the alleged discriminatory practice.

14. The Federal Fair Housing Act makes discrimination in housing illegal if it is based upon all of the following EXCEPT:
   A. Marital status.
   B. Religion.
   C. Race.
   D. Gender.

15. Under the Federal Fair Housing Act, which of the following acts would be exempt:
   A. A private club operating a commercial boarding house that it owns and exclusively supports with club dues.
   B. A religious organization that gives preference to their members in renting church-owned housing.
   C. A private seller who has listed his property with a real estate broker.
   D. The owner of a 4-unit residential property who lives in one of the units and advertises, "Married Couples Only."

16. Single-family housing that is privately owned may be sold or rented without being subject to the provisions of the Federal Fair Housing Act if:
   A. Not more than four single family houses are owned by the individual at any one time.
   B. Only one sale has occurred within any 24 month period and the owner was not the most recent resident prior to the sale.
   C. The owner uses the services of a real estate agent who has signed an affirmative marketing pact.
   D. The owner clearly advertises his preferences to avoid confrontation at the home site.

17. Which of the following statements concerning discrimination is NOT true:
   A. An owner selling his own home will be in violation of the Federal Fair Housing Act if he advertises "Persons of Irish Ancestry Preferred."
   B. No violation of the Federal Fair Housing Act has occurred if the privately-operated Buffalo's Club advertised rooms in a building it owns for rent to "Members only."
   C. A multiple listing service cannot broadcast property data to its members that suggests a preference as to the religion of purchasers.
   D. A tenant who rents a unit in a duplex may be evicted by the landlord based on the tenant's unexpected pregnancy.

18. Alice, a 23 year old single parent with three children, applies to rent an apartment located in a singles-only housing complex where she hopes to eventually meet someone with whom she can share her life. Alice's friend Betty, also a tenant, recommended the complex to her. Alice is rejected because the landlord feels that the presence of the children might discourage other "swinging singles" from locating there. After Betty complains to the Secretary of HUD, Betty is evicted. All of the following statements are true EXCEPT:
   A. The rejection of Alice violates the Federal Fair Housing Act.
   B. The landlord's actions are justifiable due to the adult-only exemption.
   C. Such reprisal action against Betty violates the Federal Fair Housing Act.
   D. Familial status is a protected classification under Federal law.

19. The prohibitions of the 1968 Fair Housing Act do not apply to privately-owned housing when:
   A. A broker or other person engaged in selling or renting dwellings is used.
   B. Discriminatory advertising is used.
   C. The owner is subject to a valid exemption.
   D. The owner holds a real estate broker's license.

20. A seller lists his home with a real estate broker. The broker begins to show the seller's home to a same-sex couple with the seller present. The seller pulls the broker to the side and whispers that he steadfastly refuses to sell the home to the buyers based on what he claims are strongly-held beliefs. Which of the following statements about this situation is most accurate?
   A. The seller has engaged in illegal discrimination, but only because the property was listed with a licensed real estate broker.
   B. There is no circumstance under which the seller has engaged in illegal discrimination.
   C. The owner has engaged in an illegal act of discrimination against the buyers if there is a local ordinance that includes sexual orientation as a protected classification.
   D. Illegal discrimination would only occur if the buyers had made a full price offer that the seller refused to accept.

21. A complainant under the Federal Fair Housing Act may undertake all EXCEPT which of the following actions?
   A. Calling on the Attorney General's office for assistance in processing the complaint.
   B. Filing a complaint with the Department of Housing and Urban Development.
   C. Filing a civil lawsuit in a U.S. District Court.
   D. Seeking damages without limit in the amount.

22. Under Federal Fair Housing, the burden to prove there was discrimination is on which of the following parties:
   A. The court in which the complaint is filed.

B. The complainant.
C. the respondent.
D. The Secretary of HUD.

23. The Civil Rights Act of 1866 prohibits discrimination in housing on the basis of:
A. Race.
B. Religion.
C. National origin.
D. Familial status.

24. A minority family is moving into an area immediately adjacent to an established subdivision. XYZ Realty enters into an advertising campaign to list homes in the subdivision at discount rates if the owners list within 45 days. There is no evidence that the broker is motivated by the minority family moving into the adjacent area. Which of the following is true?
A. The broker's license can be revoked.
B. The broker's actions amount to implied blockbusting.
C. The broker's actions are not illegal.
D. Brokers cannot lower their standard rate of commission.

25. A particular commercial bank has blocked out certain regions of the community where it will not place loans because of perceived unfavorable conditions. Such practice is called:
A. Redlining.
B. Steering.
C. Warehousing.
D. Relocating.

26. Of the following statements, which is accurate as applied to the Americans with Disabilities Act:
A. Real estate salespersons are not covered by the act since they are traditionally hired as independent contractors.
B. A person who claims that he has been discriminated against on the basis of sexual orientation is entitled to relief.
C. Employees are not covered by the act in regard to employment advancement opportunities.
D. A person who feels that he has been the object of discrimination due to the fact that he is a rehabilitated drug user is covered under the Act.

27. A broker is discussing a new listing with a prospective African-American buyer. The buyer wants to inspect the property immediately but the listing owner has instructed the broker not to show the house during the owner's three-week absence. The broker should do which of the following?
A. Show the property to avoid a violation of the Federal Fair Housing Act.
B. Request the state licensing department to arbitrate the problem.
C. Report the incident to the equal housing committee of the local real estate board.
D. Convey the owner's instructions that the home not be shown to anyone during his absence.

28. All EXCEPT which of the following acts on the part of a real estate licensee would constitute steering and thus be prohibited under the Federal Fair Housing Act?
A. Directing a prospective buyer of one national origin to work with a salesperson of the same national origin who works in the office.
B. Directing a member of one race away from properties located in areas dominated by other races.
C. Making a good-faith suggestion to a client that a neighborhood may be unsafe due to hostile attitudes toward members of a protected class who reside there.
D. Showing several homes in an integrated neighborhood that a buyer as identified as possible purchase properties.

29. A public accommodation under the Americans with Disabilities Act must comply with certain building requirements. All of the following are designated as a public accommodation under the act except:
A. A church.
B. A fast food restaurant.
C. A branch office for a real estate company under 2,000 square feet.
D. A bowling alley.

30. The Michigan Civil Rights Department and Michigan courts may do which of the following to ensure the equal enjoyment of real property:
A. Expel a broker from a multiple listing service.
B. Issue a $100,000 fine for a first offense.
C. Approve a plan to correct past discriminatory practices, but only if race is involved.
D. Issue an injunction.

31. When you are taking a listing on an owner-occupied single-family residence, if the owner states that you are not to show the property to anyone of the Irish nationality, you should:
A. Ignore the request and proceed with the listing.
B. Comply with your principal's request.
C. Make note of the fact in the listing and continue to list hoping that no Irish want to see the property.
D. Refuse to take the listing.

Chapter 19
Real Estate License Law

Understanding Michigan's statutory requirements for the real estate industry.

I. **Foreword**: By this point in the textbook, it should be clear that the real estate industry is not only essential to maintaining strong and vibrant communities, it is also vital to the United States economy. The industry supplies jobs and represents an important part of the country's workforce. While the industry is populated with honest, ethical, and hardworking brokers and salespersons, not every licensee follows the same path of professionalism. In a perfect world, there would be no need for laws and rules because everyone would abide by "The Ethics of Reciprocity" which is more commonly known as the Golden Rule.

As long as there are individuals who show little regard for the rights of others, there will be a need for laws and their enforcement. An orderly society depends on having laws that set minimum standards of acceptable practice for everyone to follow. Some industries such as real estate have an even greater need for established guidelines due to the public trust placed in its practitioners. This chapter explores one of the three primary sources of regulation for real estate professionals–real estate license law.

A. **Protects the public**: License laws are designed to protect the public from unscrupulous and dishonest real estate licensees. This is accomplished by requiring all persons who wish to practice real estate to first obtain a license and to be placed under the jurisdiction of an administrative agency. Although the intent of license law is to protect the public rather than licensees, an argument can be made that some provisions do help create a level playing field for all licensees by limiting the activities of those who choose to be dishonest.

B. **Minimum entry requirements**: Most licensed professions, including real estate, require license applicants to complete certain entry-level education requirements. Then, they are asked to pass an examination to demonstrate their understanding of the laws and regulations to which they will be bound. Completing the education and passing the required examination does not guarantee a consumer that a particular licensed professional will be a great agent. It does, however, assure the consumer that the licensee has met and will be held to minimum standards of competence.

II. **Administrative agencies**: Enforcement of license laws is typically vested in a state administrative agency known as a licensing board, real estate commission, bureau, or department. Regardless of its specific name, a licensing agency is authorized by statute to issue real estate licenses to qualified individuals and to impose disciplinary actions when warranted. These actions can include license suspension or revocation and monetary fines. If the licensing statute includes a provision that allows for a prison sentence, only a court of law can impose it (rather than the licensing agency).

A. **Michigan's licensing agency–LARA**: Presently, the official title of Michigan's licensing agency is the Michigan Department of Licensing and Regulatory Affairs, or LARA for short. According to its website, LARA's mission is to support business growth and job creation while safeguarding Michigan's citizens through a simple, fair, efficient, and transparent regulatory structure. For ease of learning, LARA will simply be referred to as the department.

B. **Authority over unlicensed persons**: Under the law, certain activities (such as receiving commissions for the sale of real estate for others) require a license. One possible violation occurs when the activities of an individual fall within the statutory definition of a broker or salesperson, but the individual does not have the required license. This is one example of how an action can be brought against an unlicensed individual, i.e., a member of the public, for violating real estate license law. A prosecuting attorney would be the likely official to pursue an action against the individual for operating without a license (since doing so is a misdemeanor offense).

III. **Source of license regulation**: All states have some form of real estate license law. The authority to pass license laws emanates from the police power of the state. As discussed in Chapter 11, all police power devices (such as license laws) are designed to promote the health, safety, and welfare of the public. Since real estate license laws protect the interests of the public from dishonest individuals, licensed or otherwise, the laws are proper tools for regulating conduct.

   A. **Components of real estate regulation**: Real estate regulations consist of a series of separate but related statutes, along with administrative rules that govern the practice of real estate. If a statute defines what is required of a licensee under certain circumstances, the administrative rules may further explain how that must be accomplished. For example, a particular statutory provision defines a real estate broker and what acts the broker can perform under his license. The administrative rules further spell out how these acts must be carried out. By analogy, if a statute requires a person to "bake a cake," the rules provide the "recipe."

      1. **Administrative rules**: An administrative rule is a statement by an agency of how it interprets the law. Administrative rules also represent how an agency intends to implement the law. In a broader sense, rules are an important set of policy statements that indicate to all interested parties, especially licensees, how the law will be applied in both general and specific terms. In Michigan, the administrative rules for the practice of real estate are promulgated (i.e., published and officially announced) pursuant to the Michigan Administrative Procedures Act of 1969.

      2. **Enforceability of administrative rules**: Although administrative rules differ from statutes, they can be enforced through hearings similar to those conducted by a court of law. Michigan's Administrative Procedures Act specifies how enforcement proceedings must be conducted before any state administrative agency such as the department. These guidelines ensure that all parties to a hearing, especially the respondent, are afforded a fair hearing (as guaranteed by the state and federal Constitutions). The substance of Michigan's administrative rules is covered in Chapter 20.

   B. **Michigan license law**: Michigan's first license law, Public Act 306, was enacted in 1919 and became effective January 1, 1920. Since then, it has been amended (i.e., modified) several times to keep pace with changes in the way business is conducted. For example, in 1994 the license law was amended to acknowledge the practice of buyer's agency. It was amended in 2008 to allow for the practice of limited service agency. In 2017, yet another amendment changed several provisions to bring license law into closer alignment with modern real estate practices.

      1. **Statutory layout**: Michigan's real estate license law experienced a sweeping overhaul in 1980 when the Michigan Legislature passed Public Act 299. Presently known as the Occupational Code, it created a statutory umbrella that consolidated many different licensed occupations, including real estate.

         a. **Articles**: The Occupational Code consists of Articles that deal with various aspects of code enforcement. Articles 1 through 6 are considered to be generic in character because they discuss matters that are general to all covered occupations. After Article 6, the balance of the Articles are individually assigned to particular occupations and address specific requirements for each one. For example, a real estate licensee is subject to the provisions of Articles 1 through 6 and Article 25.

         b. **Sections**: An Article is divided into several numbered sections (that are abbreviated in these materials as Sec.). Section numbers correspond to the specific Article in which they are located. Each section may then be divided into one or more subsections. A subsection is noted in parentheses. Fortunately for those who are using this textbook to prepare for the Michigan salesperson's or broker's examination, there is no need to memorize the numbers of Articles or sections. All that is necessary is a thorough working knowledge of the information contained in the license law and rules.

      2. **Redbook**: For many years, the department published the statutory provisions affecting the practice of real estate in a soft cover handbook officially titled the "Real Estate Law Book." Since it was published with a red cover, it was informally dubbed the "Redbook" by industry professionals. The last edition of the "Redbook" was published by the department in October, 2011. Many veteran brokers and licensees still have these older editions in their offices. They should not be used to prepare for the salesperson's or broker's examination since they are all out-of-date. Further, practitioners should not use them for guidance on license law and rules.

         As of the date of this publication, Chapters 19 and 20 of this textbook contain the most current version of real estate license laws and rules. If you are preparing for the real estate exam, check with your course provider to see if any information updates are available. The department also has a link to the most current

Chapter 19: Real Estate License Law

version of the laws and rules on its website at <michigan.gov/realestate>. There you will find "Quick Links" to Articles 1–6 of the Occupational Code, Article 25, and Administrative Rules.

C. **Other ways in which activities are regulated**: Licensed individuals must remember that they are bound by many forms of regulation that affect the practice of real estate. For example, in addition to license laws and administrative rules, licensees are bound by state and federal statutes, local municipal code provisions, and precedents established in appellate-level court cases. If the licensee is a member of a trade association and its multiple listing service, he will also be bound by the association's code of ethics and its MLS rules and regulations.

Equally important is the fact that all licensees who are affiliated with an employing broker are bound by the broker's company policies and procedures. A broker's policies and procedures manual is important because it set the scope of what each affiliated licensee must do to comply with the broker's risk management strategies. See Chapters 2 and 3 for further information about real estate company policies and procedures manuals.

IV. **Student notes**: The following notes apply to the information contained in Chapters 19 and 20 of this textbook.

  A. **Subsection and subrule references**: As these two chapters are read, you will notice numbers listed on the left side of many pages. The numbers correspond to a specific numbered subsection or subrule in the actual Occupational Code and Administrative Rules.

  1. **Study tip 1**: With some of the sections and rules, numbers and/or letters are missing from the sequence. This was done intentionally. The subsections and subrules of lesser importance, those which are repetitive, those which have little or no impact on the actual practice of real estate or the real estate examination, and those that apply to a different occupation have been omitted from this material. This is designed to make it easier to focus on the key provisions that have the highest degree of likelihood of appearing on the exam or would be vital to everyday practice. As discussed, the full text of real estate license laws and administrative rules is available on the department's website.

  As a side note, statutes are frequently amended over time by the legislature. When this occurs, entire sections of a statute may be repealed, meaning officially removed. This can create numbering gaps in the remainder of the statute or rule.

  2. **Study tip 2**: Many sections and rules contain multiple topics without setting them apart in separately numbered subsections or subrules. Long and detailed paragraphs are consistent with the drafting style used in most statutes.

    /1/ To make it easier for you when reading this textbook, sections and rules with multiple concepts have been broken apart using the special format you see here in Study tip 2.

    /2/ Whenever you encounter italicized numbers formatted with forward slashes, / /, they have been added by the author to break down complex sections or rules. These numbers, for example /4/, contain information that is actually found in the license law or rules. They have been added to assist with learning.

  3. **Study tip 3**: Other explanations are provided at the end of several subsections and rules. They are set apart from the actual law or rule as follows: (Note: ...). When you see this, it contains explanation or detail added by the author to help you understand what the subsection or subrule says, but is not actually part of the law or rule. Finally, portions of the discussion about license law and rules have been paraphrased for ease of learning. Refer to the LARA website to access the full text of the license law and rules.

  B. **Cross referencing**: Several provisions in the license law and rules make reference to other provisions. Anytime you encounter a sentence that ends with the following, "–see Sec. 519(1)" it is a cross reference recommendation. Using the example, you would compare what you are reading with the information contained in section 519, subsection (1) elsewhere in the textbook.

  C. **Broker/Associate Broker references**: For the most part, the terms "broker" and "associate broker" are used interchangeably in Chapters 19 and 20. There are circumstances, however, where the license law and rules draw distinctions between the two types of licenses. When this arises, they will be pointed out and clearly noted. Otherwise, assume that the term broker also includes associate broker.

  One particularly important difference is that a broker is licensed to conduct real estate business under the name in which the license is issued. There can only be one broker's license issued to a firm whether it is in the name of a natural person or in the name of a business entity. All other individuals who are licensed to the firm in the capacity of a broker must obtain an associate broker's license. All associate brokers are licensed under the broker and must conduct business under the name in which the broker's license is issued.

[The information in this section begins the review of Michigan License Law as contained in the Occupational Code.]

Occupational Code
P.A. 299 of 1980, as amended

ARTICLE 1
[Covers definitions.]

Sec. 101 [Short title].

Act 299 is called the Occupational Code. A code is a collection of laws and regulations that are classified according to subject matter. A statute is a type of code. The Occupational Code contains Michigan's real estate license law. As you read the Occupational Code, you will notice the frequent use of the word "shall." The word "shall" in a statute means the same thing as the word "must."

Sec. 103 [▶ Definitions; B, C.]

(Note: Most statutes have a definitions section located at or near the beginning. Sometimes definitions are contained within special subsections where the defined terms appear. Having definitions is important since technical terms can sometimes be unclear or interpreted differently by different people. For example, if a statute requires a "real estate broker" to have a license, we need to know how the term "real estate broker" is defined. The information in Sections 103, 104, and 105 contain the definitions of many terms used throughout the license law. Other subsection also contain definitions such as Sections 402, 501a, 551, 601, 2501, and 2517.)

(1) "Board" refers to an agency which is composed mostly of members of a regulated occupation.
(Note: Section 2502 of Article 25 establishes the "Board of Real Estate Brokers and Salespersons." It will be discussed in further detail there.)

(2) "Censure" is defined as an expression of disapproval of a licensee's professional conduct. It does not automatically mean that the licensee violated a law or rule, but the conduct was of such nature that an administrative reprimand or warning was appropriate.
(Note: A censure is a less strict form of discipline that is used for minor violations. It is viewed as a formal, written reprimand by an administrative body.)

(3) "Competence" means a degree of expertise by which a person practices real estate that meets or exceeds minimal standards of acceptable practice–see incompetence in Sec. 104.
(Note: Even though real estate licensees are legally considered to be professionals, they must minimally be competent as defined in this subsection. Licensees must operate at or above this legal bar.)

(4) "Complaint" means an oral or written grievance–see formal complaint in Sec. 104.
(Note: A member of the public may lodge an oral complaint to the department that alleges licensee misconduct. Upon receipt of the complaint, the department will begin an investigation. If the investigation suggests that a violation has occurred, a written formal complaint may be prepared.)

Sec. 104 [Definitions; D to K.]

(1) ▶ "Department" is the term used to refer to Michigan's real estate administrative/licensing agency (which is the Department of Licensing and Regulatory Affairs or LARA for short).
(2) "Director" means the director of the department.
(3) "Disability" refers to an infirmity that prevents a member of a board from performing his duties.
(4) "Files" refers to the records of a board.
(5) "Formal complaint" is a document that states the charges of an alleged violation–see complaint in Sec. 103.
(Note: Although Sec. 501 indicates that anyone may file a complaint with the department alleging misconduct or a violation, only the department or attorney general's office can prepare a formal complaint.)
(6) "General public" refers to an individual who resides in Michigan and is at least 18 years of age. The term does not include a person or spouse of a person who is licensed in the occupation or who has a material financial interest in the occupation being regulated by the Article in which the term "general public" is used.
(7) "Good moral character" is a term that is defined in the Occupational License For Former Offenders Act.
(Note: A person with good moral character is presumed to have a propensity, meaning natural tendency, to serve the public in the licensed area in a fair, honest, and open manner. A person who demonstrates a lack of good moral character is presumed not to have this tendency.)

Chapter 19: Real Estate License Law 335

(8) "Incompetence" is defined as a failure to conform to minimal standards of acceptable real estate practice–see competence in Sec. 103.

(9) "Knowledge and skill" refers to information, education, and practical experience, coupled with the ability to apply it.
(<u>Note:</u> The real estate exam measures if an applicant has sufficient "knowledge and skill" to practice real estate.)

Sec. 105 [Definitions; L to S.]

(1) ▶ "License" is defined as the document issued by the department which allows a person to call himself a real estate broker, associate broker, or salesperson and to practice real estate as defined in Article 25 (anywhere within Michigan). It also refers to the document that permits a real estate school to offer approved educational offerings such as broker's and salesperson's pre-license training.
(<u>Note:</u> A real estate license allows the holder-licensee to provide real estate services anywhere within the state.)

(2) ▶ "Licensee" refers to the actual person who has been issued a license.
(<u>Note:</u> Read all questions carefully since words like "license" and "licensee" are close in spelling and can be misread.)

(3) ▶ "Limitation" means a restriction attached to a license relative to the scope of practice.
(<u>Note:</u> A limitation can be issued as a form of discipline for violating license laws or rules. Of the ten possible limitations, not all are geared toward real estate. Recall that Articles 1 though 6 are generic to multiple occupations. What is a limitation for one occupation may be a requirement for another–see the Note for subsection (3)(i), below.)
A licensee may be:
(a) Limited to performing only specified functions of the occupation.
(b) Limited to performing the occupation only for a specified period of time.
(c) Limited to performing the occupation only within a specified geographical area.
(d) Required to make restitution or perform certain work before issuance, renewal, or reinstatement of a license.
(e) Required to obtain a financial statement certified by a CPA and file it with the department at regular intervals.
(f) Asked to fulfill a requirement that reasonably assures the department of his or her competence.
(g) Required to have all contracts reviewed by an attorney.
(h) Required to have a surety bond or actual cash on file with the department.
(i) Required to deposit all money received in an escrow account that can be disbursed only under certain conditions.
(<u>Note:</u> A broker must maintain an escrow or trust account for the deposit of money belonging to others–see Sec. 2512(k)(i) through (vi) and Rule 313.)
(j) Required to file regular reports with the department.

(4) "Occupation" means a regulated field of endeavor such as real estate.

(5) "Person" means a natural person or business entity such as a sole proprietorship, partnership, association, corporation, limited liability company, or common law trust.
(<u>Note:</u> Article 25 authorizes a business entity to obtain a broker's license in the actual name of the business. If so, the person, i.e., natural person, who actually controls and directs the operations of the company must obtain an associate broker's license. This is discussed later in the chapter. See also control person in Sec. 2501(e).)

(6) "Physical dominion" means control and possession.

(8) ▶ "Probation" means an evaluation of a licensee's fitness to practice real estate which is conducted over time.
(<u>Note:</u> Probation can be viewed as a lesser form of discipline for a less serious violation. Probation is usually reserved for circumstances in which it is believed that the respondent should be given another chance to prove himself worthy of continued licensure, but under the temporary supervision of a named entity.)

(9) "Public access" means the right of a person to view and copy files under Michigan's freedom of information act.

(10) "Registrant" refers to a person who is registered under Act 299.
(<u>Note:</u> One who wishes to engage in real estate activities as a vocation must obtain a license rather than a certificate of registration. Therefore, they are called licensees rather than registrants. See additional notes below.)

(11) "Registration" refers to a document, called a certificate of registration, which enables a person to use a designated title which use would otherwise have been prohibited.
(<u>Note 1:</u> Generally, licensure is reserved for more highly regulated occupations in which various requirements and qualifications must be met before a person can practice the occupation. These requirements can include pre- and post-license education and successful completion of a license examination. In the case of a broker's license, prior real estate or real estate-related experience is also required. For other occupations, registration is required before a person can publicly use certain protected titles such as Forester when performing the activities of the occupation.)
(<u>Note 2:</u> Since real estate requires a license rather than a certificate of registration, references to the terms registration and registrants contained in license law are intentionally ignored in the balance of this chapter.)

(12) "Rule" means a rule created under Michigan's Administrative Procedures Act.
(<u>Note:</u> The authority to create rules stems from license law. Chapter 20 covers Michigan's real estate rules.)

ARTICLE 2
[Covers department administrative issues.]

Sec. 201 [Department; director.]

The department consists of a director as the executive head along with other employees who are appointed or employed by the department. The director is appointed by the governor subject to the advice and consent of the senate.

Sec. 202 [Licensure; form; fees; expiration.]

(1) A license application must be completed on a form provided by the department and submitted with the required fees. A license will be issued to a person who meets all licensure requirements.
(Note: Some of the provisions in the Occupational Code may appear to be so obvious that one might wonder why they are even addressed. For example, if a person meets the licensure requirements, of course he or she should receive a license from the department. Provisions like this are included in the law to leave no doubt whatsoever about an individual's rights. Were this provision not included, the department would not have an absolute mandate to respond by issuing the license. If a provision relating to fees was not included, an applicant for a license could argue that he or she should receive it without having to pay for it.)

(2) The license expiration date is established by rule. Real estate licenses previously expired on October 31 of every third year. Licenses are now issued with staggered expiration dates 3 years from the original date of issuance.

Sec. 203 [Fees; limitation.]

(1) A license shall not be issued without payment of the appropriate fees. This subsection also allows a license to be issued to a person who successfully challenges the licensure requirements, including the examination, as not constituting a fair and adequate measure of the person's knowledge and skills.
(Note: This challenge would likely be unsuccessful since great care, including input from the Board, goes into creating a fair and adequate way to measure an applicant's knowledge and skills.)

(2) ▶ A license may be issued with a limitation. If so, the department must notify and seek approval from the board. A person who receives a limitation may have the decision reviewed (which is a type of appeal)–see also, Sec. 519(1) for more information pertaining to license limitations.

Sec. 204 [▶ Renewal; limitation; renewal as responsibility of licensee; change of address.]

(1) The department must renew the license of a person who fulfills the following requirements:
  (a) Has applied to the department on the proper form and delivers it to the department before the expiration date.
  (b) Has paid the appropriate fees.
  (c) Has met the renewal requirements. (For real estate, this includes fulfilling continuing education.)
(2) A board may waive a continuing education proof requirement if it was due to the licensee's disability, military service, absence from the continental United States, or circumstances beyond the control of the licensee.
(3) A license may be renewed with a limitation. If so, the department must notify and seek approval from the board. A person who receives a limitation may have the decision reviewed (which is a type of appeal)–see also, Sec. 519(1) for more information pertaining to license limitations.
(4) A licensee is responsible for renewing his or her own license.
  /1/ The renewal application is mailed to the licensee's last known address.
  /2/ Failure to notify the department of a change of address will not extend the expiration date and may result in discipline.
(5) Change of address or electronic mail address (see below) must be reported to the department within 30 days of the change.
(6) If a licensee agrees in writing, the department may contact the licensee using electronic mail for any communication that the department would normally serve by first-class mail.

Sec. 205 [Promulgation of rules.]

This section contains the statutory authority for the department to create the rules it believes are necessary for it to implement articles 1 to 6 and to fulfill its role under Act 299.

Sec. 206 [Examination; administration.]

(1) Before administering the real estate exam, the department and board must review it to make sure that it measures whether a person has the sufficient level of knowledge and skill to competently practice real estate–see Sec.

Chapter 19: Real Estate License Law

104(9) for the definition of knowledge and skill; see also Sec. 316(1) regarding the department's and board's right to develop an exam or outsource it to another entity.

(2) The department may either administer, score, and monitor a licensing exam or delegate the process to another entity (which it currently does to "PSI Licensure:Certification").

Sec. 207 [Approval of school; continuing education.]

(1) The department may issue an approval to a real estate school–see Rule 601.
(2) The department may grant approval to a continuing education program.
(3) School approval must be processed within 90 days.
(4) If the department asks the board to approve a school or a program, the board shall process the request within 90 days.

Sec. 208 [▶ Files of board; physical dominion.]

The department has control over the files of the board and must assure that public access laws are met.
(Note: The word "control" is also known as "physical dominion" under the Occupational Code.)

Sec. 210 [Contracting with persons or agencies.]

To fulfill its responsibilities, the department may contract with outside persons or agencies–see Rule 101(1)(a) for an example of one such outside agency, e.g., a "statewide real estate related trade association." The department currently contracts with an outside company to administer real estate license examinations.

ARTICLE 3
[Defines and delineates the Board of Real Estate Brokers and Salespersons.]

Sec. 301 [▶ Boards; composition.]

Each board has 9 voting members; 6 are currently licensed in the occupation and 3 represent the general public. A board member must be 18 years of age and a Michigan resident.

Sec. 302 [▶ Nomination and appointment of board members.]

The governor appoints board members and fills vacancies (subject to the advice and consent of the senate). In making an appointment, the governor shall seek nominations from a wide range of interested groups and persons, including appropriate professional associations.

Sec. 303 [Terms of board members; vacancy; appointment and removal.]

(1) A board member is appointed to a 4-year term. A person appointed to fill a vacancy shall serve for the balance of the term.
(2) An individual shall not serve for more than 2 consecutive terms.
(4) For members who are required to be licensed, they must possess a valid license in the occupation that the board monitors.

Sec. 304 [Compensation and expenses of board members.]

The legislature annually establishes the per diem compensation members of the board receive. Allowable travel and other expenses are payable by the department according to a standardized budget.
(Note: "Per diem" is Latin for "per day." It is an allowance given to board members for their time serving on the board.)

Sec. 305 [Board; availability of files.]

(1) A board shall meet as often as necessary to fulfill its duties, but not less than 2 times per year.
(2) Board files are open to public inspection under Sec. 208.

Sec. 306 [Board; election of officers; report.]

(1) The board shall elect a chairperson and vice-chairperson each year.
(2) A board may adopt bylaws to regulate its internal affairs.
(3) A board shall report its activities to the department.

Sec. 307 [▶ Board; creation within department; duties.]

(1) The board exists within the department.
(Note: The department has primary control over licensing activities. The board provides input and gives the department profession-related technical support from the perspectives of licensees and members of the general public.)
(2) A board's duties include: interpreting licensure requirements; furnishing aid in investigations conducted under Article 5; at its discretion, having a member attend an informal conference; and assisting the department in the implementation of Act 299.

Sec. 308 [▶ Promulgation of rules.]

(1) Each board creates its own rules to fulfill its role or mission.
(2) The board may also promulgate (meaning publish and put into effect) rules to set minimum standards of acceptable practice for a regulated occupation.

Sec. 309 [▶ Assessment of penalties.]

If a respondent is found guilty at a hearing of violating the law or rules, the board can assess a penalty under article 6. (Note: This is important since most of the board members have real estate licenses. Experienced real estate licensees are well-equipped to understand the seriousness of real estate violations and to assess the most suitable penalty.)

Sec. 313 [Recommending licensure of school.]

While the board may recommend whether to grant approval to a school or person offering certain training in real estate, the department actually approves schools and ensures compliance. The enforcement division of the department regulates schools by investigating any complaints.

Sec. 316 [Examination or test; development; closed session; alternative form of testing.]

(1) The board and the department may either develop the required written exam or adopt an exam prepared by another agency–see Sec. 206(1).
(2) Developing an exam may take place in a closed session.
(3) For persons with a disability, alternative forms of testing must be made available to enable them to demonstrate the required level of knowledge and skill.

ARTICLE 4
[Covers licensing issues such as renewal, relicensure and reinstatement.]

Sec. 401 [Specific amounts to be charged for licenses.]

The fees charged for licenses are prescribed in Michigan's State License Fee Act.

Sec. 402 [▶ Definitions.]

(a) "Expiration date" means the date set forth in the rules for license expiration.
(b) "Reinstatement" means the granting of a license, with or without limitation, to a person whose license has been revoked.
(c) "Relicensure" means the granting of a license to a person whose license has lapsed for failure to renew within 60 days after expiration.
(Note: Be aware of the difference between reinstatement and relicensure. Reinstatement is what follows the loss of a license as a result of discipline. Relicensure results from simply failing to renew in a timely fashion.)

Sec. 405 [Nonrefundable application processing fee; examination fee; fee for initial license.]

A license application must include a nonrefundable application processing fee. This is assessed in addition to the examination fee and the fee for the initial license.

Sec. 407 [Examination fee; forfeiture; reexamination fee; publication of application deadline.]

(1) An examination fee must be paid before a person can be scheduled for an examination.
(2) Failure to appear for the exam results in forfeiture of the exam fee.

Chapter 19: Real Estate License Law

(3) Reexamination requires payment of the exam fee. If a person does not receive a passing score, the entire exam must be retaken.
(4) The department must publish the deadline by which exam applications have to be received in its application instructions.

Sec. 409 [Payment of fee as condition to receive license; period for completion of requirements.]

(1) A person who completes the license or renewal requirements will not be issued a license until the license fee is paid.
(3) Application fees are good for 1 year from the date of receipt. If the license requirements are not completed by then, the fees are deemed forfeited to the department and the application is voided.

Sec. 411 [▶ Failure to renew license; conditions to relicensing.]

(1) Subject to subsection (2), a person fails to renew on or before expiration cannot practice real estate once the license actually expires. The license expires 3 years from the original date of issuance, and every 3 years thereafter.
(Note: A licensee may continue the uninterrupted practice of real estate while awaiting receipt of license renewal if the department received the renewal application on or before it lapses, and the required continuing education is completed by that date. E.g., if the original issue date is March 1, it expires on April 30 of the third year.)
(2) A person not renewing by the expiration date has up to 60 days thereafter to renew. Although the licensee can still renew any time during this late renewal period, he or she may not work after the expiration date.
(3) A person who does not renew within the 60-day late renewal period may be relicensed without examination and further education if all of the following conditions are met:
   (a) The person applies within 3 years after expiration.
   (b) An application processing fee, late renewal fee, and per year license fee are paid.
   (c) All disciplinary actions are satisfied.
   (d) One year's continuing education requirements have been met within the preceding 12 months.
(4) Relicensure (i.e., loss of license resulting from failure to renew) 3 years or more after expiration requires a person to retake the exam, complete all requirements, or meet the current education requirements for the license.
(5) In the case of reinstatement (i.e., loss of license resulting from revocation rather than failure to renew), the following must be submitted to the department:
   – An application for reinstatement;
   – The application processing fee; and
   – A petition stating the reasons for reinstatement.
   If approved, the person applying must also pay the per-year license fee.
   (Note: Under Sec. 2502a(7), the person must wait 3 years from revocation to reapply and must retake all education.)
(6) The department must issue an initial or renewal license within 90 days after an applicant files an application with the department. If the application is deficient for any reason, the department must notify the applicant of the deficiency within 30 days of receipt including what additional information is needed.
   (Note: There are 2 important caveats: This subsection does not apply to salespersons or appraisers–see subsection 10, below. And, time periods are reduced for real estate brokers and associate brokers–see subsection 7, below.)
(7) In the case of a broker's or associate broker's license, the time for approval (discussed in subsection 6, above) is reduced to 30 days and the time for notification of incomplete applications is reduced to 15 days after receipt by the department.
(8) If the department fails to issue or deny a license within the times specified in subsections 6 and 7, the department must return the license fee paid by the applicant and reduce the next renewal application (if any) by 15%.
(9) The department director must file a report with the legislature concerning the following information from the previous fiscal year:
   – The number of applications received and completed within the 90- and 30-day time periods.
   – The number of applications denied.
   – The number of applicants not issued a license within the time required and the amount of money returned as a result.
(10) Subsection 6 does not apply to certain specified licenses including real estate salespersons and appraisers.
(11) An individual or qualifying officer of a company who is a licensee and who is mobilized for military duty in the armed forces of the United States is temporarily exempt from the requirements of the Occupational Code including license renewal and continuing education.
   /1/ The licensee must inform the department via mail or e-mail of his or her desire to exercise the exemption and include proof of active duty service.

/2/ If the licensee is responsible for supervision and oversight, i.e., acted as a broker or principal associate broker, he or she must also make arrangements for someone else to assume the supervisory and oversight responsibilities of the real estate company.

/3/ The temporary exemption is valid until 90 days from release from active duty, but cannot exceed 36 months from the date of license expiration (which is the period within which any lapsed license can be relicensed without retesting–see subsection 3, above). The licensee must also fulfill all continuing education requirements that accumulated while he or she was on active duty.

ARTICLE 5
[Covers complaints, investigations, hearings, and enforcement.]

Sec. 501 [▶ Lodging or filing a complaint.]

Complaints must be lodged with the department. Although anyone can file a complaint (by either oral or written grievance), only the department or the Attorney General's office prepares the actual formal complaint after a complaint has been received and a violation established–see Sec. 104(5).

(Note: Sec. 2512(2)(a) and (b) now require that a complaint lodged under Article 5 be filed within 18 months of either the date of the alleged violation or, if a real estate transaction is involved, the date the transaction is completed.)

Sec. 501a [Definitions.]

(a) "Complainant" means a person who has filed a complaint alleging a violation of Act 299, a rule, or an order.
(b) "Respondent" means a person against whom a complaint is filed, including unlicensed members of the public.
(Note: A complainant is similar to a plaintiff in a legal action, and a respondent is similar to a defendant.)

Sec. 502 [▶ Investigation; correspondence file; complaint made by department.]

Upon receipt of a complaint, the department must begin an investigation and open a correspondence file. The department must make written acknowledgment to the complainant within 15 days of receipt.

Sec. 503 [▶ Investigation; petition to issue subpoena.]

It may be necessary to subpoena records or require the testimony of an individual as part of an investigation. Since no hearing is involved at this stage, the department must ask the attorney general to petition (i.e., request) a circuit court to issue the subpoena–see also Sec. 512.

(Note: The Attorney General safeguards against unwarranted subpoenas being issued in an investigation conducted prior to the filing of formal charges. Only a court can issue a subpoena at this point in the process.)

Sec. 504 [▶ Investigations; status; time extension; preparation of action; informal conference.]

(1) If an investigation cannot be completed within 30 days, the director may extend the time.
(2) If the investigative report does not disclose a violation, the complaint must be closed. The parties can provide additional information at this point for the purpose of having the complaint possibly reopened.
(3) If the report discloses evidence of a violation, the department or attorney general's office must take appropriate action which may include:
   (a) Preparation of a formal complaint.
   (b) Issuance of a cease and desist order.
   (c) Issuance of a notice of summary suspension.
      (Note: Summary actions are authorized if an immediate public threat exists and there is no time for a hearing.)
   (d) Issuance of a citation.
(4) The department may bring the complainant and respondent together for an informal conference during which the department attempts to resolve the issues to reach a settlement or stipulation.
(Note: A stipulation is an agreement by the parties as to a set of facts. It eliminates the need to prove uncontested facts and simplifies hearings.)

Sec. 505 [▶ Summary suspension; petition to dissolve order; hearing.]

(1) After conducting an investigation, the department may order a summary suspension of a license based on the belief that an imminent threat to the public health, safety, and welfare exists. Thereafter, any hearing shall be promptly commenced and decided.

Chapter 19: Real Estate License Law

(Note: A summary suspension in this context is a form of emergency action used to stop a serious alleged offender from further wrongful conduct while awaiting more formal and potentially time-consuming proceedings.)
(2) A person whose license is summarily suspended can petition the department for a hearing to dissolve the order.
(3) The administrative law hearings examiner must dissolve the order in the absence of evidence of an imminent threat.
(Note: An administrative law hearings examiner is an individual who works for, or is appointed by, an administrative agency to conduct a matter that requires adjudication. To adjudicate means to act as a judge.)
(4) The record created at a hearing to dissolve a summary suspension becomes part of the record to be used at any subsequent hearing based on the allegations in the complaint.

Sec. 506 [▶ Cease and desist order; hearing; application to restrain and enjoin.]

(1) The director may issue a cease and desist order after conducting an investigation.
(Note: A cease and desist order is a demand by an administrative agency or court that a person stop engaging in a certain course of action.)
(2) A person ordered to cease and desist can appeal the decision by requesting a hearing.
(3) If the cease and desist order is violated, the department or attorney general's office can apply for a restraining order or injunction.
(Note: A restraining order is a temporary court order, in the nature of an injunction, that prohibits a person from engaging in certain conduct until a hearing can be held on the injunction.)

Sec. 507 [▶ Informal conference; criminal prosecution.]

If a summary suspension order is issued, it does not replace an informal conference, prosecution, or other proceeding.
(Note: Additional action will still be taken against a respondent even though he or she is subject to summary suspension.)

Sec. 508 [▶ Formal complaint; options; methods of settlement.]

(1) After an investigation has been conducted and a violation has been substantiated, the formal complaint is prepared and then delivered to the respondent and complainant. The respondent is also given a choice of the following:
   (a) Negotiate a settlement.
   (b) Demonstrate compliance.
   (c) A contested case hearing.
(2) The respondent will have 15 days to select one of the options. If one is not selected, a contested case hearing is held.
(3) An informal conference may result in: a license revocation, suspension, or limitation; censure; probation; restitution; or other article 6 penalty (which can include up to a $10,000 civil fine for each substantiated violation).
(4) A department employee or agent may represent the department at a contested case hearing.

Sec. 510 [▶ Showing compliance.]

A respondent can always demonstrate compliance as a defense.

Sec. 511 [▶ Hearing.]

If an informal conference is not held or does not result in a settlement, a hearing must be held (which may be attended by a board member).

Sec. 512 [Subpoena.]

This section covers subpoenas issued during the course of a contested case hearing. Since the department's role in a hearing may be that of fact finder (similar to the function a court plays when hearing a case without a jury), the department may petition a circuit court directly for a subpoena.
(Note: This is contrasted with subpoena power under Sec. 503 where the department's function is merely investigative.)

Sec. 513 [▶ Findings of fact; hearing report.]

(1) When a hearing is concluded, the administrative law hearings examiner must submit a report to the department, the attorney general's office, and the board. The report may recommend Article 6 penalties, or in the case of a finding of no violation, no penalties or a recommend dismissal of the complaint.
(2) The hearing report must also be given to the complainant and respondent.

Sec. 514 [▶ Determination of penalties; hearing report; board member prohibition.]

(1) The board must meet and determine the penalties to be assessed within 60 days of receipt of an administrative law hearings examiner's report.
(2) If the board does not determine the appropriate penalties within the time required, the director may do so.
(3) A board member who participated in the investigation or attended an informal conference cannot participate in the final determination of penalties (or determination that no penalties will be assessed) on that complaint.

Sec. 515 [Petition for review generally.]

A person whose license or renewal is denied may petition (which is a form of appeal) the department and the board for a review of the denial.

Sec. 516 [Petition for review; contents.]

The appeal discussed in Sec. 515 must be in writing and state the reasons why the license should be issued.

Sec. 517 [Consideration for petition; alternative form of testing.]

Pursuant to Sec. 515 involving a denial of license or renewal, the department or board may administer an alternative form of testing or conduct a personal interview with the petitioner or both.

Sec. 518 [Issuance of license or renewal based on review of qualifications.]

Pursuant to Sec. 515, the department may issue the license or renewal if the department and board determine that the petitioner could perform the occupation with competence.

Sec. 519 [Petition to review limitation on license or renewal.]

(1) As noted at Sec. 203(2) and Sec. 204(3), a person may have a limitation imposed when a license is issued or renewed. This section affords the person an opportunity to petition the department within 30 days for a review of the decision to impose the limitation.
(2) After receiving the petition from the person, the department has 15 days to set forth the reasons for imposing the limitation.
(3) The department or board may remove the limitation if it is believed the person could perform each function of the occupation with competence in the absence of the limitation.

Sec. 520 [Petition to review decision denying person licensure.]

A school, institution, program, or other person that has been denied approval may appeal the decision within 30 days by way of a petition filed with the department.

Sec. 521 [Consideration of petition; reinvestigation; reply.]

In considering the petition, the department and board may reinvestigate the school, institution, program, or other person, including its curriculum or program before replying to the petition.

Sec. 551 [Additional definitions.]

(a) "Employee of the department" refers to any direct employee or contractor who enforces the provisions of Act 299.
(b) "Citation" is a form prepared by the department under Sec. 553.
   (Note: Since this definition is brief, refer to Sec. 553 for details.)

Sec. 553 [▶ Citation generally.]

(1) The department may issue a citation to a licensee if a violation of Act 299, the rules, or an order appears to exist.
   (Note: Citations are usually issued for minor violations of the law or rules. This allows the department to avoid holding more formal proceedings. A citation issued for a violation of Act 299 is analogous to a ticket issued for a minor traffic violation.)
(2) A citation may be sent to a respondent by certified mail or delivered in person.
(3) Among other things, the citation contains the following:
   (a) The date of the citation.
   (b) Who issued the citation.

Chapter 19: Real Estate License Law

(c) The respondent's name and address along with a statement that he or she is being cited for a violation of the act, rules, or order.
(d) A brief description of the conduct considered to be a violation.
(e) The proposed penalties, including the payment of a fine not to exceed $100 for each violation.
(f) A space for the respondent to sign as a receipt.
(g) A space where the respondent may accept the citation and agree to comply.
(h) A notice that the citation must be accepted or rejected within 30 days.
(i) A brief description of the hearing process and the process for a settlement through an informal conference.

Sec. 555 [▶ Citation; notice of acceptance or denial; disclosure; removal from records.]

(1) A respondent has 30 days to either accept the citation terms or deny the violation it cites.
(2) If the respondent accepts the citation terms, he or she must sign and return it to the department along with the fine or other required material.
  – If no further disciplinary actions are recorded for 5 years, the citation is removed from the records.
  – A 1-page explanation can be prepared by the respondent and placed in the department's files which will be provided any time the citation is disclosed.
(3) If the respondent does not admit to the violation, he or she can select a negotiated settlement, demonstrate compliance, or select a contested case hearing.

Sec. 557 [Effect of signing citation.]

The signing of a citation is only a receipt and not an admission to the violation.

ARTICLE 6
[Covers penalties, sanctions, and enumerates impermissible conduct.]

Sec. 601 [▶ Practicing regulated occupation without license; violation as misdemeanor; etc.]

(1) A person cannot engage in the practice of real estate or call himself a licensee without a current license.
(Note: This and other provisions of Article 6 emphasize the fact that real estate law applies to both licensed and unlicensed persons.)
(2) An approval is required to operate a real estate school.
(3) A person whose license is suspended, revoked, or lapsed is considered to be unlicensed.
(4) A person or school that violates subsections (1) or (2) is guilty of a misdemeanor punishable by a fine of $500 and/or 90 days imprisonment.
(Note: A misdemeanor is a breach of criminal law as opposed to civil law. Under criminal law, offenses are classified into felonies and lesser offenses called misdemeanors. Further, only a court of law can impose a prison sentence.)
(5) A second offense is a misdemeanor punishable by a fine of $1,000 and/or 1 year imprisonment.
(8) Any violation of Act 299 must include a requirement that restitution be made (if the findings substantiate its imposition)–see Sec. 602.
(9) An affected person may seek an injunction from a court to prevent someone from operating without a license or approval pursuant to subsections (1) and (2).
(11) "Affected person" is defined as anyone, including a board or private association, who has been directly impacted by the actions of one operating without a license or approval.
(12) An investigation may be conducted under article 6 to enforce its requirements.
(13) The department, attorney general, or a county prosecutor may utilize a forfeiture action as a remedy–see Sec. 606 for further details on its application.
(Note: Forfeiture relates to the loss or surrender of property as a penalty–see Sec. 606 for further information on the definition of a forfeiture action.)
(14) The remedies described in this section may be pursued independently of other remedies. They are also cumulative (which means that imposition of one form of discipline does not act as a bar to other remedies that may be warranted).
(16) Once a conviction is entered by a court under subsection (4) or (5), the department must be notified by mail, facsimile, or electronic mail.

Sec. 602 [▶ Violation of act, rule, or order; penalties.]

The following penalties can be assessed for a violation of Act 299, administrative rules, or an order:

(a) Limitation of license.
(b) Suspension of license.
(c) Denial of a license or its renewal.
(d) Revocation of license.
(e) In the case of a licensee, a maximum $10,000 civil fine paid to the department.
(f) Censure.
(g) Probation.
(h) A requirement that restitution be made based on the findings of a hearing examiner after a contested case hearing.
(Note: Restitution may take the form of money a respondent repays to an innocent party who lost it as a result of the respondent's conduct. It may also take the form of certain work that the respondent must perform.)

Sec. 603 [Restitution; suspension of license.]

If restitution is required, the respondent's license can be suspended until restitution is made.

Sec. 604 [▶ Violation of article regulating occupation; penalties.]

A person who commits 1 or more of the following acts is subject to Sec. 602 penalties.
(Note: This list is generic. Specific acts of violation by real estate licensees are noted in Sec. 2512.)
(a) Fraud or deceit in obtaining a license.
(b) Practicing fraud, deceit, or dishonesty.
(c) Violating a rule.
(d) Lacking good moral character.
(e) Gross negligence.
(f) False advertising.
(g) Committing an act of incompetence.
(h) Violating any other provision of the Occupational Code or rule for which a penalty is not otherwise prescribed.
(Note: This is a catch-all provision that closes any potential penalty loopholes.)
(i) Failing to comply with a subpoena.
(j) Failing to respond to a citation.
(k) Violating or failing to comply with a final order of the board.
(l) Aiding or abetting another person in the unlicensed practice of an occupation.

Sec. 605 [Action in name of state; intervention and prosecution by attorney general.]

(1) The department may bring an action, including mediation or other alternative dispute resolution, in the name of the people of the state of Michigan to enforce Act 299.
(2) The attorney general may prosecute any case arising under Act 299.
(Note: Every licensee has potential civil and criminal liability beyond any administrative action taken by the department. The fact that a license has been suspended or revoked will not shield the licensee from further legal action.)
(4) The department may bring an administrative action or an action directly in a court of law regarding the unlicensed practice of an occupation.
(Note: From time-to-time, individuals attempt to generate money by offering real estate services without being licensed. Some of these individuals have even used the Internet to further their illegal business objectives. Act 299 gives the department, the attorney general, and the courts the tools they need to stop such activities.)

Sec. 606 [Forfeiture.]

(1) As noted in Sec. 601(13), forfeiture may be utilized as a remedy. This section clarifies that the forfeiture pertains to items such as property that were determined to be obtained or sold through the commission of a crime, or were used in the commission of a crime. The property can be seized or taken into official custody.
(Note: The term forfeiture refers to the divestiture or loss of one's property without compensation.)

ARTICLE 25 REAL ESTATE
[Covers real estate specific issues.]

(Note: Recall that the majority of the provisions in Articles 1 through 6 are general in nature and can apply to any of the occupations governed by the Occupational Code. Article 25 is the specific Article assigned to the real estate industry. It represents what can be called real estate law or real estate license law. These laws must be taken seriously because they are part of the compiled laws of the State of Michigan.

Chapter 19: Real Estate License Law

As Article 25 is studied, notice its wide-reaching effect on nearly all real estate activities. Make sure that you have a clear understanding of how the law defines certain terms such as real estate broker. Become aware of how brokerage companies are formed and operated, including the duties that the principal broker must fulfill. Lastly, make sure that you fully grasp the many requirements that pertain to agency, contract formation, disclosures, and prohibited conduct. For ease of learning this material, the words "real estate" are not always included in front of "broker" or "salesperson." In other words, the term "broker" means "real estate broker" and the term "salesperson" means "real estate salesperson.")

Sec. 2501 [Definitions.]

(a) "Associate broker" or "associate real estate broker" means an individual who meets the requirements for licensure as a broker and is licensed as an associate broker under Sec. 2505 to provide real estate brokerage services as an employee or independent contractor of a broker.
(Note: It appears that an associate broker does not have to be designated as either a principal or a nonprincipal, but can simply perform the acts of a broker while being licensed under, and in the employ of, a broker; i.e., an associate broker does not have to be a control person in a real estate company).

(b) "Business entity" means a partnership, corporation, limited liability company, or common law trust (but, not a sole proprietorship).

(c) "Classroom course" means an educational course of instruction provided at either a:
  (i) Physical location where instruction is offered and students and an instructor are present.
  (ii) Location where a student receives instruction provided by distance learning.

(d) "Clock hour" means either of the following:
  (i) For a classroom course at a physical location, a period of 50 to 60 minutes of actual classroom instruction, not including outside assignments and reading.
  (ii) For a classroom course involving distance learning, the period required for a student to process the amount of material provided in 50 minutes of distance learning instruction.

(e) ► "Control person" means: an individual who is a sole proprietor; a partner in a partnership or limited partnership; an officer, director, or shareholder in a corporation; a member or manager in a limited liability company; or holds a responsible position in any other form of business entity authorized under the laws of Michigan or the state in which the entity is organized or formed–see also the definitions of "nonprincipal" and "principal" in this section.
(Note 1: As a partner, officer, or member, a control person holds a responsible position in the operations of a real estate company. A control person will be designated as either a principal or a nonprincipal and, therefore, must be licensed as an associate broker.
(Note 2: License law does not appear to prohibit a salesperson from owning or having an ownership interest in a real estate company as long as a control person is designated as the principal associate broker. The salesperson cannot be a control person, i.e., he or she cannot be a partner, officer or member of the real estate company.)

(f) "Distance learning" means the technology and educational process used to provide instruction to a student when the student and instructor are not physically present at the same time or place. It also includes instruction provided through an interactive classroom, computer conferencing, or an interactive computer system.

(g) "Employ" or "employment" means the relationship between a broker and an associate broker, or a broker and a salesperson, which may include an independent contractor relationship.
(Note: As a general rule, one who employs an independent contractor only controls what the independent contractor is hired to do, i.e., the end result of the work. The independent contractor controls how the job is completed. As noted in Sec. 2512f, a broker must supervise the real estate activities and provide operating policies and procedures for salespersons who are licensed under the broker.)

(h) ► "Independent contractor relationship" means a relationship between a broker and an associate broker or salesperson that satisfies both of the following conditions:
  (i) A written agreement exists in which the broker does not consider the associate broker or salesperson to be an employee for federal and state income tax purposes.
  (ii) At least 75% of the annual compensation paid by the broker to the associate broker or salesperson is derived from commissions from the sale of real estate.
    (Note 1: Even though subsection (ii) refers to "commissions from the sale of real estate," it would likely be interpreted to include compensation earned from any regulated real estate activity.)
    (Note 2: The definition in subsection (h) is important because it creates a statutory form of independent contractor for purposes of income taxation. As discussed in Chapter 15, brokers, associate brokers, and salespersons must be aware of their individual income tax reporting responsibilities as independent contractors.)

(i) "License cycle" means the term of a license issued under this article (currently, every 3 years beginning with the date the license was originally issued).

(j) ▶ "Limited service agreement" means a written service provision agreement by which the broker and client establish an agency relationship in which services are knowingly waived in whole or part by the client–see Sec. 2512d(3)(b), (c), and (d).
(Note: This definition pertains to the practice of limited service agency which is discussed further in Chapter 2.)
(k) "Negotiate the mortgage of real estate" means engaging in activity in connection with a mortgage that is not regulated under: the Mortgage Brokers, Lenders, and Servicers Licensing Act; The Secondary Mortgage Loan Act; or the Mortgage Loan Originator Licensing Act (discussed in Chapter 17).
(Note: If a real estate licensee engages in any activity regulated by one of the Acts listed in this subsection, he or she is subject to that Act in spite of the fact that the Article 25 definition of a broker or salesperson authorizes the negotiation of a mortgage of real estate. A real estate licensee should not offer or negotiate a residential mortgage loan for a fee. A real estate licensee may refer a buyer to a licensed loan officer as long as no referral fee is involved.)
(l) A "nonprincipal" of a real estate broker means a control person who is licensed as an associate real estate broker, but is not designated as a principal under section 2505(1)–see Sec. 2505(1)(d) for further details and explanation.
(m) "Place of business" means a physical location that a real estate broker, by advertisement, signage, or otherwise, represents to the public is a place where clients and customers may consult or do business with a licensee.
(Note: This definition does not allow an Internet-based company to designate their website, i.e., a cyber-office, as a "place of business" in Michigan.)
(n) "Pocket card" means the pocket card that contains information about the license that the department provides under section 2506 when it issues a license under this article–see Sec. 2506 for details.
(o) "Prelicensure course" means a course that is represented to the public as fulfilling, in whole or in part, the requirements of section 2504–see Sec. 2504 for details.
(p) A "principal" of a real estate broker means a control person who is licensed as an associate broker and is designated as a principal under section 2505(1)–see Sec. 2505(1)(d) and 2508(2) for further details and explanation.
(q) "Professional designation" means a certification from a real estate professional association demonstrating attainment of proven skills or education in a real estate occupational area and may include the right to use a title or letters after the licensee's name that represents the designation.
(Note: The National Association of REALTORS® sanctions several professional designations for its members.)
(r) ▶ "Property management" means the leasing of other's property for a fee pursuant to a management contract.
(s) ▶ "Property management account" is a non interest-bearing account, interest-bearing account, or instrument such as a certificate of deposit that is used for client funds when operating as a property manager.
(t) "Property management employment contract" is the written employment agreement entered into between a broker who is acting as a property manager and his or her client such as a landlord or other income property owner.
/1/ It sets forth the broker's duties, responsibilities, and activities as a property manager.
/2/ It also sets forth the handling, management, safekeeping, investment, disbursement and use of the property management money, funds, and accounts.
(u) ▶ "Real estate broker" is defined by the following:
/1/ A broker's license can be issued to either a natural person or a business entity.
/2/ A broker is one who collects a fee, typically a commission, for performing regulated real estate acts.
(Note: Even if a person does not charge a fee, he or she is required to possess a broker's license if he or she holds him or herself out to the public as a broker.)
/3/ The following acts require a license if they are performed with the intent of receiving a fee: Selling; Buying; Providing a market analysis; Listing; Negotiating the purchase, sale, exchange, or mortgage of real estate; and/or Negotiating the construction of a building on real estate. Even if a person merely attempts to perform any of these functions, he or she must have a broker's license.
/4/ A broker is one who leases real estate for others.
(Note: The phrase "for others" means that an unlicensed person can lease any number of personally-owned properties and even hire an unlicensed assistant to help providing the assistant only performs clerical functions and does not engage in any other act for which a broker's license is required such as serving as a rental agent.)
/5/ The broker licensing requirement for fee-based leasing and property management applies whether the services are provided on a full or part-time basis.
/6/ The definition of which leasing and property management activities require a real estate license does not depend on the length of the executed leases. Even if the leases are short-term, a real estate license is required if an individual receives a fee for renting or leasing real property for others as a whole or partial vocation.
(Note: Some individuals offer what are known as "seasonal rentals" of vacation properties on behalf of the property owners. The rental periods may be for a limited number of days, weeks, or months. According to a 2012 letter from the Michigan Attorney General's office, a real estate broker's or salesperson's license is required to collect a fee or commission for leasing such properties under these circumstances.)

Chapter 19: Real Estate License Law   347

/7/ A broker is one who sells, buys, leases, or negotiates the purchase, sale, or exchange of a business, business opportunity, or the goodwill of an existing business for others.
(Note: A Michigan Supreme Court case from 2003 held that the broker licensing requirement pertaining to the sale of a business between a buyer and a seller applies only when: (1) the purchase or sale actually involves real estate; and (2) the person who is seeking a commission actually negotiates the transaction.
For exam purposes, an individual who is involved in the listing and/or sale of a business for a fee, whether or not real estate is involved, must have a broker's license. In practice, many legal experts believe this decision may be limited to specific circumstances. Therefore, an unlicensed person should not rely on it to collect a commission or finder's fee in connection with the listing or selling of any business without first consulting an attorney.)
/8/ Engaging in the sale of real estate as a "principal vocation" also requires a license–see Sec. 2502b for the definition of principal vocation.
(v) ▶ "Real estate salesperson" is defined by license law standards that essentially parallel those of a broker with a couple of key differences.
/1/ A salesperson's license can only be issued to a natural person, not a business entity.
/2/ A salesperson may perform essentially the same functions that a broker can except that a salesperson must be licensed under a broker and, therefore, acts as an agent for the broker. As will be seen in subsequent sections and rules, there are other key differences such as a broker's responsibility for trust accounts, closing statements, and supervision of salespersons.
(w) ▶ "Service provision agreement" means a buyer agency agreement or listing agreement executed by a broker and a client that establishes an agency relationship.
(Note: This definition includes all forms of listings and other agency agreements, even a limited service agency agreement. An agreement or memorandum to act as a transaction coordinator is not included in this definition since a transaction coordinator does not provide agency-level services.)
(x) "Sponsor" means a person that represents to the public that the courses it conducts for purposes of this article fulfill the requirements of section 2504a for continuing education.

Sec. 2502 [▶ Board of real estate brokers and salespersons; creation.]

This section authorizes the creation of the Board of Real Estate Brokers and Salespersons–see Article 3 for further details.

Sec. 2502a [▶ Term of license; relicensure.]

(1) The department will establish the term of real estate licenses by rule (currently, every 3 years beginning with the date the license was originally issued). No license shall be issued to an individual who is under the age of 18.
(2) The department shall renew a broker's, associate broker's, or salesperson's license if it receives the proper application for renewal, the appropriate fee, within the time set forth in Sec. 411(1) or (2), and all continuing education requirements have been met (as set forth in Sec. 2504a).
(3) The department may relicense a business entity that fails to renew the broker's license in a timely fashion if the entity pays an application processing fee, the late renewal fee, and the per-year license fee for the upcoming license period and designates a principal as required by Sec. 2505(1)(d).
(4) The department may relicense, without examination, an individual who failed to renew in a timely fashion if all of the following are met:
 (a) The individual applies within 3 years of expiration of the last license.
 (b) The individual pays an application processing fee, the late renewal fee, and the per-year license fee for the upcoming licensure period.
 (c) The individual completes 6 hours of continuing education for each year and partial year that have elapsed since the expiration of his last license as required under Sec. 2504a.
(Note: The subsection outlines what a licensee must do to get relicensed without having to retake an exam. The 6 hours of continuing education is mandated in this subsection even though Sec. 2504a(2)(a) only requires a licensee to complete at least 2 hours of law, rules, and court cases each year of a license cycle.)
(5) The department may relicense an individual who failed to renew a broker or associate broker license within 3 years if the individual pays an application processing fee, late renewal fee, per-year license fee for the upcoming licensure period, and submits proof that the individual meets any of the following:
 (a) Has completed 6 hours of continuing education for each year (and partial year) that have elapsed since expiration.
 (b) Has completed 90 hours of prelicensure courses within one year of making application for relicensure.
 (c) Has passed the broker's license examination, i.e., successfully retakes the exam.

(Note: This subsection outlines what a broker must do to get relicensed who waited until <u>after</u> 3 years of expiration to do so. The 6 hours of continuing education is mandated in this subsection even though Sec. 2504a(2)(a) only requires a licensee to complete at least 2 hours of law, rules, and court cases each year of a license cycle.)

(6) The department may relicense an individual who failed to renew a salesperson license within 3 years if the individual pays an application processing fee, late renewal fee, per-year license fee for the upcoming licensure period, and submits proof that the individual meets any of the following:
  (a) Has completed 6 hours of continuing education for each year and partial year that have elapsed since expiration.
  (b) Has completed 40 hours of prelicensure courses within one year of making application for relicensure.
  (c) Has passed the salesperson's license examination, i.e., successful retake the exam.
  (Note: This subsection outlines what a salesperson must do to get relicensed who waited until <u>after</u> 3 years of expiration to do so.)

(7) An individual whose license is revoked must wait at least 3 years from the revocation before reapplying for a new license. To be reconsidered, the applicant must meet all existing education and examination requirements. No credit is given for education, experience, or examinations passed before the revocation.
(Note: This subsection outlines what a licensee must do to reinstate a license after it has been revoked.)

Sec. 2502b [▶ Owner engaging in sale as principal vocation; license as broker required.]

(1) A real estate broker's license is required to engage in the sale of real estate as a principal vocation.
  (Note: Alternatively, an unlicensed owner can hire a broker to assist with those sales.)
  Each of the following is considered engaging in the sale of real estate as a principal vocation:
  (a) Engaging in more than 5 real estate sales in any 12-month period.
    (Note: An unlicensed person can sell up to 5 properties in any 12-month period providing he or she owns the properties. This, essentially, sets the limit for any person selling on a for-sale-by-owner basis.)
  (b) Representing to the public that he or she is principally engaged in the sale of real estate.
  (c) Devoting over 50% of his or her working time, or more than 15 hours per week in any 6-month period, to the sale of real estate.
  (d) If he or she is a real estate salesperson, a sale of real estate other than his or her principal residence.
    (Note: A salesperson can sell his principal residence on a for-sale-by-owner basis without the assistance of a broker. All other property owned by the salesperson must be handled through a licensed broker. This subsection does not require the salesperson to list with his or her employing broker or to pay the eventual listing broker a commission. These details would be a matter of negotiation between the parties and/or brokerage company policy.)
(2) A sale of real estate that is owned by, or under option to, a broker or associate broker is subject to the provisions of this article.
  (Note: Just because a broker owns the property does not mean that he or she is exempt from license law and rules.)
(3) If a licensee sells a property that he or she owns or has an interest, the licensee must provide written disclosure of the ownership or interest and licensure status to the purchaser before an offer is signed. Written proof of this disclosure may be requested by the department.

Sec. 2503 [▶ Exemptions.]

(1) Certain activities are exempt from the requirement to obtain a real estate license:
  /1/ A state-licensed builder licensed under Article 24 of the Occupational Code may sell a detached, 1–4 family dwelling under his or her builder's license providing: (1) the builder is the owner; (2) the property has never been occupied; and (3) the builder constructed the dwelling.
  /2/ The following individuals are exempt under real estate license law providing the sales do not qualify as a principal vocation:
    – An owner (e.g., a person selling on a for-sale-by-owner basis).
    – A lessor (e.g., one acting as a landlord for his or her personally-owned property).
    – An attorney-in-fact who is acting under a signed and recorded power of attorney from an owner or lessor.
    – An individual who has been appointed by a court.
(2) Other exemptions include:
  /1/ An attorney, providing his services are part of the ordinary functions an attorney performs for his clients.
  /2/ A receiver; trustee in bankruptcy; administrator; executor; person selling under court order; and trustee selling under a deed of trust. The exemption for a trustee does not, however, apply to repeated sales (which would mean that the trustee is engaging in the sale of real estate as a principal vocation.)

Chapter 19: Real Estate License Law

(3) A person regulated under the Mortgage Brokers, Lenders, and Servicers Licensing Act is exempt from real estate license law providing no other act requiring a real estate license is performed in connection with any covered mortgage services.
(<u>Note:</u> This exemption was enacted before the passage of Michigan's Mortgage Loan Originator Licensing Act. It would likely be interpreted to exempt an individual who is licensed under the Mortgage Loan Originator Licensing Act.)

Sec. 2504 [Broker's and salesperson's license requirements; approved courses.]

(1) ▶ Both of the following requirements must be met before an applicant can receive a broker's license:
   (a) The applicant submits an application under Sec. 2505.
   (b) If the applicant is an individual, or an individual designated as a principal under Sec. 2505, he or she must complete 90 hours of approved prelicensure classroom courses including:
      (i) 9 hours of which involve civil rights law and equal opportunity in housing, i.e., fair housing laws).
      (ii) The 90 hours are in addition to the required 40 hours for a salesperson's license.
      (iii) The 90 hours must have been completed within the 36 months preceding the application (unless the applicant was actively licensed as a real estate salesperson).
      (iv) The department may allow equivalent education credit for applicants who possess the following:
         (A) A law degree.
         (B) A bachelor's degree in business or finance from a college, university, junior college, or community college.
         (C) A master's degree in business or finance from a college, university, junior college, or community college.
         (D) Any other education that the department (in consultation with the board of real estate brokers and salespersons) determines is equivalent.

(2) ▶ A salesperson applicant must complete 40 clock hours of approved real estate courses, 4 hours of which involve civil rights law and equal opportunity in housing, i.e., fair housing laws. The 40 hours must be completed within the 36 months preceding the application.

(3) Approved broker and salesperson pre-license courses meet all of the following:
   (a) It meets the department's criteria.
   (b) It covers 1 or more of the following topics:
      (i) Real estate law and regulatory laws.
      (ii) Real property law, including property interests and restrictions.
      (iii) Federal, state, and local tax laws affecting real property.
      (iv) Conveyances including contracts, deeds, and leases.
      (v) Financing including mortgages, land contracts, foreclosure, and limits on lending procedures and interest rates.
      (vi) Appraisal of real property.
      (vii) Design and construction.
      (viii) Marketing, exchanging, and counseling.
      (ix) The law of agency.
      (x) Sales and office management, including listing and selling techniques.
      (xi) Real estate securities and syndications.
      (xii) Investments, including property management.

(4) A person who offers or conducts prelicensure courses must be approved by the department and comply with rules pertaining to curriculum, instructor qualification, grading system, and other related matters. The course must be taught for at least 1 clock hour (not including breaks). The person cannot represent that his or her students are assured of passing or that the approval to teach constitutes a recommendation or indorsement by the department. The class must be conducted by 1 of the following:
   (a) A local public school district.
   (b) A community college.
   (c) An institution of higher learning that grants degrees.
   (d) Any other education provider approved by the department that meets prelicensure education requirements.

(5) A person who violates subsection (4) is subject to Article 6 penalties.

(6) The department may assist schools within Michigan in sponsoring studies, research, and programs for the purpose of raising the standards of professional real estate practice.

(7) The department may contract with a statewide real estate association representing more than 18,000 members to:
   (a) Review and approve prelicense courses.
   (b) Review prelicensure courses to determine whether the subject matter is relevant to the practice of real estate.

Sec. 2504a [▶ Continuing education.]

(1) A licensee must successfully complete at least the following number of hours of eligible continuing education courses in each license cycle:
   (a) The number of hours set by department rule.
      (<u>Note:</u> This number would begin with the license cycle after the department determines the rules required in subsection (2)(e)).
   (b) 18 clock hours in each license cycle.
      (<u>Note:</u> For state exam purposes, use 18 clock hours when asked about the number of required hours.)
(2) All of the following apply to continuing education requirements:
   (a) At least 2 hours in each year of the license cycle must involve law, rules, and court cases regarding real estate. Thereafter, the licensee may select any continuing education courses in his area of expertise to complete the remaining hours and may do so at any time during the license cycle.
   (b) The licensee must do both of the following to confirm his identity at the time he or she attends a continuing education course:
      (i) Present his or her pocket card or provide the license number.
      (ii) Present his or her operator's license or other government-issued photo identification.
   (c) Courses that a licensee completes to obtain a professional designation can be counted toward the total required continuing education credits.
   (d) No additional credit is given for repeating a continuing education course.
   (e) By rule, the department must do all of the following:
      (i) Determine and publish the number of hours of eligible continuing education courses a licensee must complete in a license cycle (currently 18 clock hours including the 2 annual hours of law, rules, and court cases). The department must determine this number by multiplying the number of years in a license cycle by 6.
      (ii) Establish the standards for determining if a continuing education course qualifies as an eligible continuing education course.
   (<u>Recap note:</u> A licensee must complete a minimum of 2 hours of "legal" continuing education content each year. This equals 6 hours which means that 12 additional hours must be completed to fulfill the total 18 hour requirement. These additional hours can be completed at any time during the 3-year cycle. For example, a licensee could complete 2 hours of "legal" in year one and an additional 2 hours of "legal" in year two, and then complete 14 more hours in year three providing at least 2 of the 14 qualify as "legal").
   (<u>Suggestion:</u> While license law does not address the issue, licensees should not procrastinate in completing their continuing education requirements. Most licensees find that it is easier to obtain 6 hours of continuing education each year. This also helps to avoid a disciplinary action flowing from a department audit that discovers a licensee inadvertently missed any of the required hours. In today's competitive world, it is critical to attend only high quality continuing education courses delivered by qualified and experienced experts in the subject matter being taught.)
(3) An applicant for license renewal shall certify compliance with all continuing education requirements to the department. The licensee must retain proof of successful completion for a minimum of 4 years from the date of completion and produce the following proof at the request of the department:
   (a) The name and contact information of the continuing education program sponsor.
   (b) The participant's name.
   (c) The course title and course field of study.
   (d) The date the course was offered or completed.
   (e) The location of the course (if applicable).
   (f) Verification by the program sponsor of the participant's completion.
   (g) The number of hours of instruction included in the course and that credits were granted on a 50-minute hour.
   (<u>Suggestion:</u> Licensees should retain all certificates in a safe location for the required 4-year period and consider using Internet-based backup storage. Further, some courses are optionally certified by the CE Marketplace which is a private entity operated by the Michigan REALTORS® that allows students to track their annual credits.)
(4) The department may audit an applicant for renewal to make sure that he or she complied with continuing education requirements. The applicant may also have to submit documentation listed in subsection (3) on request.
   (<u>Broker suggestion:</u> While not required by law, a broker may wish to consider having each affiliated licensee submit a copy of his or her certificate of completion for all continuing education courses attended. Further, a broker should talk to legal counsel before paying any commission to an affiliated licensee who has not fulfilled his or her licensure requirements.)
(5) An applicant for renewal who did not complete a sufficient number of eligible continuing education course hours will have to complete both of the following:
   (a) Completion of the required hours he or she did not attend (i.e., make up the missed hours).

Chapter 19: Real Estate License Law

(b) If the period determined by the audit to be deficient is at least 60 days, completion of additional continuing education hours in the following amounts:
   (i) If the deficiency period is at least 60 days and less than 120 days, 4 additional hours must be completed.
   (ii) If the deficiency period is 120 days or more, 8 additional hours must be completed.
(6) Additional hours required in subsection (5)(b) do not apply toward continuing education required in a current license cycle. The department may waive these additional hours if the applicant can demonstrate that it presents an undue hardship on him or her.
(7) If a license is issued after the beginning of the current license cycle, the department may prorate the required hours based on the year in which the license is actually issued.
(8) Course credits used to meet continuing education requirements do not apply toward broker's prelicensure requirements. Similarly, course credits used to fulfill broker's prelicensure requirements do not apply toward continuing education requirements.
(9) The phrase "eligible continuing education course" means a continuing education course that meets the standards set in subsection (2)(e) and counts toward a licensee's requirements for continuing education.

Sec. 2505 [▶ Broker's license; application; branch office; application for salesperson's license.]

(1) A broker applicant must provide certain information on the application including:
   (a) The applicant's current business address; if an individual, his or her home address; and the address of all former businesses and residences during the prior 5 years.
   (b) The name of the individual or business entity and the place for which the license is desired; the location for which the license is sought; and the period of time the applicant has been engaged in the business.
   (c) The application must be signed by the applicant if an individual, or by a principal of the applicant if a business entity.
   (d) If the applicant is a business entity, the application must designate which individuals who are control persons (i.e., officers, partners, members, etc.) will be engaging in real estate activities as principals. An applicant cannot designate a control person as a principal unless the control person is licensed as an associate real estate broker. (Note: To recap, a control person is defined as a sole proprietor, partner, officer, or member in a real estate business entity. The term "control person" is incorporated in the definitions of "principal" and "nonprincipal" who are licensed as associate brokers. Nevertheless, it appears that a real estate business entity can have an officer, partner, or member who does not possess a real estate license, does not perform the activities of an associate broker or salesperson, and therefore, is not a control person as defined in Sec. 2501(e); e.g., a Chief Financial Officer of a real estate corporation. A broker should verify this with legal counsel. See also, Sec. 2505(7)(b)(vii)(C) which references a real estate officer of a corporation who is not a licensed broker.)
(2) New applicants who have been convicted of embezzlement or misappropriation of funds cannot obtain a broker's license.
(3) A broker must maintain a place of business in Michigan. A branch office license is required for each branch office location. If a branch office is located more than 25 miles from the nearest boundary of the municipality in which the main office is located, the branch must be under the direct supervision of an associate broker who must be physically present on a regular basis to supervise and manage the business during ordinary business hours.
(Note 1: Notice how this subsection references 25 miles from the nearest boundary as opposed to 25 miles from the main office itself.
(Note 2: This subsection implies that a broker is the one who supervises any branch that is located within: (1) the municipality where the main office is situated; and/or (2) the 25-mile limit. It also implies that a broker can appoint a salesperson as the manager for any office within the municipality itself or the 25 mile limit (as long as the salesperson does not perform any acts that require a broker's license and the broker is physically available for supervision).
(4) A salesperson's application must be signed by the broker for whom he or she will be working. The department will only issue a salesperson's license to an individual, i.e., a natural person.
(5) Before issuing a license to an individual (or principal of a business entity), the department can require proof of business experience, competence, and good moral character. All applicants must pass an examination developed by the department or an outside testing agency that establishes a satisfactory understanding of the: fundamentals of real estate practice; laws and principles of conveyancing, deeds, mortgages, land contracts, and leases; obligations of a broker to the public and a principal; and law defining, regulating, and licensing brokers and salespersons.
(6) All of the following apply to the written examination requirement:
   (a) The department may relicense (meaning the license was not renewed within 60 days after expiration) an individual for a broker's or associate broker's license without exam, if he or she has previously held a broker's or associate broker's license that has lapsed, and has been continuously licensed as a real estate salesperson since lapse of the previous license.

(Note: This refers to a situation in which a licensed broker elects thereafter to become licensed as a salesperson by allowing his or her broker's license to lapse. He or she can return to licensure as a broker without having to retake the broker's exam.)
  (b) A passing score on an exam is valid for 1 year from taking the exam.
(7) All applicants for a broker's license must have the equivalent of 3 years full-time experience in the real estate business as determined by the following criteria:
  (a) No credit is given for any activity that was performed without a required real estate license (e.g., acting illegally).
  (b) Credit shall be granted for the following:
    (i) Licensed real estate salesperson: 1 year of credit is given for each 12-month period in which the individual closed 5 or more real estate transactions.
    (ii) Licensed builder: 1 year of credit is given for each 12-month period in which at least 5 residential, commercial, or industrial units were personally built and sold or leased.
    (iii) Investor: 6 months of credit is given for each 5 real property transactions that were personally negotiated for purchase or sale for the individual's own account; no credit is given if the investor engaged in more than 5 sales in a 12-month period (because doing would have required a broker's license–see Sec. 2502b).
    (iv) Land or condominium developer: 1 year of credit for each 2 developments or subdivisions that contain at least 10 units that he or she purchased, subdivided, and improved for sale as lots or dwellings.
    (v) Attorney: 1 year of credit for each year in which the individual acted as the attorney for at least 6 real estate transactions.
    (vi) Licensed appraiser: 1 year of credit for each 40-hour per week period (48 weeks per year) in which the individual acted as an appraiser.
    (vii) Other: 1 year of credit for each 40-hours per week period (48 weeks per year) in which the individual worked in a capacity directly related to the acquisition, financing, or conveyance of real estate, or directly involved in a real estate business including serving as the decision-making authority in any of the following:
      (A) A loan or trust officer or a federal or state-regulated depository institution.
      (B) A loan or trust officer of a mortgage company.
      (C) A real estate officer of a corporation, and who is not a licensed real estate broker.
      (D) A title insurance company officer engaged in the closing of escrow accounts and real estate closings.
    (viii) Credit for other equivalent experience that is approved by the department, in consultation with the board.

Sec. 2506 [▶ Delivering of salesperson's license to broker; display; change of location; transfer.]

(1) An individual cannot act as a broker, associate broker, or salesperson until he or she receives a license and pocket card (or a temporary license). A licensee cannot act in the capacity indicated on the card without having his or her pocket card (or temporary license) on his or her person; a photocopy or digital image of the pocket card suffices. /1/ The pocket card serves as proof of licensure and may be requested by a consumer or another licensee with whom the licensee is working in a cooperative transaction, e.g., to gain access to keys for a showing.
(2) The department shall deliver or mail the license of a salesperson to the broker who employs the salesperson, and the broker shall retain custody and control of the salesperson's certificate of license and deliver the pocket card for that license to the salesperson.
(Note: The phrase "certificate of license" merely refers to the license.)
(3) A licensee must give written notice to the department of any change of principal or branch business location.
(Note: Failure to do so constitutes a license law violation.)
(4) A salesperson or associate broker (who is not the sole associate broker for a broker that is a business entity) whose license is suspended or revoked must immediately forward his or her pocket card to the department. The broker shall immediately forward the suspended or revoked licensee's license to the department. If an individual broker (or sole associate broker for a broker that is a business entity) is suspended or revoked, he or she must immediately forward his or her pocket card along with the licenses and pocket cards of all salespersons, nonprincipal associate brokers, and branch office licenses.
(Note: This is due to the fact that salespersons and nonprincipal associate brokers are licensed under the broker whose license was suspended or revoked. These licensees will simply apply for a new license under a new broker.)
(5) If the department receives a completed application and fee for transfer of a license (under Sec. 2507 or 2508) to a new broker, the pocket card will serve as proper evidence of licensing for 45 days from the latest date written on the back of the card. If the application is incomplete or the new broker is not properly licensed, the transferring licensee must wait until the new license and pocket card are received before engaging in real estate activities.

Chapter 19: Real Estate License Law

Sec. 2507 [▶ Discharge or termination of salesperson; transfer; performing acts with a license.]

(1) Whether a salesperson is discharged or gives the broker written notice of termination, the broker must return the salesperson's license to the department within 5 days. If written notice of termination is not served on the broker by the salesperson, the department shall notify the broker (and operate as if the salesperson had served notice).

(2) The broker must send a letter to the salesperson, at his or her last known residence address, advising that the license has been returned (and include a copy of this letter when returning the salesperson's license to the department).

(3) Unless the salesperson is following the transfer process outlined in Sec. 2506(5), he or she cannot engage in real estate activities under authority of the returned license after the date of his or her termination.

(4) Not more than 1 license can be issued to a salesperson for the same period of time.
(Note: This means a salesperson cannot be licensed under and work for more than one broker at a time.)

Sec. 2508 [▶ Broker's license; entities to which issued; authorized acts; associate broker's license.]

(1) A broker's license may be issued to an individual or a business entity.
/1/ When a broker's license is issued to a natural person, the broker can conduct all of the activities authorized for brokers–see Sec. 2501(u) for the permissible activities of a broker.
/2/ When a broker's license is issued to a business entity, those persons designated as principals for the business can act as brokers. Accordingly, each principal must obtain an associate broker's license.
(Note: Refer to Sec. 2501(l) and (p) for the definitions of a nonprincipal and a principal associate broker.)
/3/ Broker's licenses are not transferable.
(Note: A broker's license is issued in a name that must be used by all affiliated licensees who conduct business and advertise. Instead of transferring, the broker can surrender the old license to the department and apply for either: (1) a new broker's license under a new name; (2) an associate broker's licensed issued under a different broker; or (3) a salesperson's license issued under a different broker.)
(Note regarding principal who does not qualify as a broker: If a person designated as a principal in the broker's license application (for a business) does not qualify for an associate broker's license (i.e., does not have 3 years relevant and related experience, or has not successfully completed the broker's examination), he or she cannot act as a principal. In other words, he or she cannot engage in any real estate activities for which a broker's license is required. As another option, a principal who does not qualify for a broker's license may sign a stipulation agreement with the department that he or she will not perform any of the regulated acts for which a broker's license is required. For example, assume that the unlicensed principal is a corporate Vice President in a real estate company. He or she may continue to hold his position as Vice President providing he or she does not engage in any real estate activities.)

(2) Before acting as a principal broker, an associate broker's license must be applied for and obtained. The requirements to obtain an associate broker's license are the same as those for obtaining a broker's license. An associate broker's license will only be issued to a natural person.
/1/ Any qualifying individual can apply for an associate broker's license.
(Note: Recall that an individual can be licensed to a company as an associate broker without having to be an owner, officer, partner, or member of that company.)
(Note regarding the difference between broker and associate broker: Essentially, there is no difference between a broker and an associate broker except that: (1) there can only be one broker in a real estate operation regardless of whether the broker's license is issued in the name of an individual or a business entity; and (2) a real estate operation can have multiple principal and nonprincipal associate brokers as affiliated licensees.

(3) If a principal associate broker ceases to be connected with a real estate business entity, his or her license (to that company) is automatically suspended.

(4) The associate broker's license of a principal is not transferable.
(Note: This is due to the fact that the principal may be the only natural person licensed to carry out the activities of a broker for the business entity. When a broker's license is issued to a business entity, there must be at least one natural person licensed to carry out the functions of a broker.)
A nonprincipal associate broker may transfer to another broker in the same manner as a salesperson–see Sec. 2507 and 2506(5).

(5) The revocation of a broker's license causes the automatic suspension of all salespersons and associate brokers because they were licensed to conduct business in the name of that broker.
(Note: Suspension in this instance is not a form of punishment. Either a new broker can be licensed to fulfill the role of the (principal) broker whose license was revoked, or the suspended salespersons and associate brokers can relocate to another broker–see also Sec. 2506(4).)

(6) If a sole principal associate broker dies or becomes disabled, the department will afford all affiliated licensees a reasonable time to either wind up the business of the broker or designate a new principal associate broker.

Sec. 2509 [▶ Associate broker's license; issuance to principal and nonprincipal; limitations.]

(1) The department may issue multiple associate broker's licenses to a real estate broker for all affiliated principals.
(2) A nonprincipal associate broker cannot have more than 1 associate broker's license as a nonprincipal (because the nonprincipal broker does not control or direct the operations of the business). However, an individual can hold more than one principal associate broker's license (because he or she may be an officer, partner, or member in more than one company and must be licensed as an associate broker under each one).
Example: "Broker A" wishes to open a residential real estate sales company. She also plans to open a separate commercial real estate company and a separate property management company. A separate broker's license is obtained for each company. As an officer and principal in each company, "Broker A" must obtain separate associate broker's license under each one.

Sec. 2510 [▶ Salesperson; commission or valuable consideration.]

(1) A salesperson can only receive compensation (for acting as a salesperson) from his or her employing broker.
(Note 1: All commissions earned by a salesperson must be paid directly and personally to the salesperson. A salesperson cannot establish a business entity and direct that his broker make the salesperson's commission checks payable to the entity. Further, Sec. 2505(4) states that a salesperson's license can only be issued to an individual.)
Example 1: In an attempt to reduce personal liability and increase business tax deductions, Salesperson X creates a Limited Liability Company (LLC) and asks his broker to make all commission checks payable to the LLC rather than to Salesperson X. The broker cannot legally comply with this request under license law. Once the broker pays the check directly to the salesperson, the salesperson can do whatever he or she wants with the money.
Example 2: Salesperson Y forms a sales team with both licensed and unlicensed (i.e., administrative) individuals. Y establishes a corporation so all commissions earned by the team can be paid to Y's corporation. It is a violation of license law for the broker to comply with this request. The fact that a team is involved is irrelevant.
(Note 2: License law is silent on the issue of how a broker or associate broker may be compensated.)
Example: John is a nonprincipal associate broker with "Bravo Realty, Inc." who regularly lists and sells real estate under Bravo Realty's name. John wants to continuing working under Bravo Realty, but for tax purposes, have his checks made payable to "Alpha Realty, LLC," a company John created for this purpose. John must: (1) obtain a broker's license in the name of Alpha Realty, LLC; (2) obtain a principal associate broker's license under Alpha Realty, LLC; and (3) maintain his nonprincipal associate broker's license with Bravo Realty, Inc. Bravo Realty can now legally pay Alpha Realty since both entities and John are licensed as brokers.
(Note regarding holding companies: If a licensee desires to maintain an active license without actually listing and selling real estate, he or she can place his license with a broker who maintains what is known in the industry as a holding company. The holding company broker typically enters into an agreement with each affiliated licensee to refer all listing and sale leads to the broker in exchange for a referral fee. Such fee can legally be paid since the licensees are active in the department's view. Affiliated licensees in a holding company are subject to all license law and rules requirements including annual continuing education.)
(2) Providing a salesperson earned a commission while employed by one broker, that broker can pay it to the salesperson without violating Sec. 2512(h) even if the salesperson is employed by another broker or is no longer licensed.
(Note: As long as the commission was "earned" while licensed, it can be paid after employment has ended. While not required, if the salesperson transferred to a new broker before the commission check was cut, the former broker may wish to pay it to the salesperson's new broker. Company policy typically defines the definition of "earned.")

Sec. 2511 [▶ Plan or scheme for selling or promoting sale of real estate.]

(1) Lotteries, contests, games, or drawings cannot be used by a broker or salesperson to promote the sale of real estate. Privately run lotteries are generally prohibited by statute in Michigan. Michigan's "Bingo Act" regulates other forms of permissible gaming such as bingo, charity games, and raffles.
(Note regarding game promotions: A game promotion may be used by a broker or salesperson for any purpose other than the direct promotion or sale of a specific piece of real estate. A raffle should not be confused with an auction sale which is permissible.)
(Note regarding lotteries: To qualify as a lottery, three elements must be present: prize (something is given away); chance (not everyone wins); and consideration (something of value has to be given to play the game). For example, an instant lottery ticket offers a $10,000 prize, not everyone wins, and it costs $1.00 to play. A game promotion differs from a lottery in that the elements of prize and chance are present, but not consideration. In other words, a participant does not have to buy something or otherwise pay for the right to play.)
(Note regarding raffles: Raffles, even those that do not involve the sale of real estate such as 50/50 drawings, may require a license issued by the Michigan Lottery, Charitable Gaming Division.)

Chapter 19: Real Estate License Law   355

Example 1: Broker X participates in a Spring Home Show to create awareness of his real estate company. He rents an exhibition booth and collects the names and addresses of attendees by holding a drawing for a mountain bike. There is no cost to attend the home show and all a person has to do to enter the broker's drawing is provide the requested contact information. Subject to the advice of legal counsel, this is likely permissible.

Example 2: Broker Z wishes to boost attendance at an upcoming open house conducted for one of his listed properties. The advertisement is sent to the prospective buyers in his database along with the neighbors of the listed property. The advertisement mentions that all in attendance can enter a drawing for a free mountain bike. All the attendee has to do is visit the property and fill out an information card. While a game promotion may be permissible, it cannot be used for the direct promotion or sale of a specific piece of real estate. Therefore, Broker Z may not promote or hold the drawing at the open house.

(Note regarding inducements: Generally, it is permissible for a licensee to offer items of value–including commission rebates/reductions, home warranties, and promotional advertising items–to induce consumers to list their homes through the licensee or hire the licensee to assist with the purchase of a home. Care must be exercised, however, to make sure that any inducement does not constitute the payment or referral of a commission to an unlicensed person or entity. In other words, commissions or fees cannot be paid to unlicensed persons or entities.)

(Note regarding advertising items: Common promotional advertising items and giveaways with the licensee's name, company name, and telephone number are also generally permitted. According to Sec. 2512e(3), all advertising by a salesperson and associate broker must be in the name of the employing broker. Therefore, licensees should also check with their employing brokers before engaging in any such promotional activities to make sure they are consistent with company policy.)

Sec. 2512 [▶ Prohibited conduct; penalties; filing complaint under Article 5.]

(1) A licensee is subject to disciplinary action for engaging in any of the following activities:
(Note: These are the real estate-specific illegal acts. Article 6, Sec. 604, contains illegal acts that are general in nature. Any violation of Sec. 604 or Sec. 2512 subjects a licensee to any of the penalties set forth in Article 6, Sec. 602.)
   (a) Representing more than one party in a transaction (i.e., acting as a dual agent) without consent from both parties. Consent should be in writing. This subsection does not apply to property managers.
   (b) Failing to provide a written agency disclosure to a prospective buyer or seller in a real estate transaction. (According to Sec. 2517(11)(b) and (h), the definition of "buyer" includes "tenant" and "seller" includes "landlord.")
   (c) A salesperson or associate broker representing a broker other than his or her employer without the employer's broker's knowledge and consent.
       (Note: This provision dates back many years. While most employing brokers would never allow their salespersons to represent other brokers, licensees should be aware of this subsection since it is part of the license law.)
   (d) Failing to account for or to remit (i.e., pay) money that belongs to others which comes into the licensee's possession.
       (Note: Mishandling of consumer funds such as earnest money deposits is a serious violation. This is why a broker must maintain a trust account. Further, according to Sec. 2505(2), a person cannot obtain a broker's license if he or she has been convicted of embezzlement or misappropriation of funds.)
   (e) Changing a business location without notifying the department.
   (f) If licensed as a broker, failing to return a salesperson's license within 5 days as required in Sec. 2507.
   (g) Violating the provisions of Sec. 2512c(2), (5), and (6) (regarding property management which require the maintenance of a separate account for client funds, maintenance of records relating to the deposit and withdrawal of client funds, and accounting to the client under the property management employment contract).
   (h) Paying a referral fee or other valuable consideration to an unlicensed person for assisting the licensee in earning a commission.
       (Note: Closing gifts to clients are generally permissible since the gift is not provided in exchange for leads.)
       Exceptions from the prohibitions of this subsection include:
       – A broker paying an earned commission to a salesperson who leaves the employ of a broker.
       – Paying for commercially prepared lists of names provided by an unlicensed person (e.g., mailing labels).
       – Payment of a referral fee by a Michigan broker to a broker licensed in another state providing the outstate broker does not conduct any of the work in Michigan for which a license is required.
   (i) Conducting a market analysis that does not comply with the appraiser licensing requirements of Article 26.
       (Note: Refer to Chapter 4 for further discussion of what constitutes a permissible market analysis or CMA.)
   (j) Fails to provide the minimum services specified in Sec. 2512d(3) pursuant to a service provision agreement, unless the client waives, in writing, those services that can be waived under the law per Sec. 2517(2).
   (k) Failing to deposit money which belongs to others in a special custodial trust or escrow account maintained by the broker.

(Note: This money is typically the earnest money deposit, i.e., EMD, paid by the buyer and held by the receiving broker pending the closing. A custodial account is a financial account established for the benefit of another. The broker is the custodian. Property management accounts are not governed by this subsection.)
- (i) If the deposit is made payable to the broker rather than another escrowee or title company, that broker (usually the broker who works with the buyer) must retain the funds in his or her trust account until the transaction is closed (i.e., consummated) or terminated.
- (ii) A salesperson must turn over any collected deposit to his or her employing broker upon receipt.
- (iii) A broker cannot commingle (i.e., combine) his or her personal or business funds with the funds received from the public.
- (iv) A broker may maintain more than 1 trust account and maintain up to $2,000 of his or her own money in each trust account to cover bank service charges, minimum balance requirements, and to keep the account open in the absence of client (EMD) funds.
- (v) In the case of an EMD check made payable to a broker, the funds must be deposited within 2 banking days after that broker receives notice that an offer to purchase has been accepted by all parties and retained pending consummation or termination of the transaction. Trust accounts must be maintained with a bank, savings and loan association, credit union, or other recognized depository.
(Note 1: The "2 banking day" time requirement is triggered (i.e., begins) when the broker "receives notice" that the offer has been accepted by all parties, not necessarily when all parties have signed the purchase agreement. The broker who retains the EMD may wish to use the date he or she receives the fully-signed copy of the acceptance from the seller (or listing agent) to mark the beginning of the two banking day requirement. In practice, the date the purchase agreement is "bottom-lined" by the buyer-offeror is frequently used to determine when the deposit time requirement begins.)
(Note 2: A banking day is that portion of a business day during which banking functions are performed and transactions are posted. Many banks stop posting after a certain time such as 4:00 p.m. Thereafter, transactions are posted to the next business day. While a bank may be open on a Saturday as a convenience, transactions are usually posted to the next business day since federal reserve banks are closed for check clearing functions on weekends and holidays.)
- (vi) A broker must maintain records of funds deposited in his trust account including the date and from whom the money was received, the date deposited, the date of withdrawal, for whose account the money is deposited, and to whom the money belongs. Records are subject to inspection by the department.
  - The broker must be designated as the trustee of the account which shall provide for withdrawal of funds without previous notice (i.e., the account must be demand in nature such as a checking account).
  - As long as the trust account is not interest-bearing, a broker can open a trust account in a savings and loan association or credit union.
- (vii) A purchaser and seller can designate in their purchase agreement that an EMD check be held by an escrowee other than the broker such as a title company. A licensee in possession of such deposit must deliver it to the title company within 2 banking days after the licensee has received notice that an offer to purchase is accepted by all parties.
(Note: This subsection uses the term "licensee" which opens the possibility that a deposit check could come into the hands of a salesperson who, in turn, delivers it directly to the escrowee rather than the broker. A broker may address this issue in the policy manual and require that EMD funds be delivered to the broker).

(2) A complaint seeking a penalty under Article 5 for violation of Sec. 2512 must be filed within 18 months after either:
  (a) The date of the alleged violation.
  (b) If the violation involves a real estate transaction, the date the transaction is completed (i.e., closed or terminated).
  (Note: This is not a general statute of limitations within which legal actions must be filed in a court of law. It only pertains to complaints filed with the department that involve license law.)

Sec. 2512a [▶ Action for collection of compensation for performance of act; allegation; proof.]

A licensee cannot sue for the nonpayment of a commission without first proving that he or she was licensed when the activity was conducted for which the commission is claimed.

Sec. 2512b [▶ Actions not constituting participation in real estate transaction.]

A landlord or his or her agent can pay a finder's fee, not to exceed the value of ½ month's rent, to existing tenants for the referral of new tenants. Conversely, the tenant can accept such a referral fee.
(Note: This is another exemption from the prohibition against paying a finder's fee to an unlicensed person–see Sec. 2512(h) for additional information.)

Chapter 19: Real Estate License Law

Sec. 2512c [Property management performed by broker.]

(1) All activities of a property manager and his employees must be reduced to a written agreement known as a property management employment contract.
(2) Property management accounts must be separate from other accounts and must be managed according to the property management employment contract.
(Note: If a broker who acts as a property manager also provides traditional brokerage services, his management and brokerage trust accounts cannot be commingled.)
(3) As long as the property management employment contract allows it, the property management account can be interest-bearing. The contract also determines how interest is managed (i.e., whether it is retained by the manager or belongs to the client).
(4) The property manager or his or her employees can serve as signatories on property management accounts.
(5) A property manager must maintain a recordkeeping system for his or her accounts including: the date of the transaction; from whom the money was received or to whom it was given; and other pertinent information.
(6) A property manager must account for and remit funds to the client according to the management agreement.
(7) Property management records are subject to inspection by the department.

Sec. 2512d [▶ Service provision agreement; conduct by broker or salesperson; waiver of services.]

(1) A broker or salesperson acting pursuant to a service provision agreement shall perform the duties imposed in subsection (2). A broker may authorize a designated agent to represent the client so long as that authorization is in writing.
(Note: Remember that a service provision agreement includes any agency agreement such as a listing agreement or buyer's agency agreement. It does not include an agreement to provide services as a transaction coordinator.)
(2) A licensee acting pursuant to a service provision agreement owes, at a minimum, the following <u>duties</u> to his or her client:
   (a) The exercise of reasonable care and skill in representing the client and carrying out the responsibilities of the agency relationship.
   (b) The performance of the terms of the service provision agreement.
   (c) Loyalty to the interest of the client.
   (d) Compliance with the laws, rules, and regulations of this state and any applicable federal statutes or regulations.
   (e) Referral of the client to other licensed professionals for expert advice related to material matters that are not within the expertise of the licensed (real estate) agent.
   (f) An accounting in a timely manner of all money and property received by the agent in which the client has or may have an interest.
   (g) Confidentiality of all information obtained in the course of the agency relationship, unless disclosed with the client's permission or as provided by law, including the duty not to disclose confidential information to any licensee who is not an agent of the client.
(Note: Taken together, subsections 2(a) through (g) represent the statutory fiduciary duties a licensee owes a client. As noted in Chapter 2, these statutory fiduciary duties are coupled with other common law fiduciary duties.)
(3) A licensee acting pursuant to a service provision agreement shall provide the following <u>services</u> to his or her client:
   (a) When the broker or salesperson is representing a seller or lessor, the marketing of the client's property in the manner agreed upon in the service provision agreement.
   (b) Acceptance of delivery and presentation of offers and counteroffers to buy, sell, or lease the client's property or the property the client seeks to purchase or lease. At the time of execution of an offer to purchase, a licensee must recommend to the purchaser that the purchaser require the seller to provide a fee title policy in the amount of the purchase price to the purchaser, issued to the approximate date of the closing.
(Note: This alerts the purchaser of the need for title insurance so he or she can include it in the offer. Even though most purchase agreements already contain this language, the licensee should point it out.)
   (c) Assistance in developing, communicating, negotiating, and presenting offers, counteroffers, and related documents or notices until a purchase or lease agreement is executed by all parties and all contingencies are satisfied or waived.
   (d) After execution of a purchase agreement by all parties, assistance as necessary to complete the transaction under the terms specified in the purchase agreement. A licensee must not close a transaction on any terms or conditions that are contrary to the terms of the purchase agreement without written permission of all parties.
(Note: This is due to the fact that the purchase agreement, in part, dictates the contents of the closing statement. Therefore, any change on the closing statement may constitute a modification of the previously agreed to purchase agreement.)

(e) For a broker or associate broker who is involved at the closing of a real estate or business opportunity transaction, furnishing or causing to be furnished to the buyer and seller, a complete and detailed closing statement signed by the broker or associate broker showing each party all receipts and disbursements affecting that party. This subsection does not apply if the closing is conducted by a licensed title insurance company or agent of the title company.

(Note: Taken together, subsections 3(a) through (e) represent the statutory services that must be provided unless some of them are waived by the client.)

(4) A broker or salesperson representing a seller under a service provision agreement shall not advertise the property to the public as "for sale by owner" or otherwise mislead the public to believe that the seller is not represented by a broker.

(5) The services described in subsection (3)(b), (c), and (d) may be waived by the client, in writing, in a limited service agreement.

(Note: While three of the statutory "services" may be waived under a written limited service agreement, the statutory "duties" can never be waived.)

Sec. 2512e [▶ Advertisement.]

(1) All broker advertising related to real estate and/or business opportunities (i.e., to buy, sell, exchange, rent, mortgage, etc.) must include the broker's name, the broker's telephone number or street address, and a statement that the person advertising is a real estate broker.

(Note: Advertising must include the actual name as it appears on the broker's license. As indicated in subsection (5), below, if the license is issued in an assumed name (i.e., d/b/a), the d/b/a can be used in advertising. Abbreviations of the broker's name or only including the name of any franchise of which the broker is a franchisee is insufficient.)

(2) A broker or associate broker can advertise personally-owned property for sale or lease, in his or her own personal name, without including the name on the broker's license, providing the advertisement affirmatively indicates that the individual who is selling or leasing is a licensed real estate broker or associate broker.

(3) Except as provided in subsections (2) and (4), advertising by a salesperson or associate broker must be in the name of, and under the supervision of, the employing broker. Beginning January 1, 2018, all advertising that includes the name of an associate broker, salesperson, or cooperating group of associate brokers or salespersons (known in the industry as a real estate team) must include all of the following:

(a) The telephone number or street address of the employing broker.
(b) The business name of the employing broker, in equal or greater type size than the associate broker, salesperson, or cooperating group (team).

(Note 1: The referenced telephone number is likely to be interpreted as a number owned by the broker. It is not sufficient for a licensee to merely use his personal cell phone number. If a licensee wishes to use his personal cell phone number, all he has to do is include the broker's address or broker's telephone number in the advertising. A broker-owned number can also be forwarded to a personal cell phone and qualify for this subsection. There are no type size requirements for phone numbers or addresses, so the licensee's personal cell phone number can be larger and more prominent. The address can be the broker's main office or (licensed) branch office since both are held out to the public for purposes of conducting business.)

(Note 2: This new provision is primarily designed to prohibit real estate teams–or affiliated licensees–from advertising or branding their names in such a manner that it appears to the public they are licensed as separate brokerage entities. Some teams, for example, have omitted the broker's name in their advertising. Others have included the broker's name, but in a type size that was small compared to the team name. This provision only refers to the actual size of the type, i.e., the letter height, not the font, color, or logo. Graphic illustrations and examples are available on the Michigan REALTORS® website at <mirealtors.com>.)

(4) A salesperson cannot advertise under his or her own name unless the property is his or her principal residence. A salesperson cannot advertise property for rent under his or her own name unless he or she owns the property.

(Note 1: Even though this rule permits a salesperson to advertise in his or her own name under these circumstances, company policy may dictate otherwise. A salesperson should check with his or her broker prior to running any such advertisements. Advertising that does not identify that the seller or landlord is a licensee is sometimes referred to as a blind advertisement.)

(Note 2: All other property owned by the salesperson must be handled through a licensed broker. This does not require the salesperson to list with his or her employing broker or to pay the eventual listing broker a commission. These details would be a matter of negotiation between the parties and/or brokerage company policy.)

(5) A broker can only conduct business or advertise under the name in which the broker's license is issued (including an assumed name). If a broker desires to use an assumed name, it must be included with the license application or within 30 days of its adoption.

Chapter 19: Real Estate License Law 359

(Note 1: If a broker applicant intends to operate as an individual or a partnership, the assumed name certificate is issued by the county clerk where it is on file. If the broker applicant intends to operate as a legal (i.e., business) entity, the certificate is issued by the Corporations Division of the department.)

(Note 2: An assumed name is a business alias, i.e., an alternate name, adopted for purposes of conducting business. A broker licensed under an assumed name must legally promote and conduct his or her business under that name. For example, John Doe wishes to do business as Doe Realty. John would file a Certificate of Assumed Name form with the state and obtain a license as "John Doe d/b/a Doe Realty.")

(Note 3: Do not confuse an individual broker's license issued under an assumed name with a broker's license issued in the name of a business entity, e.g., Doe Realty, Inc. In the latter case, John Doe obtains a associate broker's license as a principal under Doe Realty, Inc. which serves as the broker. John Doe can, instead, elect to obtain his individual broker's license with a d/b/a. Either way is a matter of preference.)

Sec. 2512f [▶ Supervision of real estate salesperson.]

(1) A broker or associate broker must supervise the work of a salesperson. Supervision must include all of the following as a minimum:
   (a) Direct and regular communication in person or by radio, telephone, or electronic communication (i.e., text or email).
   (b) Review of the practice of the salesperson.
   (c) Review of the salesperson's reports (e.g., contracts, forms, disclosures, and transaction file notes).
   (d) Analysis and guidance of the salesperson's performance in regulated activities.
   (e) Providing written operating policies and procedures to the salesperson.
   (Note: A company policies and procedures manual is only required if a broker has one or more affiliated salespersons. Nevertheless, all brokerage operations can benefit from having such a manual in existence. It helps to avoid procedural mistakes and may be required by the broker's errors and omissions insurance company.)
(2) A broker shall not enter into any contract with a salesperson or a non-principal associate broker that limits the broker's authority to supervise the licensee.
   (Note: This section is an important reminder that a broker is responsible for the actions of his affiliated licensees. A broker must minimally fulfill the supervision responsibilities set forth in this section.)

Sec. 2513 [Filing bond as condition to issuance of license; action by injured person.]

A license applicant who has been previously disciplined may be required to first obtain a bond not to exceed 5 years in term, or $5,000 in amount, in which the state is named as the insured. If imposed, the bond must be obtained before the applicant will receive a new real estate license. If the licensee violates the law thereafter, any injured party can bring a legal claim against the bond for damages (to the extent it is covered by the bond).

Sec. 2514 [Nonresident applicant; consent to service of process.]

Residency is not a condition to receiving a Michigan real estate license. The nonresident licensee must, however, agree to abide by Michigan law (including the Occupational Code and rules).

/1/ A nonresident applicant must file an irrevocable consent to service of process form which gives Michigan courts jurisdiction over the nonresident's real estate activities.
   (Note: The nonresident can be served with a copy of the complaint and a summons to appear in court, or at a hearing, in spite of the fact that the licensee is not a resident of Michigan.)
/2/ In the case of a non-Michigan corporation, the consent to service of process form must be authenticated by corporate seal or acknowledged by an officer or member of the business entity. It shall further be accompanied by a certified copy of a resolution authorizing the officer or member to execute the form.

(Note: Recall from Sec. 2505(3) that all brokers must maintain a place of business in Michigan. Further, Michigan does not have a reciprocal real estate licensing agreement with any other state, i.e., no other state's real estate license is accepted as valid in Michigan.)

Sec. 2515 [▶ Listing agreement; discrimination prohibited; burden of proof; remedies.]

(1) All listing agreements must contain a nondiscrimination clause that discrimination based on religion, race, color, national origin, age, sex, disability, familial status, or marital status on the part of the licensee, seller, or lessor is prohibited.
   (Note: Pursuant to Rule 101(s), seller listing agreements and buyer's agency agreements are both referred to as "service provision agreements." Accordingly, a broker acting as buyer's agent must also include a nondiscrimination clause in his buyer's agency agreement.)

(2) Since there is a presumption of innocence under Michigan law, the department must prove its case against a party.
(3) An injured party can go directly to a court of law to seek relief rather than to the department.
(Note: Even if the injured party elects not file a complaint with the department, and instead files a court action, the department may wait to see how the court rules and initiate its own complaint if a violation has been found.)

Sec. 2516 [▶ Interest in real property; acquisition by licensee; proof of disclosures and consents.]

(1) When a licensee directly or indirectly buys or acquires an interest in a property, he or she must disclose the fact that he is licensed to the owner before the owner signs the purchase agreement.
(2) When a licensee directly or indirectly acquires an option to purchase a property from an owner (who has requested the licensee's services), the licensee must disclose the fact that he is licensed to the owner before the owner signs the option agreement. Disclosure must be clear and in writing.
(3) A licensee who directly or indirectly buys or acquires an interest in property, and is due a commission or other fee as a result, must disclose to the seller or owner that he or she is licensed to receive the commission.
(4) On request of the department, the licensee must provide written proof of any disclosures and consents required under this section.
(Note: It is generally best if these written disclosures are included in the purchase agreement or option agreement.)

Sec. 2516a [▶ Inspection of document or record by representative of department.]

Licensees must allow an authorized representative of the department to enter its place of business to inspect any document or record deemed to be reasonably necessary for investigation of the licensee, review of the broker's business activities, or administration of the law or rules.

Sec. 2517 [▶ Disclosure of agency relationship.]

(1) A licensee shall disclose to a potential buyer or seller in a real estate transaction all types of agency relationships available and the licensee's duties that each agency relationship creates. The licensee must make this disclosure before the potential buyer or seller discloses any confidential information about himself or herself to the licensee.
(Note regarding timing: Since it is difficult to guess if, or when, a potential buyer or seller might disclose confidential information, it may be best for a licensee to make the required disclosure of agency relationships and duties at or around the time they first make contact.)
(Note regarding buyers who are unwilling to sign a buyer's agency contract: Some licensees who work with buyers who desire agency-level services, but are not willing to sign a buyer's agency agreement, merely check "Buyer's Agent" on the agency disclosure form. This is not a good practice because the agency disclosure form is not contractual in nature and should not be used as a substitute for a buyer's agency agreement. Further, the agency disclosure form could be used as evidence of an implied buyer's agency against the licensee–see Chapter 2 for further details.)
(2) Unless certain services are knowingly waived by execution of a limited service agreement, a broker or salesperson providing services under any service provision agreement shall, at a minimum, provide to the client the "duties" described in Sec. 2512d(2) and the "services" described in Sec. 2512d(3).
(Note: Recall that duties cannot be waived, only some of the services can.)
(3) The disclosure of the type of agency relationship shall be in writing, shall be provided to the client, and shall substantially conform to the language set forth in this subsection.
(Note: Refer to the copy of the "Disclosure Regarding Real Estate Agency Relationships" provided in the back of this textbook for details.)
(Note regarding changes to the form: Most legal experts feel that a broker may make slight modifications to the agency disclosure language in their company version of the form as long as it substantially complies with the language in this section. Generally, clarifying words or short statements may be added, but nothing in the statutory language should be deleted. Salespersons and non-principal associate brokers should never make any modifications without first checking with their respective broker.)
(Note regarding completion of disclosure: A licensee must disclose his status by checking the appropriate line. To be safe, only one selection should be made at any given time. If the status changes, an updated or new form should be provided. Some brokers, mostly those who practice dual agency, elect to check "Dual Agent" in addition to the form of agency entered into at first contact with the buyer or the seller. The purpose is to let the seller or buyer know at first contact that a dual agency may arise at some later time. This practice should only be adopted by a broker, and only after consultation with legal counsel. The statute is silent on the legality of this practice.)
(Note regarding refusal to sign: Licensees may encounter buyers and sellers who refuse to sign the disclosure form. If this occurs, the licensee should complete the form to the extent possible and give a copy to the buyer or seller. The

Chapter 19: Real Estate License Law

licensee should then take a copy of the form and write down the circumstances, including the time, date, location where it was provided, and that it was refused. This copy should be retained in the office files.)

(4) This subsection contains the statutorily-prescribed language to be used when a client desires to waive any of the services required under Sec. 2512(3)(b), (c), and (d) by execution of a limited service agreement.
(Note: Refer to the waiver located at the back of this textbook following the copy of the agency disclosure form.)

(5) ▶ A licensee can act as a transaction coordinator providing that proper notice is given.
(Note: A transaction coordinator is a licensee who is not an agent because agency-level services are not offered or provided. The issue of appropriate notice and permission or authorization is discussed in Chapter 3.)

(6) ▶ A broker and client may enter into a designated agency agreement. In its absence, the client has an agency relationship with the broker and all of the broker's affiliated licensees, i.e., a non-designated agency relationship exists–see Chapter 3 for a more thorough discussion of designated agency.

(7) A designated agency agreement must contain the name of all associate brokers authorized to act as supervisory brokers. If one licensee in a company is the designated agent for the seller, and another licensee in the same company is the designated agent for the buyer, the broker and named supervisory brokers are considered to be consensual dual agents for the transaction. Clients must be notified before an offer to purchase is made or presented that the broker represents both parties.
(Note: While this fact is already noted in the agency disclosure form itself, a broker may wish to have the buyer and seller execute an additional Dual Agency Agreement based on the recommendation of legal counsel.)
(Note about who the designated agent is: The designated agent is typically the salesperson or non-principal associate broker who actually procures the listing agreement with the seller-client or buyer's agent agreement with the buyer-client.)

(8) The client of a designated agent does not have an agency relationship with other affiliated licensees in the company.
(Note: Adopting a designated agency policy is a matter of preference for a broker. A broker can elect to practice traditional non-designated agency instead of designated agency. Regardless of which policy a broker adopts, it applies to the entire company. For example, if a broker practices designated agency, all affiliated licensees must follow it.)
/1/ Two affiliated designated agents can represent different parties in the same transaction without being considered dual agents themselves.
(Note: The broker and named supervisory brokers are dual agents, however.)
/2/ Confidential information about a client which is known by one designated agent is not imputed, meaning charged, to affiliated licensees that do not have an agency relationship with the client.
(Note: Other affiliated licensees in the company are not presumed to "legally" know what the designated agent knows about his client.)

(9) A designated agent must not disclose confidential information about a client to any licensee whether or not they are affiliated. The designated agent may, however, disclose confidential information to the broker or supervisory broker when seeking beneficial advice or assistance for the client. An agent does not breach any duty to his or her client by failing (or refusing) to disclose confidential information obtained through a present or prior agency relationship.
Example: A licensee is the designated agent for two buyer-clients who are both interesting in making an offer to purchase a property that is listed with another company. "Buyer-Client A" makes a full price and terms offer. "Buyer-Client B" makes an offer that exceeds the list price by $1,000. The designated agent does not breach any fiduciary duty to "Buyer-Client A" by remaining silent about "Buyer-Client B's" higher offer. This also holds true under a non-designated agency policy.

(10) A listing agreement or buyer's agency agreement may be amended to establish a designated agency relationship, change a designated agent, or change supervisory brokers pursuant to a written addendum signed by the parties.

(11) The following definitions are provided in this subsection for purposes of agency disclosure and designated agency:
  (a) "Affiliated licensee" includes all individual salespersons and associate brokers who are employed by the same broker.
  (b) "Buyer" means a purchaser, tenant, or lessee of any legal or equitable real estate interest.
  (Note: Depending on the nature of the interest, a legal interest can be obtained through a deed or contract. An equitable interest includes that which a vendee acquires in a land contract during the term of the contract.)
  (c) "Buyer's agent" means a licensee who acts on behalf of the buyer in a real estate transaction and accepts the responsibility of serving the buyer in a manner consistent with fiduciary duties existing under common law.
  (Note: Although this provision does not mention the statutory fiduciary duties set forth in Sec. 2512d(2)(a) through (g), they are also part of the overall duties an agent owes to a client.)
  (d) "Designated agent" means an individual salesperson or associate broker who is named by the broker as the client's legal agent (pursuant to a designated agency agreement and/or acknowledgment on the agency disclosure form).

(e) "Designated agency agreement" means a written agreement between a broker and client in which an individual salesperson or associate broker is named as the client's designated agent.

(f) "Dual agent" means a licensee who acts as the agent of both buyer and seller (in the same transaction) and provides services without the full range of fiduciary duties owed by a buyer's agent and a seller's agent.

(g) "Real estate transaction" means a sale or lease of any legal or equitable interest in land.

(h) "Seller" means the equitable or legal owner of real estate.

(i) "Seller's agent" means a licensee who acts on behalf of the seller in a real estate transaction and accepts the responsibility of serving the seller in a manner consistent with fiduciary duties existing under common law. (Note: Although this provision does not mention the statutory fiduciary duties set forth in Sec. 2512d(2)(a) through (g), they are part of an agent's duties to a client.)

(j) "Supervisory broker" means an associate broker designated in a written agency agreement to act in a supervisory role in an agency relationship.

(k) "Transaction coordinator" means a licensee who does not act as the agent of either the buyer or the seller.

Sec. 2518 [▶ Prohibited actions.]

An action shall not be brought against a broker, an associate broker, or a salesperson under the circumstances noted in subsections (a), (b), and (c) of this section.

(Note: The language in this section, "An action shall not be brought...," provides a potentially significant degree of protection against lawsuits brought against a licensee under the circumstances outlined in this section. Interpreting the statute literally, it does not appear to be specifically limited to actions brought by the department. If a court shares this interpretation, Sec. 2518 provides an important shield, meaning defense, against certain lawsuits. Any time a salesperson or associate broker encounters a situation having to do with the issues raised in these subsections, the employing broker should be immediately alerted.)

(a) An action cannot be brought against a licensee for failing to disclose to a buyer or tenant that a former occupant has or is suspected of having a disability.

(Note: A person with HIV/AIDS, or any other infectious disease, is deemed to have a disability for purposes of state and federal law. As a result, a licensee should never disclose such fact, even to a client, lest the licensee risk violating the civil rights of the person with a disability.)

(b) An action cannot be brought against a licensee for failing to disclose to a buyer or tenant that the property was or was suspected to have been the site of a homicide, suicide, or other occurrence prohibited by law which had no material effect on the property. Such occurrences are sometimes referred to as stigmatizing or psychologically-impacting events.

(Note regarding disclosure: As discussed in Chapter 2, a stigmatizing event or circumstance that does not affect the physical condition of the property is not generally considered to be a defect under Michigan law and does not have to be disclosed. If a prospective buyer asks a licensee about such an event or circumstance and the licensee is aware of it, Sec. 604(b) requires honesty, so the question should be answered truthfully.)

(Note regarding disclosure to buyer-client: Voluntary disclosure to a buyer-client by a buyer's agent may be prudent as part of the agent's fiduciary duty to the client. If a literal interpretation of Sec. 2518 is applied, no action can be brought against a licensee for failing to disclose a stigmatizing event, including a lawsuit for breach of fiduciary duty for failing to disclose the event to a client. However, a broker's legal counsel may recommend alerting a buyer-client in advance to prevent a lawsuit from being filed.)

(Note regarding stigmatizing events: Events that potentially stigmatize a property from a buyer's perspective include a notorious crime, murder, suicide, illegal drug activity, or an allegation of paranormal activity on the premises. If a seller-client asks his or her listing agent whether or not to disclose such an event to a buyer, the licensee should direct the seller-client to seek the advice of legal counsel.)

(c) An action cannot be brought against a licensee for not disclosing any information made available under Michigan's Sex Offenders Registration Act.

(Note: A sex offender disclosure statute is commonly referred to as Megan's Law. Real estate licensees are not obligated to provide sex offender information to prospective home buyers and are cautioned against doing so since: (1) the accuracy of the information may be an issue; and (2) the disclosure is outside of the scope of a licensee's responsibilities. Persons desiring such information should be referred to the appropriate governmental or law enforcement agency. The Michigan's Seller's Disclosure Statement also contains a clause to this effect.)

DIAGNOSTIC PRACTICE QUESTIONS – CHAPTERS 19 and 20

IMPORTANT STUDY TIP!

Step 1: Carefully review the information located in this chapter.

Step 2: Take the following Diagnostic Practice Questions. Review any question you answered incorrectly by researching the topic in this textbook. If you are still uncertain as to why the question is answered as it is, consult your program provider.

NOTE ON CHAPTER PRACTICE QUESTIONS

The following questions are representative of the type encountered on the Michigan real estate licensing examination. While some of these questions may be similar in nature and style, there is no way of predicting the exact wording of a question that will appear on the exam. Spending time memorizing these questions is, therefore, not recommended.

These questions are designed to help you determine how well you comprehend the material in this chapter. They are also intended to help you develop problem solving skills and to become comfortable with question formats.

Do not attempt to answer these questions until you have attended the lecture corresponding to this chapter and spent the appropriate time studying the material.

1. Marga Reet, a licensed salesperson, took an extended overseas vacation and forgot to send in her license renewal prior to leaving. While she was out of the country, her license expired. She came home the month following expiration and wanted to begin making prospecting calls for new business. Which statement best describes Marga's current situation?
   A. Marga may make her prospecting calls provided she does not transact any business until she first renews her license and pays a late renewal fee.
   B. Marga may not make any prospecting calls until she renews and receives her salesperson license.
   C. Marga must reinstate her license before she performs the acts of a real estate salesperson.
   D. Marga must retake the real estate salesperson's license exam and pay all required fees before making any prospecting calls.

2. Kendra, a buyer, is given an agency disclosure statement by Salesperson Shaun. Kendra does not wish to sign a buyer's agency agreement until she has had some time to "get comfortable" with her salesperson. Shaun elects to initially act as a transaction coordinator just in case Kendra changes her mind. All EXCEPT which of the following statements are correct?
   A. Shaun should seek prior authorization from Kendra to act as a transaction coordinator.
   B. Shaun cannot act as a transaction coordinator under these circumstances because once a form of agency is selected on the agency disclosure form, no changes can be made.
   C. Shaun should not provide non-agency services as a transaction coordinator to a buyer unless his company policy authorizes the practice.
   D. As a transaction coordinator, Shaun cannot provide agency-level services without risk of creating an implied agency relationship.

3. Marcus, an associate broker, works strictly as a general manager for Mastiff Properties. The brokerage is fully owned and operated by 3 other broker-partners. The 3 partners decide that Marcus' services will no longer be needed. Upon learning of this, Marcus decides to go into business for himself. Under these circumstances, which statement is most true?
   A. Marcus must make application for a broker's license under his own name and take the broker's license examination before starting his new company.
   B. Since Marcus is an associate broker, he can transfer his license to his new office and apply for a change of name with the department.
   C. Although Marcus' associate broker's license is immediately suspended, the department will permit him to make application for a broker's license.
   D. Since Marcus acted as a general manager, any application for a new license must be held pending review of Mastiff Properties' trust accounts.

4. A couple shopping for their first home stop by AAA Real Estate to see one of the new listings of the company. After reviewing the agency disclosure form, the couple wants buyer's agency. Company policy dictates that a written buyer's agency contract be executed to

provide such services. The couple does not want to sign an agreement at this point, so "Seller's Agent" is checked on the disclosure form. The agent should act in the best interests of:
A. the seller, because this is the person to whom the broker's loyalty is now owed.
B. the buyers, because this is what they really wanted in the first place.
C. neither the buyer or the seller, because the salesperson is legally operating as a transaction coordinator.
D. both the buyer and the seller, because the agency disclosure form links the salesperson to the seller and an automatic implied agency links the salesperson to the buyers.

5. A broker is contacted by the owners of a property whose live-in relative just died of HIV/AIDS. The owners want to sell the property and have asked the broker to list it for them. The broker is contacted by an investor who is not interested in representation. After seeing the property and reviewing the property condition disclosure statement, the investor asks the broker if there is anything else that the investor should know. Which of the statements below is most true?
A. The broker is under no duty to disclose the existence of the HIV/AIDS patient because such disclosure might constitute unlawful discrimination.
B. The broker is under a duty to disclose that a resident of the house had HIV/AIDS because the apprehension associated with the illness might give rise to a lawsuit against the broker.
C. The broker should refuse to answer the question, instead recommending that the investor ask the sellers if they are aware of anything else.
D. As long as the broker did not volunteer the information nor make a statement that invited the question, the broker is free to answer it truthfully.

6. All EXCEPT which of the following are punishable offenses under Article 6 of the Occupational Code?
A. Failing to comply with an order of the Board of Real Estate Brokers and Salespersons.
B. Failing to respond to a citation.
C. Failing to comply with a subpoena.
D. Failing to pass the exam by the third attempt.

7. A licensee can have his or her license suspended or revoked for all of the following EXCEPT:
A. Representing more than one party in a property management transaction without the knowledge of the parties.
B. Depositing an earnest money deposit in an interest bearing account.
C. Preparing a market analysis for a fee on a federally-related transaction.
D. Changing a business location without notification to the department.

8. If a buyer defaults and forfeits an earnest money deposit being held by the broker, the broker:
A. Must arbitrate the matter with the local Board of REALTORS®.
B. Can retain the deposit to satisfy his claim to an earned commission.
C. Must file a claim for the deposit with the department under Article 5 of the Occupational Code.
D. Is ordinarily not entitled to any of the deposit unless the sales agreement states to the contrary.

9. An interested buyer contacts a broker about a property listing that was obtained by a salesperson in the broker's firm. All EXCEPT which of the following statements regarding agency disclosure are true?
A. The broker must make an agency disclosure to the buyer before the buyer discloses any information confidential to the broker.
B. The agency disclosure cannot be properly made during a telephone conversation.
C. If the buyer refuses to sign the agency disclosure form, the broker must refer the buyer to another agent in the firm.
D. The broker must disclose all types of agency relationships even if the broker's individual policy does not permit the practice of dual agency.

10. A real estate broker accepts a listing from a homeowner that contains a handwritten clause limiting any showings to a certain named minority. Which of the following is most true?
A. This listing is void due to the existence of the clause.
B. The broker is in violation of Act 299 only if he refuses to show the property to a minority.
C. The broker may operate under the terms of the listing providing he alerts all minority prospects to the existence of the clause.
D. The seller can enforce the listing agreement if the broker agrees to accept its terms.

11. Which of the following statements regarding the license of an associate broker is most correct?
A. An associate broker's license will automatically be issued to any salesperson who has been continuously licensed for at least 3 years.
B. A principal associate broker can never hold more than one associate broker's license.
C. The license of a nonprincipal associate broker may be transferred to another real estate company.
D. An associate real estate broker's license is identical to a real estate broker's license in every respect.

12. Persons found guilty of operating in the real estate business without a license may be sent to prison by which of the following?
    A. The real estate department.
    B. The attorney general.
    C. A court of law.
    D. The deputy commissioner.

13. Which of the following persons would be exempt under Michigan real estate license law?
    A. An unlicensed builder who personally constructs homes and then handles the sales without the assistance of a real estate broker.
    B. A person who lists and sells properties only for her immediate family members.
    C. A licensed attorney who assists clients with purchase agreements and closings in her capacity as an attorney.
    D. A person who sells 6 properties during a year that he personally owns.

14. Which of the following applies to an out of state broker who wishes to conduct business in Michigan?
    A. The out of state broker must become a resident of Michigan.
    B. The non-resident broker will be required to execute an irrevocable consent.
    C. The broker must abide by the law of the primary state of residence providing they are not in conflict with Michigan.
    D. There is no difference in the license laws from one state to the next due to reciprocity rules.

15. In order to continue uninterrupted real estate practice at the end of a licensing cycle, a licensee must renew his or her license on or before the:
    A. expiration date
    B. reinstatement period
    C. late renewal period
    D. relicensure deadline

16. A broker is required to place earnest money deposits in his escrow account within two banking days after:
    A. The acceptance of a purchase agreement by all parties to the contract.
    B. Receipt of the deposit from either the buyer or cooperating broker.
    C. The broker receives notice that the purchase agreement has been accepted by all parties.
    D. The title work has been delivered to the listing broker's office.

17. An unlicensed person can receive a fee from a licensed broker for which of the following acts?
    A. Selling a commercially prepared list of names to the licensed agent.
    B. Receiving one month's rent free for referring a prospective tenant to the owner of a rental property.
    C. Providing the names of neighbors who are interested in listing providing the unlicensed person does not perform the acts of a licensee.
    D. All of the above.

18. A broker has just discharged a salesperson. The broker should:
    A. Instruct the salesperson to return the license to the department.
    B. Return the license to the department.
    C. Remove the license from the office and keep it on file until all the salesperson's transactions have closed.
    D. Give the salesperson his or her license to return to the department.

19. A three-office real estate company owned by broker Darcy has one of its branch offices located in an adjacent city. Darcy asked Ron, one of his salespersons, to manage the branch. Ron would be able to do so providing:
    A. The office is operating under a separate branch office license applied for by Ron.
    B. Ron is the principal designated agent for the office.
    C. The branch is not in excess of 25 miles from the nearest boundary of the city in which Darcy's main office is located.
    D. There are no circumstances under license law or rules in which Ron could manage the branch.

20. An active officer who engages in real estate activities for a corporation to which a broker's license has been issued must hold which license?
    A. A real estate salesperson.
    B. A residential builder.
    C. An associate broker.
    D. Either a salesperson or broker.

21. The Department is empowered by the Michigan legislature to do which of the following?
    A. Subpoena only licensees.
    B. Subpoena anyone in the state.
    C. Petition the circuit court to issue a subpoena.
    D. No subpoena power exists with respect to real estate issues.

*A mentor is someone who sees your Truth before you are
willing to accept it for yourself. Find a mentor who understands
this and you will have assembled a winning team.*

Chapter 20
Administrative Rules

Learning how the law is interpreted and applied by a licensing agency.

I. **Foreword**: Administrative law flows from the rules, orders, decrees, and decisions of an administrative agency such as Michigan's licensing department. These administrative decisions fulfill the department's function in monitoring and regulating an occupation or profession such as real estate. The foreword to Chapter 19 discusses how Michigan's license law and rules work together to create a set of standards to which real estate licensees are held. It is recommended that you review that discussion before studying this chapter on administrative rules.

II. **Chapter note**: The numbers listed in parentheses after many of the rules in this chapter correspond to a specific numbered subrule in the administrative rules. In some cases, numbers and letters will appear to be missing. This was done intentionally. The subrules of lesser importance and those which are repetitive have been omitted from this chapter. Also contributing to the appearance of missing numbers is the fact that many of the rules have been rescinded and moved to the law in Article 25 to assist the department and attorney general's office with enforcement.

To help create a more thorough understanding of Michigan real estate law and rules, this chapter contains some references to sections in the license law. Recall that license laws are referred to using section numbers. For example, a reference to Sec. 201 in this chapter means that the rule should be read in conjunction with Section 201 of the license law. Even though several rules were moved to the license law, some of the remaining rules contain parallel provisions to the law. If a contradiction exists, the license law takes precedence over the rules.

Finally, the term "code" is used in some of the rules. It refers to the license law. For ease of learning, "code" has been replaced by the term "license law" in this chapter. The full text of Michigan's administrative rules is available on the LARA website at <www.michigan.gov/realestate>. To access it, go to the website and click on the "Administrative Rules" link under the heading Quick Links.

DEPARTMENT OF LICENSING AND REGULATORY AFFAIRS
ADMINISTRATIVE RULES
REAL ESTATE BROKERS AND SALESPERSONS
PART 1. GENERAL PROVISIONS

Rule 101 [Definitions.]

(1) The following terms, as they are used in the rules, are defined as follows:
   (a) "Code" refers to Public Act 299 otherwise known as the Occupational Code (i.e., the license law).
   (b) "Department" means the department of licensing and regulatory affairs.
   (c) "Disability" refers to a determinable physical or mental characteristic that prevents a broker from performing his duties.
   (d) "Instructor" refers to the individual who is approved to teach prelicensure classes pursuant to Sec. 2504(4).
   (e) "Program coordinator" means an individual who assumes the responsibility for supervising the administration of approved courses.
   (f) "Real estate school" means an approved entity that represents to the public that any of its courses fulfill the requirements of Section 2504(1) and (2) for prelicensure education.

PART 2. LICENSING

Rule 203 [▶ Education validity.]

(1) A broker's license applicant must satisfy all code requirements including 90 hours of approved prelicensure courses in real estate (9 clock hours must be on civil rights and fair housing law). Broker prelicensure education must be completed not more than 36 months before the date of application (unless the applicant held an active real estate salesperson license during that period).

(2) Approved broker prelicensure education must meet criteria established by the department, but may be reviewed and preapproved by a statewide real estate trade association. Not more than 1 broker course on the same subject will be accepted for credit.

(3) The department shall give credit for the following:
 (a) Possession of a law degree equals 60 clock hours of education (includes 6 of the required 9 hours of fair housing).
 (b) Possession of a masters degree in business administration or finance from a college or university equals 60 clock hours.
  (Note: The applicant must also complete the required 9 clock hours of fair housing.)
 (c) Possession of a bachelor's degree in business or finance from a college or university equals 30 clock hours.
  (Note: The applicant must also complete the required 9 clock hours of fair housing.)

(4) An applicant for a salesperson's license must complete 40 clock hours of qualifying prelicensure education of which 4 hours must include civil rights and fair housing. All salesperson prelicense education must be completed within 36 months, i.e., 3 years, of making application for the license.

Rule 217 [▶ Acceptable related experience for broker applicants.]

For purposes of calculating the time a broker's license applicant has been engaged in the real estate business pursuant to Sec. 2505(7)(b)(viii), the following apply:
(a) Holding a real estate license in another state equals 1 year of credit for each year in which the applicant closed 5 or more real estate transactions.
(b) Managing at least 10 units located in Michigan for 3 years or longer equals 1 year of credit.

Rule 219 [▶ Lapse of broker's license.]

(1) If a broker's license is lapsed, the licenses of all salespersons and affiliated associate brokers are automatically suspended until that real estate broker is relicensed or there is a change of employer and the issuance of a new license.

(2) If a the license of a salesperson or affiliated associate broker whose license was suspended pursuant to subrule (1) becomes employed by a different broker, the department shall issue a new license to the salesperson or associate broker without charge for the same term.

(Note: Suspension of a salesperson or associate broker under these circumstances if not considered to be disciplinary.)

Rule 221 [▶ Death or disability of broker.]

(1) If a sole principal associate broker dies or becomes disabled, the department shall allow all affiliated real estate licensees a reasonable time (up to 1 year) to wind up the business of the real estate broker or designate a new sole principal associate broker.
(Note: A sole principal associate broker situation arises when the broker's license in issued in the name of the company and there is only one principal associate broker to control and supervise business operations.)

(2) The license of the deceased or disabled sole principal associate broker must not be used to enter into new business transactions.

(3) One year after the date of death or disability of a broker's sole associate principal broker, the licenses of all affiliated salespersons and associate brokers are automatically suspended (pending a replacement of the sole principal associate broker or change of employer).

(4) If a salesperson or affiliated associate broker whose license was suspended pursuant to subrule (3) of this rule becomes employed by a different licensed broker, the department shall issue a new license to the real estate salesperson or associate real estate broker without charge if the license is issued during the same term in which the original license was issued.

Chapter 20: Administrative Rules 369

PART 3. PRACTICE AND CONDUCT

Rule 305 [▶ Service provision agreement.]

(1) A broker (or licensee acting on behalf of the employing broker) who enters into a service provision agreement shall provide the party(s) a true executed copy at the time of signing the agreement. Every agreement must be fully completed by the licensee before the party(s) sign it.
(Note: A licensee cannot give the property owner a blank listing or buyer's agency contract and ask him or her to sign it with the understanding that the blank spaces will be filled in later by the licensee.)

(2) A service provision agreement must include a definite expiration date and must not contain a provision requiring the party signing it to notify the broker of the party's intention to cancel the agreement upon or after expiration.
(Note: No automatically renewable listing or buyer agency contracts are allowed. In other words, the agent cannot place a provision in the service provision agreement making the client responsible for calling to cancel it).

Rule 307 [▶ Delivery of offer to purchase; delivery of written offers; inclusion of terms.]

(1) A licensee must give the buyer a signed copy of the offer to purchase immediately after the buyer signs it.
(2) A licensee shall make certain that all terms and conditions of the transaction are included in the offer to purchase.
(3) A licensee shall promptly deliver all written offers to purchase to the seller upon receipt. Delivery may be made through any method acceptable to the parties including in person, by mail, or through an electronic communication pursuant to Michigan's Uniform Electronic Transactions Act. The use of electronic records or digital signatures requires the prior agreement of the parties
(Note: The agreement to use electronic agreements and signatures is obtained either through a clause in the purchase agreement or an addendum which is digitally signed by both the buyer and the seller and attached to the purchase agreement. See Chapter 12 for additional information.)
(4) Upon obtaining a proper acceptance (meaning signature of the seller), the licensee must promptly deliver true executed copies of the acceptance to the buyer and the seller.
(5) Once a seller accepts an offer to purchase from a buyer, a licensee does not have to submit to the seller subsequent offers received from other buyers, unless a service provision agreement requires it.
(Note: Most listing agreements contain a provision that parallels this subrule. Even if a service provision agreement is silent on the issue, an offer to purchase may contain a provision whereby the seller agrees not to accept further offers from other buyers.)

Rule 313 [▶ Trust accounts.]

(1) A trust or escrow account must comply with license law in addition to this rule.
(2) Trust accounts must be demand in nature (meaning the broker can withdraw the money at any time without prior notice being given to the lending institution, e.g., a checking account). Checks drawn on the account must be signed by a broker (or associate broker). Non-broker cosignatories (such as a salesperson or administrative personnel) may be used only if accompanied by the broker's signature.
(3) A broker shall deposit all funds received in a fiduciary capacity, including escrow funds and earnest money, in a non-interest-bearing demand trust account. The account must be maintained in accordance with the requirements of Sec. 2512(k).
(4) A broker shall maintain a record of all funds received. At a minimum, the record must include all of the following:
 (a) The date the funds were received and the date of deposit.
 (b) The name of the party who provided the funds.
 (c) The amount of funds received and deposited and the method of payment.
(5) A broker shall maintain a record of all funds disbursed. At a minimum, the record must include all of the following information:
 (a) The name of the party to whom funds were disbursed.
 (b) The date of the disbursement.
 (c) The check number.
 (d) The purpose of the disbursement.
 (e) The amount of the disbursement.
(6) The broker's records must reflect the current account balance of each account maintained and must be made available to the department upon request.
(7) The broker's records must reflect the receipts and disbursements as they affect a single, particular transaction between a buyer and seller and must contain, at a minimum, all of the following:
 (a) For funds received, the record must include all of the following:

(i) The names of both parties to a transaction.
(ii) The property address or brief legal description.
(iii) The dates and amounts received.
(b) For funds disbursed, the record must include all of the following:
(i) The date of the disbursement.
(ii) The name of the payee.
(iii) The check number.
(iv) The amount of the disbursement.
(8) Trust account records must be maintained for at least 3 years from the date of inception of the records.
(Note: Legal counsel may recommend that a broker retain the records for a longer period of time such as 7-to-10 years to parallel Michigan's statute of limitations pertaining to contracts, debt collection, and fraud.)
(9) A broker or associate broker's disbursement of an earnest money deposit must be made at consummation or termination of the signed agreement (pursuant to the terms of the agreement). However, if the buyer or seller make a claim to it, the deposit must remain in the broker's trust account until a civil action (i.e., interpleader) has determined to whom the deposit must be paid, or until the buyer and seller have agreed, in writing (i.e., mutual release), to the disposition of the deposit. The broker may also commence a civil action to interplead the deposit with the proper court.

Rule 315 [▶ Prohibition of licensee becoming party to a net service provision agreement.]

A net service provision agreement, also known as a net listing, is illegal if the licensee is using it as a means of securing a commission.
(Note: Even though the rule says "as a means of securing a commission," a net listing should be avoided regardless of whether the broker is using it to earn a commission or not.)

Rule 321 [▶ Licensee commissions for other services; disclosure and consent required.]

(1) A licensee who is entitled to receive (either directly or indirectly) a real estate commission from the sale of property, may not also receive a referral fee or other valuable consideration for placing a loan in connection with that transaction unless the licensee obtains the prior written consent of the buyer and seller and the fee is not prohibited by RESPA or other applicable law.
(2) The requirements of subrule (1) also apply to a referral fee or other valuable consideration obtained from an abstract, home warranty, title insurance company, or other settlement service provider. The licensee may not receive such consideration unless the licensee obtains the prior, written consent of any party with whom the licensee has an agency relationship and the fee is not prohibited by RESPA or other applicable law.
(Note regarding consent: The consent discussed in this subsection may be included in the language of the service provision agreement, purchase agreement, addendum, or a separate agreement.)
(Note regarding broker policy: Due to heightened potential for investigation and significant fines for improperly exchanging referral fees between settlement service providers, a broker may wish to prohibit his or her affiliated licensees from accepting them in all circumstances.)

Rule 333 [▶ Misrepresentation of material facts prohibited; disclosure of material facts.]

(1) A licensee must not directly or indirectly misrepresent material facts–see Chapter 2 for further discussion on what constitutes a material fact.
(2) A licensee's full disclosure of material facts which are within the licensee's knowledge about the condition of a subject property is not grounds for disciplinary action by the department despite a claim by the buyer or seller that the disclosure constituted disloyalty in violation of an agency relationship.
(Note: The prospective seller of a residential property must honestly and accurately indicate its condition on the Seller's Disclosure Statement which is then given to the prospective buyer. The seller uses the form to disclose all known defects, whether material or not. Assume, for example, that the seller refuses to properly disclose a defect of which the listing agent is aware. This subsection indicates that the department will not take action against the licensee for disclosing it to a buyer. The licensee should first bring the matter to the attention of his or her broker who will determine the best course of action.)

Chapter 20: Administrative Rules

PART 6. REAL ESTATE EDUCATION
SUBPART 1. GENERAL PROVISIONS

Rule 618 [Application for approval to offer prelicensure courses; forms; required information.]

(1) A real estate school must submit a prelicensure course approval application approved by the department. The application must include all of the following:
    (a) School name, business address, telephone number, facsimile number, website address, and e-mail address, if applicable.
    (b) Course title.
    (c) Instructor names, addresses, telephone numbers, and qualifications.
    (d) Program coordinator name.
    (e) Summary of topics for each prelicensure course to be taught with number of hours allocated to each topic.
    (f) Sample certificate (which must contain date of completion, approved course name, student name, clock hours completed by the student).
    (g) Methodology for verifying and monitoring attendance and the make up policy.
    (h) Enrollment application to be completed by prospective students that contains a statement disclosing the percentage of student who successfully completed the program in the past calendar year. The enrollment application must be updated by February 1 of each calendar year.
(2) A real estate school must report any change of information on the application form within 30 days.
(3) A real estate school must apply for and obtain approval before courses are offered to the public.
(4) The department must issue a course approval within 60 days of receipt of the application. Denials must state the reasons for the denial.
(5) The department must accept courses for approval that meet the criteria established by Sec. 2504.

Rule 619 [Expiration date for prelicensure courses; renewal.]

(1) Approval of prelicensure courses expire 1 year from the date the course was approved.
(2) A licensed proprietary real estate school must also comply with the authorizing Act to be approved under this subpart.
(3) To maintain course approval, a licensed proprietary real estate school must submit a renewal application to the department 60 days before expiration of the course approval.

Rule 620 [Program coordinator.]

Each school must designate an individual as program coordinator (who is responsible for supervising the courses and ensuring compliance with the code and rules).

Rule 621 [Instructors.]

(1) Instructors must be approved by the department prior to teaching any real estate course and possess one of the following minimum qualifications.
    (a) Teaches/has taught real estate courses at an accredited institution of higher learning.
    (b) Is licensed or certified by the department (or other governmental agency) to engage in real estate aspects of appraising, financing, marketing, brokerage management, real estate counseling, real property law, etc.
(2) Instructors are responsible for complying with all laws and rules, providing students with current and accurate information, maintaining an environment conducive to learning, assuring and certifying accurate attendance, and providing assistance to students and responding to questions relating to course materials.
(3) The school must submit instructor qualifications at least 60 days prior to scheduling them to teach.

Rule 622 [Syllabus.]

Students must be given a syllabus which contains: the course title; times, and dates of the course offering; the name, address, and telephone number of the coordinator and instructor; and a detailed outline of the subject matter to be covered.

Rule 623 [Student attendance and makeup policy.]

(1) Students must attend 100% of a course in order to receive credit for the course.
(2) Credit for distance learning courses requires completion of the entire course.
(3) Schools or sponsors must have a makeup policy for absent or late arriving students.

Rule 624 [Student records; content; inspection.]

(1) Approved schools must maintain records for each student.
(2) Student records must include the student's name and address, number of clock hours attended, student's grade (if a course completion exam is required), date of course completion, last four digits of the student's social security number, student's date of birth, and real estate identification number (if applicable).
(3) Records must be made available for inspection by the department during normal business hours.
(4) A real estate school or sponsor shall issue a proper certificate of completion to a student who successfully completes an approved course. The certificate must include the information required in Rule 618(1)(f).
(5) A student who completes a prelicensure course shall present a state-issued photo identification or acceptable alternative form of photo identification to the school before receiving the certificate of completion.
    (a) For traditional classroom settings, students must present the required identification to the school.
    (b) Online course providers must ensure that the person who receives the certificate of completion is the one who completed the course.
(6) Schools and sponsors must submit a schedule and geographic location notification to the department at least 30 days before courses are held.
(7) Within 5 business days of course conclusion, schools and sponsors must submit the names of students who have successfully completed an approved course.

Rule 625 [Denial, suspension, or rescission of approval to offer courses; violation of code or rules.]

A person, sponsor, real estate school, or institution is subject to the penalties of Sec. 602 of the license law for:
(a) Failure to comply with license law or rules.
(b) Revealing, attempting to discover, or inducing a person to reveal real estate exam questions.
(c) Making a substantial misrepresentation regarding the school or course of study.
(e) Pursuing a continued and flagrant course of misrepresentation or false promises through agents, salespersons, advertising, or otherwise.

Rule 626 [Distance learning.]

(1) Courses delivered through distance learning must be approved before being offered.
(2) A distance learning course must contain all of the following:
    (a) All requirements for approval of a prelicensure course.
    (b) The individual modules of instruction offered on a computer or other interactive program.
    (c) A list of at least 1 learning objective for each module of instruction. The learning objective must ensure that if all the objectives are met, the entire content of the course is understood.
    (d) A structured learning method to enable the student to attain each learning objective.
    (e) A method of assessment of the student's performance during each module of instruction.
    (f) A remediation for any student who is deficient in the assessment to repeat the module until the student understands the course content material.
(3) Delivery systems that meet the distance education criteria for current certification by the Association of Real Estate License Law Officials (ARELLO) are acceptable to the department, as follows:
    (a) Proof of ARELLO certification including the summary sheet and certificate.
    (b) Upon withdrawal or expiration of ARELLO certification, the approval to offer distance learning courses is suspended.
(4) Equivalent delivery systems may be used if they are approved by the department.
(5) The real estate school shall describe in detail on its application how it will remedy hardware and software failures.

Rule 627 [Advertising for approved real estate prelicensure courses.]

All advertising for approved real estate courses held out to the public as fulfilling the requirements of Sec. 2504 must include the name of the approved school.

Rule 628 [Solicitations.]

(1) Organizational membership, employment, business-related solicitations, or other non-educational presentations are prohibited during prelicensure courses and are not counted as part of the clock hours of the course.
(2) Students shall not receive credit for organizational membership, employment, business-related solicitations, or other non-educational presentations or solicitations offered in conjunction with an approved course.

SUBPART 2. CONTINUING EDUCATION

Rule 629 [Continuing education requirements for licensees.]

(1) A licensee shall complete 18 hours of continuing education in each license cycle as follows:
   (a) A minimum of 2 hours of legal education courses involving statutes, rules, and court cases must be completed during each year of a license cycle (pursuant to Sec. 2504a of license law), for a total of 6 or more hours of legal education per license cycle.
   (b) The remaining 12 hours of continuing education required for renewal may be completed at any time during the license cycle.
(2) Submission of an application for renewal constitutes the applicant's certification of compliance with the requirements of this rule.
(3) An applicant must retain acceptable evidence that he or she has met the continuing education requirements for renewal, and upon request, produce this evidence to the department.
   (Note: The evidence referred to in rule is the certificate of completion issued by the continuing education provider.)

Rule 630 [Waiver of continuing education.]

A request for a waiver of continuing education pursuant to Sec. 204(2) must be received by the department before the expiration date of the license cycle.

Rule 632 [Eligible continuing education program.]

Note: This rule sets forth several provisions pertaining to a continuing education course reviewed and certified by a statewide real estate association that has a membership representing more than 18,000 licensees. Currently, continuing education course approval and tracking is handled by the CE Marketplace. The CE Marketplace is a division of the Michigan REALTORS®.

The student who says, "I will never be able to pass the state exam," often proves him or herself right.
The student who says, "I will pass the state exam," stands the same chance of being right.
You get to chose the affirmation that fits your inner desire.

DIAGNOSTIC PRACTICE QUESTIONS – CHAPTERS 19 and 20

IMPORTANT STUDY TIP!

Step 1: Carefully review the information located in this chapter.

Step 2: Take the following Diagnostic Practice Questions. Review any question you answered incorrectly by researching the topic in this textbook. If you are still uncertain as to why the question is answered as it is, consult your program provider.

NOTE ON CHAPTER PRACTICE QUESTIONS

The following questions are representative of the type encountered on the Michigan real estate licensing examination. While some of these questions may be similar in nature and style, there is no way of predicting the exact wording of a question that will appear on the exam. Spending time memorizing these questions is, therefore, not recommended.

These questions are designed to help you determine how well you comprehend the material in this chapter. They are also intended to help you develop problem solving skills and to become comfortable with question formats.

Do not attempt to answer these questions until you have attended the lecture corresponding to this chapter and spent the appropriate time studying the material.

1. In order for a salesperson to transfer to another broker, the department must receive all of the following EXCEPT:
   A. The fee associated with transferring a salesperson's license.
   B. The salesperson's certificate of license issued in the name of the former broker.
   C. The application for transfer with signed statement.
   D. The salesperson's pocket card pending receipt of the sworn statement.

2. An associate broker has her license revoked for repeated violations of the agency disclosure provisions in the Occupational Code. Which of the statements is true?
   A. Since the agency disclosure provisions are recommendations and not statutory requirements, a license can only be suspended, but not revoked.
   B. The associate broker cannot apply for a new license for a minimum of 3 years after the revocation.
   C. If the associate broker is a non-principal, the license of all salespersons will be immediately suspended pending assignment of a new associate broker.
   D. The associate broker is entitled to a mandatory review of the decision by a representative of the attorney general's office.

3. Salesperson Dillon listed a property on behalf of his company. He received a telephone call from a buyer's agent working with another company who has an interested buyer. After the buyer saw the property, the buyer's agent called Dillon to present an offer from the buyer. Dillon said to bring it to his office and he would take it to the seller as soon as possible. Upon receiving the offer at his office, Dillon held it until the next day thereby giving him time to contact several other buyers with whom he had been working. Dillon's actions were:
   A. proper because a higher offer might have been obtained which is clearly in his seller-client's best interests.
   B. proper because the offer was from a buyer's agent and a listing agent owes no duty to a buyer's agent.
   C. improper because a listing agent must tender all offers to the seller upon receipt.
   D. improper because the listing agent should have refused the offer until the other buyers were contacted.

4. Grace, a real estate broker, is asked by her father-in-law, a builder-developer, to purchase a large tract of vacant land listed with another broker. The builder does not want to tip off his competitors regarding his interest so he asks his Grace to buy the property as if it were for her own use. Can the broker comply with the request?
   A. Yes, providing she makes written disclosure to the selling owner that she is a real estate broker and seeks written approval to collect a commission.

B. Yes, providing she makes written disclosure that she is a broker and agrees not to collect a commission from the transaction.
C. No, because a real estate broker can never purchase a property unless her name is on the title.
D. No, because she is related to the person for whom the property is ultimately being purchased.

5. The principal broker for Piper-Carson Realty promotes the fact that she is a proud member of the local Multiple Listing Service in all of her advertisements. The broker obtains a listing on a particularly nice property. In order to make a quick sale, the seller tells the broker to advertise it for 10% under market value. The broker feels that she can find a buyer herself and not have to share the commission with another broker, so she places an advertisement in the local newspaper rather than the MLS. Which of the following statements is most true?
    A. The broker has violated the license law and rules because she listed an undervalued property.
    B. The broker has violated the license law and rules because she indicated to the seller that she cooperates with other brokers.
    C. The broker has not violated the license law or rules because brokers are never required to cooperate with other brokers.
    D. The broker has not violated the license law or rules because the property was advertised through another form of advertising.

6. Broker Taylor Jacques listed a property. His seller accepted an offer from another company. The buyer applied for an FHA mortgage and was approved. All of the following statements is true EXCEPT:
    A. A HUD-1 settlement statement will be required.
    B. If the closing is held at a title company, Jacques has no further responsibility with regard to the settlement documents.
    C. Jacques must prepare a closing statement pursuant to license laws and rules.
    D. Jacques can ask his closing agent to review the settlement statements for him, but he retains responsibility for their contents.

7. A salesperson licensed in Michigan can receive a commission for performing a real estate transaction from any broker who is:
    A. licensed in any state providing the out-of-state broker does not perform any of the acts in Michigan for which a license is required.
    B. licensed in the state of Michigan.
    C. licensed in another state providing the transaction involves a corporate relocation.
    D. specifically responsible for supervision of the salesperson.

8. A broker takes the necessary closing statements to a closing that were completed by one of the broker's salespersons. All EXCEPT which of the following statements is true?
    A. All statements must have been signed by the broker prior to, or at, the actual closing.
    B. The broker can be held liable for any unintentional errors committed by the salesperson.
    C. The receipts and disbursements of both buyer and seller must be indicated on the statements.
    D. If the transaction is federally-related, a HUD-1 Statement is the only required closing statement.

9. A broker is considered to have commingled funds if he:
    A. places together the funds of his personal savings and personal checking accounts.
    B. places up to $2,000 of his own money in a trust account with the funds of his client.
    C. divides a down payment with sales commission and escrow account.
    D. mixes his personal funds with those of his clients.

10. Of all the following organizations, which requires a real estate broker to maintain a separate real estate escrow account?
    A. The local real estate board
    B. The state broker's association
    C. The multiple listing association
    D. The state licensing agency

11. Year two of a particular license cycle is coming to a close. Which of the following statements is true:
    A. A licensee must file a certificate of licensure with the department.
    B. At least 2 hours of approved continuing education must have been obtained during year two that cover laws, rules and court cases.
    C. There are no specific requirements for year two of a license cycle.
    D. At least 12 hours of approved continuing education must have been obtained by the end of year two.

12. The following advertisement appeared in a local newspaper one Sunday morning: "Beautiful 4 bedroom brick ranch, wooded lot, Pebble Farms area. Call Elizabeth Neena at 555-1212." Which of the following statements is true based upon the wording of the advertisement?
    A. If Elizabeth is a real estate broker, her advertisement might be in compliance with the law.
    B. If Elizabeth is a real estate salesperson, her advertisement might be in compliance with the law.
    C. Neither a broker or a salesperson can run such an advertisement without violating license law or rules.

Chapter 20: Administrative Rules

D. Either a broker or a salesperson can run the advertisement without violating license law or rules.

13. All EXCEPT which of the following represents a type of service provision agreement?
    A. A one-party exclusive agency agreement.
    B. A limited service listing agreement.
    C. An excluded party exclusive right to sell listing agreement.
    D. A transaction coordinator agreement.

14. The department may do all EXCEPT which of the following?
    A. Inspect a broker's business files at his place of business.
    B. Issue a citation based upon investigation of a complaint.
    C. Impose a 90-day prison sentence.
    D. Revoke a license for more than 1 year.

15. Salesperson Smith is showing property to Buyer Jones that is listed with Salesperson Judy. Jones expresses his desire to make an offer on the property. Which of the following statements is true regarding the preparation and signing of the necessary documents?
    A. Smith must give Jones a copy of the offer immediately after the seller accepts it.
    B. Smith must make certain that all terms and conditions of the sale are included in the offer.
    C. If accepted by the seller, only the buyer must be given a copy of the executed agreement.
    D. Judy will be required to continue to present backup offers pending the closing even though the listing agreement indicates no such requirement.

16. A broker is considering the purchase of a new residence for his family. He later contacts a seller who is selling on a for-sale-by-owner basis and attempts to list the property. According to license law, which of the following statements is false?
    A. The broker cannot enter into a net listing with the seller.
    B. The broker must disclose the fact that he may purchase the property at the time of listing.
    C. The broker must disclose that fact that he is a licensee before asking the seller to sign a purchase agreement.
    D. The broker needs the written consent of the owner if he anticipates using an earned commission to reduce the price of the property.

17. A seller and broker entered into a 6-month exclusive-right-to-sell listing agreement to sell her house. The seller accurately completed the seller's disclosure statement. One month later, the seller mentioned to the broker that a little water got in the basement during a storm the previous night. Power was lost to the sump pump for an hour, but it quickly drained and no damage was done. An unrepresented buyer to whom the broker was showing the home the following week asked the broker if there were any water problems with the basement. Which of the following is true?
    A. The broker can disclose the water issue without being subject to disciplinary action by the department for being disloyal to the seller under the listing agreement.
    B. The broker can tell the buyer there are no water issues since it resulted from power being lost to a sump pump rather than a structural problem.
    C. The broker tell the buyer "no" because the broker is not representing the buyer.
    D. It does not matter what the broker says since any potential problems will be handled by the broker's errors and omissions insurance policy.

18. A licensee is required to carry his or her pocket card:
    A. When acting in the capacity indicated on the card.
    B. Only while working in the office.
    C. At all times during the period for which it is issued.
    D. Only when marketing residential properties.

19. Salesperson Buddy wishes to purchase a 4 bedroom condominium from homeowner Tim who has his condominium listed with Buddy's broker, Martha. Which of the following statements is true?
    A. Any advertising by the real estate company on Tim's home must be in the name of Buddy.
    B. Buddy has to make a written disclosure of his license status to Tim prior to any sale taking place.
    C. Providing the agency disclosure was made by Buddy in a timely fashion, no further notices are required
    D. Buddy need only disclose his license status if the property was listed by another broker.

20. An applicant for a broker's license must do which of the following?
    A. Maintain a residence in the state of Michigan.
    B. Complete 90 hours of approved real estate education within no less than 30 days of successfully passing his or her exam.
    C. Have at least 3 years relevant, related experience specifically in real estate sales.
    D. If previously licensed as a broker, and currently working for another broker as a salesperson, surrender his salesperson's license and apply for a broker's license.

21. Which of the following is NOT required to be included in the bookkeeping system a broker must maintain for client funds?
    A. Records that segregate the earnest money deposit

of one transaction from that of another.
B. Records that reflect the amount and purpose of all disbursements.
C. Records that reflect the chronological sequence in which funds are received by the broker.
D. Records that reflect the amount of interest earned on receipts so it can be disbursed to the appropriate party.

Study. Study vigorously. Study often. . . . . *Ditch the excuses.*

Review. Review vigorously. Review often. . . . . *Pass the test.*

Celebrate. Celebrate vigorously. Celebrate often. . . . . *Have fun.*

Chapter 21
Michigan Specific Statutes

Understanding the specific laws that affect real estate development, leasing, financing and sales.

I. **Foreword**: Over the years, the Michigan legislature has enacted numerous statutes that regulate the development, purchase, sale, transfer, ownership, leasing, financing, and other investment aspects of real property within the state. Some statutes such as the Seller Disclosure Act actually contain sections that directly refer to real estate licensees. Statutes often target specific behaviors that, without regulation, can lead to problems for innocent and unsuspecting consumers. By regulating the conduct of certain individuals, problems relating to fraud, misrepresentation, price gouging, and environmental harm, for example, can be prevented.

A real estate licensee is not expected to be have an attorney's understanding of these Michigan-specific statutes. Nevertheless, it is still important for licensees to understand the purpose of each Act and how it potentially applies to real property and real property transactions. To make this process easier, this chapter takes each statute and divides it into four sections of coverage: (1) Purpose, (2) Application, (3) Provisions, and (4) Remedies and damages.

   A. **Purpose**: The segment titled "Purpose" examines the intent or design of the statute in clear and simple language.

   B. **Application**: The "Application" section describes the individuals, property, and/or conduct that the statute regulates.

   C. **Provisions**: The "Provisions" section describes the details of the statute's key provisions that affect, govern, or protect real property or real property transactions.

   D. **Remedies and damages**: The "Remedies and damages" section of the discussion sets forth the type of relief that each statute grants to anyone who has or may be harmed as a result of the statute being violated or ignored. Damages not only serve as a form of punishment, but also, to deter potential violators. The remedies and damages section is sometimes referred to as the "teeth" of the statute.

II. ▶ **Land Division Act** (Formerly referred to as the Subdivision Control Act): Public Act 288 of 1967. *[Uniform Standard for subdivision]*

   A. **Purpose**: As noted in the discussion of the Lot and Block method of property description in Chapter 10, a plat must be prepared and recorded before certain tracts of land can be subdivided. A plat is a scaled down representation of a subdivision which is comparable to a subdivision "blueprint." When a subdivision is created, private developers are the individuals who typically perform the tasks of subdividing and installing the infrastructure such as sewers, roads, sidewalks, and utilities. The Land Division Act regulates the subdivision of land by imposing requirements as to how it must be accomplished. This guarantees uniformity when control over certain aspects of the finished development, such as streets, is finally turned over to the local unit of government. *[Apply to the State]*

   1. **History of subdivision regulation**: The subdividing of land in Michigan was originally regulated under the Subdivision Control Act of 1967. This Act was amended with the passage of the Land Division Act in 1997. One of the most significant changes for property owners related to the formula by which exempt splits are calculated. The amended Act afforded owners and purchasers more power and flexibility to determine how many parcels they wish to create without having to first create a plat. Incentives were also built in for landowners to partition their land in a manner that preserves farmland and open spaces.

   2. **General objectives**: There are several well-defined objectives of the Land Division Act, all of which relate to the creation of functional subdivisions. These objectives include:

[The Plat is the actual Map of the subdivision]

a. To further the orderly layout of land; require that it be suitable for building sites and public improvements; and that there be adequate drainage.

b. Provide for proper ingress and egress to lots.

c. Promote proper surveying, monumenting, and conveyance by accurate legal descriptions.

d. Provide for the approvals that must be obtained before plats can be filed and recorded; establish procedures for vacating, correcting, and revising of plats; and provide for assessor's plats.

e. Provide for the establishment of special assessment districts to defray the cost of retention basins within final plats. (A "retention" basin or pond is a land depression that is excavated in the ground adjacent to a subdivision. It is designed to hold a specific amount of water for an indefinite period of time. If the land depression is designed to temporarily hold a set amount of water, it is referred to as a "detention" pond. Retention and detention ponds both help with flood control during rainy periods. A retention pond can also help preserve wetlands.)

f. Control residential building within floodplain areas.

g. Provide for reserving easements for utilities in vacated streets and alleys.

B. **Application and statutory definition of a plat**: Under the Land Division Act, plats have to be prepared, submitted for approval, and then recorded before certain lands can be subdivided and sold (whether to builders and developers or to private owners for the purpose of building). The subdivider or developer is responsible for submitting the plats to the appropriate office of the local unit of government. According to the Act, a plat is a map or chart of a subdivision of land. The Act further defines a preliminary plat as a map showing the salient (i.e., prominent) features, which map is then submitted for preliminary consideration by the appropriate authorities.

C. **Provisions**: Several key terms are defined under the Land Division Act as it relates to the parcelling of land including "subdivide or subdivision," "division," and "exempt split." Other important provisions govern a landowner's ability to split his land without having to file a plat.

1. **Subdivide/Subdivision**: To subdivide, or a subdivision, is the (1) partitioning or splitting of a parcel or tract of land by the owner for the purpose of sale, lease of more than 1 year, or building development, (2) that results in 1 or more parcels of less than 40 acres, and (3) is not exempt from platting requirements. In other words, subdividing or the subdivision of land into lots which are less than 40 acres in size must adhere to all platting requirements.

2. **Division**: A division of land is the partitioning or splitting of a parcel of land by the owner (or his heirs). A division is not subject to platting requirements as long as it qualifies under the formula for exempt splits.

3. **Exempt split**: An exempt split is any land split that results in 1 or more lots of 40 or more acres. To qualify as an exempt split, the resulting parcels must also be accessible, meaning that vehicular access to an existing public road or street must be provided. No platting is required to create exempt splits. As noted below, certain divisions may be made without having to plat.

4. **Divisions not requiring platting**: For a division (including any previous division of the same parcel) to fall outside of the platting requirements of the Act, the resulting parcels must not exceed the numbers noted in [brackets] below. The term parent parcel refers to any legally-existing parcel or tract of land that was in existence prior to March 31, 1997.

    a. For the first 10 acres (or fraction thereof) of the parent lot, [4] parcels can be created.

    b. For each whole 10 acres in the parent parcel (in excess of the first 10 acres), [1] additional lot can be created up to a maximum of [11] additional parcels.

    c. For each 40 acres in excess of the first 120 acres in the parent parcel, [1] additional parcel is allowed.

    d. If the parent parcel is at least 20 acres, [2] additional or bonus splits can be earned if one or more of the following apply: One or more new roads are established (thereby avoiding the need to create additional driveway accesses to an existing road), and/or 60% of the parcel is left intact by the owner (to preserve farmland and open space).

    e. Further splitting can occur under a slightly different formula after 10 years has lapsed. The number of splits depends on the size of the parcel.

    Example–Exempt divisions: Ms. Dee Velliper owns a 20 acre parcel of undeveloped land that has been in her family since the 1950s. Dee wants to divide the parcel and sell the lots individually as residential

Chapter 21: Michigan Specific Statutes

building sites. She decides to keep 12 acres intact as one of the lots (which represents 60% of the 20 acre parent parcel). Based on the Land Division Act formula, Dee may create a total of 7 lots without having to meet the platting requirements.

- For the first 10 acres, Dee may create [4] lots. (Note: The Act allows 4 lots for the first 10 acres or fraction thereof. Only 3 splits are actually needed to create 4 lots.)
- For the next 10 acres, she may create [1] additional lot. (This is permitted since there is another "whole" 10 acres in excess of the first 10 acres.)
- For keeping 60% of the parent parcel intact, she earns the right to create [2] additional or bonus splits.

5. **Approval of proposed divisions and plats**: A developer who wishes to subdivide must prepare and seek approval from various state and local government agencies. The Act limits the time within which splits must be approved by a municipality to 45 days. This helps developers by making sure that the approval process does not become stalled. From a practical perspective, the municipality must first approve the split before the platting process can move forward.

   a. **Plat approval requirements**: Approval of a preliminary or final plat is conditioned on review by various agencies and units of government. Depending on which agency has jurisdiction over the particular parcel, a developer will work with (1) applicable municipal or county ordinances, (2) the County Drain Commissioner, Road Commission, Health Department, and/or Plat Board, (3) the State Transportation Department, and/or (4) the Department of Environment, Great Lakes, and Energy (EGLE) Quality.

   b. **Simultaneous preliminary review and final approval**: The Land Division Act was amended in 2004 to streamline the plat approval process. Developers can request a pre-application meeting and seek informal review by the participating government entities of the proposed subdivision. The amendment also provides for simultaneous preliminary review and final plat approval. The developer may be required to post a bond to insure the completion of the project.

   c. **Lot shape requirements**: Each resulting parcel must have a depth of not more than 4 times its width. This prevents land fragmentation from occurring during the subdividing process. A local municipality also has some flexibility to establish its own stricter width-to-depth ratio.

6. **Sale of unplatted land and deed requirements**: A couple of important notices must be included in any deed that transfers title to unplatted parcels. They include a notice of any right to make splits and a notice of farm operations.

   a. **Notice of right to make splits**: A person cannot sell an unplatted parcel unless the deed contains the following statement: "THE GRANTOR GRANTS TO THE GRANTEE THE RIGHT TO MAKE [INSERT NUMBER] DIVISION(S) UNDER SECTION 108 OF THE LAND DIVISION ACT, ACT NO. 288 OF THE PUBLIC ACTS OF 1967." If this statement is not included, the right to make any such division stays with the remainder of the parent parcel retained by the grantor after the sale.

   b. **Notice of farm operations**: All deeds for parcels of unplatted land must contain the following statement: "THIS PROPERTY MAY BE LOCATED WITHIN THE VICINITY OF FARMLAND OR A FARM OPERATION. GENERALLY ACCEPTED AGRICULTURAL AND MANAGEMENT PRACTICES WHICH MAY GENERATE NOISE, DUST, ODORS, AND OTHER ASSOCIATED CONDITIONS MAY BE USED AND ARE PROTECTED BY THE MICHIGAN RIGHT TO FARM ACT."

   c. **Need for legal review**: It is essential that a real estate licensee not provide specific advice on the transfer of division or subdivision rights from a grantor to a grantee. Questions pertaining to property transfer and division rights can be highly complex, are beyond the scope of advice that a licensee should be providing, and need to be referred to legal counsel.

7. ▶ **Disclosure of private roads**: The seller of land abutting a private road must disclose this fact to a purchaser, in writing, on a separate document that is attached to the deed stating that the road is private and not required to be maintained by the county road commission. While the disclosure must be included in the attachment to the deed, it is prudent to make certain that the purchase agreement (or attached addendum) also reflects the existence of the private road.

   a. **Failure to disclose**: If the existence of a private road is not properly disclosed to a buyer, the purchase agreement is voidable at the option of the buyer and the seller must refund all of the consideration received along with any actual damages. (Note: Although the contract is considered to be voidable even after the sale is closed, Michigan case law indicates that the contract ceases to be voidable if the defect is cured without any harm to the buyer.)

  b. **Seller Disclosure Statement and private roads**: The Michigan Seller Disclosure Statement also includes an item that the seller must complete regarding private roads. The item states "FEATURES OF THE PROPERTY SHARED IN COMMON WITH THE ADJOINING LANDOWNERS, SUCH AS WALLS, FENCES, ROADS AND DRIVEWAYS, OR OTHER FEATURES WHOSE USE OR RESPONSIBILITY FOR MAINTENANCE MAY HAVE AN EFFECT ON THE PROPERTY." If the seller indicates "yes," the disclosure statement requires the seller to explain it further in writing.

D. **Remedies and damages**: Both civil remedies and criminal fines are set forth in the Act.

 1. **Civil remedies**: An action to restrain (meaning prevent) a violation, or continuance of a violation, may be brought by the Attorney General, a municipality, a board or county road commissioners, a county plat board, or a county prosecuting attorney. At his option, a buyer may void any sale that is found to be in violation of the Act. Should this occur, the seller will forfeit all consideration (which could include the down payment and purchase price) and may incur liability for any damages.

 2. **Criminal fines**: A person who sells a lot without first recording the plat is guilty of a misdemeanor. The fine for a first offense cannot exceed $1,000 and/or imprisonment for more than 180 days. Upon a second or subsequent offense, the fine cannot exceed $1,000 and/or imprisonment for more than one year.

III. ▸ **Condominium Act**: Public Act 59 of 1978. *[handwritten: Common Property / Usage / Ownership]*

 A. **Purpose**: When a condominium complex is created in Michigan by a developer, certain requirements come into play under the state's Condominium Act. For example, the Act requires the developer as the first selling party to provide certain documents to the buyer of any unit before the buyer acquires it. The Act also affords the buyer a certain time period within which to review all documents and even withdraw from the transaction if he is not satisfied.

 Relative to condominium conversions, protections are afforded to senior citizens and persons with a disability. The overriding purpose of the Act is to protect consumers of condominium units by controlling how they are developed and sold to the first buyer (as new construction). After reading this Act, it will be helpful to return to Chapter 7 and review the general discussion about condominiums.

 B. **Application**: All types of condominiums are covered in the Condominium Act including residential units, marina units known as dockominiums, mobile home units, timeshare interests, and site condominiums. It is important to remember that condominium ownership qualifies as a real property interest, so the same general laws that govern the sale of other types of properties also apply to the resale of a condominium unit by the first owner to the next buyer. Likewise, real estate license laws and rules apply to the listing and sale of existing condominium units.

 1. **Residential builder is not a "developer"**: A residential builder may wish to purchase one or more vacant lots in a site condominium development for the purpose of constructing residential units for resale. From the builder's perspective, he is constructing dwelling units as he would in any traditional land development. The only difference is that the dwelling unit must conform to the construction and appearance standards of the site condominium development and the lot is actually a limited common element.

 The Condominium Act specifically exempts residential builders from the definition of "developer." As a result, the residential builder does not have to use an escrow agent to hold earnest money deposits or honor the purchaser's 9 day right to withdraw as set forth in the Act. The residential builder is, however, still required to deliver the following required condominium documents: the qualifying purchase agreement, recorded master deed, condominium buyer's handbook, and disclosure statement.

 2. **Real estate broker is not a "developer"**: A real estate broker who acts as agent for the condominium developer in selling new condominium units is also exempt from the definition of developer. While the real estate broker is not subject to the developer's requirements, the broker (as the developer's agent) may wish to assist the developer with the prompt delivery of all required documents to prospective buyers.

 C. **Provisions**: Before the developer of a condominium project can sell any of the units, a master deed with attached bylaws and subdivision plans has to be recorded. The master deed must meet all of the recording requirements, including a tax certification stating that all real estate taxes and special assessments are current. When a buyer acquires a unit, he must receive certain documents along with a copy of the master deed. Other noteworthy

Chapter 21: Michigan Specific Statutes

provisions in the Condominium Act relate to condominium conversions, leasehold interests, and modifications for persons with a disability.

1. **Master deed**: As defined in the Act, the master deed is the document by which the condominium project is recorded. The master deed also (1) incorporates the bylaws and the condominium subdivision plan, (2) defines the co-owners' rights in the limited common elements, and (3) shows the total percentage of value for the project with separate percentages of values assigned to each individual unit.

2. **Bylaws**: The administration of a condominium project is governed by the bylaws which are recorded as part of the master deed. Condominium bylaws deal with a wide range of important issues. As it relates to the Condominium Act, certain mandatory provisions must be included in the bylaws. For example, bylaws must contain a provision for the designation of persons who will administer the affairs of the project. Such persons are required to keep books and records that detail all expenditures and receipts that affect the project.

    a. **Other specific required provisions**: Other provisions in the bylaws deal with (1) the course of action that must be taken in the event of a partial or complete destruction of the buildings; (2) that administration of the project includes costs associated with liability arising from use of the common elements and receipts from liability insurance policies; (3) that the owners' association must prepare and distribute to each owner an annual financial statement; and (4) an indemnification clause for the association's board of directors except for acts of willful misconduct or gross negligence. This last clause states that the director's legal expenses will be paid if they are sued for an action involving the condominium.

    b. **General definition of bylaws**: Bylaws are the regulations or rules that an organization adopts for its internal governance. In other words, bylaws describe and set forth how the organization is supposed to function. These rules are deemed to be so important to the organization that they may not be altered without notice and a vote by a majority of all members of the organization.

3. **Association records**: The books, records, and contracts concerning the administration of the condominium project must be available for examination by the co-owners (and their mortgagees) at convenient times. Associations of co-owners with more than $20,000 in annual revenues are required to have their books, records, and financial statements audited or reviewed by a certified public accountant on an annual basis. The association must also keep current copies of the master deed and other condominium documents (including books, records, and financial statements) available for inspection at reasonable hours by co-owners, prospective purchasers, and prospective mortgagees.

4. **Preliminary reservation agreement**: When a developer creates a new condominium project, written notice must be sent to several state and local government agencies. This must be done at least 10 days before the master deed is recorded, construction begins, or preliminary reservation agreements are taken to reserve a unit for a prospective purchaser. The developer must also have a condominium buyer's handbook available at the project site while reservations are being accepted from prospective buyers.

    a. **Escrow account**: After receipt of a preliminary reservation, any payment received must be placed in a special escrow account. Even if a purchase agreement is subsequently signed, the funds must be maintained in the escrow account.

    b. **Cancellation and refund**: A prospective purchaser who makes a payment pursuant to a preliminary reservation agreement may cancel it at any time. Upon cancellation, the developer must refund all payments received within 3 business days.

5. **Required documents**: The developer must provide a prospective purchaser of a residential condominium with (1) a qualifying purchase agreement, (2) the recorded master deed, (3) a condominium buyer's handbook, and (4) a disclosure statement with information such as the co-owner's liability as an association member, the identity and addresses of any developers, management company, real estate broker, and builder who may be involved in the project, along with a projected budget.

    a. **9-day right to withdraw**: Once a buyer executes a purchase agreement, he has 9 days from the receipt of all required documents to withdraw the purchase agreement without penalty. The 9 days is measured from actual receipt of all required documents rather than the date the purchase agreement is signed. If the developer delays in providing any of the documents, the 9 days begins when the last document has been provided to the prospective buyer. The right to terminate ends if the closing occurs and the unit is conveyed before the end of the 9-day period.

[Handwritten note at top: "Site-condos are single homes"]

b. **Additional notice**: The purchase agreement must also state that all funds paid by the prospective buyer shall be deposited in an escrow account (as stated above) and shall be returned to the buyer within 3 business days after withdrawal of the purchase agreement.

6. **Reserve fund**: The association of co-owners must maintain a reserve fund to cover major repairs and replacement of common elements in the condominium development.

7. **Condominium conversions**: A developer can establish a condominium conversion project in an existing rental facility by giving notice to all existing tenants. The lease of a person with a disability or an elderly person cannot be terminated (without cause) within 1 year of the notice. Further, such persons have up to 60 days from the notice to elect an extended lease arrangement if they choose. An extended lease allows the qualified tenant to renew his lease on a year-to-year basis for a period, depending on the age of the resident, of 4 years up to 10 years maximum. Rent increases during the extended lease period cannot exceed the fair rental value of a comparable apartment.

[Handwritten note: "Bylaws can prohibit"]

8. **Leasing of condominium units by the owners**: Unless otherwise restricted by the condominium documents, a condominium unit may be rented to a tenant by a co-owner. A co-owner who intends to rent his unit must provide the association with a review copy of the blank lease form and a subsequent copy of the actual signed lease. If no lease form is used, the co-owner must supply the association with the name and address of the tenant, the term of the lease, along with the rent amount and due date. The lease must state that the lessee agrees to comply with the condominium documents.

   a. **Violation by lessee**: If a lessee violates the condominium documents, the association must notify the co-owner and give him 15 days to investigate and correct the violation. Thereafter, the association may begin simultaneous actions for eviction and money damages against the co-owner.

   b. **Lessee can deduct assessment from rent**: Both the lessee and the condominium owner may be held liable for any damages. If the owner is in arrears with his monthly assessment, the tenant can deduct the amount from his rent payment to the owner and pay it directly to the condominium association.

9. **Modifications to provide access to persons with disabilities**: An owner may make improvements or modifications to the unit at his own expense, including the common elements and the route from the public way to the door of the unit, if the purpose is to facilitate access for persons with disabilities including persons with a disability who regularly visit the owner.

   The owner must remove any modifications when selling or leasing unless (1) the sale or lease is to a person with a disability, or (2) the owner intends to re-occupy the unit within 12 months. Proper notice to the association is required for exterior modifications. Exterior modifications cannot unreasonably prevent other condominium residents from accessing their units.

10. **Timeshares**: The Act defines a timeshare as a right to occupy a condominium unit during 5 or more separated time periods over a period of at least 5 years including renewal options. The interest is referred to as a "timeshare estate" if it is coupled with a freehold estate or an estate for years in a unit. The interest is referred to as a "timeshare license" if it is not coupled with a freehold estate or an estate for years. Refer to Chapter 7 for additional details.

D. **Remedies and damages**.

1. **Arbitration of disputes**: The condominium bylaws must contain a provision that arbitration of disputes, claims, and grievances arising out of the condominium documents or disputes between co-owners shall be submitted to arbitration and that the arbitrator's decision will be final and binding. This applies where the parties have consented in writing to arbitration.

2. **Association lien**: Failure of an owner to comply with all of the terms and conditions of the condominium documents constitutes default by the owner. In response, the association may institute legal action and may be entitled to damages, injunctive relief, or any combination thereof. The association, if successful, may also recover its costs and reasonable attorney's fees. In the case of unpaid assessments, the association may impose fines and late fees as provided in the condominium documents.

   Ultimately, unpaid assessments can result in a lien being placed on a unit. The lien may be foreclosed in the same manner as foreclosure of real estate mortgages, meaning by advertisement or judicial action. The lien may be expanded to include attorney's fees, late charges, and collection fees. If the lien is foreclosed, the association is also entitled to reasonable interest and expenses resulting from the foreclosure.

Chapter 21: Michigan Specific Statutes

3. **Civil**: In addition to the penalties already discussed, a court may grant an injunction to prevent continued violations of the Act. An individual who violates the condominium conversion requirements can be held liable for 3 times the difference by which the rental payments exceed the fair rental value of the unit.

4. **Criminal**: Sale of condominium units prior to the recording of the master deed as well as the commission of fraud or misrepresentation in a publication, advertisement, prospectus, or letter concerning a condominium project is a misdemeanor. Each violation is considered to be a separate offense punishable by a fine of $10,000 or imprisonment for not more than 1 year, or both. The court may impose prison terms that run consecutively and may allow the fines to be aggregated or combined.

IV. **Seller Disclosure Act**: Public Act 92 of 1993.

A. **Purpose**: Michigan's Seller Disclosure Act was enacted to compel sellers of certain residential properties to disclose (to prospective buyers) the existence of property defects of which the sellers are aware. This prevents a seller with a defective house from attempting to sell it without disclosing the defect. The seller may wish to remain quiet about the defect fearing that the buyer will make an offer that is contingent on the seller making repairs. The seller may also fear that the buyer will offer substantially less money for the house. In either case, the cost of a lawsuit based on fraud should be the seller's greatest concern. Note that nearly all disclosures required by this Act relate to the condition of the subject property.

Although a buyer can usually sue a seller in court if a material defect is not properly disclosed, such lawsuits can be time-consuming and expensive for the plaintiff-buyer to maintain. In an attempt to dramatically reduce lawsuits involving undisclosed defects, the Michigan Legislature enacted the Seller Disclosure Act. A real estate licensee who knowingly assists a seller in passing on false information through a seller disclosure form can also be held liable. See also Chapter 2 for additional discussion pertaining to property condition disclosure.

B. **Application and Provisions**: Due to the significance of the Seller Disclosure Act and its numerous provisions, it is covered in this section using the same format as we discussed the Occupational Code and Administrative Rules in Chapters 19 and 20. In other words, the Seller Disclosure Act is covered on a section-by-section basis to make sure that its provisions are thoroughly understood. For convenience and ease of learning, a copy of the actual Seller Disclosure Form is located in the back of this textbook. It may be helpful to refer to it as you study this material.

Sec. 1 [Short title.]

The Act is known and may be cited as the Seller Disclosure Act. (Note: The expressions "seller disclosure statement" and "seller disclosure form" are used interchangeably in this discussion.)

Sec. 2 [▶ Applicability of seller disclosure requirements.]

Disclosure is only mandated if the subject property consists of 1–4 residential units. Commercial property is exempt. Disclosure is required if the property transfer results from a sale, exchange, land contract, lease-option, ground lease to a purchaser who intends to build on the property, or a sale of stock in a cooperative.

(Note: Vacant land disclosure is not mandated by this Act. A buyer is free, however, to include a contingency in his offer to purchase vacant land requesting the seller to provide a similar type of seller disclosure form. Many real estate brokers have vacant land disclosure forms that can be used for this purpose.)

Sec. 3 [▶ Seller disclosure requirements; exceptions.]

The seller disclosure requirements of the Act do not apply to any of the following:
(a) Transfers ordered by a court (e.g., a probate court action; foreclosure; bankruptcy; or order for specific performance).
(b) Transfers to a lender by a borrower who is in default (e.g., deed in lieu of foreclosure).
(c) Transfers resulting from foreclosure (e.g., transfer to a lender via sheriff's deed. Note: This exemption is also interpreted to include any subsequent resale of a bank-owned property by the lender to a new buyer.)
(d) Transfers by a non-occupant fiduciary in the course of the administration of a decedent's estate. (Note: Since the exemption mentions "non-occupant," it only applies to a personal representative, for example, who has never personally-occupied a property that is transferred pursuant to a will.)
(e) Transfers between co-owners.
(f) Transfers to a spouse, parent, grandparent, child, or grandchild.
(g) Transfers between spouses resulting from divorce.

Exemptions cont.

(h) Transfers to a governmental entity.
(i) Transfers by a properly-licensed builder under Michigan law of newly-constructed residential property that has not been previously occupied. *A new homeowner purchases*

(Note: There is no general exemption for investor-owners or landlords who elect to sell residential properties they own. In such cases, a disclosure form must be provided. If the investor-owner or landlord is honestly unaware of any defects, he can check the box labeled "Unknown.")

Sec. 4 [Written statement; delivery; time limits; compliance; right to terminate]

(1) The seller must give a copy of the disclosure form to the buyer or the buyer's agent. Delivery to a buyer's agent is treated as if it was delivered to the prospective buyer. If the statement is given to the listing agent, the listing agent must deliver it to the buyer or buyer's agent.
   (a) In the case of a sale, disclosure must be made before the seller signs a binding purchase agreement. Although late notice creates a problem for the seller under the Act, early notice is not prohibited.
   (b) If a land contract is involved, the statement must be given to the buyer prior to the seller signing the land contract. The same applies to a lease-option, meaning that disclosure must be provided to the tenant before the landlord executes a purchase agreement.
(2) The seller must indicate on the purchase agreement, addendum, or separate writing that the statement has been provided to the buyer. A reliable and convenient way to handle this is to note that it has been provided on the actual purchase agreement, land contract, or lease, and then attach a copy of the disclosure statement to the agreement as an exhibit.
(3) If any disclosure or amendment of disclosure is delivered after the seller signs the purchase agreement (but before the closing), the purchaser has a limited right to terminate the purchase agreement. This is based on the fact that the buyer may not have made an offer to purchase the property if the form was delivered in a timely fashion and disclosed any defects. If the disclosure is delivered after a binding purchase agreement has been entered into, the buyer can terminate the purchase agreement within the following time limits:
   (a) 72 hours (i.e., 3 days) after actual delivery of the statement to the buyer or his buyer's agent if it was delivered in person.
   (b) 120 hours (i.e., 5 days) after delivery of the statement to the buyer or his buyer's agent if it were delivered by registered mail.
(4) Once the property is transferred via deed or land contract, the buyer's right to terminate the purchase agreement ends.

Sec. 5 [Liability for error; delivery as compliance; conditions.]

(1) The seller or his listing agent is not liable for inaccuracies in the disclosure statement providing (1) the seller was not aware of the inaccuracy, (2) the inaccuracy resulted from a government agency providing incorrect information on which the seller relied, or (3) the inaccurate information was provided by a professional inspector. The seller is not required to disclose unknown conditions in inaccessible areas or conditions that only an expert would be able to recognize.
(2) If a public agency or a professional (such as an engineer, surveyor, or contractor) provides information to the seller that the seller relies on to disclose a specific item in the disclosure form, the seller does not have to supply further information relating to that item. If the seller is aware of a defect not disclosed in the professional's report, the seller must disclose the defect to the purchaser.
(3) If the purchaser requests an independent inspection by an expert property inspector, the seller can rely on the information provided by this expert (in the expert's inspection report) for purposes of compliance with this Act. The expert may also specify, in writing, an understanding that his report is being used to fulfill the requirements of the Seller Disclosure Act. If so, the expert must indicate to which section(s) of the seller disclosure statement his information applies. Again, if the seller is aware of a defect not disclosed in the professional's report, the seller must disclose the defect to the purchaser.
(Note: Even in situations where a seller relies on information provided in a professional's report, it might be a good idea for the seller to fill out his own seller disclosure statement and give it to the buyer as well. This might deflect a claim by the buyer that the inspector's report was deficient in some respect. Doing so also guarantees the seller that all required items and conditions are properly disclosed.)

Sec. 6 [Disclosures; inaccuracy due to occurrence after delivery; unknown information; basis.]

The information supplied by the seller on the disclosure form (1) must be accurate at the time the form was completed, and (2) must be based on the best information available and known by the seller at that time. If a defect or other problem

Chapter 21: Michigan Specific Statutes

subsequently arises after the form has been provided to the buyer, the seller is not in violation of the Act. This presumes the seller was not aware of the problem at the time the initial disclosure was made.
(Note: If the seller is not aware of a defect in an item, but cannot attest to it being in good working, the seller can check "Unknown" on the statement. This might occur, for example, when an investor or landlord sells a rental property to a buyer after expiration of a lease.)

Sec. 7 [▶ Disclosure; form.]

Section 7 of the Act describes the actual form that must be used for property condition disclosure. Sellers must not delete or skip any of the items on the form. (Note: Letters "a." through "i." in this discussion do not correspond to a specific letter in the statute or on the disclosure form. The letters are merely used to separate the discussion points for ease of learning.)

a. The seller disclosure form indicates that it is not part of any contract between the buyer and the seller. This has been interpreted by some legal experts to mean that the seller makes no contractual promises or warranties based on the information provided in the disclosure form. Nevertheless, as will be discussed, the seller cannot use the form to further a misrepresentation.
b. The form authorizes the listing broker to give copies of it to prospective buyers.
c. The representations made on the form are those of the seller only (and not the listing licensee).
   (Note: A listing licensee must still take care when discussing the condition of a property since he could be held liable for statements he makes and knows to be false.)
d. If any changes occur in the "structural/mechanical/appliance systems" of the property, the seller must complete an amended disclosure. If the amendment is given after execution of a binding purchase agreement, the purchaser may terminate the purchase agreement according to the time frames listed in Sec. 4(3) of the Act.
   (Note: The seller can likely avoid having to give the buyer a right to rescind the purchase agreement by simply repairing a problem that surfaces between the signing of the purchase agreement and the closing. If the problem involves a section in the disclosure form that requires an historical description, such as water in the basement or insect infestation, any repair or remediation history must be disclosed. Even if the seller repairs an item on the form, he should consult with legal counsel before electing not to disclose the repair.)
e. The form was amended in 2000 to clarify and affirm that certain aspects of the property are covered by the Act including washer/dryer, crawl spaces, and wall furnaces.
f. The seller is required to disclose what he knows about the items listed on the form under the heading titled, *"Property condition, improvements and additional information"* and the items listed under the heading titled, *"Other items."*

   Property condition, improvements and additional information:
   1. Basement/Crawlspace: Has there been evidence of water? If yes, please explain. (Note: The phrase "has there been" is asking for the history of water problems whether the problems have been repaired or not.)
   2. Insulation: Describe, if known. Urea Formaldehyde Foam Insulation (UFFI) is installed? (Note: Although it is not specifically listed on the form, vermiculite insulation should probably be disclosed either here or under number 10. Environmental problems. The seller should consult with legal counsel on what to disclose.)
   3. ▶ Roof: Leaks? (Note: Since water emanating from roof leaks can appear nearly anywhere within a structure, any water intrusion into a house should be disclosed regardless of what the entry point may appear to be.)
   4. Well: Type of well (depth/diameter, age, and repair history, if known). Has the water been tested? If yes, date of last report/results.
   5. Septic tanks/drain fields: Condition, if known?
   6. ▶ Heating system: Type/approximate age?
   7. ▶ Plumbing system: Type: copper ___ galvanized ___ other ___ Any known problems?
   8. ▶ Electrical system: Any known problems?
   9. History of infestation, if any: (termites, carpenter ants, etc.): (Note: This is another item in which the history of any problems is requested whether they have been remediated, meaning repaired, or not.)
   10. ▶ Environmental problems: Are you aware of any substances, materials, or products that may be an environmental hazard such as, but not limited to, asbestos, radon gas, formaldehyde, lead-based paint, fuel or chemical storage tanks and contaminated soil on the property. (Note: Environmental problems are important to buyers for a variety of reasons. Not only are they potential health issues, but they can also lead to expensive repairs, litigation under environmental protection acts, and render the property uninsurable.)
   11. Flood insurance: Do you have flood insurance on the property?
   12. Mineral rights: Do you own the mineral rights?

Other items:

1. Features of the property shared in common with the adjoining landowners, such as walls, fences, roads and driveways, or other features whose use or responsibility for maintenance may have an effect on the property?
2. ▶ Any encroachments, easements, zoning violations, or non-conforming uses?
3. Any "common areas" (facilities like pools, tennis courts, walkways, or other areas co-owned with others), or a homeowners' association that has authority over the property? (Note: This would most likely be pertinent in a condominium, cooperative, or standard subdivision which has a homeowners' association.)
4. ▶ Structural modifications or repairs made without necessary permits or a licensed contractor? (Note: This alerts the buyer to any possible municipal code violations that could impact either the property or the buyer's ability to obtain a Certificate of Occupancy on the property. If the seller obtained a building permit, but never completed the work, the buyer may be required to complete the work and pass a final inspection before moving into the home.)
5. ▶ Settling, flooding, drainage, structural, or grading problems?
6. Major damage to the property from fire, wind, floods, or landslides? (Note: Although this does not directly indicate that the history must be disclosed, a buyer may learn after the closing that the property suffered from major fire damage. Technically, as long as the damage was properly repaired, subject to applicable permits and inspections, no disclosure of the fire may be necessary. A seller whose property was damaged by fire and repaired may wish to discuss how to answer this question with legal counsel. A real estate licensee should not advise the seller.)
7. Any underground storage tanks?
8. ▶ Farm or farm operations in the vicinity; or proximity to a landfill, airport, shooting range, etc.? (Note: The word "proximity" is not defined in the Act. However, if the seller and neighbors are generally aware of any such issue nearby, it should probably be disclosed rather than debating what "proximity" means in court.)
9. Any outstanding utility assessments or fees, including any natural gas main extension surcharge?
10. Any outstanding municipal assessments or fees?
11. Any pending litigation that could affect the property or the seller's right to convey the property?

g. Effective 2006, indoor air and water quality was added to the seller's disclosure statement. The disclosure statement contains a clause recommending that the buyer obtain professional advice and inspections to determine the physical condition of the property. Further, the inspections should take into account evidence of unusually high levels of potential allergens such as mold, mildew, and bacteria.

h. Buyers are advised to contact a law enforcement agency for information pertaining to the Sex Offenders Act rather than relying on the seller or any other party for such information. (Note: A real estate licensee should not discuss information pertaining to sex offenders. See Section 2518(c) of the license law, Chapter 19, for further details.)

i. ▶ Buyers are advised that the state equalized valuation of the property, principal residence exemption information, and other real property tax information is available from the appropriate local assessor's office. Buyers are also advised not to assume that their future property tax bills will be the same as the seller's current bill and that real property tax obligations can change significantly when property is transferred. (Note: This last statement reflects the uncapping of the seller's taxable value tax that occurs when ownership changes. See Chapter 15 for details.)

Sec. 8 [Availability of copies.]

Copies of the form must be made available to the public by real estate brokers and salespersons.

Sec. 9 [Additional disclosures.]

A local unit of government may require additional disclosures. If so, this does not relieve the seller of the duty to provide the seller disclosure statement required under this Act.

Sec. 10 [▶ Disclosure; good faith.]

Disclosures must be made in good faith which is defined as honesty-in-fact.
(Note: Honesty-in-fact represents the actual truth rather than what the law presumes the truth to be. The fact that a particular item or defect is not directly addressed on the seller disclosure statement is not an excuse to fail to inform the purchaser of its condition or existence. The disclosure form prompts a seller to explain, to provide additional information, and attach additional sheets, if necessary. This indicates that a high level of disclosure is required. For example, windows and foundations are not mentioned in the Act. However, if the seller knows that a problem exists with leaking windows or broken seals on gas-filled windows, it must be disclosed. The same applies to items such as gutters, downspouts, exterior doors, and foundations.)

Chapter 21: Michigan Specific Statutes

Sec. 11 [Other obligations created by law not limited.]

Other laws relating to fraud, misrepresentation, or deceit apply in addition to this Act. In other words, completing the form does not shield the seller from a lawsuit based on misrepresentation. (Note: Although the Act does not mention the possibility, if a seller knowingly misrepresents the condition of an item on the disclosure form, a buyer's attorney may later attempt to introduce the form as evidence in a lawsuit against the seller for misrepresentation.)

Sec. 12 [Disclosure; amendment.]

This section indicates that disclosures may be amended by the seller. Recall that Sec. 7 mandates the disclosure of any change in the structural/mechanical/appliance systems of the property. Also, review Sec. 4(3) for the ramifications of amending a disclosure after the purchase agreement is signed by the seller.

Sec. 13 [Disclosure; manner of delivery.]

Disclosure statements may be delivered to the buyer by personal delivery, facsimile, or registered mail. (Note: Although the Act does not refer to email, it would likely be interpreted that facsimile and email are acceptable methods of electronic delivery. A listing agent may wish to keep a printout of the email containing the disclosure in the transaction file as evidence that it was delivered.)

Sec. 14 [Transfer not invalidated by noncompliance.]

Once the transaction is closed and the deed or land contract is transferred to the purchaser, the provisions of this Act cannot be used to overturn the conveyance.
(Note: While the buyer's right to a disclosure form under this Act ends with the closing, the buyer may have up to 6 years under Michigan's statute of limitations to sue the seller for fraud.)

Sec. 15 [Liability of agent.] *[handwritten: Do Not assist filling out Seller Disclosure]*

A listing agent is not liable for a violation of this Act by a seller-client unless the listing agent knowingly acts in concert with the seller-client to violate the Act.

(Note 1: Acting "in concert" means acting together or in partnership with the seller to violate the Act. For example, a seller lists his property and informs the listing agent that there was a small leak in the basement several years ago. The seller tells the listing agent that he is going to mark on the disclosure form that there has not been evidence of water in the basement because it was a simple issue that was fully repaired. If the listing agent continues to market the property and provide the inaccurate disclosure statement, the agent is knowingly acting in concert with a seller to violate the Act.

Note 2: A licensee, especially one who is acting as a listing agent, should never provide any level of assistance to a seller in the completion of the seller disclosure statement. If the seller needs physical assistance filling out the form due to a disability, for example, the seller should be directed to obtain the assistance from a third party. If the seller has difficulty understanding what the disclosure form is asking, the licensee should refer the seller to the directions on the form and/or to seek the assistance of legal counsel.

Note 3: As another example, a seller is worried that he will have difficulty selling his home since the exterior finish is composed of synthetic stucco (otherwise known as EIFS or Exterior Insulation and Finish System) which has contributed to moisture problems in the exterior and interior walls. The seller does not disclose the issue on the disclosure statement and tells his listing agent not to mention it to prospective buyers if they ask about it. The listing agent must either strongly encourage the seller to disclose the defect or the listing agent should refuse to list the property and inform his broker.)

V. **Michigan Right to Farm Act**: Public Act 93 of 1981. *[handwritten: Existing farms are exempt]*

   A. **Purpose**: Agriculture is widely recognized as a leading industry in Michigan, and one that is vital to its economy. The Right to Farm Act was passed to protect farmers from complaints and lawsuits over the operation of their farms. Buyers who purchase property in rural areas often find themselves living in close proximity to active farms. The dream of a quiet, peaceful lifestyle in a rural setting may be interrupted by odors, dust, and noise generated from ordinary operations of nearby farms.

   Lawsuits from neighboring owners have been filed against adjacent farms seeking to have the farm shut down on the basis that it presents a legal nuisance. These lawsuits can result in the cessation or interruption of farming operations. Consequently, persons may be discouraged from buying and/or operating farms which would

[handwritten: Supercedes any municipality ordinances]

affect this vital state interest. By following certain established practices, farmers can now defend themselves from such suits.

B. **Application**: The Act applies to the farming of crops and food products and the marketing of produce at roadside stands. Real estate licensees who sell or rent property near a farm or farm operations should be aware of the Michigan Right To Farm Act. The seller of residential property which is located in the vicinity of a farm or farm operation must disclose such fact on the seller disclosure statement. The buyer should also be aware that farm operations may be protected under Michigan law.

1. **The Act supersedes local ordinances**: As noted, the Act was originally designed to protect farmers against suits brought on the basis of nuisance law. Some neighboring property owners found that they could "work around" the Act by instead alleging that a particular farm violated local zoning laws (instead of nuisance law). In 1999, the Act was amended to preempt local ordinances. In other words, the Act now supersedes these local zoning ordinances and farms will continue to be protected.

C. **Provisions**.

1. **Types of farming operations protected by the Act**: The following consequences of farm operations are protected under the Act: noise; odors; dust; fumes; operation of machinery; ground and aerial seeding and spraying; application of chemical fertilizers and other conditioners; treatment and care of animals; management of farm wastes and by-products; employment and use of labor; and farm management.

2. **Types of farms protected by the Act**: The definition of a farm includes the raising of plants and animals which are useful to human beings. This includes: forage and sod crops; grains and feed crops; field crops; dairy and dairy products; poultry and poultry products; livestock including breeding and grazing, equine (horses), fish and other aquatic products; apiaries (bees); fruits; berries; vegetables; flowers; herbs; seeds; grasses; nursery stock; trees and other similar products; or any other product which incorporates the use of food, feed, fiber, or fur.

VI. ▶ **Landlord And Tenant Relationships**: Public Act 348 of 1972. (Note: While this statute is generally referred to as The Landlord And Tenant Relationships Act, its actual statutory title is "Landlord And Tenant Relationships.")

A. **Purpose**: The Act was passed to regulate the relationships between landlords and tenants relative to rental agreements for residential units. It also: (1) Regulates the payment, repayment, use, and investment of security deposits; (2) Provides for commencement and termination inventories of rental units; and (3) Provides for termination arrangements on rental units. As you study this Act, keep in mind that it only applies to residential lease arrangements.

B. **Application**: A primary purpose of the Act is to control the use and handling of security deposits for residential units. It does not apply to commercial or industrial rental units. Commercial leases are normally governed by principles of contract law as well as common law. A residential rental unit is defined as any portion of a structure that is used as a home, residence, or sleeping unit by a person or household unit, or any grounds or other facilities or areas promised for the use of a residential tenant. This definition encompasses apartment units, boarding houses, rooming houses, mobile home spaces, and single and 2-family dwellings.

C. **Provisions**: The Act sets the maximum amount of security deposit and, as noted earlier, establishes the manner in which the deposits may be used by a landlord. Other provisions set forth who the deposit legally belongs to, inventory checklists, what the deposit may ultimately be used for, and the required notices relative to the deposit.

1. **Security deposit–definition**: A security deposit is any amount of money which is paid by the tenant to the landlord or the landlord's agent to be held for the term of the rental agreement or any part thereof. It also includes: (1) Any required prepayment of rent other than the first full rental period of the lease; (2) Any sum required to be paid as rent that exceeds the average rent for the term; and (3) Any amount of money or property which is returnable to the tenant on the condition that the unit is returned in the condition required in the rental agreement. (Note: This assumes the rental agreement complies with all other laws.)

   a. **Maximum amount of deposit**: The Act governs the actual amount of security deposit that a landlord may charge a tenant. A landlord may require a security deposit for each rental unit as long as it does not exceed 1½ month's rent. The definition of a security deposit is especially important in light of this 1½ month's rent limitation. Many landlords attempt to assess separate "move-in fees" under different names to avoid the appearance of an illegal security deposit. Most of these fees, however, fall under the security deposit definition and must be calculated as part of the 1½ month limit.

Chapter 21: Michigan Specific Statutes

b. **Items not considered to be a security deposit**: Security deposits do not include: (1) Any consideration paid for an option to purchase under a lease; or (2) Sums paid for the purchase of a membership in a housing cooperative association. Consequently, these amounts may be charged in addition to the 1½ month's rent.

(1) **Cleaning fees**: Michigan courts have held that a written lease can require the tenant to pay a separate, non-refundable cleaning deposit without having to add it to the amount calculated as security deposit. The cleaning fee must be reasonable in relation to the size of the unit. This is important to landlords since a security deposit cannot be used to pay for ordinary cleaning of the unit after the tenant vacates. Although the security deposit may be used to repair actual damage to the unit, normal cleaning is not considered to be a form of damage. [*can be required up front*]

(2) **Pet fees**: If a tenant wishes to have a pet on the leased premises, a landlord can likely assess a reasonable, non-refundable pet fee on a similar basis to a cleaning fee. Refer to Chapter 18 for information on pet fee limitations for tenants with disabilities. The Landlord And Tenant Relationships Act does not actually authorize the charging of cleaning fees and pet fees in residential leases. However, since such fees are not included in the definition of what constitutes a security deposit, a landlord may assess them if they are reasonable.

(3) **Example**: Rick the landlord agrees to lease a unit in a small residential apartment building to Kathy. The lease agreement is for 1 year and calls for $1,000 to be paid on the first of each month. Rick tells Kathy that she must pay a $1,500 security deposit plus the first and last month's rent in order to take possession of the unit. Rick is in violation of the Landlord And Tenant Relationships Act because the security deposit Kathy is asked to pay exceeds 1½ month's rent. In actuality, Rick is charging 2½ month's rent since the last month's rent is added in the security deposit calculation.

c. **Notice of security deposit**: Within 14 days from the date the tenant first assumes possession, and before the landlord requires a security deposit, the landlord must notify the tenant in writing of the: (1) Landlord's name and address; (2) Name and address of the financial institution where the deposit will be held; and (3) Tenant's obligation to provide the landlord with a forwarding mailing address within 4 days after the tenant terminates occupancy.

(1) **Failure to provide notice**: Failure of the landlord to provide the required notice relieves the tenant of his obligation to give the landlord a forwarding mailing address upon vacating the unit.

2. **Deposit and bonding requirements**: The security deposit must be deposited in a regulated financial institution. The landlord may use the money for any purpose he desires if he deposits a surety bond with the Secretary of State. The bond must be filed for the benefit of all persons giving security deposits to the landlord. The bond is designed to protect all tenants if the landlord disappears with their deposits. Although the landlord can use the money for any purpose (subject to the bonding requirement), the deposit is considered to be the lawful property of the tenant, at least until the landlord establishes a proper claim to it at the end of the lease.

3. **Permitted uses**: A security deposit may be used to reimburse the landlord for actual damages to the rental unit or any additional facility that directly result from conduct not reasonably expected in the normal course of habitation of a dwelling. For example, walls that are in need of painting and ordinary wear patterns in older carpet are not damages. Recall from the earlier discussion that a unit in need of normal cleaning is also not considered to be damaged.

The security deposit may also be used to pay the landlord for past due rent, rent due for early termination of the rental agreement by the tenant, and for utility bills not paid by the tenant. The Michigan Attorney General issued an opinion a number of years ago that the earning of interest on a deposit by a landlord is another permissible use. Lastly, the landlord cannot charge an existing tenant for damages caused by a previous tenant. To make sure this does not occur, the Act requires the use of inventory checklists.

4. **Inventory checklists and damages**: A landlord must use inventory checklists at the commencement of a lease and upon termination of occupancy for each rental unit. An inventory checklist is designed to detail the precise condition of the rental unit. When the lease begins, the landlord must furnish the tenant with 2 blank copies of a commencement inventory checklist which is identical to the form used on termination. The checklist must include all items in the rental unit owned by the landlord including items such as carpeting, draperies, appliances, windows, furniture, walls, closets, shelves, paint, doors, and plumbing and electrical fixtures.

On receipt, the tenant must review the checklist, note the condition of the property, and return 1 copy to the landlord within 7 days after receiving possession of the unit. At the termination or end of the lease, the landlord must complete a termination inventory checklist listing all the damages he claims were caused by the tenant. By comparing the two lists, the landlord can determine which damages resulted from the tenant's use of the unit and how much of the security deposit will be retained for repairs.

    a. **Notice of damages**: If there is any damage to the rental unit, or any other obligation that the landlord is attempting to satisfy with the deposit (such as unpaid rent), the landlord must mail to the tenant, within 30 days after termination, an itemized list of damages including the estimated cost of repair, the amount which will be withheld, and the basis on which he intends to assess the tenant. The list must be accompanied by a check or money order for the difference between the claim and the amount of deposit held by the landlord.

       The notice of damages must include a statement in boldface type telling the tenant to respond by mail within 7 days or he will lose the amount claimed for damages. If the landlord does not send the notice of damages within 30 days, it constitutes an agreement by the landlord that no damages are due. Accordingly, the landlord must return the full amount of the deposit to the tenant.

    b. **Action for damages**: The landlord cannot withhold any portion of the security deposit for damages unless he commences a court action for a money judgment within 45 days after termination of occupancy. Assuming the landlord does so, he must return the balance of the security deposit (or any other amount agreed to in writing by the parties) to the tenant.

       The landlord does not have to obtain a money judgment from the court for the disputed amount if: (1) the tenant failed to provide a forwarding address within 4 days after termination of occupancy; (2) the tenant failed to respond to the notice of damages within 7 days as required; (3) the parties agreed in writing as to how the balance of the deposit claimed by the landlord is to be handled; or (4) the amount claimed is entirely based on unpaid rent during the time the tenant had or was entitled to possession of the unit.

  D. **Remedies and damages**: To emphasize the importance of the various notice provisions, the remedies and damages have been mentioned throughout the discussion of this Act. In addition to what has already been stated, a landlord can be held liable for double the amount of a retained security deposit if he attempts to retain any portion for damages without first obtaining a money judgment. *[handwritten: voids the contract]*

VII. **Truth In Renting Act**: Public Act 454 of 1978. *[handwritten: make sure Landlord leases not illegal]*

  A. **Purpose**: The Truth In Renting Act: (1) Regulates the rental agreements of residential premises; (2) Prohibits the inclusion by lessors of certain clauses or provisions in residential rental agreements; (3) Requires the disclosure by lessors of certain information; (4) Requires the inclusion of certain provisions in residential rental agreements; and (5) Regulates the commercial sale of printed rental agreements forms. (Note: The use of the phrase "commercial sale" refers to rental agreements, meaning leases, that are commercially offered for sale. It does not refer to commercial property because the Act only applies to residential property leases.)

  B. **Application**: The Truth In Renting Act includes two key definitions that set forth the type of leases and dwellings to which it applies. These definitions include "rental agreement" and "residential premises."

    1. **Rental agreement defined**: The Act defines a residential rental agreement as a written agreement that embodies the terms and conditions regarding the use and occupancy of a residential premises.

       (Note: The Act specifically exempts the following from the statutory definition of rental agreement—"an agreement the terms of which are limited to one or more of the following: the identity of the parties, a description of the premises, the rental period, the total rental amount due, the amount of rental payments, and the times when payments are due." This appears to apply to limited circumstances in which housing is provided without the use of a separate rental agreement. The exemption does not apply to a landlord who uses a pre-printed lease agreement or a standard lease form when leasing a residential premises.)

    2. **Residential premises defined**: The term "residential premises" is defined any portion of a house, structure, or living space occupied by 1 or more human beings. Included in this definition are apartment units, boarding houses, rooming houses, and single and multiple family dwellings. It does not include any temporary accommodation such as a hotel, motel, motor home, other tourist accommodation, or dwelling which is used as the principal residence of an owner who occasionally rents it during temporary absences.

[handwritten at bottom: Cannot agree to do something illegal]

Chapter 21: Michigan Specific Statutes

C. **Provisions**: The Truth In Renting Act requires that a residential lease contain certain provisions and prohibits the inclusion of others.

1. **Required provisions**: A rental agreement must state the name and address at which any notice can be given the lessor. The following notice must also be included in the rental agreement in type not smaller than 12-point type or letters no smaller than 1/8 inch: "NOTICE: Michigan law establishes rights and obligations for parties to rental agreements. This agreement is required to comply with the Truth In Renting Act. If you have a question about the interpretation or legality of a provision of this agreement, you may want to seek assistance from a lawyer or other qualified person."

2. **Prohibited provisions**: Certain provisions cannot be included in a residential rental agreement. (Note: Any legally enforceable provision can be upheld in commercial or industrial rental agreements.) The inclusion of 1 or more of the following provisions in a residential rental agreement can void the contract.

    a. Waives or alters a remedy available to the parties when the premises violates the covenants of fitness and habitability. (Note: These covenants represent a promise by the landlord that the leased premises will be properly maintained and fit for habitation by the tenant.)

    b. Provides that the parties waive a right established in the Landlord And Tenant Relationship Act as to security deposits.

    c. Excludes or discriminates against a person in violation of the Elliott-Larsen Civil Rights Act or Michigan's Persons With Disabilities Civil Rights Act.

    d. Provides for a confession of judgment by a party. (Note: A confession of judgment in a lease is a clause through which the tenant authorizes the automatic entry of a judgment against him if he defaults in his rental payments. The purpose is to avoid costly and lengthy court proceedings. A confession of judgment is illegal in a residential lease.)

    e. Exculpates (meaning releases) the lessor from liability for his own failure to perform, or the negligent performance of, a duty imposed by law. This prohibition does not apply to a lease provision that releases a party (such as the landlord) from liability for any loss, damage, or injury providing the other party (the tenant) carries insurance (such as a renter's policy). The policy must permit the waiver of liability and must waive the insurance company's right to subrogation to the extent of recovery under the policy. (Note: A landlord cannot include a provision in a lease that relieves him of his duties to provide a premises that is both fit for the intended use and is habitable. The waiver of liability discussed in this subsection likely has limited application since insurance companies generally do not permit the advance waiver of subrogation clauses in their policies.)

    f. Waives or alters a party's right to demand a trial by jury or any other right of notice or procedure required by law in a judicial proceeding.

    g. Provides that a party is liable for legal costs or attorney's fees incurred by another party in connection with a dispute arising under the rental agreement, in excess of those specifically permitted by statute.

    h. Provides for the acquisition by the lessor of a security interest in any personal property of the tenant to assure payment of rent or other charges arising under the rental agreement, except as specifically permitted by statute. (Note: The landlord cannot require the tenant to give the landlord a lien in the tenant's personal property to secure the payment of rent.)

    i. Provides that rent may be accelerated if the rental agreement is breached by the tenant, unless the provision also includes a statement that the tenant may not be liable for the total accelerated amount because of the landlord's obligation to minimize damages, and that either party may have a court determine the actual amount owed, if any. (Note: The landlord still has a duty to mitigate damages by attempting to locate a new tenant.)

    j. Waives or alters a party's rights with respect to possession or eviction proceedings under summary proceedings to recover possession as provided by Michigan law.

    k. Releases a party from a duty to mitigate damages. (Note: See Chapter 13 for information on a landlord's duty to mitigate damages.)

    l. Provides that a lessor may alter a provision of the rental agreement after its commencement without the written consent of the tenant. However, an agreement may provide for adjustments to be made on 30 days written notice for: changes required by law; changes in property rules that are required to protect the physical health, safety, or peaceful enjoyment of tenants and guests; and changes in rental payment to cover increases in ad valorem taxes, increases in charges for utilities, or increases in liability and worker compensation insurance.

m. Violates the Michigan Consumer Protection Act. (Note: Michigan courts have held that a real estate licensee is not subject to the Consumer Protection Act. However, if the licensee is also a residential landlord, he is subject to the Consumer Protection Act as a landlord.)

n. Requires the tenant to give the lessor a power of attorney which allows the landlord to act on the tenant's behalf.

D. **Remedies and damages**: The remedies provided in the Truth In Renting Act are considered to be in addition to any other remedies provided by law.

1. **Lessor's cure of violation**: Where a rental agreement contains a prohibited provision or does not contain the required notice, the lessor may cure the violation by giving written notice to all tenants who are currently parties to the lease with the lessor. The notice must state that the prohibited provision is void and unenforceable. The lessor may also alter the provision to bring it into compliance with the Act. The notice can be personally delivered or sent by first class or certified mail to the tenant at the address of the leased premises.

2. **Lessee's notice to lessor of a violation**: If the tenant believes that the agreement contains a prohibited provision, he can give the lessor notice of the violation and allow him 20 days to cure it. If the lessor does not cure the violation, a lessee may bring an action for any of the following forms of relief:

    a. Void the rental agreement and terminate the tenancy.

    b. Enjoin (meaning prevent) the lessor from including the provision in any rental agreement subsequently entered into, and to require the lessor to exercise the notice procedure to cure the violation in all rental agreements in which the provision occurs.

    c. Recover damages in the amount of $250 per action or actual damages, whichever is greater. If the rental agreement fails to contain any required information, damages are the greater of $500 or actual damages.

3. **Attorney's fees**: A party who prevails in an action is entitled to recover court costs plus statutory attorney fees.

4. **Commercial seller of forms**: A commercial seller of a printed rental agreement form can be held liable for damages suffered by a purchaser of such form (for example, a lessor) if the lease fails to include a required provision or contains a provision that unambiguously violates the Act. If a lease provision is subsequently declared unenforceable by statute or the Supreme Court, the commercial seller must remove the offending lease or provision within 90 days.

VIII. ▶ **Usury laws**.

A. **Purpose**: The term usury means charging an illegal rate of interest. Usury laws are designed to protect financial consumers by controlling maximum interest rates and preventing acts of loansharking by lenders. In Michigan, usury regulations are contained within a series of statutes including the three listed below. The title of each act is in bold and underlined. This is tested on the broker's exam only.

   – **Interest Rates**: Public Act 326 of 1966. This Act defines and regulates the rate of interest of money in Michigan.
   – **Criminal Usury**: Public Act 259 of 1968. This Act defines and regulates the practice of criminal usury and provides for penalties.
   – **Exemption Of Loans To Business Entities From Usury Statute**: Public Act 52 of 1970. This Act exempts loans to business entities from the provisions of the usury statute.

B. **Application**: The provisions of the various usury regulations apply to nearly every extension of credit where interest is charged as a cost of borrowing money. There are also a number of detailed and sometimes complicated exemptions.

C. **Provisions**: One might wonder why there is a need for an upper interest rate limit because no sensible borrower would pay an exorbitant rate. The problem, however, is that some borrowers are so emotionally focused on the purchase of a property that they do not stop to examine the actual terms of a loan. In other cases, buyers with

Chapter 21: Michigan Specific Statutes

severe financial problems may be so desperate that they will accept whatever terms a lender is willing to offer. In both of these instances, ample opportunity exists for loansharking by an unethical lender.

1. **Statutory (legal) rate**: The maximum legal rate of interest under Michigan's general usury statute (for oral lending agreements) is 5% per annum. If the lending agreement is in writing, the parties can agree to any amount not to exceed 7%. In terms of today's financing market, few if any, financing contracts are actually capped at 7%. This is due to the numerous exemptions in the Interest Rates Act. For example, the rate of interest charged by a corporation, association, or person who is regulated by other laws of Michigan or the United States is not regulated under this provision. Nevertheless, any such corporation, association, or person must be aware of the 25% cap set under Michigan's Criminal Usury Act.

    a. **Closing costs are not interest**: For purposes of usury law, the definition of interest does not include reasonable charges necessary to make, close, disburse, extend, readjust, or renew a loan; in other words, closing costs. This exclusion only applies to a regulated state or national lender, or an insurance company. Usury law also requires most of these lenders to provide a loan settlement statement to the borrower that details all of the borrower's charges due at the time of closing.

2. **Criminal usury**: Criminal usury arises when a person (meaning, anyone acting as a lender) charges a rate of interest that exceeds 25%. When a provision calls for more than 25% interest, it renders the clause along with the entire financing contract unenforceable. Although reasonable closing costs are exempted under usury law, lenders must take care not to become too aggressive when assessing financing charges as a court can ultimately calculate them into the interest rate formula.

3. **Exemptions from Michigan's statutory cap**: Exemptions to the general usury rules have been carved out for entities such as corporations, qualified lending institutions, private lenders, and second mortgages. The following exemptions set the maximum allowable interest ceiling cap at higher levels. Without these exemptions, their loans would be subject to the 5% or 7% cap under Michigan's general usury statute.

    a. **Loans to corporations**: A corporation may enter into a written agreement to pay a rate of interest in excess of the legal rate. If so, the corporation cannot later attempt to avoid the contract on the basis of a usury violation. The exemption also pertains to nonprofit corporations. The Michigan Attorney General has interpreted this to mean any amount up to 25%. A lender may not, however, require private party borrowers to form a shell corporation for the sole purpose of charging a higher rate of interest. (A shell corporation is one that does not carry on active business operations or have assets.)

    b. **Qualified institutional lenders**: A qualified institutional lender may charge any rate of interest on a land contract or mortgage for which the bona fide primary security is a first lien on the borrower's principal residence. This provision is still subject to the criminal usury ceiling which means that the rate may not exceed 25%. A loan originated under this exemption can include an interest rate that adjusts according to a fixed formula such as an adjustable rate mortgage. The phrase "bona fide" means real, actual, and honest.

    c. **Private party lenders and land contracts**: Either a non-regulated lender who becomes a party to a purchase money mortgage or a land contract vendor may enter into a written agreement to make a mortgage loan or a land contract that provides for a rate of interest not to exceed 11% per annum. All amounts defined as finance charges under the Truth-in-Lending Act are added to interest when determining the 11% rate. The term "per annum" means for each year.

    d. **Second mortgages**: Interest rates on secondary mortgage loans may not exceed 18% per year computed by the actuarial method. This applies to a lender who makes a loan of $3,000 or more for a personal, family, or household purpose that is not to be repaid in 90 days or less and is secured by a mortgage on an interest in real property used as a dwelling. The actuarial method is the standard method lenders use when calculating compound interest.

    e. **Loans of at least $100,000**: A lender who makes a loan of at least $100,000, the primary security for which is a lien against real property other than a single family residence, or the parties to a land contract of such amount and nature, may charge any rate of interest. It is important to emphasize that this exemption does not apply to a loan or land contract for a single-family residence. Even though this has been interpreted to allow rates which are higher than the criminal usury rate of 25%, it may be a wise practice to stay within the criminal usury limit.

D. **Remedies and damages**.

1. **Criminal penalties**: A person who knowingly charges an interest rate that exceeds 25% per annum may be fined not more than $10,000 and/or be imprisoned for no longer than 5 years. A person who knowingly possesses usurious loan records may be fined not more than $1,000 and/or be imprisoned for no longer than 1 year.

2. **Civil remedies**: Usury is a defense that a borrower can use as a shield against a lender's action for collection of interest payments. As long as a usurious rate is not criminal (i.e., in excess of 25%), charging an excessive rate of interest does not make the contract illegal. Instead, the interest provisions of the contract become unenforceable and the lender cannot collect the interest due. Although the lender may not collect the interest due on the loan, the borrower must still repay the outstanding principal balance.

IX. ▶ **State Housing Development Authority Act of 1966**: Public Act 346 of 1966.

A. **Purpose**: When the State Housing Development Authority Act was passed in 1966, the legislature determined: (1) that a seriously inadequate supply of safe and sanitary dwellings for low-to-moderate income families or persons existed; (2) that a pressing need for rehabilitation of property occupied by these families and persons also existed; (3) the inability to redevelop blighted areas is detrimental to the general welfare of Michigan citizens; and (4) that economic integration promotes the financial and social stability of low-to-moderate income families.

To fulfill these objectives, a vehicle was needed to facilitate the purchase of existing housing through affordable financing and to finance the purchase and rehabilitation of existing housing, or the construction of additional housing, for low-to-moderate income families and persons. Today, the Michigan State Housing Development Authority, or MSHDA, provides financial assistance through a variety of housing-related financial products. These products are available through MSHDA's partner lenders to qualified first-time buyers, and all qualified buyers who are located in targeted economic districts. These targeted areas have been determined to be financially distressed.

B. **Application**: The Act creates and funds what is known as the Michigan State Housing Development Authority which is commonly referred to by the acronym MSHDA. MSHDA is authorized to make loans and grants to qualified individuals, lenders, and municipalities. The Act also authorizes MSHDA to issue notes and bonds which are purchased by investors. Funds from bonds and loan payments are used to finance all of MSHDA's programs.

C. **Provisions**: The State Housing Development Authority Act is comprehensive with many different provisions. Only those provisions which are of potential interest to home sellers, home buyers, and real estate licensees are covered in this chapter.

1. **First mortgage loans program**: MSHDA offers a program that makes home ownership possible for low and moderate income households. Below-market fixed rate loans as well as step loans are authorized. A step loan features a reduced interest rate for the first three years which then "steps up" for the remainder of a 30 year term. Conventional loans, FHA loans, VA loans, and Rural Development loans are all available through participating lenders under the MSHDA program for the purchase of single-family homes, condominiums, and newer, permanently-affixed, manufactured (i.e., mobile) homes.

    a. **Borrower guidelines**: To qualify, the borrower cannot exceed maximum family gross income levels, which depending on the size of the family and geographic area, may vary from approximately $59,600 to $117,880. These income limits are subject to change and should be reviewed with a representative of the participating lender prior to completion of a loan application. The borrower must (1) have acceptable credit; (2) occupy the home as his principal residence, in other words, it cannot be rented out; and (3) be a first-time buyer which is defined as not having owned a house as a principal residence within the preceding three years. The first-time buyer requirement does not apply to buyers of homes in targeted areas.

    b. **Loan limitations**: The maximum sale price for a MSHDA loan cannot exceed $224,500 regardless of area. As with income limits, the maximum sale price is subject to change and should be reviewed before applying for a MSHDA loan. Further, the borrower cannot use MSHDA's Single Family Program (1) to refinance an existing mortgage or land contract; (2) to finance rental property; or (3) in conjunction with the Michigan Mortgage Credit Certificate program.

Chapter 21: Michigan Specific Statutes

2. **Down payment assistance**: To make home purchasing easier, MSHDA makes a down payment assistance program available. A borrower may obtain up to $7,500 in a zero-interest down payment assistance loan, with no required monthly payments, on a MSHDA first mortgage. The borrower must complete a home buyer education class and contribute at least one percent to the sale price. The assistance may be applied to the down payment, closing costs, and prepaid escrow expenses.

3. **Property improvement program**: A qualified Michigan homeowner may obtain up to $25,000 in a low-interest home improvement loan to improve the livability or energy efficiency of an owner-occupied property. To qualify, household income cannot exceed $150,700 and the borrower must have a credit score of at least 620 (and up to 660 for larger loan amounts). Loan terms are up to 20 years, no appraisal is required, there are no out of pocket costs, and a lien is placed on the property only if the loan amount is $7,500 or more. Investment properties are also eligible for this program.

4. **Michigan Mortgage Credit Certificate Program**: MSHDA, in cooperation with specific local lending institutions, offers another financing option called a Michigan Mortgage Credit Certificate or MCC. A Mortgage Credit Certificate issued by MSHDA reduces the amount of federal income tax the borrower pays. As a result of paying less tax, the borrower has more money with which to qualify for a mortgage. The MCC is an annual tax credit that exists for the life of the MSHDA loan (provided the property continues to be used as a principal residence). A credit provides a dollar-for-dollar reduction in the borrower's overall federal income tax liability.

    a. **Requirements**: A Mortgage Credit Certificate can be combined with conventional, FHA, VA, and Rural Development loans. They are not, however, available with a MSHDA mortgage, refinancing loans, or rehabilitation loans. The buyer must meet MSHDA household income and sales price limits; the buyer cannot have had an ownership interest in the previous 3 years (unless the home is purchased in a targeted area); the home must be used as a single-family residence; and the borrower is potentially subject to an IRS recapture tax. The borrower should consult with a tax expert if the property is sold and a gain is realized.

    b. **Calculation**: To claim the credit in a given year, the homeowner must file IRS Form 8396. The credit is calculated by taking the Annual Interest Paid × 20% (which is the MCC rate). For example, assume the interest paid in the current year for which a credit is taken equals $3,000. The calculation is: $3,000 (interest) × .20 (20%) = $600 tax credit.

5. **Pre-Purchase Inspection Funds Program**: MSHDA has a program through which eligible homebuyers can obtain up to $750 to fund one or more home inspections on a MSHDA loan. The home buyer must have a signed purchase agreement in which a home inspection is a condition of purchase. When obtaining the inspection, the buyer must work with a MSHDA-approved agency that participates in the program. The agency pays the inspector directly. Since it is not a reimbursement program, the borrower cannot obtain an inspection from the inspector of his choice.

6. **"MI Next Home" Program**: As one of MSHDA's newest programs, repeat home buyers are eligible for down payment assistance up to (the lesser of) $7,500 or 4% of the purchase price. The credit can be applied to the down payment, closing costs, and prepaid expenses such as taxes and insurance for the purchase of a new or existing single-family home, condominium, or multiple-section manufactured home. To be eligible, the home buyer must be a previous home owner and be purchasing a principal residence. As with other MSHDA programs, there are limits pertaining to income, sales price, and credit score.

D. **Remedies and damages**.

1. **Criminal penalties**: MSHDA offers low-cost financing programs for persons who might not otherwise be able to qualify for a home loan. A person with a higher financial standing may attempt to secure a MSHDA loan by providing false information on the application. Under Michigan law, anyone who with intent to defraud or cheat obtains financing, property, or a lease by false pretenses, is guilty of a felony if the value of the money, property, or other valuable thing is more than $100. Punishment includes imprisonment not to exceed 10 years or a fine not to exceed $5,000.

2. **Foreclosure**: The circuit court is given the authority to foreclose mortgages and land contracts held by MSHDA. The foreclosure process is essentially identical to that which is used with conventional financing including judicial foreclosure or foreclosure by advertisement. Refer to Chapter 16 for details on the mortgage foreclosure process.

X. **Michigan Antitrust Reform Act**: Public Act 274 of 1984.

   A. **Purpose**: Before discussing the purpose of the Michigan Antitrust Reform Act, its underlying history will be briefly explored.

      1. **History**: Although the reach of the federal Sherman Antitrust Act of 1980 is wide, there are some business acts and arrangements that unreasonably retrain trade and are beyond federal jurisdiction because they only impact commerce within a particular state. For this reason, a model statute known as the Uniform State Antitrust Act was adopted and approved by the American Bar Association in 1974. This model statute served as the basis for the Michigan Antitrust Reform Act. Michigan's Act is also intended to reduce some of the perceived burdens in attempting to comply with federal law. However, since it does parallel federal law in its prohibitions, both federal and state law should be followed by everyone, including real estate brokers and salespersons.

      2. **Primary goal**: The primary goal of Michigan's antitrust law is the protection of competition. In furtherance of this goal, section 2 states that "A contract, combination, or conspiracy between 2 or more persons in restraint of, or to monopolize, trade or commerce in a relevant market is unlawful." Under Michigan law, some covenants (meaning agreements) not to compete are permitted. An antitrust violation typically arises when two or more competitors in a common marketplace either agree (which forms a contract) or merely meet to discuss (known as a combination) how to control prices or who else can participate within that market. Chapter 3 provides further information on antitrust law and its application to the practice of real estate brokerage.

   B. **Provisions**: The provisions of Michigan's Antitrust Reform Act include definitions for terms such as "relevant market" and "trade or commerce." The Act also includes general language that has been interpreted to prohibit a number of different practices such as price fixing and group boycotts. Monopolies, and to a certain degree, covenants not to compete are also regulated.

      1. **Meaning of relevant market**: Relevant market is defined as any geographic area of actual or potential competition in a line of trade or commerce that occurs at least partially within Michigan. The definition of this term is important because business competitors who participate within the same geographic area or market have the opportunity to "contract" or "combine" for the purpose of restricting other competitors. Such actions defeat the free enterprise system which is based on the interaction of independent businesspeople who vie for a limited number of consumers within a common market. Free and fair competition generally leads to more attractive pricing structures and better services which are in the best interests of consumers.

      The definition of relevant market also becomes important when determining if a company has sufficient monopoly power to warrant scrutiny by the U.S. Department of Justice or the Attorney General of the State of Michigan. To measure a target company's market power, the relevant market must first be defined. Companies that compete using newer technologies such as the Internet are providing interesting challenges in making this determination.

      2. **General prohibitions**: Similar to federal law, there are a number of general and specific trade practices that are against state law. Of particular concern to the real estate industry is collaboration among competitors. Examples of illegal conduct include price fixing, group boycotts, customer allocation, and certain actions that result from the interaction of competitors within a trade association. Another form of unfair and illegal trade practice is a tying arrangement.

         a. **Price fixing**: Price fixing occurs when two or more individuals or businesses combine to set minimum prices, maximum prices, competitor-negotiated list prices, or to limit production to keep supply low and prices artificially high. Interestingly, price fixing could also arise if two or more buyers combine to establish the maximum price each one will pay for something. The act of price fixing is illegal per se, which means that the guilty party cannot offer any defense or justification as to why he engaged in the act.

         b. **Group boycotts**: As a general rule, an individual is free to do business with whomever he chooses. However, when two or more competitors agree not to deal with another competitor who is outside of their group, to deal such person only on certain terms, or to pressure other customers not to deal with the boycotted competitor, there has been a combination which is in restraint of trade. This represents an illegal group boycott which, at least historically, has been held to be a per se violation of antitrust law. It is also known as a concerted refusal to deal. The word "concerted" refers to something that is done deliberately through the actions of more than one. See Chapter 3 for further discussion and specific examples.

c. **Customer allocation**: Customer allocation, or division of market, generally arises through an agreement between competing businesses that offer similar products or services. The common market in which they mutually work is divided in such a way that each business agrees and receives its own "exclusive" territory. The problem is that each business receives what amounts to a mini-monopoly in their specific division because other businesses agree not to crossover into the geographical area of another. Customer allocation is another form of unfair trade practice because it deprives customers of the benefits of competition.

[handwritten note above: "Dividing people"]

d. **Interaction through trade associations**: At one time or another, many trade associations such as those involving professional sports, stock exchanges, and real estate associations (including their multiple listing services), have come under the scrutiny of the Department of Justice and the Federal Trade Commission. The concept of a trade association is inherently positive and good for competition. Nonetheless, whenever a group of competitors meets to exchange ideas, there is a risk that illegal exchanges of other information such as pricing may result.

Members of real estate associations must take care not to let their conversations stray to certain trade practices. Group discussion of individual commission rates, cooperative sale commission splits, or other pricing structures of service provision agreements could serve as evidence of illegal price fixing. Conversations about how to pressure discount and limited service brokers to change their business practices could be used as evidence of a group boycott.

e. **Tying arrangements**: Under a tying arrangement, a seller conditions the purchase or lease of a desired product (the tying product) on the purchase of another and usually less desirable product (the tied product). Certain tying arrangements are found to be illegal, especially if they force consumers to purchase inferior items for which they have no interest or they are used to perpetuate a monopoly. For the most part, typing arrangements are not applicable to the real estate industry.

3. **Specific prohibitions–monopoly power**: Michigan's antitrust law specifically prohibits the establishment, maintenance, or use of a monopoly in a relevant market for the purpose of excluding or limiting competition or controlling (meaning fixing) prices. A monopoly is created when a business is so concentrated or dominant in a marketplace that one person or group practically controls the quantity and price of salable items. Monopoly power is detrimental to free enterprise because it chokes out competition. When this occurs, prices tend to rise, and service and quality tend to diminish.

4. **Covenants not to compete are legal**: Michigan antitrust law permits the creation and enforcement of what are known as covenants not to compete. These agreements can take several different forms. For example, covenants not to compete are frequently used in employment situations, and in the context of commercial leases.

    a. **Employment application**: Employers sometimes ask their key employees to sign promises not to compete as a condition of initial employment. Under the agreement, the employee agrees that on termination or resignation, he will not compete in similar employment or a similar line of business for a period of time and within a certain limited geographic location. To be enforceable (1) the employer must be protecting a reasonable competitive business interest, and (2) the agreement must be reasonable as to duration, geographic area, and the type of employment or line of business from which the employee will be barred during the non-compete period.

    Covenants not to compete are easier to uphold if the employee's services had some unique value to the line of work he was hired to perform, or where employment exposed the employee to highly confidential information (such as trade secrets or customer lists) that could not ordinarily be obtained through any other source. It is becoming more common for brokers who hire managers, for example, to include covenants not to compete in their employment contracts. An employee must understand that when he signs an employment contract that contains a covenant not to compete, a court will most likely uphold it if the terms are reasonable. If the terms are held not to be reasonable, the court can modify the clause and then uphold it.

    b. **Commercial lease application**: A lease of a commercial property may contain a promise by the landlord that, upon expiration of the lease, the landlord will not lease the unit to a new tenant that competes with the vacating tenant's business for a certain period of time. Another variation of the clause contains a promise by the landlord not to lease any other of his properties within a small geographic area to a competing business during the term of the lease. Courts have held these agreements to be enforceable providing they are limited in scope. This type of clause may also be referred to as a restrictive covenant.

C. **Remedies and damages**: Anyone whose business or property is injured or threatened with injury due to an unfair trade practice may bring an action for relief or damages. A nearly identical action may be brought by the state, a political subdivision, or any public agency.

1. **Civil remedies**: A court may issue an injunction or other equitable relief to avoid immediate irreparable harm. A prevailing plaintiff may receive actual damages, interest on the damages, taxable costs, and attorney's fees. If the court or jury finds that the violation was flagrant (meaning willful, shocking, or outrageous), the recovery may be increased by an amount not to exceed 3 times the actual damages. This is known as treble damages. If the action is brought by the Attorney General on behalf of the state, a civil fine of $50,000 can be assessed for each violation.

2. **Criminal fines**: Violation of the Act is a misdemeanor that can result in imprisonment for not more than 2 years and/or a criminal fine not to exceed $10,000. The fine may be up to $1,000,000 if the violator is not an individual. If criminal prosecution has been initiated under federal law, the state cannot maintain its own criminal prosecution for the same transaction or occurrence.

XI. ▶ **Michigan Environmental Protection Act (MEPA) (Part 17 of NREPA)**: The topic of environmental protection laws was introduced in Chapter 11 with discussion about wetlands protection. Wetlands regulation is covered in that chapter because it stems from federal law. This chapter covers other environmental protection laws that are more Michigan-specific. These laws span a number of different aspects of Michigan's environment.

In 1994, the Michigan Legislature brought nearly all Michigan environmental protection laws together into the Natural Resources and Environmental Protection Act, or NREPA for short, as part of a restructuring process. NREPA protects Michigan's environment and natural resources by (1) regulating the discharge of pollutants; (2) regulating the use of lands, waters, and natural resources; (3) protecting the people's right to hunt and fish; and (4) prescribing the powers and duties of certain state and local agencies.

A. **Purpose and application**: The Michigan Environmental Protection Act, or MEPA for short, was originally enacted in 1970. MEPA is an outgrowth of the Michigan Constitution that declares the conservation and development of natural resources to be in the interest of the health, safety, and general welfare of the people. The Michigan Constitution actually requires the legislature to provide for the protection of the air, water, and other natural resources of this state from pollution, impairment, and destruction.

B. **Provisions**: The Attorney general, a municipality, a state agency, or any person can bring an action in a circuit court for declaratory or equitable relief to protect the air, water, and other natural resources from pollution, impairment, or destruction regardless of whether the land is public or private. The Act defines "person" broadly to include an individual, partnership, corporation, association, governmental entity, or other legal entity.

1. **Meaning of equitable relief**: An equitable remedy is one based on justice and fairness, encompassing actions such as specific performance and injunctions. Injunctions are court orders that prohibit someone from committing a MEPA violation or compelling him to correct one. Any person or entity such as a homeowner or homeowners' association could seek injunctive relief.

2. **Meaning of declaratory judgment**: When a party is in doubt as to his legal rights, he can seek a declaratory judgment from a court. A declaratory judgment is a court decision that establishes what a party's legal rights are in a matter without awarding damages or ordering the party to do something. If the matter is later decided in court, the prior declaratory judgment will be binding on the parties.

3. **Meaning of prima facie case**: In the case of protecting the environment, the plaintiff must make a prima facie showing that the defendant has or is likely to pollute, impair, or destroy the air, water, or other natural recourses. A prima facie case consists of the minimum evidence necessary to state a case without being thrown out of court for insufficient evidence. For example, if a plaintiff is seeking an injunction against the activity of a defendant, the court will determine whether a natural resource is involved and whether the impact of the defendant's activity sufficiently impairs the resource to warrant the issuance of the injunction.

4. **Affirmative defenses**: After the plaintiff makes his case, the defendant can rebut or counter the claim. The defendant is given the opportunity to prove that there is no feasible and prudent alternative to his activities. He must also demonstrate that his conduct is consistent with the promotion of the public health, safety, and welfare in light of the state's paramount (meaning supreme) concern for the protection of the environment.

Chapter 21: Michigan Specific Statutes 401

5. **Other provisions**: Along with a temporary or permanent injunction, a court may impose a condition on the defendant that he protect the air, water, and other natural resources from pollution, impairment, or destruction. If an administrative or licensing agency is available to determine the legality of the defendant's conduct, the court may turn the case over to that agency for such determination. On completion, the court will then determine the impact of the defendant's conduct on the environment.

6. **Relationship to other laws**: MEPA is considered to be supplementary to any other administrative or regulatory procedures allowed by other state and federal laws. This means that a party may be subject to additional, and potentially more stringent, regulations.

7. **Sedimentation control**: As discussed in this chapter, when soil erosion occurs, the resulting sediment can be a source of pollution in lakes and streams and a contributor to flooding. The Michigan Department of Environment, Great Lakes, and Energy, or EGLE for short, reviews the soil and sedimentation control programs of local municipalities, imposes fines for violations, and makes violators liable for both environmental and restoration damages.

C. **Remedies and damages**: Although the relief granted must be equitable in nature, the court may apportion costs between the parties. The courts have ruled that legal fees and litigation-related costs are generally not recoverable under federal and state environmental protection laws. Damages can include compensation for remediation (meaning to remedy, correct, or repair) of a site providing the fees are closely related to actual cleanup costs.

D. ▶ **Other state environmental regulations**: Along with MEPA, Michigan's Natural Resources and Environmental Protection Act (NREPA) contains specific sections, or what the Act refers to as Parts, that deal with important issues including soil erosion, dredging and filling of inland lakes and streams and the Great Lakes, and sand dunes protection.

1. <u>**Soil Erosion and Sedimentation Control (Part 91 of NREPA)**</u>: Sediment is matter that settles to the bottom of a liquid. In the environment, sedimentation occurs from uncontrolled erosion. When sediment settles to the bottom of inland lakes, streams, and wetlands, it becomes a form of pollution. Sedimentation can result from improper planning and management of land development and construction. Part 91 of NREPA was enacted to minimize erosion and to control off-site sedimentation. This is accomplished by requiring a permit for any earth change that disturbs 1 or more acres, or any earth change that is within 500 feet of an inland lake or stream.

2. <u>**Shorelands Protection and Management (Part 323 of NREPA)**</u>: Part 323 of NREPA requires a permit for dredging or filling of bottomland; constructing a structure on bottomland; construction or expansion of a marina; creating, enlarging, or diminishing an inland lake or stream; structurally interfering with the natural flow of an inland lake or stream; or connecting a canal or similar waterways to an inland lake or stream. The Great Lakes, Lake St. Clair, and a body of water with a surface area that is less than 5 acres are excluded from the definition of an inland lake or stream.

   Bottomland is the land area of an inland lake or stream that lies below the ordinary high water mark which may or may not actually be covered by water. (Note: While Part 301 contains its own slightly different definition of ordinary high water mark, some legal experts prefer to rely on the Michigan Supreme Court definition of high water mark that is discussed in Chapter 1.)

3. <u>**Sand Dunes Protection and Management (Part 353 of NREPA)**</u>: Part 353 of NREPA protects designated critical dune areas along the Great Lakes shoreline in Michigan. It regulates any earth moving, vegetation removal, and construction within a critical dune area by requiring a permit and approval before making any such change. Local units of government are able to assume the authority to grant permits by adopting or amending their local zoning ordinances.

XII. <u>**Acts relating to child and family support and licensees**</u>: Over the years, the Michigan Legislature has enacted many statutes that regulate the payment of child and family support. Some of these important Acts provide relief to children and families that suffer from non-payment of court-ordered support. One statute in particular has the potential to affect Michigan real estate licensees who fall behind in their support payments.

Note: These statutes and the corresponding discussion are not listed in the Content Outline as possible real estate examination material. Nevertheless, a licensee who owes child or family support should be aware of the potential impact on his license for being delinquent.

A. **Support & Parenting Time Enforcement Act**: In 1982, the Michigan Legislature passed Act 295 which is known as the Support and Parenting Time Enforcement Act. Under the Act, Michigan courts have the authority to suspend any license issued by the state if child or family support payments are three months or more in arrears. Parties to a support order must provide personal information to the friend of the court including, among other things, a statement of whether the payer or payee holds an occupational license.

   An occupational license, which includes a real estate broker's, associate broker's, and salesperson's license can be suspended if an arrearage in support payment has accrued in an amount greater than 2 months, and income-withholding has been unsuccessful.

B. **Regulated Occupation Support Enforcement Act**: The Regulated Occupation Support and Enforcement Act was passed in 1996. It requires an occupational regulatory agency (such as the department) to comply with a suspension order (that was issued under the Support and Parenting Time Enforcement Act) within 7 business days after receipt of the court order. The same 7 business day time period applies in cases where the court rescinds its suspension order and mandates reinstatement of the license. The licensee must pay all department fees set forth in the Occupational Code that are associated with relicensure of an occupational license.

DIAGNOSTIC PRACTICE QUESTIONS – CHAPTER 21

IMPORTANT STUDY TIP!

Step 1: Carefully review the information located in this chapter.

Step 2: Take the following Diagnostic Practice Questions. Review any question you answered incorrectly by researching the topic in this textbook. If you are still uncertain as to why the question is answered as it is, consult your program provider.

NOTE ON CHAPTER PRACTICE QUESTIONS

The following questions are representative of the type encountered on the Michigan real estate licensing examination. While some of these questions may be similar in nature and style, there is no way of predicting the exact wording of a question that will appear on the exam. Spending time memorizing these questions is, therefore, not recommended.

These questions are designed to help you determine how well you comprehend the material in this chapter. They are also intended to help you develop problem solving skills and to become comfortable with question formats.

Do not attempt to answer these questions until you have attended the lecture corresponding to this chapter and spent the appropriate time studying the material.

1. The owner of a 2 acre lot applied for a building permit to construct a new 2,200 square foot ranch and was told that 90% of his lot, including the most buildable area, was subject to a new interpretation of what constitutes a wetland. Consequently, the owner's application was denied. Which statement best describes the owner's options?
   A. There is nothing the owner can do since wetlands are always a risk of owning property. He should have purchased the property subject to a wetlands review.
   B. The owner can establish a new wetlands in close proximity by diverting any standing water to the back of his lot and then build his home as planned.
   C. The owner can claim that the denial constitutes an inverse condemnation and seek compensation for the lost value of his lot through the court.
   D. The owner can pay a sum of money to the local building official equivalent to the time and expense of investigating the wetland and then reapply for the building permit.

2. Saul, a salesperson for Best Call Realty, conducted a listing appointment at Mr. and Mrs. Trout's home to prepare for a sale. When Saul provided a blank seller disclosure statement, Mrs. Trout mentioned the sump pump failed years earlier resulting in 2 inches of water in the basement. The pump was immediately repaired and the water removed from the basement. Must the sump problem be disclosed and why?
   A. No: Because the water resulted from a pump which is not part of the real property.
   B. No: There is no current basement water issue.
   C. Yes: The water level rose to over 1 inch.
   D. Yes: There was evidence of water in the basement.

3. The owners of a single-family residential property in which they have lived for 18 months are placing their house up for sale. They completed the Michigan Seller's Disclosure Statement to the best of their ability and provided a copy to every interested buyer. Everything was in working order including the appliances which they intended to include with the sale. An interested buyer came along who made the sellers an offer which was accepted. One week before the scheduled closing, the sellers noticed that the refrigerator suddenly quit working. The sellers should:
   A. Do nothing, instead relying on the fact that the disclosure statement was accurate at the time it was completed and delivered to the buyer.
   B. Either pay to fix the refrigerator or give an amended statement to the buyer updating the current condition of the refrigerator.
   C. Remain silent because once the transaction is closed, the buyer has no remedies under the Seller Disclosure Act.
   D. Cancel the purchase agreement so the buyer can renegotiate the purchase price to reflect the current condition of the refrigerator.

4. A prospective tenant talks to the landlord of an apartment complex about moving into one of the vacant units. The landlord tells him that the rent is $800 per

month due and payable on the 1st of each month. In order to move in, the tenant is asked to pay the first month's rent, last month's rent, an application processing fee of $400, plus a security deposit of $1,200. Has the landlord violated the Landlord And Tenant Relationships Act?
   A. Yes, because the last month's rent, when added to the $1,200.00 security deposit, exceeds the legal limit.
   B. Yes, because a landlord can never charge move-in fees in addition to a security deposit.
   C. No, because certain items are not by definition part of a security deposit and may be assessed.
   D. No, because the landlord is exempt from the Landlord And Tenant Relationships Act under these circumstances.

5. Clem Johnson, the principal associate broker for Davinchee Realty, is asked to list an existing interest in a cooperative. Which of the following statements is true?
   A. Clem may not participate in the sale unless he also possesses a license to sell securities.
   B. Clem may sell the cooperative interest providing he is also an agent for the cooperative.
   C. Clem would have to surrender his associate broker's license since the sale of an interest in a cooperative cannot be handled by a real estate broker.
   D. Clem may assist in the sale since it would be considered a resale of a real property interest and not subject to Michigan securities laws.

6. A prospective purchaser of a new residential condominium unit signed a purchase agreement with the builder/developer of the project. The builder/developer also provided the purchaser with a copy of the master deed, buyer's handbook, and disclosure statements. Which of the following statements is most accurate?
   A. The purchaser must pay one and one-half months' association fees.
   B. The purchase agreement must state that no modifications whatsoever can be made to the unit, regardless of the reason.
   C. If the unit is a timeshare, it must be purchased for a minimum of 3 years.
   D. The purchaser has 9 days within which to withdraw from the transaction.

7. In 2015, Grace purchased a 10 acre tract of land in Michigan with the intent of parceling it into 5, 2 acre lots for development and resale. Which of the following statements is accurate regarding Grace's plans:
   A. Grace must file plats with various state and local authorities prior to subdividing the tract.
   B. Grace is required to register the sales under the Interstate Land Sales Full Disclosure Act.
   C. Before any lots can be sold, final plats must be filed with the Federal Government.
   D. No Michigan laws govern Grace's actions.

8. Pete acquired a wooded lot for purposes of building a single-family residential home for his family. It abuts a 1 acre pond. Although the anticipated building site appeared dry at the time of purchase, a local official determined that the area qualified as a wetland. What are Pete's rights?
   A. Pete may begin excavating for the basement foundation but must apply for a permit to continue further construction.
   B. Pete may begin construction since the area did not give the outward appearance of a wetland at the time of sale.
   C. Pete is subject to both civil and criminal penalties if he is determined to have violated Michigan's wetlands protection laws.
   D. A one-acre pond cannot be designated as a wetland.

9. The owner of a condominium unit purchased a larger home to establish as his principal residence. Since he did not need to sell his condominium in order to purchase the new home, he is planning on using the unit as tenant-occupied income property. Which of the following statements applies to this situation:
   A. The association can require the owner to continue complying with all conditions in the condominium documents, but not the tenant since the association is not a party to the lease.
   B. The condominium association is entitled to a copy of the proposed lease for review before the unit is rented.
   C. The tenant can be held liable for damages to the common elements, but not the owner since he is no longer in possession of the unit.
   D A condominium association has no rights with respect to the lease of the condominium unit by the owner.

10. To which of the following property types does the Michigan Seller Disclosure Act apply?
    A. A property sold by a non-occupant who is carrying out the wishes of a decedent as contained in a will.
    B. A transfer of a single-family property by a husband to a wife as part of a divorce settlement.
    C. A unit in a duplex which is being sold by the owner of the unit.
    D. A transfer of a residential property to a lending institution by a borrower who is in default.

11. Which of the following statements regarding security deposits is true?
    A. A security deposit may not exceed 1½ months

Chapter 21: Michigan Specific Statutes 405

rent unless the landlord plans on using the deposit exclusively for past due rent.
B. A landlord can use a portion of the security deposit for cleaning purposes if the landlord first declares the cleaning a necessity.
C. A landlord may use a tenant's security deposit for damages caused by a past tenant if the tenant accepts possession of the unit in an as is condition.
D. The landlord can use the security deposit for personal gain during the term of the lease if he has a bond on file with the secretary of state.

12. Under Michigan law, certain clauses may not be placed in a written lease. Of the following clauses, which one could a landlord place in a lease?
A. A clause requiring payment of a non-refundable cleaning fee.
B. A clause eliminating the landlord's liability for his own acts of negligence.
C. A provision requiring the tenant to give the landlord a lien in any personal property that the tenant places in the leased premises.
D. A clause releasing the landlord from his duty to mitigate damages in the event the tenant vacates the premises prior to expiration of the lease.

13. According to Michigan law limiting the rate of interest negotiated in a contract, which of the following would be permitted?
A. No limit if a lender first requires a private party borrower to incorporate as a condition of receiving a loan.
B. A maximum of 25% in a purchase money mortgage negotiated by the seller of a property.
C. A maximum of 18% if the lender fails to extend financing pursuant to a written contract.
D. A maximum of 11% in a land contract.

14. All of the following statements apply to the Michigan State Housing Development Authority (MSHDA) EXCEPT:
A. MSHDA funds may be used for new construction or rehabilitation of an existing building
B. All MSHDA-funded properties must be owner-occupied.
C. A qualified borrower may apply for MSHDA funds to finance a condominium
D. MSHDA money is not available for the purchase of mobile homes since it does not qualify as housing under the act.

15. An investor has decided to make money by purchasing existing land contracts for $.25 on the dollar from vendors who wanted to "cash out" their contracts. The investor then sold the contracts for $.75 on the dollar to earn a profit. Which of the following Michigan acts comes into play for the investor:

A. The Mortgage Brokers, Lenders, and Servicers Licensing Act.
B. The Uniform Securities Act.
C. The Due-on-sale Clauses Act.
D. The Michigan Consumer Protection Act.

16. Which of the following trade practices may be permitted under Michigan antitrust law?
A. A local multiple listing service that limits access to brokers who agree to offer subagency, buyer's agency, and transaction coordinator compensation.
B. Two independent brokers who discuss what rates should be charged clients desiring access to their real estate-related websites.
C. A broker who pays his salespersons well in exchange for a promise not to work with another Michigan broker for at least 10 years after terminating employment.
D. None of the above acts are permissible.

*The key to unlock the door to your full potential is already within you.
If you look anywhere else, you will search for an eternity.*

Chapter 22
Real Estate Mathematics

Understanding the numerical relationships that exist in real estate.

Explanation of formulas.

I. **Foreword**: Many numerical relationships exist in the real estate industry. The ability to grasp these relationships is necessary to fully understand the practical side of real estate transactions. For instance, the terms of a listing agreement include a rate of commission to which the broker is entitled for locating a ready, willing, and able purchaser. This rate is reflected as a percent of the listing price. To calculate the dollar equivalent of this rate, the broker or his salesperson must be able to perform one or more mathematical computations.

When a buyer is located who is interested in the listed property, he may offer a purchase price which is either higher or lower than the list price. If the seller accepts the offer, the commission must be recalculated based on the actual sale price. This requires another calculation using the same formula. Using the same mathematical process, the broker or salesperson can recalculate the actual amount of commission which is due.

II. **Application**: This chapter explores the primary categories of real estate mathematics including: (1) Percentage problems; (2) Area calculations; and, (3) Prorations. Although real estate mathematics is straightforward in its application, the mere mention of the word math strikes fear in the hearts of many a test-taker. Most of this concern is unnecessary because the number of formulas that must be learned are limited. Also, the formulas tend to be repetitive in their application. For example, the same basic percentage formula is used to calculate commissions, taxes, interest, loan-to-value ratios, profits and losses, percentage leases, and capitalization.

   A. **Preparation for the real estate exam**: Those individuals who are using this textbook to prepare for the salesperson's or broker's examination should be aware that this chapter has been designed as a self-study tool. The goal of this chapter is to explore the categories of math questions that might appear on the exam. Easy-to-use formulas are provided to aid the examinee in answering these questions. Once the formulas are thoroughly understood, they can be applied to any number of different problem variations.

   B. **Overcoming apprehension**: Initial concerns over math questions can be quickly dispelled by following a systematic approach to math questions such as the one introduced in the next section. It is also important to note that mastering real estate mathematics is basically a function of memorization. To reach the desired comfort level, a sufficient amount of time must be spent practicing the sample questions (multiple times) that are located in this chapter. Take the time to learn the formulas and you will succeed.

   C. **The systematic approach to math**: A simple, four-step process can be applied to all math problems. The steps include: (1) Read the question; (2) Note the given information; (3) Select the formula; and (4) Calculate the answer. These steps will now be discussed from the perspective of the real estate examination.

      1. **Read the question**: The importance of carefully reading a math question before attempting to answer it cannot be over-emphasized. Categories of math problems tend to use common terms. These terms provide important tips as to what formula to use. For example, words such as percent, area, or prorate tell the examinee how to tackle the question. Again, careful reading of each question is essential to uncovering these word clues.

         One interesting feature of real estate mathematics is that the majority of students who think they have difficulties can trace their troubles to incomplete or careless reading. If you think that you are one of these students, please read the previous sentence at least 10 times. Careful reading uncovers the clues which are necessary to apply the correct formula. It means more than just visually scanning the question or looking at the words. Careful reading requires a clear mind; one which is free of self-defeating thoughts such as, "I don't understand math," "I'm terrible at math," or "I'll never get this problem right."

2. **Note the given information**: All math questions contain what is known as given information. This information may be supplied as numbers, words, or a combination of numbers and words. As we will see, each math problem must supply sufficient given information to answer the question. For example, a question gives the "sale price" of a property (as a dollar amount) and the "commission rate" that is charged by the broker (as a numerical percent). The question then asks the examinee to calculate the "commission" (as a dollar amount). In this example, the "sale price" and "commission rate" are the givens.

3. **Select the formula**: The third step in answering a math question requires the examinee to select the appropriate formula. By now it should be obvious that selecting the formula involves more than a lucky guess. Step 3 depends on how well steps 1 and 2 are executed. Formula selection is actually not difficult due to the limited number of problem variations.

    To master this step, spend a sufficient amount of time working with the practice questions and solutions located at the end of this chapter. The practice questions should be answered and re-answered numerous times. Make sure to follow the recommended four-step process each time you answer a question without taking any shortcuts. At this stage in your preparation, focus mostly on the "process" of answering math questions.

4. **Calculate the answer**: If the first three steps in this process are executed properly, calculating the answer will be the easiest step. This statement is often surprising, especially to new students. Each formula provided in this chapter is designed to effortlessly lead you to the correct answer. As a reminder, if you take the time to master this four-step process and learn each formula, you will be able to calculate the answer with confidence.

D. **Calculator use**: There are a couple of different calculator types that can be used to answer equations that arise in the actual practice of real estate. They range from simple four-function calculators to more sophisticated financial calculators. The more inexpensive real estate-related calculators have dedicated functions to handle loan computations involving amortization and other basic loan-related computations. At the other end of the cost spectrum, advanced business financial calculators are programmed to handle the types of complex calculations that a commercial broker or business analysis might be called on to compute.

   1. **Calculators for exam preparation**: For purposes of completing the real estate exam, most students should consider using an inexpensive, four-function calculator. Basic addition, subtraction, multiplication, and division are all that will be required. The state licensing exam may not be completed with the use of a programmable calculator or a loan calculator such as ones described in this section.

   2. **Other rules**: Exam rules require calculators to be silent, hand-held, battery-operated (solar power is permitted), and without paper or tape printing capabilities. Other functions such as square root and memory are allowed. Calculator malfunctions do not constitute grounds for challenging test scores or requesting additional testing time. Therefore, the examinee may wish to bring an additional calculator as a back-up. Test monitors have the authority to examine all calculators before or during the exam. If calculators are in a protective sleeve, the examinee may be asked to remove it prior to taking the exam.

III. ▶ **Working with percentages–The PRB Diagram**.

   A. **Largest block of questions**: Of all math questions, the examinee is likely to encounter more percentage questions than any other type. This is due to the relative number of problem variations that exist in the industry. Fortunately, a simple and reliable formula has been created to apply to each of these variations. The formula is represented in this book as a "PRB Diagram." The acronym PRB represents the three variables of the formula. It is strongly recommended that you learn how to use this important tool. Once it is learned, the PRB Diagram is incredibly easy to use and reliable. If you are already proficient with mathematical concepts, feel free to continue using whatever system works best for you.

   B. **The PRB Diagram**: The PRB Diagram is designed to solve percentage problems without the use of complicated algebraic computations. Although extremely useful, there is an occasional reluctance to learn the Diagram since many students have not been exposed to it before. Nevertheless, it can be mastered within a short period of time and is highly accurate. This is due to the fact that nearly all percentage problems involve the relationship between three distinct variables: Part, Rate, and Base.

      1. **The PRB variables**: Two of the three Diagram variables will always be given in the story problem and the examinee will be asked to solve for the third or missing variable. This can be accomplished by either multiplying or dividing the two known variables. Even though the variables remain constant, they take on different characteristics depending on the specific nature of the problem. For example, the Part and Rate in one

Chapter 22: Real Estate Mathematics

problem may represent a "Dollar Amount Of Commission" and "Commission Rate" whereas in another problem it may represent a "Dollar Amount Of Interest" and "Interest Rate." As the following three sections regarding the Diagram variables are studied, refer to *Figure 35*.

a. **The "Part"**: As a variable in the PRB Diagram, the Part is a dollar amount that represents a portion of some total figure. Note the following examples: Commission is a dollar amount that represents a portion of total sale price; Interest is a dollar amount that represents a portion of total principal; and Taxation is a dollar amount that represents a portion of the total assessed value of a property. When calculating interest rates and taxes, annual figures must be used in the Diagram. In some problems, the examinee may be presented with monthly taxes or monthly interest payments. Depending on the problem being solved for, these figures may have to be multiplied by 12 (for the number of months in a year) before being entered in the Diagram.

Figure 35

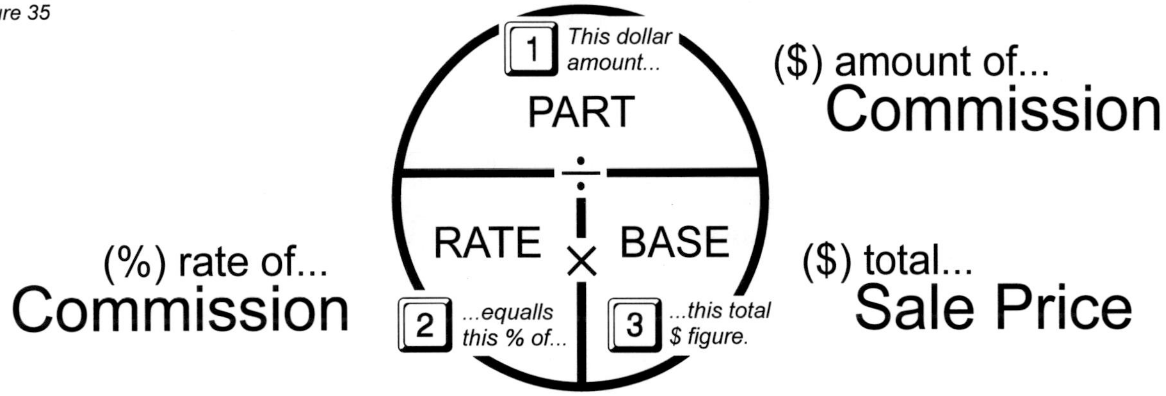

[Diagram: A circle divided into PART (top) over RATE × BASE (bottom). Labels: "1 This dollar amount...", "2 ...equalls this % of...", "3 ...this total $ figure." On the sides: "(%) rate of... Commission" on the left, "($) amount of... Commission" on the top right, "($) total... Sale Price" on the bottom right.]

b. **The "Rate"**: If the Part represents a portion of some total dollar figure, then the Rate indicates the specific percent. The percent must, however, be expressed in terms of a decimal. When converting a number from a percent to a decimal, it must be divided by 100. The quick way to do this is to move the decimal two places to the left, or away from the percent sign (%). For example, 75% would be expressed as .75 in decimal form.

If the Rate is the unknown being solved for, the answer provided by the Diagram will be the decimal equivalent of a percent which must then be converted. This can be accomplished by multiplying the number by 100. As a shortcut, the decimal can be moved two places to the right, or in the direction of the percent sign. For example, a figure of .0225 is the decimal equivalent of 2.25% or 2¼%. Even though it may require some thought to decide which variable is the Part and which is the Base, the Rate will always be easy to work with in the Diagram.

c. **The "Base"**: As a variable in the PRB Diagram, the Base represents the dollar figure from which the amount has been derived. The relationship between the Part and the Base is like a simple fraction. If in doubt as to which figure represents the Part and which represents the Base, the examinee should always ask which figure represents a percent of the other. For instance, a commission represents a percent of the sale price. Consequently, the commission is the Part (or dollar amount) and the sale price is the Base (or total dollars from which the commission is derived). In similar fashion, interest is a dollar amount that represents a percent of the total principal borrowed.

2. **Using the formula**: The PRB Diagram is represented by a simple illustration. As noted in Figure 35, the horizontal line separating the Part from the Rate and Base means that a division must take place to solve for the unknown. In other words, Part ÷ Rate = Base or Part ÷ Base = Rate. A division will always be necessary when the Part is given and the examinee is asked to solve for the Rate or the Base. The vertical line separating the Rate and the Base indicates that a multiplication is necessary. For example, Rate × Base = Part. This must be accomplished in any problem where the Rate and Base are given and the examinee is solving for the Part.

a. **Set-up**: The secret to arriving at a correct answer is to take the necessary time to correctly set up the Diagram. This is designed to insure proper placement of the Part and the Base in the Diagram. Once this has been accomplished, the Diagram indicates the appropriate math computation. It is also helpful to label the Diagram prior to actually entering any numbers.

(1) **CRITICAL POINT—Labeling**: After reading the math problem and deciding that percentages are involved, the examinee should physically draw the PRB Diagram on the exam worksheet and properly label each component immediately outside of the circle in the Diagram (as noted in Figure 35). This helps to avoid misplacement of the givens and a resulting incorrect answer. Labeling can take the form of a brief notation made immediately outside of the Diagram as to the specific nature of the Part and the Base. If commissions are being solved for, the examinee should write the word Commission outside of the Part variable. Recalling that a dollar amount of commission represents a percent of the total sale price, the examinee should then write the words Sale Price outside of the Base variable.

(2) **The relationship between Part and Rate**: As a check and balance, it is helpful to remember that a special relationship exists between the Part and the Rate. Since the Rate is the easiest variable to place correctly in the Diagram, it is best to start the labeling there. What is so helpful about the relationship between the Part and the Rate is that they are almost always labeled the same. For example, if the problem involves a commission determination, the Rate will represent the "Rate Of Commission" and the Part will represent the "Dollar Amount Of Commission."

Although simple, this is a critical step to remember since it will ultimately lead you to the correct placement of the Part and the Base. In another example, a problem may call for an interest rate determination. Beginning with the Rate, label it "Rate of Tax" (or Tax Rate). Understanding that the Part and Rate are always labeled the same, the Part is labeled "Dollar Amount Of Tax."

b. **Used in many percentage variations**: The PRB Diagram is commonly used to calculate several percentage variations. These variations include commissions, profits and losses, capitalization, taxation, percentage leases, and loan and interest calculations.

c. **Important exercise**: To improve your skills in answering percentage-based questions on the examination, complete the following exercise for each of the problem variations listed below. If you need assistance, refer to Figure 35 for guidance.

(1) First, draw a simple PRB Diagram as noted in Figure 35 in the open space to the right of each variable set listed below. Make certain to place the "divide" sign and "multiply" sign in the proper places.

(2) Next, write the title of the variable outside of the Part, Rate, and Base of the Diagram. Write it exactly as it appears in the textbook without taking shortcuts. For example, if calculating a commission-based problem, write the words "Amount of Commission" to outside of the Part variable; write the words "Rate of Commission" to the outside of the Rate variable; and then write the words "Total sale price" to the outline of the Base variable.

3. **Problem variations**.

   a. ▶ **Calculation of Commissions (and seller's proceeds of sale)**: Commission variations may ask the examinee to solve for the dollar amount of commission. The problem may also go one step further and ask for a salesperson's, broker's, or cooperating broker's share of the full commission. Regardless of the number of additional splits between brokers and/or salespersons, everything is based on the dollar amount of commission generated on the transaction. Here are the variables for a commission-based question. Two variables will be given and you will be asked to solve for the third:

   Part: **Dollar amount of commission**
   Rate: **Rate of commission**
   Base: **Total sale price**

   b. ▶ **Owner's Net calculation**: Another variation of a commission problem asks the examinee to calculate the sale price of a property based on the dollar amount an owner wants to net after paying the commission. The key to this question is using the proper rate. If the owner is charged a 6% commission, the owner's net is 94% of the sale price. Here are the variables for an owner's net calculation question. Two variables will be given and you will be asked to solve for the third:

   Part: **Dollar amount the owner wants to net (after paying a commission)**
   Rate: **Rate the owner will net (100% − Commission % = Net %)**
   Base: **Total sale price**

   c. ▶ **Calculation of Profits and Losses**: Profit and loss questions may be approached from a couple of different angles. One possible question type deals with basic net profit or net loss. The key to this question

Chapter 22: Real Estate Mathematics 411

is using the proper base. These questions may use the word appreciation instead of profit and depreciation instead of loss. Here are the variables for a profit- or loss-based question. Two variables will be given and you will be asked to solve for the third:

- Part: **Dollar amount of net profit or net loss**
- Rate: **Rate or percent of profit or loss**
- Base: **Total original investment (use purchase price or down payment if given)**

d. ▶ **Recent Sale Price versus Original Investment calculation**: In the previously discussed profit or loss question, we were only concerned with the actual dollar amount of net profit or net loss. In this variation, we use the recent sale price with the profit or loss factored into the number. The key to this question is using the proper rate. Here are the variables for a recent sale price versus original investment-based question. Two variables will be given and you will be asked to solve for the third:

- Part: **Dollar amount of recent sale price**
- Rate: **Percent of recent sale price (start with 100% and either add the % of profit or subtract the % of loss)**
- Base: **Total original investment (the base may be the purchase price or the down payment)**

e. ▶ **Calculation of Capitalization Rate**: The discussion on capitalization in Chapter 4, explains the basic process used to calculate capitalization questions. The formula is described as Value = Income ÷ Rate. Here are the variables for a capitalization-based question. Two variables will be given and you will be asked to solve for the third:

- Part: **Dollar amount of net operating income (current income stream)**
- Rate: **Capitalization rate (investment risk)**
- Base: **Market value (present value of income property)**

f. ▶ **Calculation of property taxes**: With taxation problems, keep two things in mind: (1) the amount of taxes must be expressed in annual terms; and, (2) the rate can expressed either as dollars of tax per $100 of assessed value or as millage.

Taxes/$100 of assessed valuation: When taxes are calculated per $100 of assessed valuation, the rate reflects of the amount of property taxes due for every $100 of assessed value. It also operates like a fraction. For example, $15 of tax for every $100 of assessed value is mathematically expressed as follows: $15 tax ÷ $100 assessed value = 0.15. (Hint: Move the decimal 2 places to the left to express the decimal equivalent of the rate.)

Millage: The other tax rate formula is based on millage. One mill equals one-tenth of 1 cent or 1/1000 of a dollar. Accordingly, $1 of actual tax is due for every $1,000 of assessed value or fraction thereof. For example, 15 mills is expressed as a tax rate of .015. (Hint: Since 1 mill = 1/1000 of one dollar, move the decimal 3 places to the left to express the decimal equivalent of the rate.)

Here are the variables for a property tax-based question. Two variables will be given and you will be asked to solve for the third:

- Part: **Dollar amount of tax**
- Rate: **Rate of tax**
- Base: **Assessed value**

g. **Calculation of Percentage Leases**: In percentage lease problems, a fixed minimum base rent is charged along with a percentage of the lessee's gross business profits or gross sales. The key is to remember that the base rent is added to the percentage-based portion of the rent to arrive at the total rent due. Here are the variables for a percentage lease-based question. Two variables will be given and you will be asked to solve for the third:

- Part: **Dollar amount of rent in excess of base**
- Rate: **Percent of rent charged on the excess**
- Base: **Gross excess sales**

h. ▶ **Calculation of Loans**: Loan calculation questions can appear in several different forms. For example, the examinee may be asked to calculate either the dollar amount of interest or the interest rate. Further, the interest calculation may be based on either simple interest or compound interest. Other questions may involve loan-to-value ratio determinations.

▶ **Simple Interest calculations**: As explained in Chapter 16, simple interest is calculated as a straight percent of the principal loan balance and is treated as separate from the principal. It is important to remember that interest rates are calculated on an annual basis. If the problem provides monthly interest as a variable, the figure must be multiplied by 12 months. If the examinee is asked to solve for monthly interest, the annual interest must first be calculated and then divided by 12 months to arrive at the answer. Here are the variables for a loan calculation question based on simple interest. Two variables will be given and you will be asked to solve for the third:

- Part: **Dollar amount of interest**
- Rate: **Rate of interest**
- Base: **Principal (use the loan balance if the calculation is based on an existing loan)**

▶ **Compound Interest Calculations**: Compound interest differs from simple interest in that it merges with the principal and becomes part of the base on which future interest is calculated. It will be helpful to review the written explanation of compound interest in Chapter 16 before working with the math questions. Here are the steps for a loan calculation question based on compound interest:

(1) **Step 1—Calculate the interest for month 1**: Calculate the annual amount of interest using the PRB Diagram and then divide by 12 months.

(2) **Step 2—Calculate the principal portion of the monthly payment**: Take the monthly principal and interest payment as provided in the problem and subtract the interest portion as determined in Step 1.

(3) **Step 3—Calculate the ending balance**: Take the beginning balance and subtract the principal portion as determined in Step 2. (This process can be repeated as many times as necessary to determine the loan balance at the end of month two, three, four, etc.)

i. ▶ **Loan-to-Value Ratio calculations**: A loan-to-value ratio is the maximum percent of a property's value that a lender is willing to loan to a purchaser. Providing that annual interest is used in the calculation, the answer should be easy to determine. Here are the variables for a loan-to-value ratio-based question. Two variables will be given and you will be asked to solve for the third:

- Part: **Dollar amount of loan**
- Rate: **Percent of property value that the loan represents (i.e., the LTV ratio)**
- Base: **Value of property**

j. ▶ **Financing Points calculations**: As noted in Chapter 16, a point is a fee collected by a lender when a loan is originated and closed. Points, or discount points as they may be referred to, can also be assessed when a loan is sold by a primary market participant to an investor in the secondary market. Discount points reduce the price the investor pays for the loan. Since one point equals one percent of the loan, it is important to first determine the amount of the loan. In the case of discount points, the current balance of the loan is used. Here are the variables for a points-based question. Two variables will be given and you will be asked to solve for the third:

- Part: **Dollar amount of point charge**
- Rate: **Percent of the point charge (expressed as a given number of points)**
- Base: **Total loan value (or current loan balance)**

k. ▶ **Seller's proceeds from sale**: This question variation asks the examinee to apply one or more of the individual calculations previously described in this section. The goal of the question is to arrive at the net figure a seller will receive from the sale of his home. This is similar to a question that asks for estimated closing costs, but instead of the cost to close, the examinee solves for the seller's net after deduction of his closing costs. Here are some common seller closing costs that may appear in the question:

> Mortgage payoff (first and second/HELOC)   > Mortgage payoff processing fees
> Prorated property taxes (including any special assessments and water bill/escrow)
> Commission due the broker   > Title insurance costs
> County/State real estate transfer tax   > Seller paid concessions
> Home warranty   > Other: Attorney fees, repairs, etc.

(Note: Additional information about closing costs and prorations is located in Chapter 9.)

IV. **Working with Area, Volume, and Feet-to-Yard conversions**.

A. **Introduction**: It is important for a real estate licensee to be able to handle area and volume calculations. For instance, a licensee might be called on to calculate the square footage of total living space in a house, one or more rooms in a house, or the total area of a parcel of land. Some calculations, such as those involving

Chapter 22: Real Estate Mathematics

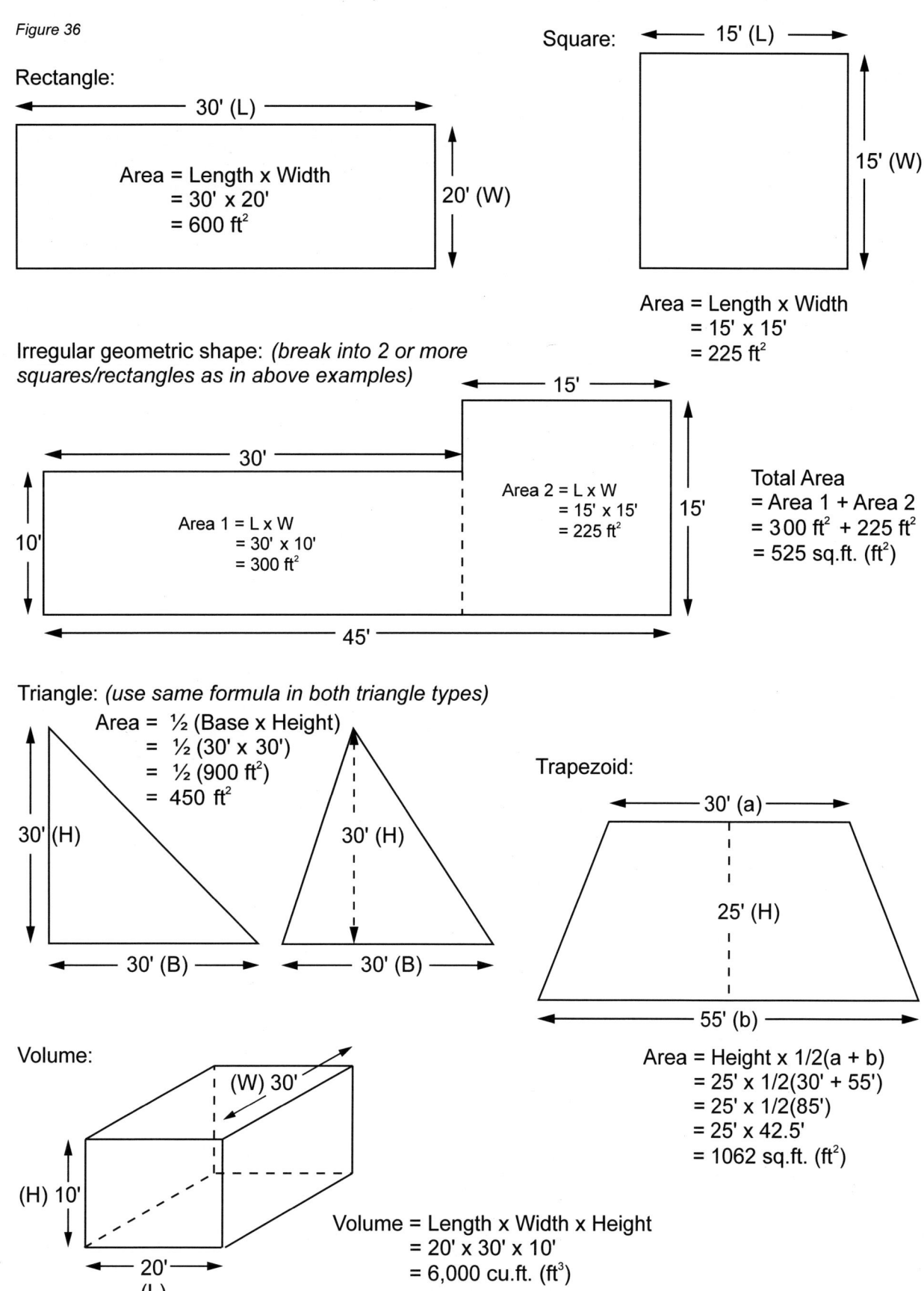

Figure 36

irregularly shaped lots or rooms with unusual layouts, can be more challenging. As the following explanations are studied, refer to the illustrations in *Figure 36*.

B. ▶ **Area calculations**: An area calculation is based on a two-dimensional representation of an object's surface. This is measured in square units such as square feet or square yards. Examples of area measurements include the total area of floor space, wall size, or lot size. In some instances, especially for triangular shapes, a different formula is necessary.

1. **Squares and rectangles**: The formula for calculating the area or square footage of a square or rectangle is exactly the same. The formula is:
   - Area = Length × Width or A = L × W.

   If the room or parcel of land being calculated is L-shaped, it should be broken into two rectangles before applying the L × W formula. The two pieces are then added together for the total square footage. *See Figure 36* for practical examples of these concepts.

2. **Triangles**: To determine the area of a triangle, use a modified version of the standard square or rectangle area formula. The formula is:
   - Area = ½ (Base × Height) or A = ½ (B × H)

   The Base is equivalent to the length of a rectangle while the Height represents the distance from the base of the triangle to its highest point. The height is roughly equivalent to the Length of a rectangle. Since a triangle is actually one-half of a square or rectangle, the B × H calculation must be halved, meaning divided by 2. *See Figure 36.*

3. **Miscellaneous shapes**: Some shapes are comprised of what looks like a rectangle combined with a triangle. By viewing these shapes as such, the areas can be computed separately using simple area formulas and then added together. Another shape that may be encountered is known as a trapezoid.

   A trapezoid is a plane figure (meaning two dimensional) with four sides. Two of the sides are parallel and of unequal length. Although complex appearing at first glance, the formula for determining the area of a trapezoid represents a modification of the basic area formula for a square or rectangle. This formula is:
   - Area = Height × ½ (a + b) or A = H × ½ (a + b)

   The Height is the distance between the two parallel sides (which remains constant because the lines are parallel). The lengths of the two parallel sides are different so they must be averaged. This is accomplished by adding the two lengths and then dividing by two (for the number of sides being added together). The variable "a" represents the length of one of the parallel sides while the variable "b" represents the length of the other parallel side. In review, the area of a trapezoid is the height × an average of the two parallel sides. An example is provided in *Figure 36*.

4. **Volume calculations**: Volume calculations are used to determine the size of a three-dimensional space. The basic formula for a volume calculation is:
   - Volume = Length × Width × Height or V = L × W × H

   Real estate licensees are seldom, if ever, asked to make volume calculations during the course of listing or selling properties. They are, however, frequently used in the construction industry for calculating things such as excavated areas. See *Figure 36*.

C. ▶ **Feet-to-Yard conversions**.

1. **Converting feet and yards**: Certain problems may provide measurements in terms of feet and ask the examinee to solve for a figure in terms of yards or vice versa. In area calculations, square feet or square yards are used. Volume calculations are made in terms of cubic yards or cubic feet.

2. **Converting linear feet and linear yards**: Single measurements are given in linear terms such as the distance between two points. Linear means extending along a straight line. Since there are 3 feet per yard, the conversion factor is 3.
   - When converting from FEET → YARDS, divide (÷) by 3.
   - When converting from YARDS → FEET, multiply (×) by 3.

   Hint: The quick way to remember when to divide and when to multiply is to think in terms of what is being converted. For example, when converting from feet to yards or 3 (feet) per 1 (yard), notice how the number of units decreases from 3 to 1. This signals the need to divide by the conversion factor of 3. Conversely, when converting from yards to feet or 1 (yard) for every 3 (feet), the number increases. This signals

Chapter 22: Real Estate Mathematics

the need to multiply by the conversion factor of 3. Simply stated, remember the following phrase, "Divide Down and Multiply Up."

3. **Converting square feet and square yards**: Once the concept of converting linear feet and yards is understood, converting square measurements is easy. Recall that a square measurement represents the multiplication of two linear measurements such as length × width; consequently, the conversion factor is 3 (feet per yard) × 3 (feet per yard) or 9.
   - When converting from FEET → YARDS, divide (÷) by 9.
   - When converting from YARDS → FEET, multiply (×) by 9.

4. **Converting cubic feet and cubic yards**: Once the concept of converting square feet and yards is understood, converting cubic measurements is equally uncomplicated. Recall that a cubic measurement represents the multiplication of three linear measurements such as length × width × height; consequently, the conversion factor is 3 (feet per yard) × 3 (feet per yard) × 3 (feet per yard) or 27.
   - When converting from FEET → YARDS, divide (÷) by 27.
   - When converting from YARDS → FEET, multiply (×) by 27.

V. ▶ **Working with prorations**.

   A. ▶ **Introduction**: Since the proration process is discussed thoroughly in Chapter 9, this chapter merely provides a few shortcuts for calculating prorations on the real estate examination. Proration is the process used to divide and then allocate part of the property taxes and other financial obligations to the appropriate party in the sale and closing of a property. The exact amount allocated to the seller and the buyer depends on the time of year the transaction is closed in relation to the due date of the prorated item. Common prorated items include: real estate property taxes; municipal utility bills such as water; insurance payments; and rent if the seller plans to retain possession for a few weeks or months after the closing.

   B. **Use a 360-day year unless instructed otherwise**: For ease of calculation on a real estate examination, you may be asked to base prorations on a 360-day year. Make sure to read each question carefully, however, as you may also be asked to prorate based on a 365-day year. In an actual closing of a real estate transaction, some real estate purchase agreements specify that a 360-day year is to be used to simplify the calculation process. In other actual closings, the individual handling the proration calculations uses a 365-day year. In such case, adjustments will be made for leap years. If you are asked to apply a 360-day year on a test question, every month will be treated as having 30 days. If not, then adjust for each specific month depending on whether it has 30 or 31 days.

   C. **Determine whether payments are due in advance or in arrears**: If obligations are due in advance, the seller is responsible for paying the taxes, insurance, or other debts at the beginning of the proration period. As a result, the seller is entitled to a credit from the purchaser for the time beginning with the closing to the end of the period. If the obligation is due in arrears, the bill will not come due until the end of the payment period. This will be after the purchaser takes title at the closing. The seller must then credit the purchaser with the time from the beginning of the period to the closing.

   D. **Responsibility for the day of closing**: As noted in Chapter 9, Michigan law indicates that in the absence of an agreement to the contrary, the buyer is responsible for the prorated costs associated with the day of the closing. Nevertheless, make sure to read the exam question carefully to see if it contains instructions on who pays for the day of closing.

   E. **Calculation steps**: Accurate proration calculation requires the determination of several items. Notice the following 5 step approach.

   1. **Step 1**: Determine what item is being prorated. (Note the due date, amount, and closing date.)

   2. **Step 2**: Determine if the item has been prepaid (in advance) by the seller or is due in arrears.

      Payments in advance: If the item has been prepaid, recall that the purchaser must credit the seller for the day of the closing until the end of the prepaid period. In some cases, the item may have been billed in advance, but the seller has not paid it on time and it is delinquent. If so, the item must be paid out of the sale proceeds as a debit to the seller.

      Payments in arrears: If the item is due in arrears, recall that the seller owes the purchaser for the beginning of the period up to, but not including, the day of closing.

   3. **Step 3**: Calculate the proration period. (The number of years, months, and days must either be calculated from the beginning of the payment period up to the closing or from the date of closing until the end of the payment period.)

4. **Step 4**: Determine the value of the payment per year, month, and day.

   Calculating the annual rate: The annual rate is important only if the payment period exceeds one year (as in the case of a multiple year insurance policy). To calculate the annual cost, divide the total cost of the obligation by the number of years it covers. For example, a $2,700, 3-year policy would be divided by 3 years to arrive at an annual rate of $900.

   Calculating the monthly rate: To calculate the monthly rate, take the cost per year and divide by 12 months. Using the figures from the prior example, $900 cost per year is divided by 12 months to arrive at a monthly expense of $75.

   Calculating the daily rate: The daily rate is calculated by taking the monthly rate and dividing it by 30 days. For example, $75 cost per month is divided by 30 days to arrive at a daily expense of $2.50.

5. **Step 5**: Calculate the proration. (Multiply the annual, monthly, and/or daily rate by the number of years, months, and/or days in the proration period. Finally, total these figures to arrive at the exact proration amount.)

VI. ▶ **Land measuring standards and devices**.

   A. **Introduction**: Throughout history, many different devices have been created to measure land boundaries and calculate the extent of its contents. The following list contains modern devices. Archaic devices are those that were used at one time, but are no longer considered standard forms of measurement.

   B. **Lineal measurements**: A lineal measurement is commonly used to determine the distance between any two points such as a boundary line. A lineal measurement is also necessary when calculating area or volume since, in the case of area, the length and width are needed.
   - 1 foot = 12 inches.
   - 1 yard = 3 feet or 36 inches.
   - 1 mile = 5,280 feet or 1,760 yards.

   C, **Area measurements**: Area measures the contents of a two-dimensional space. It is commonly used to determine things such as floor space or the square footage of a house. For example, if carpet is ordered for a room, the area or square footage is measured and then converted to square yards because carpet is typically sold by the square yard.
   - 1 square foot = 144 square inches (12 inches × 12 inches).
   - 1 square yard = 9 square feet (3 feet × 3 feet).

   D. **Volume measurements**: Volume measures the contents of a three-dimensional space. It can be indicated as either cubic feet or cubic yards. For example, in construction certain fill materials such as pea gravel will typically be ordered by the cubic yard.
   - 1 cubic foot = 1,728 cubic inches (12 inches × 12 inches × 12 inches).
   - 1 cubic yard = 27 cubic feet (3 feet × 3 feet × 3 feet).

   E. **Land measurements**: Several common land measurement tools are available including acres, sections, and townships.
   - 1 acre = 43,560 square feet (208.708 feet × 208.708 feet) or 4,840 square yards.
   - 1 section = 1 square mile or 640 acres.
   - 1 township = 36 square miles or 36 sections.

Switch your interpretation of what you experience in life from "good and bad" to "I only receive feedback." It removes all the emotional baggage and allows you to see things more clearly.

Chapter 22: Real Estate Mathematics

DIAGNOSTIC PRACTICE QUESTIONS – CHAPTERS 22

IMPORTANT STUDY TIP!

Step 1: Carefully review the information located in this chapter.

Step 2: Take the following Diagnostic Practice Questions. Review any question you answered incorrectly by researching the topic in this textbook. If you are still uncertain as to why the question is answered as it is, consult your program provider.

NOTE ON CHAPTER PRACTICE QUESTIONS

The following questions are representative of the type encountered on the Michigan real estate licensing examination. While some of these questions may be similar in nature and style, there is no way of predicting the exact wording of a question that will appear on the exam. Spending time memorizing these questions is, therefore, not recommended.

These questions are designed to help you determine how well you comprehend the material in this chapter. They are also intended to help you develop problem solving skills and to become comfortable with question formats.

Do not attempt to answer these questions until you have attended the lecture corresponding to this chapter and spent the appropriate time studying the material.

Hint: Questions 1–3 deal with Commission and Selling Price percentages [a PRB Diagram application]:

1. Frank the broker lists a house for $72,000 with a commission rate of 6.5% Helen the salesperson who is employed by Frank receives 50% of the total commission on every house she sells. If Helen sells the house for 12% less than its listing price, how much commission does she receive?
   A. $4,118
   B. $2,059
   C. $63,360
   D. $2,340

2. Nancy, a property manager, entered into a property management employment contract to receive 25% of the first month's rent and 3% of each month's rent thereafter for renting an apartment. If she rents the apartment for one year at $300 per month, what is her total commission for the year?
   A. $174
   B. $99
   C. $900
   D. $1,188

3. Ms. Taffy is employed by Zip Realty Co. on a 50/50 commission split. She sells 200 acres for $1,200 per acre listed with Tobby Realty. The commission schedule is 7% on the first $25,000, 4% on the next $25,000, and 3% on the remainder. If Tobby's offer of compensation is 50%, what is the total commission amount earned by Ms. Taffy?
   A. $2,112.50
   B. $5,700.00
   C. $8,450.25
   D. $1,750.75

Hint: Questions 4–6 deal with Profit and Loss percentages [a PRB Diagram application]:

4. Bob sells his house for a 58% profit. If his original cost basis was $35,000, for what price did he sell the house?
   A. $55,300
   B. $53,000
   C. $35,058
   D. $93,000

5. Grace pays $61,500 for a house. One year later she is transferred to Las Vegas and sells the house for $59,000. What is her percent of loss on the sale?
   A. 4.2%
   B. .0406%
   C. 4.06%
   D. 2.5%

6. Dan Seller lists his house with Lois Broker and agrees to pay her a 7% commission. Dan wants to net $8,000 on the sale after paying Lois her commission and his existing mortgage balance of $38,000. At what offering price must Lois list Dan's house?
   A. $49,220
   B. $49,462
   C. $46,000
   D. $51,000

Hint: Questions 7–9 deal with simple Appreciation and Depreciation percentages [a PRB Diagram application]:

7. A parcel of land was purchased for $12,500. If it has appreciated in value 8% per year, what is the value at the end of 5 years?
   A. $13,500
   B. $15,700
   C. $17,500
   D. $25,000

8. A seven-year old office building has depreciated in value 4% per year. If its value today is $84,000, what was its worth new?
   A. $215,080   C. $106,800
   B. $165,000   D. $116,667

9. Four years ago a house costing $45,000 was constructed on a lot valued at $9,000. What is the current value of the land and improvements if the land has appreciated 6% per year and the house has depreciated 2% per year?
   A. $11,160   C. $41,400
   B. $65,560   D. $52,560

Hint: Questions 10–15 deal with Interest Rates and Mortgage Payments [a PRB Diagram application]:

10. Mrs. Beasley applies for and receives a one-year student loan for $8,000 from University Bank. If the bank charges 14% interest, how much interest is due at the end of one year?
    A. $1,000   C. $200
    B. $1,120   D. $2,100

11. Using the facts from problem 10 above, assume that Mrs. Beasley must pay the interest monthly. How much interest is due the first month?
    A. $93.33   C. $1,200.00
    B. $30.33   D. $33.90

12. Mike and Rosalyn borrow $70,000 to purchase a home. If the monthly interest payment is $787.50, what is the rate of interest?
    A. 17½%   C. 13½%
    B. 16%   D. 12¼%

13. Lynda borrows $10,000 at an interest rate of 14.4%. Her monthly payment of $200 is applied first to interest and then to principal. How much is the principal reduced after the first payment?
    A. $117.60   C. $28.80
    B. $120   D. $80

14. Using the facts from problem number 13 above, what is the principal balance at the end of the third month?
    A. $9,920   C. $9,880
    B. $9,882   D. $9,757

15. The Clearwater Savings & Loan Association makes a loan to Mr. Buster for 80% of the appraised value of his home. The first monthly interest payment is $599.55 and the interest rate is 10½%. What is the value of the house?
    A. $68,520   C. $71,940
    B. $58,500   D. $85,650

Hint: Questions 16–17 deal with Property Taxation [a potential PRB Diagram application]:

16. A vacant lot is assessed for tax purposes at $20,000. If the tax rate is $3.60/$100, how much tax is annually due?
    A. $270   C. $720
    B. $785   D. $500

17. The tax rate in Livingston County is 65 Mills. If property is assessed at 40% of market value, what is the annual tax due on a house with a market value of $76,000?
    A. $30,400   C. $1,976
    B. $2,530   D. $1,900

Hint: Questions 18–19 deal with Property Insurance [a partial PRB Diagram application]:

18. The house in problem number 17 is insured for 80% of market value. If the annual insurance bill is $212.80, what is the rate per $1,000?
    A. $3.50/$1,000   C. $.0035/$1,000
    B. $35/$1,000   D. $350/$1,000

19. Mr. Cierstan wishes to insure his $70,000 income property with 80% coverage. The annual insurance rate is $2.80 per $1,000 coverage. If he purchases a 3-year policy, however, he can save 30% of one year's premium. What is the monthly insurance cost if he purchases a 3-year policy?
    A. $13.06   C. $35.28
    B. $47.04   D. $11.76

Hint: Questions 20–21 deal with Prorations [a partial PRB Diagram application]:

20. Using the information in problem number 19 above, assume Mr. Cierstan purchased the 3-year policy on June 1, 2008. If he sells the house and the closing takes place on September 20, 2008, how much will be credited to him if the purchaser assumes the insurance policy?
    A. $380.63   C. $282.24
    B. $153.27   D. $456.78

21. A house is purchased and the closing takes place on February 17, 2021. The annual property tax bill of $1,450, which is due on January 1 of each year has not been paid for either the current year or all of 2020. How much should be debited to the seller at the closing?
    A. $185.31   C. $1,450.00
    B. $212.78   D. $1,635.31

Hint: Questions 22–25 deal with Investment and Capitalization [a potential PRB Diagram application]:

22. A warehouse returns $18,000 per year for its owner. If this represents a 9% return, what is the value of the investment?
    A. $200,000   C. $150,000
    B. $180,000   D. $18,000

Chapter 22: Real Estate Mathematics

23. What is the gross rent multiplier for a rental property that sold for $60,000 and has a total rent of $570 per month?
    A. 137   C. 10.5
    B. 105   D. 8.7

24. Mr. Metamo owns a senior citizen apartment complex that contains 20 efficiency units each renting for $225 per month. If he can expect a 10% vacancy rate and if operating expenses are 45% of gross income, what is the net income of the property?
    A. $48,600   C. $26,730
    B. $54,000   D. $14,500

25. Using the facts from problem number 24 above, what return is Mr. Metamo receiving on his investment if he paid $121,500 for the project?
    A. 22%   C. 35%
    B. 28%   D. 42%

Hint: Questions 26–32 deal with various forms of measurement:

26. A lot measuring 60 feet by 212 feet costs $10,800. What is its cost per front foot?
    A. $51   C. $212
    B. $60   D. $180

27. Al wishes to carpet his living and dining rooms. The living room is 24 feet by 14 feet and the dining room is 13 feet square. How many square yards of carpeting does he need?
    A. 505.11 sq.yd.   C. 336 sq.yd.
    B. 169.50 sq.yd.   D. 56.11 sq.yd.

28. A triangular lot is 400 feet at its base and has a depth (height or altitude) of 300 feet. How many acres does the lot contain?
    A. 2.6 acres   C. 1.38 acres
    B. 5.5 acres   D. 2.27 acres

29. (*Note: Refer to the lot titled "Question 29" immediately preceding this question.*) If the lot sold for $3,000, what is the price per acre?
    A. $15,000   C. $1,500
    B. $315,000   D. $150

30. Blackacre is a lot with a 150' width. Greenacre is another lot with a 450' width. Both lots have the same depth. If Blackacre consists of 2 acres, how many acres does Greenacre contain?
    A. 5 acres   C. 3 acres
    B. 4 acres   D. 6 acres

31. If two dehumidifiers remove 15,000 gallons of water from a damp warehouse in 10 hours, how many hours will it take 4 dehumidifiers to remove 12,000 gallons of water from the same space?
    A. 4   C. 6
    B. 3   D. 2

32. What is the actual square footage of a lot that is shown on a blueprint as measuring 10 inches by 13 inches? (scale: ⅛ " = 1')
    A. 1,040 sq.ft.   C. 130 sq.ft
    B. 8,320 sq.ft.   D. 1,300 sq.ft.

Hint: Questions 33–36 deal with miscellaneous subjects:

33. According to the offer of cooperation and compensation in a multiple listing agreement, Brokers Smith and Jones are to receive one-half of the 8% commission paid on the sale of a house. The multiple listing service charges 3% of the total commission paid for its services. Salesperson Fred who is employed by Broker Smith receives 40% of his broker's commission upon selling a house. How much will Fred receive if he sells a $45,000 house listed by Broker Jones?
    A. $720   C. $698.40
    B. $677.45   D. $1,746

34. Mr. Piroghee is in the 28% tax bracket. What tax credit can she expect from the Internal Revenue Service if her mortgage interest payments are $212 per month?
    A. $712.32   C. $1,984.32
    B. $59.36   D. $1,831.68

35. A home was purchased for $75,000 with an 80% loan-to-value ratio. The loan was for 30 years at 12% annual interest with monthly payments of $617. How much total mortgage interest will be paid at the end of the 30-year term?
    A. $222,120   C. $216,000
    B. $147,120   D. $162,120

Hint: Questions 36–50 deal with intermediate to advanced subject matter:

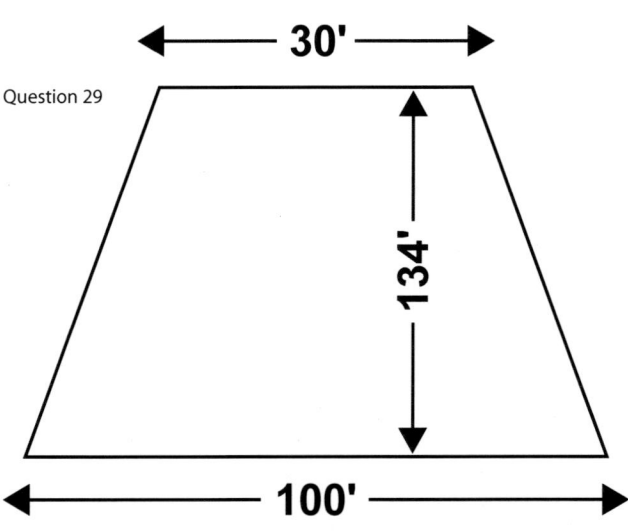
Question 29

36. Larry, a land developer, estimates that 1/10 of the land he owns is wetlands and cannot be disturbed; 1/5 must be dedicated to streets, roads, and schools; and, the remainder can be developed. If Larry develops 45 acres, what is the total size of his entire land holdings?
    A. 64 acres
    B. 128 acres
    C. 50 acres
    D. 155 acres

37. A room which is shown on a blueprint to be 6 inches by 9 inches is actually 18 feet by 27 feet. If another room on the blueprint is shown as 26 square inches, how many square feet does it contain?
    A. 212 sq.ft.
    B. 234 sq.ft.
    C. 252 sq.ft.
    D. 486 sq.ft.

38. Jack purchased 35 acres of wooded land at a cost of $12,500 per acre to develop resort properties. He spent $80,000 developing roads and installing other improvements and constructed 70 dwellings at an average cost of $52,000 per unit. What must Jack sell each improved property for if he wants to make a 15% return on his total investment?
    A. $59,393
    B. $68,302
    C. $69,874
    D. $89,089

39. Mr. Grizlie purchased a home 3 years ago for $41,000. Today, he advertises it for sale at a price 40% greater than what he paid for it. If Grizlie accepts $2,000 less than the advertised price, how much profit will he net on his investment after paying a brokerage commission of 6.5%?
    A. $70,000
    B. $120,000
    C. $10,799
    D. $18,466

40. A store in a shopping mall is leased for $1,000 per month plus 1½% of the gross sales over $50,000. If the total rent paid for the year was $17,250, what were the total gross sales for the year?
    A. $350,000
    B. $400,000
    C. $300,000
    D. $5,250

41. Joanie borrows 80% of the purchase price of a house at 9% interest. If her first month's interest payment is $330, what is the purchase price of the property?
    A. $39,600
    B. $44,000
    C. $47,520
    D. $55,000

42. What is the value of a building which has a monthly profit of $825 and is earning the owner a 14% annual return?
    A. $5,893
    B. $70,714
    C. $82,112
    D. $64,515

43. Salesperson Howard earned a total of $1,850 last month from his broker Lisa. He is paid a salary of $225 plus 45% of all commissions paid on real estate he sells. If Lisa's company charges its clients a 7% commission rate, what was the value of the real estate Howard sold?
    A. $42,208
    B. $48,052
    C. $51,587
    D. $58,730

44. A small office building is valued at $800,000 when its net operating income is capitalized at a rate of 20%. If operating expenses are 40% of gross income, what is the gross income?
    A. $266,667
    B. $312,412
    C. $400,000
    D. $507,312

45. Gina purchased a one-year homeowners insurance policy on March 7 for $188. Annual property taxes of $614.14 were paid on January 1. How much should be credited to her if a purchaser assumes the insurance policy and the closing takes place on September 20?
    A. $191.00
    B. $255.58
    C. $257.80
    D. $544.33

46. A circular room in a Victorian mansion has a diameter of 20 feet. The owner wishes to carpet the room. Calculate the total square footage of the room?
    A. 62.83 sq.ft.
    B. 225.5 sq.ft.
    C. 200 sq.ft.
    D. 314.16 sq.ft.

47. A building with walls one foot thick measures 90' × 70' around the exterior. Inside there are 20, one-foot thick support columns. What is the usable floor area of the building?
    A. 5,964 sq.ft.
    B. 5,984 sq.ft.
    C. 6,121 sq.ft.
    D. 6,280 sq.ft.

48. Mr. Heller sold his house for $48,500 which was 13% more than he paid for it. How much did he pay for the house?
    A. $42,250
    B. $42,920
    C. $54,805
    D. $55,747

49. An old warehouse has 10 dehumidifiers that remove 12,000 gallons of water in 6 hours. Eight additional dehumidifiers are being added. How many gallons will the eight additional units remove in a 12-hour day?
    A. 4,000
    B. 9,600
    C. 19,200
    D. 38,400

50. Gladys sells her house through a broker to whom she pays a 7% commission. If Gladys nets $6,500 after paying the broker, an existing mortgage balance of $23,400, and a property tax lien of $512, what was the selling price of the house?
    A. $28,422
    B. $30,412
    C. $32,701
    D. $32,540

Chapter 22: Real Estate Mathematics   421

REAL ESTATE MATH PRACTICE QUESTION SOLUTIONS

The following section contains the solutions to the 50-question set of practice math questions. It is important to note not only what the correct response is, but also, how the response was calculated. Recall from the introductory notes to this chapter that math is more process-oriented than it is answer-oriented. Although there is more than one way to answer a given math question, this section employs a common and uniform approach which is designed to walk the examinee through the solution process. All answers are assumed to be approximate.

1. $ 72,000.00 listed price
    x   .88 (100% – 12%)

       63,360.00 sale price
    x   .065 commission rate

        4,118.40 total commission
    x   .50 salesperson share

    $ 2,059.20

5. $ 61,500 purchase price
    – 59,000 sale price

    $ 2,500 net loss

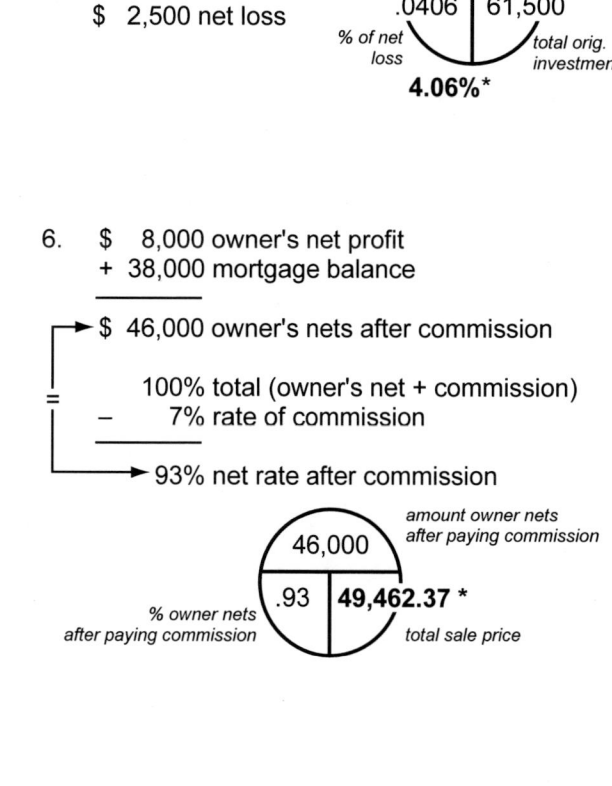

2. $ 300/mo. x .25 = $ 75.00
    $ 300/mo. x 11 mo. x .03 = $ 99.00 (+)
                             $ 174.00

6. $ 8,000 owner's net profit
    + 38,000 mortgage balance

    $ 46,000 owner's nets after commission

       100% total (owner's net + commission)
    –   7% rate of commission

       93% net rate after commission

3.   200 acres
    x   1,200 price/acre

    $ 240,000 selling price
    – 25,000 (1st)   x .07 = $ 1,750

       215,000
    – 25,000 (2nd)   x .04 =   1,000

       190,000 (remain) x .03 = 5,700 +

          Total commission $ 8,450
          ½ of broker's ½ x   .25
          (50/50 split)
                            $ 2,112.50

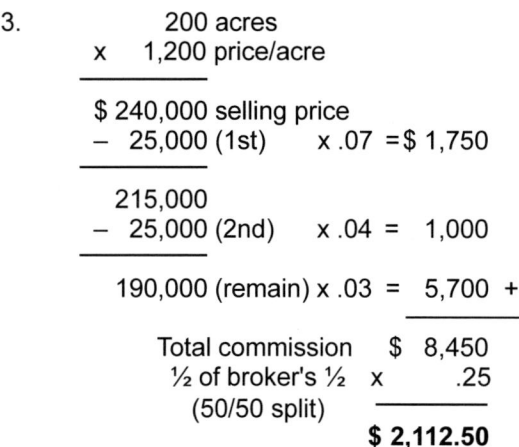

7.   40% appreciation (8%/yr. x 5 yr.)
     + 100% orig. value

       140% present value

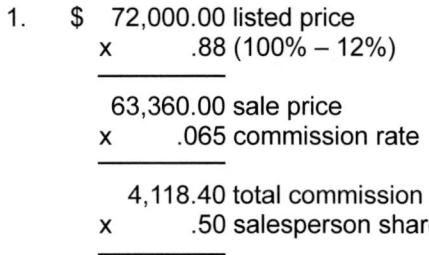

8.   100% orig. value
     – 28% depreciation (4%/yr. x 7 yr.)

        72% present value

4. 100% break even
    + 58% profit

       158%

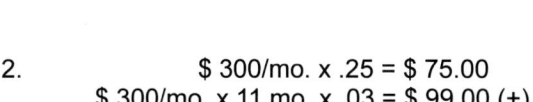

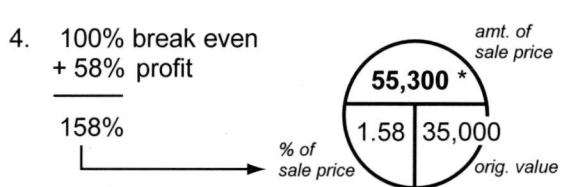

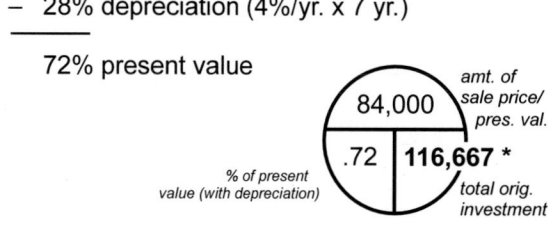

9. Land: House:
       4 years   4 years
    x 6 % appreciation   x 2 % depreciation/yr.
    ─────────────   ─────────────
      24 %   100 %
    +100 original   − 8 %
    ─────────────   ─────────────
    124 % present value   92 % present value

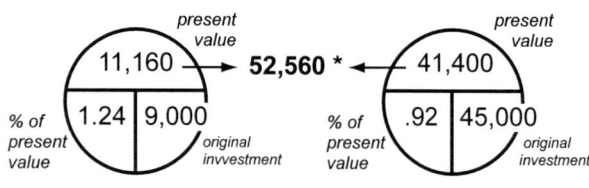
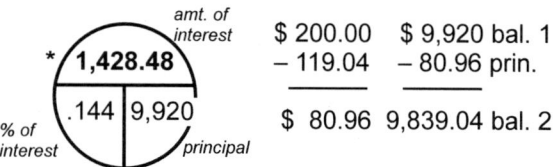
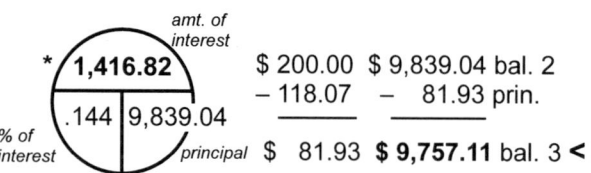

14. Hint: Apply the same steps as in problem 13 changing the principal balance each time.

                    $ 200.00 $ 9,920 bal. 1
                    − 119.04   − 80.96 prin.
                    ──────────   ──────────
                    $ 80.96   9,839.04 bal. 2

                    $ 200.00 $ 9,839.04 bal. 2
                    − 118.07   − 81.93 prin.
                    ──────────   ──────────
                    $ 81.93   **$ 9,757.11** bal. 3 <

10.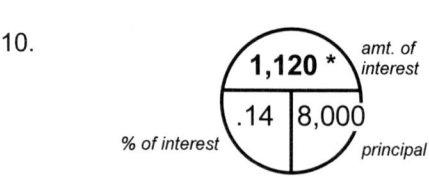

15. $ 599.55 int./mo.
     x   12 mo.
     ──────────────
     $ 7,194.60 int./yr.

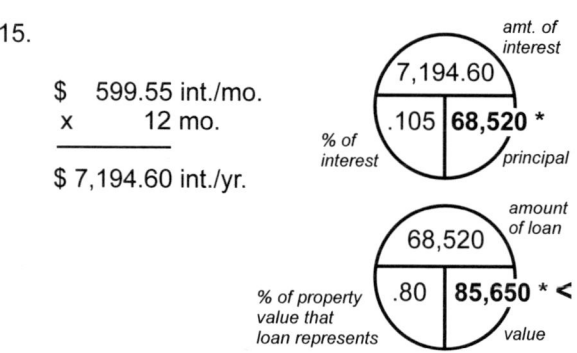

11. $ 1,120 int./yr. ÷ 12 months = **$ 93.33 int./mo.**

12. $ 787.50 int./mo.
     x   12 months
     ──────────────
     $ 9,450.00 int./yr.

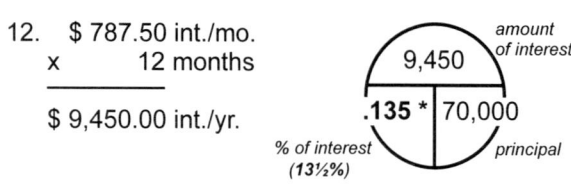

16. $ 3.60 tax rate
     ─────────────────── = .036
     $ 100 assessed value

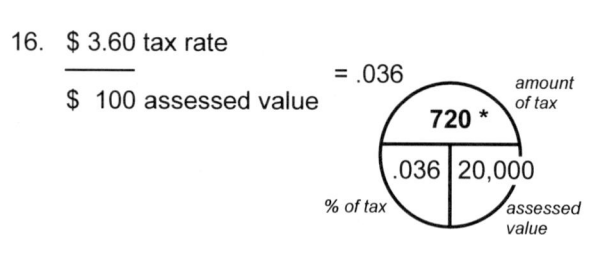

13.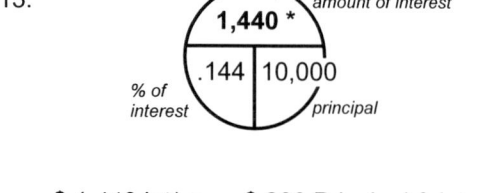

    $ 1,440 int/yr. $ 200 Principal & Interest
    ÷   12 mo.   − 120 interest
    ───────────── ─────────────────
    $ 120 int./mo. **$ 80 principal reduction**

Note: The question only $ 10,000 begin balance
calls for princ. reduction.   −   80 principal
The end bal. is provided   ──────────────────
here for illustration only. $ 9,920 bal. end month 1

17. 65 mills = 65 x .001 = .065

    $ 76,000
    x   .40
    ─────────
    $ 30,400 assessed
            value

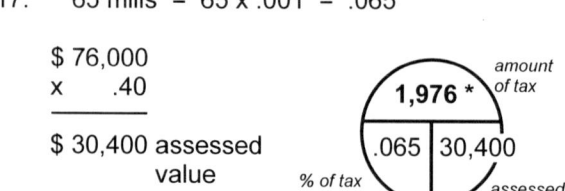

Chapter 22: Real Estate Mathematics

18.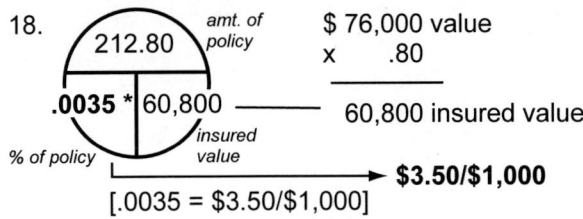

$ 76,000 value
x   .80
———
60,800 insured value

$3.50/$1,000
[.0035 = $3.50/$1,000]

19. $ 70,000 value
x   .80
———
56,000 ins'd value
x .0028
———
$ 156.80 premium/yr.
x   .30 discount
———
$ 47.04

$ 156.80 premium/yr.
x   3 years
———
470.40
− 47.04
———
423.36 3 yr. premium
÷   36 mo.
———
$ 11.76 cost/mo.

20. Hint: The buyer owes beginning the date of closing through the end of the policy period or 9-20-2008 to 6-1-2011 (2 yr., 8 mo.,10 days)

$ 423.36 3 yr. policy
÷   3 yrs.
————
   141.12 cost/yr.   x 2 yr.   = $ 282.24
÷   12 months
————
    11.76 cost/mo.   x 8 mo. =   94.08
÷   30 days
————
     .392 cost/day   x 11 days =   4.31 +
                                   ————
                                   $ 380.63

21. Hint: The seller owes from the date the tax begins to the last day before closing or Jan. 1 to Feb. 16 (1 mo., 16 days) plus the previous year

$ 1,450.00 tax/yr.
÷   12 mos.
————
   120.83 cost/mo.   x 1 mo. = $ 120.83
÷   30 days
————
    4.03 cost/day   x 16 days =   64.48 +
                                  ————
                                  $ 185.31
            previous yr. $ 1,450.00 +
                          ————
                          $ 1,635.31

22.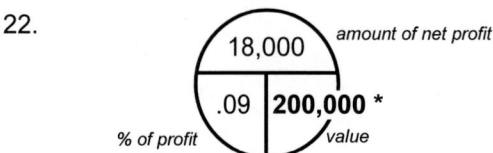

23. $ 60,000 sale price
    ÷   570 rent
         ————
         105 GRM

24. $ 225 rent/mo.
    x   20 units
         ————
         4,500 total/mo.
    x   12 months
         ————
        54,000 potential income/yr.
    x   .90 (10% vacancy = 90% occupancy)
         ————
        48,600 actual gross income
    x   .55 (45% expenses = 55% net income)
         ————
    $ 26,730 net income

25.

26. $ 10,800 cost
    ÷   60 front feet
          ————
    $ 180 per front foot

27. 24 feet x 14 feet = 336 sq.ft.
    13 feet x 13 feet = 169 sq.ft. +
                        ————
                         505 sq.ft.
                      ÷ 9 sq.ft./sq.yd.
                        ————
                      56.11 sq.yd.

28. area = length x width   ÷ 2
         = 300 ft. x 400 ft.   ÷ 2
         = 120,000 sq.ft.   ÷ 2
         = 60,000 sq.ft.
         ÷ 43,560 sq.ft./acre
         ————
         1.38 acres

29. area =
$$H\left(\frac{a+b}{2}\right) =$$
$$134'\left(\frac{30'+100'}{2}\right) =$$
134' (65') =
8,710 sq.ft.

8,710 sq.ft.
÷ 43,560 sq.ft./acre
──────────
    .20 acres

$ 3,000 sale price
÷   .20 acres
──────────
$ 15,000 price/acre

Note: The diagram in the problem is out of proportion to the scale indicated.

30.   2 acres (Blackacre)
   x 43,560 sq.ft./acre
   ──────────
       87,120 sq.ft.
   ÷   150 ft.
   ──────────
          580 ft. depth in (Blackacre)
   x   450 ft. width (Greenacre)
   ──────────
      261,000 sq.ft. (Greenacre)
   ÷   43,560 sq.ft./acre
   ──────────
   6 acres

31.   15,000 gal./10 hr./2 dehumidifiers
   ÷   2 dehumidifiers
   ──────────
        7,500 gal./10 hr./1 dehumidifier
   ÷   10 hours
   ──────────
          750 gal./hr./1 dehumidifier
   x   4 dehumidifiers
   ──────────
        3,000 gal./hr./4 dehumidifiers

       12,000 gal.
   ÷   3,000 gal./hr.
   ──────────
   4 hrs.

32. If 1/8 inch = 1 foot;
     then 1 inch = a factor of 8 feet.

     10 inches   x   13 inches (on the blueprint)
     (x 8 factor)   (x 8 factor)
     ──────────   ──────────
     80 feet   x   104 feet = **8,320 sq.ft.**

33. $ 45,000 sale price
    x   .08 commission rate
    ──────────
      3,600 total commission
    x   .97 (3% to multi-list = 97%)
    ──────────
      3,492 to brokers
    x   .50 broker split
    ──────────
      1,746 to broker A
    x   .40 salesperson/broker split
    ──────────
    $ **$698.40 to salesperson Fred**

34. $ 212 interest/month
    x   12 months
    ──────────
    $ 2,544 interest/year
    x   .28 tax bracket
    ──────────
    $ **712.32**   (Interest only is deductible)

35. $ 75,000 value
    x   .80 loan to value ratio
    ──────────
    $ 60,000 loan

    $ 617 payment/month
    x   12 months
    ──────────
      7,404 total payments/year
    x   30 years
    ──────────
    222,120 total payments over 30 years
    − 60,000 principal
    ──────────
    $162,120 total interest

Note: Interest rate is not necessary.

36. 1/5 (2/10) + 1/10 = 3/10 unusable
          10/10 − 3/10 = 7/10 usable
     45 acres ÷ 7 (tenth's) = 6.4 acres or 1/10 of the
                                          total area
                   6.4 x 10 = **64 acres**

37. 18 ft. actual = 6 inches on blueprint
           18 ÷ 6 = 3 ft. actual/1 in. on blueprint
                  = 9 sq.ft./sq.in.

     26 sq.in. x 9 = **234 sq.ft.**

Chapter 22: Real Estate Mathematics

38. Step 1: Total cost
    35 acres x $12,500 = $ 437,500
    roads   80,000
    70 x $52,000   + 3,640,000
    ─────────────────────────────
    Total investment $ 4,157,500

    Step 2:
    $ 4,157,500 total investment
    +   623,625 (15% of total investment)
    ─────────────────────────────
    $ 4,781,125 total cost
    ÷   70 lots
    ─────────────────────────────
    $ 68,302 cost per home

39. $ 41,000
    x   1.40 (100% + 40% increase)
    ─────────────────────────────
    $ 57,400 advertised price
    − 2,000
    ─────────────────────────────
    $ 55,400 sale price
    x   .065 (6.5% commission)
    ─────────────────────────────
    $ 3,601 commission

    $ 55,400 sale price
    − 3,601 commission
    ─────────────────────────────
    $ 51,799 net to seller
    − 41,000 original price
    ─────────────────────────────
    $ 10,799 net profit

40. $ 17,250 actual rent paid
    − 12,000 minimum rent ($1,000/mo. x 12)
    ─────────────────────────────
    $ 5,250 excess rent paid

    [circle: 5,250 / .015 / 350,000; amt. of excess rent; % of excess rent; i.e., gross sales over $50,000; excess gross sales]

    $ 350,000 excess gross sales
    + 50,000 minimum
    ─────────────────────────────
    $ 400,000 total sales for the year

41. $ 330 interest/month
    x   12 months
    ─────────────────────────────
    $ 3,960 interest/year

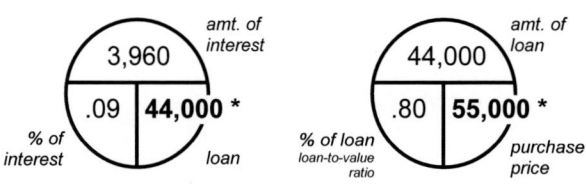

42. $ 825 monthly profit
    x   12 months
    ─────────────────────────────
    $ 9,900 annual income

    [circle: 9,900 / .14 / 70,714 *; amt. of net operating income; capitalization rate; market value]

43. $ 1,850 total earnings (salary & commissions)
    −   225 salary
    ─────────────────────────────
    $ 1,625 commissions

    [circle: 1,625 / .45 / 3,611.11 *; amt. of commissions (paid to the salesperson); % of commissions (paid to the salesperson); total commissions paid]

    [circle: 3,611.11 / .07 / 51,587 *; amt. of commissions paid; % of commissions; total sales price]

44. Step 1: Calculate the total market value using the capitalization rate formula.
    Step 2: Calculate gross income based upon the following: 100% − 40% expenses = 60%.

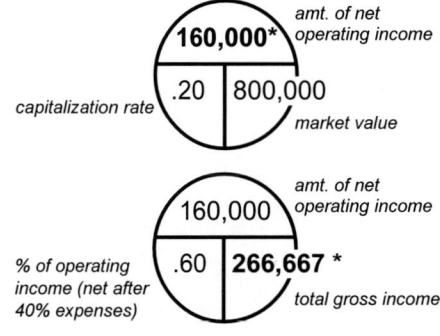

45. Property tax proration period: Buyer owes
    from Sept. 20 to Dec. 30 (3 mo., 10 days)
    $ 614.14 annual taxes
    ÷   12 months

    ─────────
    51.178 tax/month x 3 mo. = $ 153.535
    ÷   30 days
    ─────────
    1.706 tax/day   x 10 days =   17.059 +
                                 ─────────
                                 $ 170.594

Insurance proration period:
Sept. 20 to Mar. 6 (5 mo., 17 days)
$ 188.00 annual insurance
÷   12 months
─────────
15.666 ins./month x 5 mo. = $ 78.333
÷   30 days
─────────
.522 ins./day   x 17 days =   8.877 +
                              ─────────
                              $ 87.210 +
                                 170.594
                              ─────────
                              $ 257.80

46. Area = πR^2 π = 3.1416
                         R = radius (one-half of circle)

    Area = 3.1416 x 10^2
         = 3.1416 x 100
         = **314.16 square feet**

47. 90 feet x 70 feet exterior measurement
    (minus 1 foot from each of 4 walls) =
    88 feet x 68 feet =   5,984 sq.ft. interior
                        −   20 columns 1' thick
                           ─────────
                           5,964 sq.ft. usable

48. $ 48,500 = 100% orig. sale price
              13% profit   +
              ─────────────────
              113% of orig. sale price

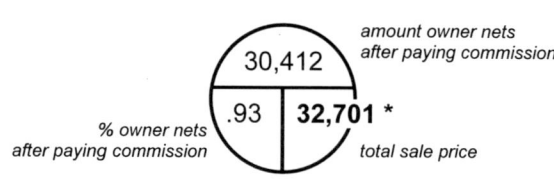
% of recent sale   total original value
amount of recent sale
48,500
1.13 | **42,920** *

49.   12,000 gal./6 hr./10 dehumidifiers
    ÷   10 dehumidifiers
    ─────────
       1,200 gal./6 hr./1 dehumidifier
    x   8 dehumidifiers
    ─────────
       9,600 gal./6 hr./8 dehumidifiers
    x   2 (6 hr. output x 2 = 12 hr. output)
    ─────────
    19,200 gal. output/12 hr.

50. $ 6,500 owner's net
      23,400 mortgage balance
    +   512 property tax lien
    ─────────
    $ 30,412 owner's net after commission

       100% total (owner's net + commission)
    −   7% rate of commission
    ─────────
       93% net rate after commission

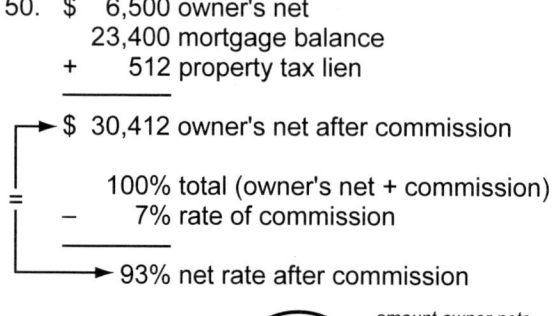
% owner nets   total sale price
after paying commission
amount owner nets
after paying commission
30,412
.93 | **32,701** *

Michigan
Real Estate Law & Practice

A Complete Guide for Exam Prep, Practitioners, and Consumers

Practice Exam
and Answer Keys

Sharpening your test-taking skills.

Confidently handle life's challenges as they arise.
The attempt to deny "what is" does not negate its existence.

Answer Key, Chapter Practice Questions

The following answer keys correspond to the questions at the end of each chapter. Each question relates to the information presented in the specific chapter. If the answer you provided to any particular question is incorrect, it is recommended that you determine the specific issues covered by the question and research it in the chapter.

Ch. 1		Ch. 2	Ch. 3	Ch. 4	Ch. 5	Ch. 6	Ch. 7	Ch. 8	Ch. 9	Ch. 10	Ch. 11
1. B	17. B	1. B	1. D	1. A	1. A	1. B	1. B	1. C	1. D	1. B	1. B
2. C	18. D	2. A	2. A	2. C	2. A	2. C	2. D	2. A	2. A	2. B	2. D
3. A	19. B	3. D	3. C	3. D	3. C	3. A	3. B	3. B	3. D	3. D	3. B
4. D	20. A	4. B	4. B	4. A	4. C	4. A	4. D	4. C	4. A	4. C	4. C
5. D		5. A	5. C	5. B	5. D	5. C	5. C	5. A	5. C	5. A	5. D
6. B		6. C	6. A	6. C	6. B	6. D	6. A	6. D	6. B	6. C	6. A
7. D		7. C	7. B	7. D	7. D	7. D	7. A	7. B	7. A	7. B	7. B
8. B		8. D	8. C	8. A	8. A	8. D	8. D	8. B	8. B	8. C	8. B
9. C		9. D	9. C	9. D	9. C	9. B	9. A	9. A	9. D	9. A	9. A
10. A		10. A	10. D	10. B	10. C	10. A	10. A	10. D	10. D	10. C	10. C
11. B		11. A	11. C	11. B	11. D	11. B	11. D	11. C	11. C	11. B	11. D
12. C		12. D	12. B	12. A	12. B	12. B	12. B	12. A	12. A	12. A	12. B
13. D		13. D	13. D	13. C	13. D	13. D	13. D	13. D	13. A	13. B	13. D
14. B		14. B	14. C	14. A	14. D	14. C	14. A	14. A	14. C	14. A	14. A
15. A		15. A	15. A	15. B	15. D	15. C	15. C	15. B	15. D	15. C	15. C
16. D		16. B	16. D	16. B	16. A	16. A	16. D	16. D	16. C	16. B	16. A

Ch. 12	Ch. 13	Ch. 14	Ch. 15	Ch. 16	Ch. 17	Ch. 18		Ch. 19	Ch. 20	Ch. 21
1. A	1. A	1. B	1. B	1. A	1. A	1. A	27. D	1. B	1. D	1. C
2. B	2. C	2. A	2. C	2. B	2. D	2. C	28. D	2. B	2. B	2. D
3. C	3. B	3. B	3. A	3. D	3. B	3. C	29. A	3. C	3. C	3. B
4. A	4. B	4. C	4. D	4. D	4. C	4. A	30. D	4. A	4. A	4. A
5. D	5. D	5. D	5. B	5. C	5. D	5. D	31. D	5. A	5. B	5. D
6. D	6. C	6. B	6. C	6. A	6. A	6. B		6. D	6. B	6. D
7. D	7. D	7. B	7. B	7. D	7. D	7. D		7. A	7. D	7. A
8. B	8. B	8. D	8. D	8. A	8. C	8. A		8. D	8. D	8. C
9. C	9. D	9. A	9. C	9. D	9. A	9. D		9. C	9. D	9. B
10. C	10. A	10. B	10. B	10. C	10. C	10. D		10. A	10. D	10. C
11. A	11. A	11. D	11. B	11. A	11. C	11. C		11. C	11. B	11. D
12. D	12. D	12. A	12. D	12. D	12. C	12. C		12. C	12. B	12. A
13. A	13. D	13. D	13. A	13. C	13. A	13. D		13. C	13. B	13. C
14. D	14. A	14. A	14. C	14. B	14. D	14. A		14. B	14. C	14. D
15. B	15. B	15. C	15. D	15. D	15. B	15. B		15. A	15. B	15. B
16. C	16. C	16. A	16. C	16. C	16. D	16. B		16. C	16. B	16. D
17. C				17. C	17. B	17. D		17. A	17. A	
18. B				18. B	18. D	18. B		18. B	18. A	
19. C				19. B	19. A	19. C		19. C	19. B	
20. D				20. C	20. B	20. C		20. C	20. D	
21. B				21. D	21. A	21. D		21. C	21. D	
					22. C	22. B				
					23. D	23. A				
					24. D	24. C				
					25. A	25. A				
					26. B	26. D				

Answer Key, Diagnostic Practice Exam

The following answer key corresponds to the 100-question Diagnostic Practice Examination at questions at the end of this textbook. If the answer you provided to any particular question is incorrect, it is recommended that you determine the specific issues covered by the question and research it in the appropriate chapter.

1. A	21. D	41. D	61. C	81. D
2. A	22. B	42. B	62. A	82. A
3. D	23. A	43. B	63. D	83. A
4. C	24. D	44. A	64. D	84. B
5. A	25. A	45. A	65. C	85. D
6. D	26. B	46. C	66. B	86. C
7. C	27. B	47. D	67. A	87. D
8. B	28. C	48. C	68. D	88. B
9. C	29. B	49. A	69. D	89. C
10. B	30. D	50. A	70. A	90. B
11. B	31. C	51. B	71. A	91. A
12. C	32. D	52. B	72. D	92. D
13. B	33. B	53. C	73. C	93. A
14. D	34. A	54. C	74. B	94. B
15. C	35. C	55. B	75. C	95. B
16. A	36. B	56. A	76. A	96. A
17. A	37. A	57. D	77. A	97. C
18. C	38. B	58. A	78. C	98. B
19. D	39. D	59. C	79. B	99. C
20. D	40. A	60. B	80. B	100. D

To create wealth, be aware of how you are using your productive time.
Success is measured by what you do in life, not what you post on social media.

Michigan
Real Estate Law & Practice

A Complete Guide for Exam Prep, Practitioners, and Consumers

Appendix

"What you see is what you get" really means...
What you project in your mind's eye is what you create and experience.

Agency Disclosure

Disclosure Regarding Real Estate Agency Relationships

Before you disclose confidential information to a real estate licensee regarding a real estate transaction, you should understand what type of agency relationship you have with that licensee. A real estate transaction is a transaction involving the sale or lease of any legal or equitable interest in real estate consisting of not less than 1 or more than 4 residential dwelling units or consisting of a building site for a residential unit on either a lot as defined in section 102 of the Land Division Act, 1967 PA 288, MCL 560.102, or a condominium unit as defined in section 4 of the Condominium Act, 1978 PA 59, MCL 559.104.

(1) An agent providing services under any service provision agreement owes, at minimum, the following *duties* to the client:
   (a) The exercise of reasonable care and skill in representing the client and carrying out the responsibilities of the agency relationship.
   (b) The performance of the terms of the service provision agreement.
   (c) Loyalty to the interest of the client.
   (d) Compliance with the laws, rules and regulations of this state and any applicable federal statutes or regulations.
   (e) Referral of the client to other licensed professionals for expert advice related to material matters that are not within the expertise of the licensed agent. *A real estate licensee does not act as an attorney, tax advisor, surveyor, appraiser, environmental expert, or structural or mechanical engineer and you should contact professionals on these matters.*
   (f) An accounting in a timely manner of all money and property received by the agent in which the client has or may have an interest.
   (g) Confidentiality of all information obtained within the course of the agency relationship, unless disclosed with the client's permission or as provided by law, including the duty not to disclose confidential information to any licensee who is not an agent of the client.

(2) A real estate broker or real estate salesperson acting pursuant to a service provision agreement shall provide the following *services* to his or her client:
   (a) When the real estate broker or real estate salesperson is representing a seller or lessor, the marketing of the client's property in the manner agreed upon in the service provision agreement.
   (b) Acceptance of delivery and presentation of offers and counteroffers to buy, sell or lease the client's property or the property the client seeks to purchase or lease.
   (c) Assistance in developing, communicating, negotiating and presenting offers, counteroffers and related documents or notices until a purchase or lease agreement is executed by all parties and contingencies are satisfied or waived.
   (d) After execution of a purchase agreement by all parties, assistance as necessary to complete the transaction under the terms specified in the purchase agreement.
   (e) For a broker or associate broker who is involved at the closing of a real estate or business opportunity transaction, furnishing, or causing to be furnished, to the buyer and seller, a complete and detailed closing statement signed by the broker or associate broker showing each party all receipts and disbursements affecting that party.

Michigan law requires real estate licensees who are acting as agents of sellers or buyers of real property to advise the potential sellers or buyers with whom they work of the nature of their agency relationship.

SELLER'S AGENTS

A seller's agent, under a listing agreement with the seller, acts solely on behalf of the seller. A seller can authorize a seller's agent to work with subagents, buyer's agents and/or transaction coordinators. A subagent of the seller is one who has agreed to work with the listing agent, and who, like the listing agent, acts solely on behalf of the seller. Seller's agents and their subagents will disclose to the seller known information about the buyer which may be used to the benefit of the seller.

Individual services may be waived by the seller through execution of a limited service agreement. Only those services set forth in paragraph (2)(b),(c) and (d above may be waived by the execution of a limited service agreement.

BUYER'S AGENTS

A buyer's agent, under a buyer's agency agreement with the buyer, acts solely on behalf of the buyer. A subagent of the buyer is one who has agreed to work with the buyer's agent with who, like the buyer's agent, acts solely on behalf of the buyer. Buyer's agents and their subagents will disclose to the buyer known information about the seller which may be used to benefit the buyer.

Individual services may be waived by the buyer through execution of a limited service agreement. Only those services set forth in paragraph (2)(b),(c) and (d) above my be waived by the execution of a limited service agreement.

DUAL AGENTS

A real estate licensee can be the agent of both the seller and the buyer in a transaction, but only with the knowledge and informed consent, in writing, or both the seller and the buyer. In such a dual agency situation, the licensee will not be able to disclose all known information to either the seller or the buyer. As a dual agent, the licensee will not be able to provide the full range of fiduciary duties to the seller or the buyer. The obligations of a dual agent are subject to any specific provisions set forth in any agreement between the dual agent, the seller and the buyer.

TRANSACTION COORDINATOR

A transaction coordinator is a licensee who is not acting as an agent of either the seller or the buyer, yet is providing services to complete a real estate transaction. The transaction coordinator is not an agent for either party and therefore owes no fiduciary duty to either party.

DESIGNATED AGENCY

A buyer or seller with a designated agency agreement is represented only by agents specifically named in the agreement. Any agents of the firm not named in the agreement do not represent the buyer or seller. The "designated" agent acts solely on behalf of his or her client and may only share confidential information about the client with the agent's supervisory broker who is also named in the agreement. Other agents in the firm have no duties to the buyer or seller and may act solely on behalf of another party in the transaction.

LICENSEE DISCLOSURE (Check one)

I hereby disclose that the agency status of the licensee named below Is:

_____ Seller's agent

_____ Seller's agent – limited service agreement

_____ Buyer's agent

_____ Buyer's agent – limited service agreement

_____ Dual agent

_____ Transaction coordinator (A licensee who is not acting as an agent of either the seller or the buyer.)

_____ None of the above

AFFILIATED LICENSEE DISCLOSURE (Check one)

_____ Check here if acting as a designated agent. Only the licensee's broker and a named supervisor broker have the same agency relationship as the licensee named below. If the other party in a transaction is represented by an affiliated licensee, then the licensee's broker and all named supervisory brokers shall be considered disclosed consensual dual agents.

_____ Check here if not acting as a designated agent. All affiliated licensees have the same agency relationship as the licensee named below.

Further, this form was provided to the buyer or seller before disclosure of any confidential information.

_____   _____
Licensee   Date

_____   _____
Licensee   Date

ACKNOWLEDGMENT

By signing below, the parties acknowledge that they have received and read the information in this agency disclosure statement and acknowledge that this form was provided to them before the disclosure of any confidential information. **THIS IS NOT A CONTRACT.**

The undersigned _____ DOES _____ DOES NOT have an agency relationship with any other real estate licensee.

If any agency relationship exists, the undersigned is represented as a _____ SELLER _____ BUYER.

_____   _____
Potential Buyer / Seller (circle one)   Date

_____   _____
Potential Buyer / Seller (circle one)   Date

Appendix: HUD-1

HUD-1
A. Settlement Statement (HUD-1)

OMB Approval No. 2502-0265

B. Type of Loan

1. ☐ FHA	2. ☐ RHS	3. ☐ Conv. Unins.	6. File Number:	7. Loan Number:	8. Mortgage Insurance Case Number:
4. ☐ VA	5. ☐ Conv. Ins.				

C. Note: This form is furnished to give you a statement of actual settlement costs. Amounts paid to and by the settlement agent are shown. Items marked "(p.o.c.)" were paid outside the closing; they are shown here for informational purposes and are not included in the totals.

D. Name & Address of Borrower:	E. Name & Address of Seller:	F. Name & Address of Lender:

G. Property Location:	H. Settlement Agent:	I. Settlement Date:
	Place of Settlement:	

J. Summary of Borrower's Transaction		K. Summary of Seller's Transaction	
100. Gross Amount Due from Borrower		**400. Gross Amount Due to Seller**	
101. Contract sales price		401. Contract sales price	
102. Personal property		402. Personal property	
103. Settlement charges to borrower (line 1400)		403.	
104.		404.	
105.		405.	
Adjustment for items paid by seller in advance		**Adjustment for items paid by seller in advance**	
106. City/town taxes to		406. City/town taxes to	
107. County taxes to		407. County taxes to	
108. Assessments to		408. Assessments to	
109.		409.	
110.		410.	
111.		411.	
112.		412.	
120. Gross Amount Due from Borrower		**420. Gross Amount Due to Seller**	
200. Amount Paid by or in Behalf of Borrower		**500. Reductions In Amount Due to seller**	
201. Deposit or earnest money		501. Excess deposit (see instructions)	
202. Principal amount of new loan(s)		502. Settlement charges to seller (line 1400)	
203. Existing loan(s) taken subject to		503. Existing loan(s) taken subject to	
204.		504. Payoff of first mortgage loan	
205.		505. Payoff of second mortgage loan	
206.		506.	
207.		507.	
208.		508.	
209.		509.	
Adjustments for items unpaid by seller		**Adjustments for items unpaid by seller**	
210. City/town taxes to		510. City/town taxes to	
211. County taxes to		511. County taxes to	
212. Assessments to		512. Assessments to	
213.		513.	
214.		514.	
215.		515.	
216.		516.	
217.		517.	
218.		518.	
219.		519.	
220. Total Paid by/for Borrower		**520. Total Reduction Amount Due Seller**	
300. Cash at Settlement from/to Borrower		**600. Cash at Settlement to/from Seller**	
301. Gross amount due from borrower (line 120)		601. Gross amount due to seller (line 420)	
302. Less amounts paid by/for borrower (line 220)	( )	602. Less reductions in amounts due seller (line 520)	( )
303. Cash ☐ From ☐ To Borrower		603. Cash ☐ To ☐ From Seller	

The Public Reporting Burden for this collection of information is estimated at 35 minutes per response for collecting, reviewing, and reporting the data. This agency may not collect this information, and you are not required to complete this form, unless it displays a currently valid OMB control number. No confidentiality is assured; this disclosure

L. Settlement Charges

700. Total Real Estate Broker Fees		Paid From Borrower's Funds at Settlement	Paid From Seller's Funds at Settlement
Division of commission (line 700) as follows:			
701. $ to			
702. $ to			
703. Commission paid at settlement			
704.			

800. Items Payable in Connection with Loan			
801. Our origination charge	$ (from GFE #1)		
802. Your credit or charge (points) for the specific interest rate chosen	$ (from GFE #2)		
803. Your adjusted origination charges	(from GFE #A)		
804. Appraisal fee to	(from GFE #3)		
805. Credit report to	(from GFE #3)		
806. Tax service to	(from GFE #3)		
807. Flood certification to	(from GFE #3)		
808.			
809.			
810.			
811.			

900. Items Required by Lender to be Paid in Advance			
901. Daily interest charges from to @ $ /day	(from GFE #10)		
902. Mortgage insurance premium for months to	(from GFE #3)		
903. Homeowner's insurance for years to	(from GFE #11)		
904.			

1000. Reserves Deposited with Lender			
1001. Initial deposit for your escrow account	(from GFE #9)		
1002. Homeowner's insurance months @ $ per month $			
1003. Mortgage insurance months @ $ per month $			
1004. Property Taxes months @ $ per month $			
1005. months @ $ per month $			
1006. months @ $ per month $			
1007. Aggregate Adjustment -$			

1100. Title Charges			
1101. Title services and lender's title insurance	(from GFE #4)		
1102. Settlement or closing fee	$		
1103. Owner's title insurance	(from GFE #5)		
1104. Lender's title insurance	$		
1105. Lender's title policy limit $			
1106. Owner's title policy limit $			
1107. Agent's portion of the total title insurance premium to	$		
1108. Underwriter's portion of the total title insurance premium to	$		
1109.			
1110.			
1111.			

1200. Government Recording and Transfer Charges			
1201. Government recording charges	(from GFE #7)		
1202. Deed $ Mortgage $ Release $			
1203. Transfer taxes	(from GFE #8)		
1204. City/County tax/stamps Deed $ Mortgage $			
1205. State tax/stamps Deed $ Mortgage $			
1206.			

1300. Additional Settlement Charges			
1301. Required services that you can shop for	(from GFE #6)		
1302.	$		
1303.	$		
1304.			
1305.			

1400. Total Settlement Charges (enter on lines 103, Section J and 502, Section K)

HUD-1, p 2

Appendix: HUD-1

Comparison of Good Faith Estimate (GFE) and HUD-1 Charrges		Good Faith Estimate	HUD-1
Charges That Cannot Increase	**HUD-1 Line Number**		
Our origination charge	# 801		
Your credit or charge (points) for the specific interest rate chosen	# 802		
Your adjusted origination charges	# 803		
Transfer taxes	# 1203		

Charges That In Total Cannot Increase More Than 10%		Good Faith Estimate	HUD-1
Government recording charges	# 1201		
	#		
	#		
	#		
	#		
	#		
	#		
	Total		
	Increase between GFE and HUD-1 Charges	$ or	%

Charges That Can Change		Good Faith Estimate	HUD-1
Initial deposit for your escrow account	# 1001		
Daily interest charges $ /day	# 901		
Homeowner's insurance	# 903		
	#		
	#		
	#		

Loan Terms

Your initial loan amount is	$
Your loan term is	years
Your initial interest rate is	%
Your initial monthly amount owed for principal, interest, and any mortgage insurance is	$ includes ☐ Principal ☐ Interest ☐ Mortgage Insurance
Can your interest rate rise?	☐ No ☐ Yes, it can rise to a maximum of %. The first change will be on and can change again every after . Every change date, your interest rate can increase or decrease by %. Over the life of the loan, your interest rate is guaranteed to never be **lower** than % or **higher** than %.
Even if you make payments on time, can your loan balance rise?	☐ No ☐ Yes, it can rise to a maximum of $
Even if you make payments on time, can your monthly amount owed for principal, interest, and mortgage insurance rise?	☐ No ☐ Yes, the first increase can be on and the monthly amount owed can rise to $. The maximum it can ever rise to is $
Does your loan have a prepayment penalty?	☐ No ☐ Yes, your maximum prepayment penalty is $
Does your loan have a balloon payment?	☐ No ☐ Yes, you have a balloon payment of $ due in years on .
Total monthly amount owed including escrow account payments	☐ You do not have a monthly escrow payment for items, such as property taxes and homeowner's insurance. You must pay these items directly yourself. ☐ You have an additional monthly escrow payment of $ that results in a total initial monthly amount owed of $. This includes principal, interest, any mortagage insurance and any items checked below: ☐ Property taxes ☐ Homeowner's insurance ☐ Flood insurance ☐ ☐

Note: If you have any questions about the Settlement Charges and Loan Terms listed on this form, please contact your lender.

TRID Rule Loan Estimate

FICUS BANK
4321 Random Boulevard • Somecity, ST 12340

Save this Loan Estimate to compare with your Closing Disclosure.

Loan Estimate

DATE ISSUED	2/15/2013
APPLICANTS	Michael Jones and Mary Stone 123 Anywhere Street Anytown, ST 12345
PROPERTY	456 Somewhere Avenue Anytown, ST 12345
SALE PRICE	$180,000

LOAN TERM	30 years
PURPOSE	Purchase
PRODUCT	Fixed Rate
LOAN TYPE	☒ Conventional ☐ FHA ☐ VA ☐ _____
LOAN ID #	123456789
RATE LOCK	☐ NO ☒ YES, until 4/16/2013 at 5:00 p.m. EDT

Before closing, your interest rate, points, and lender credits can change unless you lock the interest rate. All other estimated closing costs expire on **3/4/2013** at 5:00 p.m. EDT

Loan Terms

		Can this amount increase after closing?
Loan Amount	$162,000	NO
Interest Rate	3.875%	NO
Monthly Principal & Interest *See Projected Payments below for your Estimated Total Monthly Payment*	$761.78	NO

		Does the loan have these features?
Prepayment Penalty	YES	• As high as **$3,240** if you pay off the loan during the first 2 years
Balloon Payment	NO	

Projected Payments

Payment Calculation	Years 1-7	Years 8-30
Principal & Interest	$761.78	$761.78
Mortgage Insurance	+ 82	+ —
Estimated Escrow *Amount can increase over time*	+ 206	+ 206
Estimated Total Monthly Payment	**$1,050**	**$968**

Estimated Taxes, Insurance & Assessments *Amount can increase over time*	**$206** a month	**This estimate includes** ☒ Property Taxes ☒ Homeowner's Insurance ☐ Other: *See Section G on page 2 for escrowed property costs. You must pay for other property costs separately.*	**In escrow?** YES YES

Costs at Closing

Estimated Closing Costs	$8,054	Includes $5,672 in Loan Costs + $2,382 in Other Costs – $0 in Lender Credits. *See page 2 for details.*
Estimated Cash to Close	$16,054	Includes Closing Costs. *See Calculating Cash to Close on page 2 for details.*

Visit **www.consumerfinance.gov/mortgage-estimate** for general information and tools.

LOAN ESTIMATE   PAGE 1 OF 3 • LOAN ID # 123456789

Appendix: TRID Rule Loan Estimate

Closing Cost Details

Loan Costs

A. Origination Charges	**$1,802**
.25 % of Loan Amount (Points)	$405
Application Fee	$300
Underwriting Fee	$1,097

B. Services You Cannot Shop For	**$672**
Appraisal Fee	$405
Credit Report Fee	$30
Flood Determination Fee	$20
Flood Monitoring Fee	$32
Tax Monitoring Fee	$75
Tax Status Research Fee	$110

C. Services You Can Shop For	**$3,198**
Pest Inspection Fee	$135
Survey Fee	$65
Title – Insurance Binder	$700
Title – Lender's Title Policy	$535
Title – Settlement Agent Fee	$502
Title – Title Search	$1,261

D. TOTAL LOAN COSTS (A + B + C)	**$5,672**

Other Costs

E. Taxes and Other Government Fees	**$85**
Recording Fees and Other Taxes	$85
Transfer Taxes	

F. Prepaids	**$867**
Homeowner's Insurance Premium (6 months)	$605
Mortgage Insurance Premium (months)	
Prepaid Interest ($17.44 per day for 15 days @ 3.875%)	$262
Property Taxes (months)	

G. Initial Escrow Payment at Closing		**$413**
Homeowner's Insurance $100.83 per month for 2 mo.		$202
Mortgage Insurance per month for mo.		
Property Taxes $105.30 per month for 2 mo.		$211

H. Other	**$1,017**
Title – Owner's Title Policy (optional)	$1,017

I. TOTAL OTHER COSTS (E + F + G + H)	**$2,382**

J. TOTAL CLOSING COSTS	**$8,054**
D + I	$8,054
Lender Credits	

Calculating Cash to Close

Total Closing Costs (J)	$8,054
Closing Costs Financed (Paid from your Loan Amount)	$0
Down Payment/Funds from Borrower	$18,000
Deposit	– $10,000
Funds for Borrower	$0
Seller Credits	$0
Adjustments and Other Credits	$0
Estimated Cash to Close	**$16,054**

TRID LE, p 2

LOAN ESTIMATE

Additional Information About This Loan

LENDER	Ficus Bank	**MORTGAGE BROKER**	
NMLS/__ LICENSE ID		**NMLS/__ LICENSE ID**	
LOAN OFFICER	Joe Smith	**LOAN OFFICER**	
NMLS/__ LICENSE ID	12345	**NMLS/__ LICENSE ID**	
EMAIL	joesmith@ficusbank.com	**EMAIL**	
PHONE	123-456-7890	**PHONE**	

Comparisons
Use these measures to compare this loan with other loans.

In 5 Years	$56,582	Total you will have paid in principal, interest, mortgage insurance, and loan costs.
	$15,773	Principal you will have paid off.
Annual Percentage Rate (APR)	4.274%	Your costs over the loan term expressed as a rate. This is not your interest rate.
Total Interest Percentage (TIP)	69.45%	The total amount of interest that you will pay over the loan term as a percentage of your loan amount.

Other Considerations

Appraisal	We may order an appraisal to determine the property's value and charge you for this appraisal. We will promptly give you a copy of any appraisal, even if your loan does not close. You can pay for an additional appraisal for your own use at your own cost.
Assumption	If you sell or transfer this property to another person, we ☐ will allow, under certain conditions, this person to assume this loan on the original terms. ☒ will not allow assumption of this loan on the original terms.
Homeowner's Insurance	This loan requires homeowner's insurance on the property, which you may obtain from a company of your choice that we find acceptable.
Late Payment	If your payment is more than *15* days late, we will charge a late fee of *5% of the monthly principal and interest payment.*
Refinance	Refinancing this loan will depend on your future financial situation, the property value, and market conditions. You may not be able to refinance this loan.
Servicing	We intend ☐ to service your loan. If so, you will make your payments to us. ☒ to transfer servicing of your loan.

Confirm Receipt

By signing, you are only confirming that you have received this form. You do not have to accept this loan because you have signed or received this form.

_____ _____ _____ _____
Applicant Signature   Date   Co-Applicant Signature   Date

LOAN ESTIMATE

Appendix: TRID Rule Closing Disclosure

TRID Rule Closing Disclosure

Closing Disclosure

This form is a statement of final loan terms and closing costs. Compare this document with your Loan Estimate.

Closing Information
Date Issued	4/15/2013
Closing Date	4/15/2013
Disbursement Date	4/15/2013
Settlement Agent	Epsilon Title Co.
File #	12-3456
Property	456 Somewhere Ave Anytown, ST 12345
Sale Price	$180,000

Transaction Information
Borrower	Michael Jones and Mary Stone 123 Anywhere Street Anytown, ST 12345
Seller	Steve Cole and Amy Doe 321 Somewhere Drive Anytown, ST 12345
Lender	Ficus Bank

Loan Information
Loan Term	30 years
Purpose	Purchase
Product	Fixed Rate
Loan Type	☒ Conventional ☐ FHA ☐ VA ☐ _____
Loan ID #	123456789
MIC #	000654321

Loan Terms

		Can this amount increase after closing?
Loan Amount	$162,000	NO
Interest Rate	3.875%	NO
Monthly Principal & Interest See Projected Payments below for your Estimated Total Monthly Payment	$761.78	NO

		Does the loan have these features?
Prepayment Penalty	YES	• **As high as $3,240** if you pay off the loan during the first 2 years
Balloon Payment	NO	

Projected Payments

Payment Calculation	Years 1-7	Years 8-30
Principal & Interest	$761.78	$761.78
Mortgage Insurance	+ 82.35	+ —
Estimated Escrow Amount can increase over time	+ 206.13	+ 206.13
Estimated Total Monthly Payment	**$1,050.26**	**$967.91**

| Estimated Taxes, Insurance & Assessments
Amount can increase over time
See page 4 for details | $356.13
a month | **This estimate includes**
☒ Property Taxes
☒ Homeowner's Insurance
☒ Other: Homeowner's Association Dues
See Escrow Account on page 4 for details. You must pay for other property costs separately. | **In escrow?**
YES
YES
NO |

Costs at Closing

Closing Costs	$9,712.10	Includes $4,694.05 in Loan Costs + $5,018.05 in Other Costs – $0 in Lender Credits. See page 2 for details.
Cash to Close	$14,147.26	Includes Closing Costs. See Calculating Cash to Close on page 3 for details.

TRID CD, p 1

CLOSING DISCLOSURE PAGE 1 OF 5 • LOAN ID # 123456789

Closing Cost Details

Loan Costs		Borrower-Paid		Seller-Paid		Paid by Others
		At Closing	Before Closing	At Closing	Before Closing	
A. Origination Charges		**$1,802.00**				
01 0.25 % of Loan Amount (Points)		$405.00				
02 Application Fee		$300.00				
03 Underwriting Fee		$1,097.00				
04						
05						
06						
07						
08						
B. Services Borrower Did Not Shop For		**$236.55**				
01 Appraisal Fee	to John Smith Appraisers Inc.					$405.00
02 Credit Report Fee	to Information Inc.		$29.80			
03 Flood Determination Fee	to Info Co.	$20.00				
04 Flood Monitoring Fee	to Info Co.	$31.75				
05 Tax Monitoring Fee	to Info Co.	$75.00				
06 Tax Status Research Fee	to Info Co.	$80.00				
07						
08						
09						
10						
C. Services Borrower Did Shop For		**$2,655.50**				
01 Pest Inspection Fee	to Pests Co.	$120.50				
02 Survey Fee	to Surveys Co.	$85.00				
03 Title – Insurance Binder	to Epsilon Title Co.	$650.00				
04 Title – Lender's Title Insurance	to Epsilon Title Co.	$500.00				
05 Title – Settlement Agent Fee	to Epsilon Title Co.	$500.00				
06 Title – Title Search	to Epsilon Title Co.	$800.00				
07						
08						
D. TOTAL LOAN COSTS (Borrower-Paid)		**$4,694.05**				
Loan Costs Subtotals (A + B + C)		$4,664.25	$29.80			

Other Costs						
E. Taxes and Other Government Fees		**$85.00**				
01 Recording Fees Deed: $40.00 Mortgage: $45.00		$85.00				
02 Transfer Tax	to Any State			$950.00		
F. Prepaids		**$2,120.80**				
01 Homeowner's Insurance Premium (12 mo.) to Insurance Co.		$1,209.96				
02 Mortgage Insurance Premium (mo.)						
03 Prepaid Interest ($17.44 per day from 4/15/13 to 5/1/13)		$279.04				
04 Property Taxes (6 mo.) to Any County USA		$631.80				
05						
G. Initial Escrow Payment at Closing		**$412.25**				
01 Homeowner's Insurance $100.83 per month for 2 mo.		$201.66				
02 Mortgage Insurance per month for mo.						
03 Property Taxes $105.30 per month for 2 mo.		$210.60				
04						
05						
06						
07						
08 Aggregate Adjustment		– 0.01				
H. Other		**$2,400.00**				
01 HOA Capital Contribution	to HOA Acre Inc.	$500.00				
02 HOA Processing Fee	to HOA Acre Inc.	$150.00				
03 Home Inspection Fee	to Engineers Inc.	$750.00			$750.00	
04 Home Warranty Fee	to XYZ Warranty Inc.			$450.00		
05 Real Estate Commission	to Alpha Real Estate Broker			$5,700.00		
06 Real Estate Commission	to Omega Real Estate Broker			$5,700.00		
07 Title – Owner's Title Insurance (optional) to Epsilon Title Co.		$1,000.00				
08						
I. TOTAL OTHER COSTS (Borrower-Paid)		**$5,018.05**				
Other Costs Subtotals (E + F + G + H)		$5,018.05				

J. TOTAL CLOSING COSTS (Borrower-Paid)		**$9,712.10**				
Closing Costs Subtotals (D + I)		$9,682.30	$29.80	$12,800.00	$750.00	$405.00
Lender Credits						

CLOSING DISCLOSURE

Appendix: TRID Rule Closing Disclosure

Calculating Cash to Close

Use this table to see what has changed from your Loan Estimate.

	Loan Estimate	Final	Did this change?	
Total Closing Costs (J)	$8,054.00	$9,712.10	YES	• See **Total Loan Costs (D)** and **Total Other Costs (I)**
Closing Costs Paid Before Closing	$0	− $29.80	YES	• You paid these Closing Costs **before closing**
Closing Costs Financed (Paid from your Loan Amount)	$0	$0	NO	
Down Payment/Funds from Borrower	$18,000.00	$18,000.00	NO	
Deposit	− $10,000.00	− $10,000.00	NO	
Funds for Borrower	$0	$0	NO	
Seller Credits	$0	− $2,500.00	YES	• See Seller Credits in **Section L**
Adjustments and Other Credits	$0	− $1,035.04	YES	• See details in **Sections K and L**
Cash to Close	$16,054.00	$14,147.26		

Summaries of Transactions

Use this table to see a summary of your transaction.

BORROWER'S TRANSACTION

K. Due from Borrower at Closing		**$189,762.30**
01	Sale Price of Property	$180,000.00
02	Sale Price of Any Personal Property Included in Sale	
03	Closing Costs Paid at Closing (J)	$9,682.30
04		
Adjustments		
05		
06		
07		
Adjustments for Items Paid by Seller in Advance		
08	City/Town Taxes to	
09	County Taxes to	
10	Assessments to	
11	HOA Dues 4/15/13 to 4/30/13	$80.00
12		
13		
14		
15		
L. Paid Already by or on Behalf of Borrower at Closing		**$175,615.04**
01	Deposit	$10,000.00
02	Loan Amount	$162,000.00
03	Existing Loan(s) Assumed or Taken Subject to	
04		
05	Seller Credit	$2,500.00
Other Credits		
06	Rebate from Epsilon Title Co.	$750.00
07		
Adjustments		
08		
09		
10		
11		
Adjustments for Items Unpaid by Seller		
12	City/Town Taxes 1/1/13 to 4/14/13	$365.04
13	County Taxes to	
14	Assessments to	
15		
16		
17		

CALCULATION

Total Due from Borrower at Closing (K)	$189,762.30
Total Paid Already by or on Behalf of Borrower at Closing (L)	− $175,615.04
Cash to Close ☒ From ☐ To Borrower	**$14,147.26**

SELLER'S TRANSACTION

M. Due to Seller at Closing		**$180,080.00**
01	Sale Price of Property	$180,000.00
02	Sale Price of Any Personal Property Included in Sale	
03		
04		
05		
06		
07		
08		
Adjustments for Items Paid by Seller in Advance		
09	City/Town Taxes to	
10	County Taxes to	
11	Assessments to	
12	HOA Dues 4/15/13 to 4/30/13	$80.00
13		
14		
15		
16		
N. Due from Seller at Closing		**$115,665.04**
01	Excess Deposit	
02	Closing Costs Paid at Closing (J)	$12,800.00
03	Existing Loan(s) Assumed or Taken Subject to	
04	Payoff of First Mortgage Loan	$100,000.00
05	Payoff of Second Mortgage Loan	
06		
07		
08	Seller Credit	$2,500.00
09		
10		
11		
12		
13		
Adjustments for Items Unpaid by Seller		
14	City/Town Taxes 1/1/13 to 4/14/13	$365.04
15	County Taxes to	
16	Assessments to	
17		
18		
19		

CALCULATION

Total Due to Seller at Closing (M)	$180,080.00
Total Due from Seller at Closing (N)	− $115,665.04
Cash ☐ From ☒ To Seller	**$64,414.96**

CLOSING DISCLOSURE

Additional Information About This Loan

Loan Disclosures

Assumption
If you sell or transfer this property to another person, your lender
- ☐ will allow, under certain conditions, this person to assume this loan on the original terms.
- ☒ will not allow assumption of this loan on the original terms.

Demand Feature
Your loan
- ☐ has a demand feature, which permits your lender to require early repayment of the loan. You should review your note for details.
- ☒ does not have a demand feature.

Late Payment
If your payment is more than *15* days late, your lender will charge a late fee of *5% of the monthly principal and interest payment.*

Negative Amortization (Increase in Loan Amount)
Under your loan terms, you
- ☐ are scheduled to make monthly payments that do not pay all of the interest due that month. As a result, your loan amount will increase (negatively amortize), and your loan amount will likely become larger than your original loan amount. Increases in your loan amount lower the equity you have in this property.
- ☐ may have monthly payments that do not pay all of the interest due that month. If you do, your loan amount will increase (negatively amortize), and, as a result, your loan amount may become larger than your original loan amount. Increases in your loan amount lower the equity you have in this property.
- ☒ do not have a negative amortization feature.

Partial Payments
Your lender
- ☒ may accept payments that are less than the full amount due (partial payments) and apply them to your loan.
- ☐ may hold them in a separate account until you pay the rest of the payment, and then apply the full payment to your loan.
- ☐ does not accept any partial payments.
If this loan is sold, your new lender may have a different policy.

Security Interest
You are granting a security interest in
456 Somewhere Ave., Anytown, ST 12345

You may lose this property if you do not make your payments or satisfy other obligations for this loan.

Escrow Account

For now, your loan
- ☒ will have an escrow account (also called an "impound" or "trust" account) to pay the property costs listed below. Without an escrow account, you would pay them directly, possibly in one or two large payments a year. Your lender may be liable for penalties and interest for failing to make a payment.

Escrow		
Escrowed Property Costs over Year 1	$2,473.56	Estimated total amount over year 1 for your escrowed property costs: *Homeowner's Insurance Property Taxes*
Non-Escrowed Property Costs over Year 1	$1,800.00	Estimated total amount over year 1 for your non-escrowed property costs: *Homeowner's Association Dues* You may have other property costs.
Initial Escrow Payment	$412.25	A cushion for the escrow account you pay at closing. See Section G on page 2.
Monthly Escrow Payment	$206.13	The amount included in your total monthly payment.

- ☐ will not have an escrow account because ☐ you declined it ☐ your lender does not offer one. You must directly pay your property costs, such as taxes and homeowner's insurance. Contact your lender to ask if your loan can have an escrow account.

No Escrow		
Estimated Property Costs over Year 1		Estimated total amount over year 1. You must pay these costs directly, possibly in one or two large payments a year.
Escrow Waiver Fee		

In the future,
Your property costs may change and, as a result, your escrow payment may change. You may be able to cancel your escrow account, but if you do, you must pay your property costs directly. If you fail to pay your property taxes, your state or local government may (1) impose fines and penalties or (2) place a tax lien on this property. If you fail to pay any of your property costs, your lender may (1) add the amounts to your loan balance, (2) add an escrow account to your loan, or (3) require you to pay for property insurance that the lender buys on your behalf, which likely would cost more and provide fewer benefits than what you could buy on your own.

Appendix: TRID Rule Closing Disclosure

Loan Calculations

Total of Payments. Total you will have paid after you make all payments of principal, interest, mortgage insurance, and loan costs, as scheduled.	$285,803.36
Finance Charge. The dollar amount the loan will cost you.	$118,830.27
Amount Financed. The loan amount available after paying your upfront finance charge.	$162,000.00
Annual Percentage Rate (APR). Your costs over the loan term expressed as a rate. This is not your interest rate.	4.174%
Total Interest Percentage (TIP). The total amount of interest that you will pay over the loan term as a percentage of your loan amount.	69.46%

Questions? If you have questions about the loan terms or costs on this form, use the contact information below. To get more information or make a complaint, contact the Consumer Financial Protection Bureau at www.consumerfinance.gov/mortgage-closing

Other Disclosures

Appraisal
If the property was appraised for your loan, your lender is required to give you a copy at no additional cost at least 3 days before closing. If you have not yet received it, please contact your lender at the information listed below.

Contract Details
See your note and security instrument for information about
- what happens if you fail to make your payments,
- what is a default on the loan,
- situations in which your lender can require early repayment of the loan, and
- the rules for making payments before they are due.

Liability after Foreclosure
If your lender forecloses on this property and the foreclosure does not cover the amount of unpaid balance on this loan,
- [X] state law may protect you from liability for the unpaid balance. If you refinance or take on any additional debt on this property, you may lose this protection and have to pay any debt remaining even after foreclosure. You may want to consult a lawyer for more information.
- [ ] state law does not protect you from liability for the unpaid balance.

Refinance
Refinancing this loan will depend on your future financial situation, the property value, and market conditions. You may not be able to refinance this loan.

Tax Deductions
If you borrow more than this property is worth, the interest on the loan amount above this property's fair market value is not deductible from your federal income taxes. You should consult a tax advisor for more information.

Contact Information

	Lender	Mortgage Broker	Real Estate Broker (B)	Real Estate Broker (S)	Settlement Agent
Name	Ficus Bank		Omega Real Estate Broker Inc.	Alpha Real Estate Broker Co.	Epsilon Title Co.
Address	4321 Random Blvd. Somecity, ST 12340		789 Local Lane Sometown, ST 12345	987 Suburb Ct. Someplace, ST 12340	123 Commerce Pl. Somecity, ST 12344
NMLS ID					
ST License ID			Z765416	Z61456	Z61616
Contact	Joe Smith		Samuel Green	Joseph Cain	Sarah Arnold
Contact NMLS ID	12345				
Contact ST License ID			P16415	P51461	PT1234
Email	joesmith@ficusbank.com		sam@omegare.biz	joe@alphare.biz	sarah@epsilontitle.com
Phone	123-456-7890		123-555-1717	321-555-7171	987-555-4321

Confirm Receipt

By signing, you are only confirming that you have received this form. You do not have to accept this loan because you have signed or received this form.

_____ _____   _____ _____
Applicant Signature   Date   Co-Applicant Signature   Date

CLOSING DISCLOSURE

Seller Disclosure Statement

SELLER'S DISCLOSURE STATEMENT

Property Address: _____ _____ Michigan
                               Street   City, Village, or Township

Purpose of Statement: This statement is a disclosure of the condition of the property in compliance with the seller disclosure act. This statement is a disclosure of the condition and information concerning the property, known by the seller. Unless otherwise advised, the seller does not possess any expertise in construction, architecture, engineering, or any other specific area related to the construction or condition of the improvements on the property or the land. Also, unless otherwise advised, the seller has not conducted any inspection of generally inaccessible areas such as the foundation or roof. **This statement is not a warranty of any kind by the seller or by any agent representing the seller in this transaction, and is not a substitute for any inspections or warranties the buyer may wish to obtain.**

Seller's Disclosure: The seller discloses the following information with the knowledge that even though this is not a warranty, the seller specifically makes the following representations based on the seller's knowledge at the signing of this document. Upon receiving this statement from the seller, the seller's agent is required to provide a copy to the buyer or the agent of the buyer. The seller authorizes its agent(s) to provide a copy of this statement to any prospective buyer in connection with any actual or anticipated sale of property. The following are representations made solely by the seller and are not the representations of the seller's agent(s), if any. **THIS INFORMATION IS A DISCLOSURE ONLY AND IS NOT INTENDED TO BE A PART OF ANY CONTRACT BETWEEN BUYER AND SELLER.**

Instructions to the Seller: (1) Answer ALL questions. (2) Report known conditions affecting the property. (3) Attach additional pages with your signature if additional space is required. (4) Complete this form yourself. (5) If some items do not apply to your property, check NOT AVAILABLE. If you do not know the facts, check UNKNOWN. **FAILURE TO PROVIDE A PURCHASER WITH A SIGNED DISCLOSURE STATEMENT WILL ENABLE A PURCHASER TO TERMINATE AN OTHERWISE BINDING PURCHASE AGREEMENT.**

Appliances/Systems/Services: The items below are in working order (the items below are included in the sale of the property only if the purchase agreement so provides):

	Yes	No	Unknown	Not Available		Yes	No	Unknown	Not Available
Range/Oven					Water heater				
Dishwasher					Plumbing system				
Refrigerator					Water softener/conditioner				
Hood/fan									
Disposal					Well & pump				
TV antenna, TV rotor & controls					Septic tank & drain field				
Electrical system					Sump pump				
Garage door opener & remote control					City Water System				
					City Sewer System				
Alarm system					Central air conditioning				
Intercom									
Central vacuum					Central heating system				
Attic fan									
Pool heater, wall liner & equipment					Wall furnace				
					Humidifier				
Microwave					Electronic air filter				
Trash compactor					Solar heating system				
Ceiling fan									
Sauna/hot tub					Fireplace & chimney				
Washer									
Dryer					Wood burning system				
Lawn sprinkler system									

Explanations (attach additional sheets if necessary): _____
_____

UNLESS OTHERWISE AGREED, ALL HOUSEHOLD APPLIANCES ARE SOLD IN WORKING ORDER EXCEPT AS NOTED, WITHOUT WARRANTY BEYOND DATE OF CLOSING.

Appendix: Seller Disclosure Statement

Property conditions, improvements & additional information:
1. **Basement/crawl space**: Has there been evidence of water? . . . . yes____ no____
   If yes, please explain: _____
2. **Insulation**: Describe, if known_____
   Urea Formaldehyde Foam Insulation (UFFI) is installed? . . . . unknown____ yes____ no____
3. **Roof**: Leaks? . . . . yes____ no____
   Approximate age if known _____
4. **Well**: Type of well (depth/diameter, age, and repair history, if known): _____
   Has the water been tested? yes____ no____
   If yes, date of last report/results: _____
5. **Septic tanks/drain fields**: Condition, if known: _____
6. **Heating System**: Type/approximate age: _____
7. Plumbing system: Type: copper____ galvanized____ other____
   Any known problems? _____
8. **Electrical system**: Any known problems?_____
9. **History of infestation, if any**: (termites, carpenter ants, etc.)_____
10. **Environmental Problems**: Are you aware of any substances, materials, or products that may be an environmental hazard such as, but not limited to, asbestos, radon gas, formaldehyde, lead-based paint, fuel or chemical storage tanks and contaminated soil on the property. . . . . unknown____ yes____ no____
    If yes, please explain: _____
11. **Flood insurance**: Do you have flood insurance on the property? . . . . unknown____ yes____ no____
12. **Mineral rights**: Do you own the mineral rights? . . . . unknown____ yes____ no____

Other Items: Are you aware of any of the following:
1. Features of the property shared in common with the adjoining landowners, such as walls, fences, roads and driveways, or other features whose use or responsibility for maintenance may have an effect on the property? . . . . unknown____ yes____ no____
2. Any encroachments, easements, zoning violations, or nonconforming uses? . . . . unknown____ yes____ no____
3. Any "common areas" (facilities like pools, tennis courts, walkways, or other areas co-owned with others), or a homeowners' association that has any authority over the property? . . . . unknown____ yes____ no____
4. Structural modifications, alterations, or repairs made without necessary permits or licensed contractors? . . . . unknown____ yes____ no____
5. Settling, flooding, drainage, structural, or grading problems? . . . . unknown____ yes____ no____
6. Major damage to the property from fire, wind, floods, or landslides? . . . . unknown____ yes____ no____
7. Any underground storage tanks? . . . . unknown____ yes____ no____
8. Farm or farm operation in the vicinity; or proximity to a landfill, airport, shooting range, etc.? . . . . unknown____ yes____ no____
9. Any outstanding utility assessments or fees, including any natural gas main extension surcharge? . . . . unknown____ yes____ no____
10. Any outstanding municipal assessments or fees? . . . . unknown____ yes____ no____
11. Any pending litigation that could affect the property or the seller's right to convey the property? . . . . unknown____ yes____ no____

If the answer to any of these questions is yes, please explain.
Attach additional sheets, if necessary: _____

The seller has lived in the residence on the property from _____ (date) to _____ (date).
The seller has owned the property since _____ (date).

The seller has indicated above the condition of all the items based on information known to the seller. If any changes occur in the structural/mechanical/appliance systems of this property from the date of this form to the date of closing, seller will immediately disclose the changes to buyer. In no event shall the parties hold the broker liable for any representations not directly made by the broker or broker's agent.

Seller certifies that the information in this statement is true and correct to the best of seller's knowledge as of the date of seller's signature.

BUYER SHOULD OBTAIN PROFESSIONAL ADVICE AND INSPECTIONS OF THE PROPERTY TO MORE FULLY DETERMINE THE CONDITION OF THE PROPERTY. THESE INSPECTIONS SHOULD TAKE INDOOR AIR AND WATER QUALITY INTO ACCOUNT, AS WELL AS ANY EVIDENCE OF UNUSUALLY HIGH LEVELS OF POTENTIAL ALLERGENS INCLUDING, BUT NOT LIMITED TO, HOUSEHOLD MOLD, MILDEW AND BACTERIA.

BUYERS ARE ADVISED THAT CERTAIN INFORMATION COMPILED PURSUANT TO THE SEX OFFENDERS REGISTRATION ACT, 1994 PA 295, MCL 28.721 TO 28.732, IS AVAILABLE TO THE PUBLIC. BUYERS SEEKING THAT INFORMATION SHOULD CONTACT THE APPROPRIATE LOCAL LAW ENFORCEMENT AGENCY OR SHERIFF'S DEPARTMENT DIRECTLY.

BUYER IS ADVISED THAT THE STATE EQUALIZED VALUE OF THE PROPERTY, PRINCIPAL RESIDENCE EXEMPTION INFORMATION, AND OTHER REAL PROPERTY TAX INFORMATION IS AVAILABLE FROM THE APPROPRIATE LOCAL ASSESSOR'S OFFICE. **BUYER SHOULD NOT ASSUME THAT BUYER'S FUTURE TAX BILLS ON THE PROPERTY WILL BE THE SAME AS THE SELLER'S PRESENT TAX BILLS. UNDER MICHIGAN LAW, REAL PROPERTY TAX OBLIGATIONS CAN CHANGE SIGNIFICANTLY WHEN PROPERTY IS TRANSFERRED.**

Seller _____ Date _____

Seller _____ Date _____

Buyer has read and acknowledges receipt of this statement.

Buyer _____ Date _____ Time: _____

Buyer _____ Date _____ Time: _____

Seller's Disclosure Form, p 3

Seller Disclosure Statement

Michigan
Real Estate Law & Practice

A Complete Guide for Exam Prep, Practitioners, and Consumers

Index

Respect the creative power of your mind. Every thought you hold in the present has already shaped your future.

Index

Symbols

100-year floodplain. *See* Floodplain

A

Abandonment 204
Ability-to-Repay 299
Abstract of title 119
Acceleration clause 244
Acceleration of debt, mortgage 244
Acceptance, of contract 174
Accession 92, 201
Accommodations. *See* Reasonable accommodation
Accounting 28
Accretion 9
Acknowledgment 89
Actual notice. *See* Notice
Addenda 172
Adjustable rate mortgage 275
  Hybrid ARM 276
Adjusted basis 232
Administrative law 16
Administrative rules 367
  Defined 332
Administrator 93
Adult only housing 309, 317, 324
Ad valorem 224
Advance, payment in 136, 246
Adverse possession 91
Affiliated Business Arrangement Disclosure 138
Affiliated licensee 59, 361
  Statutory definition 361
Affirmative marketing 313
Agency
  Actual 25
  By estoppel 25
  Designated 59, 361
  Dual 24, 58, 362
  Express 25
  Implied 25
  Non-designated 59
  Single 23, 58
  Termination 56
Agent
  General agent 22
  Ostensible agent 26
  Special agent 23
  Subagent 24, 25
  Universal agent 22
Air rights. *See* Land
Alienation clause 244
Allodial system 97
Alt-A loan 273
ALTA Owner's Policy. *See* Title insurance
Amendment, of contract 173
American Dream Down-payment Initiative Act 285
Americans with Disabilities Act of 1990 (ADA) 319
Amortization 247
Amortized loan 274
Annual Percentage Rate (APR) 297
Antitrust 50. *See also* Michigan Antitrust Reform Act
Appraisal 70
  For FHA loan 282
  For VA loan 285
Appraisal Institute 71
Appraisal Management Company 70
Appraiser 70
  Certified General Real Estate 71
  Certified Residential Real Estate 71
  Limited Real Estate 71
  State Licensed Real Estate 71
Appreciation 219
APR. *See* Annual Percentage Rate (APR)
Arbitration 189
Area calculations, math 414
Arms length 69
Arrears, payment in 136, 246
Article 1 334
Article 2 336
Article 3 337
Article 4 338
Article 5 340
Article 6 343
Article 25 344
Asbestos 166
As Is clause 180
Assessed value 224
Assignment
  Of contract 184
  Of deed 84
  Of Lease 198
  Of mortgage 248
Assistance animal 198, 316. *See also* Service animal
Associate broker. *See* Broker
Assumption
  Of FHA loan 284
  Of mortgage 137, 244, 249, 297
  Of VA loan 286
Attachment 104
Attestation 89
Attorney General 72
Attorney-in-fact 22
Attorney review clause 183
Authority 21, 34
Avulsion 9

B

Bailment 101
Balloon payment 274, 299
Bank-owned property 56
Bankruptcy 57, 262
Bankruptcy Abuse Prevention and Consumer Protection Act 263
Bargain and sale deed. *See* Deed
Basis 232
Bench mark 146
Beneficiary 252
Bilateral contract. *See* Contract
Bill of sale 134
Blanket loan 278
Blockbusting 311, 316
Blue-sky laws 221
Board of review 224
Bottomland 8
Bottom lining, contract 175
Boycott 52, 398
BPO. *See* Broker's price opinion
Breach. *See also* Default
  Of contract 186
  Of lease 200, 204
Bridge loan 279
Broker
  Administration of firm 34, 41
  Associate, statutory definition 354
  Buyer's 47, 69, 361
  Full service 51
  Limited service 51
  Principal, statutory definition 354
  Seller's 362

Statutory definition 346
Supervisory 362

Broker's price opinion 76, 261

Brownfield 163

Budget mortgage 275

Builder 157, 286, 348, 382, 383

Building code 157

Building manager 212

Building permit 157

Bundle of rights 83. *See also* Ownership

Buydown 276

Buyer
Statutory definition 361

Buyer beware. *See* Caveat emptor

Buyer's broker. *See* Broker

Bylaws 113, 383

C

Calculator use, math 408

Can-Spam Act 40

Capacity. *See* Legal capacity

Capital gains. *See* Tax

Capitalization 79

Capitalization rate 79

Capital loss 232

Capped value. *See* Taxable value

Carryover provision 53

Caveat emptor 31, 180

CC&R 86

Certificate of eligibility 285

Certificate of no defense 245

Certificate of Reasonable Value 285

Certificate of reduction of mortgage 249

Certificate of use and occupancy 157

CFPB. *See* Consumer Financial Protection Bureau (CFPB)

Chain of title. *See* Title

Chattel mortgage 279

City certification requirements 133

Civil rights 307
Commission 324
History 313

Civil Rights Act of 1866 315, 319

Cleaning fees, lease 197

Clean Water Act 159

Client 23

Closed-end loan 277

Closed loan 276

Closing. *See* Settlement

Closing Disclosure 127, 129, 140

Closing statement. *See* Settlement

Cloud on the title 103

CLTV 283

Cluster zoning 156

CMA. *See* Comparative Market Analysis

Coastal regulation. *See* Shorelands Protection and Management Act

Code of Ethics 16

Collateral 241

Color 308

Commercial banks 290

Commercial Real Estate Broker's Lien Act 104

Commission 51
Contingent fee 49
Enforcement of 50
Flat rate fee 50
Non-contingent fee 50
Percentage fee 49
Programs 33
Variable rate 50

Common elements 113

Common interest ownership. *See* Ownership

Common law 16

Communication 174, 175

Community bank 290

Community property 109

Community Reinvestment Act. *See* Redlining

Comparable property 75

Comparative Market Analysis 71, 76

Compensation 49

Competitive market analysis 76

Compound interest. *See* Interest

Computer Loan Origination (CLO) 140

Concessions 284. *See also* Rent concession
Financing 287
Sales 279, 287

Condemnation 154
Inverse 154

Conditional release 57

Conditional rescission 228

Conditions, in contract. *See* Contract

Condominium 112
Application of securities law 222
Association 384
Conversion 384
Leasing of 384
Site 112, 161

Condominium Act 382

Confidentiality 28

Conformity 73

Conservatorship 93

Consideration 176
Good 85
Valuable 85

Construction loan 278

Construction types 13

Constructive notice. *See* Notice

Consumer Financial Protection Bureau (CFPB) 296

Continuing education 27, 42, 339

Contract 171
Bilateral 47, 173
Condition concurrent 183
Condition precedent 182
Condition subsequent 183
Unilateral 47, 55, 173

Controlled substance, use of 163, 198, 206

Conventional mortgage 270, 272

Cooperative 111
Application of securities law 222

Copyright 39

Corporations 110

Cost 70

Cost approach 76

Cost (price) per square foot 77

Counteroffer 175

County transfer tax. *See* Transfer tax

Courteous disregard 313

Credit 133

Credit report 273. *See also* Hard inquiries; *See also* Soft inquiries

Credit score 273
FICO 273

Credit unions 290

Crime, property 29, 41

Cul-de-sac 147

Curable 78

Customer 23

Cybersquatting 39

Index

D

Damages 186
Death
    Effect on contract 186
    Effect on lease 206
Debit 133
Debt-to-income ratios 292
Decedent 92
Declaration of Covenants, Conditions and Restrictions 86. *See also* Homeowners Association (HOA)
Deed 84
    Bargain and sale 90
    Covenants of title 89
    Lady Bird 91, 93
    Quitclaim 91
    restrictions 86
    Special warranty 90
    Validity 84
Deed in escrow. *See* Deed in trust
Deed in lieu of foreclosure 260
Deed in trust 253
Deed of trust 134, 251
Default
    In deed of trust 252
    In land contract 253
    In note (mortgage) 248
    Strategic 260
Defeasance clause 242
Defects
    Latent 31
    Material 32
    Patent 31
    Property 31
Delegation 185
Demand for possession 205
Demise 195
Demographic data 311
Department of Environment, Great Lakes, and Energy 158
Department of Licensing and Regulatory Affairs 331
Department of Natural Resources 158
Department of Veteran Affairs. *See* Veteran's Administration
Deposits
    Resolving competing claims 188
Depreciation 77
    IRS 231
Dereliction 9
Descent 93
Designated agency. *See* Agency

Destruction of subject matter 57
Development 160, 379, 382
Devise 93
Devisee 93
Devisor 93
Direct Endorsement 282
Disability 309, 316, 319
Discharge 57, 185
Disclosure
    Agency 58, 360, 443
    Dual agency 60
    Lead-paint 164
    Material facts 28
    Property defects 31
    Radon 165
    Seller, property condition 32, 180, 382, 456
Discount points. *See* Points
Disparate impact doctrine 313
Divorce, effect of 91, 109, 385
DNR. *See* Department of Natural Resources
Document preparation fees 52
Dodd Frank Act 161, 274, 298
Domestic violence, duty to pay rent 207
Dominant estate 99
Do-not-call 35
Down payment 271, 288
Down payment assistance programs 285
Draws 278
Dual agency. *See* Agency
Due diligence 180
Due-on-sale clause 244
Due process 189
Duress 180
DUST 72
Duties 31
    Agent owes third party 31
    Fiduciary 26
    Principal owes agent 31

E

Earnest money deposit 48, 187
Easement 99
    Appurtenant 99
    By implication 100
    By prescription 100
    In gross 100
    Of necessity 100

Economic cycles 73
Economic obsolescence 78
EGLE. *See* Department of Environment, Great Lakes, and Energy
EIFS 166
Electronic Communications Privacy Act 39
Electronic signature 171
Electronic transaction 171
Elliott-Larsen Civil Rights Act 322
    Exemptions 323
E-mail 39
Emblement 101
EMD. *See* Earnest money deposit
Eminent domain 92, 99, 153
Employee 32
Encroachment 101
Encumbrance 99, 121
End loan 278
Environmental cleanup 162
Environmental impact statement 162
Environmental Protection Agency 159
Environmental regulation 162
    restrictions on sale 163
    Site assessment 162
EPA. *See* Environmental Protection Agency
Equal Credit Opportunity Act (ECOA) 298
Equal Housing Opportunity Logo 312
Equitable conversion 183, 252
Equitable redemption. *See* Redemption
Equitable title 252
Equity 220
Erosion 9
Escheat 92
Escrow 87, 130, 133, 134
Escrow closing 130
Estate 97
Estate at sufferance 202
Estate at will 201
Estate for years 201
Estate from period-to-period 202
Estoppel certificate 134, 245
Eviction 204
    Actual 205
    Constructive 205
    Retaliatory 205
Excluded party listing 54

Exclusive listing 54
Exclusive right to sell listing 54
Executed agreement 182
Executor 93
Executory agreement 181
Expiration 57
Expired. *See* Listing agreement
External obsolescence. *See* Economic obsolescence

F

Facsimile 37
Fair Credit Reporting Act 215
Fair housing 307
   Advertising 312
   HUD logo. *See* Equal Housing Opportunity Logo
   Testing 312
Fair Housing Act of 1968 315
   Exemptions 316
Familial status 309
Fannie Mae 270, 294
Federal Housing Administration
   assumption of 249
   Loan 281
Federal National Mortgage Association. *See* Fannie Mae
Federal Reserve System 288
Federal Securities Act of 1933 221
Fee simple 97
   Absolute 97
   Defeasible 97
FEMA 236
Feudal system 97
FHA. *See* Federal Housing Administration
FHA Energy Efficient Mortgages 284
FHLMC. *See* Freddie Mac
FICO. *See* Credit score
Fidelity 27
Fiduciary. *See* Duties
Financial Institutions Reform, Recovery and Enforcement Act 71
Financing
   Private (seller/owner) financing 271
Financing concession. *See* Concessions
Financing contingency 183
Fire safety 157

FIRREA. *See* Financial Institutions Reform, Recovery and Enforcement Act
Fixed rate mortgage 275
Fixture 9
Flipping. *See* Property flipping
Flood insurance 235
Floodplain 161, 236, 380
Floodway. *See* Floodplain
FNMA. *See* Fannie Mae
Forbearance, of loan 259
Force-placed insurance 243
Foreclosure 92, 103, 206, 385
   Advertisement (non-judicial) 256
   Deficiency and surplus 249, 256
   Judicial 256
   Land contract 253
   Mortgage (note) 255
   Strict 255
Foreign Investment in Real Property Tax Act 233
Forfeiture
   Land contract 254
   Lease 204
Form HUD-1. *See* Settlement
For Sale By Owner 36
Fractional ownership. *See* Ownership
Fraud 32, 70, 166, 192, 221, 287, 344, 385. *See also* Misrepresentation
   Silent 180
Freddie Mac 270, 295
Freehold 97, 99
FSBO. *See* For Sale By Owner
Fully amortized loan 274. *See also* Amortized loan
Funding fee 286

G

General agent. *See* Agent
Ginnie Mae 295
GNMA. *See* Ginnie Mae
Good consideration. *See* Consideration
Good faith estimate, RESPA 138
Government National Mortgage Association. *See* Ginnie Mae
Government Sponsored Enterprise (GSE) 294
Grace period 248
Graduated lease 203
Graduated payment mortgage 277

Grantee 85, 87, 89
Grantor 87
Grantor-Grantee index 119
Greenfield 163
GRM. *See* Gross rent multiplier
Gross Income Multiplier (GIM) 79
Gross living area 80
Gross Rent Multiplier (GRM) 79
Ground lease 203
Group boycott. *See* Boycott
Growing equity mortgage 277
Guardianship 93

H

Habendum clause 89
Handicap. *See* Disability
Hard inquiries 216
Hardship, short sale 260
Heterogeneity 11
Highest and best use 73
High water mark 8
Historic preservation 160
Holdover 201
Home Affordable Modification Program. *See* HAMP
Home Affordable Refinance Program. *See* HARP
Home Equity Conversion Mortgage 284
Home equity line of credit (HELOC) 280. *See also* Home equity loan
Home equity loan 280. *See also* Home equity line of credit (HELOC)
Home inspection contingency 183
HOME Investment Partnerships Program 285
Homeowners Association (HOA) 86
Home Ownership and Equity Protections Act (HOEPA) 298
Homeowner's policy. *See* Insurance
Homeowner's warranty policy. *See* Insurance
Homestead Property Tax Credit 229
Homestead tax rate 227
Homogeneous 11
Honesty 31
Housing bubble 74
Housing cooperative. *See* Cooperative
Housing crises of the 2000s 74

Index

HUD-1 Settlement Statement. *See* Settlement
HUD logo. *See* Equal Housing Opportunity Logo

I

Immobility 11
Impairment, ADA 309, 319
Implied agency. *See* Agency
Implied/Inquiry notice. *See* Notice
Improvement 9, 73
Improvements (lease) 200
Imputed knowledge 59
Income capitalization approach 79
Income property
    Tax benefits of 230
Incorporation by reference clause 34, 243
Incurable 78
Independent contractor 32
    Statutory definition 345
Indestructibility 11
Index lease 203
Injunction 189
Innocent purchaser defense 162
Inspection
    Home (property) 132, 183, 282
    Resale 158
    Termite/Pest 133
Insurance 30, 114, 235
    Broker liability 30, 42
    Commercial property 236
    Errors and omissions 61
    General liability 236
    Home-based business 237
    Homeowner's policy 235
    Homeowner's warranty policy 235
    National flood insurance program 235
    Renter's 236
    Umbrella policy 236
    Worker's compensation 236
Insurance company, as lender 291
Integration clause 182
Interest
    Compound 246
    Defined 246
    Index and margin 275
    Rate caps 276
    Simple 246
Internet 38, 55
Interpleader 188
Interstate Land Sales Full Disclosure Act 161
Inventory checklists 391
Inverse condemnation. *See* Condemnation
Investment
    Return "of" 219
    Return "on" 219
Irrevocable offer 176
IRS Form 1099-S, transaction reporting 233
IRS Form 8300, cash reporting 53
IRS Forms 8288/8288A, FIRPTA 235
IRS Restructuring and Reform Act of 1998 233

J

Joint tenancy 108
Jones v. Mayer 314
Judicial foreclosure. *See* Foreclosure
Jumbo loan 278, 290
Junior lien. *See* Lien
Junior mortgages 280
Junk Fax Prevention Act 37
Just compensation 154

K

Kickback 139
Know Before You Owe 127

L

Laches 178
Lady Bird deed. *See* Deed
Land 7
    Air rights 7
    Mineral rights 7
    Physical characteristics 11
    Surface rights 7
    Water-related property rights 8
Land contract 99, 133, 184, 226, 252, 299
    servicing 290
    Technical requirements 252
Land contract mortgage 279
Land Division Act 379
Landlord And Tenant Relationships Act 390
Land patent 117
LARA. *See* Department of Licensing and Regulatory Affairs
Latent defect. *See* Defects
Law defined 16
Lead-based paint abatement 165
Lead-free 165
Lead-paint disclosure. *See* Disclosure
Lead-safe 165
Lead Safe Housing Registry 165
Lease 195
    Essentials 197
Leasehold 99
Lease-option 199
Legal capacity 48, 84, 178
    Loss of 57
Legal counsel, need to consult 188, 223, 316, 347
Legal description 145
Lender requirements 291
Let the buyer beware. *See* Caveat emptor
Leverage 220
Levy date 135. *See also* Tax day
License, as property right 101
License law
    Defined 332
Lien 101
    Condominium association 384
    Construction 102
    General 102
    Judgment 102
    Junior 101
    Priority 102
    Property tax 103
    Senior 101
    Specific 102
    Types 102
Lienee 102
Lienor 101
Lien theory 242
Life estate 98
    Pur autre vie 98
Like-kind exchange. *See* Section 1031 like-kind exchange
Limited common elements 113
Limited Liability Company (LLC) 111
Liquidity 221
Lis pendens 103
Listing agreement 47
    Expired 36
    Term 53
    Types of 53
List scrubbing. *See* Do-not-call

Littoral land 8
Loan
    Application procedures 291
    Modification 259
    Non-conforming 269, 290
    Origination 291
    Processing 292
    Servicing 294
    Underwriting 292
Loan Estimate 128, 138
Loan-to-value ratio 271
    FHA loan 282
Long-term capital gains 232
Lot and block 148, 149
Loyalty 27

M

MAI 71
Maintenance fee 113
Manager 34
Manufactured housing 11
Marked-up title policy. *See* Title insurance
Marketable Title Act, 40-year 118
Market cycles. *See* Economic cycles
Market data approach 75
Market value 69
Master deed 113, 383
Master listing 23, 56
Master plan 153
Material defect. *See* Defects
Material facts 28
Mathematics 407
    Land measuring standards and devices 416
    Working with Area, Volume, and Feet-to-Yard conversions 412
    Working with percentages 408
    Working with prorations 415
Maturity date 248
Measuring square footage 79
Mediation 189
Meeting of the minds 175
Megan's Law 362
Menace 180
Mental incompetence 178
Merger 186, 204
Merger clause 182
Metes and bounds 146
Meth lab, as property defect 163

Michigan Antitrust Reform Act 398
Michigan Civil Rights Department 324
Michigan Environmental Protection Act 400. *See also* NREPA
Michigan State Housing Development Authority 281, 396. *See also* State Housing Development Authority Act
Michigan Uniform Securities Act 221
Mineral rights. *See* Land
Minor 178
Misrepresentation 179, 370
    Innocent 179
    Intentional (fraud) 179
Mistake 185
Mitigate damages 159, 204, 393
MLOLA. *See* Mortgage Loan Originator Licensing Act
Mobile home. *See* Manufactured housing
Modification 186
Modular home 12
Mold 165
Monument 146
Monuments property description 147
Mortgage 134, 137
    Defined 241
    Technical aspects 242
Mortgage Assistance Relief Services (MARS) Rule 250
Mortgage-backed securities 270
Mortgage banking company 289
Mortgage broker 289
Mortgagee 242
Mortgage Electronic Registration System (MERS) 250
Mortgagee's policy. *See* Title insurance
Mortgage fraud 300
Mortgage insurance premium (MIP) 283
Mortgage Loan Originator Licensing Act 291
Mortgage securitization 294
Mortgage servicing 138, 294
Mortgagor 242
MSHDA. *See* Michigan State Housing Development Authority
Multiple Listing Service 55, 56

Municipal certification requirements. *See* City certification requirements
Municipal code 153
Mutual assent 175
Mutual consent 56
Mutual release 186, 188
Mutual savings banks 291

N

National Association of Real Estate Brokers 16
National Association of REALTORS 16, 307, 346
National flood insurance program. *See* Insurance
National origin 308
Navigable waters 159
Negative amortization 275
Negotiable instrument 245
Neighborhood Enterprise Zone (NEZ) 229
Net lease 202
Net listing 55
Net operating income 79
NOI. *See* Net operating income
Nonassignment clause, lease 198
Nonconforming use 155
Non-designated agency. *See* Agency
Non-homestead tax rate 227
Nonjudicial foreclosure. *See* Foreclosure
Nonrecourse debt 242
Note 134, 245
Notice 118
    Actual 118
    Constructive 118
    Implied/Inquiry 118
Notice to quit 205
    7 day 206
    24 hour 206
    30 day 205
Novation 249
NREPA 159. *See also* Michigan Environmental Protection Act

O

Obedience 27
Obligee 245
Obligor 245
Obsolescence 78

Index

Occupational Code 334
Offer 173
Offeree 172
Offeror 172
One-party listing 54
Open-end loan 280
Open house 29
Open listing 54
Open loan 276
Operation of law 177
Opinion of title 119
Option contract 177
Option to purchase 199
Ordinances 153
Origination. *See* Loan: Origination
Origination fee (loan) 283, 286
Ownership
　By a trust 110
　By business entities 110
　By natural persons 107
　Common interest 111
　Defined 83
　Fractional 114
　In severalty 107
Owner's policy. *See* Title insurance

P

Package mortgage 278
Panelized (prefabricated) home 12
Parcel identification number.
　See Sidwell number
Parol evidence rule 182
Partially amortized loan 274. *See also* Amortized loan
Partial release clause 278
Participation mortgages 281
Partnerships 110
Party wall 100
Patent. *See* Land patent
Patent defect. *See* Defects
Pattern or practice 318
Payoff letter (mortgage). *See* Certificate of reduction of mortgage
Percentage lease 202
Percolation test 157
Performance 185
Periodic tenancy. *See* Estate from period-to-period
Permissive waste. *See* Waste

Per se 51
Personal assistant 60
Personal property 10
Personal representative 93
Persons With Disabilities Civil Rights Act 324
　Exemptions 326
Pest inspection. *See* Inspection
Pet fees, lease 198
Physical characteristics of land.
　See Land
Physical deterioration 77
PITI/PITIA. *See* Budget mortgage
Planned unit development (PUD) 157
Planning 153
　Commission 153
Plat/Plat map 148, 161
Pledge 241
PMI. *See* Private mortgage insurance
Point of beginning 146
Points 247, 286
　determination of 248
　Discount 248, 284
Police power 153
Policies and procedures manual 34, 58, 62, 310
Pop-up tax. *See* Taxable value
Portfolio loan 278
Poverty exemption 229
Power of sale clause 257
Practice of law. *See* Unauthorized practice of law
PRE. *See* Principal Residence Exemption
Pre-approved buyer 293
Predatory loan 270
Preliminary reservation agreement, condominium 383
Prepayment of loan 276
Prepayment penalty 276
Pre-printed forms, use of 172
Pre-qualified buyer 293
Price 70
Price fixing 51, 398
Primary mortgage market 289
Principal 22
　Defined 246
Principal (associate) broker. *See* Broker
Principal Residence Exemption 226

Prior appropriation 8
Private mortgage insurance 134, 271
Private road 381
Probate 92, 93
Processing. *See* Loan: Processing
Procuring cause 56
Profit, as land right 101
Progression 73
Property. *See* Land
Property condition disclosure.
　See Disclosure
Property description methods 146
Property flipping 284
Property inspection. *See* Inspection
Property management 211
　Statutory definition 346, 357
Property manager 211, 346
Property pins 146
Property Transfer Affidavit 226
Proposal A 225, 226
Proprietary lease 111
Proration 135, 415. *See also* Mathematics: Working with prorations
Protected classes
　Federal law 308
　Generally 308
　Michigan law 310
Public accommodations 321
Puffing 32
Pur autre vie. *See* Life estate
Purchase agreement 135, 172
Purchase money mortgage 270

Q

QM. *See* Qualified Mortgage
Qualified Mortgage 275, 299
Qualified Written Request (QWR) 141
Quiet enjoyment 195
Quitclaim deed. *See* Deed

R

Race 308
Racially restrictive covenant 314
Radon 165
　mitigation 165
Range lines 147
Ratifying a contract 179
Ready, willing, and able 69

Real estate broker. *See* Broker
Real estate defined 7. *See also* Land
Real Estate Investment Trust (REIT) 223
Real estate salesperson. *See* Salesperson
Real Estate Settlement Procedures Act. *See* RESPA
Reality of consent 179
Realtist 16
REALTOR 16
Reappraisal lease 203
Reasonable accommodation 320, 321, 325, 384
Reasonable care and skill 26
Recapture clause 202
Receiver 258, 348
Reconciliation 79
Recording 118
Recourse debt 242
Recruiting 42
Rectangular Survey System. *See* U.S. Government survey system
Redemption
    Equitable 257
    Land contract 254
    Mortgage, generally 257
    Statutory 258
    Tax sale 229
Redlining 312
Reduction (of mortgage) certificate. *See* Certificate of reduction of mortgage
Referral fee 138, 355
Refinance 220, 259
Reformation 185
Register of deeds 117
Regression 73
Regulated Occupation Support Enforcement Act 402
Regulation B. *See* Equal Credit Opportunity Act
Regulation X. *See* RESPA
Regulation Z. *See* Truth-in-Lending
REIT. *See* Real Estate Investment Trust (REIT)
Rejection 177
Religion 308
Remainder interest 98
Renaissance Zone 230
Renegotiable rate mortgage 277

Rent 195, 197
Rent concession 214
REO 53, 56
Replacement cost 77
Reproduction cost 77
Rescission 185
Resignation 57
RESPA 52, 127, 128, 130, 137, 252, 291, 297, 298, 300
Retaliatory eviction. *See* Eviction
Reverse mortgage 278
Reversion interest 98
Reversion, lease 195
Revocation 176
Right of first refusal 199
Right of survivorship 109
Right to Farm Act 389
Right to renew 199
Riparian land 8
Rules. *See* Administrative Rules
Run with the land 99
Rural Housing and Economic Development (RHED) 295

S

SAFE Act 291
Safe harbor 36, 300
Safety, personal 41
Sale and leaseback 279
Sales concession. *See* Concessions
Salesperson
    Role of 33
    Statutory definition 347
Sales training 42
Sand Dudes Protection and Management Act 401
Satisfaction of mortgage 245
Savings and loan associations 291
Schedule A. *See* Title insurance
Schedule B. *See* Title insurance
Scrivener 172
Search engine optimization (SEO) 38
Seasonal rentals 346
Secondary mortgage market 294
Section 8 Housing 203
Section 203(b) loan 284
Section 203(k) loan 284
Section 234(c) loan 284

Section 245 loan 284
Section 251 loan 284
Section 1031 like-kind exchange 231
Section, as part of township 148
Securities law 112, 221
Securitized TIC 222
Security 241
Security deposit, lease 197
Self-help 206
Seller
    Statutory definition 362
Seller concessions. *See* Concessions
Seller Disclosure Act 385
Seller Disclosure Statement. *See* Disclosure
Seller financing 252, 279, 292, 299
Seller's broker. *See* Broker
Senior housing. *See* Adult only housing
Senior lien. *See* Lien
Septic system. *See* Sewage disposal permit
Service animal 198, 316. *See also* Assistance animal
Service provision agreement 21
Services 29
Services owed client 29
Servicing. *See* Loan: Servicing
Servient estate 100
Setback requirement 155
Settlement 294
    Closing statement 130
    Documents 133
    Form HUD-1 129, 130, 134, 137, 138, 140, 301, 445
Severalty. *See* Ownership
Sewage disposal permit 157
Sex, as a protected class 308
Sex Offenders Registration 362, 388
Sexual harassment 309
Sexual orientation, as a protected class 310
Shared appreciation mortgage 281
Shared listing 55
Shelley v. Kraemer 314
Sheriff's sale 257
Shorelands Protection and Management Act 401
Short sale 75, 206, 260
Short-term capital gains 232

Index

Sidwell number 149
Simple interest. *See* Interest
Single agency. *See* Agency
Site condominium. *See* Condominium
Situs 73
Slander of title 103
Social media 38
Soft inquiries 216
Soil Erosion and Sedimentation Control Act 401
Spam 40
Special agent. *See* Agent
Special assessment 228
Special use permit 156
Special warranty deed. *See* Deed
Specific performance 189
Split closings 130
Square footage, measuring 79
State Equalized Value (SEV) 224
State Housing Development Authority Act 396
State transfer tax. *See* Transfer tax
Statute 16
Statute of frauds 178, 181, 252
Statute of limitations 178, 260
Statutory cash investment 283
Statutory redemption. *See* Redemption
Steering 311
Stigmatized property 32, 164, 362
Straight-line depreciation 231
Street address 146
Strict foreclosure. *See* Foreclosure
Subagent. *See* Agent
Subdivision 160, 380
Subject to mortgage, sale 249
Sublease. *See* Sublet
Sublet 198
Subordination 103
Subordination agreement 280
Subprime
 Loan 269
  Mortgage crises 269
Subrogation clause 121
Sufficient memorandum 181
Suit to quiet title 92
Summary proceedings 205
Supervisory broker 59. *See* Broker
Supply and demand 73

Support & Parenting Time Enforcement Act 402
Surface rights. *See* Land
Surrender 204
Survey 145
 ALTA 145
 Mortgage 145
Surveyor 145
Syndicate 223
Synthetic stucco. *See* EIFS

T

Tacking 92
Target housing. *See* Disclosure: Lead-paint
Tax 223
 Abatement 229
 Capital gains 232
 Credit 231
 Deduction 231
 Exemption 229
 Foreclosure 228
 Income 33, 230
 Property 223
 Shelter 230
 Summer 135
 Winter 135
Taxable value 225
Tax day 135. *See also* Levy date
Tax Identification Number (TIN) 234
Tax per $100 of assessed valuation 225
Telemarketing. *See* Do-not-call
Tenancy by the entireties 109
Tenancy in common 108
Termite inspection. *See* Inspection
Term loan 274
Testate 93
Testator 93
Testatrix 93
Testimonium clause 89
Testing. *See* Fair housing
Third party 23
Three-day right of rescission, TILA 298
TILA. *See* Truth-in-Lending
Time is of the essence 177
Time-share condominium 114
Title 107
 Chain of 117
 Defined 83
 Examiner 117

Search 117
Title insurance 119, 130
 ALTA Owner's Policy 120
 Commitment 120
 Marked-up policy 121
 Mortgagee's policy 120
 Owner's policy 120
 Schedule A 120
 Schedule B 120
Title theory 242
Torrens system 119
Township 148
Township lines 147
Tract index 119
Trade fixture 10, 201
Trademark 16, 39
Transaction coordinator 60, 165, 361, 363
Transfer tax 87, 133
 County 88
 State 88
Trespass 8, 202
Trespasser 30
TRID 127, 131, 137, 138
True cash value (TCV) 224
Trust account 369. *See also* Earnest money deposit
 Timing for deposit 355
Trustee 251
Trustor 251
Trust ownership 110
Truth-in-Lending 127, 128, 296, 299, 300, 395
Truth In Renting Act 392

U

Unauthorized practice of law 53, 61, 107, 109, 172
Unclaimed property 92, 188
Underwriting. *See* Loan: Underwriting
Underwriting overlays 293
Undue influence 180
Unenforceable contract 178
Unilateral contract. *See* Contract
Unit deed 113
Unities of Time, Title, Interest, and Possession 108
Unity of person 109
Universal exclusion 233

Unsolicited Commercial E-mail Protection Act 41

Upside-Down, meaning of 75

U.S. Army Corps of Engineers 159

USDA Rural Development loans 295

U.S. Government survey system 147

USPAP 71

Usury 296
- Statutes 394

V

VA. *See* Veteran's Administration

Valuable consideration. *See* Consideration

Valuation
- methods 75

Value 69
- principles 69
- types and characteristics 69

VantageScore. *See* Credit score

Variable rent lease 202

Variance 156

Vendee 252

Vendor 184, 252

Vermiculite insulation 167

Veteran's Administration 285
- assumption of VA loan 249

Vicarious liability 24

Voidable 84

Voidable contract 178

Void contract 178

Voluntary waste. *See* Waste

W

Warehouse lending 289

Waste 258
- Permissive 258
- Voluntary 259

Water rights. *See* Land: Water-related property rights

Wetlands 158
- Defined 159

Will 93

Will substitute 93

Worker's compensation insurance. *See* Insurance

World Wide Web 38

Wraparound loan 280

Z

Zoning 154
- Administration 155
- Board of Appeals 156
- Buffer 155
- Challenges 156
- Cluster 156
- Contract 157
- Density 155
- Exclusionary 155
- Spot 156
- Use 155